INTRODUCTION TO mass

communication

MEDIA LITERACY AND CULTURE

UPDATED MEDIA ENHANCED THIRD EDITION

Stanley J. Baran

Bryant College

Boston   Burr Ridge, IL   Dubuque, IA   Madison, WI   New York   San Francisco   St. Louis
Bangkok   Bogotá   Caracas   Kuala Lumpur   Lisbon   London   Madrid   Mexico City
Milan   Montreal   New Delhi   Santiago   Seoul   Singapore   Sydney   Taipei   Toronto

Higher Education

INTRODUCTION TO MASS COMMUNICATION:
MEDIA LITERACY AND CULTURE: Updated Media Enhanced Third Edition
Published by McGraw-Hill, an imprint of The McGraw-Hill Companies, Inc., 1221 Avenue of the Americas, New York, NY 10020. Copyright © 2004, 2002, 2001, 1998 by The McGraw-Hill Companies. All rights reserved. No part of this publication may be reproduced or distributed in any form or by any means, or stored in a database or retrieval system, without the prior written consent of The McGraw-Hill Companies, Inc., including, but not limited to, in any network or other electronic storage or transmission, or broadcast for distance learning.

This book is printed on acid-free paper.

1 2 3 4 5 6 7 8 9 0 WCK/WCK 0 9 8 7 6 5 4

ISBN: 0-07-299837-7

Publisher and sponsoring editor: *Phillip A. Butcher*
Development editor: *Jennie Katsaros*
Editorial assistant: *Christine Fowler*
Marketing manager: *Leslie Oberhuber*
Media producer: *Erin Marean*
Production editor: *Brett Coker*
Senior production supervisor: *Richard DeVitto*
Design manager: *Cassandra Chu*
Art manager: *Robin Mouat*
Manager, photo research: *Brian J. Pecko*
Interior design: *Glenda King*
Cover design: *Joan Greenfield*
Cover illustration: *Lou Beach*
Illustration: *John and Judy Waller, Jim Dandy, Joan Carol, Robin Mouat*
Compositor: *The GTS Companies, Inc.*
Typeface: *10/13 New Aster*
Printer: *Quebecor World Versailles*

Library of Congress Cataloging-in-Publication Data

Baran, Stanley J.
  Introduction to mass communication: media literacy and culture /
  Stanley J. Baran.—
  Updated media enhanced, 3rd ed.
     p. cm.
Includes bibliographical references and index.
ISBN 0-07-299837-7
     1. Mass media. 2. Mass media and culture. 3. Media literacy. I. Title.

P90.B284 2004b
302.23—dc22   2004042576
                                             CIP

www.mhhe.com

In loving memory of my mother,
Margaret Baran

About the Author

STANLEY BARAN EARNED HIS PH.D. IN COMMUNICATION research at the University of Massachusetts after taking his M.A. in journalism at Pennsylvania State University. He taught for 4 years at Cleveland State University, eventually moving to the University of Texas. He led the Department of Radio-TV-Film's graduate program for 6 of his 9 years in Austin and won numerous teaching awards there, including the AMOCO Teaching Excellence Award as the best instructor on that 40,000 student campus, the College of Communication's Teaching Excellence Award as that college's outstanding professor, and *Utmost Magazine*'s Student Poll for best instructor. Dr. Baran moved to San Jose State University in 1987 and served 9 years as chair of the Department of Television, Radio, Film, and Theatre. At SJSU he was named President's Scholar as the university's outstanding researcher. Now, he teaches at Bryant College, where he is the founding chairman of that school's Communication Department. Among the other experiences that helped shape this book are his service as a judge for the Fulbright Scholar Awards and his many years of professional activity in audience research, writing for radio, and producing for television. Dr. Baran has published 10 books and scores of scholarly articles, and he sits or has sat on the editorial boards of five journals. His work has been translated into half a dozen languages. He is a skilled sailor and plays tenor sax in the Wakefield, Rhode Island, Civic Band. He is married to Susan Baran and has three very cool children, Simmony, Matt, and Jordan.

Brief Contents

Contents

PART two

MEDIA, MEDIA INDUSTRIES, AND MEDIA AUDIENCES   65

PART four

MASS-MEDIATED CULTURE IN THE INFORMATION AGE 413

Preface

ON SEPTEMBER 11, 2001, MILLIONS OF AMERICANS—IN FACT, millions of people around the globe—went to bed in shock. The world had changed. The United States no longer seemed invincible. Americans no longer felt safe at home. As everyone, from politicians to pundits to the people next door, said, "Nothing would ever be the same again." Much, in fact, is the same; but not our view of the mass media. The questions we were asking about media in the immediate aftermath of 9/11 and the questions we are raising now are shaped in large part by what happened on that horrific day.

At first we were impressed, even moved, by the performance of our mass media. The coverage of the attack and rescue effort in all media was thorough, knowledgeable, courageous, even-handed, and sensitive. But then we started asking, Why were we caught so badly by surprise? Why didn't we know about the anti-American feelings in much of the world? Where were the media? Then, with the war on terrorism and in Iraq, new questions arose: How many restrictions on media freedom should we accept in time of war? Should we air, unedited, the videotaped ranting of Osama bin Laden? How much should we trust reports from the Arabic television network Al Jazeera? Are reporters Americans first and journalists second, or are they journalists first and Americans second? How much or how little should the press question government policy and our elected leaders? Should the questions stop when troops enter combat?

But it did not take a cowardly terrorist attack on civilians or an invasion of a hostile country to start people thinking and talking about the media. September 11 and the war in Iraq chased from the cultural forum the relentless criticism of the media's performance in the 2000 presidential elections. Dan Rather said that media professionals did not have egg on their faces after that shameful failure of our democracy; they wore the entire omelet. People questioned the media's priorities—a missing Capitol Hill intern garnered more coverage than world events. Others were complaining that movies were starting to look like extra-long commercials, while television commercials were getting increasingly briefer and all media, even novels, were seemingly drowning in more and more advertising. Critics across the political spectrum were concerned that media companies were merging at an unhealthy-for-democracy rate. Concern about media violence and sexual content remained unabated. Furor followed a television network's proposal to air hard-liquor ads. People who had lost their life savings wanted to know what the media were doing while Enron and WorldCom were stealing from them. To First Amendment advocates, new copyright rules designed to thwart digital piracy were undoing two centuries of fair use copyright protection, with consumers and democracy poorer for it.

The media, like sports and politics, are what we talk about. Argue over. Dissect and analyze.

Those of us who teach media know that these conversations are essential to the functioning of a democratic society. We also know that what moves these conversations from the realm of chatting and griping to that of effective public discourse is media education—the systematic study of media and their operation in our political and economic system, as well as their contribution to the development and maintenance of the culture that binds us together and defines us. We now call this media education *media literacy*.

Regardless of what an individual course is called—Introduction to Mass Communication, Introduction to Mass Media, Media and Society, Media and Culture—media literacy has been a part of university media education for more than four decades. The course has long been designed to fulfill the following goals:

- to increase students' knowledge and understanding of the mass communication process and the mass media industries;
- to increase students' awareness of how they interact with those industries and with media content to create meaning;
- and to help students become more skilled and knowledgeable consumers of media content.

These are all aspects of media literacy as it is now understood. This text makes explicit what has been implicit for so long: that media literacy skills can and should be taught directly and that, as we travel through the 21st century, media literacy is an essential survival skill for everyone in our society.

Perspective

This focus on media literacy grows naturally out of a *cultural perspective* on mass communication. This text takes the position that media, audiences, and culture develop and evolve in concert. The current prevailing notion in the discipline of mass communication is that, although not all individuals are directly affected by every media message they encounter, the media nonetheless do have important cultural effects. Today, the media are accepted as powerful forces in the process through which we come to know ourselves and one another. They function both as a forum in which issues are debated and as the storytellers that carry our beliefs across time and space. Through these roles, the media are central to the creation and maintenance of both our dominant culture and our various bounded cultures.

This cultural orientation toward mass communication and the media places much responsibility on media consumers. In the past, people were considered either victims of media influence or impervious to it. The cultural orientation asserts that audience members are as much a part of the mass communication process as are the media technologies and industries. As important agents in the creation and maintenance of their own culture, audience members have an obligation not only to participate in the process of mass communication but also to participate actively, appropriately, and effectively. In other words, they must bring media literacy—the ability to effectively and efficiently comprehend and use mass media—to the mass communication process.

Features of This Text

The features that made this text successful in its earlier editions have been retained in this revision.

- **Emphasis on developing media literacy.** The pedagogical features of this book are designed to support and improve media literacy skills. Chapter 2 lays out the elements of media literacy, and an emphasis on media literacy is woven throughout the text. Each chapter from Chapter 3 to 15 contains a section, specific to that chapter's medium or issue, on developing media literacy skills. For example, Chapter 4, Newspapers, offers guidelines for interpreting the relative placement of newspaper stories. Chapter 8, Television, discusses how to identify staged news events on television. Other media literacy topics include recognizing product placements in movies, evaluating news based on anonymous sources, and protecting personal privacy on the Internet.

- **Cultural perspective.** The media—either as forums in which important issues are debated or as storytellers that carry our beliefs and values across people, space, and time—are central to the creation and maintenance of our various cultures. This book advocates the idea that media audiences can take a more active role in the mass communication process and help shape the cultures that, in turn, shape them.

- **Brief historical sections.** Historical sections at the beginning of each chapter on a medium offer relevant background information for students. By providing historical context, these sections help students understand current issues in the media landscape.

- **Focus on convergence.** Each chapter on a medium includes a section called Trends and Convergence. These sections emphasize the influence of new technologies on media and society.

- **Pedagogical boxes included throughout the text.** These boxes give students a deeper understanding of media-related issues and the role of media in society.

USING MEDIA TO MAKE A DIFFERENCE These boxes highlight interesting examples of how media practitioners and audiences use the mass communication process to further important social, political, or cultural causes. For example, Chapter 6, Film, highlights the African American films and film industry that grew up in response to the D. W. Griffith film, *The Birth of a Nation.*

CULTURAL FORUM These boxes highlight media-related cultural issues that are currently debated in the mass media. Titles include, for example, Advertorials Aimed at Young Girls; Concentration, Conglomeration, and 9/11; and Does DVR Make You a Thief?

MEDIA ECHOES These boxes demonstrate that the cultural and social debates surrounding the different media tend to be repeated throughout history, regardless of the technology or era in question. For example, the public relations chapter discusses early PR efforts to encourage women to smoke, and the advertising chapter covers advertisers' more recent attempts to attract teenage smokers.

Key Changes to the Updated Media Enhanced Third Edition

Although the book maintains its commitment to critical thinking throughout its pages, several important changes were made to enhance and update this, the third edition.

- A fourth pedagogical box, **Living Media Literacy,** has been added to each chapter. These brief, chapter-ending essays suggest ways in which students can put what they have learned into practice. They are calls to action—personal, social, educational, political. Their goal is to make media literacy a living enterprise, something that has value in how students interact with the culture and media. Several use the stories of "everyday people" who have made a difference. Indicative titles are Start a Citywide Book Conversation, Help a School Start an Online Newspaper, and Smoke-Free Movies.

- Three important changes have been made to the text's structure. First, cable is now discussed at length in its own chapter, **Cable and Other Multichannel Services.** This has been done in recognition of cable's new (and potentially greater) role in the delivery of all media to consumers' homes. Naturally, the economic, regulatory, and cultural issues surrounding this venerable medium are changing and worthy of comment. Second, mass communication theories and the effects of mass media have been combined into one chapter, producing a more seamless discussion of the relationship between *how* we think and *what* we think about media's impact. Finally, the chapter on the Internet and the World Wide Web has been moved to follow the chapters on the more traditional media, placing it in a more appropriate chronological location for studying their relationship with other forms of mass communication.

■ Every chapter has been informed by the events of September 11 and the war on terrorism and the conflict in Iraq. Chapter 10's discussion of privacy, for example, contains an examination of the difficulty in balancing privacy and security in time of war. Concentration and conglomeration and their contribution to the decline of international coverage are part of Chapter 1. The ethical questions raised by 9/11 and the war on terrorism are presented: Do a reporter's patriotism and journalism conflict? What are acceptable levels of criticism of public officials in wartime? What are acceptable levels of government censorship? How much access should media professionals have to battle zones? How should advertisers make use of the tragedy?

■ Chapters are now introduced by graphically attractive historical timelines of the medium or issue under discussion and a list of the chapter's learning objectives.

■ In previous editions each chapter closed with a chapter review, review questions, questions for discussion, and a listing of important resources. These pedagogical features are now accompanied by a list of key terms.

■ URLs of important or interesting Web sites are placed in page margins near concepts they are designed to support.

■ Boxes have been updated to cover current topics and issues. The coverage of international news, book censorship, the erosion of the firewall between newspapers' sales and news departments, the Pentagon's Office of Strategic Influence, mandatory cable access for Internet service providers, and changes in the way we think about copyright are a few examples.

■ All statistical entries have been updated. These changes include new information on Internet demographics, new media consumption statistics, and new statistics for all media sales and circulation figures.

■ Coverage of media ownership has been updated to the extent possible. Although it is challenging to keep up with changes in media ownership, we have made a diligent effort to provide the most recent information on mergers and acquisitions in media conglomerate ownership.

Learning Aids

Several types of learning aids are included in the book to support student learning and to enhance media literacy skills.

■ World Wide Web URLs in the margins of every chapter enable students to locate additional resources and encourage students to practice using the Internet.

- Photo essays raise provocative questions, encouraging students to further develop their critical thinking and analytical skills.

- Important Resources, an annotated listing of books and articles for further reading, provides additional information for students.

- Chapter Reviews allow students to make sure they have focused on each chapter's most important material.

- Questions for Review further highlight important content and provide a review of key points.

- Questions for Critical Thinking and Discussion encourage students to investigate their own cultural assumptions and media use and to engage one another in debate on critical issues.

- Margin icons throughout the text direct students to view the CD-ROM *Media Tours* and *NBC* video clips.

- Historical timelines, chapter learning objectives, and chapter-ending lists of key terms guide and focus student learning.

- An exhaustive list of references is provided at the end of the book.

Organization

Introduction to Mass Communication: Media Literacy and Culture is divided into four parts. Part One, Laying the Groundwork, as its name implies, provides the foundation for the study of mass communication. Chapter 1, Mass Communication, Culture, and Mass Media, defines important concepts and establishes the basic premises of the cultural perspective on mass communication with its focus on media literacy. Chapter 2, Media Literacy and Culture, provides an overview of the development of mass communication and the media and elaborates on the meaning and implications of media literacy.

Part Two, Media, Media Industries, and Media Audiences, includes chapters on the individual mass media technologies and the industries that have grown up around them—books (Chapter 3), newspapers (Chapter 4), magazines (Chapter 5), film (Chapter 6), radio and sound recording (Chapter 7), television (Chapter 8), cable and other multichannel services (Chapter 9) and the Internet and the World Wide Web (Chapter 10). All of these chapters open with a short history of the medium and continue with discussions of the medium and its audiences, the scope and nature of the medium, and current trends and convergence in the industry and technology. Each chapter concludes with a section on developing a media literacy skill specifically related to that medium and a call to action in the form of the Living Media Literacy essays. Throughout each chapter there is a focus not just on the industry and technology but also on cultural issues and the interaction of culture, medium, and audience. For example, in Chapter 10, advances in digital technology and computer networking are discussed in terms of our ability to maintain control of our personal data and our privacy. Chapter 3's examination of book censorship asks students to challenge their personal commitment to free expression and to reflect on how that commitment speaks to their belief in democracy. Radio and rock 'n' roll are connected to a discussion of race relations in America in Chapter 7.

Part Three, Supporting Industries, carries this same approach into two related areas—public relations (Chapter 11) and advertising (Chapter 12). As in the medium-specific chapters, each of these chapters begins with a brief history, continues with a discussion of audience, the scope of the industry, and current trends and convergence, and concludes with guidelines on developing relevant media literacy skills.

Part Four, Mass-Mediated Culture in the Information Age, tackles several important areas. Chapter 13, Theories and Effects of Mass Communication, provides a short history of mass communication theory and compares and evaluates the field's major theories. It then explores the ongoing debate over media effects. The chapter considers such topics as media and violence, media and gender and racial/ethnic stereotyping, and media and the electoral process. Chapter 14, Media Freedom, Regulation, and Ethics, provides a detailed discussion of the First Amendment, focusing on refinements in interpretation and application made over the years in response to changes in technology and culture. The chapter analyzes such topics and issues as privacy, the use of cameras in the courtroom, and changing definitions of indecency. The chapter concludes with an extended discussion of media ethics and professionalism. Chapter 15, Global Media, looks at media systems in other parts of the world and concludes with a discussion of local cultural integrity versus cultural imperialism.

New and Updated Supplements

The supplements package available with the text includes a full array of tools designed to facilitate both teaching and learning.

- An *Instructor's Resource Guide*, available on the Online Learning Center, provides teaching aids for each chapter, including learning objectives, key terms and concepts, lecture ideas, video suggestions, a guide to using the Media Literacy Worksheets, and a test bank of more than 1,000 test items.

- Questions in a computerized test bank can be edited and new questions can be added.

- The *Introduction to Mass Communication* Student CD-ROM offers students interactive quizzes, summaries, key terms flash cards, activity worksheets, Web links, and *NBC* and *Media Tours* video clips.

- Two new video tapes feature brief clips that bring to life the concepts discussed in the text. Clips are from *NBC News* and *The*

Today Show, and McGraw-Hill's *Media Tours* of a television station and *Vibe* magazine. An instructor's guide is packaged with the videos.

- The Online Learning Center (www.mhhe.com/baran3) has been thoroughly updated. The new site includes Media Literacy worksheets, PowerPoint® slides, a Web tutorial, a bulletin board, a syllabus builder for the instructor, an online study guide, chapter self-quizzes with feedback, hot links to media resources for the student, and more.

- *PowerWeb: Mass Communication* is a password-protected Web site that includes current articles from *Annual Editions: Mass Media*, curriculum-based materials, weekly updates with assessment, informative and timely world news, Web links, research tools, student study tools, interactive exercises, and much more.

- An *Instructor's CD-ROM* (compatible with both Macintosh and IBM computers) offers electronic versions of the *Instructor's Resource Guide*, PowerPoint® slides, electronic transparencies, and worksheets.

- *Media Literacy Worksheets and Journal,* now online (www.mhhe.com/baran3), has been revised to include worksheets for each chapter. Activities direct students to selected Web sites, suggest topics for entries in an ongoing Media Journal, and further explore the media literacy skills highlighted in each chapter. There are more than 75 worksheets in total.

- *PageOut: The Course Web Site Development Center.* All online content for this text is supported by WebCT, eCollege.com, Blackboard, and other course management systems. Additionally, McGraw-Hill's Page-Out service is available to get you and your course up and running online in a matter of hours, at no cost. PageOut was designed for instructors just beginning to explore Web options. Even the novice computer user can create a course Web site with a template provided by McGraw-Hill (no programming knowledge necessary). To learn more about PageOut, ask your McGraw-Hill representative for details, or fill out the form at www.mhhe.com/pageout.

Acknowledgments

Any project of this magnitude requires the assistance of many people. My colleague Bob Mendenhall of Southwestern Adventist University was particularly helpful with his sharp eyes and good suggestions.

Reviewers are an indispensable part of the creation of a good textbook. In preparing for this third edition, I was again impressed with the thoughtful comments made by my colleagues in the field. Although I didn't know them by name, I found myself in long-distance, anonymous debate with several superb thinkers, especially about some of the text's most important concepts. Their collective keen eye and questioning attitude sharpened each chapter to the benefit of both writer and reader. (Any errors or misstatements that remain in the book are of course my sole responsibility.) Now that I know who they are, I would like to thank the reviewers by name. **Third Edition Reviewers:** Jenny L. Nelson, Ohio University; Terri Toles Patkin, Eastern Connecticut State University; Alyse Lancaster, University of Miami; Deborah A. Godwin-Starks, Indiana University-Purdue University Fort Wayne; Kevin R. Slaughter, George Mason University; Enid Sefcovic, Florida Atlantic University; David Whitt, Nebraska Wesleyan University; Roger Desmond, University of Hartford; Carol S. Lomicky, University of Nebraska at Kearney; Jules d'Hemecourt, Louisiana State University; Junhao Hong, State University of New York at Buffalo; Gary J. Wingenbach, Texas A&M University. **Second Edition Reviewers:** Rob Bellamy, Duquesne University; Beth Grobman Burruss, DeAnza College; Stephen R. Curtis, Jr., East Connecticut State University; Lyombe Eko, University of Maine; Junhao Hong, State University of New York at Buffalo; Carol Liebler, Syracuse University; Robert Main, California State University, Chico; Stephen Perry, Illinois State University; Eric Pierson, University of San Diego; Ramona Rush, University of Kentucky; Tony Silvia, University of Rhode Island; and Richard Welch, Kennesaw State University. **First Edition Reviewers:** David Allen, Illinois State University; Sandra Braman, University of Alabama; Tom Grimes, Kansas State University; Kirk Hallahan, Colorado State University; Katharine Heintz-Knowles, University of Washington; Paul Husselbee, Ohio University; Seong Lee, Appalachian State University; Rebecca Ann Lind, University of Illinois at Chicago; Maclyn McClary, Humboldt State University; Guy Meiss, Central Michigan University; Debra Merskin, University of Oregon; Scott R. Olsen, Central Connecticut State University; Ted Pease, Utah State University; Linda Perry, *Florida Today* newspaper; Elizabeth Perse, University of Delaware; Tina Pieraccini, State University of New York-College at Oswego; Michael Porter, University of Missouri; Peter Pringle, University of Tennessee at Chattanooga; Neal Robison, Washington State University; Linda Steiner, Rutgers University; and Don Tomlinson, Texas A&M University.

This edition is the first I have written with the support of my new team at McGraw-Hill. My development editor, Jennie Katsaros, proved to be as polished a professional as she is a lunchtime conversationalist. She intuitively understood the soul of this text and encouraged me to write in its spirit. My editor, Phil Butcher, was questioning and imaginative. Confident in me, he let me write *my* book. I also want to acknowledge my original editor, Holly Allen. She waited for me to *want* to write this book. If I had known how skilled a colleague and delightful a friend she would have become, I would have been ready years sooner.

Finally, my most important inspiration throughout the writing of this book has been my family. My wife, Susan, is educated in media literacy and a strong disciple of spreading its lessons far and wide—which she does with zest. Her knowledge and assistance in my writing was invaluable; her love in my life is sustaining. My children—Jordan, Matthew, and Simmony—simply by their existence require that I consider and reconsider what kind of world we will leave for them. I've written this text in the hope that it helps make the future for them and their friends better than it might otherwise have been.

S.J.B.

A Visual Preview

As we travel through the twenty-first century, Media Literacy is an essential survival skill for everyone in our society.

> **Media Literacy:** the ability to effectively and efficiently comprehend and use mass media

The focus on media literacy grows out of a **cultural perspective** on mass communication. Through this cultural perspective, students learn that audience members are as much a part of the mass communication process as are the media producers, technologies, and industries.

Cultural Forum: Defining Media Literacy

Developing Media Skills: Recognizing Staged News

for viewer feedback. Fiber optic cable is making **broadband** (channels with broad information-carrying capacity) access more of a reality, and industry experts estimate that by 2005, 30 million Americans will have sufficient bandwidth for full interactivity (Amdur, 2003). Still, this is only a fraction of the total Web and television audience. Another problem potentially limiting the fuller diffusion of interactive television is that many people simply may not want it. As technology writer Bill Syken observed, "Television and work do not go together as naturally as, say, television and beer" (2000, p. 27). See Chapter 9 for more on broadband and interactive television.

DEVELOPING MEDIA LITERACY SKILLS
Recognizing Staged News

For years studies have shown that a majority of the American public turns to television as [the source of most of its news and that viewers accept it as] the most believ[able ...] dramatic, espec[...] images. But wh[...] news is also a [...] vision newspeo[...] the public, but [...] people so their [...]

Even the b[...] not tune in, an[...] als, driven to g[...] that is, re-creat[...] Sometimes new[...] narrate an acc[...] that event is pl[...] scene. What ha[...] U.S. television [...] ABC's 1994 bro[...] ter clothes, see[...] night when she[...] "presence" at t[...]

The broadc[...]
event was stage[...]

Did Geraldo Rivera engage in permissible or impermissible news staging when he reported from "sacred ground" although he was miles from the actual spot?

the spot? What was reported actually did happen." If you accept this view (the event *did* happen, therefore it's not news staging), how would you evaluate Fox News's Geraldo Rivera's reporting from "sacred ground," the scene of a battle in Afghanistan in which U.S. forces suffered heavy losses, even though he was miles from the actual spot? And if you accept digital alteration of news scenes to place network reporters "at the scene," how would you evaluate CBS's common practice of digitally inserting its network logo on billboards and buildings that appear behind its reporters and anchors (Poniewozik, 2000)? If this staging is acceptable to you, why not OK the digital enhancement of fires and explosions in the news?

Some media literate viewers may accept the-event-did-happen argument, but another form of news staging exists that is potentially more troublesome—re-creation. In 1992 the producers of *Dateline NBC* re-created the explosion of a GMC truck, justifying the move with the argument that similar explosions "had happened" (Chapter 14). In the mid-1990s a Denver news show ran footage of a pit bull fight it had arranged and defended its action on the ground that these things "do happen." *ABC Evening News* simulated surveillance camera recordings of U.S. diplomat Felix Bloch handing [...] on the street to accompan[...]

Cultural Forum

Defining Media Literacy

Media literacy takes on slightly different meanings depending on the orientation of the person or organization doing the defining. In a special issue of the *Journal of Communication* dedicated to media literacy, media researcher Alan Rubin cited these definitions of media literacy.

> From the National Leadership Conference on Media Literacy: *the ability to access, analyze, evaluate, and communicate messages* (1998, p. 3).

> From media scholar Paul Messaris: *knowledge about how media function in society* (1998, p. 3).

> From mass communication researchers Justin Lewis and Sut Jhally: *understanding cultural, economic, political, and technological constraints on the creation, production, and transmission of messages* (1998, p. 3).

> Rubin went on to provide his own definition of media literacy:

[...] out understanding the sources [...] unication, the codes that are [...] re produced, and the selection, [...] of those messages. (p. 3)

[...] cation scholars William Christ [...] their view of media literacy:

[...] f media literacy) include the fol- [...] are constructed and construct [...] ercial implications; media have

ideological and political implications; form and content are related in each medium, each of which has a unique aesthetic, codes, and conventions; and receivers negotiate meaning in media. (1998, pp. 7–8)

The Cultural Environment Movement ("The People's Communication Charter," 1996), a public interest group devoted to increasing literacy as a way to combat corporate takeover of media, suggests this definition:

> The right to acquire information and skills necessary to participate fully in public deliberation and communication. This requires facility in reading, writing, and storytelling; critical media awareness; computer literacy; and education about the role of communication in society. (p. 1)

The National Communication Association (1996), a professional scholarly organization composed largely of university academics, offers this description of media literacy:

> Being a critical and reflective consumer of communication requires an understanding of how words, images, graphics, and sounds work together in ways that are both subtle and profound. Mass media such as radio, television, and film and electronic media such as the telephone, the Internet, and computer conferencing influence the way meanings are created and shared in contemporary society. So great is this impact that in choosing how to send a message and evaluate its effect, communicators need to be aware of the distinctive characteristics of each medium. (p. 2)

These definitions are currently in play in the cultural forum. How would you assess the worth of each? Identify the one most useful for you and defend your choice.

[...] *the impact of media.* Writing and the printing [...] e world and the people in it. Mass media do the [...] impact of media on our lives, we run the risk of [...] along by that change rather than control[...]

For more information on this topic, see NBC Video Clip #8 on the CD—*Author James Steyer Discusses His Book*

Introduction to Mass Communication offers a rich selection of examples and features that increase students' knowledge and understanding of the mass communication process and mass media industries.

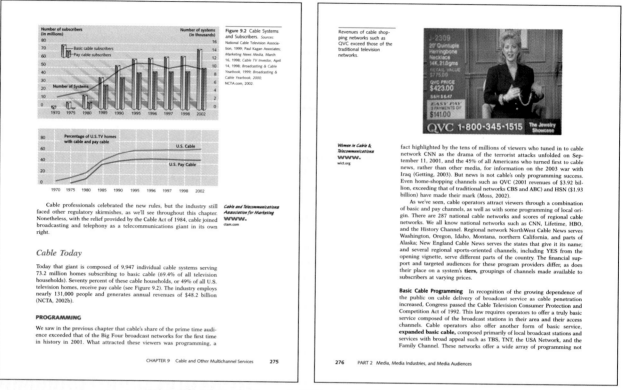

New Chapter: Cable and Other Multichannel Services

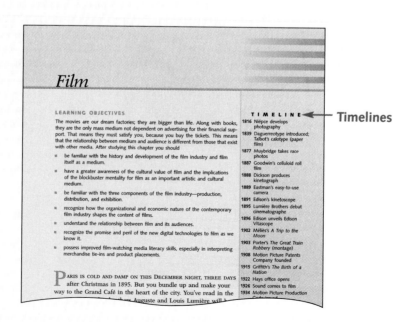

Timelines

Rock 'n' Roll and Radio

NYPD Blue *and* Buffy the Vampire Slayer *are only two of the many television shows that use government-approved antidrug messages in their stories.*

The Television Industry

Reprinted with permission. Reprinted with permission.

Two of the more successful online newspapers.

Public Journalism Network
WWW.
pjnet.org

Newspapers: Convergence with the Internet

The **Global Media** chapter examines the changing media systems and their impact on world economic, political, and cultural environments.

Cultural Forum: U.S. as International Propagandist

Cultural Forum

The United States as International Propagandist

September 11, 2001, and the subsequent war on terrorism thrust the VOA into the cultural forum, although it was rarely free of controversy before its October 2001 broadcast of an interview with Taliban leader Mullah Mohammad Omar—the equivalent, according to North Carolina Republican Senator Jesse Helms, of granting "equal time for Hitler" (in Wenner, 2001, p. 11).

The VOA offers Afghanistan and Pakistan services in two languages, Dari and Pashto (the language of the Taliban). Eighty percent of all Afghan men listen to the transmissions (Wenner, 2001). Just as the VOA-conducted interview with Omar was to be broadcast, the U.S. State Department stopped it. Taking the words of acting director Myrna Whitworth to heart—she urged her staff "*not* to fall under the spell of 'self-censorship.' If you do, 'they have won.' Continue to interview, *anyone, anywhere*" (quoted in Hentoff, 2001, p. 26)—VOA reporters and editors threatened mass resignation. The State Department relented, and the interview, in part, was eventually aired.

The difficulty that repeatedly returns the VOA to the cultural forum resides in the question of whether it should operate as an independent news organization or as an arm of American foreign policy. When it went on the air in the 1940s, its pledge to foreign listeners was straightforward: The news may be good. The news may be bad. We shall tell you the truth. Even today, VOA external affairs director Joseph O'Connell says that the best way to present the United States in the "best possible light" is "by telling the whole story. That by itself says something about us as a country. We're not afraid to let people make up their own minds." Robert Reilly, who replaced Myrna Whitworth soon after her demand for independence for her staff, agrees, telling the *American Journalism Review* that he'd be "stupid to squander the reputation and trust that almost 60 years of accurate news reporting has created around the world" (both quoted in Wenner, 2001, pp. 10–11). Still, incidents such as the interference with the Omar interview and practices such as mandatory State Department approval of all VOA editorials lead critics, such as former VOA Moscow bureau chief Mark Hopkins to charge that the VOA consistently places "the truth" second to "political programming with clear ideological agendas" (1999, p. 44). Current VOA news director Andre de Nesnera says he feels the pressure: "There are quite a lot of people on Capitol Hill who would like this to be the office of war information" (quoted in Wenner, 2001, p. 10).

The argument of a VOA language service director that "as a government broadcaster, you can't be neutral" (quoted in Hopkins, 1999, p. 46) is unconvincing to those who want America's premier surrogate service, the VOA, to be more like the highly regarded BBC World Service or the smaller but respected German Deutsche Welle. These critics want a unified, objective American international radio and television service, free of political objectives, that commands an audience because of its reliability and credibility.

Their arguments are several. First, a worldwide propaganda system is unnecessary in an era of global telecommunications. Why would anyone tune in to a propaganda channel when they can receive objective, high-quality content not only from the BBC World Service but from other American and Western sources? Critics point to Radio and TV Marti, both of which are ignored by a Cuban audience within easy reach of American commercial broadcasters. Second, propagandistic broadcasts can alienate the leadership of targeted countries. The president of the VOA's Radio Free Europe/Radio Liberty, Thomas Dine, says that his service aims to "foster democracy, promote free market reforms"; indeed, Radio Free Asia focuses its news reports on dissidents who challenge regimes considered unfriendly to the United States (Hopkins, 1999, p. 46). Neither RFE/RL's goals nor Radio Free Asia's practice endear the United States to leaders in eastern Europe and China who, regardless of their political orientations, are our global neighbors. Finally, the cost—nearly $400 million a year—is simply too high to engage in practices that would not only be considered offensive at home but also belie the American ideal of free media open to all shades of opinion.

Enter your voice in the cultural forum. Is $400 million not a particularly steep price to ensure that people around the world have access to the American point of view? Do you think any international service, commercial or surrogate, should produce and distribute content specifically designed to transmit its government's "official" viewpoint? Does it concern you that Congress, in exchange for its funding, requires the VOA to broadcast U.S. State Department-approved editorials? How free of government influence should any taxpayer-supported international telecommunications service be? Would you have run the Mullah Mohammad Omar interview? If yes, what defense would you offer to those who said you were giving equal time to Hitler?

506

---

of Man, and Radio Veronica, broadcasting from a ship off the coast of the Netherlands.

These pirates, unlike their politically motivated clandestine cousins, were powerful and well subsidized by advertisers and record companies. Moreover, much like the commercial radio stations with which we are now familiar, they broadcast 24 hours a day, every day of the year. These pirates offered listeners an alternative to the controlled and low-key programming of the British Broadcasting Corporation's (BBC) stations. Because the BBC was noncommercial, pirate stations represented the only opportunity for advertisers who wanted to reach British consumers. Record companies intent on introducing Britain's youth to their artists and to rock 'n' roll also saw the pirates as the only way to reach their audience, which the staid BBC all but ignored.

For more information on this topic, see NBC Video Clip #19 on the CD—*Why Is the United States Viewed So Poorly in the Arab World?*

Enterprising broadcasters also made use of foreign locales to bring commercial television to audiences otherwise denied. The top-rated network in Germany today, for example, is RTL. Now broadcasting from the German city of Cologne, it began operations in January 1984 in Luxembourg, transmitting an American-style mix of children's programming, sports, talk shows, and action-adventure programming into Germany to compete with that country's two dominant public broadcasters, ARD and ZDF.

The United States as International Broadcaster World War II brought the United States into the business of international broadcasting. Following the lead of Britain, which had just augmented its colonial broadcast system with an **external service** called the BBC World Service, the United States established in 1940 what would eventually be known as the Voice of America (VOA) to counter enemy propaganda and disseminate information about America. The VOA originally targeted countries in Central and South America friendly to Germany, but as the war became global, it quickly began broadcasting to scores of other nations, attracting, along with Britain's World Service, a large and admiring listenership, first in countries occupied by the Axis powers, and later by those in the Soviet sphere of influence.

Voice of America
WWW.
voa.gov

It was this Cold War with the Soviets that moved the United States into the forefront of international broadcasting, a position it still holds today. To counter the efforts of the Soviet Union's external service, Radio Moscow, the United States established three additional services. Radio in the American Sector (RIAS), broadcasting in German, served people inside East Berlin and East Germany; Radio Free Europe (RFE) broadcast to all of the other Communist-bloc Eastern European countries in their native languages; and Radio Liberty (RL) was aimed at listeners in the Soviet Union itself. When these services were initiated, people in both the United States and abroad were told that they were funded by contributions from American citizens. However, as a result of the furor that arose when it was revealed in 1971 that they were in fact paid for by the Central Intelligence Agency, they were brought openly under

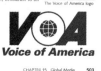

The Voice of America logo

VOA
Voice of America

CHAPTER 15 Global Media 503

Voice of America

Using Media to Make a Difference: Satellite Television in Bhutan

Using Media to Make a Difference

Maintaining Gross National Happiness

High in the Himalayas, in a country half the size of Indiana, the 600,000 citizens of the monarchy of Bhutan try to eke out an existence. The country is poor—the majority of its people are yak herders and monks—and anxious to maintain its Buddhist culture and identity. But global media, as they have everywhere else, are coming to this tiny land sitting between China and India. King Jigme Singye Wangchuck has declared that he intends to bring modern technology to his country while at the same time preserving its guiding principle, Gross National Happiness. The king's goal is to bring his "spartan rural society into the high-tech world without surrendering its soul." In calling for Gross National Happiness, the king hopes to ensure the "equitable distribution of health care and education; environmental protection; and, good government" (Zielenziger, 2000, p. 6AA). To accomplish his goals he wants his people to use media, rather than be used by them. "We felt the compulsion of globalization," explains Foreign Minister Jigme Thinley. "We see ourselves as a society that must change. [But] we are very conscious of the fact that certain aspects of our culture need to be preserved. Culturally we are changing, but we want to remain Bhutanese" (as quoted in Zielenziger, 2000, p. 6AA).

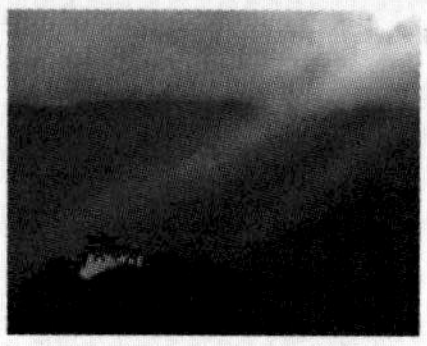

Remote and picturesque, the tiny nation of Bhutan sees the new communication technologies as its avenue to involvement with the larger world.

This is a country whose capital, Thimphu, has no traffic lights. Not a single McDonald's or Starbucks is to be found anywhere in Bhutan. It is a nation that strictly limits the number of foreign visitors it allows inside its borders, charging those who do come $200 a day just for the honor. But it is also a land that offers its citizens free public education in English and sends its best students overseas to do advanced study. When they have completed their studies, 99% return home to render service, along with compassion and individual enlightenment, a primary precept of the country's Mahayanan Buddhism.

E.R. earns Warner Brothers $1.4 million per episode from foreign broadcasters.

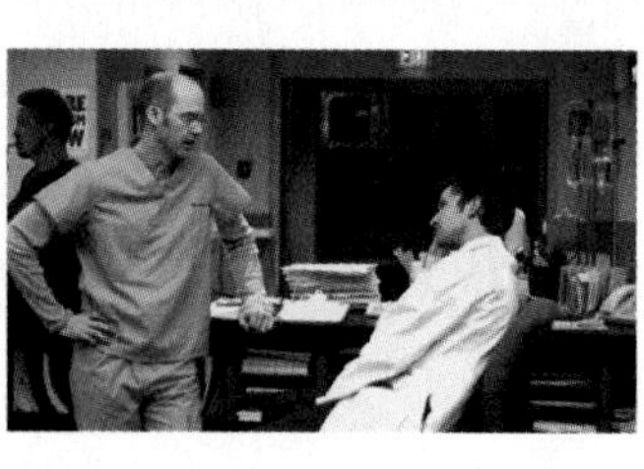

510 PART 4 Mass-Mediated Culture in the Information Age

Foreign Distribution of U.S. Television Programs

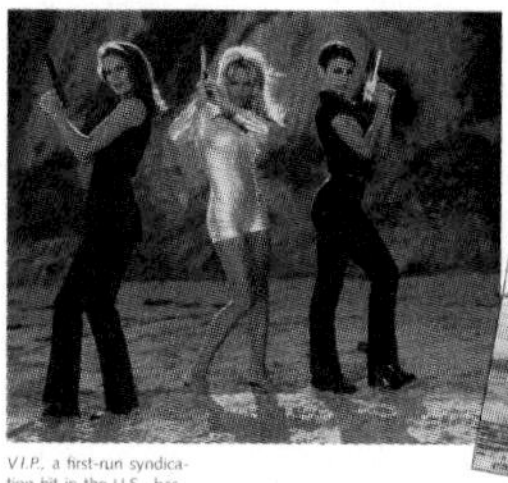

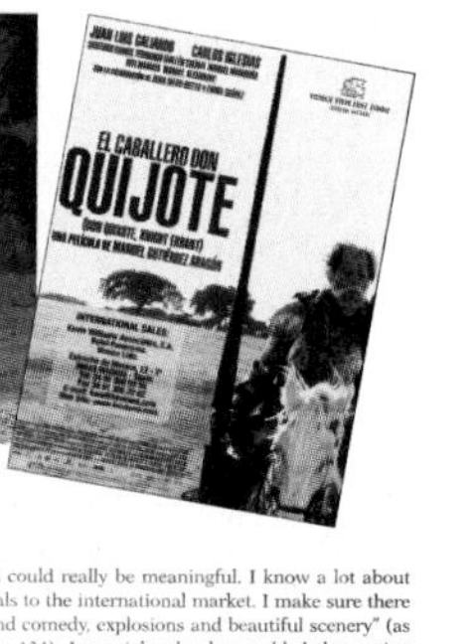

V.I.P., a first-run syndication hit in the U.S., has been quite successful in foreign distribution, largely because it requires little dubbing of dialogue, and it offers its international audiences "a lot of physical gags and comedy, explosions, and beautiful scenery." Other countries export their media too. Here is an ad for a Spanish distribution company that appeared in *Variety*.

because I felt the back end could really be meaningful. I know a lot about syndication and what appeals to the international market. I make sure there are a lot of physical gags and comedy, explosions and beautiful scenery" (as quoted in J. Stein, 1999, p. 134). Lee might also have added that action shows such as *V.I.P.* are easily dubbed into local languages.

Naturally, programming varies somewhat from one country to another. The commercial television systems of most South American and European countries are far less sensitive about sex and nudity than are their counterparts in the United States. In Brazil, for example, despite a constitutional requirement that broadcasters "respect society's social and ethical values" (Epstein, 1999, p. A11), television networks such as SBT, TV Record, and TV Globo compete in what critics call the *guerra da baixaria*, the war of the lowest common denominator. Guests on variety shows wrestle with buxom models dressed only in bikinis and eat sushi off other women's naked bodies. On game shows, male contestants who give wrong answers can be punished by having patches of leg hair ripped out, while those who answer correctly are ...ded by having a nearly naked model sit in th...

Thought provoking **boxed features and photo essays** support and improve media literacy skills.

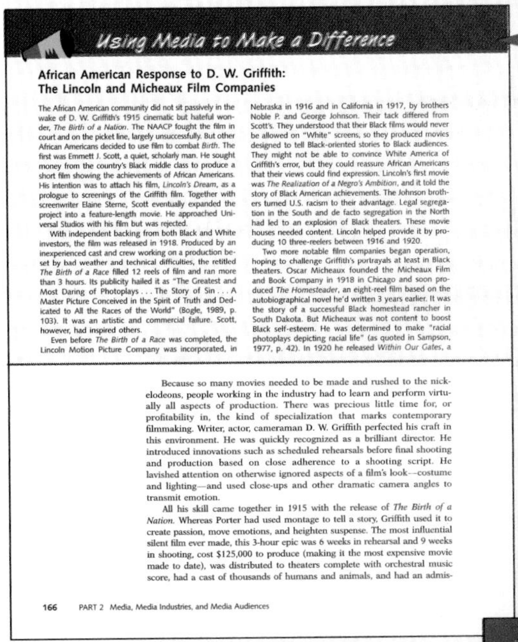

Using Media to Make a Difference

African American Response to D. W. Griffith: The Lincoln and Micheaux Film Companies

The African American community did not sit passively in the wake of D. W. Griffith's 1915 cinematic but hateful wonder, *The Birth of a Nation*. The NAACP fought the film in court and on the picket line, largely unsuccessfully. But other African Americans decided to use film to combat *Birth*. The first was Emmett J. Scott, a quiet, scholarly man. He sought money from the country's Black middle class to produce a short film showing the achievements of African Americans. His intention was to attach his film, *Lincoln's Dream*, as a prologue to screenings of the Griffith film. Together with screenwriter Elaine Sterne, Scott eventually expanded the project into a feature-length movie. He approached Universal Studios with his film but was rejected.

With independent backing from both Black and White investors, the film was released in 1918. Produced by an inexperienced cast and crew working on a production beset by bad weather and technical difficulties, the retitled *The Birth of a Race* filled 12 reels of film and ran more than 3 hours. Its publicity hailed it as "The Greatest and Most Daring of Photoplays . . . The Story of Sin . . . A Master Picture Conceived in the Spirit of Truth and Dedicated to All the Races of the World" (Bogle, 1989, p. 103). It was an artistic and commercial failure. Scott, however, had inspired others.

Even before *The Birth of a Race* was completed, the Lincoln Motion Picture Company was incorporated, in Nebraska in 1916 and in California in 1917, by brothers Noble P. and George Johnson. Their tack differed from Scott's. They understood that their Black films would never be allowed on "White" screens, so they produced movies designed to tell Black-oriented stories to Black audiences. They might not be able to convince White America of Griffith's error, but they could reassure African Americans that their views could find expression. Lincoln's first movie was *The Realization of a Negro's Ambition*, and it told the story of Black American achievements. The Johnson brothers turned U.S. racism to their advantage. Legal segregation in the South and de facto segregation in the North had led to an explosion of Black theaters. These movie houses needed content. Lincoln helped provide it by producing 10 three-reelers between 1916 and 1920.

Two more notable film companies began operation, hoping to challenge Griffith's portrayals at least in Black theaters. Oscar Micheaux founded the Micheaux Film and Book Company in 1918 in Chicago and soon produced *The Homesteader*, an eight-reel film based on the autobiographical novel he'd written 3 years earlier. It was the story of a successful Black homestead rancher in South Dakota. But Micheaux was not content to boost Black self-esteem. He was determined to make "racial photoplays depicting racial life" (as quoted in Sampson, 1977, p. 42). In 1920 he released *Within Our Gates*, a

Because so many movies needed to be made and rushed to the nickelodeons, people working in the industry had to learn and perform virtually all aspects of production. There was precious little time for, or profitability in, the kind of specialization that marks contemporary filmmaking. Writer, actor, cameraman D. W. Griffith perfected his craft in this environment. He was quickly recognized as a brilliant director. He introduced innovations such as scheduled rehearsals before final shooting and production based on close adherence to a shooting script. He lavished attention on otherwise ignored aspects of a film's look—costume and lighting—and used close-ups and other dramatic camera angles to transmit emotion.

All his skill came together in 1915 with the release of *The Birth of a Nation*. Whereas Porter had used montage to tell a story, Griffith used it to create passion, move emotions, and heighten suspense. The most influential silent film ever made, this 3-hour epic was 6 weeks in rehearsal and 9 weeks in shooting, cost $125,000 to produce (making it the most expensive movie made to date), was distributed to theaters complete with orchestral music score, had a cast of thousands of humans and animals, and had an admis-

166 PART 2 Media, Media Industries, and Media Audiences

"Using Media to Make a Difference" boxes highlight examples of how practitioners and audiences use the mass communication process to further social, political, or cultural causes.

"Cultural Forum" boxes examine media-related issues currently debated in the mass media.

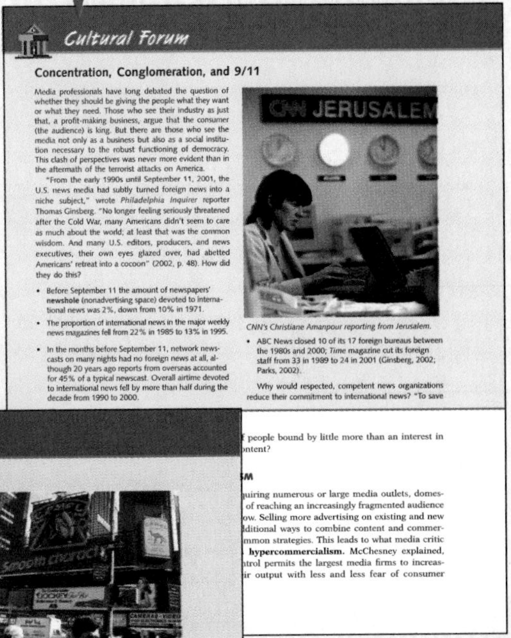

Cultural Forum

Concentration, Conglomeration, and 9/11

Media professionals have long debated the question of whether they should be giving the people what they want or what they need. Those who see their industry as just that, a profit-making business, argue that the consumer (the audience) is king. But there are those who see the media not only as a business but also as a social institution necessary to the robust functioning of democracy. This clash of perspectives was never more evident than in the aftermath of the terrorist attacks on America.

"From the early 1990s until September 11, 2001, the U.S. news media had subtly turned foreign news into a niche subject," wrote *Philadelphia Inquirer* reporter Thomas Ginsberg. "No longer feeling seriously threatened after the Cold War, many Americans didn't seem to care as much about the world; at least that was the common wisdom. And many U.S. editors, producers, and news executives, their own eyes glazed over, had abetted Americans' retreat into a cocoon" (2002, p. 48). How did they do this?

- Before September 11 the amount of newspapers' **newshole** (nonadvertising space) devoted to international news was 2%, down from 10% in 1971.
- The proportion of international news in the major weekly news magazines fell from 22% in 1985 to 13% in 1995.
- In the months before September 11, network newscasts on many nights had no foreign news at all, although 20 years ago reports from overseas accounted for 45% of a typical newscast. Overall airtime devoted to international news fell by more than half during the decade from 1990 to 2000.

CNN's Christiane Amanpour reporting from Jerusalem.

- ABC News closed 10 of its 17 foreign bureaus between the 1980s and 2000; *Time* magazine cut its foreign staff from 33 in 1989 to 24 in 2001 (Ginsberg, 2002; Parks, 2002).

Why would respected, competent news organizations reduce their commitment to international news? "To save

...people bound by little more than an interest in ...ntent?

...iring numerous or large media outlets, domes... of reaching an increasingly fragmented audience ...ow. Selling more advertising on existing and new ...ditional ways to combine content and commer... ...mmon strategies. This leads to what media critic ... **hypercommercialism.** McChesney explained, ...trol permits the largest media firms to increas...ir output with less and less fear of consumer

"Media Echoes" boxes demonstrate that the cultural and social debates surrounding the different media tend to be repeated throughout history regardless of the technology or era in question.

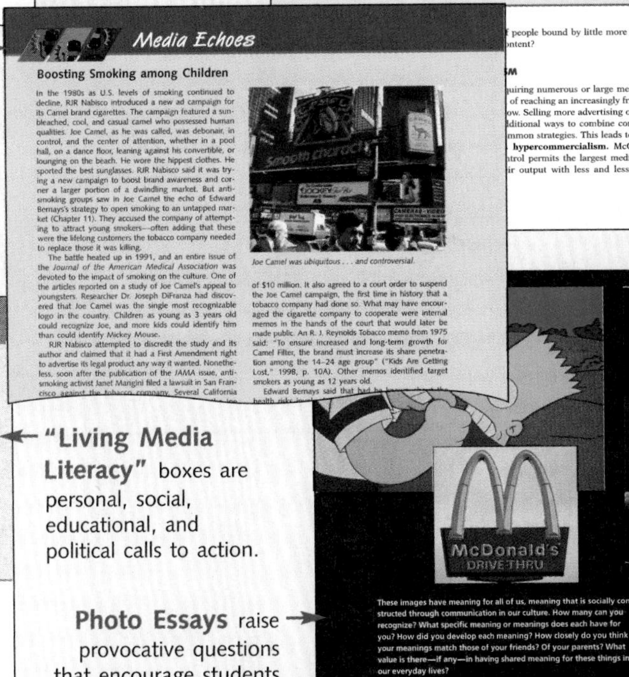

Media Echoes

Boosting Smoking among Children

In the 1980s as U.S. levels of smoking continued to decline, RJR Nabisco introduced a new ad campaign for its Camel brand cigarettes. The campaign featured a sun-bleached, cool, and casual camel who possessed human qualities: Joe Camel, as he was called, was debonair, in control, and the center of attention, whether in a pool hall, on a dance floor, leaning against his convertible, or lounging on the beach. He wore the hippest clothes. He sported the best sunglasses. RJR Nabisco said it was trying a new campaign to boost brand awareness and corner a larger portion of a dwindling market. But anti-smoking groups saw in Joe Camel the echo of Edward Bernays's strategy to open smoking to an untapped market (Chapter 11). They accused the company of attempting to attract young smokers—often adding that these were the lifelong customers the tobacco company needed to replace those it was killing.

The battle heated up in 1991, and an entire issue of the *Journal of the American Medical Association* was devoted to the impact of smoking on the culture. One of the articles reported on a study of Joe Camel's appeal to youngsters. Researcher Dr. Joseph DiFranza had discovered that Joe Camel was the single most recognizable logo in the country. Children as young as 3 years old could recognize Joe, and more kids could identify him than could identify Mickey Mouse.

RJR Nabisco attempted to discredit the study and its author and claimed that it had a First Amendment right to advertise its legal product any way it wanted. Nonetheless, soon after the publication of the *JAMA* issue, anti-smoking activist Janet Mangini filed a lawsuit in San Francisco against the tobacco company. Several California

Joe Camel was ubiquitous . . . and controversial.

of $10 million. It also agreed to a court order to suspend the Joe Camel campaign, the first time in history that a tobacco company had done so. What may have encouraged the cigarette company to cooperate were internal memos in the hands of the court that would later be made public. An R. J. Reynolds Tobacco memo from 1975 said: "To ensure increased and long-term growth for Camel Filter, the brand must increase its share penetration among the 14–24 age group" ("Kids Are Getting Lost," 1998, p. 10A). Other memos identified target smokers as young as 12 years old.

Edward Bernays said that had he...

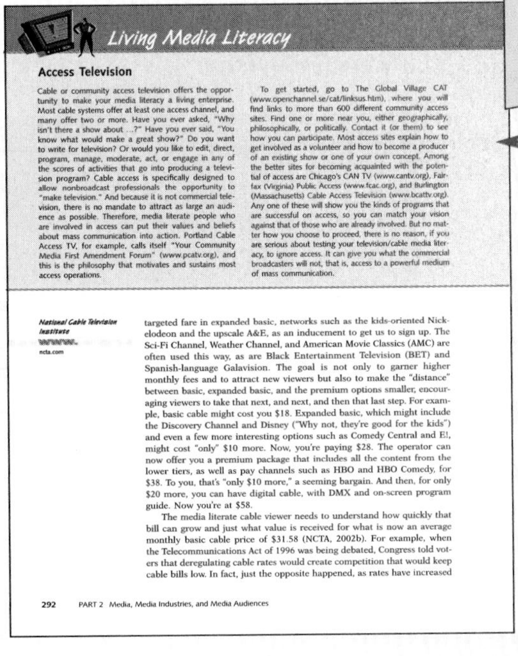

Living Media Literacy

Access Television

Cable or community access television offers the opportunity to make your media literacy a living enterprise. Most cable systems offer at least one access channel, and many offer two or more. Have you ever asked, "Why isn't there a show about . . .?" Have you ever said, "You know what would make a great show?" Do you want to write for television? Or would you like to edit, direct, program, manage, moderate, act, or engage in any of the scores of activities that go into producing a television program? Cable access is specifically designed to allow nonbroadcast professionals the opportunity to "make television." And because it is not commercial television, there is no mandate to attract as large an audience as possible. Therefore, media literate people who are involved in access can put their values and beliefs about mass communication into action. Portland Cable Access TV, for example, calls itself "Your Community Media First Amendment Forum" (www.pcatv.org), and this is the philosophy that motivates and sustains most access operations.

To get started, go to The Global Village CAT (www.openchannel.se/cat/linksus.htm), where you will find links to more than 600 different community access sites. Find one or more near you, either geographically, philosophically, or politically. Contact it (or them) to see how you can participate. Most access sites explain how to get involved as a volunteer and how to become a producer of an existing show or one of your own concept. Among the better sites for becoming acquainted with the potential of access are Chicago's CAN TV (www.cantv.org), Fairfax (Virginia) Public Access (www.fcac.org), and Burlington (Massachusetts) Cable Access Television (www.bcattv.org). Any one of these will show you the kinds of programs that are successful on access, so you can match your vision against that of those who are already involved. But no matter how you choose to proceed, there is no reason, if you are serious about testing your television/cable media literacy, to ignore access. It can give you what the commercial broadcasters will not, that is, access to a powerful medium of mass communication.

National Cable Television Institute
www.
ncta.com

targeted fare in expanded basic, networks such as the kids-oriented Nickelodeon and the upscale A&E, as an inducement to get us to sign up. The Sci-Fi Channel, Weather Channel, and American Movie Classics (AMC) are often used this way, as are Black Entertainment Television (BET) and Spanish-language Galavision. The goal is not only to garner higher monthly fees and to attract new viewers but also to make the "distance" between basic, expanded basic, and the premium options smaller, encouraging viewers to take that next, and next, and then that last step. For example, basic cable might cost you $18. Expanded basic, which might include the Discovery Channel and Disney ("Why not, they're good for the kids") and even a few more interesting options such as Comedy Central and E!, might cost "only" $10 more. Now, you're paying $28. The operator can now offer you a premium package that includes all the content from the lower tiers, as well as pay channels such as HBO and HBO Comedy, for $38. To you, that's "only $10 more," a seeming bargain. And then, for only $20 more, you can have digital cable, with DMX and on-screen program guide. Now you're at $58.

The media literate cable viewer needs to understand how quickly that bill can grow and just what value is received for what is now an average monthly basic cable price of $31.58 (NCTA, 2002b). For example, when the Telecommunications Act of 1996 was being debated, Congress told voters that deregulating cable rates would create competition that would keep cable bills low. In fact, just the opposite happened, as rates have increased

292 PART 2 Media, Media Industries, and Media Audiences

"Living Media Literacy" boxes are personal, social, educational, and political calls to action.

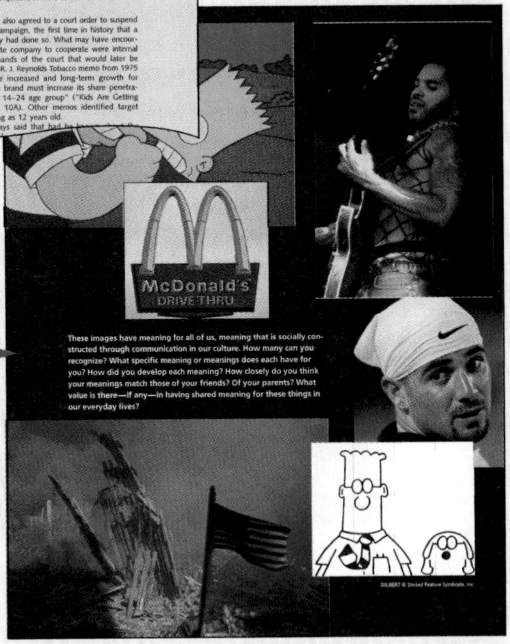

These images have meaning for all of us, meaning that is socially constructed through communication in our culture. How many can you recognize? What specific meaning or meanings does each have for you? How did you develop each meaning? How closely do you think your meanings match those of your friends? Of your parents? What value is there—if any—in having shared meaning for these things in our everyday lives?

DILBERT © United Feature Syndicate, Inc.

Photo Essays raise provocative questions that encourage students to develop their critical thinking and analytical skills.

New Videos! McGraw-Hill's unique *Media Tours: An Inside Look at the Mass Media* and *NBC: News Archives* and *The Today Show* feature brief clips that bring to life the concepts discussed in the text. They are available on the student CD-ROM and in VHS format. CD icons in the text margins direct students to the appropriate video clips.

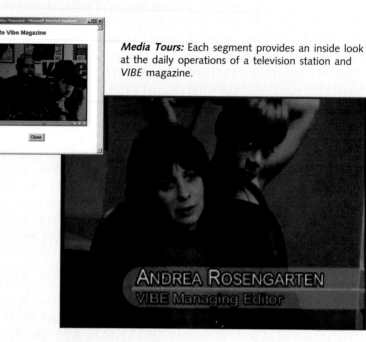

Media Tours: Each segment provides an inside look at the daily operations of a television station and *VIBE* magazine.

Clips from *NBC News* and *The Today Show* serve as lecture launchers and generate class discussion.

Future Television

PART one

Laying the Groundwork

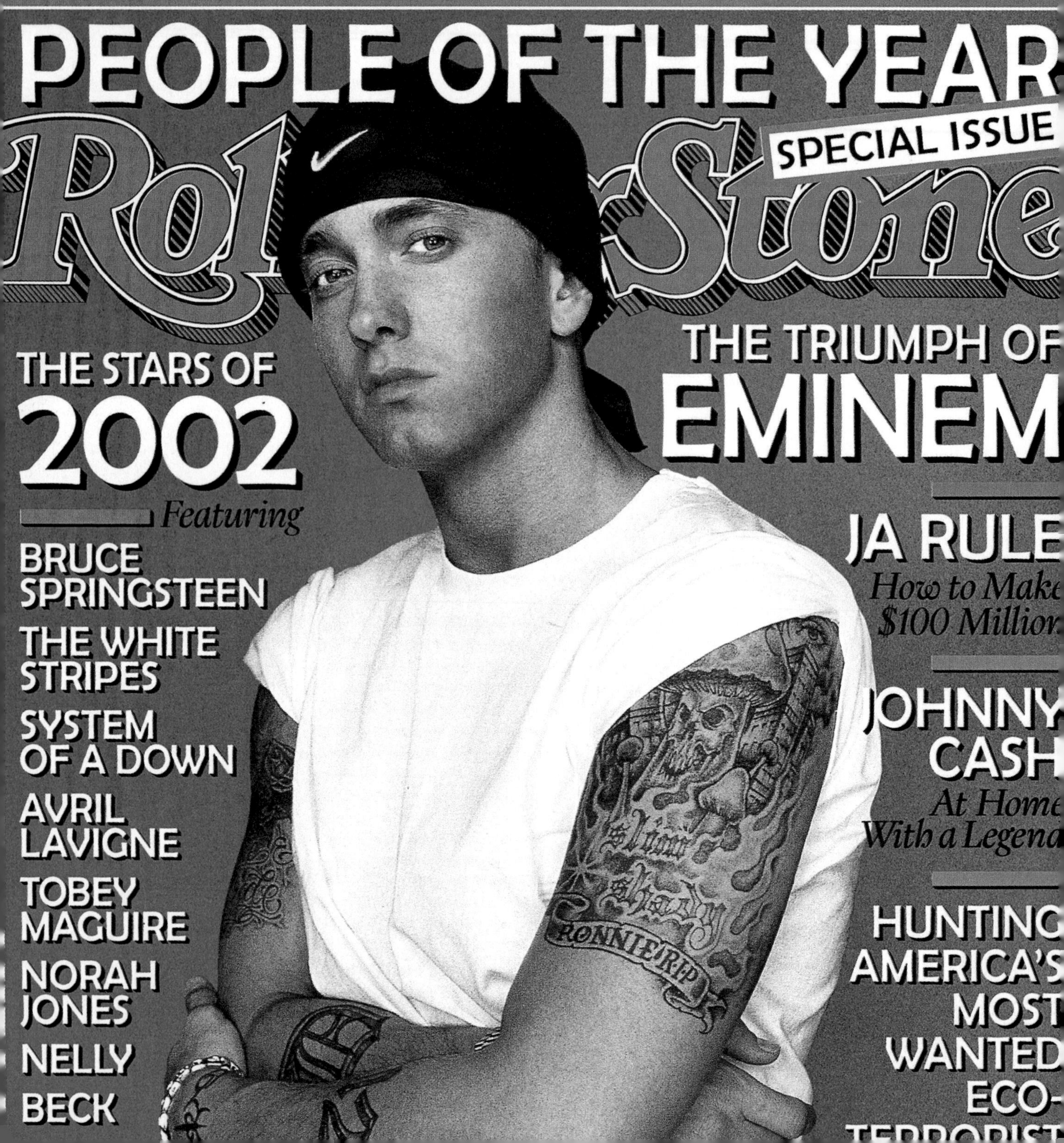

CHAPTER 1

PEOPLE OF THE YEAR

Rolling Stone

SPECIAL ISSUE

THE STARS OF
2002
Featuring

BRUCE
SPRINGSTEEN

THE WHITE
STRIPES

SYSTEM
OF A DOWN

AVRIL
LAVIGNE

TOBEY
MAGUIRE

NORAH
JONES

NELLY

BECK

THE TRIUMPH OF
EMINEM

JA RULE
*How to Make
$100 Million*

JOHNNY
CASH
*At Home
With a Legend*

HUNTING
AMERICA'S
MOST
WANTED
ECO
TERRORIST

Mass Communication, Culture, and Mass Media

LEARNING OBJECTIVES

Mass communication, mass media, and the culture that shapes us (and that we shape) are inseparable. After studying this chapter you should

- know the definitions of communication, mass communication, mass media, and culture.

- understand the relationships among communication, mass communication, culture, and those who live it.

- have a basis for evaluating the impact of technology and economics on those relationships.

- be aware of the scope and nature of the different mass media industries.

- have a broad overview of current trends in mass communication, especially concentration of ownership and conglomeration, globalization, audience fragmentation, hypercommercialism, and convergence.

THE CLOCK RADIO JARS YOU AWAKE. IT'S THE DAVE Matthews Band, the last few bars of "I Did It." The laughing deejay shouts at you that it's 7:41 and you'd better get going. But before you do, he adds, listen to a few words from your friends at Fry's Electronics, home of fast, friendly, courteous service—"We will beat any competitive price!"

In the living room, you find your roommate has left the television on. You stop for a moment and listen: The Supreme Court has refused to hear an affirmative action appeal, your U.S. representative is under investigation for sexual harassment, and you deserve a break today at McDonald's. As you head toward the bathroom, your bare feet slip on some magazines littering the floor—*Wired, Rolling Stone, Newsweek.* You need to talk to your roommate about picking up!

After showering, you quickly pull on your Levi's, lace up your Nike cross-trainers, and throw on a FUBU pullover. No time for breakfast; you grab a Nature Valley granola bar and the newspaper and head for the bus stop. As the bus rolls up, you can't help but notice the giant ad on its side: *Die Hard IX—Kill Before You're Killed.* Rejecting that as a movie choice for the weekend, you sit down next to a teenager listening to music on his headphones and playing a video game. You bury yourself in the paper, scanning the lead stories and the local news and then checking out *Doonesbury* and *Dilbert*.

Hopping off the bus at the campus stop, you run into Chris from your computer lab. You walk to class together, talking about last night's *Simpsons* episode.

It's not yet 9:00, and already you're awash in media messages.

In this chapter we define communication, interpersonal communication, mass communication, media, and culture and explore the relationships among them and how they define us and our world. We investigate how communication works, how it changes when technology is introduced into the process, and how differing views of communication and mass communication can lead to different interpretations of their power. We also discuss the opportunities mass communication and culture offer us and the responsibilities that come with those opportunities. Always crucial, these issues are of particular importance now, when we find ourselves in a period of remarkable development in new communication technologies.

Finally, we discuss the changing nature of contemporary mass communication and its implications for both communication industries and media consumers.

What Is Mass Communication?

More on McLuhan
WWW.
mcluhan.ca/

"Does a fish know it's wet?" influential cultural and media critic Marshall McLuhan would often ask. The answer, he would say, is "No." The fish's existence is so dominated by water that only when water is absent is the fish aware of its condition.

So it is with people and mass media. The media so fully saturate our everyday lives that we are often unconscious of their presence, not to mention their influence. Media inform us, entertain us, delight us, annoy us. They move our emotions, challenge our intellects, insult our intelligence. Media often reduce us to mere commodities for sale to the highest bidder. Media help define us; they shape our realities.

A fundamental theme of this book is that media do none of this alone. They do it *with* us as well as *to* us through mass communication, and they do it as a central—many critics and scholars say *the* central—cultural force in our society.

COMMUNICATION DEFINED

In its simplest form **communication** is the transmission of a message from a source to a receiver. For nearly 60 years now, this view of communication has been identified with the writing of political scientist

Harold Lasswell (1948). He said that a convenient way to describe communication is to answer these questions:

- *Who?*
- Says *what?*
- Through *which* channel?
- To *whom?*
- With *what effect?*

Expressed in terms of the basic elements of the communication process, communication occurs when:

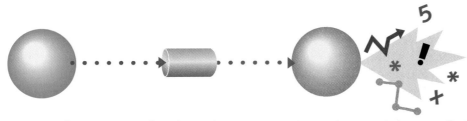

A source sends a message   through a medium   to a receiver   producing some effect

Straightforward enough, but what if the source is a professor who insists on speaking in a technical language far beyond the receiving students' level of skill? Obviously, communication does not occur. Unlike mere message-sending, communication requires the response of others. Therefore, there must be a *sharing* (or correspondence) of meaning for communication to take place.

A second problem with this simple model is that it suggests that the receiver passively accepts the source's message. However, if our imaginary students do not comprehend the professor's words, they respond with "Huh?" or look confused or yawn. This response, or **feedback,** is also a message. The receivers (the students) now become a source, sending their own message to the source (the offending professor), who is now a receiver. Hence, communication is a *reciprocal* and *ongoing process* with all involved parties more or less engaged in creating shared meaning. Communication, then, is better defined as *the process of creating shared meaning.*

Communication researcher Wilbur Schramm, using ideas originally developed by psychologist Charles E. Osgood, developed a graphic way to represent the reciprocal nature of communication (Figure 1.1, p. 6). This depiction of **interpersonal communication**—communication between two or a few people—shows that there is no clearly identifiable source or receiver. Rather, because communication is an ongoing and reciprocal process, all the participants, or "interpreters," are working to create meaning by *encoding* and *decoding* messages. A message is first **encoded,** that is, transformed into an understandable sign and symbol system. Speaking is encoding, as are writing, printing, and filming a television program. Once received, the message is **decoded;** that is, the signs and symbols are

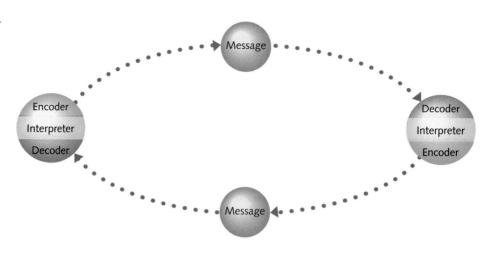

Figure 1.1 Osgood and Schramm's Model of Communication. *Source:* From *The Process and Effects of Mass Communication.* Copyright © 1954 by the Board of Trustees of the University of Illinois. Used with the permission of the University of Illinois Press.

interpreted. Decoding occurs through listening, reading, or watching that television show.

The Osgood-Schramm model demonstrates the ongoing and reciprocal nature of the communication process. There is, therefore, no source, no receiver, and no feedback. The reason is that, as communication is happening, both interpreters are simultaneously source and receiver. There is no feedback because all messages are presumed to be in reciprocation of other messages. Even when your friend starts a conversation with you, for example, it can be argued that it was your look of interest and willingness that communicated to her that she should speak. In this example, it is improper to label either you or your friend as the source—Who really initiated this chat?—and, therefore, it is impossible to identify who is providing feedback to whom.

Not every model can show all aspects of a process as complex as communication. Missing from this representation is **noise**—anything that interferes with successful communication. Noise is more than screeching or loud music when you are trying to read. Biases that lead to incorrect decoding, for example, are noise, as is newsprint that bleeds through from page 1 to page 2.

Encoded messages are carried by a **medium,** that is, the means of sending information. Sound waves are the medium that carries our voice to friends across the table; the telephone is the medium that carries our voice to friends across town. When the medium is a technology that carries messages to a large number of people—as newspapers carry the printed word and radio conveys the sound of music and news—we call it a **mass medium** (the plural of medium is **media**). The mass media we use regularly include radio, television, books, magazines, newspapers, movies, sound recordings, and computer networks. Each medium is the basis of a giant industry, but other related and supporting industries also serve them and us—advertising and public relations, for example. In our culture we use the words *media* and *mass media* interchangeably to refer to the communication industries themselves. We say, "The media entertain" or "The mass media are too conservative (or too liberal)."

MASS COMMUNICATION DEFINED

We speak, too, of mass communication. **Mass communication** is the process of creating shared meaning between the mass media and their audiences. Schramm recast his and Osgood's general model of communication to help us visualize the particular aspects of the mass communication process (Figure 1.2). This model and the original Osgood and Schramm scheme have much in common—interpreters, encoding, decoding, and messages—but it is their differences that are most significant for our understanding of how mass communication differs from other forms of communication. For example, whereas the original model includes "message," the mass communication model offers "many identical messages." Additionally, the mass communication model specifies "feedback," whereas the interpersonal communication model does not. When two or a few people communicate face-to-face, the participants can immediately and clearly recognize the feedback residing in the reciprocal messages (our boring professor can see and hear the students' disenchantment as they listen to the lecture). Things are not nearly as simple in mass communication.

In Schramm's mass communication model, feedback is represented by a dotted line labeled delayed **inferential feedback.** This feedback is indirect rather than direct. Television executives, for example, must wait a day, at the very minimum, and sometimes a week or a month, to discover the ratings for new programs. Even then, the ratings only measure how many sets are tuned in, not whether people liked or disliked the programs. As a result, these executives can only infer what they must do to improve programming; hence the term *inferential feedback.* Mass communicators are also subject to additional feedback, usually in the form of criticism in other media, such as a television critic writing a column in a newspaper.

TV Critics Assn.
www.
tvcritics.org/

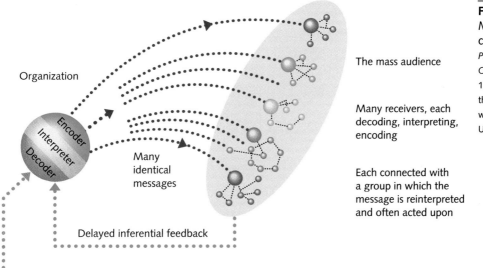

Organization

Encoder
Interpreter
Decoder

Many
identical
messages

The mass audience

Many receivers, each
decoding, interpreting,
encoding

Each connected with
a group in which the
message is reinterpreted
and often acted upon

Delayed inferential feedback

Input from news sources, art sources, etc.

Figure 1.2 Schramm's Model of Mass Communication. *Source:* From *The Process and Effects of Mass Communication.* Copyright © 1954 by the Board of Trustees of the University of Illinois. Used with the permission of the University of Illinois Press.

	Interpersonal Communication You invite a friend to lunch.		**Mass Communication** David E. Kelley produces *The Practice*	
	Nature	**Consequences**	**Nature**	**Consequences**
Message	Highly flexible and alterable	You can change it in midstream. If feedback is negative, you can offer an alternative. Is feedback still negative? Take a whole new approach.	Identical, mechanically produced, simultaneously sent Inflexible, unalterable The completed *The Practice* episode that is aired.	Once production is completed, *The Practice* cannot be changed. If a plot line or other communicative device isn't working with the audience, nothing can be done.
Interpreter A	One person—in this case, you	You know your mind. You can encode your own message to suit yourself, your values, your likes and dislikes.	A large, hierarchically structured organization—in this case, David E. Kelley Productions and the ABC television network	Who really is Interpreter A? David E. Kelley? The writers? The director? The actors? The network and its standards and practices people? The sponsors? All must agree, leaving little room for individual vision or experimentation.
Interpreter B	One or a few people, usually in direct contact with you and, to a greater or lesser degree, known to you—in this case, Chris	You can tailor your message specifically to Interpreter B. You can make relatively accurate judgments about B because of information present in the setting. Chris is a vegetarian; you don't suggest a steak house.	A large, heterogeneous audience known to Interpreter A only in the most rudimentary way, little more than basic demographics—in this case, several million viewers of *The Practice*	Communication cannot be tailored to the wants, needs, and tastes of all audience members or even those of all members of some subgroup. Some more or less generally acceptable standard is set.
Feedback	Immediate and direct yes or no response	You know how successful your message is immediately. You can adjust your communication on the spot to maximize its effectiveness.	Delayed and inferential Even overnight ratings too late for this episode of *The Practice* Moreover, ratings limited to telling the number of sets tuned in	Even if the feedback is useful, it is too late to be of value for this episode. In addition, it doesn't suggest how to improve the communication effort.
Result	Flexible, personally relevant, possibly adventurous, challenging, or experimental		Constrained by virtually every aspect of the communication situation A level of communication most likely to meet the greatest number of viewers' needs A belief that experimentation is dangerous A belief that to challenge the audience is to risk failure	

Figure 1.3 Elements of Interpersonal Communication and Mass Communication Compared.

The differences between the individual elements of interpersonal and mass communication change the very nature of the communication process. How those alterations influence the message itself and how the likelihood of successfully sharing meaning varies are shown in Figure 1.3. For example, the immediacy and directness of feedback in interpersonal communication free communicators to gamble, to experiment with different approaches. Their knowledge of one another enables them to tailor their messages as narrowly as they wish. As a result, interpersonal communication is often personally relevant and possibly even adventurous and challenging. In contrast, the distance between participants in the mass communication process, imposed by the technology, creates a sort of "communication conservatism." Feedback comes too late to enable corrections or alterations in communication that fails. The sheer number of people in many mass communication audiences makes personalization and specificity difficult. As a result, mass communication tends to be more constrained, less free. This does not mean, however, that it is less potent than interpersonal communication in shaping our understanding of ourselves and our world.

Media theorist James W. Carey (1975) recognized this and offered a **cultural definition of communication** that has had a profound impact on the way communication scientists and others have viewed the relationship between communication and culture. Carey wrote, *"Communication is a symbolic process whereby reality is produced, maintained, repaired and transformed"* (p. 10).

Carey's definition asserts that communication and reality are linked. Communication is a process embedded in our everyday lives that informs the way we perceive, understand, and construct our view of reality and the world. Communication is the foundation of our culture.

What Is Culture?

Culture is the learned behavior of members of a given social group. Many writers and thinkers have offered interesting expansions of this definition. Here are four examples, the first three from anthropologists, the last from a performing arts critic. These definitions highlight not only what culture *is* but also what culture *does*:

Culture is the learned, socially acquired traditions and lifestyles of the members of a society, including their patterned, repetitive ways of thinking, feeling and acting. (M. Harris, 1983, p. 5)

Culture lends significance to human experience by selecting from and organizing it. It refers broadly to the forms through which people make sense of their lives, rather than more narrowly to the opera or art of museums. (R. Rosaldo, 1989, p. 26)

Culture is the medium evolved by humans to survive. Nothing is free from cultural influences. It is the keystone in civilization's arch and is the medium through which all of life's events must flow. We are culture. (E. T. Hall, 1976, p. 14)

Culture is an historically transmitted pattern of meanings embodied in symbolic forms by means of which [people] communicate, perpetuate, and develop their knowledge about and attitudes toward life. (C. Geertz, as cited in Taylor, 1991, p. 91)

CULTURE AS SOCIALLY CONSTRUCTED SHARED MEANING

Virtually all definitions of culture recognize that culture is *learned*. Recall the opening vignette. Even if this scenario does not exactly match your early mornings, you probably recognize its elements. Moreover, all of us are familiar with most, if not every, cultural reference in it. *The Simpsons*, *Rolling Stone*, McDonald's, Nike, *Dilbert*, the Dave Matthews Band—all are points of reference, things that have some meaning for all of us. How did this come to be?

Creation and maintenance of a more or less common culture occurs through communication, including mass communication. When we talk to our friends; when a parent raises a child; when religious leaders instruct their followers; when teachers teach; when grandparents pass on recipes; when politicians campaign; when media professionals produce content that we read, listen to, and watch, meaning is being shared and culture is being constructed and maintained.

FUNCTIONS AND EFFECTS OF CULTURE

Culture serves a purpose. It helps us categorize and classify our experiences; it helps define us, our world, and our place in it. In doing so, culture can have a number of sometimes conflicting effects.

Limiting and Liberating Effects of Culture   A culture's learned traditions and values can be seen as patterned, repetitive ways of thinking, feeling, and acting. Culture limits our options and provides useful guidelines for behavior. For example, when conversing, you do not consciously consider, "Now, how far away should I stand? Am I too close?" You just stand where you stand. After a hearty meal with a friend's family, you do not engage in mental self-debate, "Should I burp? Yes! No! Arghhhh. . . ." Culture provides information that helps us make meaningful distinctions about right and wrong, appropriate and inappropriate, good and bad, attractive and unattractive, and so on. How does it do this?

Obviously, through communication. Through a lifetime of communication we have learned just what our culture expects of us. The two examples given here are positive results of culture's limiting effects. But culture's limiting effects can be negative, such as when we are unwilling or unable to move past patterned, repetitive ways of thinking, feeling, and acting, or when we entrust our "learning" to teachers whose interests are selfish, narrow, or otherwise not consistent with our own.

These images have meaning for all of us, meaning that is socially constructed through communication in our culture. How many can you recognize? What specific meaning or meanings does each have for you? How did you develop each meaning? How closely do you think your meanings match those of your friends? Of your parents? What value is there—if any—in having shared meaning for these things in our everyday lives?

DILBERT © United Feature Syndicate, Inc.

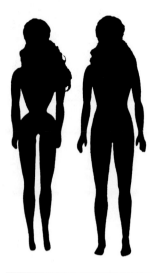

The Barbie doll (*left*) represents an unattainable ideal for American girls. In 1991, a rival, the Happy to Be Me doll (*right*), appeared on the scene. Happy's creator wanted to present a more realistic image to young, impressionable minds. Do you think the American public was ready for Happy?

U.S. culture, for example, values thinness in women. How many women endure weeks of unhealthy diets and succumb to potentially dangerous surgical procedures in search of a body that for most is physically unattainable? How many men (and other women) never get to know, like, or even love those women who cannot meet our culture's standards of thinness and beauty? Why are 81% of all 10-year-old girls "afraid of being fat," and why do 42% of girls in grades 1 to 3 "want to be thinner"? (Kirk, 2003, p. 9)

Now consider how this situation may have come about. Our mothers did not bounce us on their knees when we were babies, telling us that thin was good and fat was bad. Think back, though, to the stories you were told and the television shows and movies you watched growing up. The heroines (or, more often, the beautiful love interests of the heroes) were invariably tall and thin. The bad guys were usually mean and fat. From Disney's depictions of Snow White, Cinderella, Beauty, Tinker Bell, and Pocahontas to the impossible dimensions of Barbie, the message is embedded in the conscious (and unconscious) mind of every girl and boy. Thin is in! In a recent reversal—either because it tired of the controversy or because it finally understood its possibly negative contribution to young girls' self-concept—Mattel, Barbie's manufacturer, announced in 1997 that it would henceforth give the doll more realistic body proportions.

This message—thin is in—and millions of others come to us primarily through the media, and although the people who produce these media images are not necessarily selfish or mean, their motives are undeniably financial. Their contribution to our culture's repetitive ways of thinking, feeling, and acting is most certainly not primary among their concerns when preparing their communication.

Culture need not only limit. That media representations of female beauty often meet with debate and disagreement points up the fact that culture can be liberating as well. This is so because cultural values can be contested.

Especially in a pluralistic, democratic society such as ours, the **dominant culture** (sometimes **mainstream culture**)—the one that seems to hold sway with the majority of people—is often openly challenged. People do meet, find attractive, like, and even love people who do not fit the standard image of beauty. Additionally, media sometimes present images that suggest different ideals of beauty and success. Actress Janeane Garofalo; television star Camryn Manheim; singer/actress Jennifer Lopez; talk show host and influential broadcasting executive Oprah Winfrey; and singer-actress Bette Midler all represent alternatives to our culture's idealized standards of beauty, and all have undeniable appeal (and power) on the big and small screens. Liberation from the limitations imposed by culture resides in our ability and willingness to learn and use *new* patterned, repetitive ways of thinking, feeling, and acting; to challenge existing patterns; and to create our own.

Defining, Differentiating, Dividing, and Uniting Effects of Culture Have you ever made the mistake of calling a dolphin, porpoise, or even a whale a fish? Maybe you have heard others do it. This error occurs because when

Camryn Manheim of *The Practice*, Oprah Winfrey, and Jennifer Lopez are prominent women whose presentation in the media suggests different cultural ideals of beauty and success. Each represents an alternative to our culture's idealized standards of beauty. How attractive do you find each woman to be? What is it about each that appeals to you?

we think of fish we think, "lives in the water" and "swims." Fish are defined by their "aquatic culture." Because water-residing, swimming dolphins and porpoises share that culture, we sometimes forget that they are mammals, not fish.

We, too, are defined by our culture. We are citizens of the United States; we are Americans. If we travel to other countries, we will hear ourselves labeled "American," and this label will conjure up stereotypes and expectations in the minds of those who use and hear it. The stereotype, whatever it may be, will probably fit us only incompletely, or perhaps hardly at all—perhaps we are dolphins in a sea full of fish. Nevertheless, being American defines us in innumerable important ways, both to others (more obviously) and to ourselves (less obviously).

Within this large, national culture, however, there are many smaller, **bounded cultures** (sometimes **co-cultures**). For example, we speak comfortably of Italian neighborhoods, fraternity row, the South, and the suburbs. Because of our cultural understanding of these categories, each expression communicates something about our expectations of these places. We think we can predict with a good deal of certainty the types of restaurants and shops we will find in the Italian neighborhood, even the kind of music we will hear escaping from open windows. We can predict the kinds of clothes and cars we will see on fraternity row, the likely behavior of shop clerks in the South, and the political orientation of the suburb's residents.

Friends, JAG, and *Sabrina the Teenage Witch*—these three television programs are aimed at different audiences, yet in each the characters share certain traits that mark them as attractive. Must people in real life look like these performers to be considered attractive? Successful? Good? The 12 people shown are all slender, tall, and young. Yes, they are just make-believe television characters, but the producers of the shows on which they appear chose these people—as opposed to others—for a reason. What do you think it was? How well do you measure up to the cultural standard of beauty and attractiveness represented here? Do you ever wish that you could be just a bit more like these people? Why or why not?

What is it about these Muslim-Americans that "communicated disloyalty" to the U.S. in the wake of the September 11, 2001, terrorist attacks on New York and Washington?

Moreover, the people within these cultures usually identify themselves as members of those bounded cultures. An individual may say, for example, "I am Italian American" or "I'm from the South." These smaller cultures unite groups of people and enable them to see themselves as different from other groups around them. Thus culture also serves to differentiate us from others.

In the United States, we generally consider this a good thing. We pride ourselves on our pluralism and our diversity and on the richness of the cultural heritages represented within our borders. We enjoy moving from one bounded culture to another or from a bounded culture to the dominant national culture and back again.

Problems arise, however, when differentiation leads to division. All Americans were traumatized by the horrific events of September 11, 2001, but that tragedy was compounded for Muslim Americans who had their patriotism challenged simply because of membership in their particular bounded culture. The Arab-American Anti-Discrimination Committee reported more than 500 post–9/11 incidents of threats, beatings, arsons, shootings, and at least six murders (Levitas, 2002). For these good Americans, regardless of what was in their hearts or minds, their religion, skin color, maybe even their clothing "communicated" disloyalty to the United States to many other Americans. Just as culture is constructed and maintained through communication, it is also communication (or miscommunication) that turns differentiation into division.

Yet, U.S. citizens of all colors, ethnicities, genders and gender preferences, nationalities, places of birth, economic strata, and intelligences often get along; in fact, we *can* communicate, *can* prosper, *can* respect one another's differences. Culture can divide us, but culture also unites us. Our culture represents our collective experience. We converse easily with strangers because we share the same culture. We speak the same language, automatically understand how far apart to stand, appropriately use titles or first or last names, know how much to say, and know how much to leave unsaid. Through communication with people in our culture, we internalize cultural norms and values—those things that bind our many diverse bounded cultures into a functioning, cohesive society.

Defining Culture   From this discussion of culture comes the definition of culture on which the remainder of this book is based:

> Culture is the world made meaningful; it is socially constructed and maintained through communication. It limits as well as liberates us; it differentiates as well as unites us. It defines our realities and thereby shapes the ways we think, feel, and act.

Mass Communication and Culture

Culture defines our realities, but who contributes to the construction and maintenance of culture? Because culture is constructed and maintained through communication, it is in communication that cultural power resides. And because mass media are such a significant part of the modern world, more and more attention is being paid to the interaction between mass communication and culture.

EXAMINING MASS COMMUNICATION AND CULTURE

Since the introduction of the first mass circulation newspapers in the 1830s, media theorists and social critics have argued about the importance and power of the media industries and mass communication. In their most general form, these debates have been shaped by three closely related dichotomies.

Micro- Versus Macro-Level Effects   People are concerned about the effects of media. Does television cause violence? Do beer ads cause increased alcohol consumption? Does pornography cause rape? The difficulty here is with the word *cause*. Although there is much scientific evidence that media cause many behaviors, there is also much evidence that they do not.

As long as we debate the effects of media only on individuals, we remain blind to media's greatest influences (both positive and negative) on the way we live. For example, when the shootings at Littleton, Colorado's Columbine High School in 1999 once again brought public debate on the issue of media effects, USA Network copresident Steve Brenner was forced to defend his industry. "Every American has seen hundreds of films, hundreds of news stories, hundreds of depictions, thousands of cartoons," he said, "Millions don't go out and shoot people" (as quoted in Albiniak, 1999, p. 8).

Who can argue with this? For most people, media have relatively few *direct* effects at the personal or **micro level.** But we live in a culture in

which people *have* shot people or are willing to use violence to settle disputes, at least in part because of the cultural messages embedded in our media fare. The hidden, but much more important, impact of media operates at the cultural or **macro level.** Violence on television contributes to the cultural climate in which real-world violence becomes more acceptable. Sure, perhaps none of us have gone out and shot people. But do you have bars on the windows of your home? Are there parts of town where you would rather not walk alone? Do you vote for the "tough on crime" candidate over the "education" candidate?

The micro-level view is that televised violence has little impact because most people are not directly affected. The macro-level view is that televised violence has a great impact because it influences the cultural climate.

Administrative Versus Critical Research   **Administrative research** asks questions about the immediate, observable influence of mass communication. Does a commercial campaign sell more cereal? Does an expanded Living Section increase newspaper circulation? Did *Mortal Kombat* inspire the killings at Columbine High School? For decades the only proofs of media effects that science (and therefore the media industries, regulators, and audiences) would accept were those with direct, observable, immediate

What are the effects of televised violence? The debate swirls as different people mean different things by "effects." This violent scene is from *Oz*.

Read about Lazarsfeld
www.
Columbia.edu/cu/news/01/10/
lazarsfeld.html

effects. Sixty years ago, however, Paul Lazarsfeld, the "Father of Social Science Research" and possibly the most important mass communication researcher of all time, warned of the danger of this narrow view. He believed **critical research**—asking larger questions about what kind of nation we are building, what kind of people we are becoming—would serve our culture better. Writing long before the influence of television and information access through the World Wide Web, he stated:

> Today we live in an environment where skyscrapers shoot up and elevateds (commuter trains) disappear overnight; where news comes like shock every few hours; where continually new news programs keep us from ever finding out details of previous news; and where nature is something we drive past in our cars, perceiving a few quickly changing flashes which turn the majesty of a mountain range into the impression of a motion picture. Might it not be that we do not build up experiences the way it was possible decades ago . . . ? (1941, p. 12)

Administrative research concerns itself with direct causes and effects; critical research looks at larger, possibly more significant cultural questions. As Figure 1.4 shows, cartoon character Calvin understands the distinction well.

Transmissional Versus Ritual Perspective Last is the debate that led Professor Carey to articulate his cultural definition of communication. The **transmissional perspective** sees media as senders of information for the purpose of control; that is, media either have effects on our behavior or they do not. The **ritual perspective,** Carey wrote, views media not as a means of transmitting "messages in space" but as central to "the maintenance of society in time." Mass communication is "not the act of imparting information but the representation of shared beliefs" (1975, p. 6). In other words, the ritual perspective is necessary to understand the *cultural* importance of mass communication.

Consider an ad for Skyy malt beverage. What message is being transmitted? Buy Skyy, of course. So people either do or do not buy Skyy. The message either controls or does not control people's alcohol-buying behavior. That is the transmissional perspective. But what is happening culturally in that ad? What reality about alcohol and socializing is shared? Can young people really have fun in social settings without alcohol? What constitutes a good-looking man or woman? What does success look like

More on Carey
www.
65.107.211.206/Post/Poldiscourse/2views.html

in the United States? The ritual perspective illuminates these messages—the culturally important content of the ad.

MASS COMMUNICATION OPPORTUNITIES AND RESPONSIBILITIES

Because culture can limit and divide or liberate and unite, it offers us infinite opportunities to use communication for good—if we choose to do so. Carey wrote,

> Because we have looked at each new advance in communication technology as opportunities for politics and economics, we have devoted them, almost exclusively, to government and trade. We have rarely seen them as opportunities to expand [our] powers to learn and exchange ideas and experience. (1975, pp. 20–21)

Who are "we" in this quote? *We* are everyone involved in creating and maintaining the culture that defines us. *We* are the people involved in mass media industries and the people who compose their audiences. Together we allow mass communication not only to occur but also to contribute to the creation and maintenance of culture.

Everyone involved has an obligation to participate responsibly. For people working in the media industries, this means professionally and ethically creating and transmitting content. For audience members, it means behaving as critical and thoughtful consumers of that content. Two ways to understand our opportunities and our responsibilities in the mass communication process are to view the mass **media as our cultural storytellers** and to conceptualize **mass communication as a cultural forum.**

The transmissional message in this liquor ad is obvious—buy Skyy. The ritual message is another thing altogether. What is it?

Mass Media as Cultural Storytellers A culture's values and beliefs reside in the stories it tells. Who are the good guys? Who are the bad guys? How many of your childhood heroines were chubby? How many good guys dressed in black? How many heroines lived happily ever after without marrying Prince Charming? Probably not very many. Our stories help define our realities, shaping the ways we think, feel, and act. Storytellers have a remarkable opportunity to shape culture (Figure 1.5, p. 20). They also have a responsibility to do so in as professional and ethical a way as possible.

At the same time, you, the audience for these stories, also have opportunities and responsibilities. You use these stories not only to be entertained but to learn

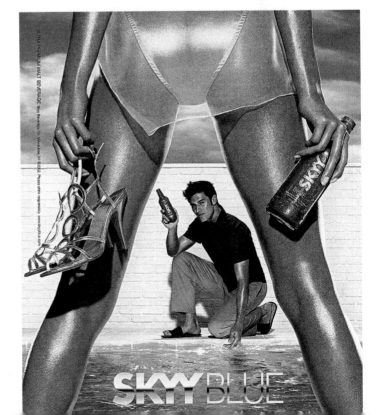

There we are, huddled around the tribal campfire, telling and retelling the stories of our people.

Figure 1.5 Storytellers play an important role in helping us define ourselves. By permission of Jerry Van Amerongen and Creators Syndicate, Inc.

about the world around you, to understand the values, the way things work, and how the pieces fit together. You have a responsibility to question the tellers and their stories, to interpret the stories in ways consistent with larger or more important cultural values and truths, to be thoughtful, to reflect on the stories' meanings and what they say about you and your culture. To do less is to miss an opportunity to construct your own meaning and, thereby, culture.

For example, the 1992 animated Disney movie, *Aladdin*, presented Arabs and Arabic culture in ways that many people found far too narrow, stereotypic, and even offensive. They demanded that the tellers (Disney) reconstruct their story. And that's just what that media giant did. When the film first appeared, the song "Arabian Nights" contained these lyrics:

Oh, I come from a land from a faraway place,
where the caravan camels roam,
where they cut off your ear if they don't like your face.
It's barbaric, but hey, it's home.

But when the movie was released on home video and DVD, these lyrics replaced the original:

Oh, I come from a land from a faraway place,
where the caravan camels roam.
Where it's flat and immense and the heat is intense.
It's barbaric, but hey, it's home.

In a cultural conversation with Disney, audiences questioned and rejected that company's animated story of a violent, inhumane people. Disney listened.

Mass Communication as Cultural Forum   Imagine a giant courtroom in which we discuss and debate our culture—what it is, and what we want it to be. What do we think about welfare? Single motherhood? Labor unions? Nursing homes? What is the meaning of "successful," "good," "loyal," "moral," "honest," "beautiful," "patriotic"? We have cultural definitions or understandings of all these things and more. Where do they come from? How do they develop, take shape, and mature?

Mass communication has become a primary forum for the debate about our culture. Logically, then, the most powerful voices in the forum have the most power to shape our definitions and understandings. Where should that power reside—with the media industries or with their audiences? If you answer "media industries," you must demand that members

When viewers complained that Disney's *Aladdin* presented a stereotypical image of Arabs and Arabic culture, Disney listened.

of these industries act professionally and ethically. If you answer "audiences," you must insist that individual audience members be thoughtful and critical of the media messages they consume. The forum is only as good, fair, and honest as those who participate in it.

Scope and Nature of Mass Media

No matter how we choose to view the process of mass communication, it is impossible to deny that an enormous portion of our lives is spent in interaction with mass media. On a typical Sunday night, 37 million people in the United States will tune in a prime-time television show. Television sets are in 98% of all our homes, VCRs in over 80%. The television set is on for more than 7½ hours a day in a typical U.S. household. Two-thirds of all U.S. adults will read a newspaper each day; two-thirds will listen to the radio for some part of every day. The World Wide Web is growing at the rate of 7.3 million pages a day ("Web Pages Grow," 2000). Ninety-eight percent of all American teens have used a computer; 32% spend at least 5 hours a week on the Net; 55% rate the Internet above the phone for communicating ("The Future of Communication," 2001). Twenty-five percent of American kids under 2 years old have a television in their room. Those 6 years old and under sit in front of a television or computer screen for nearly two hours a day (McConnell, 2003). Americans spend more on entertainment media than they do on clothes and health care. The average person spends 3,700 hours a year—65% of his or her waking hours—consuming mass media content. (Figure 1.6 on page 22 provides data on several individual media.)

Despite the pervasiveness of mass media in our lives, many of us are dissatisfied with or critical of the media industries' performance and much

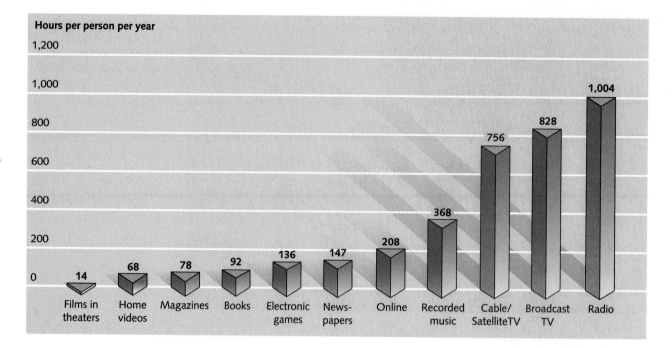

Hours per person per year

Films in theaters	14
Home videos	68
Magazines	78
Books	92
Electronic games	136
Newspapers	147
Online	208
Recorded music	368
Cable/SatelliteTV	756
Broadcast TV	828
Radio	1,004

Figure 1.6 United States Media Consumption, 2003. *Source:* U.S. Census, <www.census.gov/statab>

of the content provided. For example, in November 2001 the Gallup organization measured Americans' esteem for essential social institutions in the wake of the September 11 terrorist attacks. Its findings? Fifty-four percent of the respondents expressed disrespect for the media. Even the politicians in Congress enjoyed wider approval (Kelly, 2002, p. 18).

Our ambivalence—we criticize, yet we consume—comes in part from our uncertainties about the relationships among the elements of mass communication. What is the role of technology? What is the role of money? And what is *our* role in the mass communication process?

THE ROLE OF TECHNOLOGY

To some thinkers, it is machines and their development that drive economic and cultural change. This idea is referred to as **technological determinism.** Certainly there can be no doubt that movable type contributed to the Protestant Reformation and the decline of the Catholic Church's power in Europe or that television changed the way members of American families interact. Those who believe in technological determinism would argue that these changes in the cultural landscape were the inevitable result of new technology.

But others see technology as more neutral and claim that the way people *use* technology is what gives it significance. This perspective accepts technology as one of many factors that shape economic and cultural change; technology's influence is ultimately determined by how much power it is given by the people and cultures that use it.

This disagreement about the power of technology is at the heart of the controversy surrounding the new communication technologies. Are we more or less powerless in the wake of advances such as the Internet, the World Wide Web, and instant global audio and visual communication? If we are at the mercy of technology, the culture that surrounds us will not be of our making, and the best we can hope to do is make our way reasonably well in a world outside our own control. But if these technologies are indeed neutral and their power resides in *how* we choose to use them, we can utilize them responsibly and thoughtfully to construct and maintain whatever kind of culture we want. As film director and technophile Steven Spielberg explained, "Technology can be our best friend, and technology can also be the biggest party pooper of our lives. It interrupts our own story, interrupts our ability to have a thought or daydream, to imagine something wonderful because we're too busy bridging the walk from the cafeteria back to the office on the cell phone" (quoted in Kennedy, 2002, p. 109). Or, as Dr. Ian Malcolm (Jeff Goldblum) said in Spielberg's 1997 *The Lost World: Jurassic Park*, "Oooh! Ahhh! That's how it always starts. Then later there's running and screaming."

Technology does have an impact on communication. At the very least it changes the basic elements of communication (see Figure 1.3). What technology does not do is relieve us of our obligation to use mass communication responsibly and wisely.

More on Spielberg
www. filmmakers.com/artists/spielberg

THE ROLE OF MONEY

Money, too, alters communication. It shifts the balance of power; it tends to make audiences products rather than consumers.

The first newspapers were financially supported by their readers; the money they paid for the paper covered its production and distribution. But in the 1830s a new form of newspaper financing emerged. Publishers began selling their papers for a penny—much less than it cost to produce and distribute them. Because so many more papers were sold at this bargain price, publishers could "sell" advertising space based on their readership. What they were actually selling to advertisers was not space on the page—it was readers. How much they could charge advertisers was directly related to how much product (how many readers) they could produce for them.

This new type of publication changed the nature of mass communication. The goal of the process was no longer for audience and media to create meaning together. Rather, it was to sell those readers to a third participant—advertisers.

Some observers think this was a devastatingly bad development, not only in the history of mass communication but in the history of democracy. It robbed people of their voice, or at least made the voices of the advertisers more powerful. Others think it was a huge advance for both mass communication and democracy because it vastly expanded the media, broadening and deepening communication. Models showing these two different ways of viewing mass communication are presented in the box "Audience as Consumer or Audience as Product?" Which model makes the most sense to you? Which do you think is the most accurate?

The goals of media professionals will be questioned repeatedly throughout this book. For now, keep in mind that ours is a capitalist economic system and that media industries are businesses. Movie producers must sell tickets, book publishers must sell books, and even public broadcasting has bills to pay.

This does not mean, however, that the media are or must be slaves to profit. Our task is to understand the constraints placed on these industries by their economics and then demand that, within those limits, they perform ethically and responsibly. We can do this only by being thoughtful, critical consumers of the media.

For more information on this topic, see NBC Video Clip #7 on the CD—*Media Professionals Discuss State of the Media.*

Changes

Today, technology and money continue to alter the mass communication process. There is a growing **concentration of ownership** and conglomeration, rapid globalization, increased audience fragmentation, hypercommercialism, and a steady erosion of traditional distinctions among media—that is, **convergence.** We will return to these themes in later chapters, but here we will discuss them in terms of their impact on the mass communication process.

CONCENTRATION OF OWNERSHIP AND CONGLOMERATION

Ownership of media companies is increasingly concentrated in fewer and fewer hands. Through mergers, acquisitions, buyouts, and hostile takeovers, a very small number of large conglomerates is coming to own more and more of the world's media outlets. For example, in 2003 General Electric—owner of the NBC television network and cable's CNBC and MSNBC—bought the media holdings of France's Vivendi, adding Universal movie studios and the USA, Trio, and Sci-Fi cable channels to its $43 billion global media empire. In 2001, cable giant Comcast paid $72 billion for cable giant AT&T Broadband, creating the world's largest cable operator (22 million subscribers). In 1996, Disney bought Capital Cities/ABC, and Time Warner bought Turner Broadcasting. News Corporation, owner of the Fox Television Network, reaches 40% of all U.S. homes with its 35 owned and operated television stations and virtually the entire country with its broadcast and cable networks.

More on Concentration
WWW.
cjr.org/owners

Concentration is a reality in nonbroadcast media as well. In June 1998 Disney bought Internet search engine Infoseek, and in 1999 NBC bought a share of search engine Snap! As 1998 closed, AOL paid $4.2 billion for the Internet's premier browser, Netscape. And just after 1999 opened, @Home, the high-speed Internet access company that uses cable television lines to serve its subscribers, bought Web search engine Excite for $6.7 billion, both now controlled by major stockholder AT&T.

Cultural Forum

Audience as Consumer or Audience as Product?

People base their judgments of media performance and content on the way they see themselves fitting into the economics of the media industry. Businesses operate to serve their consumers and make a profit. The consumer comes first, then, but who *is* the consumer in our mass media system? This is a much debated issue among media practitioners and media critics. Consider the following models.

	Producer	Product	Consumer
Basic U.S. Business Model	A manufacturer . . .	produces a product . . .	for consumers who choose to buy or not. The manufacturer must satisfy the consumer. Power resides here.
Basic U.S. Business Model for Cereal: Rice Krispies as Product, Public as Consumer	Kellogg's . . .	produces Rice Krispies . . .	for us, the consumers. If we buy Rice Krispies, Kellogg's makes a profit. Kellogg's must satisfy us. Power resides here.
Basic U.S. Business Model for Television (A): Audience as Product, Advertisers as Consumer	NBC . . .	produces audiences (using its programming) . . .	for advertisers. If they buy NBC's audiences, NBC makes a profit. NBC must satisfy its consumers, the advertisers. Power resides here.
Basic U.S. Business Model for Television (B): Programming as Product, Audience as Consumer	NBC . . .	produces (or distributes) programming . . .	for us, the audience. If we watch NBC's shows, NBC makes a profit. NBC must satisfy us. Power resides here.

The first three models assume that the consumer *buys* the product; that is, the consumer is the one with the money and therefore the one who must be satisfied. The last model makes a different assumption. It sees the audience, even though it does not buy anything, as sufficiently important to NBC's profit-making ability to force NBC to consider its interests above others' (even those of advertisers). Which model do you think best represents the economics of U.S. mass media?

Media observer Ben Bagdikian reported that in 1997 the number of media corporations with "dominant power in society" was 10 (in March 2000, *Harper's* set the number at just 6: AOL Time Warner, News Corporation, Sony, Viacom, Disney, and Vivendi Universal), and this "new communications cartel" has the power to "surround almost every man, woman, and child in the country with controlled images and words." This places in their hands, Bagdikian argues, the "ability to exert influence that in many ways is greater than that of schools, religion, parents, and even government itself" (as quoted in Goldstein, 1998, p. 52). To critic Eric Effron, the "serious consequence" of concentration is "the story not told, the questions not asked, the power not challenged" (1999a, p. 47). Journalist and social critic Bill Moyers calls this concentration of media ownership "the central issue that faces us as a democratic society" (as quoted in Moore, 1999, p. A11).

Media critic Douglas Dowd explained this threat to our democratic society, writing:

The media giants are . . . at the very heart of economic power—with a handful of companies dominating the main flow of information and entertainment. Their political and economic interests are no different in general from those of General Motors, EXXON, USX, or DuPont. Their two principal sources of income are from advertising, designed and paid for by the latter, and from the major political parties and their candidates. Does this suggest a conspiracy to shape opinion and polls and politics and society? Doubtless such a conspiracy could be arranged, were it seen as necessary. It does not seem to be necessary. There is instead an "innocent" confluence of interests as when tiny streams pulled by gravity ultimately form a great river. (1997, pp. 26–27)

And media legal scholar Charles H. Tillinghast helped identify those tiny streams: "One need not be a devotee of conspiracy theories to understand that journalists, like other human beings, can judge where their interests lie, and what risks are and are not prudent, given their desire to continue to eat and feed the family" (2000, pp. 145–146).

There is no more obvious example of media concentration than what was at the time the largest corporate merger in history, the $184 billion uniting in January 2000 of the world's largest producer of "traditional" media content, Time Warner, and the world's largest-by-far Internet provider, America Online (AOL). Speaking specifically of the merger's impact on the Internet, *Washington Post* media writer Howard Kurtz wrote, "The creation of the world's largest media and cyberspace company seems to muddy the original dream of the Internet as a democratizing force that would enable thousands of individual voices to compete with major media organs. But the rapid expansion of newspaper, magazine, and network (television) sites on the Web has given it a decidedly corporate cast" (2000, p. 7). Kurtz quoted Mark Crispin Miller, director of New York University's Project on Media Ownership, "Is there something good about one very large entity being able to reach everybody?" and James Ledbetter, New York bureau chief of *Industry Standard* magazine, "The wonders of the information age are in the hands of very few companies" (Kurtz, 2000, p. 7).

Closely related to concentration is **conglomeration,** the increase in the ownership of media outlets by larger, nonmedia companies. "The threat is clear," wrote media critic Steven Brill:

The bigger these conglomerates get, the less important their journalism gets and the more vulnerable that journalism becomes to the conglomerate's other interests. . . . These mega-companies, therefore, present a new, sweeping, and unprecedented threat to free expression, independent journalism, and a vibrant, free marketplace of ideas. Their sheer enormity makes it almost routine that they are covering a subject involving one of their own divisions or some competitor to one of their enterprises. And their involvement in so much other than journalism threatens to water down the values that would assure that they deal with those conflicts honorably. (2000, pp. 26–27)

Conflict of interest is only one presumed problem with conglomeration. The other is the dominance of a bottom-line mentality and its inevitable degradation of media content. *Variety's* Peter Bart explained, "Hence atop every corporation there sits a functionary who is empowered to set a number for every unit of every company. That functionary may in fact have no knowledge whatsoever of the market conditions affecting that entity and no interest in the product it produces. Nonetheless, everyone dances to his tune" (2000, p. 95). Bart was speaking of media in general. As for journalism, CBS anchor Dan Rather added, "The larger the entities that own and control the news operations, the more distant they become" (quoted in Auletta, 2001, p. 60). New York University law professor Burt Neuborne warned:

> The press has been subsumed into a market psychology, because they are now owned by large conglomerates, of which they are simply a piece. And they (news organizations) are expected to contribute their piece of the profit to the larger pie. You don't have people controlling the press anymore with a fervent sense of responsibility to the First Amendment. Concentrating on who's sleeping with whom, on sensationalism, is concentrating on essentially irrelevant issues. (as quoted in Konner, 1999, p. 6)

Here, for example, is *Los Angeles Times* reporter Steve Lopez's analysis of a typical evening of news on one of that city's major television stations 6 weeks after the terrorist attacks of September 11:

> The first story on the 10 o'clock news was about a Britney Spears concert in Anaheim. . . . The next story on KCAL 9 that night was about another concert. Jennifer Lopez this time. . . . The third story . . . finally mentioned Afghanistan . . . a strip club laywer . . . said with a straight face that Americans want Afghan women to come out from under the veil, but at the same time we're asking American women to cover up. . . . The fourth story of the night . . . was about shopping for lingerie. . . . The fifth story was about . . . Operation Playmate, in which Playboy bunnies entertain the troops. (2002, p. 14)

For more information on this topic, see NBC Video Clip #19 on the CD—*Why Is the United States Viewed So Poorly in the Arab World?*

We have entered an era, according to the critics of concentration and conglomeration, of 24-hour OJ, Monica, missing interns, and celebrity gossip. You can read more about this issue in the box titled "Concentration, Conglomeration, and 9/11."

There are, however, less dire observations on concentration and conglomeration. Many telecommunications professionals argue that concentration and conglomeration are not only inevitable but necessary in a telecommunications environment that is increasingly fragmented and internationalized; companies must maximize their number of outlets to reach as much of the divided and far-flung audience as possible. If they do not, they will become financially insecure, and that is an even greater threat to free and effective mediated communication because advertisers and other well-monied forces will have increased influence over them.

Another defense of concentration and conglomeration has to do with **economies of scale;** that is, bigger can in fact sometimes be better because the relative cost of an operation's output declines as the size of that endeavor grows. For example, the cost of collecting the news or producing a television program does not increase significantly when that news report or television program is distributed over 2 outlets, 20 outlets, or 100 outlets. The additional revenues from these other points of distribution can then be plowed back into even better news and programming. In the case of conglomeration, the parallel argument is that revenues from a conglomerate's nonmedia enterprises can be used to support quality work by its media companies.

The potential impact of this **oligopoly**—a concentration of media industries into an ever smaller number of companies—on the mass communication process is enormous. What becomes of shared meaning when the people running communication companies are more committed to the financial demands of their corporate offices than they are to their audiences, who are supposedly their partners in the communication process? What becomes of the process itself when media companies grow more removed from those with whom they communicate? And what becomes of the culture that is dependent on that process when concentration and conglomeration limit the diversity of perspective and information?

GLOBALIZATION

Closely related to the concentration of media ownership is **globalization.** It is primarily large, multinational conglomerates that are doing the lion's share of media acquisitions. The potential impact of globalization on the mass communication process speaks to the issue of diversity of expression. Will distant, anonymous, foreign corporations, each with vast holdings in a variety of nonmedia businesses, use their power to shape news and entertainment content to suit their own ends? Opinion is divided. Some observers feel that this concern is misplaced—the pursuit of profit will force these corporations to respect the values and customs of the nations and cultures in which they operate. Some observers have a less optimistic view. They point to the 1998 controversy surrounding the publication of *East and West* as a prime example of the dangers of media globalization.

HarperCollins, a subsidiary of News Corporation, decided not to publish this book from the last Governor of Hong Kong, Chris Patten, even though the publisher had given Patten a hefty advance and early reviews of the manuscript were glowing. Internal memos made it clear that News Corporation executives, including Chairman Rupert Murdoch, thought the text was too critical of the Chinese government because Patten faulted Beijing for its lack of commitment to democracy. News Corporation had significant business dealings with the Chinese government and had ambitions of even more. In addition, News Corporation had already pulled BBC World Television from its Asian television service because that respected news source had aired a speech critical of China's human rights record.

More on Globalization
WWW.
unescosources.org/

The world's largest untapped audience again figured in a scenario that frightened critics of globalization. Just weeks after his company bought CBS, Viacom CEO Sumner Redstone attended the celebration of the 50th anniversary of Communism in China, where he announced, "Journalistic integrity must prevail in the final analysis. But that doesn't mean that journalistic integrity should be exercised in a way that is unnecessarily offensive to the countries in which you operate" (as quoted in Baker, 1999, p. 6B). Globalization's opponents fairly asked the question, What message has the boss just sent his new employees at historically respected CBS News? What stories will go untold, what questions unasked, what power unchallenged?

Yet defenders of increased globalization point to the need to reach a fragmented and widespread audience—the same factor that fuels concentration—as encouraging this trend. They also cite the growing economic clout of emerging democracies (and the need to reach the people who live in them) and the increasing intertwining of the world's economies as additional reasons globalization is necessary for the economic survival of media businesses.

AUDIENCE FRAGMENTATION

The nature of the other partner in the mass communication process is changing too. The **audience** is becoming more **fragmented,** its segments more narrowly defined. It is becoming less of a mass audience.

Before the advent of television, radio and magazines were national media. Big national radio networks brought news and entertainment to the entire country. Magazines such as *Life, Look,* and the *Saturday Evening Post* once offered limited text and many pictures to a national audience. But television could do these things better. It was radio with pictures; it was magazines with motion. To survive, radio and magazines were forced to find new functions. No longer able to compete on a mass scale, these media targeted smaller audiences that were alike in some important characteristic and therefore more attractive to specific advertisers. So now we have magazines such as *Ski* and *Internet World,* and radio station formats such as Country, Urban, and Lithuanian. This phenomenon is known as **narrowcasting, niche marketing,** or **targeting.**

Technology has wrought the same effect on television. Before the advent of cable television, people could choose from among the three commercial broadcast networks—ABC, CBS, NBC—one noncommercial public broadcasting station, and, in larger markets, maybe an independent station or two. Now, with cable, satellite, and VCRs, people have literally thousands of viewing options. The television audience has been fragmented. To attract advertisers, each channel now must find a more specific group of people to make up its viewership. Nickelodeon targets kids, for example; Nick at Night appeals to baby boomers; Fox Television aims at young urban viewers; and Bravo seeks upper-income older people.

If the nature of the media's audience is changing, then the mass communication process must also change. The audience in mass communication is typically a large, varied group about which the media industries know only the most superficial information. What will happen as smaller, more specific audiences become better known to their partners in the process of making meaning? What will happen to the national culture that binds us as we become increasingly fragmented into demographically targeted **taste publics**—groups of people bound by little more than an interest in a given form of media content?

Concentration, Conglomeration, and 9/11

Media professionals have long debated the question of whether they should be giving the people what they want or what they need. Those who see their industry as just that, a profit-making business, argue that the consumer (the audience) is king. But there are those who see the media not only as a business but also as a social institution necessary to the robust functioning of democracy. This clash of perspectives was never more evident than in the aftermath of the terrorist attacks on America.

"From the early 1990s until September 11, 2001, the U.S. news media had subtly turned foreign news into a niche subject," wrote *Philadelphia Inquirer* reporter Thomas Ginsberg. "No longer feeling seriously threatened after the Cold War, many Americans didn't seem to care as much about the world; at least that was the common wisdom. And many U.S. editors, producers, and news executives, their own eyes glazed over, had abetted Americans' retreat into a cocoon" (2002, p. 48). How did they do this?

- Before September 11 the amount of newspapers' **newshole** (nonadvertising space) devoted to international news was 2%, down from 10% in 1971.

- The proportion of international news in the major weekly news magazines fell from 22% in 1985 to 13% in 1995.

- In the months before September 11, network newscasts on many nights had no foreign news at all, although 20 years ago reports from overseas accounted for 45% of a typical newscast. Overall airtime devoted to international news fell by more than half during the decade from 1990 to 2000.

CNN's Christiane Amanpour reporting from Jerusalem.

- ABC News closed 10 of its 17 foreign bureaus between the 1980s and 2000; *Time* magazine cut its foreign staff from 33 in 1989 to 24 in 2001 (Ginsberg, 2002; Parks, 2002).

Why would respected, competent news organizations reduce their commitment to international news? "To save

HYPERCOMMERCIALISM

The costs involved in acquiring numerous or large media outlets, domestic and international, and of reaching an increasingly fragmented audience must be recouped somehow. Selling more advertising on existing and new media and identifying additional ways to combine content and commercials are the two most common strategies. This leads to what media critic Robert McChesney calls **hypercommercialism.** McChesney explained, "Concentrated media control permits the largest media firms to increasingly commercialize their output with less and less fear of consumer reprisal" (1999a, pp. 34–35). The rise in the number of commercial minutes in a typical broadcast or cable show is evident to most viewers. The American Association of Advertising Agencies reported that in 1999 there

More on Hypercommercialism
www.
commercialalert.org/

money," argues Scottie Williston, former Cairo bureau chief for CBS (quoted in McClellan, 2001, p. 24). Reporter Ginsberg elaborates, "By the end of the '90s, with cable TV and the Internet splintering audiences, and media conglomerates demanding news divisions make more money, broadcasters and some publications gradually changed formats to cover more scandal, lifestyle, personalities. There simply were fewer shows and pages where hard news, much less foreign news, could find a home" (Ginsberg, 2002, p. 50).

The question now in the cultural forum, then, is, Might 9/11 have been averted if American media and their audiences had been more aware of the larger world (and its view of our country)? It is not as though there were no hints of growing anti-American sentiment. Former *Los Angeles Times* editor Michael Parks enumerated them:

> The terrorist threat from radical Islamic fundamentalists had been clear for years—attacks on the World Trade Center in 1993, on apartments housing U.S. Air Force personnel in Saudi Arabia in 1996, on the U.S. embassies in Kenya and Tanzania in 1998, and on the U.S.S. Cole in the Yemeni port of Aden in 2000. Coverage of these attacks was largely episodic with limited investigative reporting and few follow-up stories even when participants were brought to trial. The (media's) failure was sweeping. (quoted in Parks, 2002, p. 52)

"While we can debate whether this failure played a role in our national lack of preparedness, there is no question that we failed our readers," added Edward Seaton, editor-in-chief of the *Manhattan* (Kansas) *Mercury* (quoted in Parks, 2002, pp. 52–53).

Enter your voice into the cultural forum. Do you blame the media conglomerates, agreeing with CNN chief international correspondent Christiane Amanpour, who declared, "It's time the cost-cutters, the money-managers and the advertisers . . . gave us room to operate in a way that's meaningful" (quoted in Ginsberg, 2002, p. 53)? Or do you side with CNN's chairman Walter Isaacson, who argued that blame must be shared by audiences *and* media: "I think this has been a wake-up call to the public and to all of us in the news business that there are certain things that really matter more than the latest trivial thing that can cause a ratings boost" (quoted in Ginsberg, 2002, p. 52)?

What would you do if you ran a news operation? You need to make a profit, but international news is expensive and people just do not seem to want it (audience research demonstrates that readership and viewing consistently decline when international news is printed or broadcast; Auletta, 2001). But you have a privileged place in our society. The Constitution grants you special freedoms because you are understood to be essential to the public's right and need to know; you are indispensable to democracy. Do you give the people what they need (and maybe reduce profits a bit), or do you give them what they seem to want (and boost revenues)? Do you have an obligation—through your coverage of important, if less profitable, news—to educate your audiences about what it is they *should* want? Is there a proper balance between the two? Can you find it? Is it harder to find that balance if your news organization is just one more profit center in a large, international conglomerate?

were 16 minutes and 43 seconds of advertising in an average network television prime-time hour, a 21.8% increase from 1991 (Jessell, 2000).

The sheer growth in the amount of advertising is one troublesome aspect of hypercommercialism. But for many observers the increased mixing of commercial and noncommercial media content is even more troubling. For example, in March 2002 ABC announced that it would begin writing Revlon cosmetics into the storyline of its popular soap opera *All My Children*. In that same month an episode of ABC's *My Wife and Kids* centered on the re-release of the movie *E.T. the Extra-Terrestrial* in exchange for "a big commercial buy" on the network (Flint & Nelson, 2002, p. G-12). In May 2002 it was revealed that WBBH-TV in Fort Myers, Florida, was offering advertisers, for $5,000, "a news story on you or your family and how they have impacted Southwest Florida, which will air in the Monday–Friday 5 p.m.–6 p.m. newscast." KOLO-TV in Reno, Nevada, presented its advertisers with a similar deal, and WSTM-TV in Syracuse, New York, promised "positive special-events news coverage of lottery events" to that state's lottery commission as part of a 3-year advertising contract ("Clueless," 2002, p. 50). The 2002 NFC Championship football telecast on ESPN employed Microsoft's Xbox game system rather than actual video footage to illustrate team play and strategy ("Jeers," 2002). NBC sells guest spots for advertiser executives and products on its talk show *The Other Half* without identifying these segments as part of an advertising arrangement. In 2001 ABC sold eight episodes of its talk show *The View*, featuring news personality Barbara Walters, to Campbell's Soup, requiring hosts "to weave a soup message into their regular on-air banter" (Jackson & Hart, 2001, p. 15). Virtually all the major Internet search engines sell top placement in search results to advertisers without informing users (Enns, 2001). A poll of 287 journalists in 2000 indicated that 41% censor themselves or otherwise reshape or soften stories rather than produce content that might offend advertisers because they "get signals from their bosses to avoid such stories or ignore them based on how they think their bosses would react" (Kohut, 2000, p. 43). Many radio stations now accept payment from record promoters to play their songs, an activity once illegal and called **payola.** It is now quite acceptable as long as the "sponsorship" is acknowledged on the air.

Again, as with globalization and concentration, where critics see damage to the integrity of the media themselves and disservice to their audiences, defenders of hypercommercialism argue that it is simply the economic reality of today's media world.

EROSION OF DISTINCTIONS AMONG MEDIA: CONVERGENCE

Beginning with his 1996 hit "Telling Lies," David Bowie and his label, Virgin Records, have released the rocker's music online before doing so on disc in record stores. HBO produces first-run films for its own cable television channel, immediately releasing them on tape for VCR rental. Both former *New Republic* editor Michael Kinsley and former Republican presidential hopeful Pete DuPont publish political magazines exclusively on the Web. There are more than 4,200 U.S. commercial, nearly 1,200 U.S. noncommercial, and more than 3,000 non-U.S. radio stations delivering their broadcasts over the Web. *Pokémon* is as much a 30-minute TV commercial for licensed merchandise as it is a cartoon.

You can read the *New York Times* or *Time* magazine and hundreds of other newspapers and magazines on your computer screen. Manufacturers now produce WebTV, allowing families to curl up in front of the big screen for online entertainment and information. And what will "newspapers, magazines, and books," "radio and recordings," and "television and film" really mean (or more accurately, *really be*) when people can access printed texts, audio, and moving images virtually anyplace, anytime via **Wi-Fi** (wireless Internet)? Today there are 54 million Wi-Fi users worldwide; there will be 75 million by 2008 (Yi, 2003). This erosion of distinctions among media is called *convergence.*

The traditional lines between media are disappearing. Concentration is one reason. If one company owns newspapers, an online service, television stations, book publishers, a magazine or two, and a film company, it has a strong incentive to get the greatest use from its content, whether news, education, or entertainment, by using as many channels of delivery as possible. The industry calls this **synergy,** and it is the driving force behind several recent mergers and acquisitions in the media and telecommunications industries. In 1997, for example, computer software titan Microsoft paid $1 billion for a 6% interest in cable television operation US West. Microsoft's goal in this and other similar purchases (it already owned part of cable giant Comsat Corporation and, at the time, was negotiating for a one-third stake in TCI Cable) is to make cable and the Internet indistinguishable.

Another reason for convergence is audience fragmentation. A mass communicator who finds it difficult to reach the whole audience can reach its component parts through various media. A third reason is the audience itself. We are becoming increasingly comfortable receiving information and entertainment from a variety of sources. Will this expansion and blurring of traditional media channels confuse audience members, further tilting the balance of power in the mass communication process toward the media industries? Or will it give audiences more power—power to choose, power to reject, and power to combine information and entertainment in individual ways?

Concentration of ownership, globalization of media, audience fragmentation, hypercommercialism, and convergence are forcing all parties in the mass communication process to think critically about their positions in it. Those in the media industries face the issue of professional ethics, discussed in Chapter 14. Audience members confront the issue of media literacy, the topic at the core of Chapter 2.

Chapter Review

Communication is the process of creating shared meaning. All communication is composed of the same elements, but technology changes the nature of those elements. Communication between a mass medium and its audience is mass communication, a primary contributor to the construction and maintenance of culture. James Carey's articulation of the "cultural defi-nition" of communication enriched our understanding of how mass communication functions in our lives.

As the learned behavior of a given social group, culture is the world made meaningful. It resides all around us; it is socially constructed and is

maintained through communication. Culture limits as well as liberates us; it differentiates as well as unites us. It defines our realities and shapes the ways we think, feel, and act.

Although culture and communication are interrelated, the influence of mass communication has long been in dispute. Still debated are micro- versus macro-level effects, administrative versus critical research, and the transmissional versus the ritual perspective.

Because we construct and maintain our culture largely through mass communication, mass communication offers us remarkable opportunities, but with them come important responsibilities. As our culture's dominant storytellers or as the forum in which we debate cultural meanings, media industries have an obligation to operate professionally and ethically. Audience members, likewise, have the responsibility to consume media messages critically and thoughtfully.

The proponents of technological determinism argue that technology is the predominant agent of social and cultural change. Opponents of this view believe technology is only one part of the mix and that how people use technology is the crucial factor in determining its power. The new communication technologies, which promise to reshape our understanding of mass communication, are controversial for that very reason.

Money, too, shapes the mass communication process. Questions arise about the nature of the partnership between media professionals and their audiences when audiences are seen as products to be sold to a third party (advertisers) rather than as equal members in the process. Ultimately, however, ours is a capitalist economic system, and the media, as profit-making entities, must operate within its limits and constraints. Our task is to understand this and demand that, within these limits, media operate ethically and responsibly. This is especially crucial today as technological and economic factors— concentration of ownership and conglomeration, globalization of media, audience fragmentation, hypercommercialism, and convergence—promise to further alter the nature of mass communication.

Key Terms

Use the text's CD-ROM and the Online Learning Center at www.mhhe.com/baran to further your understanding of the following terminology.

communication, 4
feedback, 5
interpersonal communication, 5
encoding, 5
decoding, 5
noise, 6
medium (pl. *media*), 6
mass medium, 6
mass communication, 7
inferential feedback, 7
cultural definition of
   communication, 9
culture, 9
dominant culture (mainstream
   culture), 12

bounded culture (co-culture), 13
micro-level media effects, 16
macro-level media effects, 17
administrative research, 17
critical research, 18
transmissional perspective, 18
ritual perspective, 18
media as cultural storyteller, 19
mass communication as
   cultural forum, 19
technological determinism, 22
audience as consumer/as
   product, 23
concentration of ownership, 24
convergence, 24

conglomeration, 26
economies of scale, 27
oligopoly, 28
globalization, 28
audience fragmentation, 29
narrowcasting, 29
niche marketing, 29
targeting, 29
newshole, 30
taste publics, 30
hypercommercialism, 30
payola, 32
wi-fi, 32
synergy, 33

Questions for Review

Go to the self-quizzes on the CD-ROM and the Online Learning Center to test your knowledge.

1. What is culture? How does culture define people?
2. What is communication? What is mass communication?
3. What are encoding and decoding? How do they differ when technology enters the communication process?
4. What does it mean to say that communication is a reciprocal process?
5. What is James Carey's cultural definition of communication? How does it differ from other definitions of that process?
6. What three dichotomies define the debate surrounding media effects?
7. What do we mean by mass media as cultural storyteller?

8. What do we mean by mass communication as cultural forum?
9. How did the advent of penny newspapers in 1830 change the nature of the mass communication process?

10. What is concentration of ownership? Conglomeration? Media globalization? Audience fragmentation? Hypercommercialism? Convergence?

Questions for Critical Thinking and Discussion

1. Do you feel inhibited by your bounded culture? By the dominant culture? How so?
2. Have the events of September 11, 2001 caused you to look at your own culture differently? Amid all the flags and patriotism, are we, as Americans, undergoing a reassessment of the meaning of "American culture"? If so, can you predict the outcome of this reassessment? In addition, what did you know of "Muslim culture" before that fateful day? Where did that knowledge come from? Now

that there is more information about that culture available, how different is your understanding of it?
3. Who were your childhood heroes and heroines? Why did you choose them? What cultural lessons did you learn from them?
4. Critique the definition of culture given in this chapter. What would you personally add? Subtract?
5. What are the qualities of a thoughtful and reflective media consumer? Do you have these characteristics? Why or why not?

Important Resources

Carey, J. W. (1989). *Communication as culture: Essays on media and society.* **Boston, MA: Unwin Hyman.** A collection of essays and lectures from the "founder" of the cultural approach to media studies in the United States. Taken together, they present a strong basis for approaching mass communication and technology from the cultural or ritual perspective.

Compaine, B. M., & Gomery, D. (2000). *Who owns the media? Competition and concentration in the mass media industry.* **Mahwah, NJ: Lawrence Erlbaum.** In its third edition, this comprehensive and data-heavy book provides a thorough discussion of the question posed in its title. The impact of convergence on concentration makes up an important part of this latest edition, and the impact of concentration on culture and society is given full play. Boxes dispersed throughout the text offer profiles of media's biggest owners.

McChesney, R. W. (1999). *Rich media, poor democracy: Communication politics in dubious times.* **Urbana, IL: University of Illinois Press.** This important book presents in great detail the threat to democracy posed by media concentration, globalization, and hypercommercialism. The potential of the Internet and public broadcasting to return control of the media to the people is discussed (albeit not optimistically). Bill Moyers said, "If Thomas Paine were around, he would have written this book."

Real, M. R. (1996). *Exploring media culture: A guide.* **Thousand Oaks, CA: Sage.** Examines the interaction between popular culture and mass media. Investigates the cultural role of media and content, such as Hollywood movies, the Internet, and MTV, as a means of helping the public become more skilled "readers" of the media.

More on McLuhan
TV Critics Assn.
Read about Lazarsfeld
More on Carey
More on Spielberg
More on Concentration
More on Globalization
More on Hypercommercialism

www.mcluhan.ca/
www.tvcritics.org/
Columbia.edu/cu/news/01/10/lazarsfeld.html
65.107.211.206/Post/Poldiscourse/2views.html
www.filmmakers.com/artists/spielberg
www.cjr.org/owners
www.unescosources.org/
www.commercialalert.org/

CHAPTER 2

Media Literacy and Culture

LEARNING OBJECTIVES

Literacy has historically been associated with power and success. Literate people have the advantage in the cultures in which they live. With the coming of mass communication, the definition of literacy has been broadened, but its value has not changed. After studying this chapter you should

- be familiar with the development of written and mass-mediated communication.

- understand the relationship between communication and culture.

- understand the relationship between literacy and power.

- recognize how technologies change the cultures that use them.

- recognize how mass media technologies have changed the definition of literacy.

- be aware of the overarching relationships between different mass media and culture, themes to be examined in detail in later chapters.

- understand media literacy.

- possess the basis for developing good media literacy skills.

- be encouraged to practice media literacy.

BABY-SITTING YOUR 3-YEAR-OLD NIECE WAS *NOT* HOW YOU wanted to spend your Saturday night. But family is family, so here you are, watching television with a little kid.

"What do you want to watch?" you ask.

"MTV!" she cheers.

"No. You're too young."

"Friends!"

"No. It's too sexy for little kids like you."

"Mommy lets me watch."

"Are you telling me the truth?"

"No. How 'bout HBO?"

"Compromise. How about Disney?"

"What means *compromise?*"

"It means we'll watch Disney." You punch up the Disney Channel with the remote and settle in to watch what looks like an adolescent action show. Three preteen sleuths are in a low-speed car chase, pursuing a bad guy of some sort.

When the chase takes them into a car wash, your niece asks, "Why are they dreaming?"

"What?!"

"Why are those people dreaming?"

"They're not dreaming."

"Then why is the picture going all woosie-like?"

"That's not woosie-like. That's the brushes in the car wash going over the windshield. The camera is showing us what they're seeing. It's called POV, point of view. It's when the camera shows what the characters are seeing."

"I know that! But why are they dreaming? When the picture goes all woosie-like, it means that the people are dreaming!"

"Says who?"

"Says everyone. And when the music gets louder, that means the show's gonna be over. And when the man talks real loud, that means it's a commercial. And when stars and moons come out of the kitty's head, that means it hurts."

"Can we just be quiet for a little bit?"

"And when there's blood, it's really catsup. And when the . . ."

"If I let you watch MTV, will you quiet down?"

"Cool. Deal."

"Are you really only 3?"

"And a half."

In this chapter we investigate how we can improve our media literacy skills. Before we can do this, however, we must understand why literacy, in and of itself, is important. Throughout history, literacy has meant power. When communication was primarily oral, the leaders were most often the best storytellers. The printing press ushered in the beginnings of mass communication, and in this primarily print-based environment, power and influence migrated to those who could read.

As literacy spread through various cultures, power began to fragment. The world became increasingly democratic. In today's modern, mass mediated cultures, literacy is still important, but there are now two forms of literacy—literacy as traditionally understood (the ability to read) and media literacy.

Let's begin by looking at the development of writing and the formation of **literate culture.** An expanding literate population encouraged technological innovation; the printing press transformed the world. Other communication technology advances have also had a significant impact; however, these technologies cannot be separated from how people have used them. Technology can be used in ways beneficial and otherwise. The skilled, beneficial use of media technologies is the goal of media literacy.

A Cultural History of Mass Communication

Our quick trip through the history of mass communication begins at the beginning, in cultures whose only form of communication was oral.

ORAL CULTURE

Oral or **preliterate cultures** are those without a written language. Virtually all communication must be face-to-face, and this fact helps to define the culture, its structure, and its operation. Whether they existed thousands of years ago before writing was developed or still function today (for example, among certain Eskimo peoples and African tribes where **griots,** or "talking chiefs," provide oral histories of their people going back hundreds of years), oral cultures are remarkably alike. They share these characteristics:

More on Storytelling
www.
storynet.org

The meaning in language is specific and local. As a result, communities are closely knit, and their members are highly dependent on each other for all aspects of life.

Knowledge must be passed on orally. People must be *shown* and *told* how to do something. Therefore, skilled hunters, farmers, midwives, and the like hold a special status; they are the living embodiments of culture.

Memory is crucial. As repositories of cultural customs and traditions, elders are revered; they are responsible for passing knowledge on to the next generation.

Myth and history are intertwined. Storytellers are highly valued; they are the meaning makers, and, like the elders, they pass on what is important to the culture.

What does the resulting culture look like? People know each other intimately and rely on one another for survival. Roles are clearly defined. Stories teach important cultural lessons and preserve important cultural traditions and values. Control over communication is rarely necessary, but when it is, it is easily achieved through social sanctions.

THE INVENTION OF WRITING

Writing, the first communication technology, complicates this simple picture. More than 5,000 years ago, alphabets were developed independently in several places around the world. **Ideogrammatic** (picture-based) **alphabets** appeared in Egypt (as hieroglyphics), Sumeria (as cuneiform), and urban China.

Ideogrammatic alphabets require a huge number of symbols to convey even the simplest idea. Their complexity meant that only a very select few,

This Sumerian cuneiform dates from 700 years before the birth of Christ.

an intellectual elite, could read or write. For writing to truly serve effective and efficient communication, one more advance was required.

The Sumerians were international traders, maintaining trade routes throughout known Europe, Africa, and Asia. The farther the Sumerian people traveled, the less they could rely on face-to-face communication and the greater their need for a more precise writing form. Sumerian cuneiform slowly expanded, using symbols to represent sounds rather than objects and ideas. Appearing around 1800 B.C., these were the first elements of a **syllable alphabet**—an alphabet employing sequences of vowels and consonants, that is, words.

The syllable alphabet as we know it today slowly developed, aided greatly by ancient Semitic cultures, and eventually flowered in Greece around 800 B.C. Like the Sumerians long before them, the Greeks perfected their easy alphabet of necessity. Having little in the way of natural resources, the Greek city-states depended and thrived on bustling trade routes all around the Aegean and Mediterranean Seas. For orders to be placed, deals arranged, manifests compiled, and records kept, writing that was easy to learn, use, and understand was required.

A medium was necessary to carry this new form of communication. The Sumerians had used clay tablets, but the Egyptians, Greeks, and Romans eventually employed **papyrus,** rolls of sliced strips of reed pressed together. Around 100 B.C. the Romans began using **parchment,** a writing material made from prepared animal skins, and in A.D. 105 midlevel Chinese bureaucrat Ts'ai Lun perfected a paper-making process employing a mixture of pressed mulberry tree bark, water, rags, and a sophisticated frame for drying and stretching the resulting sheets of paper. This technology made its way to Europe through various trade routes some 600 years later.

LITERATE CULTURE

With the coming of **literacy**—the ability to effectively and efficiently comprehend and use written symbols—the social and cultural rules and structures of preliterate times began to change. People could accumulate a permanent body of knowledge and transmit that knowledge from one generation to another. Among the changes that writing brought were these:

Meaning and language became more uniform. The words "a bolt of cloth" had to mean the same to a reader in Mesopotamia as they did to one in Sicily. Over time, communities became less closely knit and their members less dependent on one another. The definition of "community" expanded to include people outside the local area.

This Egyptian funeral papyrus depicts the weighing of a heart when a person dies.

Communication could occur over long distances and long periods of time. With knowledge being transmitted in writing, power shifted from those who could show others their special talents to those who could write and read about them.

The culture's memory, history, and myth could be recorded on paper. With written histories, elders and storytellers began to lose their status, and new elites developed. Homer (some historians believe he was actually several scribes), for example, compiled in written form several generations of oral stories and histories that we know as the *Iliad* and the *Odyssey.*

What did the resulting culture look like? It was no longer local. Its members could survive not only by hunting or farming together but by commercial, political, or military expansion. Empires replaced communities. There was more compartmentalization of people based on what they did to earn a living—bakers baked, herders herded, merchants sold goods. Yet, at the same time, role and status were less permanently fixed. Slaves who learned to read to serve their masters took on new duties for those masters and rose in status.

Power and influence now resided not in the strongest hunter, wisest elder, or most engaging storyteller but in those who could read and write; that is, power and influence now rested with those who were literate. They could best engage in widespread official communication, and they wrote the histories and passed on cultural values and lessons. With this change from preliterate to literate culture, the first stirrings of a new political philosophy were born. Reading and writing encouraged more open and robust debate, political exchange, and criticism of the powerful; in other words, it fostered democracy.

It is important to remember that in the newly literate cultures, communication was still quite limited. An orator could address at most a few hundred people at a time. Writers could reach only those literate few who held their handwritten scrolls or letters. The printing press would change this, making it possible to duplicate communication, thereby expanding our ability to communicate with one another.

THE GUTENBERG REVOLUTION

Project Gutenberg
WWW.
promo.net/pg/

It is impossible to overstate the importance of Johannes Gutenberg's development of movable metal type. Historian S. H. Steinberg wrote in *Five Hundred Years of Printing:*

> Neither political, constitutional, ecclesiastical, and economic, nor sociological, philosophical, and literary movements can be fully understood without taking into account the influence the printing press has exerted upon them. (1959, p. 11)

Marshall McLuhan expressed his admiration for Gutenberg's innovation by calling his 1962 book *The Gutenberg Galaxy.* In it he argued that the advent of print is the key to our modern consciousness. Why was Gutenberg's invention so important? Simply, because it allowed *mass* communication.

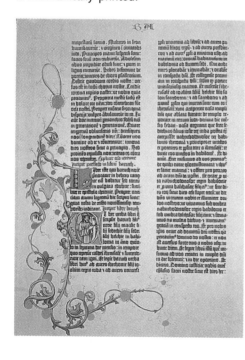

This page from a Gutenberg Bible shows the exquisite care the printer used in creating his works. The artwork in the margins is handpainted, but the text is mechanically printed.

The Printing Press   Printing and the printing press existed long before Gutenberg perfected his process in or around 1446. The Chinese were using wooden block presses as early as A.D. 600 and had movable clay type by A.D. 1000. A simple movable metal type was even in use in Korea in the 13th century. Gutenberg's printing press was a significant leap forward, however, for two important reasons.

Gutenberg was a goldsmith and a metallurgist. He hit upon the idea of using metal type crafted from lead molds in place of type made from wood or clay. This was an important advance. Not only was movable metal type durable enough to print page after page, but letters could be arranged and rearranged to make any message possible. And Gutenberg was able to produce virtually identical copies.

In addition, Gutenberg's advance over Korean metal mold printing was one of scope and intention. The Korean press was used to produce attractive artwork. Gutenberg saw his invention as a way to produce books—many books—for profit. He was, however, a poor businessman.

Johannes Gutenberg takes the first proof from his printing press.

He stressed quality over quantity, in part because of his reverence for the book he was printing, the Bible. He used the highest quality paper and ink and turned out far fewer volumes than he otherwise could have.

Other printers, however, quickly saw the true economic potential of Gutenberg's invention. The first Gutenberg Bible appeared in 1456. By the end of that century, 44 years later, printing operations existed in 12 European countries, and the continent was flooded with 20 million volumes of 7,000 titles in 35,000 different editions (Drucker, 1999).

The Impact of Print   Although Gutenberg developed his printing press with a limited use in mind, printing Bibles, the cultural effects of mass printing have been profound.

Handwritten or hand-copied materials were expensive to produce, and the cost of an education, in time and money, had made reading an expensive luxury. However, with the spread of printing, written communication was available to a much larger portion of the population, and the need for literacy among the lower and middle classes grew. The ability to read became less of a luxury and more of a necessity; eventually literacy spread, as did education. Soldiers at the front needed to be able to read the emperor's orders. Butchers needed to understand the king's shopping list. So the demand for literacy expanded, and more (and more types of) people learned to read.

Tradespeople, soldiers, clergy, bakers, and musicians all now had business at the printer's shop. They talked. They learned of things, both in conversation and by reading printed material. As more people learned to read, new ideas germinated and spread and cross-pollination of ideas occurred.

More material from various sources was published, and people were freer to read what they wanted when they wanted. Dominant authorities—the Crown and the Church—were now less able to control communication and, therefore, the culture. New ideas about the world appeared; new understandings of the existing world flourished.

In addition, duplication permitted standardization and preservation. Myth and superstition began to make way for standard, verifiable bodies of knowledge. History, economics, physics, and chemistry all became part of the culture's intellectual life. Literate cultures were now on the road to modernization.

Printed materials were the first mass-produced product, speeding the development and entrenchment of capitalism. We live today in a world built on these changes. Use of the printing press helped fuel the establishment and growth of a large middle class. No longer were societies composed of rulers and subjects; printing sped the rise of democracy. No longer were power and wealth functions of birth. Power and wealth could now be created by the industrious. No longer was political discourse limited to accepting the dictates of Crown and Church. Printing had given ordinary people a powerful voice.

THE INDUSTRIAL REVOLUTION

More on the Industrial Revolution
WWW.
fordham.edu/halsall/mod/modsbook14.html

By the mid-18th century the printing press had become one of the engines driving the Industrial Revolution. Print was responsible for building and disseminating bodies of knowledge, leading to scientific and technological developments and the refinement of new machines. In addition, industrialization reduced the time necessary to complete work, and this created something heretofore unknown to most working people—leisure time.

Industrialization had another effect as well. As workers left their sunrise-to-sunset jobs in agriculture, the crafts, and trades to work in the newly industrialized factories, not only did they have more leisure time but they had more money to spend on their leisure. Farmers, fishermen, and tile makers had to put their profits back into their jobs. But factory workers took their money home; it was spendable. Combine leisure time and expendable cash with the spread of literacy and the result is a large and growing audience for printed *information* and *entertainment*. By the mid-19th century, a mass audience and the means to reach it existed.

"Modern" Communication Technologies: The Printing Press of Their Time

Every major advance in mass communication technology has affected the cultures that used it, just as the printing press changed Western Europe. Today, many experts argue that television and computers are equal in influence to Gutenberg's marvel. Whether you agree or not, there is no doubt that the introduction of mass market newspapers and magazines, motion pictures, radio, television, and computers has created a world markedly different from that which existed before their arrival. All media will be examined in detail in upcoming chapters, but here are thumbnail sketches of the tremendous, but often overlooked, restructuring of everyday life that these media fostered.

NEWSPAPERS, MAGAZINES, MOTION PICTURES, AND RADIO

The printing press made newspapers and magazines possible, but it was technological and social changes brought about by industrialization that gave us *mass market* newspapers and magazines. As these media were flourishing in the late 19th and early 20th centuries, motion pictures and radio were also developing. Taken together, these communication technologies spoke to and for the growing lower- and middle-class populations of the United States. This was a time of remarkable transformation.

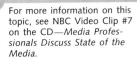

For more information on this topic, see NBC Video Clip #7 on the CD—*Media Professionals Discuss State of the Media.*

The westward migration that had begun in the 1840s was in full force, and immigrants from Asia and Europe were pouring into the United States in search of jobs and opportunity. Former slaves and their children began moving north to the great industrial cities in the late 1860s, looking for freedom and dignity as well as work. Industry was producing consumer products such as electric lights and telephones that once were only dreams. Organized labor was agitating for a greater say in workers' lives.

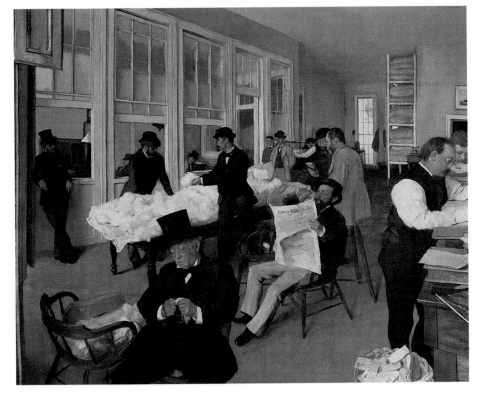

Mass circulation newspapers brought everyday people into the cultural dialogue, as depicted in this 1873 painting by Edgar Degas, *The Interior of the Cotton Market in New Orleans.*

Government was struggling to deal with duties and responsibilities unimagined 20 years earlier.

Into the middle of this volatile brew came the new mass market media. Foreign-speaking immigrants and unschooled laborers could be informed and entertained by movies or radio; minimal reading skill was required. Mass market newspapers and magazines were simple to read and full of pictures and cartoons, accessible even to newly literate immigrants and un-educated former slaves. Movies were silent, requiring no reading ability at all, and radios in the 1920s were inexpensive to own and demanded nothing more of listeners than the ability to hear. For the first time in history, an entire population was able to participate in cultural communication.

Mass market newspapers and magazines, motion pictures, and radio helped unify a rapidly expanding, pluralistic, multiethnic country; created and nourished the U.S. middle class; and established, supported, and solidified the roots of the U.S. consumer economy.

TELEVISION

Television was no less influential than these media. Its diffusion throughout U.S. homes was phenomenal. Figure 2.1 shows this remarkable rate of growth.

Television was virtually nonexistent in 1945 at the end of World War II, with only 10,000 sets in people's homes, and those exclusively in major urban areas. A short 14 years later, 54 million households had televisions.

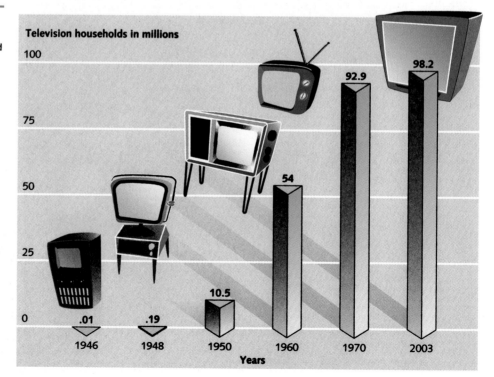

Figure 2.1 Growth of Television in the United States. *Source:* Census data and *Broadcasting & Cable Yearbook;* various years.

Television households in millions

100 · 75 · 50 · 25 · 0

.01 (1946) · .19 (1948) · 10.5 (1950) · 54 (1960) · 92.9 (1970) · 98.2 (2003)

Years

The country that welcomed television was as much in a state of transformation as the one that had already greeted mass market newspapers, magazines, movies, and radio.

World War II further removed the United States from its primarily rural, small-town identity. It was fast becoming a global industrial giant. More people now worked shorter weeks (40 hours) and had increased leisure time—and money to spend. The manufacturing capabilities refined for the war effort were retooled for the manufacture of consumer products—cars, golf clubs, sportswear—that took advantage of this free time and money. Because people needed to know about these new products in order to buy them, advertising expanded.

Minorities who had fought for freedom in Europe and Asia demanded it at home. Some women who had entered the workforce while the men were at war remained on the job, but many others returned to their homes in the 1950s. However, by the 1960s and 1970s women were questioning their domestic role. This, as well as economic necessity, contributed to the reentry of women into the workforce in even greater numbers. The trend toward both Mom and Dad working outside the home was set. People left their small towns to move nearer the factories, and traditional communities began to dissolve. Historically important anchors such as school and church lost their hold over children, and thanks to the postwar baby boom, there were teenagers aplenty when television became a mass medium.

Television became a true mass medium in 1960, reaching into 90% of all U.S. homes. At that time the United States was characterized by social and racial unrest. The youth revolution of "sex, drugs, and rock 'n' roll" took hold in that decade, as did economic growth accompanied by rampant commercialism and consumerism. There were dramatic rises in violence of all kinds, especially teen violence and juvenile delinquency. Television was smack in the middle of this social and cultural sea change.

Television may not have "caused" the Civil Rights movement, but Dr. Martin Luther King Jr.'s adroit use of the medium's ability to bring scenes like this into people's homes surely aided the cause.

Did the new medium *cause* this transformation? No, television did not cause these profound alterations in our culture. To make that argument is to take the transmissional view. But if we apply Carey's ritual perspective (see Chapter 1) to one example from that era—the success of the Civil Rights movement—it is easy to understand the cultural importance of mass communication in our lives.

It is impossible to imagine the Civil Rights movement succeeding without the ugly televised pictures of Southern cops and their dogs descending on Dr. Martin Luther King, Jr. and his peaceful marchers. The ability of television to convey "representations of shared belief" was central to Dr. King's strategy. He believed Americans were basically good and fair and that they shared a fundamental belief in freedom and equality. Dr. King's plan worked; people of conscience were shocked at scenes of nonresisting marchers being bludgeoned. After seeing televised news reports from Selma, Alabama, President John F. Kennedy is reported to have turned to his brother, Attorney General Robert Kennedy, and said, "We must now act. The American people will not stand for this." He then dedicated the power of his office to the movement.

COMPUTER NETWORKS

Among the overlooked cultural changes wrought by the Internet is the explosion of home offices and telecommuting. These phenomena, in turn, produced their own effect, the emergence of the office supply super store.

The United States in the first decade of the new century, much like the country that greeted television, is a nation in transition. It has "won" the Cold War, but its citizens are not coming home to a changed culture as they did in 1945; they never left. Yet the rules have changed anyway. The United States exists in a different world than that which followed World War II. It is one player in the global economy, and the nature of work has changed. The service industries—retailing, telecommunications, social services—now provide more jobs than manufacturing.

In the midst of this change are the new computer technologies. The information society, the electronic superhighway, the information infrastructure, and virtual reality were dreams 30 years ago. Individuals can communicate electronically in an instant with one person or 10 million people. People search for and retrieve information from the world's most sophisticated libraries, newspapers, and databases without ever leaving their homes. Many workers telecommute, rarely visiting the office. More and more, homes are *becoming* people's offices. We are an **information society**—a society wherein the creation and exchange of information is the dominant social and economic activity.

We cannot be certain yet how this information society will evolve, but many issues are already being debated, as you will see in virtually every chapter that follows. For example, what becomes of those who cannot afford to be

The Dangers of Papyrus

New communication technologies invariably are met with concern. Today's debate surrounds the impact of the Internet and the World Wide Web. On April Fools' Day 1997, the *ABC Evening News* offered this report:

> WORLD NEWS NOW (THEN) Egypt's emerging papyrus technology continues to alarm parents and law enforcement. A new bill introduced today would let the government regulate material found on papyrus. Legislators said paperspace, as it is known to so-called writers, is becoming a haven for monotheists, con artists, and worse, hoping to prey on the young and the gullible. A little bit later in the broadcast we will have some tips on how to shield your children from offensive and dangerous material found on the papyrus.

Clearly, this is a humorous take on the current debate in our cultural forum over the Internet. What is your own opinion?

linked, wired, and online? Will computer technologies divide the nation into information haves and have-nots? What new communities will develop? Who owns information? What skills will be needed to succeed professionally and personally? To what extent should government be involved in creating and maintaining computer networks? Should there be official policing of content?

These are questions about the use and control of a new medium. Throughout history, whenever new communication technologies have been introduced, societies have inevitably confronted similar questions (see the box "The Dangers of Papyrus"). The concern, obviously, is with how best to use the strengths of the emerging medium and how to minimize its disruptive potential. This is just one element, albeit an important one, of media literacy.

Media Literacy

Television influences our culture in innumerable ways. One of its effects, according to many people, is that it has encouraged violence in our society. For example, American television viewers overwhelmingly say there is too much violence on television. Yet almost without exception, the local television news program that has the largest proportion of violence in its nightly newscast is the ratings leader. "If it bleeds, it leads" has become

Center for Media Literacy
www.
medialit.org/

For more information on this topic, see NBC Video Clip #14 on the CD—*Debating the Effects of TV Violence.*

the motto for much of local television news. It leads because people watch.

So, although many of us are quick to condemn improper media performance or to identify and lament its harmful effects, we rarely question our own role in the mass communication process. We overlook it because we participate in mass communication naturally, almost without conscious effort. We possess high-level interpretive and comprehension skills that make even the most sophisticated television show, movie, or magazine story understandable and enjoyable. We are able, through a lifetime of interaction with the media, to *read media texts*. Recall the opening vignette. That 3-year-old was already exhibiting a fairly high level of skill at reading television texts. Maybe her skills are not as sophisticated as yours—she did not know POV, for example—but in her short life she has already become a fairly skilled viewer.

Media literacy is a skill we take for granted, but like all skills, it can be improved. And if we consider how important the mass media are in creating and maintaining the culture that helps define us and our lives, it is a skill that *must* be improved.

Media Education Foundation
www.
igc.org/mef

Hunter College media professor Stuart Ewen emphasized this point in comparing media literacy with traditional literacy. "Historically," he wrote, "links between literacy and democracy are inseparable from the notion of an informed populace, conversant with the issues that touch upon their lives, enabled with tools that allow them to participate actively in public deliberation and social change. . . . Literacy was about crossing the lines that had historically separated men of ideas from ordinary people, about the enfranchisement of those who had been excluded from the compensations of citizenship" (2000, p. 448). To Ewen, and others committed to media literacy, media literacy represents no less than the means to full participation in the culture.

ELEMENTS OF MEDIA LITERACY

Center for Media Education
www.
cme.org/cme

Earlier we defined literacy as the ability to effectively and efficiently comprehend and use written symbols. With the development of nonprint-based media, however, that definition must be expanded to include the ability to effectively and efficiently comprehend and utilize *any form of communication*. When speaking specifically of participation in mass communication, this ability is called **media literacy.**

Media literacy can mean somewhat different things to different observers, as shown in the box "Defining Media Literacy." What each of its definitions has in common, however, is the idea that media consumers must develop the "ability" or "facility" to better interpret media content. So, for our purposes, media literacy is the ability to effectively and efficiently comprehend and utilize mass media content.

Media scholar Art Silverblatt (1995) identified five fundamental elements of media literacy. To these we will add two more. Media literacy includes these characteristics:

Defining Media Literacy

Media literacy takes on slightly different meanings depending on the orientation of the person or organization doing the defining. In a special issue of the *Journal of Communication* dedicated to media literacy, media researcher Alan Rubin cited these definitions of media literacy.

From the National Leadership Conference on Media Literacy: *the ability to access, analyze, evaluate, and communicate messages* (1998, p. 3).

From media scholar Paul Messaris: *knowledge about how media function in society* (1998, p. 3).

From mass communication researchers Justin Lewis and Sut Jhally: *understanding cultural, economic, political, and technological constraints on the creation, production, and transmission of messages* (1998, p. 3).

Rubin went on to provide his own definition of media literacy:

Media literacy, then, is about understanding the sources and technologies of communication, the codes that are used, the messages that are produced, and the selection, interpretation, and impact of those messages. (p. 3)

In that same issue, communication scholars William Christ and W. James Potter offered their view of media literacy:

Most conceptualizations (of media literacy) include the following elements: Media are constructed and construct reality; media have commercial implications; media have ideological and political implications; form and content are related in each medium, each of which has a unique aesthetic, codes, and conventions; and receivers negotiate meaning in media. (1998, pp. 7–8)

The Cultural Environment Movement ("The People's Communication Charter," 1996), a public interest group devoted to increasing literacy as a way to combat corporate takeover of media, suggests this definition:

The right to acquire information and skills necessary to participate fully in public deliberation and communication. This requires facility in reading, writing, and storytelling; critical media awareness; computer literacy; and education about the role of communication in society. (p. 1)

The National Communication Association (1996), a professional scholarly organization composed largely of university academics, offers this description of media literacy:

Being a critical and reflective consumer of communication requires an understanding of how words, images, graphics, and sounds work together in ways that are both subtle and profound. Mass media such as radio, television, and film and electronic media such as the telephone, the Internet, and computer conferencing influence the way meanings are created and shared in contemporary society. So great is this impact that in choosing how to send a message and evaluate its effect, communicators need to be aware of the distinctive characteristics of each medium. (p. 2)

These definitions are currently in play in the cultural forum. How would you assess the worth of each? Identify the one most useful for you and defend your choice.

---

1. *An awareness of the impact of media.* Writing and the printing press helped change the world and the people in it. Mass media do the same. If we ignore the impact of media on our lives, we run the risk of being caught up and carried along by that change rather than controlling or leading it.

2. *An understanding of the process of mass communication.* If we know the components of the mass communication process and how they relate to one another, we can form expectations of how they can serve us. How do the various media industries operate? What are their obligations to us? What are the obligations of the audience? How do different media limit or enhance messages? Which forms of feedback are most effective, and why?

3. *Strategies for analyzing and discussing media messages.* To consume media messages thoughtfully, we need a foundation on which to

For more information on this topic, see NBC Video Clip #8 on the CD—*Author James Steyer Discusses His Book The Other Parent.*

Media Awareness Network
www.
schoolnet.ca/medianet

The Sopranos is a television program about the Mob. It has all the things you wo
from a Mafia show—violence, sex, and betrayal. Yet its drama revolves around Ca
Soprano, a mobster who sees a psychiatrist and who lives in an upscale New Jers
with his wife and two kids. Why do you think the producers have gone to the tro
give Tony these trappings of a more or less normal life? And what's going on in
Report? Is it a good piece of cinematic science fiction or an updated example of t
Or is it a commentary on holding and detaining "suspected" individuals, say, terr
s it a reflection on the fairness of the judicial system, especially in capital cases?
ask us how much freedom are we willing to give up to feel safe? Both are fine ex
content designed expressly to be read from multiple points of access.

base thought and reflection. If *we* make meaning, we must possess the tools with which to make it (for example, understanding the intent and impact of film and video conventions like camera angles and lighting, or the strategy behind the placement of photos on a newspaper page). Otherwise, meaning is made for us; the interpretation of media content will then rest with its creator, not with us.

4. *An understanding of media content as a text that provides insight into our culture and our lives.* How do we know a culture and its people, attitudes, values, concerns, and myths? We know them through communication. For modern cultures like ours, media messages increasingly dominate that communication, shaping our understanding of and insight into our culture. Some groups feel so strongly about the potential of the media to shape culture that they have attempted to take back some of that power themselves. See the box "Media Literacy as the Struggle for Power" on page 54 for more information about media literacy as a power issue.

5. *The ability to enjoy, understand, and appreciate media content.* Media literacy does not mean living the life of a grump, liking nothing in the media, or always being suspicious of harmful effects and cultural degradation. We take high school and college classes to enhance our understanding and appreciation of novels; we can do the same for media texts.

Learning to enjoy, understand, and appreciate media content includes the ability to use **multiple points of access**—to approach media content from a variety of directions and derive from it many levels of meaning. Thus, we control meaning making for our own enjoyment or appreciation. For example, we can enjoy the 2002 Steven Spielberg movie *Minority Report* as an exciting piece of cinematic science fiction. But we can also understand it as a thrilling whodunit in the film noir tradition. Or we can access it at the point of its cultural meaning. What, for example, does the operation of the precrime unit have to say about the holding and detaining of "suspected" individuals, say, terrorists? How does the erasure of the many minority reports reflect on the fairness of the judicial system, especially in capital cases? Just how much freedom are we willing to give up to feel safe?

In fact, television programs such as *Arli$$, Sex and the City, The Simpsons, Malcolm in the Middle,* and *Star Trek: The Next Generation* are specifically constructed to take advantage of the media literacy skills of sophisticated viewers while providing entertaining fare for less skilled consumers. The same is true for such films as *Pulp Fiction, Dogma,* and *Being John Malkovich,* magazines such as *Mondo 2000,* and the best of jazz, rap, and rock. *Arli$$* and *Sex and the City* are produced as television comedies, designed to make people laugh. But they are also intentionally produced in a manner that provides more sophisticated, media literate viewers with opportunities to make more personally interesting or relevant meaning. Anyone can laugh while watching these programs, but

Some people see media literacy as essential if the public is to be fully engaged in our democracy. As such, they see media literacy as a struggle for power. How might these people interpret this cartoon? How do you interpret it?

Media Literacy as the Struggle for Power

Some approaches to media literacy are avowedly political; that is, they see media literacy in terms of the struggle between disadvantaged audiences and powerful media industries. Media historian and critic Robert McChesney has written passionately on this issue. The Cultural Environment Movement, a coalition of 150 independent organizations with supporters in 64 countries, and Paper Tiger Television, a group that uses public access television to boost media literacy, also address this issue. Here are their approaches to media literacy. Are these the rantings of paranoid, antimedia zealots, or do these approaches have merit?

The Cultural Environment Movement ("The People's Communication Charter," 1996, p. 4) issued its *Viewers' Declaration of Independence* at its founding convention. Here are excerpts:

Viewers' Declaration of Independence

This declaration originated at the Founding Convention of the Cultural Environment Movement (CEM) in St. Louis, Missouri, U.S.A., on March 17, 1996. It was revised following suggestions by a committee elected at the convention.

> We hold these truths to be self-evident:
> That all persons are endowed with the right to live in a cultural environment that is respectful of their humanity and supportive of their potential.
> That all children are endowed with the right to grow up in a cultural environment that fosters responsibility, trust, and community rather than force, fear, and violence.
> That when the cultural environment becomes destructive of these ends, it is necessary to alter it.

Such is the necessity that confronts us. Let the world hear the reasons that compel us to assert our rights and to take an active role in the shaping of our common cultural environment.

1. Humans live and learn by stories. Today they are no longer hand-crafted, home-made, community-inspired. They are no longer told by families, schools, or churches but are the products of a complex mass-production and marketing process. Scottish patriot Andrew Fletcher once said, "If one were permitted to make all the ballads, one need not care who should make the laws of a nation." Today most of our "ballads"—the myths and stories of our culture—are made by a small group of global conglomerates that have something to sell.

2. This radical transformation of our cultural environment has changed the roles we grow into, the way we employ creative talent, the way we raise our children, and the way we manage our affairs. Communication channels proliferate but technologies converge and media merge. Consolidation of ownership denies entry to newcomers, drives independents out of the mainstream, and reduces diversity of content. Media blend into a seamless homogenized cultural environment that constrains life's choices as much as the degradation of the physical environment limits life's chances.

3. This change did not come about spontaneously or after thoughtful deliberation. It was imposed on an uninformed public and is enshrined in legislation rushed through Congress without any opportunity for public scrutiny or debate about its consequences and worldwide fallout. The airways, a global commons, have been given away to media empires.

4. In exchange for that give-away, we are told, we get "free" entertainment and news, but in truth, we pay dearly, both as consumers and as citizens. The price of soap we buy includes a surcharge for the commercials that bring us the "soap opera." We pay when we wash, not when we watch. And we pay even if we do not watch or do not like the way of life promoted. This is

Alliance for a Media Literate America
www.
nmec.org/medialit.html

some people can investigate hypocrisy in professional sports *(Arli$$)*, or they can examine what goes on inside the heads of young and middle-aged women looking for love *(Sex and the City)*.

6. *An understanding of the ethical and moral obligations of media practitioners.* To make informed judgments about the performance of the media, we also must be aware of the competing pressures on practitioners as they do their jobs. We must understand the media's official and unofficial rules of operation. In other words, we must know, respectively, their legal and ethical obligations. Return, for a moment, to the question

taxation without representation. Furthermore, the advertising expenditures that buy our media are a tax-deductible business expense. Money diverted from the public treasury pays for an invisible, unelected, unaccountable, private Ministry of Culture making decisions that shape public policy behind closed doors.

5. The human consequences are also far-reaching. They include cults of media violence that desensitize, terrorize, brutalize and paralyze; the promotion of unhealthy practices that pollute, drug, hurt, poison, and kill thousands every day; portrayals that dehumanize, stereotype, marginalize and stigmatize women, racial and ethnic groups, gays and lesbians, aging or disabled or physically or mentally ill persons, and others outside the cultural mainstream.

6. These distortions of the democratic process divert attention from the basic needs, problems and aspirations of people. They conceal the drift toward ecological suicide; the silent crumbling of our vital infrastructure; the cruel neglect of children, poor people, and other vulnerable populations; the invasions of privacy at home and in the workplace; the growing inequalities of wealth and opportunity; the profits made from throwing millions of people on the scrapheap of the unemployed; the commercialization of the classroom; and the downgrading of education and the arts.

7. Global marketing formulas, imposed on media workers and foisted on the children of the world, colonize, monopolize and homogenize cultures everywhere. Technocratic fantasies mask social realities that further widen the gaps between the information rich and the information poor.

8. Repeated protests and petitions have been ignored or dismissed as attempts at "censorship" by the media magnates who alone have the power to suppress and to censor. No constitutional protection or legislative prospect will help us to loosen the noose of market censorship or

to counter the repressive direction the "culture wars" are taking us. We need a liberating alternative.

We, therefore, declare our independence from a system that has drifted out of democratic reach. Our CEM offers the liberating alternative: an independent citizen voice in cultural policymaking, working for the creation of a free, fair, diverse, and responsible cultural environment for us and our children.

Paper Tiger Television was founded in 1981, and at that time issued its *Manifesto*, which reads in part:

> The power of mass culture rests on the trust of the public. This legitimacy is a paper tiger. Investigation into the corporate structures of the media and critical analysis of their content is one way to demystify the information industry. Developing a critical consciousness about the communications industry is a necessary first step toward democratic control of information resources. (online: <http://www.papertiger.org>)

McChesney bases his call for more widespread and sophisticated media literacy on the threat posed by the "corporate takeover" of our media system. He writes:

> The very issue of who controls the media system and for what purposes is not part of contemporary political debate. Instead, there is the presumption that a profit-seeking, commercial media system is fundamentally sound, and that most problems can be resolved for the most part through less state interference or regulation, which (theoretically) will produce the magic elixir of competition. In view of the extraordinary importance of media and communication in our society, I believe that the subject of how media are controlled, structured, and subsidized should be at the center of democratic debate. Instead, this subject is nowhere to be found. This is not an accident; it reflects above all the economic, political, and ideological power of the media corporations and their allies. And it has made the prospect of challenging corporate media power, and of democratizing communication, all the more daunting. (1999a, p. 7)

of televised violence. It is legal for a station to air graphic violence. But is it ethical? If it is unethical, what power, if any, do we have to demand its removal from our screens? Dilemmas such as this are discussed at length in Chapter 14.

7. *Development of appropriate and effective production skills.* Traditional literacy assumes that people who can read can also write. Media literacy also makes this assumption. Our definition of literacy (of either type) calls not only for effective and efficient comprehension of content but for its effective and efficient *use*. Therefore, media literate individuals

Paper Tiger TV
www.
papertiger.org

should develop production skills that enable them to create useful media messages. If you have ever tried to make a narrative home video—one that tells a story—you know that producing content is much more difficult than consuming it. Even producing a taped answering machine message that is not embarrassing is a daunting task for many people.

This element of media literacy may seem relatively unimportant at first glance. After all, if you choose a career in media production, you will get training in school and on the job. If you choose another calling, you may never be in the position of having to produce content. But most professions now employ some form of media to disseminate information, for use in training, to enhance presentations, or to keep in contact with clients and customers. The Internet and the World Wide Web, in particular, require effective production skills of their users—at home, school, and work—because online receivers can and do easily become online creators.

MEDIA LITERACY SKILLS

Consuming media content is simple. Push a button and you have television pictures or music on a radio. Come up with enough cash and you can see a movie or buy a magazine. Media literate consumption, however, requires a number of specific skills:

1. *The ability and willingness to make an effort to understand content, to pay attention, and to filter out noise.* As we saw in Chapter 1, anything that interferes with successful communication is called noise, and much of the noise in the mass communication process results from our own consumption behavior. When we watch television, often we are also doing other things, such as eating, reading, or chatting on the phone. We drive while we listen to the radio. Obviously, the quality of our meaning making is related to the effort we give it.

2. *An understanding of and respect for the power of media messages.* The mass media have been around for more than a century and a half. Just about everybody can enjoy them. Their content is either free or relatively inexpensive. Much of the content is banal and a bit silly, so it is easy to dismiss media content as beneath serious consideration or too simple to have any influence.

We also disregard media's power through the **third person effect**—the common attitude that others are influenced by media messages but that we are not. That is, we are media literate enough to understand the influence of mass communication on the attitudes, behaviors, and values of others but not self-aware or honest enough to see it in our own lives.

3. *The ability to distinguish emotional from reasoned reactions when responding to content and to act accordingly.* Media content is often designed to touch us at the emotional level. We enjoy losing ourselves in

a good song or in a well-crafted movie or television show; this is among our great pleasures. But because we react emotionally to these messages does not mean they don't have serious meanings and implications for our lives. Television pictures, for example, are intentionally shot and broadcast for their emotional impact. Reacting emotionally is appropriate and proper. But then what? What do these pictures tell us about the larger issue at hand? We can use our feelings as a point of departure for meaning making. We can ask, "Why does this content make me feel this way?"

4. *Development of heightened expectations of media content.* We all use media to tune out, waste a little time, and provide background noise. When we decide to watch television, we are more likely to turn on the set and flip channels until we find something passable than we are to read the listings to find a specific program to view. When we are at the video store, we often settle for anything because "It's just a rental." When we expect little from the content before us, we tend to give meaning making little effort and attention.

Media Alliance **www.** media-alliance.org

5. *A knowledge of genre conventions and the ability to recognize when they are being mixed.* The term **genre** refers to the categories of expression within the different media, such as "the evening news," "documentary," "horror movie," or "entertainment magazine." Each genre is characterized by certain distinctive, standardized style elements—the **conventions** of that genre. The conventions of the evening news, for example, include a short, upbeat introductory theme and one or two good-looking people sitting at a space-age desk. When we hear and see these style elements, we expect the evening news. We can tell a documentary film from an entertainment movie by its more serious tone and the number of "talking heads." We know by their appearance—the use of color and the amount of text on the cover—which magazines offer serious reading and which provide entertainment.

Knowledge of these conventions is important because they cue or direct our meaning making. For example, we know to accept the details in a documentary film about the sinking of the *Titanic* as more credible than those found in a Hollywood movie about that disaster.

This skill is also important for a second reason. Sometimes, in an effort to maximize audiences (and therefore profits) or for creative reasons, media content makers mix genre conventions. Are Oliver Stone's *Nixon* and *JFK* fact or fiction? Is Geraldo Rivera a journalist, a talk show host, or a showman? Is *G.I. Joe* a kid's cartoon or a 30-minute commercial? *Extra!* and *E! Daily News* look increasingly like *Dateline NBC* and the *CBS Evening News.* Reading media texts becomes more difficult as formats are co-opted.

6. *The ability to think critically about media messages, no matter how credible their sources.* It is crucial that media be credible in a democracy in which the people govern because the media are central to the governing process. This is why the news media are sometimes referred to as the fourth branch of government, complementing the executive, judicial,

The sets of each of these newscasts share certain characteristics. Yet we know them to be very different types of programs with quite different definitions of what constitutes news. Why do you think the producers of *Extra!* work to make their set look like that of NBC's *The Brokaw Report*? Or are the producers of Tom Brokaw's show trying to make it look more like *Extra!*?

and legislative branches. This does not mean, however, that we should believe everything they report. But it is often difficult to arrive at the proper balance between wanting to believe and accepting what we see and hear unquestioningly, especially when frequently we are willing to suspend disbelief and are encouraged by the media themselves to see their content as real and credible.

Consider the *New York Times* motto, "All the News That's Fit to Print," and the title "Eyewitness News." If it is all there, it must all be real, and who is more credible than an eyewitness? But if we examine these media, we would learn that the *Times* in actuality prints all the news that fits (in its pages) and that the news is, at best, a very selective eyewitness.

7. *A knowledge of the internal language of various media and the ability to understand its effects, no matter how complex.* Just as each media genre has its own distinctive style and conventions, each medium also has its own specific internal language. This language is expressed in **production values**—the choice of lighting, editing, special effects, music, camera angle, location on the page, and size and placement of headline. To be able to read a media text, you must understand its language. We learn the grammar of this language automatically from childhood—for example, "the picture going all woosie-like" from the opening vignette.

Let's consider two versions of the same movie scene. In the first, a man is driving a car. Cut to a woman lying tied up on a railroad track. What is the relationship between the man and the woman? Where is he going? With no more information than these two shots, you know automatically that he cares for her and is on his way to save her. Now, here

It is one thing to understand the importance of being a media literate individual, of knowing its fundamental elements and necessary skills. It is quite another to live a media literate life. This is not as difficult as it may seem at first. For one thing, we live lives that are virtually awash in media and their messages, so the opportunities to practice media literacy are always there. But we can (and should) do more. We can live a media literate life *and* make media literacy a living enterprise. We can encourage and even teach others its value.

The margins of this text are replete with URLs that connect us to educational, professional, scholarly, public interest, governmental, and industry groups that, either directly or indirectly, contribute to our ability to be media literate. This chapter alone offers links to a dozen sites specifically devoted to advancing the cause of media literacy. In addition, a majority of states maintain standards for teaching media literacy in their schools. Montana and Massachusetts are notable examples. Get a copy of the standards used where you live. Read them and, if need be, challenge them.

Look, too, at the media literacy efforts in other countries. Media literacy is a mandatory part of the school curriculum in Canada, Great Britain, and Australia. The Bertelsmann Foundation has long sponsored media education programs in Germany (and recently in the United States). The British Film Institute and CLEMI in France underwrite similar efforts in their respective countries. The Australian Teachers of Media encourage media education in Australia, New Zealand, and Southeast Asia.

The American media industry, too, is committing itself to the effort. Many contemporary television programs, such as public broadcasting's adolescent reading show *Wishbone*, regularly close with a behind-the-scenes, how-did-we-produce-that-shot feature in an attempt to teach television "readers" the "grammar" of video narrative. The cable network Court TV runs a classroom-style program called *Choices and Consequences* designed to help students read the difference between negative and positive media images. Cable network Odyssey runs a public service campaign featuring "Spokesfrog" Kermit aimed at instructing parents how to pass media literacy skills on to their children. The Discovery Channel offers *Assignment: Media Literacy*, separate kits for elementary, middle, and high school students designed to impart critical viewing skills for all electronic media. The cable industry, in conjunction with the national PTA, sponsors an annual nationwide media literacy event called *Take Charge of Your TV Week*, typically in October. Almost every newspaper of any size in America now produces a weekly "young person's section" to encourage boys and girls to read the paper and differentiate it from the other news media. Even controversial in-school news/advertising network Channel One (Chapter 12) offers a media literacy course to schools free of charge.

Again, there is no shortage of ways to improve your own media literacy and to advance that of others. This text will help you get started. Each chapter ends with two sections. The first, *Developing Media Literacy Skills,* focuses on improving our personal media literacy. The second, *Living Media Literacy,* offers suggestions for using our media literacy skills in the larger culture—making media literacy a living enterprise.

The PBS young people's reading show *Wishbone* always closes with an explanation of how some part of the program was technically produced.

is the second version. The man is driving the car. Fade to black. Fade back up to the woman on the tracks. Now what is the relationship between the man and the woman? Where is he going? It is less clear that these two people even have anything to do with each other. We construct completely different meanings from exactly the same two pictures because the punctuation (the quick cut/fade) differs.

Media texts tend to be more complicated than these two scenes. The better we can handle their grammar, the more we can understand and appreciate texts. The more we understand texts, the more we can be equal partners with media professionals in meaning making.

"Complete" media literacy is difficult to achieve, but it is a worthy goal. Reading and understanding the model of media literacy shown in Figure 2.2 is a good place to start your own personal journey toward fuller media literacy.

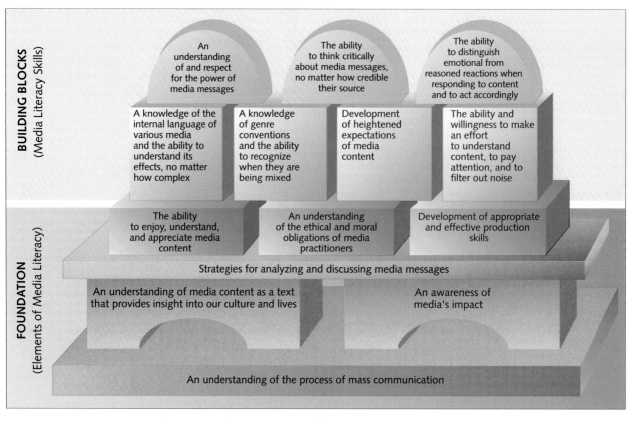

Strategies for Media Literacy
www.
swamp.org/mediasites.html

Figure 2.2 A Model of Media Literacy. This model graphically represents some of the themes investigated in this chapter. The entire media literacy enterprise has at its base *an understanding of the process of mass communication.* Upon this rests its second most fundamental set of elements, *an understanding of media content as a text that provides insight into our culture and lives,* and *an awareness of media's impact.* Once media message consumers acquire these three elements, the remainder should logically follow. Individuals may alter the relative position of the remaining foundational elements and building blocks to suit their personally determined consumption strategies.

Chapter Review

In oral or preliterate cultures language was local and specific; knowledge, history, and myth were transmitted orally; memory was crucial; and elders and storytellers, as repositories of cultural values and beliefs, occupied positions of elevated status.

Writing changed the way cultures are organized and the way they function. Meaning and language became more uniform. When knowledge, history, and myth were transmitted in writing, the literate became the new elite. With writing also came the beginnings of democracy.

Gutenberg's invention of the printing press around 1446 gave writing new power. The ability to read became a necessity for people at all levels of society; literacy and education spread. The newly literate began to interact, both as people and in their ideas. As more material was published, people had more variety of thought presented to them, and they were freer to read what they wanted when they wanted.

The Industrial Revolution spread the power of print, but it also helped create a middle class with discretionary income to spend on information and entertainment. By the end of the 19th century a mass audience and the means to reach it existed.

The communication technologies that followed the printing press—newspapers, magazines, motion pictures, radio, television, and computer networks— had their own impacts. Mass market newspapers, magazines, motion pictures, and radio helped to geographically and culturally unify the rapidly expanding, pluralistic, multiethnic United States; aided in the creation and nourishment of its middle class; and helped establish, support, and solidify the roots of our consumer economy.

Television was central to the transformation of the United States into a true consumer economy after World War II. But the influence and power of all the mass media, as well as the new computer communication technologies, raise questions about their use and control. People who are more media literate can better answer these questions for themselves and their culture.

Media literacy is composed of an awareness of the impact of the media on individuals and society; an understanding of the process of mass communication; strategies for analyzing and discussing media messages; an awareness of media content as a "text" that provides insight into contemporary culture; cultivation of enhanced enjoyment, understanding, and appreciation of media content; development of an understanding of the ethical and moral obligations of media practitioners; and development of appropriate and effective production skills.

Media literacy requires mastery of several skills: the ability and willingness to make an effort to understand content, to pay attention, and to filter out noise; an understanding of and respect for the power of media messages; the ability to distinguish emotional from reasoned reactions when responding to content and to act accordingly; development of heightened expectations of media content; a knowledge of genre conventions and the ability to recognize when conventions are being mixed; the ability to think critically about media messages, no matter how credible their source; and a knowledge of the internal language of various media and the ability to understand its effects, no matter how complex.

Key Terms

Use the text's CD-ROM and the Online Learning Center at www.mhhe.com/baran to further your understanding of the following terminology.

literate culture, 38
oral (or preliterate) culture, 39
griots, 39
ideogrammatic alphabet, 39
syllable alphabet, 40

papyrus, 40
parchment, 40
literacy, 40
information society, 48
media literacy, 50

multiple points of access, 53
third person effect, 56
genre, 57
conventions, 57
production values, 58

Questions for Review

 Go to the self-quizzes on the CD-ROM and the Online Learning Center to test your knowledge.

1. Characterize the communication and organizational styles of preliterate cultures. Where does power reside in these cultures?
2. What social, cultural, and economic factors boosted the development and spread of writing?
3. How did literacy change communication and the organization of preliterate cultures? Characterize the newly literate cultures.
4. How did the printing press make possible mass communication?
5. What was the impact of printing on the culture of Western Europe?
6. What was the role of the Industrial Revolution in furthering literacy? The development of the middle class? Democracy?
7. What is media literacy? What are its components?
8. What is meant by multiple points of access? What does it have to do with media literacy?
9. What are some specific media literacy skills?
10. What is the difference between genres and production conventions? What do these have to do with media literacy?

Questions for Critical Thinking and Discussion

1. Consider the changes brought about by the shift from oral to literate cultures. How similar or different do you think the changes will be as we move to a more fully computer literate culture?
2. The Gutenberg printing press had just the opposite effect from what was intended. What optimistic predictions for the cultural impact of the Internet and the World Wide Web do you think will prove as inaccurate as Gutenberg's hopes for his innovation? What optimistic predictions do you think will be realized? Defend your answers.
3. How media literate do you think you are? What about those around you—your parents, for example, or your best friend? What are your weaknesses as a media literate person?
4. Can you take a piece of media content from your own experience and explain how you approach it from multiple points of access?
5. How do you choose which television programs you watch? How thoughtful are your choices? How do you choose videos? Movies? How thoughtful are you in these circumstances?

Important Resources

Davis, R. E. (1976). *Response to innovation: A study of popular argument about new mass media.* New York: Arno Press. A fascinating examination of popular press reaction to the introduction of movies, talkies, radio, and television. Thousands of quotes are used to demonstrate that concern greeting these technologies varied very little.

Eisenstein, E. L. (1979). *The printing press as an agent of change: Communications and cultural transformations in early-modern Europe.* Cambridge: Cambridge University Press. The classic work on the impact of printing. Even though it is serious scholarship, it is a readable look at and analysis of Gutenberg's technology and its cultural impact.

Innis, H. A. (1972). *Empire and communications.* Toronto: University of Toronto Press. A classic work examining how the spread of communication facilitated the spread of political and military influence. It is serious scholarship but well written and accessible to college-level readers.

Potter, W. J. (1998). *Media literacy.* Thousand Oaks, CA: Sage. A detailed and thorough discussion of media literacy—what it is, how to develop it, and how to teach it.

Silverblatt, A. (1995). *Media literacy.* Westport, CN: Praeger. Portions of Chapter 2 in this book depend heavily on the ideas expressed clearly and intelligently by Silverblatt in this excellent primer.

Together with the Potter book mentioned above, these are two of the best sources on media literacy available anywhere.

Silverblatt, A., & Enright Eliceiri, E. M. (1997). *Dictionary of media literacy.* **Westport, CT: Greenwood Press.** A reference book containing concepts, terms, organizations, and issues important to media literacy.

Silverblatt, A., Ferry, J., & Finan, B. (1999). *Approaches to media literacy: A handbook.* **Armonk, NY: Sharp.** A how-to book for building strong media literacy skills across all media, including public relations and advertising.

More on Storytelling	www.storynet.org
Project Gutenberg	www.promo.net/pg/
More on the Industrial Revolution	www.fordham.edu/halsall/mod/modsbook14.html
Center for Media Literacy	www.medialit.org
Center for Media Education	www.cme.org/cme
Media Awareness Network	www.schoolnet.ca/medianet
Media Education Foundation	www.igc.org/mef
Alliance for a Media Literate America	www.nmec.org/medialit.html
Media Education	www.mediaeducation.com
Association for Media Literacy	www.aml.ca
Paper Tiger TV	www.papertiger.org
Media Alliance	www.media-alliance.org
Strategies for Media Literacy	www.swamp.org/mediasites.html

PART two

Media, Media Industries, and Media Audiences

CHAPTER 3

Books

Books were the first mass medium and are, in many ways, the most personal. They inform and entertain. They are repositories of our pasts and agents of personal development and social change. Like all media, they mirror the culture. After studying this chapter you should

- be familiar with the history and development of the publishing industry and the book itself as a medium.

- recognize the cultural value of books and the implications of censorship for democracy.

- understand how the organizational and economic nature of the contemporary book industry shapes the content of books.

- be a more media literate consumer of books, especially in recognizing their uniqueness in an increasingly mass mediated world.

THE VIDEO BEGAN WHEN YOU HIT THE PLAY BUTTON ON the remote control. But the folks who rented the movie before you failed to rewind. So there you were, watching an arresting scene from François Truffaut's 1967 adaptation of Ray Bradbury's (1953/1981) science fiction classic *Fahrenheit 451*.

At first you couldn't make out what was happening. A group of people were wandering about, and each person was talking to him- or herself. You recognized actress Julie Christie, but the other performers and what they were saying were completely unfamiliar. You stayed with the scene. The trees were bare. Snow was falling, covering everything. Puffs of steam floated from people's mouths as they spoke, seemingly to no one. As you watched a bit more, you began to recognize some familiar phrases. These people were reciting passages from famous books! Before you could figure out why they were doing this, the film ended.

So you rewound and watched the entire video, discovering that these people *were* the books they had memorized. In this

1456 First Gutenberg Bible

1638 First printing press in the Colonies

1644 *The Whole Booke of Psalms*, first book printed in the Colonies

1732 *Poor Richard's Almanack*

1765 Stamp Act

1774 *Common Sense*

~1800 Continuous roll paper

1807 John Wiley & Sons established

1811 Steam-powered printing press

1817 Harper Brothers established

1830 Improved pulp making

1860 Dime novels appear

1861 U.S. achieves highest literacy rate in the world

1884 Linotype machine

~1885 Offset lithography

1926 Book of the Month Club begins

1935 Penguin Books (first paperbacks) established in London

1939 Pocket Books (paperbacks) established in the U.S.

1960 Paperback sales surpass hardback sales for first time

1995 Amazon.com goes online

In the now not-so-distant future of *Fahrenheit 451*, people must memorize the content of books because to own a book is illegal.

near-future society, all books had been banned by the authorities, forcing these people—book lovers all—into hiding. They hold the books in their heads because to hold them in their hands is a crime. If discovered with books, people are jailed and the books are set afire—Fahrenheit 451 is the temperature at which book paper burns.

Moved by the film, you go to the library the next day and check out the book itself. Bradbury's main character, Guy Montag, a fireman who until this moment had been an official book burner himself, speaks a line that stays with you, even today. After he watches an old woman burn to death with her forbidden volumes, he implores his ice-cold, drugged, and television-deadened wife to understand what he is only then realizing. He pleads with her to see: "There must be something in books, things we can't imagine, to make a woman stay in a burning house; there must be something there" (1981, pp. 49–50).

More on Ray Bradbury
www.
raybradbury.com

In this chapter we examine the history of books, especially in terms of their role in the development of the United States. We discuss the importance that has traditionally been ascribed to books, as well as the scope and nature of the book industry. We address the various factors that shape the contemporary economics and structures of the book industry, examining at some length the impact of convergence, concentration, and hypercommercialism on the book industry and its relationship with its readers. Finally, we discuss the media literacy issues inherent in the wild success of the Harry Potter books.

A Short History of Books

As we saw in Chapter 2, use of Gutenberg's printing press spread rapidly throughout Europe in the last half of the 15th century. But the technological advances and the social, cultural, and economic conditions necessary for books to become a major mass medium were three centuries away. As a result, it was a printing press and a world of books not unlike that in Gutenberg's time that first came to the New World in the 17th century.

More on Ben Franklin
WWW.
english.udel.edu/lemay/franklin

BOOKS IN COLONIAL NORTH AMERICA

The earliest colonists came to America primarily for two reasons—to escape religious persecution and to find economic opportunities unavailable to them in Europe. Most of the books they carried with them to the New World were religiously oriented. Moreover, they brought very few books at all. Better-educated, wealthier Europeans were secure at home. Those willing to make the dangerous journey tended to be poor, uneducated, and largely illiterate.

There were other reasons early settlers did not find books central to their lives. One was the simple fight for survival. In the brutal and hostile land to which they had come, leisure for reading books was a luxury for which they had little time. People worked from sunrise to sunset just to live. If there was to be reading, it would have to be at night, and it was folly to waste precious candles on something as unnecessary to survival as reading. In addition, books and reading were regarded as symbols of wealth and status and therefore not priorities for people who considered themselves to be pioneers, servants of the Lord, or anti-English colonists. The final reason the earliest settlers were not active readers was the lack of portability of books. Books were heavy, and few were carried across the ocean. Those volumes that did make it to North America were extremely expensive and not available to most people.

The first printing press arrived on North American shores in 1638, only 18 years after the Plymouth Rock landing. It was operated by a company called Cambridge Press. Printing was limited to religious and government

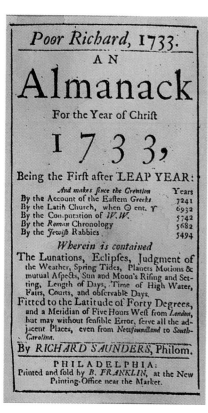

First published in 1732, Benjamin Franklin's *Poor Richard's Almanack* offered readers a wealth of information for the upcoming year.

documents. The first book printed in the Colonies appeared in 1644—*The Whole Booke of Psalms,* sometimes referred to as the *Bay Psalm Book.* Among the very few secular titles were those printed by Benjamin Franklin 90 years later. *Poor Richard's Almanack,* which first appeared in 1732, sold 10,000 copies annually. The *Almanack* contained short stories, poetry, weather predictions, and other facts and figures useful to a population more in command of its environment than those first settlers. As the Colonies grew in wealth and sophistication, leisure time increased, as did affluence and education. Franklin also published the first true novel printed in North America, *Pamela,* written by English author Samuel Richardson. Still, by and large, books were religiously oriented or pertained to official government activities such as tax rolls and the pronouncements of various commissions.

The primary reason for this lack of variety was the requirement that all printing be done with the permission of the colonial governors. Because these men were invariably loyal to King George II, secular printing and criticism of the British Crown or even of local authorities was never authorized, and publication of such writing meant jail. Many printers were imprisoned—including Franklin's brother James—for publishing what they believed to be the truth.

The printers went into open revolt against official control in March 1765 after passage of the Stamp Act. Designed by England to recoup money it spent waging the French and Indian War, the Stamp Act mandated that all printing—legal documents, books, magazines, and newspapers—be done on paper stamped with the government's seal. Its additional purpose was to control and limit expression in the increasingly restless Colonies. This affront to their freedom, along with the steep cost of the tax—sometimes doubling the price of a publication—was simply too much for the colonists. The printers used their presses to run accounts of antitax protests, demonstrations, riots, sermons, boycotts, and other antiauthority activities, further fueling revolutionary and secessionist sympathies. In November 1765—when the tax was to take effect—the authorities were so cowed by the reaction of the colonists that they were unwilling to enforce it.

Anti-British sentiment reached its climax in the mid-1770s, and books were at its core. Short books, or pamphlets, motivated and coalesced political dissent. In 1774 England's right to govern the Colonies was openly challenged by James Wilson's *Considerations on the Nature and Extent of the Legislative Authority of the British Parliament,* John Adams's *Novanglus Papers,* and Thomas Jefferson's *A Summary View of the Rights of British America.* Most famous of all was Thomas Paine's 47-page *Common Sense.* It sold 120,000 copies in the first 3 months after its release to a total population of 400,000 adults. Between 1776 and 1783 Paine also wrote a series of pamphlets called *The American Crisis. Common Sense* and *The American*

Crisis made Paine the most widely read colonial author during the American Revolution.

The Early Book Industry After the War of Independence, printing became even more central to political, intellectual, and cultural life in major cities like Boston, New York, and Philadelphia. To survive financially, printers also operated as booksellers, book publishers, and sometimes as postmasters who sold stationery and even groceries. A coffee house or tavern often was attached to the print shop. The era was alive with political change, and printer/bookshops became clearinghouses for the collection, exchange, and dissemination of information.

The U.S. newspaper industry grew rapidly from this mix, as we will see in Chapter 4. The book industry, however, was slower to develop. Books were still expensive, often costing the equivalent of a working person's weekly pay, and literacy remained a luxury. However, due in large measure to a movement begun before the Civil War, compulsory education had come to most states by 1900. This swelled the number of readers, which increased demand for books. This increased demand, coupled with a number of important technological advances, brought the price of books within reach of most people. In 1861 the United States had the highest literacy rate of any country in the world (58%), and 40 years later at the start of the 20th century, 9 out of every 10 U.S. citizens could read.

Improving Printing The 1800s saw a series of important refinements to the process of printing. Continuous roll paper, which permitted rapid printing of large numbers of identical, standardized pages, was invented in France at the very beginning of the century. Soon after, in 1811, German inventor Friedrich Koenig converted the printing press from muscle to steam power, speeding production of printed material and reducing its cost. In 1830 Americans Thomas Gilpin and James Ames perfected a wood-grinding machine that produced enough pulp to make 24 miles of paper daily, further lowering the cost of printing. The final pieces of this era's rapid production–cost reduction puzzle were fit in the later part of the century. German immigrant Ottmar Mergenthaler introduced his **linotype** machine in the United States in 1884. Employing a typewriter-like keyboard, the linotype enabled printers to set type mechanically rather than manually. Near the same time, **offset lithography** was developed. This advance made possible printing from photographic plates rather than from heavy and relatively fragile metal casts.

British-born writer, patriot, and revolutionary leader Thomas Paine wrote *Common Sense* and *The American Crisis* to rally his colonial compatriots in their struggle against the British.

The Flowering of the Novel The combination of technically improved, lower-cost printing (and therefore lower-cost publications) and widespread literacy produced the flowering of the novel in the 1800s. Major U.S. book publishers Harper Brothers and John Wiley & Sons—both in business today—were established in New York in 1817 and 1807, respectively. And books such as Nathaniel Hawthorne's *The Scarlet Letter* (1850), Herman Melville's *Moby Dick* (1851), and Mark Twain's *Huckleberry Finn* (1884) were considered by their readers to be equal to or better than the works of famous European authors such as Jane Austen, the Brontës, and Charles Dickens.

The growing popularity of books was noticed by brothers Irwin and Erastus Beadle. In 1860 they began publishing novels that sold for 10 cents. These **dime novels** were inexpensive, and because they concentrated on frontier and adventure stories, they attracted growing numbers of readers. Within 5 years of their start, Beadle & Company had produced over 4 million volumes of what were also sometimes called **pulp novels** (Tebbel, 1987). Advertising titles like *Malaeska: Indian Wife of the White Hunter* with the slogan "Dollar Books for a Dime!" the Beadles democratized books and turned them into a mass medium.

The Coming of Paperback Books Dime novels were "paperback books" because they were produced with paper covers. But publisher Allen Lane invented what we now recognize as the paperback in the midst of the Great Depression in London when he founded Penguin Books in 1935. Four years later, publisher Robert de Graff introduced the idea to the United States. His Pocket Books were small, inexpensive (25 cents) reissues of books that had already become successful as hardcovers. They were sold just about everywhere—newsstands, bookstores, train stations, shipping terminals, and drug and department stores. Within weeks of their introduction, de Graff was fielding orders of up to 15,000 copies a day (Tebbel, 1987). Soon, new and existing publishers joined the paperback boom. Traditionalists had some concern about the "cheapening of the book," but that was more than offset by the huge popularity of paperbacks and the willingness of publishers to take chances. For example, in the 1950s and '60s, African American writers such as Richard Wright and Ralph Ellison were published, along with controversial works such as *Catcher in the Rye*. Eventually, paperback books became the norm, surpassing hardcover book sales for the first time in 1960. Today, more than 60% of all books sold in the United States are paperbacks.

Paperbacks are no longer limited to reprints of successful hardbacks. Many books now begin life as paperbacks. The John Jakes books *The Americans* and *The Titans*, for example, were issued initially as paperbacks and later reissued in hardcover. Paperback sales today top 1 million volumes a day, and bookstores generate half their revenue from these sales.

Books and Their Audiences

The book is the least "mass" of our mass media in audience reach and in the magnitude of the industry itself, and this fact shapes the nature of the relationship between medium and audience. Publishing houses, both large and small, produce narrowly or broadly aimed titles for readers, who buy and carry away individual units. This more direct relationship between publishers and readers renders books fundamentally different from other mass media. For example, because books are less dependent than other mass media on attracting the largest possible audience, books are more able and more likely to incubate new, challenging, or unpopular ideas. As the medium least dependent on advertiser support, books can be aimed at extremely small groups of readers, challenging them and their imaginations in ways that many sponsors would find unacceptable in advertising-based mass media. Because books are produced and sold as individual units—as opposed to a single television program simultaneously distributed to millions of viewers or a single edition of a mass circulation newspaper—more "voices" can enter and survive in the industry. This medium can sustain more voices in the cultural forum than can other mass media.

THE CULTURAL VALUE OF THE BOOK

The book industry is bound by many of the same financial and industrial pressures that constrain other media, but books, more than the others, are in a position to transcend those constraints. In *Fahrenheit 451* Montag's boss, Captain Beatty, explains why all books must be burned. "Once," he tells his troubled subordinate, "books appealed to a few people, here, there, everywhere. They could afford to be different. The world was roomy. But then the world got full of eyes and elbows and mouths" (Bradbury, 1981, p. 53). Bradbury's firemen of the future destroy books precisely because they *are* different. It is their difference from other mass media that makes books unique in our culture. Although all media serve the following cultural functions to some degree (for example, people use self-help videos for personal development and popular music is sometimes an agent of social change), books traditionally have been seen as a powerful cultural force for these reasons:

- *Books are agents of social and cultural change.* Free of the need to generate mass circulation for advertisers, offbeat, controversial, even revolutionary ideas can reach the public. For example, Andrew MacDonald's *Turner Diaries* is the ideological and how-to bible of the antigovernment militia movement in the United States. Nonetheless, this radical, revolutionary book is openly published, purchased, and discussed. This controversial work is at the heart of the box titled "You Be the Censor" (p. 93), and for a look at the role of other books in social movements, see the box "The Role of Books in Social Movements" (p. 74).
- *Books are an important cultural repository.* Want to definitively win an argument? Look it up. We turn to books for certainty and truth

The Role of Books in Social Movements

In the 15th and 16th centuries, reformers used one book—the Bible—to create one of history's most important revolutions, the Protestant Reformation. Of course, the reformers did not write this book, but their insistence that it be available to people was a direct challenge to the ruling powers of the time. Englishman John Wycliffe was persecuted and burned at the stake in the mid-1300s for translating the Bible into English. Two hundred years later, another Englishman, William Tyndale, so angered Church leaders with his insistence on printing and distributing English-language Bibles that the Church had his dead body exhumed, strangled, burned at the stake, and thrown in a river.

Before printed Bibles became generally available in the 16th and 17th centuries, Bibles and other religious tracts were typically chained to some unmovable piece of the church. Church leaders said this was done because people desperate for the Word of God would steal them, denying others access. If this was true, why were Wycliffe and Tyndale persecuted for trying to *expand* access? Historians, both secular and religious, now believe that the reason **chained Bibles** existed was to ensure that reading and interpreting their contents could be supervised and controlled. The established elites feared the power of the printed word.

This was also the case during the American Revolution, as we have seen in this chapter, as well as when the country rejected a 200-year evil, slavery. Harriet Beecher Stowe published the realistically painful story of slavery in America in 1852. Her *Uncle Tom's Cabin* had first appeared in two parts in an antislavery magazine, but its greatest impact was as a book hungrily read by a startled public. *Uncle Tom's Cabin* sold 20,000 copies in its first 3 weeks on the market, and 300,000 copies in its first year, eventually reaching sales of 7 million.

It was the tale of a kind, literate slave, Uncle Tom. Tom's reward for his intelligence and his goodness was

Chained Bibles and other handprinted books in England's Hereford Cathedral.

about the world in which we live and the ones about which we want to know. Which countries border Chile? Find the atlas. Stevie Nicks' band before Fleetwood Mac? Look in *The Rolling Stone Illustrated History of Rock and Roll*.

- *Books are our windows on the past*. What was the United States like in the 19th century? Read Alexis de Tocqueville's *Democracy in America*. England in the early 1800s? Read Jane Austen's *Pride and Prejudice*. Written in the times they reflect, these books are more accurate representations than are available in the modern electronic media.

More on Our Bodies, Ourselves
www.
ourbodiesourselves.org

- *Books are important sources of personal development*. The obvious forms are self-help and personal improvement volumes. But books also speak to us more individually than advertiser-supported media because of their small, focused target markets. For example, *Our Bodies, Ourselves*, introduced by the Boston Women's Health Book Collective in the very earliest days of the modern feminist movement, is still published today. (For more on this influential book, see the box "Our

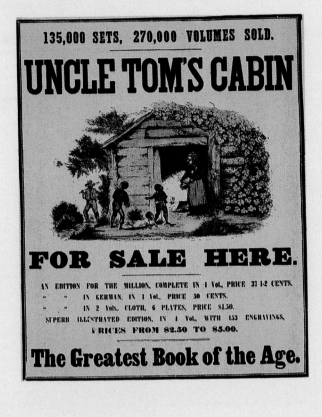

135,000 SETS, 270,000 VOLUMES SOLD.

UNCLE TOM'S CABIN

FOR SALE HERE.

AN EDITION FOR THE MILLION, COMPLETE IN 1 Vol., PRICE 37 1-2 CENTS.

" " IN GERMAN, IN 1 Vol., PRICE 50 CENTS.

" " IN 2 Vols. CLOTH, 6 PLATES, PRICE $1.50.

SUPERB ILLUSTRATED EDITION, IN 1 Vol., WITH 153 ENGRAVINGS,

PRICES FROM $2.50 TO $5.00.

The Greatest Book of the Age.

This promotional flier calls Uncle Tom's Cabin *"the greatest book of the age," a fair assessment, given its impact on the times and U.S. history.*

death at the hands of evil slave owner Simon Legree. A fine work of literature, *Uncle Tom's Cabin* galvanized public feelings against slavery. Abolitionist sentiment was no longer the domain of the intellectual, social, and religious elite. Everyday people were repulsed by the horrors of slavery. One of Stowe's most ardent readers was Abraham Lincoln, who, as president, abolished slavery.

Books have traditionally been at the center of social change in the United States. Horatio Alger's rags-to-riches stories excited westward migration in the 1800s. Upton Sinclair's *The Jungle* and other muckraking books brought about significant health and labor legislation in the early 1900s. John Steinbeck's *The Grapes of Wrath* took up the cause of migrant farmers in the post-Depression 1930s. Alex Haley's *The Autobiography of Malcolm X* and Ralph Ellison's *Invisible Man* were literary mainstays of the 1960s Civil Rights era, as was Betty Friedan's *The Feminine Mystique* for the women's movement. In the 1970s, the paperback publication of *The Pentagon Papers* hastened the end of the Vietnam War.

The role of books in important social movements is echoed in Chapter 5 in the discussion of magazine muckrakers.

Bodies, Ourselves" on p. 76.) *Dr. Spock's Baby and Child Care* has sold more than 30 million copies. J. D. Salinger's *Catcher in the Rye* was the literary anthem for the baby boomers in their teen years, as is William Gibson's *Neuromancer* for many of today's cyber-youth. It is unlikely that any of these voices would have found their initial articulation in commercially sponsored media.

■ *Books are wonderful sources of entertainment, escape, and personal reflection.*
Arthur C. Clarke, John Grisham, Judith Krantz, J. R. R. Tolkien, and Stephen King all specialize in writing highly entertaining and imaginative novels. The enjoyment found in the works of writers Joyce Carol Oates (*On Boxing, We Were the Mulvaneys*), John

Our Bodies, Ourselves

Books have been central to many of the most important social and political movements in our nation's history. *Our Bodies, Ourselves,* a book for and about women, is credited with beginning the women's health movement. The profits this book generates—some 30 years after its first appearance—continue to support what has become a worldwide undertaking. How did this influential book, with more than 4 million copies sold in 20 different languages, come into being, and how does it continue to be so influential?

The story of *Our Bodies, Ourselves* begins in 1969. That year several women, aged 23 to 39, were attending a workshop on "Women and Their Bodies" at a women's liberation conference in Boston. They began exchanging "doctor stories." They readily came to the conclusion that most women were relatively ignorant about their bodies (and by extension, their sexuality) and that the male-dominated medical profession was not particularly receptive to their needs. So they gave themselves a "summer project." As explained by the women, who began identifying themselves as the Boston Women's Health Book Collective (Norsigian et al., 1999):

> We would research our questions, share what we learned in our group, and then present the information in the fall as a course "by and for women." We envisioned an ongoing process that would involve other women who would go on to teach such a course in other settings. In creating the course, we learned that we were capable of collecting, understanding, and evaluating medical information; that we could open up to one another and find strength and comfort through sharing some of our most private experiences; that what we learned from one another was every bit as important as what we read in medical texts; and that our ex-

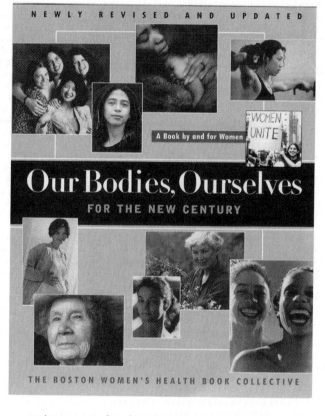

perience contradicted medical pronouncements. Over time these facts, feelings, and controversies were intertwined in the various editions of *Our Bodies, Ourselves.*

Those various editions offered a woman's perspective on issues such as reproductive health, sexuality, envi-

Irving *(The World According to Garp, Hotel New Hampshire, A Prayer for Owen Meany),* Pat Conroy *(The Prince of Tides, Beach Music),* and J. K. Rowling (the *Harry Potter* series) is undeniable.

- *The purchase and reading of a book is a much more individual, personal activity than consuming advertiser-supported (television, radio, newspapers, and magazines) or heavily promoted (popular music and movies) media.* As such, books tend to encourage personal reflection to a greater degree than these other media. We are alone when we read a book; we are part of the tribe, as McLuhan would say, when we engage other media. As such, in the words of author Julius Lester *(Look Out, Whitey! Black Power's Gon' Get Your Mama!; Why Heaven is Far Away):*

ronmental and occupational health, menopause and aging, poverty, racism, hunger, homelessness, and the overmedicalization of "women's lives that turn normal events such as childbearing and menopause into disabling conditions requiring medical intervention" (Norsigian et al., 1999).

Profits from *Our Bodies, Ourselves* were used to create the Women's Health Information Center and to fund numerous local, national, and international women's health advocacy groups and movements. Among the achievements of the resulting women's health movement that the Women's Health Information Center lists are women's ability to obtain more and better information about oral contraceptives and other drugs, the eradication of forced sterilization for poor women, improved treatment of breast cancer and increased awareness of nonsurgical treatments for this disease, the growth of women-controlled health centers, and the reinforcement of women's reproductive rights in the form of access to safe and legal abortion.

How does *Our Bodies, Ourselves* continue to make a difference? One of the original Boston Women's Health Book Collective members, Jane Pincus, explains in her introduction to the latest edition:

> Unlike most health books on the market, *Our Bodies, Ourselves for the New Century* is unique in many respects: It is based on, and has grown out of, hundreds of women's experiences. It questions the medicalization of women's bodies and lives, and highlights holistic knowledge along with conventional biomedical information. It places women's experiences within the social, political, and economic forces that determine all of our lives, thus going beyond individualistic, narrow, "self-care" and self-help approaches, and views health in the context of the sexist, racist, and financial pressures that affect far too many girls, women, and families adversely. It condemns medical corporate misbehavior driven by "bottom-line" management philosophy and the profit motive. Most of all, *Our Bodies, Ourselves* encourages you to value and share your own insights and experiences, and to use its information to question the assumptions underlying the care we all receive so that we can deal effectively with the medical system and organize for better care.

> We have listed and critiqued online health resources for women. The chapters "Body Image" and "Sexuality" deal for the first time with issues of racism. We emphasize overwork, violence, and girls' increasing use of tobacco as major threats to women's health, and we highlight more than ever the importance of good food and exercise. We explore the new issues that arise as more lesbians choose to have children. We include transgender and transsexual issues, and discuss women living with HIV as well as the most recent safer sex advice. We explore more extensively the connections between race, class, and gender-based oppressions as they affect the health of women. We offer tools for negotiating the complex and often unregulated "managed care" system, which affects women's lives much more profoundly than men's, and discuss its advantages and disadvantages. Most important, we advocate for an equitable, single-payer national health care system. (1998, p. 21)

You may disagree with some (or all) of the philosophy and goals of the Boston Women's Health Book Collective, but there is no argument that its book, *Our Bodies, Ourselves,* has made—and continues to make—a difference in the health of women around the world.

The mystery and miracle of a book is found in the fact that it is a solitary voice penetrating time and space to go beyond time and space, and to alight for a moment in that place within each of us which is also beyond time and space. . . . Books are the royal road that enable us to enter the realm of the imaginative. Books enable us to experience what it is to be someone else. Through books we experience other modes of being. Through books we recognize who we are and who we might become. . . . Books invite us into realms of the soul by asking us to imagine that we are someone other than who we are. Books require that we temporarily put our egos in a box by the door and take on the spirit of others. . . . This is what a book, any book, offers us the opportunity to do: confess and recognize ourselves. To confess and recognize our fantasies, our joys, and griefs, our aspirations and failures, our hopes and our fears. Deep within the solitary wonder in which we sit alone with a book, we confess and recognize

For more information on this topic, see NBC Video Clip #9 on the CD—*Publishers of Wind Done Gone Ordered to Stop Publication.*

what we would be too ashamed to tell another—and sometimes we are as ashamed of joy and delight and success as we are of embarrassment and failure. (2002, pp. 26–29)

■ *Books are mirrors of culture.* Books, along with other mass media, reflect the culture that produces and consumes them.

CENSORSHIP

American Library Association
WWW.
ala.org

Because of their influence as cultural repositories and agents of social change, books have often been targeted for censorship. A book is censored when someone in authority limits publication of or access to it. Censorship can and does occur in many situations and in all media (more on this in Chapter 14). But because of the respect our culture traditionally holds for books, book banning takes on a particularly poisonous connotation in the United States.

American Booksellers Foundation for Free Expression
WWW.
abffe.org

Reacting to censorship presents a dilemma for book publishers. Publishers have an obligation to their owners and stockholders to make a profit. Yet, if responsible people in positions of authority deem a certain book unsuitable for readers, shouldn't publishers do the right thing for the larger society and comply with demands to cease its publication? This was the argument presented by morals crusader Anthony Comstock in 1873 when he established the New York Society for the Suppression of Vice. It was the argument used on the evening of May 10, 1933, in Berlin when Nazi propaganda chief Joseph Goebbels put a torch to a bonfire that consumed 20,000 books. It was the argument made in 1953 when U.S. Senator Joseph McCarthy demanded the removal of more than 100 books from U.S. diplomatic libraries because of their "procommunist" slant. (Among them was Thomas Paine's *Common Sense.*)

American Civil Liberties Union
WWW.
aclu.org

According to the American Library Association Office of Intellectual Freedom and the American Civil Liberties Union, among the library and school books most frequently targeted by modern censors are the *Harry Potter* series, Mark Twain's *The Adventures of Huckleberry Finn*, Harper Lee's *To Kill a Mockingbird*, John Steinbeck's *Of Mice and Men*, the *Goosebumps* series, Alice Walker's *The Color Purple*, and children's favorite *In the Night Kitchen* by Maurice Sendak. The 50 most frequently banned books in the United States are shown in Figure 3.1. With how many are you familiar? Which ones have you read? What is it about each of these books that might have brought it to the censors' attention?

Book publishers can confront censorship by recognizing that their obligations to their industry and to themselves demand that they resist censorship. The book publishing industry and the publisher's role in it is fundamental to the operation and maintenance of our democratic society. Rather than accepting the censor's argument that certain voices require silencing for the good of the culture, publishers in a democracy have an obligation to make the stronger argument that free speech be protected and encouraged. The short list of frequently censored titles in the previous paragraph should immediately make it evident why the power of ideas

BANNED BOOKS

- *Harry Potter* (series), by J. K. Rowling
- *Of Mice and Men*, by John Steinbeck
- *The Catcher in the Rye*, by J. D. Salinger
- *The Adventures of Huckleberry Finn*, by Mark Twain
- *The Chocolate War*, by Robert Cormier
- *Bridge to Terabithia*, by Katherine Paterson
- *Scary Stories in the Dark*, by Alvin Schwartz
- *More Scary Stories in the Dark*, by Alvin Schwartz
- *Scary Stories 3: More Tales to Chill Your Bones*, by Alvin Schwartz
- *The Witches*, by Roald Dahl
- *Daddy's Roommate*, by Michael Willhoite
- *A Wrinkle in Time*, by Madeleine L'Engle
- *Forever*, by Judy Blume
- *Blubber*, by Judy Blume
- *Deenie*, by Judy Blume
- *The Giver*, by Lois Lowry
- *Anastasia Krupnik* (series), by Lois Lowry
- *Halloween ABC*, by Eve Merriam
- *A Day No Pigs Would Die*, by Robert Peck
- *Heather Has Two Mommies*, by Leslea Newman
- *It's Perfectly Normal*, by Robbie Harris
- *I Know Why the Caged Bird Sings*, by Maya Angelou
- *Fallen Angels*, by Walter Myers
- *Goosebumps* (series), by R. L. Stine

- *Sex*, by Madonna
- *Go Ask Alice*, by Anonymous
- *The Stupids* (series), by Harry Allard
- *Bumps in the Night*, by Harry Allard
- *My House*, by Nikki Giovanni
- *The New Joy of Gay Sex*, by Charles Silverstein
- *The Goats*, by Brock Cole
- *The Color Purple*, by Alice Walker
- *Kaffir Boy*, by Mark Mathabane
- *Killing Mr. Griffin*, by Lois Duncan
- *We All Fall Down*, by Robert Cormier
- *Final Exit*, by Derek Humphry
- *My Brother Sam Is Dead*, by James Lincoln Collier and Christopher Collier
- *Julie of the Wolves*, by Jean Craighead George
- *The Bluest Eye*, by Toni Morrison
- *Beloved*, by Toni Morrison
- *The Great Gilly Hopkins*, by Katherine Paterson
- *What's Happening to My Body?* by Lynda Madaras
- *To Kill a Mockingbird*, by Harper Lee
- *In the Night Kitchen*, by Maurice Sendak
- *The Outsiders*, by S. E. Hinton
- *Annie on My Mind*, by Nancy Garden
- *The Pigman*, by Paul Zindel
- *Flowers for Algernon*, by Daniel Keyes
- *The Handmaid's Tale*, by Margaret Atwood
- *The Boy Who Lost His Face*, by Louis Sachar

is worth fighting for. You can read why some people feel the need to censor in Figure 3.2, "Reasons for Banning Books."

Figure 3.1 Most Frequently Banned Books in the Past 10 Years. Shown here are the 50 books most frequently challenged in U.S. schools and public libraries during the past decade.

Scope and Structure of the Book Industry

More than 120,000 new and reprinted book titles are issued in the United States each year (Surowiecki, 2001), and each American spends, on average, $97.69 a year buying them (Statistical Abstracts of the United States, 2002).

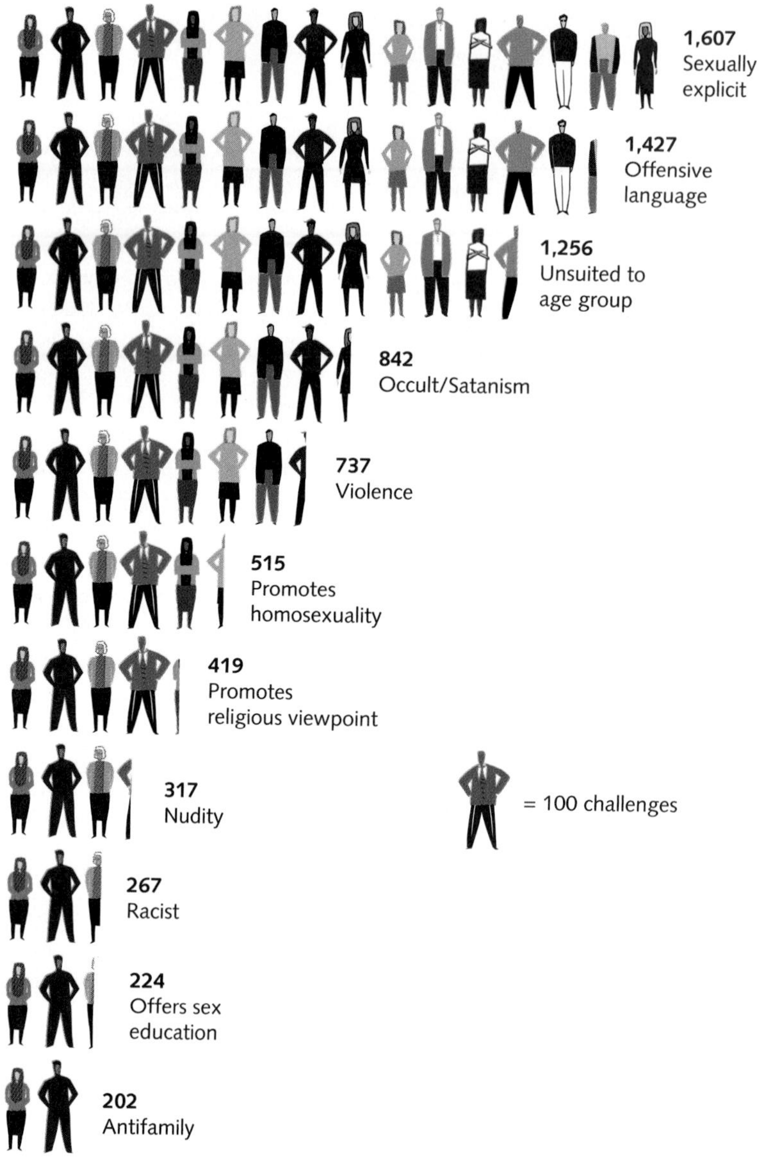

Banned Books
WWW.
ala.org/bbooks

Figure 3.2 Reasons for Banning Books. The American Library Association Office for Intellectual Freedom tallied the reasons that specific books were banned from 1990 to 2000 in America's schools and libraries. Of the 6,364 challenges reported to its offices during that decade, these were the reasons given. The number of reasons exceeds 6,364 because books were often challenged for more than one reason. Source: American Library Association Office for Intellectual Freedom (www.ala.org/bbooks/bbwdatabase.html)

1,607 Sexually explicit

1,427 Offensive language

1,256 Unsuited to age group

842 Occult/Satanism

737 Violence

515 Promotes homosexuality

419 Promotes religious viewpoint

317 Nudity

267 Racist

224 Offers sex education

202 Antifamily

= 100 challenges

CATEGORIES OF BOOKS

Association of American Publishers
WWW.
publishers.org

The Association of American Publishers divides these books into several sales categories:

- *Book club editions* are books sold and distributed (sometimes even published) by book clubs. There are currently more than 300 book clubs in the United States. These organizations offer trade, professional, and more specialized titles, for example, books for aviation aficionados and expensive republications of classic works. The Book of the Month Club, started in 1926, is the best known; the Literary Guild and the Reader's Digest Book Club are also popular.

- *El-hi* are textbooks produced for elementary and high schools.

- *Higher education* are textbooks produced for colleges and universities.

- *Mail order books,* such as those advertised on television by Time-Life Books, are delivered by mail and usually are specialized series *(The War Ships)* or elaborately bound special editions of classic novels.

- *Mass market paperbacks* are typically published only as paperbacks and are designed to appeal to a broad readership; many romance novels, diet books, and self-help books are in this category.

- *Professional books* are reference and educational volumes designed specifically for professionals such as doctors, engineers, lawyers, scientists, and managers.

- *Religious books* are volumes such as Bibles, catechisms, and hymnals.

- *Standardized tests* are guide and practice books designed to prepare readers for various examinations such as the SAT or the bar exam.

- *Subscription reference books* are publications such as the *Encyclopedia Britannica,* atlases, and dictionaries bought directly from the publisher rather than purchased in a retail setting.

- **Trade books** can be hard- or softcover and include not only fiction and most nonfiction but also cookbooks, biographies, art books, coffee-table books, and how-to books.

- *University press* books come from publishing houses associated with and often underwritten by universities. They typically publish serious nonfiction and scholarly books. The University of Chicago Press and the University of California Press are two of the better-known university presses, and the Oxford University Press is the oldest publisher in the world.

Internet Book Information Center **www.** internetbookinfo.com

In 2001, total U.S. book sales reached $25.4 billion, a mere 0.1% increase over the previous year (Figure 3.3). Several categories—mass market paperbacks (−0.8%), mail order (−18%), professional (−7.6%), Bibles (−2.6%), adult hardcover (−2.2%), and juvenile hardcover (−22.7%), showed declines in the number of books sold, some quite serious. In fact, worldwide, book sales were down 1% ("Worldwide Media Monies," 2002) in 2001.

FROM IDEA TO PUBLICATION

The ideas that ultimately become the books that fit these different categories reach publishers in a number of ways. Sometimes they reach an **acquisitions editor** (the person charged with determining which books a publisher will publish) unsolicited. This means that ideas are mailed or

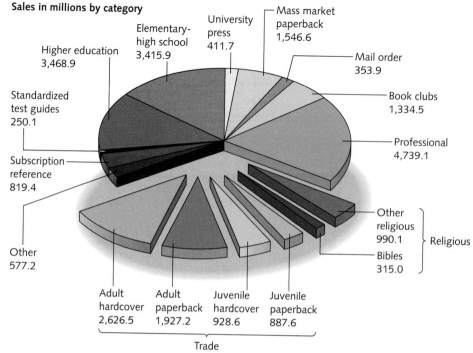

Figure 3.3 Book Sales in the United States, 2001.

Source: Publishers Weekly, March 4, 2002, p. 16

Sales in millions by category

Higher education 3,468.9

Elementary-high school 3,415.9

University press 411.7

Mass market paperback 1,546.6

Mail order 353.9

Book clubs 1,334.5

Professional 4,739.1

Standardized test guides 250.1

Subscription reference 819.4

Other 577.2

Other religious 990.1

Bibles 315.0

Religious

Adult hardcover 2,626.5

Adult paperback 1,927.2

Juvenile hardcover 928.6

Juvenile paperback 887.6

Trade

phoned directly to the acquisitions editor by the author. Many of the larger and better publishers will not accept unsolicited ideas from aspiring writers unless they first secure the services of an agent, an intermediary between publisher and writer. Increasingly, acquisitions editors are determining what books *they* think will do well and seeking out writers who can meet their needs.

At some publishing houses, acquisitions editors have the power to say "Yes" or "No" based on their own judgment of the value and profitability of an idea. At many others, these editors must prepare a case for the projects they want to take on and have them reviewed and approved by a review or proposal committee. These committees typically include not only "book people" but marketing, financial, production, and administrative professionals who judge the merit of the idea from their own perspectives. Once the acquisitions editor says "Yes," or is given permission by the committee to do so, the author and the publisher sign a contract.

Now the book must be written (if it is not already completed). An editor (sometimes the acquiring editor, sometimes not) is assigned to assist the author in producing a quality manuscript. Some combination of the publisher's marketing, promotions, and publicity departments plans the advertising campaign for the book. When available, review copies are sent to appropriate reviewers in other media. Book tours and signings are planned and scheduled. Copy for sales catalogues is written to aid salespeople in their attempts to place the book in bookstores.

American Booksellers Association
www.
ambook.org

All this effort is usually aimed at the first few months of a book's release. The publisher will determine in this time if the book will succeed or fail with readers. If the book appears to be a success, additional printings will be ordered. If the book has generated little interest from buyers, no additional copies are printed. Bookstores will eventually return unsold copies to the publisher to be sold at great discount as **remainders.**

Trends and Convergence in Book Publishing

The contemporary book industry is characterized by several important economic and structural factors. Among the most important are convergence, conglomeration, hypercommercialism and demand for profits, the growth of small presses, restructuring of retailing, and changes in readership.

CONVERGENCE

Convergence is altering almost all aspects of the book industry and its relationship with its readers. Most obviously, the Internet is changing the way books are distributed and sold. But this new technology, in the form of **e-publishing,** the publication of books initially or exclusively online, offers a new way for writers' ideas to be published. Even the physical form of books is changing—many of today's books are no longer composed of paper pages snug between two covers. E-publishing can take the form of d-books and **print on demand (POD),** and many d-books are designed to be read on handheld computers called **e-books.**

DiskUs Publishing
www.
diskuspublishing.com

D-books   Manu Herbstein could not find a publisher for his book, *Ama: A Story of the Atlantic Slave Trade.* In fact, several houses had rejected it. But he did find an outlet in the e-publisher E-Reads. In April 2002 his **d-book,** a book downloaded in electronic form from the Internet to a computer or handheld device such as a Palm Pilot, won the prestigious Commonwealth Prize in the category of best first book from the African region. The better-known Stephen King sold 400,000 digital copies (at $2.50 each) of his novella *Riding the Bullet* in 24 hours on Amazon.com's d-book service in March 2000. King followed this success later that same year with the serialized release of *The Plant.* In June 2002 John Dean of Watergate fame released his d-book through Salon.com's service, promising to reveal the identity of Deep Throat (a promise he did not keep!).

E-Reads
www.
ereads.com

Despite the presence of heavyweights like King and Dean, many book industry observers feel that e-publishing will have its greatest impact with the Herbsteins, rather than the Kings, of the literary world. Because anyone with a computer and a novel to sell can bypass the traditional book publishers, first-time authors or writers of small, niche books now have

Stephen King's *Riding the Bullet*

Xlibris
www.
xlibris.com

an outlet for their work. An additional advantage of e-publishing, especially for new or small-market authors, is that d-books can be published almost instantly. Stephen King has made enough money selling his books that he can wait the 1 to 2 years it typically takes for a traditional novel to be produced once it is in the publisher's hands. Rarely can new authors afford this luxury.

Another advantage is financial. Even though many e-publishers require payment of as much as $300 or $400 to carry the work of new or unproven novelists, authors who distribute their work through an established e-publisher usually get royalties of 40% to 70%, compared to the 5% to 10% offered by traditional publishers. (Traditional publishers say that the difference is due to the absence of services, such as editorial assistance and marketing, that authors face when using an e-publisher.) Writers who use the Web to self-publish and sell their work keep 100% of the income. For example, in June 1998 Melisse Shapiro, after being rejected by a number of traditional publishing houses, began selling her book *Lip Service* online through her own Web site. She quickly sold 1,500 copies at $12.95 each. Not only did she get to keep every penny, but her good fortune demonstrates another advantage of e-publishing. Success online can attract the attention of paper-based publishers. *Lip Service* was quickly signed by the Doubleday Book Club and the Literary Guild.

The advantages of d-books and e-publishing for readers are in time and money. Most d-books can be downloaded for as little as $3, with the average cost being around $10. And the electronic bookstore never closes. No matter what time of day or night, readers can download their next book and begin reading immediately.

Print on demand (POD) is another form of e-publishing. Companies such as Xlibris, 1stBooks, Toby Press, and iUniverse are POD publishers. They store works digitally and, once ordered, a book can be instantly printed, bound, and sent. Alternatively, once ordered, that book can be printed and bound at a bookstore that has the proper technology. The advantage for publisher and reader is financial. POD books require no warehouse for storage, there are no remainders to eat into profits, and the production costs, in both personnel and equipment, are tiny when compared to traditional publishing. These factors not only produce less expensive books for readers but greatly expand the variety of books that can and will be published. A POD operation can make a profit on as few as 100 orders. Large traditional publishers have also found a place for POD in their business, using the technology to rush hot, headline-inspired books to readers. For example, Pocket Books produced a POD version of *Knockdown*, Martin Dugard's account of the tragic 1998 Sydney-to-Hobart boat race, getting it into the hands of readers months before the paper version became available.

Industry insiders believe POD is here to stay. After all, it reduces production and distribution costs, and it gets more books to readers faster and cheaper than can the current publishing business model. D-books, however, may not fare as well. The question of their future is a simple one: Will readers read books off computer screens? As best-selling author Jane Smiley *(A Thousand Acres, Horse Heaven, Moo, Ordinary Love & Goodwill)* explained, "Our economy has a way of getting rid of perfectly good and useful items and processes without any of us ever giving permission, just as it is right now trying to get rid of the . . . book. You can't read a novel on the Internet while taking a bath" (1999, p. 10B).

E-books What Ms. Smiley is referring to is readers' willingness to read books in a form other than what we traditionally think of as a book. One way books can be read in their electronic form is to download them to your computer. Microsoft offers free software called Reader that improves the appearance of text on computer screens. But a number of companies, most notably NuvoMedia (with its Rocket eBook) and Thomson Multimedia (makers of the SoftBook), now offer devices that look pretty much like books as we know them but have the ability to store thousands of pages of downloaded text.

E-books weigh less than 2 pounds and are the size of a standard paperback. Depending on what a reader is willing to pay, e-books can offer color and full graphic presentation capabilities, including 3-D. A number of online publishers and booksellers now make their titles available for e-books (overcoming the problem of lack of available titles that delayed fuller diffusion of e-books in their early days), and text gets to e-books through the Internet, CD-ROM, and even satellite. E-book readers can underline favorite passages or write notes in the margins with a stylus and find those notations still there the next time that page is accessed. E-books have the additional advantage of easily becoming "e-magazines" and "e-newspapers," as media companies are increasingly making all forms of printed content available for downloading.

Still, relatively few people have been charmed by the e-book. Today there are fewer than 75,000 e-book readers in the United States, and industry predictions say that number will grow to only 2 million by the end of 2005. Even optimistic estimates predict that e-books will generate only about $500 million in sales by 2004, compared to today's $8 billion paperback book market (Tessler & Heim, 2000).

CONGLOMERATION

More than any other medium, the book industry was dominated by relatively small operations. Publishing houses were traditionally staffed by fewer than 20 people, the large majority by fewer than 10. Today, however, although more than 20,000 businesses call themselves book publishers, only 2,000 produce four or more titles a year. The industry is dominated

Knockdown is a POD success, and *Timeline* is a successful d-book meant to be read off a computer screen.

1st Books
www.
1stbooks.com

iUniverse
www.
iUniverse.com

now by a few giants: Hearst Books, the Penguin Group, Bantam Double-day Dell, Time Warner Publishing, Farrar, Straus & Giroux, Harcourt General, HarperCollins, and Simon & Schuster. Each of these giants was once, sometimes with another name, an independent book publisher. All are now part of large national or international corporate conglomerates. These major publishers control more than 80% of all U.S. book sales (Schiffrin, 1999). Even e-publishing, heralded by some as the future of book publishing, is dominated by the big companies. Not only do all the major houses and booksellers maintain e-publishing units, but even POD sites such as Xlibris (Random House) and iUniverse (Barnes & Noble) are wholly or part owned by these giants.

Opinion is divided on the benefit of corporate ownership. The positive view is that the rich parent company can infuse the publishing house with necessary capital, enabling it to attract better authors or to take gambles on new writers that would, in the past, have been impossible. Another plus is that the corporate parent's other media holdings can be used to promote and repackage the books for greater profitability.

The negative view is that as publishing houses become just one in the parent company's long list of enterprises, product quality suffers as important editing and production steps are eliminated to maximize profits. Before conglomeration, publishing was often described as a **cottage industry;** that is, publishing houses were small operations, closely identified with their personnel—both their own small staffs and their authors. The cottage imagery, however, extends beyond smallness of size. There was a quaintness and charm associated with publishing houses—their attention to detail, their devotion to tradition, the care they gave to their façades (their reputations). The world of corporate conglomerates has little room for such niceties, as profit dominates all other considerations.

Random House, once an independent book publisher, is now owned by the German conglomerate Bertelsmann, owner of scores of other media outlets such as RCA Records and *McCall's* magazine. A former editor, Andre Schiffrin (1996), wrote of the change from independent to subsidiary, "The drive for profit fits like an iron mask on our cultural output" (p. 29).

DEMAND FOR PROFITS AND HYPERCOMMERCIALISM

The threat from conglomeration is seen in the parent company's overemphasis on the bottom line—that is, profitability at all costs. Unlike in the days when G. P. Putnam's sons and the Schuster family actually ran the houses that carried their names, critics fear that now little pride is taken in the content of books and that risk-taking (tackling controversial issues, experimenting with new styles, finding and nurturing unknown authors) is becoming rarer and rarer.

Chairperson of the Writing Seminars at Johns Hopkins University, Mark Miller (1997), wrote, "This is the all important difference between then and now: As book lovers and businessmen, [publishers] did the

Toby Press
www.
tobypress.com

high-yield trash so as to subsidize the books they loved (although those books might also sell). No longer meant to help some finer things grow, the crap today is not a means but (as it were) the end" (p. 14). Jason Epstein, long-time editor at Random House and founder of Anchor Books, writes that his is an "increasingly distressed industry" mired in "severe structural problems." Among them are the chain-driven bookselling system that favors "brand name" authors and "a bestseller-driven system of high royalty advances." He says that contemporary publishing is "over-concentrated," "undifferentiated," and "fatally rigid" (quoted in Feldman, 2001, p. 35). To Miller, Epstein, and other critics of conglomeration, the industry seems overwhelmed by a blockbuster mentality—lust for the biggest selling authors and titles possible, sometimes with little consideration for literary merit. In 2001, for example, Justin Timberlake of the pop group 'N Sync received a seven-figure advance for his first novel, *Crossover Dribble*. Michael Crichton got $40 million for a two-book deal from HarperCollins; Tom Clancy, $45 million for two books from Penguin Putnam; Mary Higgins Clark, $64 million for five books from Simon & Schuster; and Hillary Rodham Clinton scored an $8 million advance from that same company. Husband Bill collected $12 million. In 2002, Charles Frazier, whose first novel was the best-seller *Cold Mountain*, received an $8 million advance for his second book from Random House, based on a one-page outline. "Where the [small] houses prized the subtle labor of their editors, the giants want their staff not poring over prose but signing big names over lunch" (Miller, 1997, p. 13). As the resources and energies of publishing houses are committed to a small number of superstar writers and blockbuster books, smaller, more interesting, possibly more serious or important books do not get published. If these books cannot get published, they will not be written. We will be denied their ideas in the cultural forum.

Publishers attempt to offset these large investments through the sale of **subsidiary rights,** that is, the sale of the book, its contents, and even its characters to filmmakers, paperback publishers, book clubs, foreign publishers, and product producers like T-shirt, poster, coffee cup, and greeting card manufacturers. Frazier's one-page proposal for his second novel, for example, earned his publisher $3 million for the film rights alone from Paramount Pictures. The industry itself estimates that many publishers would go out of business if it were not for the sale of these rights. Writers such as Michael Crichton *(Jurassic Park),* John Grisham *(The Client),* and Gay Talese *(Thy Neighbor's Wife)* can command as much as $2.5 million for the film rights to their books. Although this is good for the profitability of the publishers and the superstar authors, critics fear that those books with the greatest subsidiary sales value will receive the most publisher attention.

As greater and greater sums are tied up in blockbusters, and as subsidiary rights therefore grow in importance, the marketing, promotion, and public relations surrounding a book become crucial. This leads to the additional fear that only the most promotable books will be published—

FRONTLIST

THE COMPLETE IDOIT'S GUIDE FOR DUMIES
The Fun and Easy Way to Achieve Total Stupidity
by Thomas Dolt and Ian Dullard

WHO CUT THE CHEESE?
A Cultural History of the Fart
by Jim Dawson

KOKIGAMI
Performance Enhancing Adornments for the Adventurous Man
by Burton Silver and Heather Busch

Typical of thousands of small publishing houses, Ten Speed Press offers an array of interesting, odd, or otherwise "small" books that larger publishers may ignore.

Powell's Books
WWW.
powells.com

The television show *Survivor* became the subject of an instant book within weeks of the program's initial airing.

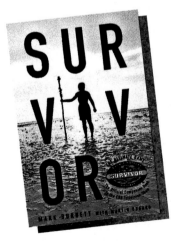

the stores are flooded with Princess Diana books, celebrity picture books, unauthorized biographies of celebrities, and tell-all autobiographies from the children of famous people.

The importance of promotion and publicity has led to an increase in the release of **instant books.** What better way to unleash millions of dollars of free publicity for a book than to base it on an event currently on the front page and the television screen? Publishers see these opportunities and then initiate the projects. Several instant books were on the shelves within days of the O. J. Simpson verdict and the death of Princess Diana. September 11, 2001, produced the instant book *In the Line of Duty*. Even the television show *Survivor* spawned a flood of instant books. Lost in the wake of instant books, easily promotable authors and titles, and blockbusters, critics argue, are books of merit, books of substance, and books that make a difference.

Several other recent events suggest that the demand for profits is bringing even more hypercommercialism to the book business. One trend is flooding the market; that is, "whenever you have a hit, milk it for all it's worth" (Streitfeld, 1998, p. 9E). Hit authors such as Anne Rice (recently averaging a novel a year), Patricia Cornwell (two a year), and Stephen King (three a year) have become virtual franchises. *Washington Post* book critic David Streitfeld offered this evidence: "None of the authors of the top 10 fiction bestsellers of 1965 (Michener, Bellow, Le Carré, etc.) reappeared on the list in 1966 (Susann, Robbins, Malamud, etc.), nor did any of those 20 appear on the list for 1967 (Kazan, Styron, Potok, etc.). The lists for the '90s, however, are dominated by the same names over and over again: King, Clancy, Grisham, Danielle Steel" (p. 9E). This, according to critics, creates two problems: most publishers' promotional and production resources go to an ever-smaller number of authors, and the books that are pumped out simply do not have the depth and quality that initially made these authors popular. As Streitfeld lamented, "When historians assign blame for the collapse of reading in America, successful writers' mad desire to capitalize will make up a significant part of it" (p. 9E).

A second trend involves the payment of as much as $10,000 by publishers to online booksellers for their recommendations. Reader outcry like the one that greeted the revelation in early 1999 that Amazon.com's "What We're Reading," "Destined for Greatness," and even author profile sections were, in fact, paid commercials may have slowed the practice somewhat for now. Amazon.com apologized to its customers and promised in the future to call an ad, an ad (actually, it calls them **co-op placements**). Critics claim, however, that Amazon.com and other online sellers continue to accept money for book ads and that they continue to give those books greater prominence on their sites than they do other, possibly more worthy books.

Bookwire
www.
bookwire.com

Another trend that has created much angst among book traditionalists is the paid product placement. Movies and television have long accepted payments from product manufacturers to feature their brands in their content (see Chapter 6), but it was not until May 2000 that the first paid-for placement appeared in a fiction novel. Bill Fitzhugh's *Cross Dressing*, published by Avon, contains what are purchased commercials for Seagram liquor. Fay Weldon followed suit in 2001, even titling her book *The Bulgari Connection*, after her sponsor, a jewelry company by the same name. As with other media that accept product placements, critics fear that content will be bent to satisfy sponsors rather than serve the quality of the work itself.

Demand for profit has also led to the invention of what *Boston Globe* critic Alex Beam (2002) calls "teeny books," very short books designed to appeal to readers with television-shortened attention spans and those who read primarily when traveling. Beam wrote, "There was a time when the standard writers contract called for a manuscript of 75,000 words, or about 300 printed pages," he wrote. But this is no longer the case. Beam quotes George Gibson, president of publishing house Walker & Company: "Of the books over 300 pages, the vast majority are either never read or never understood, because they are read over a long period of time and they are never reread" (2002, p. D1). Some popular current teeny books are Susan Minot's *Rapture* (115 pages; $18), Nick Tosches's *The Last Opium Den* (74 pages; $12.95), and Ken Blanchard and Spencer Johnson's *Who Moved My Cheese?* (77 pages; $19.95).

GROWTH OF SMALL PRESSES

The overcommercialization of the book industry is mitigated somewhat by the rise in the number of smaller publishing houses. Although these smaller operations are large in number, they account for a very small proportion of books sold (remember the 18,000 houses that annually

imprint fewer than four titles). They cannot compete in the blockbuster world. By definition *alternative,* they specialize in specific areas such as the environment, feminism, gay issues, and how-to. They can also publish writing otherwise uninteresting to bigger houses, such as poetry and literary commentary. Relying on specialization and narrowly targeted marketing, books such as Ralph Nader and Clarence Ditlow's *The Lemon Book,* published by Moyer Bell, Claudette McShane's *Warning! Dating May Be Hazardous to Your Health,* published by Mother Courage Press, and *Split Verse,* a book of poems about divorce published by Midmarch Arts, not only can earn healthy sales but also can make a difference in their readers' lives.

Many major chain bookstores now emulate the comfort and charm of an independent store. Barnes & Noble's bookstores offer customers a clean, well-lighted place to peruse their products and sip a latté.

RESTRUCTURING OF BOOK RETAILING

There are approximately 20,000 bookstores in the United States, but the number is dwindling as small independent operations find it increasingly difficult to compete with such chains as Bookstop, Barnes & Noble, Borders, and Books-A-Million. These larger operations are typically located in malls that have heavy pedestrian traffic. Their size enables them to purchase inventory cheaply and then offer discounts to shoppers. Because their location attracts shoppers, they can also profitably stock nonbook merchandise such as audio- and videotapes, CDs, computer games, calendars, magazines, and greeting cards for the drop-in trade. But

Innovations originally instituted by independent booksellers have redefined "the bookstore." Copyright © Hilary B. Price. Reprinted with special permission of King Features Syndicate.

high-volume, high-traffic operations tend to deal in high-volume books. To book traditionalists, this only encourages the industry's blockbuster mentality. When the largest bookstores in the country order only the biggest sellers, the small books get lost. When floor space is given over to Garfield coffee mugs and pop star calendars, there is even less room for small but potentially interesting books. Although big bookselling chains have their critics, they also have their defenders. At least the big titles, CDs, and cheap prices get people into bookstores, the argument goes. Once folks begin reading, even if it is trashy stuff, they might move on to better material. People who never buy books will never read books.

Although their share of total U.S. retail sales fell from about 33% in the early 1990s to about 15% today, many independent bookstores continue to prosper. Using their size and independence to their advantage, they counter the chains with expert, personalized service provided by a reading-loving staff, coffee and snack bars, cushioned chairs and sofas for slow browsing, and intimate readings by favorite authors. In fact, so successful have these devices been that the big stores now are copying them. Barnes & Noble, for example, sponsors a program it calls Discover to promote "gemlike first novels," and Borders does the same with Original Voices. Not only do these efforts emulate services more commonly associated with smaller independents, but they also help blunt some of the criticism suffered by the chains, specifically that they ignore new and smaller selling books (Allen, 2001, p. 149). Still, the big operations cannot or will not emulate some strategies. Specialization is one. Religious, feminist, and animal-lover bookstores exist. The in-store book club for children or poetry fans, for example, is another small-store strategy.

Another alternative to the big mall chain store is buying books online. Amazon of Seattle is the best known of the online book sales services. Thorough, fast (it guarantees 2-day delivery), and well stocked (it lists 2.5 million titles and its motto is "Every Book Under the Sun"), Amazon boasts low overhead, and that means better prices for readers. In addition, its Web site offers book buyers large amounts of potentially valuable information. Once online, customers can identify the books that interest them, read synopses, check reviews from multiple sources, and read comments not only from other readers but sometimes from the authors and publishers as well. Of course, they can also order books. Some other popular online bookstores can be found at <http://powells.com> and <http://www.books.com>. Ninety percent of all online book sales are made by <amazon.com> and <www.books.com> (Ross, 2000).

www.
amazon.com

www.
books.com

The best-known and most successful of the online booksellers, Amazon.com offers potential buyers a wealth of information and services.

You Be the Censor

The death of William Luther Pierce in July 2002 put censorship squarely in the cultural forum. Pierce was better known by the pseudonym Andrew MacDonald, under which he authored *The Turner Diaries*. First released in 1976, this underground tract has sold more than half a million copies, primarily through nonbookstore outlets such as gun and survivalist shows. Both "MacDonald" and *The Turner Diaries* became much more widely known after murderer Timothy McVeigh was found with seven strategically highlighted pages of the book in his car after he bombed the Murrah Building in Oklahoma City in 1995.

The American mainstream press called *The Turner Diaries*, with its precise descriptions of how to wreak mayhem, the Bible of the anti-government militia movement. The FBI, more accurately, labeled it "the

The aftermath of the Oklahoma City bombing.

Bible of the racist right," a **shoutline** that Pierce proudly added to the cover of editions that followed McVeigh's outrage (Sutherland, 2002). It tells the tale of Earl Turner, a lifelong warrior against people of color, the Jewish religion, and mixing of the races. Turner becomes a martyr when he dies in a suicide bombing on "the Jewish capital," Washington, DC. In fact, when press accounts claimed that the September 11 attack on the Pentagon was anticipated by the work of writer Tom Clancy, Pierce went public, indignantly claiming that dubious honor.

When Pierce died, antiterrorist professionals, civil rights groups, and free-speech advocates debated the propriety of selling the work, not at small venues such as gun shows or out of the trunks of cars, as McVeigh himself had done, but online at Amazon.com. Why would Amazon "shout 'Hebe!' 'Yid!' and 'Kike!' in the public's face? Shame on you Jeff Bezos (Amazon's founder)," wrote British literary critic John Sutherland (2002, p. 7). For Sutherland and many antidiscrimination and antiterrorist organizations, a book that is so closely linked to racism, discrimination, and even terrorism and death has no place on the sales list of a legitimate bookseller. They called, too, for the removal from Amazon of Pierce's other tome, *Hunter*, first published in 1989, and an even more poisonous work. Hunter is a vigilante who kills Jews, African Americans, Irish Americans, and interracial couples and their children. He rails against "race mixing" and "mud mongrels."

Add your voice to the cultural forum. Of course, you have to agree that a legitimate, global bookseller such as Amazon.com has no business selling such racist, violent trash. Especially after Oklahoma City and September 11, any book that glorifies racial or cultural antagonism and terrorism must be controlled. But then again, look at Figure 3.2. There are people, just as thoughtful and serious as you, who would argue that any book that is sexually explicit, or contains offensive language, or presents the occult, or is violent, or promotes homosexuality, or presents nudity, or offers sex education, or is antifamily, or presents a religious viewpoint should be controlled. Where do you draw the line? Who decides? If you were an online bookseller, would you offer the work of Pierce? If not, how would you explain your decision to those who asked you to stop selling the *Harry Potter* and *Goosebumps* series, *To Kill a Mockingbird*, and *In the Night Kitchen*? How would you make them understand that their values and concerns were not of sufficient interest to you to heed their calls for control?

DEVELOPING MEDIA LITERACY SKILLS:
The Lessons of Harry Potter

The excitement surrounding the release in July 2003 of the fifth installment of J. K. Rowling's series on youthful British sorcerer Harry Potter offers several important lessons for the media literate person. Publication of *Harry Potter and the Order of the Phoenix* highlighted several elements of media literacy and called into play a number of media literacy skills. For example, its huge appeal to young people can be used to examine one element of media literacy, understanding content as a text providing insight into our culture and lives. Just why have these books resonated so strongly with young readers? The controversy surrounding the numerous efforts to have the series banned from schools and libraries as antireligious and anti-Christian and its status as the "most challenged" (censored) children's literature in the United States call into play the particular media literacy skill of developing the ability and willingness to effectively and meaningfully understand content (Bronski, 2003).

The publishing industry classifies the Harry Potter books as children's literature. But their phenomenal reception by readers of all ages suggests these works not only have broader appeal but are in themselves something very special. The initial U.S. printing of the 870-page *The Order of the Phoenix* was 8.5 million copies—80 times that of a normal best-seller and the largest initial print run in publishing history. The book sold five million copies in the U.S. on its first day of release (Blais, 2003). At the time of the release of *The Order of the Phoenix,* the first four installments—*The Sorcerer's Stone, The Chamber of Secrets, The Prisoner of Azkaban,* and *The Goblet of Fire*—had sold more than 200 million copies worldwide, and two-thirds of all American children had read at least one edition. The Potter series has been published in over 55 languages (including Greek, Latin, and "Americanized English") in more than 200 countries (Italie, 2003).

With the publication of each installment, talk about the "rebirth of the book" and a "reverse in the decline of reading by young people" heated up. Harry had not only defeated the evil Lord Voldemort (a wizard so evil his name could not be uttered), but he had banished **aliteracy,** wherein people possess the ability to read but are unwilling to do so.

A 1999 survey of U.S. reading habits found that only 45% of readers read anything (books, newspapers, magazines, cereal boxes) for more than 30 minutes a day (Quindlen, 2000). And the 92 hours a year that the average American spends reading books (Chapter 1) amounts to 15 minutes a day. Aliteracy is as problematic for a robust culture as Lord Voldemort is for the wizard culture for two reasons. First, given the role books play as a major force in the social, political, and intellectual development of the cultures that use them, can any people afford to ignore them? Second, totalitarian governments ban and burn books because they are repositories of ideas, ideas that can be read and considered with limited outside influence or official supervision. What kind of culture develops when, by

Harry Potter, the little wizard who launched a million readers.

their own refusal to read books, people figuratively save the dictators the trouble of striking the match?

What has been Harry Potter's impact on reading? In 1963 the Gallup polling organization found that fewer than half of all Americans said they had read a book all the way through in the previous year. But soon after the release of *The Prisoner of Azkaban* in 1999, that number was 84% (Quindlen, 2000). Nobody would claim that Harry alone was responsible, but *Newsweek*'s Anna Quindlen speculated that he had helped "create a new generation of inveterate readers" (p. 64). Fright master Stephen King agreed, writing, "If these millions of readers are awakened to the wonders and rewards of fantasy at 11 or 12 . . . well, when they get to age 16 or so, there's this guy named King" (as quoted in Garchik, 2000, p. D10). Caroline Ward, president of the American Library Association's Services to Children, said, "It's hard to believe that one series of books could almost turn an entire nation back to reading, but that is not an exaggeration," and Diane Roback, children's book editor at *Publishers Weekly*,

Start a Citywide Book Conversation

You can help fight aliteracy, find new works, and maybe even meet some interesting people by involving yourself in one of the many citywide book-reading clubs that now exist. The movement, begun in 1998 by Nancy Pearl of Seattle's Washington Center for the Book, calls on reading groups in a city to choose one book to be read by everyone in that town. The idea, naturally, is to encourage reading, but also to get people talking about books and the ideas they hold (Angell, 2002).

These readings are organized in Chicago by One Book One Chicago and in New York City by Literary New York. Other towns with established programs are San Francisco, Los Angeles, Palm Beach, Cleveland, Colorado Springs,

and Valparaiso, Indiana. Check with your local library to see who in your area is running a similar program. If no one is, begin one yourself. The Washington Center for the Book has a how-to Web page at <www.spl.org/booklists/bookclubs.html>. You can access the Live Literature Network (<www.liveliterature.net>) to see where there might be a live author's reading near you and tie your selection to that event. Another possibility is to involve one or more area schools in a school-system-wide rather than citywide reading. National Children's Book Week in November is a good time to do it if you choose this path. The Children's Book Council (<www.cbc-books.org>) can help.

cited "'the Harry Potter halo effect,' in which children come into stores and libraries asking for books that resemble the Rowling series" (*USA Today*, 2000, p. E4). Neal Coonerty, owner of the independent Bookshop Santa Cruz in California, enthused, "The great thing about these books is they're read by both boys and girls alike, with equal enthusiasm" (as quoted in Beck, 2000, p. 17A).

One element of media literacy is the development of an awareness of the impact of media, and the Harry Potter series has amply demonstrated its influence. But its wild success was used by many media critics to castigate both media professionals who underestimate their audiences *and* audience members who encourage that underestimation. In other words, the success (and profitability) of this well-written, thoughtful, high-quality content stood in stark contrast to what critics contend is a steady decline in quality in other media, particularly advertiser-supported media such as radio and television. The argument is simple: Broadcasters, especially the major national television networks, respond to falling viewership not by improving content but by lowering its intelligence and worth. Whereas the Harry Potter books get better (and longer) in response to reader enthusiasm, network television dumbs down, giving its audience *Fear Factor, Survivor*, and other so-called reality programming.

And radio, as you will see in Chapter 7, has responded to 10 years of declining levels of listenership and the loss of interest among its young core audience not with new, imaginative programming but with more homogenization, automation, and the disappearance of local programming and news. The pressures on advertiser-supported media are somewhat different from those on books and film; with the latter two, readers and moviegoers express their desires and tastes directly through the purchase of content (the books themselves and tickets, respectively). But media literate people must ask why their exodus from a particular medium is not more often met with the presentation of better fare. Harry Potter shows that an audience that develops heightened expectations can and will have those expectations met.

Chapter Review

The colonists, due to widespread illiteracy, high cost, and official control, were not a book-oriented population. The American Revolution changed that and ushered in the beginnings of the book industry. The combination of technical advances such as roll paper, the steam printing press, linotype, offset lithography, and increased literacy after the Civil War produced the flowering of the novel in the 1800s, firmly establishing the relationship between readers and medium.

Books are divided into several categories (trade, professional, el-hi, higher ed, standardized tests, religious, book club, mail order, subscription reference, mass market paperbacks, and university press). Although more than 20,000 companies call themselves book publishers, only 2,000 produce four or more titles a year. The scope and structure of the contemporary book industry is characterized by convergence, conglomeration, hypercommercialism

and demand for profits, the growth of small presses, and the restructuring of book retailing.

Convergence manifests itself primarily through the marriage of books and the Internet. Digital books, e-publishing, print on demand, and e-books blur the distinction between the Web and the book while providing a number of benefits to the industry and readers alike. The Internet, too, is reshaping book retailing, as is the growth of the giant chain bookstores. Hypercommercialism, an issue for some time in the book industry's affection for blockbuster titles, finds recent form in flooding the market with the works of a few well-known authors, co-op placements on the pages of online booksellers, paid product placements in novels, and the flood of "teeny books." The huge success of the Harry Potter books not only demonstrates that the book is healthy as a mass medium, but it also raises a number of important media literacy issues.

Key Terms

Use the text's CD-ROM and the Online Learning Center at www.mhhe.com/baran to further your understanding of the following terminology.

linotype, 71
offset lithography, 71
dime novels, 72
pulp novels, 72
chained Bibles, 74
trade books, 81

acquisitions editor, 81
remainder, 83
e-publishing, 83
print on demand (POD), 83
e-book, 83
d-book, 83

cottage industry, 86
subsidiary rights, 87
instant book, 88
co-op placement, 89
shoutline, 93
aliteracy, 94

Questions for Review

Go to the self-quizzes on the CD-ROM and the Online Learning Center to test your knowledge.

1. What were the major developments in the modernization of the printing press?

2. Why were the early colonists not a book-reading population?

3. What was the Stamp Act? Why did colonial printers object to it?
4. What factors allowed the flowering of the American novel, as well as the expansion of the book industry, in the 1800s?
5. Who developed the paperback in England? In the United States?
6. Name six reasons books are an important cultural resource.
7. What are the major categories of books?
8. What is the impact of conglomeration on the book industry?
9. What are the products of increasing hypercommercialism and demands for profit in the book industry?
10. What are d-books, e-books, and e-publishing?
11. What two forms do e-books take? What are the advantages and disadvantages of each?
12. What particular cultural values are served by independent booksellers?
13. What is product placement?

Questions for Critical Thinking and Discussion

1. Do you envision books ever again having the power to move the nation as they did in Revolutionary or antislavery times? Why or why not?
2. How familiar are you with the early great American writers such as Hawthorne, Cooper, and Thoreau? What have you learned from these writers?
3. Are you proud of your book-reading habits? Why or why not?
4. Where do you stand in the debate on the overcommercialization of the book? To what lengths should publishers and booksellers go to get people to read?
5. Under what circumstances is censorship permissible? Whom do you trust to make the right decision about what you should and should not read? If you were a librarian, under what circumstances would you "pull" a book?

Important Resources

Epstein, J. (2001). *Book business: Publishing past, present, and future.* **New York: Norton; Korda, M. (1999).** *Another life: A memoir of other people.* **New York: Random House; Schiffrin, A. (2000).** *The business of books: How the international conglomerates took over publishing and changed the way we read.* **New York: Verso.** Three fine books from long-time publishing industry pros. None welcomes publishing's evolution from cottage industry to conglomerate profit center.

Publishers Weekly. The "bible" of the book publishing and selling industries. It typically contains a wealth of facts and figures, much inside industry information, and numerous readable feature articles.

Tebbel, J. (1972, 1975, 1978, 1981). *A history of book publishing in the United States,* **4 vols. New York: Bowker.** Everything you ever wanted to know about the book industry and readership in four excellently researched and documented volumes.

***The writers market.* Cincinnati, OH: F & W Publishing.** Indispensable for would-be writers and successful authors alike. Contains the names and addresses of all the nation's leading publishers and offers valuable how-to and insider essays on making a career as an author.

More on Ray Bradbury   www.raybradbury.com

More on Ben Franklin   www.english.udel.edu/lemay/franklin

More on Our Bodies, Ourselves   www.ourbodiesourselves.org

American Library Association   www.ala.org

American Civil Liberties Union   www.aclu.org

Banned Books   www.ala.org/bbooks

American Booksellers Foundation for Free Expression	abffe.org
Association of American Publishers	publishers.org
Internet Book Information Center	www.internetbookinfo.com
American Booksellers Association	ambook.org
E-Reads	ereads.com
DiskUs Publishing	diskuspublishing.com
Xlibris	xlibris.com
1st Books	1stbooks.com
iUniverse	iUniverse.com
Toby Press	www.tobypress.com
Powells Books	powells.com
Bookwire	www.bookwire.com
Barnes & Noble	www.books.com
Amazon.com	amazon.com
Support Harry	www.mugglesforharrypotter.org

CHAPTER 4

Newspapers

TIMELINE

100 B.C.E. Acta Diurna in Caesar's Rome

1620 Corantos

~1625 Broadsides

1641 Diurnals

1665 *Oxford Gazette*

1690 *Publick Occurrences Both Foreign and Domestick*

1704 *Boston News-Letter*

1721 *New-England Courant's* James Franklin jailed for "scandalous libels"

1729 Benjamin Franklin's *Pennsylvania Gazette*

1734 The Zenger trial

1765 The Stamp Act

1791 The First Amendment to the Constitution

1798 The Alien and Sedition Acts

1827 The first African American newspaper, *Freedom's Journal*

1828 *Cherokee Phoenix*

1833 The penny press

1844 Introduction of the telegraph

1847 Frederick Douglass's *North Star*

1856 The New York Associated Press

1883 Pulitzer's *New York World*, yellow journalism

1889 *Wall Street Journal*

1905 *Chicago Defender*

1907 United Press International

1908 *Christian Science Monitor*

1909 International News Service

1970 Newspaper Preservation Act

1982 *USA Today*

LEARNING OBJECTIVES

Newspapers were at the center of our nation's drive for independence and have a long history as the people's medium. The newspaper was also the first mass medium to rely on advertising for financial support, changing the relationship between audience and media from that time on. After studying this chapter you should

- be familiar with the history and development of the newspaper industry and the newspaper itself as a medium.

- understand how the organizational and economic nature of the contemporary newspaper industry shapes the content of newspapers.

- understand the relationship between the newspaper and its readers.

- be familiar with changes in the newspaper industry brought about by emerging technologies and how those alterations may affect the medium's traditional role in our democracy.

- possess improved newspaper-reading media literacy skills, especially in interpreting the relative placement of stories and use of photos.

NEW AT THE NEWSPAPER, YOU REALLY WANT TO MAKE YOUR mark. You go to your boss, the city editor, in hopes of enlisting his support for your plan. He is enthusiastic, and together you pitch your idea to the executive editor. The three of you sit at a worktable in her cluttered office. She asks the city editor to explain the proposal, but he defers to you. The pressure weighs on your lungs, but there's an excitement in your heart that reminds you of why you wanted to be a journalist in the first place. You begin.

"We're always being criticized for doing too much soft news, not enough depth and detail."

She nods.

"We're accused of covering political campaigns like horse races. Who's in front, who's running well—that sort of thing."

She nods again.

"People claim we in the media, especially newspapers, don't listen to them enough."

101

More nods.

"Circulation figures have been flat for some time." This was a risk—the boss could take it as a criticism of her work—but being a journalist is about putting yourself on the line. You wait for, and receive, a begrudging nod. So you continue, "We need to give people a reason to read us."

"Good setup," says the executive editor. "Now get to the point."

"I'm proposing an exercise in civic journalism, using the paper as a proactive force in the community."

"OK. Shoot."

"We have a big gubernatorial election coming up, right? So let's poll a thousand registered voters and ask what issues they most care about. Then we take the top three or four issues and create a series of questions we can ask the candidates in interviews. Then we write stories based on their responses to the very issues the people want to know about." After a pause that strikes you as a bit too long, you begin to weaken. "OK, maybe it needs some work. It was just an idea. Maybe if we can . . ."

"Stop," she interrupts, "I think it's an excellent idea. You can serve as a researcher for the team that manages the project. We'll call it 'Your Voice, Your Vote' and run the stories on the front page for a month before the election. Good work!"

For weeks you're the paper's hotshot young go-getter. Although you didn't get to write them, the reports on crime, drugs, education, and taxes are sharply crafted and well received. The readers like what you're doing; so do the politicians, who seem relieved to be spared a "personalities" campaign. Circulation, both newsstand and subscription, climbs a bit; ad revenues rise even more.

Then journalists from around the country offer their opinions. The paper has abdicated its professional responsibility by allowing a poll to dictate coverage. It's pandering to readers by allowing them to dictate newsworthiness. You've undermined candidates' personal political judgment. You've ignored issues that are equally or more important. What about race, for example? Your newspaper is accused of limiting public debate, engaging in self-serving pseudojournalism for the purpose of boosting revenues, and attempting to control the public agenda.

It may or may not be true, but your star seems to be shining a bit less brightly now. And all you wanted was to do good newspaper work.

In this chapter we examine the relationship between the newspaper and its readers. We start with a look at the medium's roots, beginning with the first papers, following them from Europe to colonial America, where many of the traditions of today's free press were set. We study the cultural changes that led to creation of the penny press and to competition between these mass circulation dailies that gave us "yellow journalism."

We then review the modern newspaper in terms of its size and scope. We discuss different types of newspapers and the importance of newspapers as an advertising medium. The wire and feature services, important providers of newspaper content, are also highlighted.

We then detail how the relationship between medium and audience is shifting as a result of the loss of competition within the industry, hyper-commercialism in the guise of commercial pressure on papers' editorial content, attempts at civic journalism, the positive and negative impacts of technology, the rise of online newspapers, and changes in the nature of newspaper readership. Finally, we test our media literacy skill through a discussion of how to read the newspaper, for example, interpreting the relative positioning of stories.

A Short History of Newspapers

The opening vignette makes an important point about contemporary newspapers—they are working hard to secure new identities for themselves in an increasingly crowded media environment. As a medium and as an industry, newspapers are poised at the edge of a significant change in their role and operation. The changing relationship between newspapers and readers is part of this upheaval. Newspapers have faced similar challenges more than once in the past and have survived.

THE EARLIEST NEWSPAPERS

In Caesar's time Rome had a newspaper. The **Acta Diurna** (actions of the day), written on a tablet, was posted on a wall after each meeting of the Senate. Its circulation was one, and there is no reliable measure of its total readership. However, it does show that people have always wanted to know what was happening and that others have helped them do so.

The newspapers we recognize today have their roots in 17th-century Europe. **Corantos,** one-page news sheets about specific events, were printed in English in Holland in 1620 and imported to England by British booksellers who were eager to satisfy public demand for information about Continental happenings that eventually led to what we now call the Thirty Years' War.

Englishmen Nathaniel Butter, Thomas Archer, and Nicholas Bourne eventually began printing their own occasional news sheets, using the same title for consecutive editions. They stopped publishing in 1641, the same year that regular, daily accounts of local news started appearing in other news sheets. These true forerunners of our daily newspaper were called **diurnals.**

Political power struggles in England at this time boosted the fledgling medium, as partisans on the side of the monarchy and those on the side of Parliament published diurnals to bolster their positions. When the monarchy prevailed, it granted monopoly publication rights to the *Oxford Gazette,* the official voice of the Crown. Founded in 1665 and later renamed the *London Gazette,* this journal used a formula of foreign news, official information, royal proclamations, and local news that became the model for the first colonial newspapers.

Colonial Newspapers   In Chapter 3 we saw how bookseller/print shops became the focal point for the exchange of news and information and how this led to the beginning of the colonial newspaper. It was at these establishments that **broadsides** (sometimes referred to as **broadsheets**), single-sheet announcements or accounts of events imported from England, would be posted. In 1690 Boston bookseller/printer (and coffee house owner) Benjamin Harris printed his own broadside, *Publick Occurrences Both Foreign and Domestick*. Intended for continuous publication, the country's first daily lasted only one day. Harris had been critical of local and European dignitaries, and he had also failed to obtain a license.

More successful was Boston Postmaster John Campbell, whose 1704 *Boston News-Letter* survived until the Revolution. The paper featured foreign news, reprints of articles from England, government announcements, and shipping news. It was dull, and it was also expensive. Nonetheless, it established the newspaper in the Colonies.

The *Boston News-Letter* was able to survive in part because of government subsidies. With government support came government control, but the buildup to the Revolution helped establish the medium's independence. In 1721 Boston had three papers. James Franklin's *New-England Courant* was the only one publishing without authority. The *Courant* was popular and controversial, but when it criticized the Massachusetts governor, Franklin was jailed for printing "scandalous libels." When released, he returned to his old ways, earning himself and the *Courant* a publishing ban, which he circumvented by installing his younger brother Benjamin as nominal publisher. Ben Franklin soon moved to Philadelphia, and without his leadership the *Courant* was out of business in 3 years. Its lasting legacy, however, was in proving that a newspaper with popular support could indeed challenge authority.

In Philadelphia, Benjamin Franklin established a print shop and later, in 1729, took over a failing newspaper, which he revived and renamed the *Pennsylvania Gazette*. By combining the income from his book shop and printing businesses with that from his popular daily, Franklin could run the *Gazette* with significant independence. Even though he held the contract for Philadelphia's official printing, he was unafraid to criticize those in authority. In addition, he began to develop advertising support, which also helped shield his newspaper from government control by decreasing its dependence on official printing contracts for survival. Ben Franklin demonstrated that financial independence could lead to editorial independence. It was not, however, a guarantee.

In 1734 *New York Weekly Journal* publisher John Peter Zenger was jailed for criticizing that Colony's royal governor. The charge was seditious libel, and the verdict was based not on the truth or falsehood of the printed words but on whether they had been printed. The criticisms had been published, so Zenger was clearly guilty. But his attorney, Andrew Hamilton,

The first daily newspaper to appear in the 13 Colonies, *Publick Occurrences Both Foreign and Domestick*, lasted all of one edition.

Early Newspaper History
WWW.
bl.uk/collections/britnews.html

Benjamin Franklin published America's first political cartoon—"Join, or Die," a rallying call for the Colonies—in his *Pennsylvania Gazette* in 1754.

argued to the jury, "For the words themselves must be libelous, that is, false, scandalous and seditious, or else we are not guilty." Zenger's peers agreed, and he was freed. The case of Peter Zenger became a symbol of colonial newspaper independence from the Crown, and its power was evident in the refusal by publishers to accept the Stamp Act in 1765 (see Chapter 3). For more on this colonial newspaperman, see the box "Truth as a Defense Against Libel: The Zenger Trial."

Newspapers After Independence After the Revolution, the new government of the United States had to determine for itself just how free a press it was willing to tolerate. When the first Congress convened under the new Constitution in 1790, the nation's founders debated, drafted, and adopted the first 10 amendments to the Constitution, called the **Bill of Rights.** The **First Amendment** reads:

> Congress shall make no law respecting an establishment of religion, or prohibiting the free exercise thereof; or abridging the freedom of speech, or of the press; or the right of the people peacefully to assemble, and to petition the Government for a redress of grievances.

But a mere 8 years later, fearful of the subversive activities of foreigners sympathetic to France, Congress passed a group of four laws known collectively as the **Alien and Sedition Acts.** The Sedition Act made illegal writing, publishing, or printing "any false scandalous and malicious writing" about the president, Congress, or the federal government. So unpopular were these laws to a people who had just waged a war of independence against similar limits on their freedom of expression that they were not

Truth as a Defense against Libel: The Zenger Trial

Young German immigrant John Peter Zenger started publishing New York's second paper, the *Weekly Journal*, in 1733 with encouragement from several anti-Crown merchants and businesspeople who wanted a voice to counter William Bradford's Crown-supported *Gazette.* Zenger had been an apprentice under Bradford, whose official title was "King's Printer to the Province of New York."

Zenger did his new job well. He was constantly and openly critical of New York's British-born governor, William Cosby. Soon he was arrested and jailed for seditious libel. For the 9 months he was imprisoned, he continued to edit his paper, run on the outside by his wife.

This trial began on August 4, 1735, and at first it did not go well for Zenger. His two original lawyers were disbarred because they argued that the judge, appointed by Cosby, should step down. Zenger's supporters then hired 80-year-old Philadelphia attorney Andrew Hamilton. Hamilton was not only a brilliant lawyer and orator but an astute reader of contemporary political sentiment. He built his defense of the accused printer on growing colonial anger toward Britain. Actually he had little choice. As the law stood, Zenger *was* guilty. British law said that printed words could be libelous, even if true, if they were inflammatory or negative. Truth, Hamilton argued, is a defense against libel. Otherwise, how could anything other than favorable material about government ever be published? Moreover, he added, why should the colonists be bound by a British law they had not themselves approved?

To make his point Hamilton said, "Power may justly be compared to a great river; while kept within its due bounds, it is both beautiful and useful. But when it over-

John Peter Zenger, sitting in the dock, is defended by Andrew Hamilton.

flows its banks, it is then too impetuous to be stemmed, it bears down all before it, and brings destruction and desolation wherever it comes."

The jury ruled Zenger not guilty, making it clear to the British and their colonial supporters that the colonists would no longer accept their control of the press.

Two hundred and seventy-five years later, different people are still fighting for press freedom. The Zenger trial is echoed in Chapter 14 in the travails of Larry Flynt and in Chapter 15 in the account of the suppression of the reformist press in Iran.

renewed when Congress reconsidered them 2 years later in 1800. We will examine in detail the ongoing commitment to the First Amendment, freedom of the press, and open expression in the United States in Chapter 14.

THE MODERN NEWSPAPER EMERGES

At the turn of the 19th century, urbanization, growing industries, movement of workers to the cities, and increasing literacy combined to create an audience for a new kind of paper. Known as the **penny press,** these one-cent newspapers were for everyone. Benjamin Day's September 3, 1833, issue of the *New York Sun* was the first of the penny papers. Day's innovation was to sell his paper so inexpensively that it would attract a large readership, which could then be "sold" to advertisers. Day succeeded because he anticipated a new kind of reader. He filled the *Sun*'s pages with police and court reports, crime stories, entertainment news, and human interest stories. Because the paper lived up to its motto, "The Sun shines for all," there was little of the elite political and business information that had characterized earlier papers.

Soon there were penny papers in all the major cities. Among the most important was James Gordon Bennett's *New York Morning Herald.* Although more sensationalistic than the *Sun,* the *Herald* pioneered the correspondent system, placing reporters in Washington, D.C., and other major U.S. cities as well as abroad. Correspondents filed their stories by means of the telegraph, invented in 1844.

Horace Greeley's *New York Tribune* was an important penny paper as well. Its nonsensationalistic, issues-oriented, and humanitarian reporting established the mass newspaper as a powerful medium of social action.

The People's Medium People typically excluded from the social, cultural, and political mainstream quickly saw the value of the mass newspaper. The first African American newspaper was *Freedom's Journal,* published initially in 1827 by John B. Russwurum and the Reverend Samuel Cornish. Forty others soon followed, but it was Frederick Douglass who made best use of the new mass circulation style in his newspaper, *The Ram's Horn,* founded expressly to challenge the editorial policies of Benjamin Day's *Sun.* Although this particular effort failed, Douglass had established himself and the minority press as a viable voice for those otherwise silenced. Douglass's *North Star,* founded in 1847 with the masthead slogan "Right is of no Sex—Truth is of no Color—God is the Father of us all, and we are all Brethren," was the most influential African American newspaper before the Civil War.

The most influential African American newspaper after the Civil War, and the first Black paper to be a commercial success (its predecessors typically were subsidized by political and church groups), was the *Chicago Defender.* First published on May 5, 1905, by Robert Sengstacke Abbot, the *Defender* eventually earned a nationwide circulation of more than 230,000. Especially after Abbot declared May 15, 1917, the start of "the Great Northern Drive," the *Defender's* central editorial goal was to encourage southern Black people to move north.

"I beg of you, my brothers, to leave that benighted land. You are free men. . . . Get out of the South," Abbott editorialized (as quoted in Fitzgerald, 1999, p. 18). The paper would regularly contrast horrific accounts of southern lynchings with northern African American success stories. Within 2 years

Volume 1, Number 1 of Benjamin Day's *New York Sun,* the first of the penny papers.

History of African American Newspapers
WWW.
iath.virginia.edu/vcdh/afam/reflector/newspaper.html

For more information on this topic, see NBC Video Clip #11 on the CD—*College Newspaper Under Fire for Controversial Advertorial.*

of the start of the Great Drive, more than 500,000 former slaves and their families moved north. Within 2 more years, another half million followed.

Native Americans found early voice in papers such as the *Cherokee Phoenix*, founded in 1828 in Georgia, and the *Cherokee Rose Bud*, which began operation 20 years later in Oklahoma. The rich tradition of the Native American newspaper is maintained today around the country in publications such as the Oglala Sioux *Lakota Times* and the Shoshone-Bannock *Sho-Ban News*, as well as on the World Wide Web. For example, the *Cherokee Observer* is at <http://www.cherokeeobserver.org>; the *Navajo Times* is at <http://www.navajo.com>; and *Indian Country Today* can be found at <http://www.indiancountry.com>.

Throughout this early period of the popularization of the newspaper, numerous foreign language dailies also began operation, primarily in major cities in which immigrants tended to settle. Sloan, Stovall, and Startt (1993) report that in 1880 there were more than 800 foreign-language newspapers publishing in German, Polish, Italian, Spanish, and various Scandinavian languages.

The First Wire Services   In 1848 six large New York papers, including the *Sun*, the *Herald*, and the *Tribune*, decided to pool efforts and share expenses collecting news from foreign ships docking at the city's harbor. After determining rules of membership and other organizational issues, in 1856 the papers established the first news-gathering (and distribution) organization, the New York Associated Press. Other domestic **wire services** followed—the Associated Press in 1900, the United Press in 1907, and the International News Service in 1909.

This innovation, with its assignment of correspondents to both foreign and domestic bureaus, had a number of important implications. First, it greatly expanded the breadth and scope of coverage a newspaper could offer its readers. This was a boon to dailies wanting to attract as many readers as possible. Greater coverage of distant domestic news helped unite an expanding country while encouraging even more expansion. The United States was a nation of immigrants, and news from people's homelands drew more readers. Second, the nature of reporting began to change. Reporters could now produce stories by rewriting—sometimes a little, sometimes a lot—the actual on-the-spot coverage of others. Finally, newspapers were able to reduce expenses (and increase profits) because they no longer needed to have their own reporters in all locations.

Yellow Journalism   In 1883 Hungarian immigrant Joseph Pulitzer bought the troubled *New York World*. Adopting a populist approach to the news, he brought a crusading, activist style of coverage to numerous turn-of-the-century social problems—growing slums, labor tensions, and failing farms, to name a few. The audience for his "new journalism" was the "common man," and he succeeded in reaching readers with light, sensationalistic news coverage, extensive use of illustrations, and circulation-building

MAINE EXPLOSION CAUSED BY BOMB OR TORPEDO

Capt. Sigsbee and Consul-General Lee Are in Doubt---The World Has Sent a Special Tug, With Submarine Divers, to Havana to Find Out---Lee Asks for an Immediate Court of Inquiry---Capt. Sigsbee's Suspicions.

CAPT. SIGSBEE, IN A SUPPRESSED DESPATCH TO THE STATE DEPARTMENT, SAYS THE ACCIDENT WAS MADE POSSIBLE BY AN ENEMY.

Dr. E. C. Pendleton, Just Arrived from Havana, Says He Overheard Talk There of a Plot to Blow Up the Ship---Capt. Zallinski, the Dynamite Expert, and Other Experts Report to The World that the Wreck Was Not Accidental---Washington Officials Ready for Vigorous Action if Spanish Responsibility Can Be Shown---Divers to Be Sent Down to Make Careful Examinations.

Several of yellow journalism's excesses—dramatic graphics, bold headlines, the reporting of rumor—are evident in this front page from Joseph Pulitzer's *New York World.* Many historians believe that the sinking of the Maine was engineered by yellow journalist William Randolph Hearst, publisher of the *New York Morning Journal,* in order to create a war that his papers could cover as a way to build circulation.

Yellow Journalism
www.humboldt.edu/~jcb10/yellow.html

stunts and promotions (for example, an around-the-world balloon flight). Ad revenues and circulation figures exploded.

Soon there were other new journalists. William Randolph Hearst applied Pulitzer's successful formula to his *San Francisco Examiner,* and then in 1895 he took on Pulitzer himself in New York. The competition between Hearst's *Morning Journal* and Pulitzer's *World* was so intense that it debased newspapers and journalism as a whole, which is somewhat ironic in that Pulitzer later founded the prize for excellence in journalism that still bears his name.

Drawing its name from the Yellow Kid, a popular cartoon character of the time, **yellow journalism** was a study in excess—sensational sex, crime, and disaster news; giant headlines; heavy use of illustrations; and reliance on cartoons and color. It was successful at first, and other papers around the country adopted all or part of its style. Although public reaction to the excesses of yellow journalism soon led to its decline, traces of its popular features remain. Large headlines, big front-page pictures, extensive use of photos and illustrations, and cartoons are characteristic even of today's best newspapers.

The years between the era of yellow journalism and the coming of television were a time of remarkable growth in the development of newspapers. From 1910 to the beginning of World War II, daily newspaper subscriptions doubled, and ad revenues tripled. In 1910 there were 2,600 daily papers in the United States, more than at any time before or since. In 1923, the American Society of Newspaper Editors issued the "Canons of Journalism and Statement of Principles" in an effort to restore order and respectability after the yellow era. The opening sentence of the Canons was, "The right of a newspaper to attract and hold readers is restricted by nothing but considerations of public welfare." The wire services internationalized. United Press International started gathering news from Japan in 1909 and was covering South America and Europe by 1921. In response to the competition from radio and magazines for advertising dollars, newspapers began consolidating into **newspaper chains**—papers in different cities across the country owned by a single company. Hearst and Scripps were among the most powerful chains in the 1920s. But the next major shift in newspapers as a medium was brought about by television.

Newspapers and Their Audiences

Nearly 56 million newspapers are sold daily in the United States, and 6 of 10 people report reading a paper every day. The industry that produces those newspapers looks quite different from the one that operated before television became a dominant medium. There are now fewer papers. There are now different types of papers. More newspapers are part of large chains. What has not changed is why people read the newspaper. Researcher Bernard Berelson's classic 1949 study of what missing the paper means speaks for today's newspaper readers as well. Readers use the newspaper:

- To get information about and interpretation of public affairs
- As tools for daily living (for example, advertising, radio and movie listings, and announcements of births, deaths, and weddings)
- For relaxation and escape
- For prestige (newspaper content is raw material for conversation)
- For social contact (from human interest stories and advice columns)

As we saw in Chapter 2, the advent of television coincided with several important social and cultural changes. Shorter work hours, more leisure, more expendable cash, movement to the suburbs, and women joining the workforce in greater numbers all served to alter the newspaper–reader relationship. Overall, circulation rose from 48 to 62 million between 1945 and 1970, but the amount of time people spent reading their papers decreased. People were reading only 20% of the stories, spending less than 30 minutes a day with the paper, and only 15 minutes was focused primarily on the paper itself. Circulation for big city papers dropped, and many closed shop. As newspapers struggled to redefine themselves in the expanding television era, the number of chains grew from 60, controlling 42% of the daily circulation in 1945, to 126, controlling 76% of the total number of dailies and 82% of the daily circulation in 1996 (Compaine & Gomery, 2000, p. 8).

Scope and Structure of the Newspaper Industry

Today there are 9,813 newspapers operating in the United States. Of these 1,661 (17%) are dailies, 7,594 (77%) are weeklies, and 558 (6%) are semi-weekly (U.S. Census Bureau, 2001, p. 706). The dailies have a combined circulation of 55.8 million, the weeklies more than 70 million. The average weekly has a circulation of just over 9,000. **Pass-along readership**—readers who did not originally purchase the paper—brings 132 million people a day in touch with a daily and 200 million a week in touch with a weekly. However, overall circulation has remained stagnant despite a growing population. In 1990 there was only 0.7 newspaper subscription per U.S. household compared to 1.12 in 1960 (*Editor & Publisher International Yearbook*, 1998). To maintain their success and to ensure their future, newspapers have had to diversify.

TYPES OF NEWSPAPERS

We've cited statistics about dailies and weeklies, but these categories actually include many different types of papers. Let's take a closer look at some of these types of papers.

National Daily Newspapers   We typically think of the newspaper as a local medium, our town's paper. But three national daily newspapers enjoy large circulations and significant social and political impact. The oldest and most respected is the *Wall Street Journal*, founded in 1889 by Charles Dow and Edward Jones. Today, as then, its focus is on the world of business, although its definition of business is broad. With a circulation of 1.8 million, the *Journal* is the biggest daily in the United States, and an average household income of its readers of $150,000 makes it a favorite for upscale advertisers.

The *Christian Science Monitor*, begun in 1908, continues to hold to its founding principle as a paper of serious journalism. Begun as a high-minded alternative to Boston's yellow papers by Mary Baker Eddy, founder of the Christian Science religion, it was international in coverage and national in distribution from the start. Today, dwindling subscribership totals about 70,000.

The newest and most controversial national daily is *USA Today*. It calls itself "The Nation's Newspaper," but its critics derisively call it

For more information on this topic, view *Newspapers: Inside the Record*, #2 on the CD *Media Tours*.

USA Today offers brief reports for people on the go. Despite its great commercial success, its critics referred to it as McPaper. But recently the paper has begun to offer longer, more detailed reporting.

"McPaper" because of what they see as its lack of depth, apparent dependence on style over substance, and early reliance on stories of no more than a dozen sentences. The paper's daily circulation of 1.7 million suggests that, critics aside, readers welcome its mix of short, lively, upbeat stories; full-color graphics; state-by-state news and sports briefs; and liberal use of easy-to-read illustrated graphs and tables. Begun in 1982 to appeal to business travelers and others on the run, *USA Today* depends primarily on single-issue rather than subscriber sales, with airport news racks a primary sales point. And, possibly in response to its critics, *USA Today* has begun offering stories of greater length and depth.

Large Metropolitan Dailies   To be a daily, a paper must be published at least five times a week. As we can see in Figure 4.1 (p. 189), the circulation of big city dailies has dropped a bit over the past 30 years, with the heavy losses of the evening papers offsetting increases for the morning papers. Many old, established papers, including the *Philadelphia Bulletin* and the *Washington Star*, have stilled their presses in recent years. When the *Chicago Daily News* closed its doors, it had the sixth highest circulation in the country.

As big cities cease to be industrial centers, homes, jobs, and interests have turned away from downtown. Those large metropolitan dailies that are succeeding have used a number of strategies to cut costs and to attract and keep more suburban-oriented readers. Several papers, such as the *Boston Globe*, produce an "all-day newspaper," with multiple editions throughout the day, accommodating everyone's work, commute, or home schedule.

Almost all papers publish **zoned editions**—suburban or regional versions of the paper—to attract readers and to combat competition for advertising dollars from the suburban papers. Many big city dailies have gone as far as to drop the city of their publication from their name. Where is *The Tribune* published? Oakland, California, and Scranton, Pennsylvania, and Warren, Ohio, and Wisconsin Rapids, Wisconsin, each produces a paper called *The Tribune*, but these papers have dropped the city name from their mastheads.

The *New York Times* is a special large metropolitan daily. It is a paper local to New York, but the high quality of its reporting and commentary, the reach and depth of both its national and international news, and the solid reputations of its features (such as the weekly *Times*

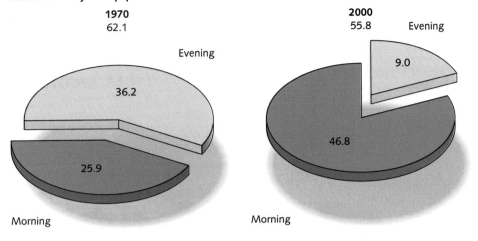

Number of Daily Newspaper Readers (in millions)

1970
62.1

Evening
36.2

25.9

Morning

2000
55.8

Evening
9.0

46.8

Morning

Figure 4.1 Daily Newspapers Circulation, 1970–2000 Source: Adapted from U.S. Census Bureau, 2001.

Magazine and the *Book Review*) make it the nation's newspaper of record.

Suburban and Small Town Dailies As the United States has become a nation of transient suburb dwellers, so too has the newspaper been suburbanized. Since 1985 the number of suburban dailies has increased by 50%, and one, Long Island's *Newsday,* is the eighth largest paper in the country, with a circulation of nearly 600,000.

Small town dailies operate much like their suburban cousins if there is a nearby large metropolitan paper; for example, the *Lawrence Eagle-Tribune* publishes in the shadow of Boston's two big dailies. Its focus is the Merrimack River Valley in Massachusetts, 25 miles northwest of Boston. If the small town paper has no big city competition, it can serve as the heart of its community.

Weeklies and Semiweeklies Many weeklies and semiweeklies have prospered because advertisers have followed them to the suburbs. Community reporting makes them valuable to those people who identify more with their immediate environment than they do with the neighboring big city. Suburban advertisers like the narrowly focused readership and more manageable advertising rates.

Many weeklies and semiweeklies, although not suburban, prosper through this same combination of meeting the needs of both readers and advertisers. Certainly there are daily ethnic newspapers, but ethnic newspapers typically tend to be weeklies. Especially in urban areas, where the big dailies are scurrying to attract and hold the suburban readers, Spanish-language and African American weeklies are operating profitably. There are approximately 540 Spanish-language and 170 African American newspapers publishing today (Garriga, 2001).

Another common type of weekly operates as the alternative press. The offspring of the underground press of the 1960s antiwar, antiracism, prodrug culture, the alternative press is redefining itself. The most successful

The *San Francisco Chronicle* uses its "Peninsula" zoned edition to compete with its rival to the south, the *San Jose Mercury News.* The *Merc,* in turn uses its "Northern California" zoned edition to compete with its rival to the south, the *Santa Cruz Sentinel.*

Weeklies typically come in tabloid form, but their look and contents can vary greatly.

among them—*The Village Voice,* the *L.A. Weekly,* the *Boston Phoenix,* and the *Seattle Weekly*—succeed by attracting upwardly mobile young people and young professionals, not the disaffected counterculture readers who were their original audiences. The Association of Alternative Newsweeklies (AAN) now represents 118 established alternative papers with a readership of more than 20 million (Moses, 2002).

THE NEWSPAPER AS AN ADVERTISING MEDIUM

The reason we have the number and variety of newspapers we do is that readers value them. When newspapers prosper financially, it is because advertisers recognize their worth as an ad medium. Newspapers account for more than 55% of all advertising spending in the United States. That is more than $50 billion a year, more than all other media combined. The biggest newspaper advertisers are retail stores (such as Macy's) and telecommunications, auto, computer, and entertainment brands (Moses, 2001).

Why do so many advertisers choose newspapers? The first reason is their reach. Six out of ten Americans read a paper every day, 85% in a week. Newspapers "deliver the equivalent of the Super Bowl every day," offers Nicholas Cannistraro of the Newspaper National Network (quoted in Case, 2001, p. SR18). The second is good demographics—newspaper readers tend to be better educated, better off financially, and have more disposable income than the audiences of other media. Third, newspapers are the most

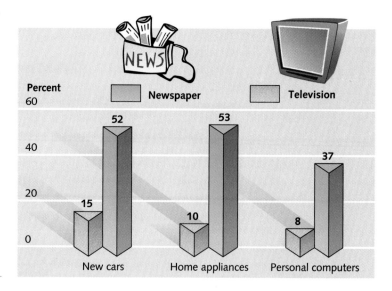

Figure 4.2 Newspaper as a Primary Advertising Source. When asked where they go for information on new product purchases, Americans most favor the newspaper for these big purchases. Source: Newspaper Association of America/American Society of Newspapers (Case, 2001).

trusted, credible ad medium when readers are looking to make a specific product purchase (Case, 2001). Figure 4.2 demonstrates newspapers' dominance in this regard. Finally, newspapers are local in nature. Supermarkets, local car dealers, department stores, movie theaters, and other local merchants who want to offer a coupon turn automatically to the paper. Approximately 65% of daily newspaper space is given to advertising. Of that space, 60% is devoted to local retail advertising and another 25% to classified, which is overwhelmingly local. This localization is further enhanced by the use of zoned editions, which allow advertisers to place their ads in editions designed for readers' specific locales, that is, closer to the point of sale.

THE WIRE AND FEATURE SERVICES

Much of the 35% of the newspaper that is not advertising space is filled with content provided by outside sources, specifically the wire and feature services. Wire services, as we've already seen, collect news and distribute it to their members. (They draw their name from the way they originally distributed material—by telephone wire. Today material is more likely to come by computer network or satellite.) Unlike the early days of the wire services, today's member is three times more likely to be a broadcast outlet than a newspaper. These radio and television stations receive voice and video, as well as written copy. In all cases, members receive a choice of material, most commonly national and international news, state and regional news, sports, business news, farm and weather reports, and human interest and consumer material.

The feature services, called **feature syndicates,** do not gather and distribute news. Instead, they operate as clearinghouses for the work of columnists, essayists, cartoonists, and other creative individuals. Among the material provided (by wire, by computer, or physically in packages) are opinion pieces such as commentaries by Ellen Goodman or Molly Ivins; horoscope, chess, and bridge columns; editorial cartoons, such as the work

American Association of Newspapers
www.
aan.org

of Scott Willis and Ben Sergeant; and comics, the most common and popular form of syndicated material. Among the major syndicates, the best known are *The New York Times* News Service, King Features, Newspaper Enterprise Association (NEA), and the *Washington Post* News Service.

Trends and Convergence in Newspaper Publishing

Loss of competition within the industry, hypercommercialism, civic journalism, convergence, and the evolution of newspaper readership are altering not only the nature of the medium but also its relationship with its audiences.

LOSS OF COMPETITION

The newspaper industry has seen a dramatic decline in competition. This has taken two forms: loss of competing papers and concentration of ownership. In 1923, 502 American cities had two or more competing (having different ownership) dailies. Today, only 20 have separate competing papers. With circulation and advertising revenues leveling out for urban dailies, very few cities can support more than one paper. Congress attempted to reverse this trend with the 1970 Newspaper Preservation Act, which allowed **joint operating agreements (JOAs).** A JOA permits a failing paper to merge most aspects of its business with a successful local competitor as long as their editorial and reporting operations remain separate. The philosophy is that it is better to have two more or less independent papers in one city than to allow one to close. Today, 12 cities have JOAs, including Seattle, Albuquerque, Detroit, and Cincinnati.

The concern is editorial diversity. Cities with only one newspaper have only one newspaper editorial voice. This runs counter to two long-held American beliefs about the relationship between a free press and its readers:

- Truth flows from a multitude of tongues.
- The people are best served by a number of antagonistic voices.

What becomes of political, cultural, and social debate when there are neither multiple nor antagonistic (or at least different) voices? Media critic Robert McChesney (1997) offered this answer: "As ownership concentrated nationally in the form of chains, journalism came to reflect the partisan interests of owners and advertisers, rather than the diverse interests of any given community" (p. 13).

The trend toward newspaper concentration is troubling to many observers. The nation's 126 newspaper chains control 82% of daily newspaper circulation, own the 9 biggest circulation papers in the country, and own 1,200 of the nation's 1,600 dailies.

Chains are not new. Hearst owned several big city papers in the 1880s, but at that time most cities enjoyed significant competition between papers. Now that most communities have only one paper, nonlocal chain or conglomerate control of that voice is more problematic. Among the larger chains are Gannett (74 dailies), Knight-Ridder (33), Newhouse (23), Hearst (12), New York Times (20), E. W. Scripps (20), and MediaNews Group (51). Additional concern is raised about chain ownership when the chain is also a media conglomerate, owning several different types of media outlets, as well as other nonmedia companies. Will the different media holdings speak with one corporate voice? Will they speak objectively, and will they cover at all the doings of their nonmedia corporations?

Chains do have their supporters. Although some critics see big companies as more committed to profit and shareholder dividends, others see chains such as Knight-Ridder, winner of numerous Pulitzer prizes and other awards, as turning expanded economic and journalistic resources toward better service and journalism. Some critics see outside ownership as uncommitted to local communities and issues, but others see balance and objectivity (especially important in one-paper towns). Ultimately, we must recognize that not all chains operate alike. Some operate their holdings as little more than profit centers; others see profit residing in exemplary service. Some groups require that all their papers toe the corporate line; others grant local autonomy. Gannett, for example, openly boasts of its dedication to local management control.

HYPERCOMMERCIALISM AND THE EROSION OF THE FIREWALL

As in other media, conglomeration has led to increased pressure on newspapers to turn a profit, sometimes at the expense of their journalistic mission. The past decade has seen papers laying off staff, closing state and regional bureaus, hiring younger and less experienced reporters, and shrinking their newsholes. Many papers, such as *USA Today*, the *Orange County Register*, the *Oakland Press*, and the *Macomb Daily* (the latter two in Michigan), have begun selling ad space on the front page, once the exclusive province of the news. Some papers now permit (and charge for) the placement of pet obituaries alongside those of deceased humans. But the greatest fear expressed by critics of concentration and conglomeration is that the quest for profits at all costs is eroding the firewall, the once inviolate barrier between newspapers' editorial and advertising missions. They point to the experience of the *Los Angeles Times* as a negative model of the hypercommercialized newspaper.

Editor & Publisher
www.
mediainfo.com

In 1996, the *Times* hired former General Mills cereal executive Mark Willes as its publisher. Willes immediately appointed a business manager to the new position of "general manager for news" for the purpose of ensuring that the paper's "editorial content conformed to the best commercial interests of the newspaper" (Peterson, 1997, p. C1). Willes then told *Forbes* magazine that he intended to break down the "Chinese wall between editors and business staffers" with "a Bazooka if necessary" (as quoted in Marsh, 1998, p. 47). On October 10, 1999, the *Times* ran a special 164-page issue of its Sunday magazine dedicated to the opening of the Staples Center, the new Los Angeles sports arena. This magazine, which was filled with flattering, upbeat stories about the facility, generated $2 million in advertising revenue. But the *Times* failed to tell its reporters or its readers that it had struck a deal with the Staples Center to split the income. As *Times* city hall reporter Jim Newton said, "If I had a financial arrangement with Mayor Riordan and wrote about him, I'd be fired. It's a conflict of interest" (as quoted in Booth, 1999, p. 79).

A firestorm of criticism greeted the deal's revelation, and *Times* executives and editors apologized for the secrecy, but Mr. Willes (now Times Mirror Corporation CEO) and publisher Kathryn Downing continued to "maintain the policy that businesspeople will share in the selection of the news," a situation, according to media critic Ben Bagdikian, that leaves "a blot on the idea that readers can trust journalists" (as quoted in "*L.A. Times Takes,*" 1999, p. A3).

American Society of Newspaper Editors **WWW.** asne.org

But the *Times* is not alone. "The wall is a myth," says former *Times* publisher David Laventhol (in Winokur, 1999, p. D3). "There's definitely more interaction as newspapers have come under more financial pressure," said Steve Proctor, deputy managing editor for sports and features at the *Baltimore Sun*. "It used to be if you had a newspaper in town you were able to make a steady profit. Now, like so many other things in the world, newspapers are more at the whim of the opinions of Wall Street analysts. There's a lot more pressure to increase the profit margin of the paper, and so that has led to a lot more interplay between the newsroom and the business side of the paper" (quoted in Vane, 2002, pp. 60–61). American Society of Newspaper Editors president Tim McGuire added, "Editors and staff feel scared. Editors and staff feel powerless. Editors and staff feel isolated. We must decide today whether we are going to take newspapers forward with a genuine sense of values and commitment or if we are going to choose the path of milking our companies of every last dime. If we do that, we will die" (quoted in Strupp, 2002, p. 3). The Cultural Forum box "A Sacred Profession?" presents one professional journalist's reaction to conglomerate-enforced demands for higher and higher profits.

For critics of conglomeration and its attendant hypercommercialization of the newspaper, there can be no more damaging blow to the newspaper's role in our democracy than the loss of readers' confidence. As Leo Wolinsky, the *L.A. Times*'s managing editor, confessed in the paper's postcrisis self-examination, "Money is the first thing we talk about. The readers are always the last thing we talk about" (as quoted in Risser, 2000, p. 26).

For more information on this topic, see NBC Video Clip #10 on the CD—*Journalism Students Free Wrongly Accused Death Row Inmate.*

CIVIC JOURNALISM

This chapter's opening vignette was based on an actual example of **civic journalism** (sometimes referred to as **public journalism**)—a newspaper actively engaging the community in reporting important civic issues—which was attempted in 1996 by a group of newspapers in North Carolina (Effron, 1997). These efforts at "interactive journalism" are motivated in part by a

A Sacred Profession?

Jay T. Harris, publisher of the profitable *San Jose Mercury News,* resigned his post in March 2001 specifically to place rising demands for profit on newspapers by their corporate parents in the cultural forum. "I stepped down," wrote the much respected and very successful Harris in a memo to his staff, "in the hope that doing so will cause them [parent company Knight-Ridder] to closely examine the wisdom of the profit targets we've been struggling to find a way to meet." Because these goals would have required severe cutbacks in staff, they risked "significant and lasting harm to the *Mercury News*" (quoted in Jackson, 2001b, p. 20). In a later speech to the American Society of Newspaper Editors (ASNE), Harris elaborated, "I resigned because I was concerned about the future of the whole of the paper, the business side and the news side. I resigned because I could no longer live with the widening gap between creed and greed" (quoted in Fitzgerald, Shields, & Strupp, 2001, p. 7). By *creed,* Harris meant the newspaper as a public trust. By *greed,* he meant the demands for ever-greater profits. In speaking to the ASNE, he was addressing an audience that shared his concerns (Mitchell, 2001):

- 42% felt that parent company management of profit margins was bad for newspapers.

- 51% felt that the long-term impact on the newspaper industry would be negative.

- 41% had made staff cutbacks in the previous 3 months.

- 60% of those cuts had been ordered by the parent company.

- 75% had reduced the number of pages in their papers; 25% had eliminated entire sections.

Knight-Ridder executive Tony Ridder addressed the Harris resignation in a column in the *Mercury News.* "Times are a lot harder in 2001 in the newspaper industry . . . than they have been for a long time. . . . Nobody knows how long the downturn will last. Nor, in the early stages, how severe it will be. So you trim your sails to be ready for whatever rough weather may come your way" (2001, p. 21).

But to critics of concentration and conglomeration of the newspaper, this explanation rang hollow. They cited the fact that Knight-Ridder was a profitable company, having an operating profit margin of 20.8% in 2000,

compared with 13.6% in 1991 (Fogel, 2001). Newspaper analyst John Morton estimated that the *Mercury News* itself earned "a profit of better than 30 percent of sales" in 2000, Harris's last full year at its helm ("News and Profits," 2001, p. 3). In fact, average newspaper industry profit margins of more than 20% far exceed those expected of just about any other industry.

As Harris himself explained in his ASNE address:

Most businesses can reduce expenses more or less proportionately with demand and revenue without doing irreparable damage to their core capabilities, their market position or their mission. Manufacturing businesses are a good example. When fewer items are bought fewer items need to be made and layoffs in various areas are possible. But news and readers' interests do not contract with declining advertising. Nor does our responsibility to the public get smaller as revenue declines or newsprint becomes more expensive. That is where the balancing act comes in. That is where the character of leaders comes in and the priorities they set. (Harris, 2001, p. 21)

The conflict between creed and greed in the newspaper industry is in the public forum. What do you think? Should profits be newspapers' sole goal? After all, newspapers are a business, and all businesses seek profit. But are newspapers somehow different from other businesses? Is the newspaper business, in the words of Melvin Claxton, reporter for the *Detroit News,* "a sacred profession" (quoted in Rieder, 2001, p. 6)?

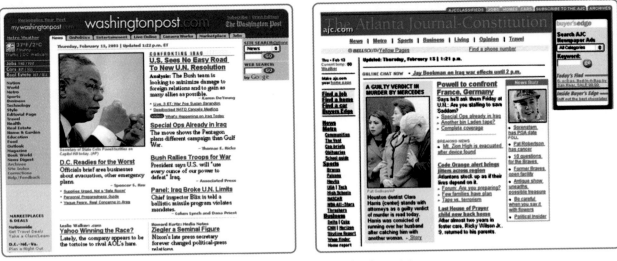

Reprinted with permission.　　Reprinted with permission.

Two of the more successful online newspapers.

drive to strengthen the identity of the paper as an indispensable local medium, thereby attracting readers and boosting revenues. This activism further differentiates newspapers from other media in the chase for advertising dollars. But papers are also trying civic journalism specifically to do good for the communities of which they themselves are members.

Civic journalism happens in a number of ways. Some newspapers devote significant resources to in-depth and long-running coverage of crucial community issues, interviewing citizens as subjects of the stories and inviting comment and debate through various "Hotline" or "Open Forum" sections of their papers. Other newspapers establish citizen councils to advise them on missed opportunities for coverage. Others assemble citizen panels that meet at regular intervals throughout a political campaign or other ongoing story. Citizen reaction to developments in those events is reported as news. Still others establish citizen roundtables to provide insight on crucial issues, for example, race and education. In these discussions people from different constituencies in the community—often holding quite conflicting perceptions of the problem—come together to talk out their differences. This interaction is reported as news, and the papers' editorial writers offer commentary and suggestions for solution.

As we also saw in the vignette, civic journalism is not universally embraced by the newspaper community. Critics contend that too much professional journalistic judgment is given away to people whose interests and concerns are too personal and too narrow. Others claim that the heavy focus on a particular issue in civic journalism distorts the public agenda (see the box "Covering the Issue of Race"). Still, the civic journalism "experiment" continues.

Public Journalism Network
www.
pjnet.org

CONVERGENCE WITH THE INTERNET

Technology has been both ally and enemy to newspapers. Television forced newspapers to change the way they did business and served their readers.

Covering the Issue of Race

Wichita Falls, Texas, has a population of about 100,000, 81% of whom are White and 11% of whom are African American. However, Carroll Wilson, editor of the daily 38,000 circulation *Times Record News*, was dismayed that the races seemed separate, distrustful of one another, and, in the case of the African Americans, embittered. His solution was to use his paper to not only "dig beneath the deceptively calm state of race relations" in the community but also to "provide context for a conversation about race" (Dalton, 1997, p. 54).

Here are a few of the problems his community faced:

- The town was still battling to meet the demands of a 1970 federal court-ordered school desegregation plan.

- African American unemployment was 14.3%, compared with 5.4% for nonminorities.

- Only 3 of the town's 178 police officers were Black.

- The large majority of African Americans left town soon after high school graduation.

Wilson chose Leah Quin, a 25-year-old reporter 3 years out of college, to head a project the paper called "About Face: Wichita Falls in Black & White." The result was a series of 17 stories that ran on 9 consecutive days in March 1997. The opening headline set the tone for what was to come: Silent Divide: Thirty Years After Integration, Blacks and Whites in Wichita Falls Still Are Leading Separate Lives, Divided Not by Laws But by Mutual Misunderstanding.

The paper did not spare itself scrutiny. One part of the series examined the contribution of the *Times Record News* to the chasm—all 12 reporters were White—and Wilson promised to correct the imbalance. As late as 1968 the paper refused to publish photographs of Blacks. Dr. Martin Luther King, Jr.'s photo wasn't shown, even after his assassination; White losers to Black boxers Sugar Ray Robinson and Joe Louis were pictured, not their Black victors. Among its other stories were reports on interracial relationships in business and religion, school imbalance, Black distrust of the local criminal justice system, and racism at nearby Sheppard Air Force Base.

Did the paper make a difference? African American Brenda Jarrett, executive director of a community youth center, felt it did: "We pulled our heads out of the sand and I think that's wonderful. The first step to recovery is admitting, and yes, racism is a disease" (Dalton, 1997, p. 55). Claude Foster, president of the local NAACP, agreed, praising the paper for "regenerating the discussion" on community race relations (p. 55). Mayor Kay Yeager, however, felt differently, complaining that the stories were written from "a pretty one-sided point of view" and that they exaggerated racial difficulties in Wichita Falls (p. 55).

Editor Wilson's own evaluation was mixed: "Nothing's happened, nothing's changed and yes, I'm disappointed. I'm proud of us, we did what a good newspaper should have done—raise hell and do the traditional things that many of us have lost sight of" (p. 55).

Now, online computer networks pose the greatest challenge to this medium. Online job hunting and auto sales services are already cutting into classified advertising profits of newspapers. The Internet and the World Wide Web provide readers with more information and more depth, and with greater speed, than the traditional newspaper. As a result, the traditional newspaper is reinventing itself by converging with these very same technologies.

The marriage of newspapers to the Web has not yet proved financially successful for the older medium, but there are encouraging signs. And in fact, the newspaper industry recognizes that it must accept economic losses while it is building online readers' trust, acceptance, and above all regular and frequent use.

Only one online newspaper, *USA Today*, makes the list of the Web's most visited news, information, and entertainment sites, and only two papers, the *Washington Post* (at number 8) and the *Atlanta Journal-Constitution* (at number 10), appear in the top 10 sites visited by people who live in those cities (Kirsner, 1999). Statistics such as these have generated some pessimistic comment. Mike Moran, CEO of KOZ Inc., a publishing software company, said, "A year ago, newspapers were worried about losing the classifieds. Today, they're worried about losing the franchise." And Scott Cohen, former director of content for the *Boston Globe*'s Boston.com, added, "Newspapers have a bullet in their heads and they don't even know it. They have a damaged brand. No one would buy a new car from [bicycle maker] Schwinn, and right now, few people think of newspapers as relevant on the Internet" (both quotes from Kirsner, 1999, p. 6).

Still, Onlinenewspapers.com lists and provides Web links to 3,000 online newspapers in the United States, including online papers in every state. These papers have adopted a variety of strategies to become "relevant on the Internet." The *Washington Post*, for example, has joined with *Newsweek* magazine, cable television channel MSNBC, and television network NBC to share content among all the parties' Web sites and to encourage users to link to their respective sites. Others have adopted just the opposite approach, focusing on their strength as local media. The *Boston Globe*, for example, offers readers Boston.com, the *Miami Herald* Miami.com, and the *Kansas City Star* KansasCity.com. Each offers not only what readers might expect to find in these sites' parent newspapers but also significant additional information on how to make the most of the cities they represent. These sites are as much city guides as they are local newspapers.

The local element offers several advantages. Local searchable and archivable classified ads offer greater efficiency than do the big national classified ad Web sites such as Monster.com (jobs) and Cars.com (automobiles). No other medium can offer news on crime, housing, neighborhood politics, zoning, school lunch menus, marriage licenses, and bankruptcies—all searchable by street or zip code. Local newspapers can use their Web sites to develop their own linked secondary sites, thus providing impressive detail on local industry. At the *Detroit Free Press*, for example, Auto.com focuses on car manufacturing, while the *San Jose Mercury News*'s SiliconValley.com focuses on the digital industries. Some newspaper Web sites even encourage **community publishing,** that is, they provide their own linked sites, such as New Jersey's *Bergen Record*'s NJCommunity.com, containing pages built by local schools, clubs, and nonprofit groups. Another localizing strategy is for online papers to build and maintain message boards and chat groups on their sites that deal with important issues.

Not all papers see their online operations as mere adjuncts to their "real" newspapers. Launching what *Editor & Publisher* called "the second act in the life of the online newspaper" (Robins, 2001, p. 17), in October 2001, the *New York Times* began **digital delivery daily,** delivering the paper, as it looks in print, to home and office computers. Some other papers that can be downloaded in their entirety are the *Akron Beacon Journal*, the *Philadelphia Enquirer*, the *Atlanta Constitution*, the *Boston Globe*, and the *International Herald Tribune*. Any online user who has News-Stand Reader, NewspaperDirect, or other appropriate software on his or her computer can buy a single copy or subscribe to these papers from any-place in the world. For readers, no more missed deliveries, papers thrown in puddles, and ink-stained fingers. For publishers, newsprint (paper) and delivery costs decline, remote areas can be served, and a paper's "circulation area" can be expanded infinitely.

For now, digital delivery daily papers can be read on home screens, laptops, handheld devices such as Palm Pilots, and as e-books. But that may soon change, as advances in transistor technology make flexible screens a very real possibility. In December 2001, for example, Dutch researchers announced the development of a computer screen with the properties of paper; that is, it is light, flexible, and offers sharp contrast (Pope, 2001). Once perfected, this technology would make reading online newspapers even more convenient, further ensuring the success of digital delivery daily.

Technology serves both online and traditional newspapers in other ways. Computers and satellites greatly aid collection and distribution of news. News copy and other content, complete with appropriate layout, is now sent from editor to printing plants (and to online data services), both locally and over distances, with the stroke of a computer key. Computers have made layout and printing faster and more accurate, helping to control newspaper production costs.

To the chagrin of the established papers, readily available, easy-to-use, and inexpensive computer hardware and software can now be combined to do **desktop publishing,** small-scale print design, layout, and production. The medium is decentralized and more varied, giving readers more and better choices of news sources and coverage. Either because of or in spite of these technological developments, traditionalists believe that there will always be paper newspapers. They cite the portability of newspapers, their ability to provide a large amount of different kinds of clearly categorized content in one place, and their relative permanence (you can start a story, put it down, read it later, then reread it after that) as major reasons newspapers will continue to find an audience.

CHANGES IN NEWSPAPER READERSHIP

A more pessimistic view of the future of newspapers is that as newspapers have reinvented themselves and become more user-friendly, more casual, more lifestyle-oriented, and more in touch with youth, they have become inessential and unimportant, just another commodity in an overcrowded marketplace of popular, personality-centered media. The shift in tone of the modern newspaper is a direct result of another force that is altering the medium–audience relationship—changes in the nature of newspaper readership.

Publishers know well that newspaper readership in the United States is least prevalent among younger people. Fewer than 30% of 18- to 29-year-olds read a daily paper. Fewer than 50% of 30- to 44-year-olds do so (in 1972 the proportion was 75%). The number of 25- to 34-year-olds who read the paper has fallen 20% in the past 5 years alone (Moses, 2002b). Look at Figure 4.3 on page 126. Note the decline in newspaper readership as people get younger. Note, too, the low interest in overall attention to the news in younger Americans. How do you feel about the fact that 25% of all people

Does this front page represent soft news run amok or an effort to give readers what they want? On a day when top Republican leaders demanded that President Bush seek Congressional approval for war with Iraq, the widening financial scandal saw the indictment of two World-Com executives, anti-globalization protests in South Africa disrupted a UN summit on development, and the son of Dr. Martin Luther King, Jr. formally petitioned the Justice Department to remove J. Edgar Hoover's name from the FBI building, two of the top stories in an August edition of this respected central New England paper were Little Leaguers visit Fenway Park and the upcoming birthday, in November, of 104-year-old Justine Girouard.

aged 18 to 24 from a national sample of your fellow Americans sought no news at all? How do you react to media analyst Michael Wolff's assertion that the flight of young readers away from the newspaper means that "if you own a newspaper, you can foresee its almost-certain end"? (quoted in Alterman, 2002, p. 10). The problem facing newspapers, then, is how to lure young people (readers of the future) to their pages. Online papers might be one solution, but the fundamental question remains: Should newspapers give these readers what they *should* want or what they *do* want?

Some newspapers confront this problem directly. They add inserts or sections directed toward, and sometimes written by, teens and young people. This is good business. But traditionalists disagree with another youth-targeted strategy—altering other, more serious (presumably more important) parts of the paper to cater to the infrequent and nonnewspaper reader. As more newspaper professionals adopt a market-centered approach in their pursuit of what media ethicist Jay Black (2001, p. 21) calls (fairly or unfairly?) the "bifurcating, self-indulgent, highly transient,

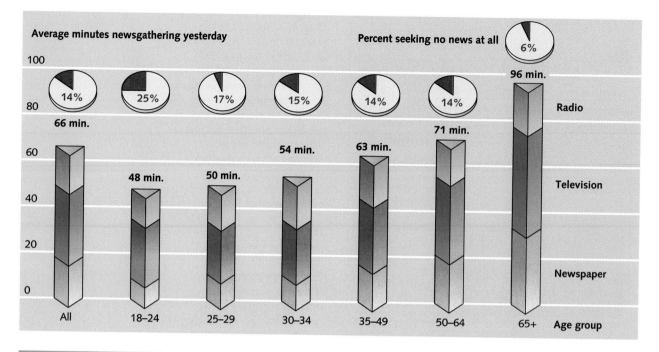

Figure 4.3 How Much Time Did You Spend Newsgathering Yesterday? Source: Pew Center for the People and the Press (Moses, 2002b).

and significantly younger audiences whose pocketbooks are larger than their attention spans"—using readership studies, focus groups, and other tests of customer satisfaction to design their papers—they increasingly find themselves criticized for "cheapening" both the newspaper as a medium and journalism as an institution.

What happens to journalistic integrity, critics ask, to community service, to the traditional role of newspapers in our democracy, when front pages are given over to reports of starlets' affairs, sports heroes' retirements, and full-color photos of plane wrecks because this is what younger readers want? As topics of interest to the 18- to 35-year-old reluctant reader and nonreader are emphasized, what is ignored? What happens to depth, detail, and precision as stories get shorter and snappier? What kind of culture develops on a diet of **soft news** (sensational stories that do not serve the democratic function of journalism; see Scott & Gobetz, 1992) rather than **hard news** (stories that "help people to make intelligent decisions and/or keep up with important issues of the day"; Wulfemeyer, 1982, p. 483)?

The "softening" of newspapers raises a potential media literacy issue. The media literate person has an obligation to be aware of the impact newspapers have on individuals and society and to understand how the text of newspapers offers insight into contemporary culture. We might ask ourselves: Are we getting what we asked for? What do we as a people and as individuals want from our newspaper? Do we understand the role newspapers play in our democratic process? Are we fully aware of how newspapers help shape our understanding of ourselves and our world?

In a 1787 letter, Thomas Jefferson wrote to a colleague, "Were it left to me to decide whether we should have a government without newspapers or newspapers without government, I should not hesitate to prefer the latter." Would he write that about today's newspaper, a newspaper increasingly designed to meet the wants, needs, and interests of younger, occasional newspaper readers or those who do not read at all?

There is the alternative view, however—that there is no problem here at all. Ever since the days of the penny press, newspapers have been dominated by soft news. All we are seeing today is an extension of what has always been. Moreover, nonreaders are simply going elsewhere for the hard news and information that were once the sole province of newspapers. They're going online, to television, and to specifically targeted sources, including magazines and newsletters.

DEVELOPING MEDIA LITERACY SKILLS
Interpreting *Relative Placement of Stories*

Newspapers tell readers what is significant and meaningful through their placement of stories in and on their pages. Within a paper's sections (for

In July, 2002, a federal judge ruled the death penalty unconstitutional, "tantamount to foreseeable, state-sponsored murder of innocent human beings." Two papers, the *Boston Globe* and the *Providence Journal,* published in cities a mere 50 miles apart and sold in one another's geographic areas, chose to report the news somewhat differently. The *Globe* put the story on page 1, the *Journal* on page 5. Would you be surprised to learn that even though both papers have consistently editorialized against capital punishment, the *Journal* is considered a more conservative paper? What can you tell about the importance assigned to this story by each of these papers from its respective placement?

Help a School Start an Online Newspaper

Newspaper circulation has held steady or declined for the past decade and a half; it has not even come close to keeping up with the growth of the American population. But as we have seen in this chapter, many people believe that the newspaper is essential to the operation of our democracy—a sacred profession. We have also seen that the greatest decline in paper readership is among young people. What can you do to support newspaper literacy?

Here are two facts that suggest one solution. One of the surest predictors of newspaper readership is parental newspaper readership. That is, "children born into newspaper-reading families tend to keep up the tradition; those born in non-newspaper families tend to become non-readers" (Morton, 2002, p. 64). We also know that many information-seeking young people ignore the newspaper in favor of "the Internet and personal digital assistants" (Moses, 2002b, p. 13). One way, then, to encourage newspaper literacy is to create a situation that involves the technology young people seem to prefer, while offering the newspaper experience that might be absent in their homes. Help a high school start an online newspaper.

Two fine examples are *The Beak* at Greenwich (Connecticut) High School (www.greenwichschools.org/ghs/beak) and *The Arrow* at Flathead High School in Kalispell, Montana (www.netrix.net/fhspub). Both offer just what you would expect from a school newspaper—news, sports, entertainment, and opinion. Many other schools around the country offer online newspapers as part of their curricula as a means of enhancing awareness of technology, media, and information literacies (information seeking, fact checking, referencing, and so on).

There is a wealth of help available to you. Most useful is the National Scholastic Press Association (www.studentpress.org). Founded in 1921 for the express purpose of supporting high school newspapers, this organization offers competitions, critiques of student work, high school newspaper news, First Amendment counsel, and conventions. Of particular value here is its online school newspaper advisory services.

Also of value is the Newspaper Association of America Foundation (www.naa.org/foundation/nie.html), which administers over 700 Newspaper-in-Education programs (www.vermonttoday.com/nie/nieinfo.html) designed to encourage use of newspapers in schools. Among its services are discounted newspapers, teacher guides, and other community newspaper education assistance. Finally, the ASNE (www.asne.org/ideas/highschools.htm), whose affiliation includes major papers such as the *Boston Globe*, the *Chicago Tribune*, the *Washington Post*, and the *Seattle Times*, maintains programs offering high school journalism students, teachers, and advisors internships, real-world newspaper experiences, and instruction.

Helping a school lay the groundwork for an online paper encourages readership among youth, promotes civic journalism, and gives students increased knowledge about issues such as First Amendment rights, current events, democratic uses of the media, making news (value) judgments, journalistic ethics, and effective communication. Perhaps more important, it unites the school with its community, teaching students that they, their school, their community, and the larger world are all inevitably linked—further reinforcing the need to develop strong newspaper and information-seeking literacy.

*Journalism Education
Association*
www.
jea.org

*High School
Journalism Institute*
www.
journalism.indiana.edu/workshops/
HSJI

example, front, leisure, sports, and careers), readers almost invariably read pages in order (that is, page 1, then page 2, and so on). Recognizing this, papers place the stories they think are most important on the earliest pages. Newspaper jargon for this phenomenon has even entered our everyday language. "Front page news" means the same thing in the pressroom as in the living room.

The placement of stories on a page is also important. English readers read from top to bottom and from left to right. Stories that the newspaper staff deem important tend to be placed "above the fold" and toward the left of the page. This is an important aspect of the power of newspapers to influence public opinion and of media literacy. As you'll see in Chapter 13, relative story placement is a factor in **agenda setting**—the way newspapers and other media influence not only what we think but what we think about.

Two pages from different newspapers published on the same day in nearby cities are shown on page 127. Both chose to report on the legal fight over the death penalty. But notice the different treatments given this story in these newspapers. What judgments can you make about the importance each daily placed on this story? How might *Globe* readers have interpreted this event differently from readers of the *Journal*?

A media literate newspaper reader should be able to make similar judgments about other layout decisions. The use of photos suggests the importance the editors assign to a story, as do the size and wording of headlines, the employment of jumps (continuations to other pages), and placement of a story in a given section. A report of a person's death on the front page, as opposed to the international section or in the obituaries, carries a different meaning, as does an analysis of an issue placed on the front page as opposed to the editorial page.

The Newseum
www.
newseum.org

Chapter Review

In this chapter we examined how European corantos and diurnals led to the creation of what we now know as the newspaper. In the Colonies, broadsides posted at print shops developed into the first American newspaper, *Publick Occurrences,* in 1690.

Pre-Revolution America saw the development of many contemporary press traditions—criticism of public officials, advertising as a financial base, and independence from government control. The commitment to newspaper freedom was codified in the United States in the First Amendment and tested in the Alien and Sedition Acts of 1798.

The modern newspaper emerged in 1833 when Benjamin Day published the *New York Sun* and sold copies for one cent. His penny press took advantage of important cultural and social change in the United States and ushered in the era of mass circulation newspapers. However, competition for that circulation led to much journalistic abuse in the form of yellow journalism. Still, the newspaper had become established as a medium for all the people, a fact capitalized on by Native American and foreign-language publishers and African American publishers such as Robert Jengstake Abbot and Frederick Douglass.

Between the era of yellow journalism and World War II, newspaper chains developed, the ASNE wrote its Canons, and the wire services internationalized. But it was war-wrought social and cultural change, coupled with the advent of television, that provided the next big shift in the newspaper–reader relationship. Although overall newspaper circulation now holds steady, the number of urban daily papers is falling, as is their circulation. Their loss is a gain for suburban and small town dailies and weeklies, reflecting changes in our lifestyle and work habits. National daily newspapers also drain readers and advertising revenue from big city dailies. Nevertheless, newspapers still attract the greatest amount of ad revenue of all the media and are the medium of choice for many advertisers. Up to 65% of newspaper space may be given over to advertising, with the remainder filled out with content often provided by wire services and feature syndicates.

The newspaper–reader relationship is again on the brink of a major change. Competition is declining in the industry because few cities have competing papers. Where competing papers do exist, they sometimes operate under joint operating agreements. Chains now dominate the medium, controlling fully 80% of all circulation. Conglomeration, too, has become a concern, as it has fueled hypercommercialism in newspapers. Many papers are experimenting with civic journalism to reinforce their commitment to their local communities.

Technology in the form of computers, satellite, and online information services not only helps reduce cost and inefficiency in newspaper production and distribution but promises to reshape the information collection and distribution functions of newspapers. Online newspapers, too, are remaking the industry.

Finally, declining readership among younger people poses an important dilemma for professionals who produce the newspaper. Should they give readers (and nonreaders) what they want or what they should want? A related literacy issue arises as media literate readers are obligated to make themselves aware of the impact newspapers have on individuals and society and to understand how the newspaper text offers insight into contemporary culture.

Key Terms

 Use the text's CD-ROM and the Online Learning Center at www.mhhe.com/baran to further your understanding of the following terminlology.

Acta Diurna, 103
corantos, 103
diurnals, 103
broadsides (broadsheets), 104
Bill of Rights, 105
First Amendment, 105
Alien and Sedition Acts, 105
penny press, 106

wire services, 108
yellow journalism, 109
newspaper chains, 110
pass-along readership, 111
zoned editions, 112
feature syndicates, 116
joint operating agreements (JOAs), 117

civic journalism (public journalism), 119
community publishing, 123
digital delivery daily, 123
desktop publishing, 124
soft news, 126
hard news, 126
agenda setting, 128

Questions for Review

Go to the self-quizzes on the CD-ROM and the Online Learning Center to test your knowledge.

1. What are Acta Diurna, corantos, diurnals, and broadsheets?
2. What is the significance of *Publick Occurrences Both Foreign and Domestick*, the *Boston News-Letter*, the *New-England Courant*, the *Pennsylvania Gazette*, and the *New York Weekly Journal*?
3. What factors led to development of the penny press? To yellow journalism?
4. What are the similarities and differences between wire services and feature syndicates?
5. When did newspaper chains begin? Can you characterize them as they exist today?
6. What are the different types of newspapers?
7. Why is the newspaper an attractive medium for advertisers?
8. What is a JOA?
9. What is the firewall? Why is it important?
10. How do online papers hope to succeed?
11. What is hard and soft news?

Questions for Critical Thinking and Discussion

1. Compare your reasons for using the newspaper to Berelson's list. Do his reasons people use the paper reflect your own use?
2. What are your favorite syndicated features? Why?
3. Does your town have competing dailies? If yes, how does that competition manifest itself? If not, what do you think you're missing? Does your town have a JOA situation? If yes, can you describe its operation?
4. Where do you stand on the debate over chains? Are they good or bad for the medium?
5. Have you ever used an online newspaper? How would you describe your experience?

Important Resources

American Journalism Review. A quarterly review of journalism in the United States, this magazine pays particular attention to issues of news coverage of national events.

Columbia Journalism Review. A quarterly magazine of reporting and commentary on issues in journalism. Covering all media, not only newspapers, it is lively and provocative.

Editor & Publisher. This weekly magazine bills itself as the bible of "the Fourth Estate" and "the only independent weekly journal of newspapering." It typically offers interesting stories about the business side of newspapering, valuable statistics, and commentary on contemporary issues.

Harris, M., & O'Malley, T. (1997). *Studies in newspaper and periodical history.* **Westport, CT: Greenwood Press.** A collection of essays and research reports that examine newspaper history from 1770 to 1970. Chapters deal with international as well as U.S. publications.

Journalism History. A scholarly but readable quarterly focusing primarily on U.S. journalism history. It has fine review sections on books and media about the subject.

Quill. Published by the Society of Professional Journalists, *Quill* calls itself "a magazine that surveys and interprets today's journalism while stimulating its readers to collective and individual action for the good of our profession." As such, in addition to timely reporting and commentary, it offers several excellent professionally oriented features such as regular columns on freedom of information, technology, and improving writing.

Kunkel, T., & Layton, C. (2001/2002). *Leaving readers behind.* **Fayetteville, AR: University of Arkansas Press.** Published in two volumes, this work is subtitled "The Age of Corporate Newspapering." It is a compilation of stories from the *American Journalism Review* series on what it calls the "relentless corporatization" of the newspaper industry that leaves "American communities in danger of becoming less informed than ever."

Squires, J. D. (1993). *Read all about it! The corporate takeover of America's newspapers.* **New York: Times Books.** A novel-like account of changes in the operation of newspapers and how they serve their readers by the former editor of the *Orlando Sentinel* and the *Chicago Tribune.*

Tebbel, J. (1969). *The compact history of the American newspaper.* **New York: Hawthorn.** Now a bit dated, but an invaluable guide to early newspaper history.

Lambeth, E. B., Meyer, P. E., & Thorson, E. (2000). *Assessing public journalism.* **Columbia, MO: University of Missouri Press.** The essays in this readable collection offer a wide-ranging evaluation of the civic journalism movement. They cover how civic journalism is practiced, some of its outcomes, and the disagreement over its worth.

Early Newspaper History	www.bl.uk/collections/britnews.html
History of African American Newspapers	www.iath.virginia.edu/vcdh/afam/reflector/newspaper.html
Yellow Journalism	www.humboldt.edu/~jcb10/yellow.html
Newspaper Association of America	www.naa.org
Links to National Newspapers	www.all-links.com/newscentral
American Association of Newspapers	www.aan.org
Editor & Publisher	www.mediainfo.com
American Society of Newspaper Editors	www.asne.org
Pew Center for Civic Journalism	www.pewcenter.org
Online Newspapers	www.onlinenewspapers.com
Journalism Education Association	www.jea.org
High School Journalism Institute	www.journalism.indiana.edu/workshops/HSJI
The Newseum	www.newseum.org

Magazines

LEARNING OBJECTIVES

Magazines were once a truly national mass medium, the television of their time. But changes in the nature of American society and the economics of mass media altered their nature. They are the medium that first made specialization a virtue, and they prosper today by speaking to ever more narrowly defined groups of readers. After studying this chapter you should

- be familiar with the history and development of the magazine industry and the magazine itself as a medium.

- recognize how the organizational and economic nature of the contemporary magazine industry shapes the content of magazines.

- understand the relationship between magazines and their readers.

- be familiar with the successes and failures of Web magazines and the reasons for both.

- possess improved magazine-reading media literacy skills, especially when interpreting advertorials and digitally altered images.

IT'S NOVEMBER 1994, AND YOU ARE WORKING AT THE NEWS-paper. It's an entry-level job, but you're excited about your career prospects. Your paper has been around for most of the century, and its reporters either build good names for themselves in town or move on to bigger markets. You have a lot of responsibility and freedom, but you are admittedly sick and tired of the ongoing battles with management. As it is, you and your colleagues are embroiled in yet another labor dispute.

The arts and features editor, however, impressed by what he's seen from you, offers you an out. It's still early in the history of online publishing, he says, but that's an opportunity, not a problem. Together you can define what an online publication should be. Here's the deal, he tells you. He has $100,000 in start-up money from Apple Computer and wants to be online in a year. Rather than take on the grind of a daily newspaper, he envisions a free biweekly magazine featuring a hip, West Coast mix of cultural criticism, political and social commentary, interviews with

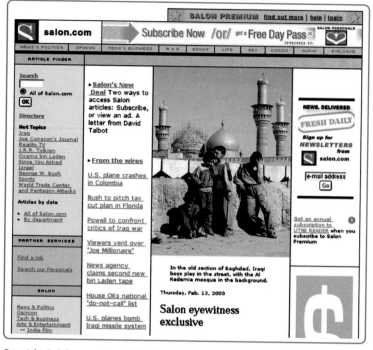

authors, and book reviews. You ask, "How will the magazine make money?" (though what you really mean is, "How will I get paid?"). As bad as management–labor relations are at the paper, at least you earn a living. "Not to worry," he assures you. "Advertisers will line up to get access to the kinds of people who'll read our little online magazine. And I need your answer," he adds, "by tomorrow."

Had you been at the *San Francisco Examiner* with David Talbot (the arts and features editor mentioned above) in 1994, you might have found yourself having to make this decision. Do you stay at a traditional paper-based publication that has many benefits and some drawbacks, or do you gamble on the convergence of magazines and the growing but still new Internet?

Salon
www.
salon.com

Talbot called his online magazine *Salon* and took the *Examiner*'s Gary Kamiya (*Salon*'s executive editor), Andrew Ross (vice president of business and strategic development), Scott Rosenberg (senior technology editor), and Mignon Khargie (design editor) with him to his new venture. And together with Microsoft-backed *Slate*, *Salon* defined (and continues to define) the world of online magazines.

For example, Talbot discovered that users would visit the magazine but disappear until new material was posted. So in early 1997, *Salon* began posting a new issue every weekday. Traffic rose dramatically to 400,000 unique visitors per month (Stein, 1999). As the Net matured, helping usher in the 24-hour-a-day, 7-day-a-week reporting cycle for all news media, the magazine increased its emphasis on breaking news, a smooth transition for an online publication staffed by refugees from a daily newspaper. Today, *Salon* draws 3.5 million unique visitors a month, but, like almost all other content providers, it has suffered from declining Internet advertising revenues. Now, in addition to its free pages, it offers a "premium service" for $30 a year. "Premium affiliates" receive content unavailable on the free site, absent all advertising. About 10% of *Salon*'s readers are affiliates, and although this has helped stem the flow of red ink somewhat, this old-line (by Internet standards) online magazine continues to lose money (Farhi, 2001). So, knowing this, would you make the move from a daily newspaper to Talbot's new venture?

In this chapter we examine the dynamics of the contemporary magazine industry—paper and online—and its audiences. We study the medium's beginnings in the Colonies, its pre–Civil War expansion, and its explosive growth between the Civil War and World War I. This was the era of great mass circulation magazines, but it was also the era of powerful writers known as muckrakers.

Influenced by television and by the social and cultural changes that followed World War II, the magazine took on a new, more narrowly focused nature, which provided the industry with a growing readership and increased profits. We detail the various categories of magazines, discuss circulation research, look at the ways the industry protects itself from competition from other media, and how advertisers influence editorial decisions. Finally, we investigate some of the editorial decisions that should be of particular interest to media literate magazine consumers.

A Short History of Magazines

Magazines were a favorite medium of the British elite by the mid-1700s, and two prominent colonial printers hoped to duplicate that success in the New World. In 1741 in Philadelphia, Andrew Bradford published *American Magazine, or a Monthly View of the Political State of the British Colonies*, followed by Benjamin Franklin's *General Magazine, and Historical Chronicle, for All the British Plantations in America*. Composed largely of reprinted British material, these publications were expensive and aimed at the small number of literate colonists. Lacking an organized postal system, distribution was difficult, and neither magazine was successful. *American Magazine* produced three issues, *General Magazine*, six. Yet between 1741 and 1794, 45 new magazines appeared, although no more than 3 were published in the same time period. Entrepreneurial printers hoped to attract educated, cultured, moneyed gentlemen by copying the successful London magazines. Even after the Revolutionary War, U.S. magazines remained clones of their British forerunners.

Magazine History
WWW.
well.com/user/art/maghist01.html

THE EARLY MAGAZINE INDUSTRY

In 1821 the *Saturday Evening Post* appeared; it was to continue for the next 148 years. Among other successful early magazines were *Harper's* (1850) and *Atlantic Monthly* (1857). Cheaper printing and growing literacy fueled expansion of the magazine as they had the book (see Chapter 3). But an additional factor in the success of the early magazines was the spread of social movements such as abolitionism and labor reform. These issues provided compelling content, and a boom in magazine publishing began. In 1825 there were 100 magazines in operation; by 1850 there were 600. Because magazine articles increasingly focused on matters of importance to U.S. readers, magazines such as the *United States Literary Gazette* and *American Boy* began to look less like London publications and more like a new and unique product. Journalism historians John Tebbel and Mary Ellen Zuckerman (1991) called this "the time of significant beginnings" (p. 13); it was during this time that the magazine developed many of the characteristics we associate with it even today. Magazines and the people who staffed them began to clearly differentiate themselves from other publishing endeavors (such as books and newspapers). The concept of specialist writers took hold, and their numbers rose. In addition, numerous and detailed illustrations began to fill the pages of magazines.

Still, these early magazines were aimed at a literate elite interested in short stories, poetry, social commentary, and essays. The magazine did not become a true national mass medium until after the Civil War.

This *McClure's* cover captures the spirit of the Roaring Twenties as well as the excitement of the burgeoning magazine industry.

THE MASS CIRCULATION ERA

The modern era of magazines can be divided into two parts, each characterized by a different relationship between medium and audience.

Mass circulation popular magazines began to prosper in the post–Civil War years. In 1865 there were 700 magazines publishing; by 1870 there were 1,200; by 1885 there were 3,300. Crucial to this expansion was the women's magazine. Suffrage—the right to vote for women—was the social movement that occupied its pages, but a good deal of content could also be described as how-to for homemakers. Advertisers, too, were anxious to appear in the new women's magazines, hawking their brand name products. First appearing at this time are several magazines still familiar today, including *Ladies' Home Journal* and *Good Housekeeping*.

There were several reasons for this phenomenal growth. As with books, widespread literacy was one reason. But the Postal Act of 1879, which permitted mailing magazines at cheap second-class postage rates, and the spread of the railroad, which carried people and publications westward from the East Coast, were two others. A fourth was the reduction in cost. As long as magazines sold for 35 cents—a lot of money for the time—they were read largely by the upper class. However, a circulation war erupted between giants *McClure's, Munsey's Magazine,* and *The Saturday Evening Post.* Soon they, as well as *Ladies' Home Journal, McCall's, Woman's Home Companion, Collier's,* and *Cosmopolitan,* were selling for as little as 10 and 15 cents, which brought them within reach of many working people.

This 1870s price war was made possible by the newfound ability of magazines to attract growing amounts of advertising. As we'll see in Chapter 12, social and demographic changes in the post–Civil War era—urbanization, industrialization, the spread of roads and railroads, and development of consumer brands and brand names—produced an explosion in the number of advertising agencies. These agencies needed to place their messages somewhere. Magazines were the perfect outlet because they were read by a large, national audience. As a result, circulation—rather than reputation, as had been the case before—became the most important factor in setting advertising rates. Magazines kept cover prices low to ensure the large readerships coveted by advertisers. The fifth reason for the enormous growth in the number of magazines was industrialization, which provided people with leisure and more personal income.

The first issue of *Time*

Magazines were truly America's first *national* mass medium, and like books they served as an important force in social change, especially in the **muckraking** era of the first decades of the 20th century (see the box "Taking On the Giants: Muckraking in the Magazines"). Theodore Roosevelt coined this label as an insult, but the muckrakers wore it proudly, using the pages of *The Nation, Harper's Weekly, The Arena,* and even mass circulation publications such as *McClure's* and *Collier's* to agitate for change. Their targets were the powerful. Their beneficiaries were the poor.

The mass circulation magazine grew with the nation. From the start there were general interest magazines such as *The Saturday Evening Post,* women's magazines such as *Good Housekeeping,* pictorial magazines such as *Life* and *Look,* and digests such as *Reader's Digest,* which was first published in 1922 and offered condensed and tightly edited articles for people on the go in the Roaring Twenties. What these magazines all had in common was the size and breadth of readership. They were mass market, mass circulation publications, both national and affordable. As such, magazines helped unify the nation. They were the television of their time—the dominant advertising medium, the primary source for nationally distributed news, and the preeminent provider of visual, or photo, journalism.

Taking On the Giants: Muckraking in the Magazines

At the start of the 20th century, corruption and greed in business and politics were creating some of the worst abuses this country had ever seen—unsafe food, inhumane child labor practices, unregulated drug manufacture and sale, exploitation of workers, a lack of safety standards in the workplace, blatant discrimination against African Americans, and a disregard for human and civil rights. Industrial giants, the so-called Robber Barons, amassed fortunes through mammoth monopolies controlling mining, manufacturing, banking, railroads, food packing, and insurance.

Why didn't the government step in and stop these abuses? Local politicians and police were in the pay of the industries. The federal government was also hamstrung. At the time, U.S. senators were selected by the legislatures of the individual states. For the right price, an industry could make sure that people favorable to its interests were selected by those legislatures to serve in the Senate. The buying and selling of seats ensured that the Senate would block any attempts to pass legislation designed to break up monopolies or remedy social ills.

Echoing the role of books in social change, magazines, particularly popular mass market magazines, took leader-

ship in challenging these powerful interests and advocating reform. Reaching a nationwide audience, *McClure's*, *American Magazine*, and *Collier's* shocked and outraged the public with their exposés. Historian Louis Filler (1968) called the crusading magazine articles of writers such as Ida Tarbell, Upton Sinclair, Lincoln Steffens, Jack London, and others "literary rather than yellow"(p. 31). That is, rather than adopting the overexcited, excessive tone of the yellow journalism of the day, these were well written, well researched, and well argued. Articles and series such as Steffens's "The Shame of the Cities," Tarbell's "The History of the Standard Oil Company," Sinclair's novel *The Jungle* (on unclean food and abuse of workers), and Edwin Markham's "The Hoe-Man in the Making" (on unsafe and inhumane child labor practices) galvanized the nation.

One of the greatest successes of magazine journalism was spurred by what we would now consider an unlikely source. However, it produced an amendment to the U.S. Constitution.

A series of articles begun in *Cosmopolitan* in March 1906 changed the way U.S. senators were elected, ensuring passage of reform legislation. "The Treason of the

Between 1900 and 1945, the number of families who subscribed to one or more magazines grew from 200,000 to more than 32 million. New and important magazines continued to appear throughout these decades. For example, African American intellectual W. E. B. DuBois founded and edited *The Crisis* in 1910 as the voice of the National Association for the Advancement of Colored People (the NAACP). *Time* was first published in 1923. Its brief review of the week's news was immediately popular (it was originally only 28 pages long). It made a profit within a year. *The New Yorker*, "the world's best magazine," debuted in 1925.

THE ERA OF SPECIALIZATION

In 1956 *Collier's* declared bankruptcy and became the first mass circulation magazine to cease publication. But its fate, as well as that of other mass circulation magazines, had actually been sealed in the late 1940s and 1950s following the end of World War II. Profound alterations in the nation's culture—and, in particular, the advent of television—changed the relationship between magazines and their audience. No matter how large their circulation, magazines could not match the reach of television. Magazines did not have moving pictures or visual and oral storytelling. Nor could magazines match television's timeliness. Magazines were weekly,

Though President Roosevelt meant the epithet as an insult, the Muckrakers wore the title with pride.

Senate" accused U.S. senators of treason for giving aid and comfort to "the enemies of the nation." Within days of hitting the newsstands, every issue of *Cosmopolitan* had been sold, and President Teddy Roosevelt was compelled to respond to the charges. In a speech delivered on March 17, Roosevelt condemned "the man with the muckrake [who in] magazines makes slanderous and mendacious attack upon men in public life and upon men engaged in public work" (Filler, 1968, p. 252). Thus did the crusading writers and journalists come to be known as "muckrakers." Roosevelt's anguish was no match for the public's anger. In 1913 the 17th Amendment, mandating popular election of senators, was ratified.

The efforts of the muckrakers and the magazines that spread their writing produced legislation and policies that have helped define the world as we know it. They were influential in passage of the Pure Food and Drug Act and the Hepburn Railroad Bill in 1906, the Federal Reserve Bill in 1913, the Clayton Anti-Trust Act in 1914, and numerous child labor laws.

A wide array of specialized magazines exists for all lifestyles and interests. Here are only 5 of the 17,000 special interest consumer magazines available to U.S. readers.

A change in people's tastes in magazines reflects some of the ways the world changed after World War II. Norman Rockwell's America was replaced by that of *GQ* and *People*.

whereas television was continuous. Nor could they match television's novelty. In the beginning, *everything* on television was of interest to viewers. As a result, magazines began to lose advertisers to television.

The audience changed as well. As we've seen, World War II changed the nature of American life. The new, mobile, product-consuming public was less interested in the traditional Norman Rockwell world of *The Saturday Evening Post* (closed in 1969) and more in tune with the slick, hip world of narrower interest publications such as *GQ* and *Self*, which spoke to them in and about their new and exciting lives. And because World War II had further urbanized and industrialized America, people—including millions of women who had entered the workforce—had more leisure and more money to spend. They could spend both on a wider array of personal interests *and* on magazines that catered to those interests. Where there were once *Look* (closed in 1971) and *Life* (closed in 1972), there were now *Flyfishing, Surfing, Ski,* and *Easyrider.* The industry had hit on the secret of success: specialization and a lifestyle orientation.

Magazines and Their Audiences

Exactly who are the audiences for magazines? Magazine industry research indicates that among people with at least some college, 94% read at least one magazine and average more than 11 different issues a month. Nearly the same figures apply for households with annual incomes of over $40,000 and for people in professional and managerial careers, regardless of educational attainment. The typical magazine reader is at least a high school graduate, is married, owns his or her own house, is employed full time, and has an annual household income of just under $40,000. Advertisers find magazine readers an attractive, upscale audience for their pitches.

American Society of Magazine Editors **www.** asme.magazine.org

How people use magazines also makes them an attractive advertising medium. People report:

- Reading magazines as much for the ads as for the editorial content, keeping them available for up to four months
- Passing them along to an average of four similar adults
- Being very loyal, which translates into increased esteem for those advertisers in the pages of their favorite publications

Scope and Structure of the Magazine Industry

In 1950 there were 6,950 magazines in operation. The number now exceeds 22,000, some 17,000 of which are general interest consumer magazines. Of these, 800 produce three-fourths of the industry's gross revenues. Ten new magazine titles are launched every week (Magazine Publishers of America, 2002). Contemporary magazines are typically divided into three broad types:

For more information on this topic, view *Magazines: Inside Vibe Magazine, #1* on the CD Media Tours.

- *Trade, professional, and business magazines* carry stories, features, and ads aimed at people in specific professions and are either distributed by the professional organizations themselves *(American Medical News)* or by media companies such as Whittle Communications and Time Warner *(Progressive Farmer)*.

- *Industrial, company, and sponsored magazines* are produced by companies specifically for their own employees, customers, and stockholders, or by clubs and associations specifically for their members. *Friendly Exchange*, for example, is the magazine of the Fireman's Fund insurance company. *Modern Maturity* is the magazine for members of the American Association of Retired Persons (AARP).

- *Consumer magazines* are sold by subscription and at newsstands, bookstores, and other retail outlets, including supermarkets, garden shops, and computer stores. *Sunset Magazine* and *Wired* fit here, as do *Road & Track, US, TV Guide,* and *The New Yorker* (Figure 5.1).

CATEGORIES OF CONSUMER MAGAZINES

The industry typically categorizes consumer magazines in terms of their targeted audiences. Of course, the wants, needs, interests, and wishes of those readers determine the content of each publication. Although these categories are neither exclusive (where do *Chicago Business* and *Sports Illustrated for Women* fit?) nor exhaustive (what do we do with *Hot Rod* and *National Geographic*?), they are at least indicative of the cascade of options. Here is a short list of common consumer magazine categories, along with examples of each type.

Magazine Publishers of America
www.
magazine.org

Alternative magazines: *Mother Jones, The Utne Reader*
Business/money magazines: *Money, Black Enterprise*
Celebrity and entertainment magazines: *People, Entertainment Weekly*
Children's magazines: *Highlights, Ranger Rick*
Computer magazines: *Internet, PC World*
Ethnic magazines: *Hispanic, Ebony*
Family magazines: *Fatherhood, Parenting*
Fashion magazines: *Bazaar, Elle*
General interest magazines: *Reader's Digest, Life*
Geographical magazines: *Texas Monthly, Bay Area Living*
Gray magazines: *Modern Maturity*
Literary magazines: *Atlantic Monthly, Harper's*
Men's magazines: *GQ, Field & Stream, Playboy*
News magazines: *Time, U.S. News & World Report, Newsweek*
Political opinion magazines: *The Nation, National Review*
Sports magazines: *Sport, Sports Illustrated*
Sunday newspaper magazines: *Parade, USA Weekend*
Women's magazines: *Working Woman, Good Housekeeping, Ms.*
Youth magazines: *Seventeen, Tiger Beat*

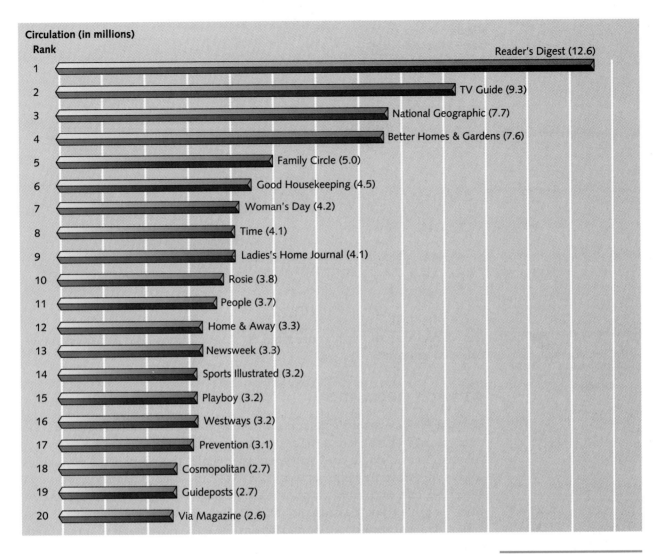

Circulation (in millions)

Rank

Rank	Magazine
1	Reader's Digest (12.6)
2	TV Guide (9.3)
3	National Geographic (7.7)
4	Better Homes & Gardens (7.6)
5	Family Circle (5.0)
6	Good Housekeeping (4.5)
7	Woman's Day (4.2)
8	Time (4.1)
9	Ladies's Home Journal (4.1)
10	Rosie (3.8)
11	People (3.7)
12	Home & Away (3.3)
13	Newsweek (3.3)
14	Sports Illustrated (3.2)
15	Playboy (3.2)
16	Westways (3.2)
17	Prevention (3.1)
18	Cosmopolitan (2.7)
19	Guideposts (2.7)
20	Via Magazine (2.6)

Figure 5.1 The 20 Consumer Magazines with the Highest Paid Circulation (2001). *Source:* Magazine Publishers of America, Dec. 2002.

Magazine Advertising

Magazine specialization exists and succeeds because the demographically similar readership of these publications is attractive to advertisers who wish to target ads for their products and services to those most likely to respond to them. This is a lucrative situation for the magazine industry. American magazines carried 237,612,500,000 ad pages in 2001, worth over $12 billion (Magazine Publishers of America, 2002). (But for the story of a magazine with no advertising, see the box "Suzuki Samurai versus *Consumer Reports.*") Eight and a quarter percent of all advertising expenditures in U.S. media is placed with magazines. How those billions of dollars are spread among different types of advertisers is shown in Figure 5.2 (p. 144).

Magazines are often further specialized through **split runs,** special versions of a given issue in which editorial content and ads vary according to some specific demographic or regional grouping. *Time,* for example, has at

Figure 5.2 Top 10 Magazine Advertiser Categories, 2002. *Source:* Publishers Information Bureau 2002.

Rank	Category
1	Technology
2	Automotive
3	Apparel and Accessories
4	Toiletries and Cosmetics
5	Home Furnishings and Supplies
6	Media
7	Financial, Insurance, and Real Estate
8	Food and Food Products
9	Drugs and Remedies
10	Retail

For more information on this topic, see NBC Video Clip #7 on the CD—*Media Professionals Discuss State of the Media.*

least 8 regional editions, more than 50 state editions, and 8 professionally oriented editions.

TYPES OF CIRCULATION

Magazines price advertising space in their pages based on **circulation,** the total number of issues of a magazine that are sold. These sales can be either subscription or single-copy sales. On the whole, the number of magazines sold is fairly evenly split between the two, but some magazines, *Woman's Day, TV Guide,* and *Penthouse,* for example, rely heavily on single-copy sales, whereas others, such as *Reader's Digest,* earn as much as 60% of their revenues from subscriptions. Subscriptions have the advantage of an assured, ongoing readership, but they are sold below the cover price and have the additional burden of postage included in their cost to the publisher. Single-copy sales are less reliable, but to advertisers they are sometimes a better barometer of a publication's value to its readers. Single-copy readers must consciously choose to pick up an issue, and they pay full price for it.

A third form of circulation, **controlled circulation,** refers to providing a magazine at no cost to readers who meet some specific set of advertiser-attractive criteria. Free airline and hotel magazines fit this category. Although they provide no subscription or single-sales revenue, these magazines are an attractive, relatively low-cost advertising vehicle for companies seeking narrowly defined, captive audiences.

MEASURING CIRCULATION

Audit Bureau of Circulations
WWW.
accessabc.com

Regardless of how circulation occurs, it is monitored through research. The Audit Bureau of Circulations (ABC) was established in 1914 to provide reliability to a booming magazine industry playing loose with self-

Suzuki Samurai versus *Consumer Reports*

Very few magazines survive today without accepting advertising. Those that are ad-free insist that freedom from commercial support allows them to make a greater difference in the lives of their readers. *Ms.*, for example, cannot advocate development of strong, individual females if its pages carry ads that suggest beauty is crucial for women's success. But it is *Consumer Reports* that makes this case most strongly—it must be absolutely free of outside influence if its articles about consumer products are to maintain their well-earned reputation for fairness and objectivity. This reputation was put to the test when automobile manufacturer Suzuki went to war with the magazine and its publisher, Consumer Union.

In 1988 *Consumer Reports* tested a number of sports utility vehicles for safety. Several passed the magazine's difficult evaluation, but the Suzuki Samurai did not. The Samurai tipped up severely and repeatedly in a series of avoidance-maneuver tests. *Consumer Reports* rated the Samurai "not acceptable" in its July 1988 issue. Later that same year, the National Highway Transportation and Safety Administration (NHTSA) accepted Consumer Union's petition that it develop minimum stability standards to prevent rollover in all vehicles. Six years later, in 1994, the NHTSA abandoned its plans to develop such a standard, citing the high cost to manufacturers in meeting proposed rules. Instead, argued the NHTSA, an "informed public" would, through its purchases of certain vehicles rather than others, produce the necessary change.

Grudgingly accepting the NHTSA market-based solution, *Consumer Reports* continued its testing as a way to inform the public, despite lawsuits and attacks from Suzuki. Those attacks, and *Consumer Reports*' reputation, were challenged in a 1997 lawsuit.

A 31-year-old Samurai passenger, Katie Rodriguez, was paralyzed from the neck down in a rollover accident on a Missouri highway. She sued Suzuki. Despite testimony from its own expert witnesses that there had been 147 deaths and 7,000 injuries resulting from Samurai rollover accidents, the manufacturer made the "unscientific and rigged" *Consumer Reports* research the center of its defense. In its closing arguments, Suzuki lawyers claimed that Rodriguez's suit and other suits against the company (more than 175 to that date) had been the direct result of the magazine's unfair rating in 1988.

But when the jury began its deliberations, one of the first exhibits it asked for was that same 1988 *Consumer Reports* article. When they returned their verdict, jurors awarded Ms. Rodriguez $25 million in compensatory damages and another $11.9 million in punitive damages.

Did the magazine make a difference? Although the NHTSA has yet to develop mandatory antirollover safety standards, *Consumer Reports* believes that the unanimous jury verdict against the Suzuki Samurai shows that it did.

Two other magazines that, like *Consumer Reports*, eschew advertising because they see it as inimical to their larger mission of making a difference with their particular category of reader are *Adbusters* and *Ms. Adbusters*, founded in 1989, boasts a worldwide circulation of 50,000 and won the *Utne Reader* Award for General Excellence three times in its first 6 years of operation. It aims to help stem the erosion of the world's physical and cultural environments by what it views as greed and commercial forces. Its online version <www.adbusters.org> allows users to download spoofs of popular ad campaigns and other anti-consumerism spots for use as banner ads on their own sites. The more well-known *Ms.* began life in 1972 as a Warner Communications publication and has gone through several incarnations as both a for-profit and a not-for-profit publication. Today it is published every other year, carries no advertising, and remains committed to advancing the cause of women and feminism on a global scale. It, too, maintains an online version <www.msmagazine.com>.

Source: This box was developed from material available on *Consumer Reports'* Web site <http://www.consumer.org>.

---

announced circulation figures. The ABC provides reliable circulation figures, as well as important population and demographic information. Other research companies, including Simmons Market Research Bureau and Standard Rate and Data Service, also generate valuable data for advertisers and magazines. Circulation data are often augmented by measures of *pass-along readership,* which refers to readers who neither subscribe nor buy single copies but who borrow a magazine or read one in a doctor's office or library.

Magazine CyberCenter
www.
magamall.com

Controlled circulation magazines, like American Airlines' in-flight publications *American Way* and *Nexos*, and Raddison Hotels' *Voyageur*, take advantage of readers' captivity.

Trends and Convergence in Magazine Publishing

The forces that are reshaping all the mass media have had an impact on magazines as well. Alterations in how the magazine industry does business are primarily designed to help magazines compete with television in the race for advertising dollars. Convergence, too, has its impact.

ONLINE MAGAZINES

Another category, **Webzines,** or online magazines, has emerged, made possible by convergence of magazines and the Internet. Many magazines, among them *Time* and *Mother Jones,* now produce online editions offering special interactive features not available to their hard copy readers. In addition, several strictly online magazines have been attempted. For example, former *New Republic* editor Michael Kinsley moved from Washington (D.C.) to Washington (state) to publish the exclusively online magazine *Slate* for Microsoft (http://www.slate.com). And as we saw in this chapter's opening vignette, *Salon* has become quite popular. Also attracting large numbers of users is the satirical *The Onion* at <http://www.theonion.com>.

Online magazines have yet to succeed financially. Those produced by existing paper magazine publishers serve primarily as an additional outlet for existing material, a way to extend the reach of the parent publication. Exclusively online magazines have yet to produce a profit, and many industry analysts think it will be a long time before they do.

There are several hurdles specific to purely online magazines. First, because Web users have become accustomed to free access to sites, Webzines

For more information on this topic, view *Television: Inside WSEE-TV,* #4 on the CD *Media Tours.*

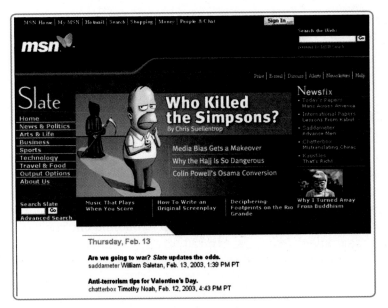

Copyright © Slate. Distributed by United Feature Syndicate.

have yet to find a successful means of charging for subscriptions. *Slate* dropped its plan to do so when faced with a 1997 reader revolt, and, as we saw earlier, *Salon* has instituted a two-tier, both free and subscription, model. Second, as opposed to Webzines produced by paper magazines, purely online magazines must generate original content, an expensive undertaking, yet they compete online for readers and advertisers as equals with Webzines subsidized by paper magazines. In addition, purely online magazines must also compete with all other Web sites on the Internet. They are but one of an infinite number of choices for potential readers. And finally, of the total annual U.S. expenditure on advertising ($200 billion), only $154 million is spent on online magazine advertising (McNamara, 2000). At least for now, there may simply be too little commercial support to sustain this new form of magazine.

Top 100 Computer Magazines **www.** internetvalley.com/ top100mag.html

NEW TYPES OF MAGAZINES

A new form of magazine is the **brand magazine,** a consumer magazine, complete with a variety of general interest articles and features, published by a retail or other business for readers having demographic characteristics similar to those of consumers with whom it typically does business. These publications carry ad pages not only for the products of its parent business, but for others as well. Benetton publishes *Colors*, and computer networker Cisco Systems offers *iQ* (for Internet Quotient).

Closely related to the brand magazine is the **magalogue,** a designer catalogue produced to look like a consumer magazine. Abercrombie & Fitch, J. Crew, Harry Rosen, and Diesel all produce catalogues in which models wearing the for-sale designer clothes "frolic along sketchily drawn plotlines" (Klein, 1999, p. 41).

A third new form, the **synergistic magazine,** may or may not take hold. These are magazines designed explicitly to generate stories that will become movies, television programs, or content for other media. The most heralded entry into this new field was *Talk*. A joint venture of Hearst Magazines and Miramax Films, it was launched in 1999 amid much fanfare. It closed shop after its February 2002 issue. Industry insiders are uncertain over the future of the form. After all, many successful magazines already rely heavily on synergy for some of their profits. CBS's 2002 broadcast of a September 11 memorial based on documentary footage from inside the North Tower of the World Trade Center came to the network's attention via *Vanity Fair*'s feature story on its creators, filmmakers Gedeon and Jules Naudet. *Proof of Life* (2000) also came from *Vanity Fair;* all the Chevy Chase *Vacation* movies come from *National Lampoon;* the 2002 summer movie *Blue Crush* came from "Surf Girls of Maui" in *Outside*. Those optimistic about the future of synergistic magazines say it was the poor economic environment, not lack of merit, that killed *Talk* (a nearly 12% drop in total ad pages sold from 2000 to 2001 produced a 5% drop in industry revenues). Also closing in that year, for example, were *Brill's Content, Mademoiselle, Working Woman,* and *Industry Standard,* the latter the industry leader in ad pages in 2000 (Poniewozik, 2002). Critics contend that magazine readers seek specific magazines for specific reasons and that the synergistic magazine cannot serve two masters—reader and film, video, and book producers.

MEETING COMPETITION FROM TELEVISION

As we've seen, the move toward specialization in magazines was forced by the emergence of television as a mass-audience national advertising medium. Ironically, it is television that once again threatens the preeminence of magazines as a specialized advertising medium. Specifically, the challenge comes from cable television. Advertiser-supported cable channels survive using precisely the same strategy as magazines—they deliver to advertisers a relatively large number of consumers who have some important demographic trait in common. Similar competition, although still insignificant, is also coming from specialized online content providers such as ESPNET SportsZone and The Discovery Channel Online. Magazines are well positioned to fend off these challenges for several reasons.

First is internationalization, which expands a magazine's reach, making it possible for magazines to attract additional ad revenues for content that, essentially, has already been produced. Internationalization can happen in one of several ways. Some magazines, *Time* and *Newsweek*, for example, produce one or more foreign editions in English. Others enter cooperative agreements with overseas companies to produce native-language versions of essentially U.S. magazines. For example, Time Warner and the French company Hachette cooperate to publish a French-language *Fortune*. Often U.S. magazines prepare special content for foreign-language editions. *Cosmopolitan*, for example, produces 50 worldwide editions in 28 languages. The internationalization of magazines will no doubt increase as conglomeration and globalization continue to have an impact on the magazine industry as they have on other media businesses.

Movies *Blue Crush*, *Proof of Life*, and *National Lampoon's Vacation* were each born as a magazine article.

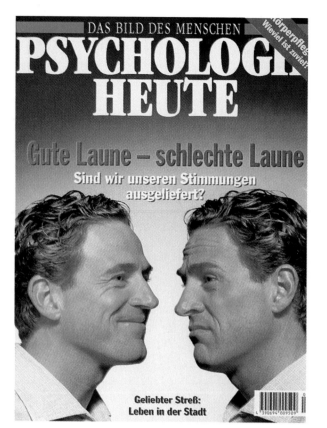

The look alone of this magazine's cover makes it clear that it is the German version of what we know in the U.S. as *Psychology Today*.

How to Start a Magazine
WWW.
laughingbear.com/magazine.html

Second is technology. Computers and satellites now allow instant distribution of copy from the editor's desk to printing plants around the world. The result—almost immediate delivery to subscribers and sales outlets—makes production and distribution of even more narrowly targeted split runs more cost-effective. This is an efficiency that cable television has yet to match.

Third is the sale of subscriber lists and a magazine's own direct marketing of products. Advertisers buy space in specialized magazines to reach a specific type of reader. Most magazines are more than happy to sell those readers' names and addresses to those same advertisers, as well as to others who want to contact readers with direct mail pitches. Many magazines use their own subscriber lists for the same purpose, marketing products of interest to their particular readership. Cable television, even the most specialized channels, cannot easily identify individual audience members; therefore, they cannot sell their names.

ADVERTORIALS

Publishers and advertisers increasingly use advertorials as a means of boosting the value of a magazine as an advertising medium. **Advertorials** are ads that appear in magazines that take on the appearance of genuine editorial content. Sometimes they are a page or less, sometimes inserts composed of several pages. They frequently carry the disclaimer "Advertisement," but it is usually in small print. Sometimes the disclaimer is no more than the advertiser's logo in a page corner. The goal is to put commercial content before readers, cloaked in the respectability of editorial content. Advertorial-generated revenue in the magazine industry more than doubled in the 1990s, as did the number of ad pages given over to their use. Advertorials now account for 10% of all magazine advertising income (Kim, Pasadeos, & Barban, 2001). The question for media literate magazine readers is clear: Is an item journalism or is it advertising?

Critics of advertorials argue that this blurring of the distinction between editorial and commercial matter is a breach of faith with readers (see the box "Advertorials Aimed at Young Girls"). Moreover, if the intent is not deception, why is the disclaimer typically small; why use the editorial content format at all? Defenders contend that advertorials are a well-entrenched aspect of contemporary magazines. The industry considers them not only financially necessary in an increasingly competitive media market but proper as well. No one is hurt by advertorials. In fact, they often deliver useful information. Advertisers are free in America to use whatever legal and truthful means are available to sell their products.

Magazines always label the paid material as such. And readers aren't idiots, defenders claim. They know an ad when they see one.

ADVERTISER INFLUENCE OVER MAGAZINE CONTENT

Controversial, too, is the influence that some advertisers attempt to exert over content. This influence is always there, at least implicitly. A magazine editor must satisfy advertisers as well as readers. One common way advertisers' interests shape content is in the placement of ads. Airline ads are moved away from stories about plane crashes. Cigarette ads rarely appear near articles on lung cancer. In fact, it is an accepted industry practice for a magazine to provide advertisers with a "heads up," alerting them that soon-to-be-published content may prove uncomfortable for their businesses. Advertisers can then request a move of their ad, or pull it and wait to run it in the next issue.

Complementary copy—content that reinforces the advertiser's message, or at least does not negate it—is problematic when creating such copy becomes a major influence in a publication's editorial decision making. This happens in a number of ways. Editors sometimes engage in self-censorship, making decisions about how stories are written and which stories appear based on the fear that specific advertisers will be offended. Some magazines, *Architectural Digest*, for example, identify companies by name in their picture caption copy only if they are advertisers. But many critics inside and outside the industry see increased crumbling of the wall between advertising demands and editorial judgment.

They point to the growing practice of advertisers demanding (and magazines granting) the right to prescreen content. Colgate-Palmolive, for example, refuses to place ads in a "media context" containing "offensive" sexual content or other material it feels is "antisocial or in bad taste." It requires its advertising agencies to prescreen content for these taboos, but those agencies need not define them for the magazines (Baker, 1997, p. 31). In February 1997 Chrysler's advertising agency, PentaCom, mailed a letter to all the magazines in which it places ads, stating, "In an effort to avoid potential conflicts, it is required that Chrysler Corporation be alerted in advance of any and all editorial content that encompasses sexual, political, social issues or any editorial that might be construed as provocative or offensive. Each and every issue that carries Chrysler advertising requires a written summary outlining major theme/articles appearing in upcoming issues" (p. 30). PentaCom, which annually places more than $270 million of Chrysler advertising in 100 magazines, demanded that executives of those publications sign and return its letter as acknowledgment of their acceptance of this requirement. Chrysler's head of consumer media relations said all publications agreed (p. 30).

The question raised by critics is, "How can a magazine function, offering depth, variety, and detail, when Colgate-Palmolive and Chrysler are joined by dozens of other advertisers, each demanding to preview content, not for its direct comment on matters of importance to their businesses, but for controversy and potential offensiveness?" Milton Glaser, cofounder

Advertorials Aimed at Young Girls

The issue of development of healthy self-esteem and body image for young girls is frequently debated in the cultural forum. We saw in Chapter 1, for example, that Mattel, manufacturer of the popular Barbie, has changed the doll's physique in response to complaints that it fosters unrealistic standards and expectations in children. Consider your attitudes on this debate as you evaluate the following situation.

Chicago-based 'Teen magazine's 1993 media kit makes the case for the use of advertorials. Read their presentation, aimed at prospective advertisers, and think about how comfortable you are with the practice.

'TEEN's advertorial services are top-notch! Last year we produced 150 advertorial pages . . . that's more advertorial pages than any other national magazine. 'TEEN has its own advertorial staff: three editors whose only responsibility is the creation and production of advertorial pages. We work with both client and agency from preliminary layouts through the day of the shoot to the final selection of film, copy and color corrections.

Why Advertorials Will Work For You

- 'TEEN advertorials are designed to look like our editorial pages. Our editors know the looks our readers like and the advertorial pages are presented in this style.
- The advertorials can take your campaign one step further by providing additional information that is not provided in your advertisement. Additionally, they dramatically increase the frequency of your advertising message. (as cited in Silverblatt, 1995, p. 138)

Are you at all troubled that this potentially misleading content appears in a magazine aimed at young, relatively unsophisticated media consumers? Why, or why not?

Do you think the first explanation of why advertorials work—advertorials are designed to look like editorial pages—implies an overt effort to deceive readers?

Examine the advertorial's construction. What physical attributes characterize the models? How quickly did you find the "advertisement" disclaimer?

Imagine yourself as a 12-year-old. Do you think you could tell the difference between this advertisement and other editorial content in the magazine? Do you think you would have associated the Sears logo on the second page with the pictures and text on the first? Do you think this is an important issue? Why, or why not?

An article or an ad? Can you tell? Could a 12-year-old reader make the distinction?

of *New York* magazine, offered one answer, "It will have a devastating effect on the idea of a free press and of free inquiry" (Baker, 1997, p. 30).

Recognizing the Power of Graphics

Detecting the use of and determining the informational value of advertorials is only one reason media literacy is important when reading magazines. Another necessary media literacy skill is the ability to understand how graphics and other artwork provide the background for interpreting stories. Three recent incidents suggest why.

The notorious June 27, 1994, *Time* O. J. Simpson cover—for which artists altered Simpson's facial tones on an L.A. police department mug shot—is one controversial example of how graphics are used to create meaning. The magazine said it wanted to show the "real" O. J., free of the glamour and hype that usually surround him. Critics claimed that darkening Simpson's face was designed to play to the ugly stereotype of African Americans as criminals. Media literate readers might also ask, "How does changing what was a 'real' photograph make the subject seem more real?"

The December 1, 1997, cover of *Newsweek* offered a less well known but equally compelling example of graphics sleight-of-hand. That issue featured Bobbi McCaughey, mother of the Iowa septuplets born November

This February, 2003 British *GQ* cover put the alteration of magazine graphics squarely in the cultural forum when actress Kate Winslet complained that her body had been digitally altered to make her thin. "This is me. Like it or leave it. I'm not a twig and I refuse to be one," she said. "I'm happy with the way I am!"

Teach Teens about Magazines

Cosmo Girl is a magazine aimed at the 12- to 16-year-old girl audience. As such, its February 2002 edition featured the teen pop band 'N Sync. That seems natural. But look a bit closer at that cover. Labeled "the love issue," this issue includes articles such as *Hot Guy Centerfold, Are You His Type? 145 Ways to Look Sexy, Your 6 Most Private Body Questions, Your Ultimate Guide to Guys,* and *Make $100 This Weekend.* Love, sex, centerfolds, beauty, money. Are these themes of interest to pre- and early teens? Should they be?

Child psychologists, educators, even many parents lament the "adultification" of childhood, and they see our mass media as central to the trend. Criticism aside, *Cosmo Girl*—as well as magazines such as *Seventeen, YM,* and *'Teen*—contribute to, as well as prosper by, promoting topics not significantly different from those found in adult women's magazines. As such, "tweens" must deal with information they may not understand or, worse, may apply incorrectly to their everyday lives (see Chapter 13's discussion of the *early window*). Talking to young people in your area is an effective tool in assuring responsible consumption of magazines and in making media literacy a living enterprise. These three steps can assist you in your efforts:

1. Introduce young people to publications that are specifically designed for them and that place emphasis on art, education, storytelling, community service, current events, and opinion. In addition to offering appropriate content, these magazines are interactive, that is, they encourage participation and editorial submissions from their young readers. Start with *Teen Voices* <www.teenvoices.com> and *Teen Ink* <www.teenink.com>.

2. Help young people understand the structure of the magazine industry. Being knowledgeable about why and how the media industries work, as you know from Chapter 2, makes for more critical, literate media users. Three Web sites provide useful magazine information, including industry trends, advertising facts, magazine terminology, and useful links. Try www.magazine.org, www.asme.magazine.org, and www.pib@magazine.org.

3. Ask questions and/or suggest exercises that will prompt young teens to think about magazine issues related to them and their lives:

- Ask them to count the number of ad and editorial pages in their favorite magazines. Have them comment on what this tells them about the true consumer in the magazine–reader interaction.

- Ask them to identify visual tactics such as celebrity endorsements, advertorials, and other selling devices. Ask them to comment on their propriety.

- Ask them to make a list of gender stereotypes found in their favorite magazines. How are boys and girls (and their interests and abilities) portrayed? Ask them to comment on how these images reflect them and their lives. Ask them if they ever feel pressure to behave in a certain way that they might not want.

- Encourage them to introduce their younger siblings to magazines (and other media) that promote literacy and introduce them to current events in comprehensible and age-appropriate ways. Suggest *Time For Kids* <www.timeforkids.com/TFK/> and *Highlights* <www.highlights.com>.

19, 1997. Artists at that magazine "repaired" McCaughey's teeth. Their intent was to present the new mother in the best possible light. There was no inflammatory issue of racial stereotyping in this instance, but the Iowa woman's multiple birth was not without controversy. Although much of the media treated her as a hero and the babies' births as a wonderful event, many observers took a different view. Doctors had advised McCaughey against the dangerous and premature births. The event was not a miracle of nature—as much of the media had packaged it—but the result of taking fertility drugs. Questions were raised about the ability of a working-class family to support such a large number of children. Media critics complained that the alteration in McCaughey's appearance helped shape people's interpretation of the event and mask a number of other important issues.

Finally, a more recent example of digital fakery that raised a somewhat different question was the electronic beheading of Prince William, son of the deceased Princess Diana and nephew of England's Prince Edward. Edward felt that William did not look sufficiently happy in the official wedding photo of Edward's marriage to Sophie Rhys-Jones in 1999. As a result, Edward ordered photographer Geoffrey Shakerley to digitally remove William's glum visage and replace it with a smiling face from another photograph before the picture was made available to the press. This raises two issues for literate readers. First, should news media use the "real" photograph (which presumably gave an accurate impression of the moment) or the one sanctioned by the main subject of the wedding photograph? In other words, how far should media outlets go in accepting altered renditions of an event at the request of those they are charged with covering? What becomes of journalistic independence in situations such as this? The second question has to do with maintaining the confidence of audience members. As digital altering of images becomes more widespread—and its occurrence better known—will viewers and readers come to question the veracity of even unaltered images and the reports that employ them?

What do you think? Did you see any of these images? Did you know they had been altered? If you did, would that have changed your reading of the stories or events that they represented? Does the fact that major media outlets sometimes alter the images they present to you as news lead you to question their overall performance? Do you believe that media outlets that use altered images have an obligation to inform readers and viewers of their decision to restructure reality? How does it feel to know that "almost all of the images that we see in our daily newspapers and newsmagazines today are digitized" (Huang, 2001, p. 149)?

Chapter Review

The colonial magazine was not particularly successful, and those that did exist were copies of popular British magazines. But in the years after the Revolutionary War, the magazine as we know it today had its start. After the Civil War, a great explosion in popular magazines occurred. The Postal Act of 1879, widespread literacy, a price war among the leading magazines, industrialization, and urbanization combined to fuel growth in this industry.

As the first national mass medium in the United States, magazines were an important force in the social change of the progressive era of the first decades of the 20th century, due to the writings and successes of the muckrakers. The giant mass circulation magazines of the time were the dominant advertising medium, the primary outlet for nationally distributed news, and the sole national provider of photojournalism.

After the coming of television, magazines changed. Despite the death of once powerful publications such as *Collier's* and *The Saturday Evening Post*, the industry prospered. The keys to its success were specialization and development of a lifestyle orientation.

The 22,000 magazines in operation today include trade, professional, and business magazines; industrial, company, and sponsored magazines; and consumer magazines. The top 800 consumer magazines account for three-fourths of the industry's revenues and exist in a variety of categories, from alternative to youth magazines. Webzines, or online magazines, are now appearing as well.

Magazines flourish because advertisers value their homogeneous audiences. Magazines further narrow their readership through split runs, special versions of the same issue targeted toward specific geographic areas or professions.

Space is sold in magazines on the basis of circulation. Magazines circulate through subscriptions, single-copy sales, and controlled circulation.

Whatever the means of distribution, research groups such as the Audit Bureau of Circulations and Simmons Market Research Bureau determine and verify the true circulation numbers, taking care to include pass-along readership.

Other media, particularly cable television and certain online content providers, currently challenge the preeminence of magazines as a specialized advertising medium. But the industry meets this competition through internationalization of its publications, improved production and distribution technologies, use of its own computer networks, and sale of lists of subscribers.

New forms of magazines are developing. Webzines have become popular, if not yet profitable. Synergistic magazines are produced specifically to generate material for other media. Brand magazines are published by retailers for readers with demographics similar to those of their customers. And magalogues blur the distinction between designer catalogues and consumer magazines.

Many magazines attract additional advertising by offering advertorials, ads that appear to be editorial content. This practice is of importance to the literate media consumer. Advertorials, as well as a variety of other editorial decisions, shape the meaning of all content. The use of artwork and graphics is intended to convey specific impressions. Several recent examples of altered images offer excellent but controversial examples of this technique.

Key Terms

muckraking, 137
split runs, 143
circulation, 144
controlled circulation, 144

Webzine, 146
brand magazine, 147
magalogue, 147
synergistic magazine, 147

advertorial, 150
complementary copy, 151

Questions for Review

1. How would you characterize the content of the first U.S. magazines?

2. Who were Ida Tarbell, Upton Sinclair, Lincoln Steffens, and Jack London? What movement did

they represent, and what were some of its accomplishments?

3. What factors fueled the expansion of the magazine industry at the beginning of the 20th century?

4. What factors led to the demise of the mass circulation era and the development of the era of specialization?

5. What are the three broad types of magazines?

6. Why do advertisers favor specialization in magazines?

7. In what different ways do magazines internationalize their publications?

8. Which two media currently challenge the preeminence of magazines as a specialized advertising medium? Why?

9. What is an advertorial? What is its function?

10. What is complementary copy? Why does it trouble critics?

11. What factors limit the success and profitability of online magazines?

12. What are synergistic magazines? Why do they trouble critics?

13. What are brand magazines? Magalogues?

Questions for Critical Thinking and Discussion

1. Can you think of any contemporary crusading magazine or muckraking writers? Compared with those of the progressive era, they are certainly less visible. Why is this the case?

2. Are you troubled by trends such as synergistic, brand, and magalogue magazines? Why or why not?

3. Which magazines do you read? Draw a demographic profile of yourself based only on the magazines you regularly read.

4. Which side do you take in the advertorial debate? Why?

5. Are you troubled by the practice of altering photographs? Can you think of times when it might be more appropriate than others?

Important Resources

Janello, A., & Jones, B. (1991). *The American magazine.* **New York: Harry N. Abrams.** A thorough examination of the operation of the magazine industry and an interesting study of how magazines develop their particular look and style.

Nourie, A., & Nourie, B. (Eds.). (1990). *American mass market magazines.* **Westport, CT: Greenwood Press.** A collection of essays and reports covering many important issues in contemporary magazines, including minority magazines and internationalization.

Tebbel, J. (1969). *The American magazine: A compact history.* **New York: Hawthorn Books.** Written by an eminent print historian, this book is considered by many to be the definitive popular discussion of the development of magazines in the United States.

Winship, J. (1987). *Inside women's magazines.* **London: Pandora Press.** The style and content of women's magazines are examined from a critical perspective in this readable, picture-filled book.

Salon	www.salon.com
Magazine History	www.well.com/user/art/maghist01.html
American Society of Magazine Editors	www.asme.magazine.org
Magazine Publishers of America	www.magazine.org
Audit Bureau of Circulations	www.accessabc.com
Magazine CyberCenter	www.magamall.com
Top 100 Computer Magazines	www.internetvalley.com/top100mag.html
How to Start a Magazine	www.laughingbear.com/magazine.html

CHAPTER 6

Film

The movies are our dream factories; they are bigger than life. Along with books, they are the only mass medium not dependent on advertising for their financial support. That means they must satisfy you, because you buy the tickets. This means that the relationship between medium and audience is different from those that exist with other media. After studying this chapter you should

- be familiar with the history and development of the film industry and film itself as a medium.

- have a greater awareness of the cultural value of film and the implications of the blockbuster mentality for film as an important artistic and cultural medium.

- be familiar with the three components of the film industry—production, distribution, and exhibition.

- recognize how the organizational and economic nature of the contemporary film industry shapes the content of films.

- understand the relationship between film and its audiences.

- recognize the promise and peril of the new digital technologies to film as we know it.

- possess improved film-watching media literacy skills, especially in interpreting merchandise tie-ins and product placements.

PARIS IS COLD AND DAMP ON THIS DECEMBER NIGHT, THREE DAYS after Christmas in 1895. But you bundle up and make your way to the Grand Café in the heart of the city. You've read in the morning paper that brothers Auguste and Louis Lumière will be displaying their new invention that somehow makes pictures move. Your curiosity is piqued.

Tables and chairs are set up in the basement room of the café, and a white bedsheet is draped above its stage. The Lumières appear to polite applause. They announce the program: *La Sortie des usines Lumière (Quitting Time at the Factory); Le Repas de bébé,* featuring a Lumière child eating; *L'Arroseur arrosé,* about a practical joking boy and his victim, the gardener; and finally *L'Arrivée d'un train en gare,* the arrival of a train at a station.

The lights go out. Somewhere behind you, someone starts the machine. There is some brief flickering on the suspended sheet and then . . . you are completely awestruck. There before you—bigger than life-size— photographs are really moving. You see places you know to be miles away. You spy on the secret world of a prankster boy, remembering your own childhood. But the last film is the most impressive. As the giant locomotive chugs toward the audience, you and most of the others are convinced you are about to be crushed. There is panic. People are ducking under their chairs, screaming. Death is imminent!

The first paying audience in the history of motion pictures has just had a lesson in movie watching.

The Lumière brothers were excellent mechanics, and their father owned a factory that made photographic plates. Their first films were little more than what we would now consider black-and-white home movies. As you can tell from their titles, they were simple stories. There was no editing; the camera was simply turned on, then turned off. There were no fades, wipes, or flashbacks. No computer graphics, no dialogue, and no music. And yet much of the audience was terrified by the oncoming cinematic locomotive. They were illiterate in the language of film.

The Cult Film Site
www.
sepnet.com/rcramer/index.htm

We begin our study of the movies with the history of film, from its entrepreneurial beginnings, through introduction of its narrative and visual language, to its establishment as a large, studio-run industry. We detail Hollywood's relationship with its early audiences and changes in the structure and content of films resulting from the introduction of television. We then look at contemporary movie production, distribution, and exhibition systems and how convergence is altering all three, the influence of the major studios, and the economic pressures on them in an increasingly multimedia environment. We examine the special place movies hold in our culture and how ever-younger audiences and the films that target them may affect our culture. Recognizing the use of product placement in movies is the basis for improving our media literacy skill.

A Short History of the Movies

We are no longer illiterate in the grammar of film, nor are movies as simple as the early Lumière offerings. Consider the sophistication necessary for filmmakers to produce a computer-generated movie such as *Ice Age* and the skill required for audiences to read *Memento*'s shifts in time, unconventional camera angles, and other twists and turns. How we arrived at this contemporary medium–audience relationship is a wonderful story.

Early newspapers were developed by businesspeople and patriots for a small, politically involved elite that could read, but the early movie industry was built largely by entrepreneurs who wanted to make money entertaining everyone. Unlike television, whose birth and growth were predetermined and guided by the already well-established radio industry (see Chapter 7), there were no precedents, no rules, and no expectations for movies.

The Lumière's *L'Arrivée d'un train en gare*. As simple as early films were, their viewers did not have sufficient film literacy to properly interpret, understand, and enjoy them. This scene supposedly sent people screaming and hiding to avoid being crushed by the oncoming train.

Return to the opening vignette. The audience for the first Lumière movies did not "speak film." Think of it as being stranded in a foreign country with no knowledge of the language and cultural conventions. You would have to make your way, with each new experience helping you better understand the next. First you'd learn some simple words and basic customs. Eventually, you'd be able to better understand the language and people. In other words, you'd become increasingly literate in that culture. Beginning with that Paris premiere, people had to become film literate. They had to develop an understanding of cinematic alterations in time and space. They had to learn how images and sound combined to create meaning. But unlike visiting in another culture, there was no existing cinematic culture. Movie creators and their audiences had to grow up together.

Hollywood Online
www.
hollywood.com

THE EARLY ENTREPRENEURS

In 1873 former California Governor Leland Stanford needed help winning a bet he had made with a friend. Convinced that a horse in full gallop had all four feet off the ground, he had to prove it. He turned to well-known photographer Eadweard Muybridge, who worked on the problem for four years before finding a solution. In 1877 Muybridge arranged a series of still cameras along a stretch of race track. As the horse sprinted by, each camera took its picture. The resulting photographs won Stanford his bet, but more important, they sparked an idea in their photographer. Muybridge was intrigued by the appearance of motion created when photos are viewed sequentially. He began taking pictures of numerous kinds of human and animal action. To display his work, Muybridge invented the **zoopraxiscope,** a machine for projecting slides onto a distant surface.

Muybridge's horse pictures. When these plates were placed sequentially and rotated, they produced the appearance of motion.

Worst Movies Ever
www.
ohthehumanity.com

When people watched the rapidly projected, sequential slides, they saw the pictures as if they were in motion. This perception is the result of a physiological phenomenon known as **persistence of vision,** in which the images our eyes gather are retained in the brain for about $1/24$ of a second. Therefore, if photographic frames are moved at 24 frames a second, people perceive them as actually in motion.

Muybridge eventually met the prolific inventor Thomas Edison in 1888. Edison quickly saw the scientific and economic potential of the zoopraxiscope and set his top scientist, William Dickson, to the task of developing a better projector. But Dickson correctly saw the problem as one of developing a better system of *filming*. He understood that shooting numerous still photos, then putting them in sequential order, then redrawing the images they held onto slides was inherently limiting. Dickson combined Hannibal Goodwin's newly invented celluloid roll film with George Eastman's easy-to-use Kodak camera into a motion picture camera that took 40 photographs a second. He used his **kinetograph** to film all types of theatrical performances, some by unknowns and others by famous entertainers such as Annie Oakley and Buffalo Bill Cody. Of course, none of this would have been possible had it not been for photography itself.

The Development of Photography The process of photography was first developed by French inventor Joseph Nicéphore Niépce around 1816. Although there had been much experimentation in the realm of image making at the time, Niépce was the first person to make practical use of a camera and film. He photographed natural objects and produced color prints. Unfortunately, his images would last only a short time.

Niépce's success, however, attracted the attention of countryman Louis Daguerre, who joined with him to perfect the process. Niépce died before the 1839 introduction of the **daguerreotype,** a process of recording images on polished metal plates, usually copper, covered with a thin layer of silver iodide emulsion. When light reflected from an object passed through a lens and struck the emulsion, the emulsion would etch the image on the plate. The plate was then washed with a cleaning solvent, leaving a positive or replica image.

In the same year as Daguerre's first public display of the daguerreotype, British inventor William Henry Fox Talbot introduced a paper film process. This process was actually more important to the development of photography than the metal film system, but the daguerreotype received widespread attention and acclaim and made the public enthusiastic about photography.

The **calotype** (Talbot's system) used translucent paper, what we now call the negative, from which several prints could be made. In addition, his film was much more sensitive than Daguerre's metal plate, allowing for exposure times of only a few seconds as opposed to the daguerreotype's 30 minutes. Until calotype, virtually all daguerreotype images were still lifes and portraits, a necessity with long exposure times.

The final steps in the development of the photographic process necessary for true motion pictures were taken, as we've just seen, by Goodwin in 1887 and Eastman in 1889 and were adapted to motion pictures by Edison scientist Dickson.

Typical of daguerreotypes, this plate captures a portrait. The method's long exposure time made all but the most stationary subjects impossible to photograph.

Thomas Edison Edison built the first motion picture studio near his laboratory in New Jersey. He called it Black Maria, the common name at that time for a police paddy wagon. It had an open roof and revolved to follow the sun so the performers being filmed would always be illuminated.

The completed films were not projected. Instead, they were run through a **kinetoscope,** a sort of peep show device. Often they were accompanied by music provided by another Edison invention, the phonograph. Patented in 1891 and commercially available 3 years later, the kinetoscope quickly became a popular feature in penny arcades, vaudeville halls, and big city Kinetoscope Parlors. This marked the beginning of commercial motion picture exhibition.

The Lumière Brothers The Lumière brothers made the next advance. Their initial screenings demonstrated that people would sit in a darkened room to watch motion pictures projected on a screen. The brothers from Lyon envisioned

Movie News
www.
enn2.com/movies.htm

great wealth in their ability to increase the number of people who could simultaneously watch a movie. In 1895 they patented their **cine-matographe,** a device that both photographed and projected action. Within weeks of their Christmastime showing, long lines of enthusiastic moviegoers were waiting for their makeshift theater to open. Edison recognized the advantage of the cinematographe over his kinetoscope, so he acquired the patent for an advanced projector developed by U.S. inventor Thomas Armat. On April 23, 1896, the Edison Vitascope premiered in New York City, and the American movie business was born.

THE COMING OF NARRATIVE

The Edison and Lumière movies were typically only a few minutes long and showed little more than filmed reproductions of reality—celebrities, weight lifters, jugglers, and babies eating. They were shot in fixed frame (the camera did not move), and there was no editing. For the earliest audiences, this was enough. But soon the novelty wore thin. People wanted more for their money. French filmmaker Georges Méliès began making narrative motion pictures, that is, movies that told a story. At the end of the 1890s he was shooting and exhibiting one-scene, one-shot movies, but soon he began making stories based on sequential shots in different places. He simply took one shot, stopped the camera, moved it, took another shot, and so on. Méliès is often called the "first artist of the cinema" because

Movie Guide
www.
allmovie.com

Scene from *A Trip to the Moon.* Narrative came to the movies through the inventive imagination of Georges Méliès.

he brought narrative to the medium in the form of imaginative tales such as *A Trip to the Moon* (1902).

Méliès had been a magician and caricaturist before he became a filmmaker, and his inventive movies showed his dramatic flair. They were extravagant stage plays in which people disappeared and reappeared and other wonders occurred. *A Trip to the Moon* came to America in 1903, and U.S. moviemakers were quick not only to borrow the idea of using film to tell stories but also to improve on it.

Edwin S. Porter, an Edison Company cameraman, saw that film could be an even better storyteller with more artistic use of camera placement and editing. His 12-minute *The Great Train Robbery* (1903) was the first movie to use editing, intercutting of scenes, and a mobile camera to tell a relatively sophisticated tale. It was also the first Western. This new narrative form using **montage**—tying together two separate but related shots in such a way that they took on a new, unified meaning—was an instant hit with audiences. Almost immediately hundreds of **nickelodeons,** some having as many as 100 seats, were opened in converted stores, banks, and halls across the United States. The price of admission was one nickel, hence the name. By 1905 cities such as New York were opening a new nickelodeon every day. From 1907 to 1908, the first year in which there were more narrative than documentary films, the number of nickelodeons in the United States increased tenfold. With so many exhibition halls in so many towns serving such an extremely enthusiastic public, many movies were needed. Literally hundreds and hundreds of new **factory studios,** or production companies, were started.

Movie News
www.
movies.go.com

Scene from *The Great Train Robbery.* Porter's masterpiece introduced audiences to editing, intercutting of scenes, moving cameras . . . and the Western.

African American Response to D. W. Griffith: The Lincoln and Micheaux Film Companies

The African American community did not sit passively in the wake of D. W. Griffith's 1915 cinematic but hateful wonder, *The Birth of a Nation*. The NAACP fought the film in court and on the picket line, largely unsuccessfully. But other African Americans decided to use film to combat *Birth*. The first was Emmett J. Scott, a quiet, scholarly man. He sought money from the country's Black middle class to produce a short film showing the achievements of African Americans. His intention was to attach his film, *Lincoln's Dream*, as a prologue to screenings of the Griffith film. Together with screenwriter Elaine Sterne, Scott eventually expanded the project into a feature-length movie. He approached Universal Studios with his film but was rejected.

With independent backing from both Black and White investors, the film was released in 1918. Produced by an inexperienced cast and crew working on a production beset by bad weather and technical difficulties, the retitled *The Birth of a Race* filled 12 reels of film and ran more than 3 hours. Its publicity hailed it as "The Greatest and Most Daring of Photoplays . . . The Story of Sin . . . A Master Picture Conceived in the Spirit of Truth and Dedicated to All the Races of the World" (Bogle, 1989, p. 103). It was an artistic and commercial failure. Scott, however, had inspired others.

Even before *The Birth of a Race* was completed, the Lincoln Motion Picture Company was incorporated, in Nebraska in 1916 and in California in 1917, by brothers Noble P. and George Johnson. Their tack differed from Scott's. They understood that their Black films would never be allowed on "White" screens, so they produced movies designed to tell Black-oriented stories to Black audiences. They might not be able to convince White America of Griffith's error, but they could reassure African Americans that their views could find expression. Lincoln's first movie was *The Realization of a Negro's Ambition*, and it told the story of Black American achievements. The Johnson brothers turned U.S. racism to their advantage. Legal segregation in the South and de facto segregation in the North had led to an explosion of Black theaters. These movie houses needed content. Lincoln helped provide it by producing 10 three-reelers between 1916 and 1920.

Two more notable film companies began operation, hoping to challenge Griffith's portrayals at least in Black theaters. Oscar Micheaux founded the Micheaux Film and Book Company in 1918 in Chicago and soon produced *The Homesteader*, an eight-reel film based on the autobiographical novel he'd written 3 years earlier. It was the story of a successful Black homestead rancher in South Dakota. But Micheaux was not content to boost Black self-esteem. He was determined to make "racial photoplays depicting racial life" (as quoted in Sampson, 1977, p. 42). In 1920 he released *Within Our Gates*, a

Because so many movies needed to be made and rushed to the nickelodeons, people working in the industry had to learn and perform virtually all aspects of production. There was precious little time for, or profitability in, the kind of specialization that marks contemporary filmmaking. Writer, actor, cameraman D. W. Griffith perfected his craft in this environment. He was quickly recognized as a brilliant director. He introduced innovations such as scheduled rehearsals before final shooting and production based on close adherence to a shooting script. He lavished attention on otherwise ignored aspects of a film's look—costume and lighting—and used close-ups and other dramatic camera angles to transmit emotion.

All his skill came together in 1915 with the release of *The Birth of a Nation*. Whereas Porter had used montage to tell a story, Griffith used it to create passion, move emotions, and heighten suspense. The most influential silent film ever made, this 3-hour epic was 6 weeks in rehearsal and 9 weeks in shooting, cost $125,000 to produce (making it the most expensive movie made to date), was distributed to theaters complete with orchestral music score, had a cast of thousands of humans and animals, and had an admis-

drama about the southern lynching of a Black man. Censored and denied a screening in dozens of cities both North and South, Micheaux was undeterred. In 1921 he released the eight-reeler *The Gunsaulus Mystery*, based on a well-known murder case in which a Black man was convicted.

These early film pioneers used their medium to make a difference. They challenged the interpretation of history being circulated by the most popular movie in the world, and they provided encouragement and entertainment to the African American community. Equally important, they began the long tradition of Black filmmaking in the United States. In fact, "Black film" has become so routine a part of our movie experience that Hollywood now differentiates *Black films* (titles whose casts, themes, writers, directors, and target audiences are Black; e.g., *Waiting to Exhale*), *Black star-driven films* (e.g., *Dr. Doolittle*), *buddy movies with a Black lead* (e.g., *Rush Hour*), and *major studio releases with one or more Black leads* (e.g., *High Crimes*). In 2000 alone, "Black films" grossed over $600 million in domestic box office (Hayes, 2002). "It used to be a fight to get a black character into a movie," said MTV Films executive David Gale. "Now the studios are all saying, 'How can we find more black actors?'" (quoted in Goldstein, 2002a, p. G14).

A scene from The Realization of a Negro's Ambition.

sion price well above the usual 5 cents—$3. It was the most popular and profitable movie made until unseated in 1939 by *Gone with the Wind*. Along with other Griffith masterpieces, *Intolerance* (1916) and *Broken Blossoms* (1919), *The Birth of a Nation* set new standards for the American film. They took movies out of the nickelodeons and made them big business. At the same time, however, *The Birth of a Nation* represented the basest aspects of U.S. culture because it included an ugly, racist portrayal of African Americans and a sympathetic treatment of the Ku Klux Klan. The film inspired protests in front of theaters across the country and criticism in some newspapers and magazines, and African Americans fought back with their own films (see the box "African American Response to D. W. Griffith: The Lincoln and Micheaux Film Companies"). Nevertheless, *The Birth of a Nation* found acceptance by the vast majority of people.

THE BIG STUDIOS

In 1908 Thomas Edison, foreseeing the huge amounts of money that could be made from movies, founded the Motion Picture Patents Company

The Ku Klux Klan was the collective hero in D.W. Griffith's *The Birth of a Nation.* This cinematic masterpiece and groundbreaking film employed production techniques never before used; however, its racist theme mars its legacy.

(MPPC), often called simply the Trust. This group of 10 companies under Edison's control, holding the patents to virtually all existing filmmaking and exhibition equipment, ran the production and distribution of film in the United States with an iron fist. Anyone who wanted to make or exhibit a movie needed Trust permission, which typically was not forthcoming. In addition, the MPPC had rules about the look of the movies it would permit: they must be one reel, approximately 12 minutes long, and must adopt a "stage perspective"; that is, the actors must fill the frame as if they were in a stage play.

Many independent film companies sprang up in defiance of the Trust, including Griffith's in 1913. To avoid MPPC scrutiny and reprisal, these companies moved to California. This westward migration had other benefits. Better weather meant longer shooting seasons. Free of MPPC standards, people like Griffith who wanted to explore the potential of film in longer than 12-minute bits and with imaginative use of the camera were free to do so.

The new studio system, with its more elaborate films and big-name stars, was born, and it controlled the movie industry from California. Thomas H. Ince (maker of the William S. Hart westerns), Griffith, and comedy genius Mack Sennett formed the Triangle Company. Adolph Zukor's Famous Players in Famous Plays—formed when Zukor was denied MPPC permission to distribute one of his films—joined with several other independents and a distribution company to become Paramount. Other independents joined to create the Fox Film Company (soon called 20th Century Fox) and Universal. Although films were still silent, by the mid-1920s there were more than 20,000 movie theaters in the United States, and more than 350,000 people were making their living in film production. More than 1,240,000 feet of film was shot each year in Hollywood, and annual domestic U.S. box office receipts exceeded $750 million.

The industry prospered not just because of its artistry, drive, and inno-vation but because it used these to meet the needs of a growing audience. At the beginning of the 20th century, generous immigration rules, com-bined with political and social unrest abroad, encouraged a flood of Euro-pean immigrants who congregated in U.S. cities where the jobs were and where people like themselves who spoke their language lived. American farmers, largely illiterate, also swarmed to the cities as years of drought and farm failure left them without home or hope. Jobs in the big mills and factories, although unpleasant, were plentiful. These new city dwellers had money and the need for leisure activities. Movies were a nickel, required no ability to read or to understand English, and offered glam-orous stars and wonderful stories from faraway places.

Foreign political unrest proved to be a boon to the infant U.S. movie business in another way as well. In 1914 and 1915, when the California stu-dios were remaking the industry in their own grand image, war raged in Europe. European moviemaking, most significantly the influential French, German, and Russian cinema, came to a halt. European demand for movies, however, did not. American movies, produced in huge numbers for the hun-gry home audience, were ideal for overseas distribution. Because so few in the domestic audience could read English, few printed titles were used in the then-silent movies. Therefore, little had to be changed to satisfy foreign moviegoers. Film was indeed a universal language, but more important, the American film industry had firmly established itself as the world leader, all within 20 years of the Lumière brothers' first screening.

Film History
WWW.
filmsite.org/filmh.html

Al Jolson, in blackface, and May McAvoy starred in the 1927 *The Jazz Singer*, one of three claimants to the title of first sound movie.

CHANGE COMES TO HOLLYWOOD

As was the case with newspapers and magazines, the advent of television significantly altered the movie–audience relationship. But the nature of that relationship had been shaped and reshaped in the three decades between the coming of sound and the coming of television.

The Talkies   The first sound film was one of three films produced by Warner Brothers. It may have been *Don Juan* (1926), starring John Barrymore, dis-tributed with synchronized music and sound effects. Or perhaps Warner's more famous *The Jazz Singer* (1927), starring Al Jolson, which had sev-eral sound and speaking scenes (354 words in all) but was largely silent. Or it may have been the

1928 all-sound *Lights of New York*. Historians disagree because they cannot decide what constitutes a sound film.

There is no confusion, however, about the impact of sound on the movies and their audiences. First, sound made possible new genres—musicals, for example. Second, as actors and actresses now had to really act, performance aesthetics improved. Third, sound made film production a much more complicated and expensive proposition. As a result, many smaller filmmakers closed shop, solidifying the hold of the big studios over the industry. In 1933, 60% of all U.S. films came from Hollywood's eight largest studios. By 1940, they were producing 76% of all U.S. movies and collecting 86% of the total box office. As for the audience, in 1926, the year of *Don Juan's* release, 50 million people went to the movies each week. In 1929, at the onset of the Great Depression, the number had risen to 80 million. By 1930, when sound was firmly entrenched, the number of weekly moviegoers had risen to 90 million (Mast & Kawin, 1996).

Scandal   The popularity of talkies, and of movies in general, inevitably raised questions about their impact on the culture. In 1896, well before sound, *The Kiss* had generated a great moral outcry. Its stars, John C. Rice and May Irwin, were also the leads in a popular Broadway play, *The Widow Jones*, which closed with a climactic kiss. The Edison Company asked Rice and Irwin to re-create the kiss for the big screen. Newspapers and politicians were bombarded with complaints from the offended. Kissing in the theater was one thing; in movies it was quite another! The then-newborn industry responded to this and other calls for censorship with various forms of self-regulation and internal codes. But in the early 1920s more Hollywood scandals forced a more direct response.

In 1920 "America's Sweetheart" Mary Pickford obtained a questionable Nevada divorce from her husband and immediately married the movies' other darling, Douglas Fairbanks, himself newly divorced. In 1920 and

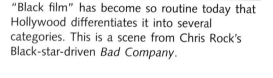
"Black film" has become so routine today that Hollywood differentiates it into several categories. This is a scene from Chris Rock's Black-star-driven *Bad Company*.

1921 comedian Fatty Arbuckle was involved in police problems on two coasts. The first was apparently hushed up after a $100,000 gift was made to a Massachusetts district attorney, but the second involved a murder at a San Francisco hotel party thrown by the actor. Although he was acquitted in his third trial (the first two ended in hung juries), the stain on Arbuckle and the industry remained. Then, in 1922, actor Wallace Reid and director William Desmond Taylor both died in what the newspapers referred to as "a mysterious fashion" in which drugs and sex were thought to have played a part. The cry for government intervention was raised. State legislatures introduced more than 100 separate pieces of legislation to censor or otherwise control movies and their content.

Hollywood responded in 1922 by creating the Motion Picture Producers and Distributors of America (MPPDA) and appointing Will H. Hays—chairman of the Republican party, a Presbyterian church elder, and a former postmaster general—president. The Hays Office, as it became known, undertook a vast effort to improve the image of the movies. Stressing the importance of movies to national life and as an educational medium, Hays promised better movies and founded a committee on public relations that included many civic and religious leaders. Eventually, in 1934, the Motion Picture Production Code (MPPC) was released. The MPPC forbade the use of profanity, limited bedroom scenes to married couples, required that skimpy outfits be replaced by more complete costumes, delineated the length of screen kisses, ruled out scenes that ridiculed public officials or religious leaders, and outlawed a series of words from "God" to "nuts," all enforced by a $25,000 fine (see the box "Self-Censorship in Hollywood: The Movie Ratings").

New Genres, New Problems By 1932 weekly movie attendance had dropped to 60 million. The Depression was having its effect. Yet the industry was able to weather the crisis for two reasons. The first was its creativity. New genres held people's interest. The feature documentaries such as *The Plow That Broke the Plains* (1936) spoke to audience needs to understand a world in seeming disorder. Musicals such as *42nd Street* (1933) and screwball comedies such as *Bringing Up Baby* (1938) provided easy escapism. Gangster movies such as *Little Caesar* (1930) reflected the grimy reality of Depression city streets and daily newspaper headlines. Horror films such as *Frankenstein* (1931) articulated audience feelings of alienation and powerlessness in a seemingly uncontrollable time. Socially conscious comedies such as *Mr. Deeds Goes to Town* (1936) reminded moviegoers that good could still prevail, and the **double feature** with a **B-movie**—typically a less expensive movie—was a welcome relief to penny-pinching working people.

Motion Picture Association of America
www.
mpaa.org

The movie business also survived the Depression because of its size and power, both residing in a system of operation called **vertical integration.** Using this system, studios produced their own films, distributed them through their own outlets, and exhibited them in their own theaters. In effect, the big studios controlled a movie from shooting to screening, guaranteeing distribution and an audience regardless of quality.

Self-Censorship in Hollywood: The Movie Ratings

In 1952 in *Burstyn v. Wilson* the Supreme Court declared that film is "a significant medium for the communication of ideas" designed to "entertain as well as to inform." Movies were finally granted First Amendment protection (undoing the 1915 Supreme Court judgment in *Mutual Film Corp. v. Ohio Industrial Commission*, which had ruled that movies were merely novelty and entertainment, unworthy of protection as expression).

The Supreme Court decision did not affect the industry's own censorship, however. In 1953 director Otto Preminger and United Artists decided to challenge that self-imposed denial of freedom. Preminger and his studio sought the MPPC certificate of approval for *The Moon Is Blue*, a saucy sex comedy starring William Holden and David Niven. Adapted from a popular Broadway play, it was the tale of a woman who flaunted her virginity, and its humor resided in its double entendre and innuendo. Because the film contained words like "virgin" and "mistress," the MPPC denied Preminger and United Artists, forbidding them to release the movie. They released it anyway. Audiences were not overly fond of *The Moon Is Blue*, but the MPPC had not halted its distribution or exhibition, nor did it punish the filmmakers in any effective manner.

In 1955 Preminger and United Artists again battled the MPPC, this time over *The Man with the Golden Arm*, a stark and powerful film starring Frank Sinatra as a drug addict and Eleanor Parker as his crippled wife. The MPPC denied the movie permission to be released because of its portrayal of unsavory morals. Director and studio again defied the industry censors, putting the film in theaters. It was a smash hit, both critically and at the box office. The MPPC was proven powerless, its control of movie content broken for good.

During this time, Hollywood was challenging television with the production of message movies about controversial social problems including racism, juvenile delinquency, and alcohol abuse. But despite *Burstyn v. Wilson*, the industry still feared government intrusion. Its solution was to develop a different kind of self-regulation, and in 1966 the Motion Picture Association of America's (MPAA) rating system was born.

No longer were moviemakers told what they could and could not do. Instead, audiences were being alerted

Film Ratings
WWW.
filmratings.com

When the 1930s ended, weekly attendance was again over 80 million, and Hollywood was churning out 500 pictures a year. Moviegoing had become a central family and community activity for most people. Yet the end of that decade also brought bad news. In 1938 the Justice Department challenged vertical integration, suing the big five studios—Warner Brothers, MGM, Paramount, RKO, and 20th Century Fox—for restraint of trade; that is, they accused the studios of illegal monopolistic practices. The case would take 10 years to decide, but the movie industry, basking in the middle of its Golden Age, was under attack. Its fate was sealed in 1939 when the Radio Corporation of America (RCA) made the first public broadcast of television from atop the Empire State Building. The impact of these two events was profound, and the medium would have to develop a new relationship with its audience to survive.

Television When World War II began, the government took control of all patents for the newly developing technology of television as well as of the materials necessary for its production. The diffusion of the medium to the public was therefore halted, but its technological improvement was not. In addition, the radio networks and advertising agencies, recognizing that the war would eventually end and that their futures were in television, were preparing for that day. When the war did end, the movie industry

to what filmmakers were doing. The idea was to give filmmakers as much artistic freedom as they wanted, but to provide moviegoers with some indication of the nature of a film's content. The rating system, which has seen some alteration since its introduction, is familiar today to everyone who goes to a movie or rents a video:

G   general audiences

PG   parental guidance; for mature audiences

PG–13   parental guidance advised for children under 13 years old

R   restricted; no one under 17 years old admitted unless accompanied by an adult

NC–17   no children under 17; replaces the old X rating

Development of an informational rating system is echoed in the online world (Chapter 10) and in music (Chapter 7) and television (Chapter 8).

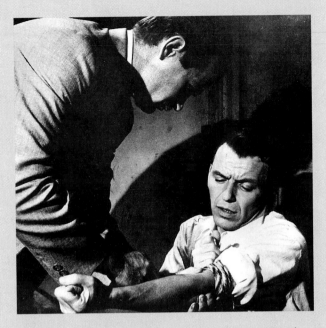

Frank Sinatra shoots heroin into his arm in the 1955 The Man with the Golden Arm.

found itself competing not with a fledgling medium but with a technologically and economically sophisticated one. As we saw in Chapter 1, the number of homes with television sets grew from 10,000 in 1946 to more than 10 million in 1950 and 54 million in 1960. Meanwhile, by 1955 movie attendance was down to 46 million people a week, fully 25% below even the worst attendance figures for the Depression years.

The Paramount Decision   In 1948, 10 years after the case had begun, the Supreme Court issued its Paramount Decision, effectively destroying the studios' hold over moviemaking. Vertical integration was ruled illegal, as was **block booking,** the practice of requiring exhibitors to rent groups of movies, often inferior, to secure a better one. The studios were forced to sell off their exhibition businesses (the theaters). Before the Paramount Decision, the five major studios owned 75% of the first-run movie houses in the United States; after it, they owned none. Not only did they no longer have guaranteed exhibition, but other filmmakers now had access to the theaters, producing even greater competition for the dwindling number of movie patrons.

Red Scare   The U.S. response to its postwar position as world leader was fear. So concerned were some members of Congress that communism would steal the people's rights that Congress decided to steal them first.

For more information on this topic, see NBC Video Clip #12 on the CD—*Are Movie Ratings Effective?*

The Hollywood chapter of the virulent anticommunism movement we now call McCarthyism (after the Republican senator from Wisconsin, Joseph McCarthy, its most rabid and public champion) was led by the House Un-American Activities Committee (HUAC) and its chair, J. Parnell Thomas (later imprisoned for padding his congressional payroll). First convened in 1947, HUAC had as its goal to rid Hollywood of Communist influence. The fear was that communist, socialist, and "leftist" propaganda was being inserted secretly in entertainment films by "reds," "fellow travelers," and "pinkos." Many of the industry's best and brightest talents were called to testify before the committee and were asked, "Are you now or have you ever been a member of the Communist Party?" Those who came to be known as the Hollywood 10, including writers Ring Lardner, Jr., and Dalton Trumbo and director Edward Dmytryk, refused to answer the question, accusing the committee, by its mere existence, of being in violation of the Bill of Rights. All were jailed. Rather than defend its First Amendment rights, the film industry abandoned those who were even mildly critical of the "red scare," jettisoning much of its best talent at a time when it could least afford to do so. In the fight against television, movies became increasingly tame for fear of being too controversial.

The industry was hurt not only by its cowardice but also by its shortsightedness. Hungry for content, the television industry asked Hollywood to sell it old features for broadcast. The studios responded by imposing on themselves the rule that no films could be sold to television and no working film star could appear on "the box." When it could have helped to shape early television viewer tastes and expectations of the new medium, Hollywood was absent. It lifted its ban in 1958.

Fighting Back   The industry worked mightily to recapture audiences from television using both technical and content innovations. Some of these innovations remain today and serve the medium and its audiences well. These

Warren Beatty eats some lead in the climax of the 1967 hit movie *Bonnie and Clyde*.

include more attention to special effects, greater dependence on and improvements in color, and CinemaScope (projecting on a large screen two and one-half times wider than it is tall). Among the forgettable technological innovations were 3-D and smellovision (wafting odors throughout the theater).

Innovation in content included spectaculars with which the small screen could not compete. *The Ten Commandments* (1956), *Ben Hur* (1959), *El Cid* (1960), and *Spartacus* (1960) filled the screen with many thousands of extras and lavish settings. Now that television was catering to the mass audience, movies were free to present challenging fare for more sophisticated audiences. The "message movie" charted social trends, especially alienation of youth (*Blackboard Jungle*, 1955; *Rebel Without a Cause*, 1955) and prejudice (*12 Angry Men*, 1957; *Imitation of Life*, 1959; *To Kill a Mockingbird*, 1962). Changing values toward sex were examined (*Midnight Cowboy*, 1969; *Bob and Carol and Ted and Alice*, 1969), as was the new youth culture's rejection of middle-class values (*The Graduate*, 1967; *Goodbye Columbus*, 1969) and its revulsion/attraction to violence (*Bonnie and Clyde*, 1967). The movies as an industry had changed, but as a medium of social commentary and cultural impact, they may have grown up.

Movies and Their Audiences

We talk of Hollywood as the "dream factory," the makers of "movie magic." We want our lives and loves to be "just like in the movies." The movies are "larger than life," and movie stars are much more glamorous than television stars. The movies, in other words, hold a very special place in our culture. Movies, like books, are a culturally special medium, an important medium. In this sense the movie–audience relationship has more in common with that of books than with that of television. Just as people buy books, they buy movie tickets. Because the audience is in fact the true consumer, power rests with it in film more than it does in television.

For better or worse, today's movie audience is increasingly a young one. The typical moviegoer in the United States is a teenager or young adult. These teens and 20-somethings, although making up less than 20% of the total population, represent more than 30% of the tickets bought. It's no surprise, then, that new screens sprout at malls, where teens and even younger people can be dropped off for a day of safe entertainment. Many movies are aimed at kids—*Hey Arnold! The Movie, Ice Age, Lilo & Stitch*, and *Scooby-Doo;* all the *Toy Story, Rush Hour*, and *American Pie* films; all the movies based on television shows, computer games, and comic books. Look at the top 10 domestic grossing movies of all time in Figure 6.1 (p. 176). With the exception of *Titanic* (1997) and *Forrest Gump* (1994), all are fantastic adventure films that appeal to younger audiences. The question asked by serious observers of the relationship between film and culture is whether the medium is increasingly dominated by the wants, tastes, and needs of what amounts to an audience of children. What becomes of film as an important medium, one with something to say, one that challenges people?

Hollywood Reporter
www.
hollywoodreporter.com

Internet Movie Database
www.
imdb.com

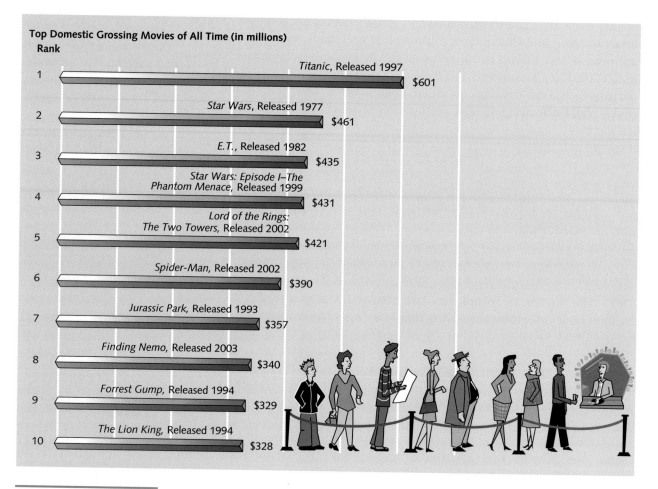

Top Domestic Grossing Movies of All Time (in millions)

Rank

1 — *Titanic*, Released 1997 — $601

2 — *Star Wars*, Released 1977 — $461

3 — *E.T.*, Released 1982 — $435

4 — *Star Wars: Episode I—The Phantom Menace*, Released 1999 — $431

5 — *Lord of the Rings: The Two Towers*, Released 2002 — $421

6 — *Spider-Man*, Released 2002 — $390

7 — *Jurassic Park*, Released 1993 — $357

8 — *Finding Nemo*, Released 2003 — $340

9 — *Forrest Gump*, Released 1994 — $329

10 — *The Lion King*, Released 1994 — $328

Figure 6.1 Top 10 All-time Domestic Box Office Hits. *Source:* Internet Movie Database, online, 2003.

Movie News
www.
movieweb.com

What becomes of film as an important medium, say the movies' defenders, is completely dependent on us, the audience. "It's the public," explains popular and distinguished actor John Malkovich. "The public gets the kind of politics, movies, and culture it deserves. The current state of affairs [in American filmmaking] is the result of the lack of [a] fundamental and essential trait, which is curiosity" (as quoted in McKenna, 2000, p. 70).

Industry defenders argue that films aimed at young people aren't necessarily movies with nothing to say. *Election* (1999) and *Drop Dead Gorgeous* (1999) are "teen films" offering important insight into American society and youth culture, as well as into the topics they explicitly examine, namely, elections and beauty pageants, respectively. In addition, despite Hollywood's infatuation with younger moviegoers, it still produces scores of movies of merit for a wider audience—*Minority Report* (2002), *Road to Perdition* (2002), *About Schmidt* (2003), *Mystic River* (2003), *The Human Stain* (2003). Four of the five Oscar nominees for best picture in 2002 were adult, important movies that had much to say about us as a people and as a culture: *Chicago, Gangs of New York, The Hours,* and *The Pianist.* Films whose talent was nominated for best actress and actor were equally grown-up: *Adaptation, The Quiet American, Far From Heaven, Unfaithful, About Schmidt.*

If Hollywood is fixated on kid and teen movies, why does it give us such treasures? True, Michael Eisner, as president of Paramount Pictures and now CEO of Disney, wrote in an internal memo, "We have no obligation to make history. We have no obligation to make art. We have no obligation to make a statement. Our only obligation is to make money" (as quoted in Friend, 2000, p. 214). Nevertheless, the movie industry continues to produce films that indeed make history, art, and a statement while they make money. It does so because we buy tickets to those movies.

Scope and Nature of the Film Industry

Hollywood's record year of 1946 saw the sale of more than 4 billion tickets. Today, about 1.6 billion people a year will see a movie in a U.S. theater. Domestic box office in 2002 was a record $9.1 billion, a 9% increase over 2001. Twenty-five movies in 2002, including *8 Mile, XXX, Die Another Day, A Beautiful Mind,* and *Lilo & Stitch,* exceeded $100 million in U.S.-only box office. Eleven exceeded $300 million worldwide.

THREE COMPONENT SYSTEMS

The movie business today enjoys significant financial health for two reasons. The first is improvements in its three component systems—production, distribution, and exhibition. The second, discussed in the next section, is that the movie industry has learned to live with television.

Production   Production is the making of movies. Between 600 and 700 feature-length films are produced in the United States each year, a large increase over the early 1980s, when, for example in 1985, 288 features were produced. As we'll see later in this chapter, significant revenues from home video are one reason for the increase, as is growing conglomerate ownership that demands more product for more markets.

Technology, too, has affected production. Many Hollywood films are shot on videotape. In most cases this taping is done in conjunction with shooting the movie on film and is used as a form of immediate feedback for directors and cinematographers. However, the success of *The Blair Witch Project* (1999), shot on videotape for $35,000, may move even more filmmakers to greater use of videotape as a primary shooting format.

Another influence of technology can be seen in films such as *Minority Report* (2002) and *The Sum of All Fears* (2002). Digital filmmaking has made grand special effects not only possible but expected. Stunning special effects, of which *Titanic* (1997) is a fine example, can make a good movie an excellent one. The downside of computer-generated special effects is that they can greatly increase production costs. *The Adventures of Pluto Nash*, for example, cost more than $100 million to make; *Titanic*, more than $200 million. The Motion Picture Association of America reports that the *average* cost of today's Hollywood feature is $89 million, a figure inflated, in large part, by the demands of audience-expected digital legerdemain

Critics assailed *Titanic* for its weak story line and two-dimensional characters—the real stars of the highest grossing movie of all time were the special effects. But grand special effects are no guarantee of success. Fx laden *Pluto Nash* was on all-time box office stinker, costing $100 million to make and earning only $14 million in 2002, while the *Blair Witch Project,* devoid of technical legerdemain and made for $35,000, made $220 million in box office worldwide.

(Numbers, 2003). Many observers see this large increase in production costs as a major reason studios are less willing to take creative chances in a big-budget film. As film critic Stephen Whitty explained, "Producers have to sell more tickets than ever. So they have to entertain as many people as they can. They try to offend as few as possible. They try to make things easy to understand, easy to forget. And we end up with callow, contrived $160 million losers like *Wild Wild West*" (1999, p. 9G).

Distribution   Distribution was once as simple as making prints of films and sending them to theaters. Now it means supplying these movies to television networks, cable and satellite networks, and makers of videocassettes and videodiscs. The sheer scope of the distribution business ensures that large companies (most typically the big studios themselves) will dominate. In addition to making copies and guaranteeing their delivery, distributors now finance production and take responsibility for advertising and promotion and for setting and adjusting release dates. The advertising and promotion budget for a Hollywood feature usually equals 50% of the production costs. Sometimes, the ratio of promotion to production costs is even higher. *Pearl Harbor* (2001), for example, cost $140 million to make. Its studio, Disney, spent $70 million in promotion in the United States and another $50 million overseas; in other words, the two sets of costs were nearly equal. Was it worth it? *Pearl Harbor* returned more than $450 million in worldwide box office. So spending $40 to $50 million to tout a

Hollywood movie (the industry average; DiOrio, 2002a) is not uncommon, and the investment is seen as worthwhile, if not necessary. In fact, so important has promotion become to the financial success of a movie that studios such as Universal and MGM include their advertising and marketing people in the **green light process,** that is, the decision whether or not to make a picture in the first place. These promotion professionals can say yes or no to a film's production, and they must also declare how much money and effort they will put behind the film if they do vote yes.

Another important factor in a film's promotion and eventual financial success is the distributor's decision to release it to a certain number of screens. One strategy, called the **platform rollout,** is to open a movie on a few screens and hope that critical response, film festival success, and good word-of-mouth reviews from those who do see it will propel it to success. Naturally, the advantage of this approach for the distributor is that it can greatly reduce the cost of promotion. Sony Picture Classics, for example, opened critically acclaimed *Crouching Tiger, Hidden Dragon* on only 16 screens. Films that may suffer at the hands of critics or from poor word-of-mouth, for example *Mission Impossible* 2 (2000, 3,500 screens) and *Lost World: Jurassic Park* 2 (1997, 3,565 screens) typically open in a lot of theaters simultaneously. However, it is not uncommon for a potential hit to open on many screens, as *Spider-Man* did in 2002—more than 6,000.

Exhibition   There are currently about 35,400 movie screens in the United States, down from 37,000 two years ago. More than 80% of theaters have two or more screens and average 340 seats in front of each. In the wake of the Reagan administration policy to deregulate the business, which undid the Paramount Decision in the 1980s, one-half of all screens are now owned by a studio, a trend that is continuing. For example, Sony owns Sony/Loews Theaters, Sony-IMAX Theaters, Magic Johnson Theaters, and Loews-Star Theaters and their 3,000 screens, and Warner Brothers International Theaters has more than 1,000 screens in 12 countries. In 1990 they owned none. Screens not owned by a studio are typically part of larger theater chains, for example, Century Theaters, with 800 screens and plans for 400 more in 11 Western American states, and Regal Entertainment Group (Regal Cinemas, United Artist Theaters, Edwards Theaters) with 5,800 screens in 26 states. Together, the seven largest chains, including studio-owned chains, control more than 80% of U.S. ticket sales.

It is no surprise to any moviegoer that exhibitors make much of their money on concession sales of items that typically have an 80% profit margin, accounting for 25% of a theater's total revenue (DiOrio, 2002a). This is the reason that matinees and budget nights are attractive promotions for theaters. A low-priced ticket pays dividends in overpriced popcorn and Goobers.

THE STUDIOS

Studios are at the heart of the movie business and increasingly are regaining control of the three component systems of the industry. There are

Indie film *Being John Malkovich* was a critical and box office hit.

major, minimajor, and independent studios. The majors, who finance their films primarily through the profits of their own business, include Warner Brothers, Columbia, Paramount, 20th Century Fox, Universal, MGM/UA, and Disney. The minimajors include Miramax, Artisan, Cannon, Lorimar, and New Line. These companies combine their own money with outside financing to make movies. Together the majors and minimajors account for 80% to 90% of annual U.S. movie revenue. Although the majors each produce 15 to 20 films of their own every year, one-half to two-thirds of the movies on U.S. theater screens come from the independents. The majors, however, finance much of the independent film companies' production and control distribution of their films, not only to domestic and foreign theaters but to television and home video as well. For example, Fireworks Films teamed with Paramount to bring *Rat Race* to theaters around the world.

Although independents provide the majority of our movies, they produce only about 10% of the box office revenue. Independent studios find the money to make their movies from outside sources. If they are successful, like Spike Lee (*Do the Right Thing*, 1989; *Malcolm X*, 1992; *Jungle Fever*, 1991; *Crooklyn*, 1994) or Quentin Tarantino (*Pulp Fiction*, 1994; *Jackie Brown*, 1997), for example, much of that funding can come from the major studios. More often funding is obtained from a distribution company, bank, or other outside sources. Lee himself raised the entire $175,000 needed for the production of *She's Gotta Have It* (1986), a movie that eventually made $8 million at the box office. The phenomenal success of *The Blair Witch Project*, which cost $35,000 and grossed $200 million worldwide, excited independent filmmakers as much as it frightened the big studios, ever reliant on big budgets and big stars.

Independent films tend to have smaller budgets. Often this leads to much more imaginative filmmaking and more risk taking than the big studies are willing to undertake. The 1969 independent film *Easy Rider*, which cost $370,000 to produce and made over $50 million in theater rentals, began the modern independent film boom. *My Big Fat Greek Wedding* cost $5 million to make and earned over $300 million in global box office receipts. Some independent films with which you might be familiar are *The English Patient* (1997), *Fargo* (1997), *Crouching Tiger, Hidden Dragon* (2000), *Traffic* (2000), *Being John Malkovich* (1999), *Boys Don't Cry* (1999), and *The Quiet American* (2003). Describing independent films, *Entertainment Weekly* Hollywood reporter Lisa Schwarzbaum (1997) said,

> At its simplest, an independent film can be defined as one made outside the Hollywood system. On the one hand this means there's no Paramount or Warner Bros. safety net to catch a falling director. On the other, it ensures that no pinhead business-school grad can reduce a director to nervous tics with notes about "third act problems." Independent films are not only independent of big publicity departments to help sell the wares, but they're also free from the kind of audience testing, second-guessing, and endemic messing around that so regularly make big-budget movies so safely *boring*. (pp. 8–9)

For more on independent filmmaking, read the box, "Will We Accept the Dogme Dogma?"

Trends and Convergence in Moviemaking

Reporter Schwarzbaum's affection for independent films is shared by many contemporary film critics who see several trends—especially increased conglomeration and the influence of television—reshaping the film industry in ways not to their liking. Other critics, however, point to record box office figures as a sign of the economic and artistic health of this industry. Convergence, too, is changing the movies' three component systems.

CONGLOMERATION AND THE BLOCKBUSTER MENTALITY

Indiewire
www.
indiewire.com

Other than MGM, each of the majors is a part of a large conglomerate. Paramount is owned by Viacom, 20th Century Fox is part of the Rupert Murdoch collection of companies, Warner Brothers is part of the huge Time Warner/Turner merger discussed in Chapter 1, Universal is now General Electric's property, and Disney is now part of the giant conglomerate formed in the 1996 Disney/Capital Cities/ABC union. Much of this conglomeration takes the form of international ownership. Columbia is owned by Japanese Sony and Fox by Murdoch's Australian company. According to many critics, this combination of conglomeration and foreign ownership forces the industry into a **blockbuster mentality**—filmmaking characterized by reduced risk taking and more formulaic movies. Business concerns are said to dominate artistic considerations as accountants and

Will We Accept the Dogme Dogma?

The 2002 independent hit *Full Frontal*, with big-name stars—Julia Roberts, David Duchovny, Blair Underwood—and a big-name director—Steven Soderbergh (*Erin Brockovich, Traffic, Ocean's Eleven*)—put the Dogme movement in the cultural forum during the summer of that year. In its sparseness—photographed in video; shot in 3 weeks on a $2 million budget; actors being responsible for their own makeup; no limos or trailers allowed—led critics to hail it as proof of the movement's impact on Hollywood moviemaking, even though *Full Frontal* itself was not a Dogme film. After all, if it were, it would have borne a Dogme number like its contemporaries *Reunion* (2001, Dogme #17), *Bad Actors* (2000, Dogme #16) and *Amerikana* (2001, Dogme #13). The irreverent documentary *The Name of the Film Is Dogme95* (2000) also served to get people talking about what one Internet Movie Database critic called "the most influential movement in world cinema for a generation."

Rebelling at the excesses of big-budget Hollywood moviemaking that were, in their view, destroying film as an art form, a small group of Danish filmmakers in 1995 issued a manifesto entitled Dogme95; they called it "a vow of chastity." A number of small, independent movies were produced under its rules, but with the huge success of *The Blair Witch Project* and the digital and Internet-inspired microcinema movement attracting artists and financial backing, Dogme95 became "the hot word in serious film circles," according to *Time* film critic Richard Corliss (1999, p. 84). Even Steven Spielberg said he'd like to make a film under Dogme's rules. These rules are as follows:

1. All shooting must be on location; no outside props can be transported into a scene.

2. Sound and images can never be produced independently of one another; in other words, there can be no soundtrack music that is not created in the scene itself (as in a radio playing) and there can be no post-production dubbing of sound effects and dialogue.

3. Cameras must be handheld. No tripods or dollies.

4. Shooting must be in color.

5. Optics, such as special lenses and filters, are forbidden.

6. There can be no superficial or unnecessary action or violence.

7. The setting of the film must be here and now; historical dramas are outlawed.

8. Genre movies, for example Westerns or hard-boiled detective stories, are not permitted.

9. Film must be 35 mm (but digital video is now permitted).

10. The director must not be credited on the film.

Original Dogme95 directors Lars von Trier (*The Idiots*, 1998, Dogme #2) and Thomas Vinterberg (*The Celebration*, 1998, Dogme #1) produced early Dogme-certified films. In fact, if a movie is made under its rules, it may run the Dogme "seal of approval" at its start: "This is to certify that the following motion picture has been produced in compliance with the rules and intentions set forth in the Dogme95 manifesto" (in Denby, 1999, p. 107). When a director who signs on to the manifesto strays, he or she must sign a confession indicating which of the commandments were broken.

Other, more recent movies produced in the Dogme spirit are Soren Kragh-Jacobsen's *Mifune* (1999, Dogme #3), about a young man returning home to settle his father's estate, Kristian Levring's *The King Is Alive* (1999, Dogme #4) with Jennifer Jason Leigh in the lead role, and *julien donkey-boy* (1999, Dogme #6), from American director Harmony Korine (*Gummo*, 1997), featuring well-known actors Ewen Bremner, Werner Herzog, and Chloë Sevegny.

Cinematographer Anthony Dod Mantle, who worked on *The Celebration, Mifune,* and *julien donkey-boy*, explains the need for Dogme, "Filmmakers and filmgoers are yearning for something else. But not necessarily something new. A revival. A renaissance. A refocusing on the story. The nakedness and simplicity of Dogme has put us back in touch with the essentials of filmmaking" (as quoted in Corliss, 1999, p. 84). The Dogme95 Web site (http://www.dogme95.dk/) adds, "Today a technological

How to Make a Dogme Film
www.
dogme95.com

financiers make more decisions once made by creative people. The global conglomerates, said Tom Pollock, former head of Universal's movie operations, "measure their income in the multiple tens of billions of dollars. And you have this annoying and pesky little division that does nothing but eat capital that could just as easily be spent on more cable channels" (quoted in Cieply, 2001, p. 49). The common outcomes of this blockbuster mentality are several.

storm is raging, the result of which will be the ultimate democratization of the cinema. For the first time, anyone can make movies."

Dogme films have been the subject of film festivals, such as those sponsored by New York's Lincoln Center Film Society and the Danish Film Institute, but there is disagreement among critics as to the movement's worth. *Time*'s Corliss praises it: "Dogme is a call to disarm, to strip away the veneer, to walk without crutches supplied by Industrial Light & Magic. Unabashedly reactionary, Dogme loves innocence; it aims for primitive purity" (1999, p. 84). *The New Yorker*'s David Denby disagrees: "They banned artifice in a medium in which all expression depends on artifice of one sort or another. The manifesto seemed naive or disingenuous—a kind of perverse Lutheran publicity stunt, in which austerity was praised as ostentatiously as possible" (1999, p. 107).

Are you as dissatisfied with Hollywood movies as this movement implies? Why or why not? If you are "yearning for something else," is that something else movies constructed according to the Dogme95 manifesto? Do you see Dogme95 as an important movement, or a naive publicity stunt? At the very minimum, what the Dogme95 movement does is force film fans to face up to their own beliefs about movies. Americans may complain about the current state of Hollywood moviemaking, but they attend in record numbers. Dogme95 was developed expressly as an antidote to Hollywood's blockbuster mentality. But do you think it is too bitter a pill? As a media literate moviegoer, you should see at least one Dogme film to determine for yourself the movement's worth. At the same time, you might further refine your feelings toward and expectations of film as a medium.

The Idiots (Dogme #2) and Dogme-inspired indie *Full Frontal*.

Concept Movies   The marketing and publicity departments of big companies love **concept films**—movies that can be described in one line. *Twister* is about a giant, rogue tornado. *The Lost World* is about giant, rogue dinosaurs. *Like Mike* (2002) is about an orphan who finds magic sneakers.

International ownership and international distribution contribute to this phenomenon. High-concept films that depend little on characterization, plot development, and dialogue are easier to sell to foreign exhibitors

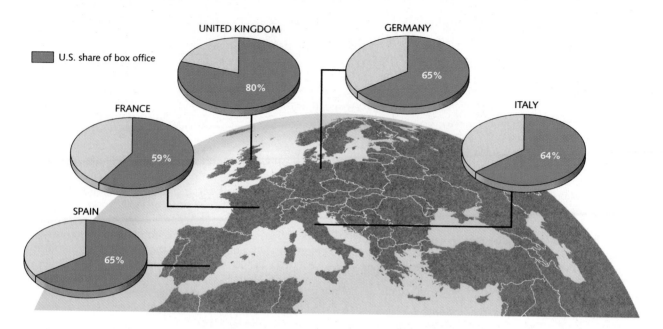

UNITED KINGDOM

GERMANY

FRANCE

ITALY

SPAIN

Figure 6.2 U.S. Filmmakers' Share of Foreign Box Office, 2001. *Source: Variety, October 22–28, 2001).*

than are more sophisticated films. *Twister* and *Jurassic Park* play well everywhere. Big-name stars also have international appeal. That's why they can command huge salaries. The importance of foreign distribution cannot be overstated. Only 2 in 10 U.S. features make a profit on U.S. box office. Much of their eventual profit comes from overseas sales. For example, 2001 domestic dud *A.I. Artificial Intelligence* ($78.6 million) made $156.4 million overseas. Likewise *Moulin Rouge* ($57 domestic vs. $113 million overseas), *Miss Congeniality* ($60.4 million vs. $105.3 million), and *Vertical Limit* ($16.6 vs. $126 million). Overseas box office accounts for 55% of the U.S. movie industry's income (Germain, 2000), and American studios will account for more than 40% of the projected $24 billion global box office in 2010 (Guider, 2001). Figure 6.2 shows the current proportion of several countries' box office that is controlled by U.S. moviemakers.

Ain't It Cool
www.
aint-it-cool.com

Audience Research   Before a movie is made, its concept, plot, and characters are subjected to market testing. Often multiple endings are produced and tested with sample audiences by companies such as National Research Group and Marketcast. MGM went as far as to reedit *Rollerball* (2002) after a test screening before an audience of one, "Ain't It Cool" webmaster Harry Knowles (Lawson, 2002). Despite being "voodoo science, a spin of the roulette wheel," says *Chicago Reader* film critic Jonathan Rosenbaum, audience testing is "believed in like a religion at this point. It's considered part of filmmaking" (quoted in Scribner, 2001, p. D3). The question raised by film purists is what has become of the filmmaker's genius? What separates these market-tested films from any other commodity?

Sequels, Remakes, and Franchises   Nothing succeeds like success. How many *Mighty Ducks* have there been? *Sister Acts? Die Hards? Lethal Weapons?*

Aliens? Beverly Hills Cops? Jerry Lewis's 1963 *The Nutty Professor* was reborn as Eddie Murphy's 1996 *The Nutty Professor*. Disney remade its own *101 Dalmatians*. The 1998 *Thin Red Line* is a remake of a 1964 film. *Mr. Deeds* (2002) is a modern-day knockoff of the 1936 Frank Capra classic, *Mr. Deeds Goes to Town*. Hollywood, too, is making increasing use of **franchise films**, movies that are produced with the full intention of producing several more sequels. The first James Bond film (1962) has had 21 sequels, *Star Wars* (1977) 4 and counting, *Harry Potter* (2001) will have as many as there are Potter books, and *The Matrix* put multiple sequels in production at once for 2003 release.

Television, Comic Book, and Videogame Remakes   Nothing succeeds like success. That, and the fact that teens and preteens make up the largest proportion of the movie audience, is the reason so many movies are adaptations of television shows, comic books, and video games. In the last few years *Inspector Gadget, Dudley Do-Right, The Flintstones, My Favorite Martian, The Fugitive, The Saint, Mission: Impossible, George of the Jungle, Leave It to Beaver, Lost in Space* (and its sequel), *Charlie's Angels, Beavis and Butthead, McHale's Navy, Mr. Magoo, The Brady Bunch, Dragnet,* and *Wayne's World* have moved from small to big screen. *The Addams Family, Dennis the Menace, Richie Rich, Spider-Man, Batman,* and *Superman* have traveled from the comics, through television, to the silver screen. *Tank Girl, Barb Wire, Spawn, X Men, Men in Black, Kull the Conqueror, Steel,* and *The Crow* have moved directly from comics to movies. *Tomb Raider, Resident Evil, Mortal Kombat, Final Fantasy,* and *Grand Theft Auto* went from game box to box office. Movies from comics and video games are especially attractive to studios because of their built-in merchandise tie-in appeal.

Merchandise Tie-Ins   Films are sometimes produced as much for their ability to generate interest for nonfilm products as for their intrinsic value as movies. The Licensing Industry Merchandisers' Association reports that toy and product tie-ins accounted for $2.5 billion in payments to the studios in 2001 (on retail sales of $42 billion; Goldsmith, 2002). *Star Wars: Episode I—The Phantom Menace* alone accounted for more than $1 billion in merchandise sales in the year after its 1999 release (Palmeri, 2001). And as almost all of us know, it is nearly impossible to buy a meal at McDonalds, Burger King, or Taco Bell without being offered a movie tie-in product. Studios often believe it is riskier to make a $7 million film with no merchandising potential than a $100 million movie with greater merchandising appeal.

Product Placement   Many movies are serving double duty as commercials. We'll discuss this phenomenon in detail later in the chapter as a media literacy issue.

CONVERGENCE RESHAPES THE MOVIE BUSINESS

So intertwined are today's movie and television industries that it is often meaningless to discuss them separately. As much as 70% of the production done by the studios is for television, Paramount's various *Star Trek* series and Fox's entire television network being two prime examples. But the growing relationship between **theatrical films**—those produced originally for theater exhibition—and television is the result of technological changes in the latter. The convergence of film with satellite, cable, pay-per-view, digital videodisc (DVD), and videocassette has provided immense distribution and exhibition opportunities for the movies. Fifty percent of studio revenues come from domestic VCR, cable, and satellite rentals alone (Hettrick, 2002). Today's distributors make three times as much from domestic home entertainment (DVD, videotapes, and network and cable television) as they do from rentals to movie houses. Video sales (to individuals and tape rental stores) are a lucrative business as well. The studios maximize their tape profits with trailers for their other video and in-theater films and with commercials. Box office failures can turn loss to profit with good video sales. Even box office hits such as *The Fast and the Furious* (2001) and *Training Day* (2001) earn more from DVD release *alone* than they do from ticket sales (Lyman, 2002).

The convergence of film with digital technologies is beginning to reshape production, distribution, *and* exhibition. In early 1999, three companies, Kodak, Texas Instruments, and CineComm, began demonstrations of their digital distributions of films to theaters via satellite. Should this advance take hold, exhibitors will no longer have to physically receive film cans and load their contents onto projectors. For now, though, even though producers are excited about the promise of saving hundreds of millions of dollars on the production of prints, questions remain about how many theaters will convert to digital delivery, how quickly they will do it, how much it will cost, and who will pay for it. "Projectors last forever. Why buy a new (digital) projector if it won't sell more tickets?" asks technology consultant Larry Gleason (quoted in Graser, 2001, p. 7). Frustrated by exhibitors' unwillingness to convert to digital satellite delivery and display of their films, the major studios, with the approval of the U.S. Justice Department, formed a consortium in 2001 to set industry standards and develop a plan that spreads the cost of conversion across film's three component systems.

The surprise 1999 hit *The Blair Witch Project* is the most visible success of the growing **microcinema** movement, through which filmmakers using digital video cameras and desktop digital editing machines are finding audiences, both in theaters and online, for their low-budget (sometimes as little as $10,000) features. *Silence,* a short film produced for $100, was screened at the 1998 Cannes Film festival to positive reviews, and the 1998 digital feature, *The Celebration,* grossed more than $1 million in its first year of distribution.

But arguably the biggest boost given to digital production of theatrical films (if they can still be called *films*) came in April 2000 when, after a trial run of the equipment, George Lucas announced that he would shoot the live action scenes for the sequel to the *Phantom Menace* using digital video cameras. Soon after, New Line Cinema announced that it had signed

Atom Films
www.
atomfilms.com

IFilm
www.
ifilm.com

Spike Lee to do *Bamboozled* on digital video. Purists were aghast, but the shift is inevitable, say supporters, given not only the Lucas/Lee blessing but also the high cost of making movies on celluloid, roughly 100 times that of an equivalent digital video production. As if to prove digital cinema's supporters correct, 25% of the dramatic feature films and 40% of the documentaries screened at the annual Sundance Film Festival are being shot digitally (Spector, 2001).

As digitalization and convergence are changing exhibition and production, they are also changing distribution. Despite predictions by legendary Hollywood actor and director Warren Beatty of a digital dream world "in which a severely reduced number of theaters equipped with startlingly high-end technology will open films on much smaller advertising budgets, sending them (directly) into homes equipped with yet another layer of technology approaching that of most theaters today" (in Cieply, 2001, p. 53), the distribution of motion pictures by Internet to individual viewers has been slowed by the lack of widespread availability of high-speed modems and audio and video Internet streaming technology (Chapter 10). Still, two of 2001's Oscar-nominated short films, *The Periwig Maker* and *Una Historia de Futebol*, were original Web releases, and a number of Web film distribution and/or production sites

The 2002 remake *(Mr. Deeds)* of the 1936 classic original *(Mr. Deeds Goes to Town)* was a critical and box office success.

have opened since the high-profile closings of Digital Entertainment Network and Steven Spielberg and Ron Howard's Pop.com in 2000. Francis Ford Coppola runs a virtual studio and writers' workshop at www.Zoetrope.com, and Atomfilms.com, IFilm.com, and Inzide.com, all offer independent filmmakers worldwide distribution of their works. There are even Web script sites. For example, ScriptShark offers script analysis for newcomers and even optioned a Western script, *The Devil's Kiss,* to Mel Gibson's production company in 2001. "Online film's time is coming," says *Guardian* technology writer Matthew Ford. "The dot.com crash is beginning to fade from memory, investors are once again showing a cautious interest in Internet film, and members of the Hollywood elite are following the indie hopefuls online" (2001, p. 11). That optimism was demonstrated in November 2002 when IBM and its Hollywood partners (MGM, Paramount, Sony, Universal, and Warner Brothers) launched an online video-on-demand movie distribution system—Movielink. Much more will be said about Internet distribution of film and video content in Chapter 9.

Online Script Help
WWW.
scriptshark.com

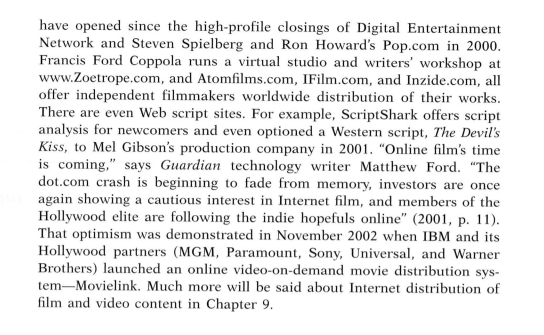

DEVELOPING MEDIA LITERACY SKILLS
Recognizing Product Placements

Inzide.com
WWW.
inzide.com

The Gap and Lexus have nearly as much screen time as Tom Cruise in *Minority Report* (2002). *What Woman Want* (2000) is a movie about making a Nike commercial. FedEx and Wilson have major roles in *Cast Away* (2001). A UPS delivery starts the action in *Lara Croft: Tomb Raider* (2001) and fuels much of the drama in *I Am Sam* (2002). The Pentagon is a proud sponsor of *The Sum of All Fears* (2002). So heavy with product placement (more than $100 million worth) was the 1997 James Bond thriller *Tomorrow Never Dies* that critics labeled it a 2-hour commercial and retitled it *Endorsements Never Die.*

The practice of placing brand-name products in movies is not new; Katharine Hepburn throws Gordon's gin into the river in the 1951 *The African Queen,* and Spencer Tracy is splashed with Coca-Cola in the 1950 *Father of the Bride.* But in today's movie industry product placement has expanded into a business in its own right. There are approximately 92 product placement agencies operating in Hollywood, and even an industry association, the Entertainment Resources and Marketing Association (ERMA). The attraction of product placements for sponsors is obvious. For one flat fee paid up front, a product that appears in a movie is in actuality a commercial that lives forever—first on the big screen, then on television and cable, and then on purchased and rented videotapes and discs. The commercial is also likely to have worldwide distribution. And, say their supporters, movie placements work. For example, in the 30 days after the release of the summer hit *Goldmember* in 2002, American sales of Jaguar automobiles were 73% higher than they were the previous June. The spy spoof featured a Union Jack XK8 Jaguar (Shaguar in the movie).

Is *Austin Powers in Gold-member* a movie or car commercial? Ask the folks at Jaguar what they think!

Said an official for the company, "Austin Powers seems to have made Jaguar an even cooler car" (Gow, 2002, p. 20).

Many people in and outside the movie industry see product placement as inherently deceptive. "Why not identify the ads for what they are?" they ask. From a media literacy standpoint, the issue is the degree to which artistic decisions are being placed second to obligations to sponsors. Film critic Glenn Lovell (1997) wrote, "Scripts are being doctored and camera angles changed to accommodate manufacturers paying for props or promotional campaigns. It's a classic case of the tail wagging the dog" (p. 7G). David Peoples, the screenwriter for *Blade Runner,* a cinematic testimonial to product placement, calls the practice a "racket . . . a horrifying compromise" (p. 7G). A "hot" Hollywood director who asked critic Lovell not to use his name said, "I've worked with producers who would sell their soul to get a major placement. I say, 'Forget it.' If movie stars want to do commercials, they should do them, and get paid" (p. 7G). One famous example of a sponsor dictating content is Reebok's lawsuit against Sony's TriStar Pictures. The shoe maker was angry that a mock ad for its product did not appear in the 1996 hit *Jerry Maguire,* as originally called for in the script. The producers said that the film-ending spot did not test well with audiences and was cut for "creative reasons." But rather than fight the suit, TriStar settled out of court, agreeing that all subsequent television and video versions of the movie would carry the excised footage.

Smoke-Free Movies

Product placement vexes its critics because of its threat to the integrity of film. But when it comes to the placement of cigarettes, the problem is compounded by the fact that this frequently placed product kills. According to the American Lung Association, in 1990 America's top-grossing films contained 0 to 1 tobacco scene per hour. In 2001 smoking was "depicted in 64 percent . . . of the top-grossing films—including an average 4.2 incidents of smoking per hour in G-rated films. During the 1990s, nearly 85% of top-grossing Hollywood films featured tobacco use. Nearly one in three showed specific cigarette brand logos—including one in five children's movies" (McCowan, 2002, p. 1). Statistics such as these moved throat cancer sufferer and screenwriter Joe Eszterhas (*Basic Instinct, Flashdance*) to apologize for putting so much smoking in his movies. "A cigarette in the hands of a Hollywood star onscreen," he said, "is a gun aimed at a 12- or 14-year-old" ("Verbatim," 2002, p. 16). Once-secret tobacco industry documents indicate that cigarette companies "aggressively pursued product placement in films—even as they told Congress they would not . . . (and) undertook an extensive campaign to hook Hollywood on tobacco by providing free cigarettes to actors" (Smoke Free Movies, 2002).

If you are troubled by this deception (the tobacco companies pledged in 1989 to cease movie product placements), or if you are bothered by the fact that both *Variety* and *Hollywood Reporter* recently refused to sell space to Smoke Free Movies for its antismoking ads (Goldstein, 2002b), or if you dislike the practice of product placement itself, or if you understand that tobacco is "the all-time leading cause of early death" (Goldstein, 2002b, p. G-3), you can act; you can make your own media literacy a living enterprise.

Smoke Free Movies provides information and an action agenda on its Web site <smokefreemovies.ucsf.edu>. It recommends:

- Contacting the MPAA <www.mpaa.org> and asking that it change its ratings system to give an R to movies that depict smoking

- Contacting the studios themselves (as well as their parent companies) and telling them that you will not attend smoke-filled films (Smoke Free Movies' Web site provides links)

- Demanding that local theaters and video stores show strong antismoking ads; organize people in your community to make in-person visits to the managers of these establishments to make these requests

- Contacting the actors themselves and letting them know how much they, as people, disappoint you

- Writing letters to the editors of your local papers. When you see a film that glamorizes smoking or pushes a particular brand, tell the world. Make those responsible answer for their actions.

But you love film, respect it as a medium of expression. You don't want to be involved in what looks like censorship. If smoking is integral to the filmmaker's vision, so be it. But why, for example, does Sissy Spacek, descending into madness over the murder of her son in *In the Bedroom* (2001), brood over a strategically placed pack of Marlboros? Why does she order that specific brand, by name, from a shop clerk? Why does a walk-on actor, incidental to the story, request a pack of Marlboros by name? As cancer researcher Stanton Glantz asks, "If smoking in a movie is about free expression, why do all the characters smoke the same brand?" (quoted in McCowan, 2002, p. 2).

Knowing how media content is funded and how that financial support shapes content is an important aspect of understanding the mass communication process. Therefore, an awareness of the efforts of the movie industry to maximize income from their films is central to good film literacy.

Consider, for example, the following product placements. If you saw these movies, did you recognize the placements?

Cadillac in *The Matrix Reloaded*
Jeep in *Lara Croft Tomb Raider: The Cradle of Life*

Reddi Wip in *Boys Don't Cry*
Miller Beer in *The Shipping News*
Gummi Bears in *Hedwig and the Angry Inch*
Pizza Hut in *The Fast and the Furious*

Does it trouble you that content is altered, even if sometimes only minimally, to allow for these brand identifications? To what extent would script alterations have to occur to accommodate paid-for messages before you find them intrusive? Do you think it is fair or honest for a moviemaker who promises you film content in exchange for your money to turn you into what amounts to a television viewer by advertising sponsors' products? At least in television, by law, all commercial messages must be identified as such, and the sponsors of those messages must be identified. Do you think such a rule ought to apply to movies?

Literate film consumers may answer these questions differently, especially as individuals hold film in varying degrees of esteem—but they should answer them.

Product Placement Organization
WWW.
erma.org

Chapter Review

The movies were developed by entrepreneurs, people seeking to earn profits by entertaining audiences. Among the first to make a movie was Eadweard Muybridge, whose sequential action photographs inspired Edison laboratory scientist William Dickson to develop a better filming system, the kinetograph. The next advance came from the Lumière brothers, whose cinematographe allowed projection of movies. Another Frenchman, Georges Méliès, brought narrative to movies, and the medium's storytelling abilities were heightened by Americans Edwin S. Porter and D. W. Griffith.

Film soon became a large, studio-controlled business on the West Coast, where it had moved to take advantage of good weather and to escape the control of the Motion Picture Patents Company. The industry's growth was a product of changes in the U.S. population, political turmoil overseas, the introduction of sound, and the development of new, audience-pleasing genres.

After World War II the industry underwent major changes due to the loss of audience to television, the red scare, and the Paramount Decision. The industry was forced to remake itself. At first Hollywood resisted television, but soon studios learned that television could be a profitable partner. Today, the major studios are responsible for much of the film industry's production and distribution. They are also involved in exhibition.

The modern film industry is experiencing the same trend toward conglomeration and internationalization as are other media, and content is influenced by that fact. A blockbuster mentality leads to reliance on concept films; audience research; sequels, franchise films, and remakes; movies based on comic books, video games, and television shows; merchandise tie-ins; and product placements. Profits are additionally boosted by distribution overseas and through other media such as videocassettes, DVD, satellite, pay-per-view, and television. Convergence and digital technology are reshaping production, distribution, and exhibition.

The audience for the movies is increasingly a young one, and movie content reflects this reality. Many observers fear that the traditional, elevated role movies have played in our culture is in danger as a result. The same pressures for profit that raise this fear also lead to the potentially misleading practice of product placement and, therefore, to the increased importance of media literacy.

Key Terms

zoopraxiscope, 161
persistence of vision, 162
kinetograph, 162
daguerreotype, 163
calotype, 163
kinetoscope, 163
cinematographe, 164

montage, 165
nickelodeons, 165
factory studios, 165
double feature, 171
B-movie, 171
vertical integration, 171
block booking, 173

green light process, 179
platform rollout, 179
blockbuster mentality, 181
concept film, 183
franchise film, 185
theatrical film, 186
microcinema, 187

Questions for Review

1. What is the significance of these people to film history? Leland Stanford, Eadweard Muybridge, William Dickson, the Lumière brothers, Louis Daguerre, Joseph Niépce, William Henry Fox Talbot, Hannibal Goodwin, George Eastman.
2. What are the kinetograph, kinetoscope, cinematographe, daguerreotype, calotype, and nickelodeon?
3. What were Méliès's, Porter's, and Griffith's contributions to film as a narrative medium?
4. What was the Motion Picture Patents Company, and how did it influence the content and development of the movie industry?
5. What societal, technical, and artistic factors shaped the development of movies before World War II?

6. How did Hollywood scandals and the red scare shape the medium's content?
7. What is vertical integration? How was it ended and reinstated?
8. What are the three component systems of the movie industry?
9. What are major and minimajor studios? What is an independent?
10. What are concept films? Product tie-ins? Product placement?
11. What is platform rollout? When and why is it used?
12. How are digitalization and convergence reshaping exhibition? Distribution? Production?
13. Why has the distribution of films to individual viewers by Internet not yet become commonplace?

Questions for Critical Thinking and Discussion

1. How do you think the entrepreneurial motivation of the early movie pioneers shaped the relationship of the medium with its audience?
2. Hollywood was an open propaganda agent for the military during World War II. Do you think a mass medium should serve a government in this way? Why or why not?
3. Hollywood suffered under strict content control and now has shed those restrictions. What restrictions do you think are reasonable for the movies? Why?

4. What do you think of the impact of the blockbuster mentality on movies? Should profit always be the determining factor in producing movie content? Why or why not?
5. Are you a fan of independent movies? When you are watching a movie, how can you tell that it's an independent? If you are an indie fan, do you welcome the microcinema and Dogme95 movements? Why or why not?

Important Resources

Balio, T. (1979). *The American film industry*. Madison, WI: University of Wisconsin Press. The classic history of the film industry through World War II and the coming of television.

Ceplair, L., & Englund, S. (1980). *The inquisition in Hollywood: Politics in the film community*. New York: Doubleday. A look at the red scare's corrosive influence on Hollywood, on both the personal and the professional levels.

Cineaste. A quarterly calling itself "America's magazine for the art and aesthetics of the cinema," its pages focus on film criticism and theory. It offers reviews, interviews, and essays on contemporary issues of film narrative and look.

Film Comment. Published by the Film Society of Lincoln Center, this bimonthly features essays, reviews, and commentary on contemporary movies, as well as essays on film theory and criticism. It also covers many of the world's important film festivals.

Film Culture. Calling itself "America's independent motion picture magazine," this magazine is published "irregularly." When it does come out, it frequently devotes all or a large part of an issue to articles and essays on one topic, following them with an in-print debate by appropriate filmmakers and critics.

Film Quarterly. For readers serious about film, this magazine specializes in interviews, history, and aesthetic theory. It also presents well-informed reviews of books about film.

Rosenbaum, J. (2001). *Movie wars*. Chicago: A Cappella Books. In this book, subtitled "How Hollywood and the Media Conspire to Limit What Films We Can See," *Chicago Reader* film critic Rosenbaum levels a sharp eye (and wit) at those he believes are killing film as an important medium of expression—studios desperate for that next big, easily promoted concept film, test audiences, and a host of other usual Hollywood suspects. Passionately written and readable.

Sklar, R. (1994). *Movie-made America: A cultural history of American movies*. New York: Vintage Books. Considered the authoritative history of the social and cultural impact of movies since its first edition in 1974, this book is readable but intellectually challenging. It has long earned rave reviews from popular as well as scholarly critics.

The Cult Film Site	www.sepnet.com/rcramer/index.htm
Hollywood Online	www.hollywood.com
Worst Movies Ever	www.ohthehumanity.com
Movie News	www.enn2.com/movies.htm
Movie Guide	www.allmovie.com
Movie News	www.movies.go.com
Film History	www.filmsite.org/filmh.html
Film Ratings	www.filmratings.com
Motion Picture Association of America	www.mpaa.org
Hollywood Reporter	www.hollywoodreporter.com
Internet Movie Database	www.imdb.com
Movie News	www.movieweb.com
Indiewire	www.indiewire.com
How to Make a Dogme Film	www.dogme95.com
Ain't It Cool	www.aint-it-cool.com
Atom Films	www.atomfilms.com
IFilm	www.ifilm.com
Online Script Help	www.scriptshark.com
Inzide.com	www.inzide.com
Product Placement Organization	www.erma.org

CHAPTER **7**

Radio and Sound Recording

LEARNING OBJECTIVES

Radio was the first electronic mass medium; it was the first national broadcast medium. It produced the networks, program genres, and stars that made television an instant success. But for many years radio and records were young people's media; they gave voice to a generation. As such, they may be our most personally significant mass media. After studying this chapter you should

- be familiar with the history and development of the radio and sound recording industries and radio and sound recording themselves as media.

- recognize the importance of early financing and regulatory decisions regarding radio and how they have shaped the nature of contemporary broadcasting.

- recognize how the organizational and economic natures of the contemporary radio and sound recording industries shape the content of both media.

- understand the relationship between radio and sound recording and their listeners.

- be aware of new and emerging radio and recording technologies and their potential impact on music, the industries themselves, and listeners.

- be familiar with the economic and ethical controversies surrounding music file sharing on the Internet.

- possess improved radio-listening media literacy skill, especially in assessing the cultural value of shock jocks.

"CAN WE LISTEN TO THE RADIO?"

"We are listening to the radio."

"I mean something other than this."

"You want music?"

"Yes, please, anything but public radio. Too much talk."

"OK. Here."

"What! That's the classical music station!"

"What's wrong with that?"

"Nothing . . . much."

"What's that supposed to mean, 'Nothing . . . much?'"

"Nothing . . . much. Let me choose."

"OK. You find a station."

"Fine. Here."

"What's that?!"

"It's the New Hot One. KISS 100. All the hits all the time."

"That's not music."

"You sound like my parents."

"I don't mean the stuff they play isn't music, I mean the deejay is yammering away."

"Hang on. A song is coming up. Anyway, this is funny stuff."

"I don't find jokes about minority wheelchair races funny."

"It's all in fun."

"Fun for whom?"

"What's *your* problem today?"

"Nothing, I just don't find that kind of stuff funny. Here, I'll find something."

"What's that?"

"The jazz station."

"Give me a break. How about Sports Talk?"

"Nah. How about All News?"

"No way. How about the All Talk station?"

"Why, you need another fix of insulting chatter?"

"How about silence?"

"Yeah, how about it?"

In this chapter we study the technical and social beginnings of both radio and sound recording. We revisit the coming of broadcasting and see how the growth of regulatory, economic, and organizational structures led to the medium's golden age.

The heart of the chapter covers how television changed radio and produced the medium with which we are now familiar. We review the scope and nature of contemporary radio, especially its rebirth as a local, fragmented, specialized, personal, and mobile medium. We examine how these characteristics serve advertisers and listeners. The chapter then explores the relationship between radio and the modern recording industry and the way new technologies serve and challenge both media. The popularity of shock jocks inspires our discussion of media literacy.

A Short History of Radio and Sound Recording

The particular stations you disagree about may be different, but almost all of us have been through a conversation like the one in the opening vignette. Radio, the seemingly ubiquitous medium, matters to us. Because we often listen to it alone, it is personal. Radio is also mobile. It travels with us in the car, and we take it along in our Walkmans. Radio is specific as well. Stations aim their content at very narrowly defined audiences. But these are characteristics of contemporary radio. Radio once occupied a very different place in our culture. Let's see how it all began.

EARLY RADIO

The "Father of Radio," Guglielmo Marconi, son of a wealthy Italian businessman and his Irish wife, had taken to reading scientific reports about the sending of signals through the air without wires. But unlike the early pioneers whom he studied, for example, James Clerk Maxwell and Heinrich Hertz, the young Marconi was interested not in the theory of sending signals through the air but in actually doing it. His improvements over earlier experimental designs allowed him to send and receive telegraph code over distances as great as 2 miles by 1896. His native Italy was not interested in his invention, so he used his mother's contacts in Great Britain to find support and financing there. England, with a global empire and the world's largest navy and merchant fleets, was naturally interested in long-distance wireless communication. With the financial and technical help of the British, Marconi successfully transmitted across the English Channel in 1899 and across the Atlantic in 1901. Wireless was now a reality. Marconi was satisfied with his advance, but other scientists saw the transmission of *voices* by wireless as the next hurdle, a challenge that was soon surmounted.

In 1903 Reginald Fessenden, a Canadian, invented the **liquid barretter,** the first audio device permitting reception of wireless voices. His 1906 Christmas Eve broadcast from Brant Rock, a small New England coastal village, was the first public broadcast of voices and music. His listeners were ships at sea and a few newspaper offices equipped to receive the transmission.

Later that same year American Lee DeForest invented the **audion tube,** a vacuum tube that improved and amplified wireless signals. Now the reliable transmission of clear voices and music was a reality. But

Marconi
WWW.
etedeschi.ndirect.co.uk/marconi/
index.htm

Guglielmo Marconi

DeForest
www.
northstar.k12.ak.us/schools/ryn/
projects/inventors/deforest/
deforest/html

DeForest's second important contribution was that he saw radio as a means of *broadcasting*. The early pioneers, Marconi included, had viewed radio as a device for point-to-point communication, for example, from ship to ship or ship to shore. But in the 1907 prospectus for his radio company DeForest wrote, "It will soon be possible to distribute grand opera music from transmitters placed on the stage of the Metropolitan Opera House by a Radio Telephone station on the roof to almost any dwelling in Greater New York and vicinity. . . . The same applies to large cities. Church music, lectures, etc., can be spread abroad by the Radio Telephone" (as quoted in Adams, 1996, pp. 104–106). Soon, countless "broadcasters" went on the air. Some broadcasters were giant corporations, looking to dominate the medium for profit; some were hobbyists and hams, playing with the medium for the sheer joy of it. There were so many "stations" that havoc reigned. Yet the promise of radio was such that the medium continued to mature until World War I, when the U.S. government ordered "the immediate closing of all stations for radio communications, both transmitting and receiving."

EARLY SOUND RECORDING

The late 1800s also saw the beginning of sound recording. In 1877 prolific inventor Thomas Edison patented his "talking machine," a device for duplicating sound that used a hand-cranked grooved cylinder and a needle. The mechanical movement caused by the needle passing along the groove of the rotating cylinder and hitting bumps was converted into electrical energy

Lee DeForest

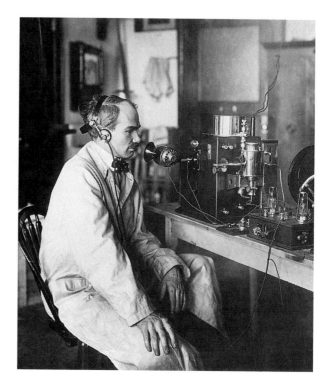

In 1887 Emile Berliner developed the flat disc gramophone and a sophisticated microphone, both important to the widespread public acceptance of sound recordings for the home. Nipper, the trademark for his company, RCA Victor, is on the scene even today.

that activated a diaphragm in a loudspeaker and produced sound. The drawback was that only one "recording" could be made of any given sound; the cylinder could not be duplicated. In 1887 that problem was solved by German immigrant Emile Berliner, whose gramophone used a flat, rotating, wax-coated disc that could easily be copied or pressed from a metal master. Two equally important contributions to recording made by Berliner were development of a sophisticated microphone and (through his company, RCA Victor Records) the import from Europe of recordings by famous opera stars. Now people had not only a reasonably priced record player but records to play on it. The next advance was introduction of the two-sided disc by the Columbia Phonograph Company in 1905. Soon there were hundreds of phonograph or gramophone companies, and the device, by either name, was a standard feature in U.S. homes by 1920. More than 2 million machines and 107 million recordings were sold in 1919 alone. Public acceptance of the new medium was enhanced even more by development of electromagnetic recording in 1924 by Joseph P. Maxwell at Bell Laboratory.

The parallel development and diffusion of radio and sound recording is significant. For the first time in history radio allowed people to hear the words and music of others who were not in their presence. On recordings they could hear words and music that may have been created days, months, or even years before.

THE COMING OF BROADCASTING

The idea of broadcasting—that is, transmitting voices and music at great distances to a large number of people—predated the development of radio. Alexander Graham Bell's telephone company had a subscription music service in major cities in the late 1800s, delivering music to homes and businesses by telephone wires. A front-page story in an 1877 edition of the *New York Daily Graphic* suggested the possibilities of broadcasting to its readers. The public anticipated and, after DeForest's much publicized successes, was eager for music and voices at home. Russian immigrant David

THE DAILY GRAPHIC

An Illustrated Evening Newspaper.

39 & 41 Park Place.

VOL. XIII.   NEW YORK. THURSDAY, MARCH 15, 1877.   NO. 1246.

This cover of an 1877 newspaper proved prophetic in its image of speakers' ability to "broadcast" their words.

Sarnoff, then an employee of American Marconi, recognized this desire and in 1916 sent his superiors what has become famous as the "Radio Music Box Memo." In this memo Sarnoff wrote of

> a plan of development which would make radio a "household utility" in the same sense as the piano or phonograph. The idea is to bring music into the house by wireless. . . . The receiver can be designed in the form of a simple "Radio Music Box" and arranged for several different wavelengths, which should be changeable with the throwing of a single switch or pressing of a single button. (Sterling & Kitross, 1990, p. 43)

The introduction of broadcasting to a mass audience was delayed in the first two decades of the 20th century by patent fights and lawsuits. DeForest and Fessenden were both destroyed financially by the conflict. Yet when World War I ended, an enthusiastic audience awaited what had become a much improved medium. In a series of developments that would be duplicated for television at the time of World War II, radio was transformed from an exciting technological idea into an entertainment and commercial giant. To aid the war effort, the government took over the patents relating to radio and continued to improve radio for military use. Thus, refinement and development of the technical aspects of radio continued throughout the war. Then, when the war ended in 1919, the patents were returned to their owners—the bickering was renewed.

Concerned that the medium would be wasted and fearful that a foreign company (British Marconi) would control this vital resource, the government forced the combatants to merge. American Marconi, General Electric, American Telephone & Telegraph, and Westinghouse (in 1921)—each in control of a vital piece of technology—joined to create the Radio Corporation of America (RCA). RCA was a government-sanctioned monopoly, but its creation avoided direct government control of the new medium. Twenty-eight-year-old David Sarnoff, author of the Radio Music Box Memo, was made RCA's commercial manager. The way for the medium's popular growth was paved; its success was guaranteed by a public that, because of the phonograph, was already attuned to music in the home and, thanks to the just concluded war, was awakening to the need for instant, wide-ranging news and information.

On September 30, 1920, a Westinghouse executive, impressed with press accounts of the number of listeners who were picking up broadcasts from the garage radio station of company engineer Frank Conrad, asked him to move his operation to the Westinghouse factory and expand its power. Conrad did so, and on October 27, 1920, experimental station 8XK in Pittsburgh, Pennsylvania, received a license from the Department of Commerce to broadcast. On November 2 this station, KDKA, made the first commercial radio broadcast, announcing the results of the presidential election that sent Warren G. Harding to the White House. By mid-1922, there were nearly 1 million radios in American homes, up from 50,000 just a year before (Tillinghast, 2000, p. 41).

THE COMING OF REGULATION

As the RCA agreements demonstrated, the government had a keen interest in the development, operation, and diffusion of radio. At first government interest focused on point-to-point communication. In 1909 almost all the passengers on the wireless-equipped *Republic* were saved as the ship sank off the east coast of the United States. The vessel had used its radio to call for help from nearby ships. Soon after, Congress passed the Wireless Ship Act of 1910, requiring that all ships using U.S. ports and carrying more than 50 passengers have a working wireless and operator. Of course, the wireless industry did not object, as the legislation boosted sales. After the *Titanic* struck an iceberg in the North Atlantic in 1912 and it was learned that hundreds of lives were lost needlessly because many ships in the area had left their radios unattended, Congress passed the Radio Act of 1912, which not

The wireless-telegraphy room of the *Titanic*. Despite the heroic efforts of wireless operator Jack Philips, scores of people died needlessly in the sinking of that great ocean liner because the ships in its vicinity did not man their receivers.

only strengthened the rules regarding shipboard wireless but also required that wireless operators be licensed by the Secretary of Commerce and Labor.

The Radio Act of 1912 established spheres of authority for both federal and state governments, provided for allocating and revoking licenses and fining violators, and assigned frequencies for station operation. The government was in the business of regulating what was to become broadcasting.

The 1910 Act had boosted sales. But the 1912 Act imposed control, and many broadcasters objected. Two legal challenges to government regulatory authority eventually followed, *Hoover v. Intercity Radio Co., Inc.* in 1923 and *U.S. v. Zenith Radio Corp. et al.* in 1926. The broadcasters won both, effectively negating the federal government's power to license. President Calvin Coolidge ordered the cessation of government regulation of radio despite his belief that chaos would descend on the medium.

Coolidge proved prophetic. The industry's years of flouting the 1912 Act had led it to the brink of disaster. Radio sales and profits dropped dramatically. Listeners were tired of the chaos. Stations arbitrarily changed frequencies, power, and hours of operation, and there was constant interference between stations, which was often intentional. Radio industry leaders petitioned Commerce Commissioner Herbert Hoover and, according to historian Erik Barnouw (1966)—who titled his book on radio's early days *A Tower in Babel*—"encouraged firmness" in government efforts to regulate and control the competitors. The government's response was a series of four National Radio Conferences involving industry experts, public officials, and government regulators. These conferences produced the Radio Act of 1927. Order was restored, and the industry prospered. But the broadcasters had made an important concession to secure this saving intervention. The 1927 Act authorized them to *use* the channels, which belonged to the public, but not to *own* them. Broadcasters were thus simply the caretakers of the airwaves, a national resource.

Federal Communications Commission **www.** fcc.gov

The Act further stated that when a license was awarded, the standard of evaluation would be the *public interest, convenience, or necessity.* The Federal Radio Commission (FRC) was established to administer the provisions of the Act. This **trustee model** of regulation is based on two premises (Bittner, 1994). The first is the philosophy of **spectrum scarcity.** Because broadcast spectrum space is limited and not everyone who wants to broadcast can, those who are granted licenses to serve a local area must accept regulation. The second reason for regulation revolves around the issue of influence. Broadcasting reaches virtually everyone in society. By definition, this ensures its power.

The Communications Act of 1934 replaced the 1927 legislation, substituting the Federal Communications Commission (FCC) for the FRC and cementing its regulatory authority, which continues today.

ADVERTISING AND THE NETWORKS

While the regulatory structure of the medium was evolving, so were its financial bases. The formation of RCA had ensured that radio would be a commercial, profit-based system. The industry supported itself through the sale of receivers; that is, it operated radio stations in order to sell radios. The problem was that once everybody had a radio, people would stop buying them. The solution was advertising. On August 22, 1922, New York station WEAF accepted the first radio commercial, a 10-minute spot for Long Island brownstone apartments. The cost of the ad was $50.

The sale of advertising led to establishment of the national radio networks. Groups of stations, or **affiliates,** could deliver larger audiences, realizing greater advertising revenues, which would allow them to hire bigger stars and produce better programming, which would attract larger audiences, which could be sold for even greater fees to advertisers. RCA set up a 24-station network, the National Broadcasting Company (NBC), in 1926. A year later it bought AT&T's stations and launched a second network, NBC Blue (the original NBC was renamed NBC Red). The Columbia Broadcasting System (CBS) was also founded in 1927, but it struggled until 26-year-old millionaire cigar maker William S. Paley bought it in 1928, making it a worthy competitor to NBC. The fourth network, Mutual, was established in 1934 largely on the strength of its hit Western, *The Lone Ranger.* Four midwestern and eastern stations came together to sell advertising on it and other shows; soon Mutual had 60 affiliates. Mutual differed from the other major national networks in that it did not own and operate its own flagship stations (called **O&O**s, for owned and operated). By 1938 the four national networks had affiliated virtually all the large U.S. stations and the majority of smaller operations as well. These corporations grew so powerful that in 1943 the government forced NBC to divest itself of one of its networks. It sold NBC Blue to Life Saver candy maker Edward Noble, who renamed it the American Broadcasting Company (ABC).

The fundamental basis of broadcasting in the United States was set:

- Radio broadcasters were private, commercially owned enterprises, rather than government operations.
- Governmental regulation was based on the public interest.
- Stations were licensed to serve specific localities, but national networks programmed the most lucrative hours with the largest audiences.
- Entertainment and information were the basic broadcast content.
- Advertising formed the basis of financial support for broadcasting.

THE GOLDEN AGE

The networks ushered in radio's golden age. Although the 1929–1939 Great Depression damaged the phonograph industry, with sales dipping to as few as 6 million records in 1932, it helped boost radio. Phonographs and records cost money, but once a family bought a radio, a whole world of entertainment and information was at its disposal, free of charge. The number of homes with radios grew from 12 million in 1930 to 30 million in 1940, and half of them had not one but two receivers. Ad revenues rose from $40 million to $155 million over the same period. Between them, the four national networks broadcast 156 hours of network-originated programming a week. New genres became fixtures during this period: comedy *(The Jack Benny Show, Fibber McGee and Molly)*, audience participation *(Professor Quiz, Truth or Consequences, Kay Kyser's Kollege of Musical Knowledge)*, children's shows *(Little Orphan Annie, The Lone Ranger)*, soap operas *(Oxydol's Ma Perkins, The Guiding Light)*, and drama (Orson Welles's *Mercury Theater of the Air*). News, too, became a radio staple. Prior to the 1933 **Biltmore agreement,** newspapers, fearing competition from the powerful new medium, refused to make their stories available to radio stations, and many would not carry radio schedules. The Biltmore agreement settled the war, limiting radio to brief news reports at specific, limited times of the day, ensuring the dominance of newspapers as a journalistic medium. Still, news had come to the airwaves.

Radio and Sound Recording in World War II The golden age of radio shone even more brightly after Pearl Harbor was bombed by the Japanese in 1941, propelling the United States into World War II. Radio was used to sell war bonds, and much content was aimed at boosting the nation's morale. The war increased the desire for news, especially from abroad. The war also caused a paper shortage, reducing advertising space in newspapers. No new stations were licensed during the war years, and the 950 existing broadcasters reaped all the broadcast advertising revenues, as well as additional ad revenues that otherwise would have gone to newspapers. Ad revenues were up to $310 million by the end of World War II in 1945.

Sound recording benefited from the war as well. Prior to World War II, recording in the United States was done either directly to master metal disc or on wire recorders, literally magnetic recording on metal wire. But GIs brought a new technology back from occupied Germany, a tape recorder that used an easily handled plastic tape on a reel. In 1947, Columbia Records introduced a new $33\frac{1}{3}$ rpm (rotations-per-minute) long-playing plastic record perfected by Peter Goldmark. A big advance over the previous standard of 78 rpm, it was more durable than the older shellac discs and played for 23 rather than $3\frac{1}{2}$ minutes. Columbia offered the technology free to all other record companies. RCA refused the offer, introducing its own 45 rpm disc in 1948. It played for only $3\frac{1}{3}$ minutes and had a huge center hole requiring a special adapter. Still, RCA persisted in its marketing, causing a speed war that was settled in 1950 when the two giants compromised on $33\frac{1}{3}$ as the standard for classical music and 45 as the standard for pop. And it was the 45, the single, that sustained the music business until the mid-1960s, when the Beatles not only ushered in the "British invasion" of rock 'n' roll but also transformed popular music into a $33\frac{1}{3}$ album-dominant cultural force, shaping today's popular music and helping reinvent radio.

Television Arrives When the war ended and radio licenses were granted again, the number of stations grew rapidly to 2,000. Annual ad revenues

George Burns and Gracie Allen were CBS comedy stars during radio's Golden Age. They were among the many radio performers to move easily and successfully to television.

reached $454 million in 1950. Then came television. Network affiliation dropped from 97% in 1945 to 50% by the mid-1950s, as stations "went local" in the face of television's national dominance. National radio advertising income dipped to $35 million in 1960, the year that television found its way into 90% of U.S. homes. If radio were to survive, it would have to find new functions.

Radio and Its Audiences

Radio has more than survived; it has prospered by changing the nature of its relationship with its audiences. The easiest way to understand this is to see pretelevision radio as television is today—nationally oriented, broadcasting an array of recognizable entertainment program formats, populated by well-known stars and personalities, and consumed primarily in the home, typically with people sitting around the set. Posttelevision radio is local, fragmented, specialized, personal, and mobile. Whereas pretelevision radio was characterized by the big national networks, today's radio is dominated by formats, a particular sound characteristic of a local station.

Who are the people who make up radio's audience? In an average week, 226 million people, 95% of all Americans 12 and over, will listen to the radio. Between the weekday hours of 6:00 and 10:00 a.m., 81% of all 12-year-olds and older will tune in. The majority of Americans, 60%, get their first news of the day from radio, and the large majority of all listening, 83%, occurs in cars (Arbitron, 2002).

Radio's audience, though, is not growing. In fact, it is declining. The annual *MTV Networks/Viacom Study of Media, Entertainment, and Leisure Time* released in June 2000 showed a sharp decline from the previous year's level of listening among teens and young adults ("Poll says," 2000). Radio industry data also indicate a steady decline in listenership. In 1989, 17.5% of the population listened regularly to commercial radio. Today, the proportion is 15.4% (Fonda, 2003). Overall time spent listening to radio decreased 9% between 1993 and 1999, or approximately 2 hours a week (Rathburn, 2000). The primary factors in this loss of audience, according to the industry itself, are the availability of online music, listener dissatisfaction with unimaginative programming ("McRadio" to critics), and hypercommercialization—on average about 12 minutes of commercials an hour for a typical station, a 6% increase between 1998 and 1999 alone (Rathburn, 2000).

Scope and Nature of the Radio Industry

There are 13,012 radio stations operating in the United States today: 4,727 commercial AM stations; 6,051 commercial FM stations; and 2,234 noncommercial FM stations.

There are two radios for every person in the United States. The industry as a whole sells more than $22 billion a year of ad time (*International Marketing Data and Statistics*, 2002).

FM, AM, AND NONCOMMERCIAL RADIO

Although FMs constitute only 56% of all commercial stations (to AMs' 44%), they attract many more listeners. This has to do with the technology behind each. The FM (frequency modulation) signal is wider, allowing the broadcast not only of stereo but also of better fidelity to the original sound than the narrower AM (amplitude modulation) signal. As a result, people attracted to music, a radio staple, gravitate toward FM. People favoring news, sports, and information tend to find themselves listening to the AM dial. AM signals travel farther than FM signals, making them perfect for rural parts of the country. But rural areas tend to be less heavily populated, and most AM stations serve fewer listeners. The FCC approved stereo AM in 1985, but relatively few people have AM stereo receivers. There seems to be little demand for news, sports, and information in stereo.

FM came about as a result of the work begun in 1923 by inventor-innovator Edwin Armstrong. By 1935 Armstrong was demonstrating his technology, as well as stereo radio, to his financial benefactor, RCA's David Sarnoff. But RCA rejected this potential competitor to its AM domain to focus on television instead. So Armstrong turned to GE, and together they put the first FM station, W2XMN, on the air in 1939.

In 1961, in an attempt to help FM compete more strongly with AM, the FCC approved FM stereo broadcasts. In 1962 it imposed a partial freeze on the allocation of new AM licenses, making the freeze permanent in 1968. And from 1963 to 1967 the FCC put its **nonduplication rule** into action. Until that time, most FMs were part of **AM/FM combos,** wherein two stations simultaneously broadcast identical content. The AM licensees were content just to keep the FM stations out of the hands of potential competitors. Under the nonduplication rules, holders of an AM and an FM license in the same market were forced to broadcast different content at least 50% of the time. The AMs were already successful, so the content was changed on the FMs, typically to rock 'n' roll, which attracted a growing audience of portable transistor radio listeners. In 1945 there were 50 FM stations on the air; in 1960 there were 785; in 1965 there were 1,300. By the mid-1970s FM had 70% of the audience and 70% of radio ad revenues. Today more than 75% of the total radio audience listens to FM radio.

Many of the stations audiences tune in to are noncommercial—that is, they accept no advertising. When the national frequency allocation plan was established during the deliberations leading to the 1934 Communications Act, commercial radio broadcasters persuaded Congress that they alone could be trusted to develop this valuable medium. They promised to make time available for religious, children's, and other educational programming. No frequencies were set aside for noncommercial radio to fulfill these functions. At the insistence of critics who contended that the commercial broadcasters were not fulfilling their promise, in 1945 the FCC set aside all FM frequencies between 88.1 and 91.9 megahertz for noncommercial radio. Today these noncommercial stations not only provide local service but many also offer national network quality programming through affiliation with National Public Radio (NPR), Public Radio International (PRI), or through a number of smaller national networks, for example, Pacifica Radio.

National Public Radio
www.
npr.org

Public Radio International
www.
pri.org

Pacifica Radio
www.
pacifica.org

RADIO IS LOCAL

No longer able to compete with television for the national audience in the 1950s, radio began to attract a local audience. Because it costs much more to run a local television station than a local radio station, advertising rates on radio tend to be much lower than on television. Local advertisers can afford radio more easily than they can television, which increases the local flavor of radio.

RADIO IS FRAGMENTED

Radio stations are widely distributed throughout the United States. Virtually every town—even those with only a few hundred residents—has at least one station. The number of stations licensed in an area is a function of both population and proximity to other towns. Tiny Long Beach, Mississippi, has one FM station. White Bluff, Texas, has one AM station. Chicago has 19 AMs and 30 FMs, and New York City has 17 AM and 28 FM stations. This fragmentation—many stations serving many areas—makes possible contemporary radio's most important characteristic, its ability to specialize.

RADIO IS SPECIALIZED

When radio became a local medium, it could no longer program the expensive, star-filled genres of its golden age. The problem now was how to program a station with interesting content and do so economically. A disc jockey playing records was the best solution. But stations soon learned that a highly specialized, specific audience of particular interest to certain advertisers could be attracted with specific types of music. **Format** radio was born. Of course, choosing a specific format means accepting that many potential listeners will not tune in. But in format radio the size of the audience is secondary to its composition.

Broadcasting & Cable Yearbook annually recognizes about 90 different formats, from the most common, which include Country, Top 40, Album-Oriented Rock, and All Talk, to the somewhat uncommon, for example, Ukrainian and Bluegrass. Many stations, especially those in rural areas, offer **secondary services** (formats). For example, a country station may broadcast a religious format for 10 hours on Saturday and Sunday.

Format radio offers stations many advantages beyond low-cost operations and specialized audiences that appeal to advertisers. Faced with falling listenership or declining advertising revenues, a station can simply change deejays and discs. Neither television nor the print media have this content flexibility. When confronted with competition from a station with a similar format, a station can further narrow its audience by specializing its formula even more. Many mid-size and large markets have Album-Oriented Rock (AOR), Hard Rock, Alternative Rock, Classic Rock, Heavy Metal, and Soft Rock stations. There are Country, Contemporary Country, Outlaw Country, Album Country, Spanish Country, and Young Country (YC) stations.

Music format radio requires a disc jockey. Someone has to spin the discs and provide the talk. The modern DJ is the invention of Todd Storz, who bought KOHW in Omaha, Nebraska, in 1949. He turned the radio personality/music formula on its head. Before Storz, radio announcers would talk most of the time and occasionally play music to rest their voices. Storz wanted more music, less talk. He thought radio should sound like a jukebox—the same few songs people wanted to hear played over and over again. His Top 40 format, which demanded strict adherence to a **playlist** (a predetermined sequence of selected records) of popular music for young people, up-tempo pacing, and catchy production gimmicks, became the standard for the posttelevision popular music station. Gordon McLendon of KLIF in Dallas refined the Top 40 format and developed others, such as Beautiful Music, and is therefore often considered, along with Storz, one of the two pioneers of format radio.

Fans debate whether Todd Storz or Gordon McClendon first invented the DJ. But there is no dispute that Alan Freed, first in Cleveland and then in New York, established the DJ as a star. Freed, here in a 1958 photo, is credited with introducing America's White teenagers to rhythm 'n' blues artists like Chuck Berry and Little Richard, and ushering in the age of rock 'n' roll.

RADIO IS PERSONAL

With the advent of television, the relationship of radio and its audience changed. Whereas families had gathered around the radio set to listen together, we now listen to the radio alone. We select personally pleasing formats, and we listen as an adjunct to other personally important activities. Radio personalities talk to us personally as well. They play our requests, wish us happy birthday, and play contests with us.

RADIO IS MOBILE

The mobility of radio accounts in large part for its personal nature. We can listen anywhere, at any time. We listen at work, while exercising, while sitting in the sun. By 1947 the combined sale of car and alarm clock radios exceeded that of traditional living-room receivers, and in 1951 the annual production of car radios exceeded that of home receivers for the first time. It has continued to do so every year since.

For more information on this topic, view *Radio: Inside WKNE-FM*, #3 on the CD *Media Tours*.

The Business of Radio

The distinctive characteristics of radio serve its listeners, but they also make radio a thriving business.

RADIO AS AN ADVERTISING MEDIUM

Advertisers enjoy the specialization of radio because it gives them access to homogeneous groups of listeners to whom products can be pitched. Since the entrenchment of specialized formats, there has not been a year in which annual **billings**—dollars earned from the sale of airtime—have declined. Advertisers buy local time (80% of all billings), national spots (for example, Prestone Antifreeze buys time on several thousand stations in winter areas), and network time. The cost of time is based on the ratings, an often controversial reality in radio (see the box "Problems with Radio Ratings").

Arbitron
www.
arbitron.com

Radio is an attractive advertising medium for reasons other than its delivery of a homogeneous audience. Radio ads are inexpensive to produce and therefore can be changed, updated, and specialized to meet specific audience demands. Ads can also be specialized to different times of the day. For example, a hamburger restaurant may have one version of its commercial for the morning audience, in which its breakfast menu is touted, and a different version for the evening audience driving home, dreading the thought of cooking dinner. Radio time is inexpensive to buy, especially when compared with television. An audience loyal to a specific format station is presumably loyal to those who advertise on it. Radio is the listeners' friend; it travels with them and talks to them personally.

DEREGULATION AND OWNERSHIP

The business of radio is being altered by deregulation and changes in ownership rules. To ensure that there were many different perspectives in the cultural forum, the FCC had long limited the number of radio stations one person or company could own to one AM and one FM locally and seven AMs and seven FMs nationally. These numbers were revised upward in the late 1980s, and controls were almost totally eliminated by the Telecommunications Act of 1996. Now, thanks to this **deregulation** there are no national ownership limits, and one person or company can own as many as eight stations in one market, depending on the size of the market. This situation has allowed **duopoly**—one person or company owning and managing multiple radio stations in a single market—to explode. Since the passage of the 1996 Act, more than 10,000 radio stations have been sold, and there are now 1,100 fewer station owners, a 30% decline. The vast majority of these sales have been to already large radio groups such as Clear Channel, Infinity, and Cox. Clear Channel alone owns 1,240 stations. As a result, in 25 of the 50 largest radio markets, three companies claim 80% of all listeners (W. Baker, 2002). All of Boston's 15 FMs and 14 of Seattle's 17 FMs, for example, are owned by only four companies (compared with Toronto, Canada's, 12 FMs, each with different ownership).

John Lennon could imagine a world at peace. Apparently, Clear Channel could not.

This concentration is a source of concern for many radio professionals. Local public affairs shows now make up less than one-half of one percent of all commercial broadcast time in this country. Thirty-five percent of all commercial stations have no local news, and 25% have no local public affairs programming at all (FAIR, 2000). The American Federation of Television and Radio Artists has charged that giant group owners such as Clear Channel have "forever transformed and destroyed the radio and recording industries" (quoted in McConnell, 2002b, p. 34). In fact, Clear Channel was the subject of both Congressional and criminal investigations in 2002 for alleged antitrust practices such as refusing to air the music of artists who are not represented by its concert tour division (Albiniak, 2002a) and for engaging in "de facto payola" (McConnell, 2002a). And it was Clear Channel that became the subject of national derision for having instructed its more than 1,200 stations to stop playing some 162 songs—including music such as the Beatles' "Ob-La-Di, Ob-La-Da" and "Ticket to Ride," John Lennon's "Imagine," Frank Sinatra's "New York, New York," Neil Diamond's "America," Don McLean's "American Pie," and all

Problems with Radio Ratings

Once radio became an advertising-based medium, some way was needed to count listeners so advertising rates could be set. The first rating system, the Crossleys, was begun in 1930 at the behest of the Association of National Advertisers, a group suspicious of broadcasters' own self-serving, exaggerated reports of audience size. Within 10 years, Hooper and Pulse were also offering radio ratings. All used random telephone calls, a method that ignored certain segments of the population (the rich and the poor, for example) and that could not accurately tap mobile use of the medium (such as listening in the car). In 1949 these companies and their methods were replaced by the American Research Bureau, later renamed Arbitron.

Arbitron mails diaries to willing listeners in every local market in the country and asks them to note what they listen to every 15 minutes for a period of one week. Arbitron reports:

- **Average quarter-hour:** the number of people listening to a station in each 15-minute segment
- **Cume:** the cumulative audience or number of people listening to a station for at least 5 minutes in any one day
- **Rating:** the percentage of the total population of a market reached
- **Share:** the percentage of people listening to radio who are tuned in to a particular station

These measures are sophisticated, but the use of diaries incurs some problems. Lying is one; forgetting is another. Uneven diary return rates among different types of audiences is a third. Yet advertisers and radio stations need some standard measure of listenership to set rates. Therefore, the ratings—flaws and all—are accepted as the final word, and both ratings service and broadcasters profit from their use.

As soon as a medium encounters a dip in audience numbers, however, the ratings come under scrutiny and are blamed for the problem. This was the case for radio, and it is the case for television, as you'll see echoed in Chapter 8.

When it first began losing audience to television, radio tried to ignore the problem. The cover from the August 12, 1953, issue of *Broadcasting/Telecasting* vividly demonstrates this technique—the medium is said to be as strong as ever, as central to people's lives as always. But there was no ignoring the continuing and growing loss of listeners. At the September 17 meeting of the NBC Radio Affiliates in Chicago, and after 15 years of using the ratings to make huge profits, new NBC President David Sarnoff (1953) offered this analysis of the dramatic drop in radio listenership:

> Our industry from the outset has been plagued by rating systems which do not say what they mean and do not mean what they say. They develop figures which give an appearance of precision, even unto decimal points, until you read the fine print.
>
> Unhappily these figures are seized upon by the advertising community as a substitute for analysis and judgment. They are used as the main standard for advertising values in broadcasting, and millions of dollars are spent or withheld each year on the basis of a drop or rise of a few ratings points! . . . Ratings, today, simply do not reflect the *real* audience. (p. 108)

The problem, in other words, was not the television-fueled exodus of millions of listeners—it was the ratings!

The Iowa radio station that bought space on the cover of the industry's "bible," Broadcasting/Telecasting, *wanted readers to believe all was well in radio-land in 1953.*

Rage Against the Machine songs—in the aftermath of the September 11 terrorist attack on America for fear of offending listeners.

As radio executive William O'Shaughnessy wrote, "Independent voices are being replaced by cookie-cutter cacophony of the same old music, often accompanied by vulgar, outrageous, and tasteless stunts. The old-time local broadcaster is being replaced by 'asset managers' beholden to corporate masters a whole continent away" (2003, p. 36). The resulting sound has "much higher commercial loads and not as much programming innovation," according to radio industry analyst Thom Moon (as quoted in Kiesewetter, 2000, p. E1)—prime factors, as we've seen, in the drop-off in radio's audience.

Scope and Nature of the Recording Industry

When the DJs and Top 40 formats saved radio in the 1950s, they also changed for all time popular music and, by extension, the recording industry. Disc jockeys were color-deaf in their selection of records. They introduced record buyers to rhythm 'n' blues in the music of African American artists such as Chuck Berry and Little Richard. Until the mid-1950s the work of these performers had to be **covered**—rerecorded by White artists such as Perry Como—before it was aired. Teens loved the new sound, however, and it became the foundation of their own subculture, as well as the basis for the explosion in recorded music. See the box "Rock 'n' Roll, Radio, and Race Relations" for more on rock's roots.

Today more than 5,000 U.S. companies are annually selling 1.15 billion tapes and discs of recorded music (worth $12.3 billion in 2002) on more than 2,600 labels. More than 60,000 stores sell recorded music, and U.S. customers annually buy one-third of the world's recorded music. See Figure 7.1 for an idea of what types of music are most popular.

THE MAJOR RECORDING COMPANIES

Five major recording companies control nearly 90% of the recorded music market in the United States. Each is part of a larger conglomeration of media and other businesses, and all but one are foreign owned:

- **Sony** is a Japanese-owned electronics conglomerate releasing music on labels such as Columbia and Epic.
- **BMG** is owned by Germany's Bertlesmann and has labels such as RCA and Arista.
- **Universal Music Group** is owned by Canadian/French conglomerate Vivendi Universal and controls labels such as MCA.
- **Warner Brothers Music Group,** owned by U.S. media giant AOL Time Warner, releases music on labels such as Atlantic, Electra, and Warner Brothers.
- **EMI Records** is owned by England's EMI Group and owns labels such as BMI, Capitol, and Def Jam Records.

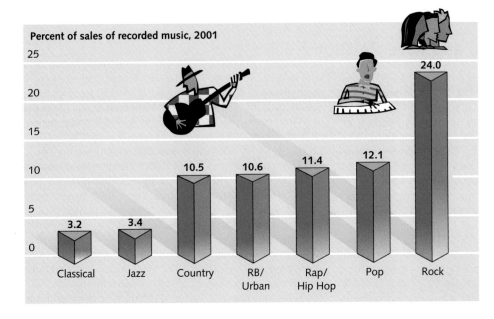

Percent of sales of recorded music, 2001

Classical	Jazz	Country	RB/Urban	Rap/Hip Hop	Pop	Rock
3.2	3.4	10.5	10.6	11.4	12.1	24.0

Figure 7.1 Sales of Recorded Music by Type, 2001. *Source:* Record Industry Association of America; www.riaa.com

Critics voice concern over conglomeration and internationalization in the music business, a concern that centers on the traditional cultural value of music, especially for young people. Multibillion-dollar conglomerates typically are not rebellious in their cultural tastes, nor are they usually willing to take risks on new ideas. These duties have fallen primarily to the independent labels, companies such as Real World Records and IRS. Still, problems with the music industry–audience relationship remain.

Cultural homogenization is the worrisome outcome of virtually all the world's influential recording being controlled by a few profit-oriented giants. If bands or artists cannot immediately deliver the goods, they aren't signed. So derivative artists and manufactured groups dominate, for example, Britney Spears, and 'N Sync. In fact, when Universal bought Polygram in 1998, it immediately announced that it would drop 250 artists from both companies' lists to focus on teen pop bands such as the Backstreet Boys. Epic Records' Harvey Leeds, senior vice president of artist development, explained, "The days of developing a band are gone. They're manufactured, not developed on the street. Instead of 'There's a new band that's huge in Gainesville, we'd better pay attention,' today they're created in a laboratory" (as cited in Waller, 2000, p. 1).

The *dominance of profit over artistry* worries many music fans. When a major label must spend millions to sign a bankable group such as R.E.M. ($80 million), Mariah Carey ($80 million) or Whitney Houston ($100 million), it typically pares lesser-known, potentially more innovative artists from its roster. EMI, for example, dropped 400 artists from its various labels in early 2002 in order to come up with the $57 million, five-album deal it thought it needed to keep British pop star Robbie Williams from defecting to another company. Critics fear that the tenuous relationship that "minor" artists have with their conglomerated labels leads to *infringement of artistic*

Rock 'n' Roll, Radio, and Race Relations

After World War II African Americans in the United States refused to remain invisible. Having fought in segregated units in Europe and proven their willingness to fight and die for freedom abroad, they openly demanded freedom at home. Some Whites began to listen. President Harry Truman, recognizing the absurdity of racial separation in the self-proclaimed "greatest democracy on earth," desegregated the armed forces by executive order in 1948. These early stirrings of equality led to a sense among African Americans that anything was possible, and that feeling seeped into their music. What had been called *cat, sepia,* or *race music* took on a new tone. While this new sound borrowed from traditional Black music—gospel, blues, and sad laments over slavery and racial injustice—it was different, much different. Rock historian Ian Whitcomb called it music about "gettin' loaded, wantin' a bow-legged woman, and rockin' all night long" (1972, p. 212). Music historian Ed Ward said that this bolder, more aggressive music "spoke to a shared experience, not just to Black (usually rural Black) life," and it would become the "truly biracial popular music in this country" (Ward, Stokes, & Tucker, 1986, p. 83).

But before this new music could begin its assault on the cultural walls that divided Americans, it needed a new name (so as to differentiate itself from older forms of race music and to appear "less Black" to White listeners). Hundreds of small independent record companies sprang up to produce this newly labeled rhythm and blues (R&B), music focusing on Americans' shared experience, and sex and alcohol were part of life for people of all colors. Songs such as Wynonie Harris's "Good Rockin' Tonight," Amos Milburn's "Chicken Shack Boogie," Stick McGhee's "Drinkin' Wine, Spo-De-O-Dee," and Wild Bill Moore's "We're Gonna Rock, We're Gonna Roll" (a song not about dancing) were, for their time, startlingly open in their celebration of sex (not to be confused with love) and drink. With its earthy lyrics and thumping dance beat, R&B very quickly found an audience in the 1950s, one composed largely of urban Blacks (growing in number as African Americans increasingly fled the South) and White teenagers.

The major record companies took notice, and rather than sign already successful R&B artists, they had their White artists cover the Black hits. The Penguins' "Earth Angel" was covered by the reassuringly named Crew Cuts, who also covered the Chords' "Sh-Boom." The McGuire Sisters covered the Spaniels' "Goodnight Sweetheart, Well It's Time to Go." Chuck Berry's "Maybellene" was covered by both the Johnny Long and Ralph Marterie Orchestras. Even Bill Haley and the Comets' youth anthem "Shake, Rattle and Roll" was a cover of a Joe Turner tune.

But these covers actually served to introduce even more White teens to the new music, and these kids demanded the original versions. This did not escape the attention of Sam Phillips, who in 1952 founded Sun Records in an effort to bring Black music to White kids ("If I could find a White man who had the Negro sound, I could make a billion dollars," he is reported to have mused; "Why Elvis," 2002, p. 9). In 1954 he found that man: Elvis Presley.

The situation also caught the attention of Cleveland DJ Alan Freed, whose nationally distributed radio (and later television) show featured Black R&B tunes, never covers. Freed began calling the music he played rock 'n' roll (to signify that it was Black *and* White youth music), and by 1955, when Freed took his show to New York, the cover business was dead. Black performers were recording and releasing their own music to a national audience, and people of all colors were tuning in.

Now that the kids had a music of their own, and now that a growing number of radio stations were willing to program it, a youth culture began to develop, one that was antagonistic toward their parents' culture. The music was central to this antagonism, not only because it was gritty and nasty but also because it exposed the hypocrisy of adult culture. Nowhere was this more apparent than in Freed's 1953 rock 'n' roll concert at the Cleveland Arena. Although Cleveland was a segregated city, Freed opened the 9,000-seat venue to all the fans of his *Moondog's Rock and Roll Party* radio show. A racially mixed crowd of more than 18,000 teens showed up, forcing the cancellation of the concert. But the kids partied. They sang. They cheered. Not a single one asked for a refund. They had come—Black kids and White kids—to celebrate *their* music, *their* culture.

For young people of the mid-1950s and 1960s, the music of Little Richard, Fats Domino, Ray Charles, and Chuck Berry made a lie of all that their parents, teachers, and government leaders had said about race, the inferiority of African Americans, and Blacks' satisfaction with the status quo. As social critic Robert Pielke wrote,

A different and conflicting set of fundamental values was introduced into American culture, acquainting white adolescents with the black side of America in the process. But more important than even this was the fact of communication itself: the years of slavery and segregation had made it virtually impossible for the races to communicate honestly face to face. Now, for the first time in American history, whites were authentically hearing what blacks were saying. . . . To be more accurate, it was principally white youth who were doing the listening.

Prejudice, ignorance, superstition, hatred, and fear can only exist in the absence of genuine communication. . . . I don't mean to give the impression that white adolescents,

The music of Chuck Berry, Bo Diddley, and Little Richard may have been covered by White performers, but its passion and soul soon attracted young listeners of all races, making a lie of their parents' racial intolerance.

en masse bought into black culture. Hardly . . . [But] what was really significant was the fact that they were truly listening. It shouldn't seem so strange, then, that it was precisely this generation that found itself uncomfortable with the whole ideology of racism and all its attendant beliefs. Not that racism immediately came to an end with the listening to black music. Far from it. But white youth could no longer feel secure with the attitudes bequeathed to them; they now knew too much. (1986, p. 87)

Ralph Bass, a producer for independent R&B label Chess Records, described the evolution to historian David Szatmary. When he was touring with Chess's R&B groups in the early 1950s, "they didn't let whites into the clubs. Then they got 'white spectator tickets' for the worst corner of the joint. They had to keep the white kids out, so they'd have white nights sometimes, or they'd put a rope across the middle of the floor. The blacks on one side, the whites on the other, digging how the blacks were dancing and copying them. Then, hell, the rope would come down, and they'd all be dancing together. Salt and pepper all mixed together" (Szatmary, 2000, p. 21).

R&B and rock 'n' roll did not end racism. But the music made a difference, one that would eventually make it possible for Americans who wanted to do so to free themselves of racism's ugly hold. Rock music (and the radio stations that played it) would again nudge the nation toward its better tendencies during the antiwar and civil rights movements of the late 1960s. And it is against this backdrop, a history of popular music making as real a difference as any piece of official legislation, that contemporary critics lament the homogenizing of popular music (see page 213). Music can and has made a difference. Can and will it ever again? they ask.

What band has sold the most albums in the United States? The Beatles, 106 million albums.

Who is the top solo artist? Garth Brooks, 89 million albums

Who has the fastest-selling album in U.S. history? 'N Sync, *No Strings Attached* sold 2.4 million discs in its first week of release.

Who recorded the single biggest-selling album of the twentieth century? The Eagles, *Their Greatest Hits 1971–1975*, 26 million albums.

Source: Recording Industry Association of America, <http://www.riaa.com/Gold-Intro.cfm>, October 1, 2000.

freedom. Said Phyllis Pollack, press agent for rap groups such as NWA and Geto Boys, "It's like we almost have a McCarthyism in the business. But the censorship isn't new; what's new is the fear and the compliance going on to this extent. And I think a lot of artists go along with it because they're afraid of being lost in the corporate shuffle and falling out of favor with their labels" (quoted in Strauss, 2000, p. 5G).

Critics and industry people alike see the ascendance of profits over artistry as a problem for the industry itself, as well as for the music and its listeners. The industry released 14% fewer titles in 2002 than it did in 1999, and sales dropped 31%—a $2 billion loss—in that span (Kava, 2003; Harper, 2003), but what kept the red ink from flowing even faster was strong sales in **catalogue albums** (more than 30% of all discs sold), albums more than 3 years old. **Recent catalogue albums,** that is, those that have been out for 15 months to 3 years, have plunged more than 20%. Tower Records' sales manager Bob Feterl explains, "Catalogue is built on the Beatles, Bob Marley, Miles Davis, John Coltrane—music that will sell forever. How many albums in the past 15 months will be like that? I'm not sure the industry is developing careers, giving artists three or four albums to grow." Bertis Downs, R.E.M.'s manager, adds, "Our first hit record was really on our fifth album (the 1987 hit "The One I Love" on *Document*). We had the luxury of growing up, of incubating and maturing. I don't know that that's really possible anymore" (both quotes in Boucher, 1999, p. 12E).

Promotion overshadows the music, say the critics. If groups or artists don't come across well on MTV or otherwise are a challenge to promote (for example, they do not fit an easily recognizable niche), they aren't signed. Again, the solution is to create marketable artists from scratch, such as 'N Sync and the Backstreet Boys. Promoting tours is also an issue. If bands or artists do not have corporate sponsorship for their tours, there is no tour. If musicians do not tour, they cannot create an enthusiastic fan base. But if they do not have an enthusiastic fan base, they cannot attract the corporate sponsorship necessary to mount a tour. This makes radio even more important for the introduction of new artists and forms of music, but radio, too, is increasingly driven by profit-maximizing format narrowing and therefore dependent on the major labels' definition of playable artists. This situation led radio critic Brad Kava (1996, p. 22) to call today's DJs and program directors "little more than trained monkeys working for the record companies" because of their penchant for playing only those artists behind whom the big companies have put their full promotional weight.

Trends and Convergence in Radio and Sound Recording

Emerging and changing technologies have affected the production and distribution aspects of both radio and sound recording.

Album Warning Labels: Child Protection or Censorship?

An FTC report on the effectiveness of the entertainment industries' various content ratings systems thrust the issue of album warning labels into the public forum in late 2000. President Clinton ordered the study after the killings at Columbine High School in April 1999, and what the FTC found angered parents and politicians while putting media industry executives on the defensive. Record company leaders were hard pressed to explain why the marketing plans for 27% of the albums carrying warning labels that the FTC studied spoke of reaching the "12–34 [year old] market" (Lohse, 2000b).

The report stated that data such as these "undermine the credibility" of record industry self-regulation and "frustrate parents' attempts to make informed decisions about their children's exposure" to offensive or objectionable content (Lohse, 2000b, p. 10A). Syndicated columnist Ellen Goodman was more blunt, noting that the people who produce and sell albums "deliberately executed an end run around parents to market no-nos to kids" (2000, p. 10B).

Once again in the public forum, what had become known as Tipper Stickers, the product of a group known as the Parents' Music Resource Center (PMRC), were under renewed scrutiny. The PMRC was founded in 1985 by the wives of several prominent Washington politicians. Most visible were Tipper Gore, wife of then Senator Al Gore, and Susan Baker, wife of Ronald Reagan's Secretary of State, James Baker. The PMRC's particular concern was the danger posed to young people by heavy metal and rap music. In newspaper essays, television and radio talk shows, and congressional testimony, it argued that youths were being negatively affected by popular music lyrics centering on eroticism, homosexuality, sadism, sex, violence, and suicide. Teens, and even younger children, were particularly susceptible to these influences because of how they listened—repetitively and through headphones. Together, the PMRC claimed, this created "a direct, unfettered freeway straight to the mind" (Walser, 1993, p. 141).

Despite their calls for "cleaning up" rock and rap lyrics, PMRC leaders Gore and Baker remained committed to freedom of expression. "We are strong advocates of [the First Amendment and] its protection of free speech and free expression," they wrote. "We do not and have not advocated or supported restrictions on those rights. We have never proposed government action" (Rock Out Censorship, 1998).

The record industry's response to the PMRC, coming in 1990, mirrored that of the movie industry. It chose self-regulation and placed warning labels on the front of albums and CDs to alert buyers and listeners to the presence of potentially offensive lyrics.

Although endorsed by the music industry's umbrella organization (the Record Industry Association of America) and the PMRC, and sufficient to forestall even the most unobtrusive federal legislation, the labels remained controversial even before the FTC report was issued. One reason resides in rap and rock's particular role in the culture. An editorial in *Rolling Stone* argued:

> Viewed in the context of the past 30 years, these activities can be seen as just another attempt to muzzle rock 'n' roll by people who neither like the music nor understand it. As a vital and often raw form of expression, rock tends to dance on the outer edge of what society finds acceptable. It always has. We must make sure that it always does. (Rock Out Censorship, 1998)

A second reason for the controversy surrounding the stickers is the suspicion that labeling will lead to other, more restrictive control. The Web pages of Rock Out Censorship (ROC) (http://www.theroc.org) offer the

THE IMPACT OF TELEVISION

We have seen how television fundamentally altered radio's structure and relationship with its audiences. Television, specifically cable channel MTV, changed the recording industry too. MTV's introduction in 1981 helped pull the industry out of its disastrous 1979 slump. However, it altered the radio–record company relationship, and many hits are now introduced on MTV rather than on radio. In addition, the look of concerts has changed. No longer is it sufficient to pack an artist or group into a hall or stadium with a few thousand screaming fans. Now a concert must be an extravagant multimedia event approximating the sophistication of an MTV video.

A third reason is the simple rejection of censorship. *Chicago Tribune* columnist Clarence Page writes on the ROC Web site, "I think the republic will survive *Me So Horny*. Whether it will survive efforts by overzealous lawmakers to 'protect' us is less certain." On the same Web site, *New York Times* writer Tom Wicker comments, "States moving toward record labeling laws may protest that they are not trying to restrict artists or expression. But freedom of expression is surely diminished if the freedom to listen is limited."

Critics of the stickers have had their worst fears confirmed. Soon after labeling began, the state of Washington passed a restrictive Erotic Music Bill (which was immediately declared unconstitutional). The Pennsylvania House of Representatives debated a bill that would have outlawed the sale of stickered albums. Other states have taken up similar legislation. None has yet been successful, but in response to the FTC report detailing the record industry's abuse of its sticker-based rating system, several state and federal politicians, even many typically pro-business conservatives, called for greater government oversight of content.

Enter your voice in the cultural forum. Is there anything wrong with warning labels on albums such as Marilyn Manson's *Antichrist Superstar*, the discs of defiantly homophobic and misogynistic rapper Eminem, or the allegedly racist and violent works of many "gangsta rappers"? Shouldn't people be alerted to the presence of potentially troublesome material? Eminem's *The Marshall Mathers LP* disc sold over 1.5 million copies in its first week of release, making it the fastest-selling album in history by a solo artist. Stickers didn't hurt this White rapper's sales. But do labels encourage a form of self-censorship? Will artists intentionally limit what they write and sing to avoid a sticker that might hurt sales? Finally, how important is popular music as a cultural force? Does music deserve the same protections as other forms of media content?

Homophobic and misogynistic, Eminem's albums invariably receive warning labels. His defenders argue, however, that the rapper's albums—such as The Marshall Mathers LP—are stigmatized as much for their unpopular politics as for their raunchy lyrics.

warning of rocker John "Cougar" Mellencamp: "They've started with the pretense that it's sex and violence they're after. But in the long run they're going to start censoring anything political." And the funkadelic rhythm 'n' blues singer George Clinton adds:"Think! It ain't illegal yet!"

This means that fewer acts take to the road, changing the relationship between musicians and fans.

SATELLITE AND CABLE

The convergence of radio and satellite has aided the rebirth of the radio networks. Music and other forms of radio content can be distributed quite inexpensively to thousands of stations. As a result, one "network" can provide very different services to its very different affiliates. ABC, for example, maintains several different radio networks under its own name, as well as that of Disney and ESPN. Together, the ABC networks have 3,050 affiliate stations reaching an audience of 50 million listeners. Westwood One, which bought the NBC Radio network in 1987 and added it to its already large and varied networking and program **syndication** operations, counts among its affiliates 60% of all the commercial stations in the United States. The low cost of producing radio programming, however, makes the establishment of other, even more specialized networks possible. Satellites, too, make access to syndicated content and formats affordable for many stations. Syndicators can deliver news, top 10 shows, and other content to stations on a market-by-market basis. They can also provide entire formats, requiring local stations, if they wish, to do little more than insert commercials into what appears to listeners to be a local broadcast.

Satellite has another application as well. Many listeners now receive "radio" through their cable televisions in the form of satellite-delivered **DMX (Digital Music Express),** and the technology exists for direct satellite home and automobile delivery of audio by **digital audio radio service (DARS).** There are two U.S. DARS providers. XM Satellite Radio began national service in November 2001, and Sirius Satellite Radio's national service debuted in July 2002. Costing from $10 to $13 per month, each offers about 100 commercial-free digital channels, as well as standard AM and FM radio and shortwave communications in addition to DARS (Figure 7.2).

XM Radio
www.
xmradio.com

DIGITAL TECHNOLOGY

In the 1970s the basis of both the recording and radio industries changed from analog to **digital recording.** That is, sound went from being preserved

Figure 7.2 The operation of DARS provider XM Satellite Radio.

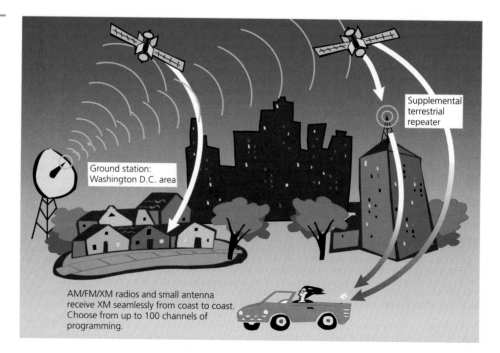

Ground station: Washington D.C. area

Supplemental terrestrial repeater

AM/FM/XM radios and small antenna receive XM seamlessly from coast to coast. Choose from up to 100 channels of programming.

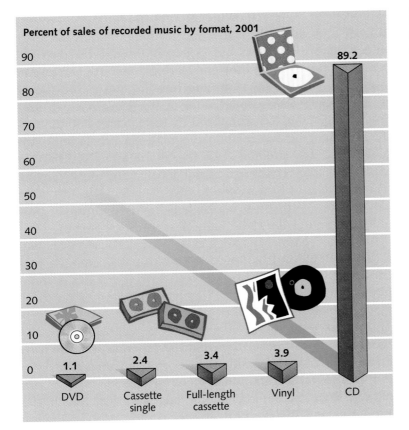

Percent of sales of recorded music by format, 2001

Format	Percent
DVD	1.1
Cassette single	2.4
Full-length cassette	3.4
Vinyl	3.9
CD	89.2

Figure 7.3 Sales of Recorded Music by Format, 2001. *Source:* Record Industry Association of America; www.riaa.com

as waves, whether physically on a disc or tape or through the air, to conversion into 1s and 0s logged in millisecond intervals in a computerized translation process. When replayed at the proper speed, the resulting sound was not only continuous but pristine—no hum, no hiss. The CD, or compact disc, was introduced in 1983 using digital coding on a 4.7 inch disc read by a laser beam. In 1986 *Brothers in Arms* by Dire Straits became the first million-selling CD. In 1988 the sale of CDs surpassed that of vinyl discs for the first time, and today CDs account for nearly 90% of all music sales (Figure 7.3).

Digital audio tape (DAT), introduced in the early 1970s, offers digital quality sound purity on minicassettes, not only to buyers of manufactured tapes but to home tapers as well. Although DAT tapes must be played on DAT recorders that cost about $1,000, the price of those machines is falling. DAT makes high-fidelity taping of complete digitally recorded albums on digitally broadcast radio stations and taping of borrowed CDs a threat to the recording industry's profits. At the insistence of the recording industry, the government kept DAT out of the United States for years after its development. In 1992 Congress passed a "taping tax," now 2%, on all sales of blank tapes, DAT and otherwise, that is to be paid to music rights holders to compensate for revenues ostensibly lost to home taping.

Convergence with computers and the Internet offers other challenges and opportunities to the radio and recording industries. The way the recording

Sirius Radio
www.
siriusradio

industry operates is likely to be altered by the Internet. Traditionally, a record company signs an artist, produces the artist's music, and promotes the artist and music through a variety of outlets but primarily through the distribution of music to radio stations. Then listeners, learning about the artist and music through radio, go to a record store and buy the music. But this is rapidly changing. David Schwartz, former editor of *Mix Magazine*, explains, "There is a seismic change going on stimulated by the Internet and the digital evolution that is changing the relationship between artists and consumers. For the first time in a hundred years (of recording) we are moving away from the idea of packaged goods to a model of delivering music directly to the consumer" (as quoted in Kava, 1999, p. 6E).

Today, the Internet and Web are increasingly being used for music promotion (potentially disrupting the radio station–recording company relationship) and distribution. Numerous sites exist at which users can buy recorded music. Music Boulevard (cdnow.com) and Amazon.com are two of the better known. With the appropriate software, users can sample music before they buy it.

Music Boulevard
www.
cdnow.com

In addition, as improvements in the Internet transmission of high-quality audio continue to come, these and similar sites will be used for the direct online digital release of music, recorded directly onto CD, DAT, or computer hard drives and disks, bypassing the record companies and radio stations altogether. An increasing number of performers themselves are using the Internet and Web to communicate directly with their fans in the production, promotion, and distribution of their music. Public Enemy became the first major musical act to release an album exclusively online. It joined with Atomic Pop (http://www.atomicpop.com) in April 1999 for the release of *There's a Poison Going On*. Downloads cost $10, significantly less than the $18 price in stores. Other big-name bands soon followed.

The Internet and the Future of the Recording Industry

MP3
www.
MP3.com

MP3 (for MPEG-1, Audio Layer 3) is compression software that shrinks audio files to less than a tenth of their original size. Originally developed in 1987 in Germany by computer scientist Dieter Seitzer at the University of Erlangen in conjunction with the Fraunhofer Institute Integrierte Schaltungen, it began to take off in the early 1990s as more users began to hook up to the Net with increasingly faster **modems.** This **open source software,** or freely downloaded software, permits users to download recorded music, and it is available at sites such as <http://www. MP3.com> and <http://www.MP3.box.sk>. So popular has MP3 become that in July 1999 it surpassed "sex" as the most frequently searched-for term on the Web and, in the first 6 months of that year, nearly 3 billion MP3 files were downloaded from the Net, or 17 million every day (Peraino, 1999). In addition to "brandless" MP3, users can access commercial versions of the software such as MusicMatch, which offers additional features such as selectable levels of audio quality, the capacity to turn music from home CDs into computer files, and compatibility with other audio streaming technology such as Liquid Audio, a2b, MS Audio, and G2. When RealNetworks (now Netster.com) made JukeBox available in May 1999, 350,000 users downloaded the software in $2\frac{1}{2}$ days, the fastest download of free software in Internet history (Quittner, 1999).

In either its open source or commercial format, MP3 is controversial, and the furor surrounding this convergence of digital and recording technologies is captured by the *New York Times'* Jon Pareles (1998):

> For Utopians, MP3 is a way to liberate music from the clutches of gatekeepers and profiteers, and perhpas to return music to its intangible essence. But the recording business sees MP3 as a Pandora's box of copyright destruction, unleashing anarchy and piracy while robbing musicians of royalties and record labels of capital.
>
> In effect, both sides are correct. There's bound to be serious legal scuffling between people who own copyrights and people who believe in the hacker credo that information wants to be free.
>
> Yet recorded music is considerably more than a corporate revenue source, and the implications of digital distribution go far beyond the particulars of software and gadgets and royalty collection. For listeners, music has never been about its physical form, but about what's in the grooves or magnetic particles or digital bits; it's the information, not the plastic. Digital distribution can turn that sentiment into a reality. And that shift could alter the way music is made, released, sold, stored, and valued. (p. 1, Section 2)

The crux of the problem for recording companies is that they sell music "in its physical form," whereas MP3 permits music's distribution in a nonphysical form. First conceived of as a means of allowing independent bands and musicians to post their music online where it might attract a following, MP3 became a headache for the recording industry when music from the name artists they controlled began appearing on MP3 sites, making **piracy,** the illegal recording and sale of copyrighted material and high-quality recordings, a relatively simple task. Not only could users listen to their downloaded music from their hard drives, but they could make their own CDs from MP3 files and play those discs wherever and whenever they wished. Matters were made even worse for the recording companies when manufacturers such as Diamond Multimedia introduced portable MP3 players, freeing downloaded music from users' computers. And as software such as Napster became popular, users could easily search for and retrieve individual songs and artists from one another's hard drives.

Rather than embrace MP3, the Recording Industry Association of America (RIAA), representing all of the United States' major labels, responded to the threat with a technological solution. But by the time the industry's "secure" technology was ready for release, it was too late—MP3 had become the technology of choice among digital audio fans. The RIAA went to court in January 2000, and it was victorious. Citing MP3.com's database of more than 80,000 albums, a federal judge in New York ruled that the primary application of MP3 was copying and distributing copyrighted material, not simply storing already purchased music. Soon after, the RIAA and MP3.com (the Net's primary distributor of MP3 files) reached a settlement in which the online company paid $100 million to the record companies in exchange for the right to legally distribute their music.

In 1999, a 19-year-old Massachusetts college student, Shawn Fanning, released Napster, software allowing registered users to search one another's hard drives for MP3-stored music files and transport them to their own computers. Ten million users downloaded Napster in the first nine months it was available (Surowiecki, 2000, p. 35).

The extent of Napster's success quickly drew the attention of the recording industry. If listeners could freely share music of even the biggest acts, record companies would potentially lose billions of dollars in sales. In mid-2000 the record companies went to court to shut Napster down, and even with financial backing from global media giant Bertelsmann, Napster's legal travails eventually brought it to bankruptcy in 2002. Now, downloading primarily takes two forms—from industry-approved and **P2P** sites.

Industry-Approved Downloading   Napster's 2.8 billion downloads a month (Oppelaar, 2001) before its collapse proved the popularity of downloading music from the Internet. So the five major labels combined to offer three "approved" music download sites—pressplay.com (Sony, Universal), emusic.com (Universal), and musicnet.com (Warner, EMI, BMG). All three were operative by 2002, yet their success is still in doubt. They offer downloads by subscription; that is, so many downloads per month or year for a monthly or annual fee. In addition, they provide downloads that either expire at the end of a specified period of time or cannot be burned to CD or transferred to MP3 players or cannot be played on any technology other than the one used for the original download—making listening to downloaded music in your car, for example, impossible, not to mention eliminating file sharing.

It is precisely these limitations that hinder the appeal of these sites. *Wall Street Journal* personal technology writer Walter Mossberg (2002b, p. E4) explains, "Some in the industry drew only one lesson from Napster: that consumers want to steal music. But the real lesson was different. For most Napster users, the thrill wasn't that their favorite songs were free, but that they were available in one location, liberated from costly CDs filled with other tracks they never wanted to buy." The industry-run sites reflect that false "lesson—all people are thieves, much more than the true lesson, that there's a huge business in selling downloadable songs for a modest price." As a result, numerous unauthorized music-file-sharing sites have developed despite the record industry's strenuous efforts to eliminate them. It is their difference from, rather than their similarity to, Napster that protects them.

P2P Downloading   Napster was a company that maintained servers containing lists of its subscribers' holdings (and therefore an entity that could be identified and sued). But sites such as Gnutella, Freenet, Limewire,

Morpheus, BearShare, and eDonkey use P2P technologies, that is, person-to-person software that permits direct Internet-based communication or collaboration between two or more personal computers while bypassing centralized servers. P2P allows users to visit a constantly and infinitely changing network of machines through which file sharing can occur. And there are no limits on how long the downloaded music can be heard, or with whom it can be shared, or on what technology (car CD player, home stereo system) it can be played. The RIAA has responded to P2P by suing the makers of its software (as it did in 2002 with KaZaa), but as much P2P software is open source (that is, it is freely downloaded, owned by no one, and continually altered and improved by its users), they may have little success.

In late 2003 the labels rolled out two nontechnological responses to piracy and declining sales. First, they reduced the price of CDs from an average of $19 to about $10. Second, they started suing some of the country's 67 million individual music-downloaders, a public relations disaster. "You might wanna stop suing your customers," wrote *Wired*'s Rebecca Harper (2003, p. 58). There was a technological response as well, but from a computer company. In April of that year Apple Computers unveiled its iTunes Music Store, featuring the simple sale of albums and individual songs for as little as 99 cents. Apple controlled only 5% of the PC market, yet it sold over a million tunes in its first week of operation. The company immediately announced an upcoming Windows version, and similar services quickly hit the Web, buymusic.com and Listen.com's Rhapsody were two. This activity led Warner Brothers CEO Tom Whalley to enthuse, "This is what the people who are willing to pay for music have been looking for all along" (quoted in Oppelaar, 2003, p. 42). For many observers, CEO Whalley's comments signaled the industry's recognition of the inevitability of the cyber revolution. The distribution and sale of music by Internet would soon be the standard. That future is at hand: in the first half of 2003, more than 600 U.S. brick-and-mortar music stores closed their doors (Kava, 2003).

No matter what model of music production and distribution eventually results from this technological and financial tumult, serious questions about the Net's impact on **copyright** (protecting content creators' financial interest in their product) will remain. There is more on copyright in Chapter 14. But for now, the labels are seeking technological solutions to the piracy they say is costing their industry $4.2 billion a year (Warner, 2002). We've already seen how they limit use of their music on their download sites. But the 50 million CD burners (copiers) anticipated to be available in 2005 (Krantz, 2000) pose an additional threat. As it is, 40% of today's CD buyers already own this technology, and just under 1.25 billion blank CDs are sold in North America every year (Cohen, 2002); 6 billion worldwide (Boutin, 2002). The labels' response to this threat is copy-proof CDs. The first of these were released in early 2002 to negative reaction from buyers and even from some in the recording industry. "I don't think the technology is perfected to a point where it can prevent copying," said Eminem's manager Paul Rosenberg. "The only thing it's going to do is get the fans angry. People who spend money won't be able to play the disc everywhere they want to, and that isn't fair."

Gnutella
WWW.
gnutella.wego.com

Freenet
WWW.
freenetproject.org

One of several Philips CD logos familiar to music fans.

This sentiment was echoed by a spokeswoman for Philips, the Dutch electronic company that invented the CD. "We are concerned about technology that limits the playability of the CD, because multiple uses of the CD in devices has been the foundation of its success," said Jeannet Harpe (both quoted in Cohen, 2002, pp. 43–44). Philips told the labels that it could not use its familiar CD logo on any copy-protected discs.

DIGITAL RADIO

Several technologies exist for the digital broadcast of traditional, terrestrial radio stations. But because no one technology has yet been deemed the standard by the FCC, broadcasters are hesitant to invest in the conversion from analog. The favored technology is called **in-band-on-channel (IBOC).** It employs digital compression to "shrink" both digital and analog signals, allowing them to occupy the same single channel. This technology permits stations to broadcast in both formats without acquiring additional spectrum space and without losing existing listeners. The Commission began issuing experimental IBOC station licenses in August 1999, and the first IBOC channels went into operation in late 2002.

WEB RADIO

Web Radio
www.
radio-directory.com

Radio's convergence with digital technologies is nowhere more pronounced and potentially profound than in **Web radio,** the delivery of "radio" directly to individual listeners over the Internet. Some 40,000 "radio stations" exist on the Web in one of two forms and are listened to by 13 million Americans every week (Arbitron, 2001):

Radio simulcast—traditional, over-the-air stations that are simulcast on the Web. Sometimes the Web-delivered signal is little more than the original broadcast re-created online. But more often, the simulcast includes additional information, for example, the lyrics of the song being played, biographical information on the artist, and concert dates. There are more than 20,000 stations online worldwide. Simply search the Web using a station's call letters to see if your favorite is online or go to <http:/radio-directory.com> or <http://www.live365.com>.

Web-only radio—"radio stations" (or more precisely **bitcasters**) that can be accessed only over the Web. The thousands of Web-only stations deliver two distinct services. Commercial sites such as <http://www.spinner.com> offer listeners a choice of more than 100 different channels of music, everything from Jazz to Celtic to New Age, all free of commercials and DJ chatter. All users have to do is click on the type of "station" they want to hear and they can hear it. And there are also more narrowly targeted Web-only stations, such as <www.khaha.com>, a comedy station out of Los Angeles, and <www.cprxtreme.com>, a "pirate Christian" station Webcasting from Glendale, California.

For more information on this topic, see NBC Video Clip #13 on the CD—*Radio of the Future May Be on the Internet.*

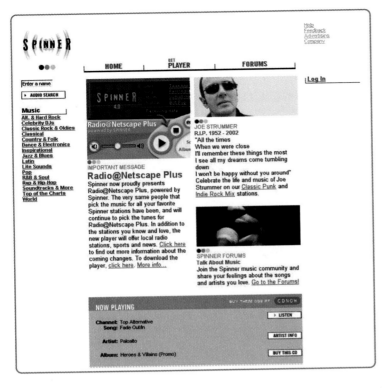

To access Web radio, users must have some form of file compression software such as Real Player. It permits **streaming** (the simultaneous downloading and accessing—playing—of digital audio or video data), and is available for free downloading at <http://www.real.com>. But even streaming software can't give all users the full-Web radio experience. Users who have dial-up access to the Internet experience a hum when listening, a sound analogous to that heard on AM radio. Perfectly clear sound is possible only with very fast cable and DSL modems not yet in widespread use.

Real Player
www.
real.com

DEVELOPING MEDIA LITERACY SKILLS

Listening to Shock Jocks

The proliferation of shock jocks—outrageous, rude, crude radio personalities—offers an example of the importance of media literacy that may not be immediately apparent. Yet it involves four different elements of media literacy: development of an awareness of media's impact, cultivation of an understanding of media content as a text that provides insight into our culture and our lives, awareness of the process of mass communication, and an understanding of the ethical demands under which media professionals operate (Chapter 2). Different media literate radio listeners judge the shock jocks differently, but they all take time to examine their work and their role in the culture.

The literate listener asks this question of shock jocks and the stations that air them: "At what cost to the culture as a whole, and to individuals

College Radio

There are few better ways to make media literacy a living enterprise than by becoming a mass communicator yourself—in other words, by engaging in the media. The Internet does indeed make us all potential mass communicators (see Chapter 10), but it does not require us to work within a larger organization, to produce content as part of a group, to meet pre-existing audience expectations, or to conform to formal and informal rules and regulations of operation, all those things identified in Chapter 1 as giving mass communication its essential nature. So, if you want to test your own media literacy values in a true mass media setting, check out college radio.

Most colleges and universities have a radio station. In fact, many have two—a student-run noncommercial station and an NPR affiliate. For example, Southampton College in New York has WLIU-AM and WPBX-FM; the University of Massachusetts in Amherst has WMUA-FM and WFCR-FM. Naturally, the student-oriented stations may offer more freedom, whereas an NPR station may offer a more formal professional experience, but both are com-

mitted to programming that prioritizes *public interest* over *what the public is interested in.* In other words, noncommercial college radio offers real media experience with content variety and diversity, the opportunity to program for bounded cultures, extended freedom of speech and expression, and, very often, more individual creative control.

There are numerous sources to which you can turn to help you use college radio to bring your media literacy to life. Metal Index (www.metalindex.com/bands/M/) and the Intercollegiate Broadcast System (www.ibsradio.org) offer information on starting, operating, and improving college radio. In addition, the British Broadcasting Corporation (www.bbc.co.uk/info/), NPR (www.npr.org), and Public Radio International (www.pri.org/PublicSite/home.html) provide information on how to do public service broadcasting. If you are not on a campus that has a station, use any of the online radio station sites identified earlier in this chapter to search for a college station near you. Virtually all college stations welcome volunteers from the community, especially other college students.

living in it, should a radio station program an offensive, vulgar personality to attract listeners and, therefore, profit?" Ours is a free society, and freedom of expression is one of our dearest rights. Citing their First Amendment rights, as well as strong listener interest, radio stations have made Howard Stern and other shock jocks like him the fashion of the day. Stern, for example, took poorly rated WXRX in New York to Number 1, and, as Infinity Broadcasting's top attraction, he is syndicated throughout the country. He is free to pray for cancer to kill public officials he does not like; to joke constantly about sexual and other body functions; to make sexist, homophobic, and misogynistic comments; and to insult guests and callers. The FCC has fined stations that carry his show more than $1 million, a move called harassment and censorship by his supporters, but one that boosts Stern's public profile and profits.

Media literate listeners must ask themselves if Stern's "Guess the Jew" contest is just a joke. They must ask themselves if his public prayer for the spread of an FCC commissioner's prostate cancer is just hyperbole. When he teases female guests about the size and shape of their body parts, is this just an example of his provocative interviewing style? When he speaks dismissively about Hispanics and African Americans, is this just a device to tease listeners? Media literate listeners ask if Opie and Anthony's having-sex-in-risky-places contest is simply good fun, even as the Infinity Broadcasting's afternoon shock jocks broadcast, live, a couple's coupling from inside New York's St. Patrick's Cathedral ("N.Y. shock jocks," 2002).

If you're Jewish, if one of your parents has cancer, if you're a member of a minority group targeted by Stern, if you're a Catholic (or respect religion), the answer to these questions may not make a difference. But you have a choice, say shock jock defenders: You can switch the station or turn off the radio. This poses a problem for the media literate listener. Literacy demands an understanding of the importance of freedom not only to the operation of our media system but also to the functioning of our democracy. Yet literacy also means that you cannot discount the impact of the shock jocks. Nor can you assume that their expression does not represent a distasteful side of our culture and ourselves.

Literate media consumers also know that Howard Stern, Opie and Anthony, and the other shock jocks exist because people listen to them. They are popular for a reason. Are programs such as Stern's merely a place in which the culture is contested (Chapter 1)? Are they a safe place for the discussion of the forbidden, for testing cultural limits? In fact, a literate listener can make the argument that Stern and others like him play an important cultural role.

Do you listen to shock jocks? If you do, how do you justify that listenership? Media literate radio listeners ask and answer these questions.

Chapter Review

The roots of radio lie in science and technology. The long search for wireless telephony and wireless telegraph culminated in Guglielmo Marconi's success around 1896. Marconi's wireless was in turn improved by Reginald Fessenden and Lee DeForest. At about the same time, sound recording was also being perfected. Thomas Edison patented a cylinder sound recorder in 1877, and Emile Berliner introduced the gramophone 10 years later. Both technologies soon found their way into U.S. homes, with broadcasting becoming firmly established at the end of World War I.

Advertising had become the economic base of radio by the 1920s. Regulation of the airwaves came in the form of the Radio Acts of 1910, 1912, and 1927. The Communications Act of 1934 formalized the core concepts of the spectrum as a national resource and radio as a public service medium. The organizational structure of the new industry also was formed early, as national networks CBS, NBC Red and Blue, and Mutual soon provided the content for most U.S. stations. These came together in the 1930s to create the golden age of radio. But the social changes that followed the war, as well as the introduction of television, changed almost every aspect of radio.

The 13,012 radio stations operating in the United States today are either commercial FM, commercial AM, or noncommercial FM stations. Whatever its form, radio survives today because it is local, fragmented, specialized (dominated by formats), personal, and mobile. These characteristics make it an attractive medium for advertisers, and recent deregulatory moves have made radio even more successful commercially.

The same youth culture that helped radio succeed in the postwar era also fueled the growth and success of the recording industry. Today there are 5,000 recording companies in the United States, but 90% of the market for recorded music is controlled by five major companies, four of which are under international ownership. This concentration has raised concern over cultural homogenization, the dominance of profit over artistry, and an emphasis on promotion rather than the music itself.

Both radio and the recording industry have prospered due to technological advances. Television gave radio its new personality and, through MTV, reinvigorated the music business. Satellite delivery of music directly to radio stations, homes, and cars has made possible the proliferation of radio networks. Convergence of radio and the Internet promises to bring further change to the radio and recording industries. In fact, it promises to completely reinvent the recording business. The large audience for shock jocks poses a dilemma for media literate listeners who must remain aware of the impact of the media and what the content of shock jock shows says about us as a culture and as individuals.

Key Terms

 Use the text's CD-ROM and the Online Learning Center at www.mhhe.com/baran to further your understanding of the following terminology.

liquid barretter, 197
audion tube, 197
trustee model, 202
spectrum scarcity, 202
affiliates, 203
O&O, 203
Biltmore agreement, 204
nonduplication rule, 207
AM/FM combo, 207
format, 208
secondary services, 208
playlist, 208
billings, 209
deregulation, 210

duopoly, 210
average quarter-hour, 211
cume, 211
rating, 211
share, 211
cover, 212
catalogue album, 217
recent catalogue album, 217
syndication, 220
DMX (Digital Music Express), 220
digital audio radio service (DARS), 220
digital recording, 220

digital audio tape (DAT), 221
MP3, 222
modem, 222
open source software, 222
piracy, 223
P2P, 224
copyright, 225
in-band-on-channel (IBOC), 226
Web radio, 226
bitcaster, 226
streaming, 227

Questions for Review

Go to the self-quizzes on the CD-ROM and the Online Learning Center to test your knowledge.

1. Who were Guglielmo Marconi, Reginald Fessenden, and Lee DeForest?
2. How were the sound recording developments of Thomas Edison and Emile Berliner similar? How were they different?
3. What is the significance of KDKA and WEAF?
4. How do the Radio Acts of 1910, 1912, and 1927 relate to the Communications Act of 1934?
5. What were the five defining characteristics of the American broadcasting system as it entered the golden age of radio?
6. How did World War II and the introduction of television change radio and recorded music?
7. What are the nonduplication rule and duopoly?

8. What does it mean to say that radio is local, fragmented, specialized, personal, and mobile?
9. What are the five major recording companies in the United States?
10. What are catalogue sales? Recent catalogue sales?
11. How have cable and satellite affected the radio and recording industries? Computers and digitalization?
12. Is the size of radio's audience in ascendance or in decline? Why?
13. What are the two forms of Web radio?
14. What is streaming audio?
15. What was Napster? How did it work?
16. What is P2P technology?

Questions for Critical Thinking and Discussion

1. Would you have favored a noncommercial basis for our broadcasting system? Why?
2. Are you primarily a commercial AM, commercial FM, or noncommercial FM listener? Which are your favorite formats? Why?
3. What do you think of the argument that control of the recording industry by a few multinational conglomerates inevitably leads to cultural homogenization and the ascendance of profit over music?

4. Have you ever been part of a radio ratings exercise? If yes, how honest were you?
5. How much regulation do you believe is necessary in U.S. broadcasting? If the airwaves belong to the people, how can we best ensure that license holders perform their public service functions?

Important Resources

Billboard. The weekly business guide of the record industry, it is typically full of short, interesting stories and great statistics.

Broadcasting & Cable Magazine. This weekly magazine for radio, television, and cable offers insightful articles on regulation, economics, programming, technology—virtually every aspect of contemporary broadcasting.

Downbeat. Written for the listener rather than for industry professionals, this weekly covers the recording and music scenes with flair and depth. Particularly strong in its jazz coverage.

Szatmary, D. P. (1991). *Rockin' in time: A social history of rock and roll.* **Englewood Cliffs, NJ: Prentice Hall.** A social and cultural history of rock, it is detailed and well researched and provides a good foundation for placing various artists in the "big picture" of popular music of the last 40 years.

Neer, R. (2001). FM: *The rise and fall of rock radio.* **New York: Villard.** This colorful, idiosyncratic but definitive look at FM radio "before the days of trashy, hedonistic dumbspeak and disposable three-minute ditties," by a man who was a DJ when radio and rock 'n' roll actually meant something to young people, will make younger students jealous and their older faculty nostalgic.

Radio History	www.radiohistory.org
Radio's First 100 Years	www.alpcom.it/hamradio/
Marconi	www.etedeschi.ndirect.co.uk/marconi/index.htm
DeForest	www.northstar.k12.ak.us/schools/ryn/projects/ inventors/deforest/deforest/html
Federal Communications Commission	www.fcc.gov
National Public Radio	www.npr.org
Public Radio International	www.pri.org
Pacifica Radio	www.pacifica.org
Arbitron	www.arbitron.com
Record Industry Association of America	www.riaa.com
Billboard magazine	www.billboard.com
Rock Out Censorship	www.theroc.org
XM Radio	www.xmradio.com
Sirius Radio	www.siriusradio
Music Boulevard	www.cdnow.com
MP3	www.MP3.com
Download Central	www.MP3downloadcentral.com
pressplay.com	www.pressplay.com
emusic.com	www.emusic.com
musicnet.com	www.musicnet.com
Gnutella	www.gnutella.wego.com
Freenet	www.freenetproject.org
Web Radio	www.radio-directory.com
Real Player	www.real.com

CHAPTER 8

Television

No one is neutral about television. We either love it or hate it. Many of us do both. The reason is that it is our most ubiquitous and socially and culturally powerful mass medium. After studying this chapter you should

- be familiar with the history and development of the television industry and television itself as a medium.

- understand in detail how television programs move from concept to broadcast.

- recognize how the organizational and economic nature of the contemporary television industry shapes the content of television.

- understand the relationship between television and its viewers.

- be aware of new and emerging video technologies and their potential impact on the television industry and its audience.

- have a clearer concept of the digital television "revolution."

- possess improved television-viewing media literacy skills, especially in recognizing staged news and testing your personal level of control over your viewing.

Two years out of college, you're assistant producer of the 6 o'clock news in a medium-sized city. Your professors told you that if you wanted to make it in broadcasting, you had to begin in smaller markets and work your way up. The wisdom of that advice hits you when the station manager at the network affiliate for which you work appoints (actually, you see it as "anoints") you the station's representative to the Association for Local Television Stations. You're in with the big boys; you are hot, the next big thing in television.

At your first meeting, however, you're brought back to earth. The Board of Directors is seeking comment on their intention to fold the organization. It seems that since the organization was founded in 1996 to represent the needs and interests of local broadcasters, the number of actual local broadcasters has dwindled to so few that the group no longer has any reason to exist (Albiniak, 2002b). You listen as the scenario is explained. As

TIMELINE

- **1884** Nipkow invents his disc
- **1923** Zworykin demonstrates electronic iconoscope tube
- **1927** Farnsworth demonstrates electronically scanned television images
- **1928** Baird transmits mechanical video image across Atlantic
- **1939** Sarnoff introduces regular television broadcasting at World's Fair
- **1941** First two commercial stations approved
- **1948** Television freeze; first cable TV system
- **1950** *Red Channels;* Nielsen ratings
- **1951** U.S. wired coast-to-coast, *I Love Lucy*
- **1954** Army–McCarthy Hearings telecast
- **1959** Quiz show scandal
- **1962** All-channel legislation
- **1976** VCR introduced
- **1994** DBS service introduced
- **1996** DVD introduced
- **1998** First digital TV broadcast
- **1999** DVR introduced
- **2002** FCC mandates digital receivers by 2007

concentration in television intensified in the wake of the Telecommunications Act of 1996, more and more stations were bought up by big corporations—global conglomerate Viacom owns 35 stations; global conglomerate News Corporation, 35; Paxon, soon to be owned by NBC (itself a subsidiary of General Electric), 68; newspaper and magazine giant Hearst-Argyle, 27, Sinclair Broadcasting, 59. And although licensed to serve their particular locales, their mandate to serve those communities has come to take a back seat to corporate demands to increase profits. Several stations, primarily in small and medium markets like your own, are even dropping local news and public affairs altogether in favor of profit-heavy reruns and *Hollywood Squares,* further reducing the emphasis on *local* in *local broadcaster* (Trigoboff, 2002). You listen, but you know it's a done deal. The board votes. You return to your station, representative to a group that no longer exists. The industry to which you thought you would devote your career is changing.

This chapter details that change, from early experiments with mechanical scanning to the electronic marvel that sits in virtually all our homes. We trace the rapid transformation of television into a mature medium after (and because of) World War II and examine several events early in its existence that changed and cemented its character—the quiz show scandal, *I Love Lucy,* McCarthyism, and reliance on the Nielsen ratings.

The remarkable reach of television accounts for its attractiveness as an advertising medium. We discuss this reach, and we explore the network–affiliate relationship, program producers, how a show gets on the air, and the syndication business. We consider new television technologies and the convergence of the Internet and television and how it promises to change the interaction between medium and audience. Finally, we discuss television literacy in terms of the practice of staging the news.

Inexpensive syndicated programming such as *Hollywood Squares* is replacing local news on many small and medium market television stations.

A Nipkow disc.

A Short History of Television

After the printing press, the most important invention in communication technology to date has been television. Television has changed the way teachers teach, governments govern and religious leaders preach and the way we organize the furniture in our homes. Television has changed the nature, operation, and relationship to their audiences of books, magazines, movies, and radio. The computer, with its networking abilities, may overtake television as a medium of mass communication, but television defines even its future. Will the promise of the Web be drowned in a sea of commercials? Can online information services deliver faster and better information than television? Even the computer screens we use look like television screens, and we await better Internet video, Web-TV, online video conferencing, and the new and improved computer video game. Before we delve deeper into the nature of this powerful medium and its relationship with its audience, let's examine how television developed as it did.

Television History
www.
mediahistory/umn.edu

MECHANICAL AND ELECTRONIC SCANNING

In 1884 Paul Nipkow, a Russian scientist living in Berlin, developed the first workable device for generating electrical signals suitable for the transmission of a scene that people could see. His **Nipkow disc** consisted of a rotating scanning disc spinning in front of a photoelectric cell. It produced 4,000 picture dots **(pixels)** per second, producing a picture composed of 18 parallel lines. Although his mechanical system proved too limiting, Nipkow demonstrated the possibility of using a scanning system to divide a scene into an orderly pattern of transmittable picture elements that could

Philo Farnsworth and Vladimir Zworykin, pioneers in the development of television.

Zworykin

www.

ieee.org/organizations/
history_center/oral_histories/
transcripts/zworykin21.html

Farnsworth

www.

invent.org/hall_of_fame/56.html

be recomposed as a visual image. (This is still the operational basis for modern television.) British inventor John Logie Baird was able to transmit moving images using a mechanical disc as early as 1925, and in 1928 he successfully sent a television picture from London to Hartsdale, NY.

Electronic scanning came either from another Russian or from a U.S. farm boy; historians disagree. Vladimir Zworykin, an immigrant living near Pittsburgh and working for Westinghouse, demonstrated his **iconoscope tube,** the first practical television camera tube, in 1923. In 1929 David Sarnoff lured him to RCA to head the electronics research lab, and it was there that Zworykin developed the **kinescope,** an improved picture tube. At the same time, young Philo Farnsworth had moved from Idaho to San Francisco to perfect an electronic television system, the design for which he had shown his high school science teacher when he was 15 years old. In 1927, at the age of 20, he made his first public demonstration—film clips of a prize fight, scenes from a Mary Pickford movie, and other graphic images. The "Boy Wonder" and Zworykin's RCA spent the next decade fighting fierce patent battles in court. In 1939 RCA capitulated, agreeing to pay Farnsworth royalties for the use of his patents.

In April of that year, at the World's Fair in New York, RCA made the first true public demonstration of television in the form of regularly scheduled 2-hour NBC broadcasts. These black-and-white telecasts consisted of cooking demonstrations, singers, jugglers, comedians, puppets—just about anything that could fit in a hot, brightly lit studio and demonstrate motion. People could buy television sets at the RCA Pavilion at prices ranging from $200 for the 5-inch screen to $600 for the deluxe 12-inch screen model. The FCC granted construction permits to the first two commercial stations in 1941, but World War II intervened. As we saw in Chapter 2, however, technical development and improvement of the new medium continued.

THE 1950s

In 1952, 108 stations were broadcasting to 17 million television homes. By the end of the decade, there were 559 stations, and nearly 90% of U.S. households had televisions. In the 1950s more television sets were sold in the United States (70 million) than there were children born (40.5 million) (Kuralt, 1977). The technical standards were fixed, stations proliferated and flourished, the public tuned in, and advertisers were enthusiastic. The content and character of the medium were set in this decade as well:

- Carried over from the radio networks, television genres included variety shows, situation comedies, dramas (including westerns and cop shows), soap operas, and quiz shows.
- Two new formats appeared: feature films and talk shows. Talk shows were instrumental in introducing radio personalities to the television audience, which could see its favorites for the first time.
- Television news and documentary remade broadcast journalism as a powerful force in its own right, led by CBS's Edward R. Murrow (*See It Now*, 1951) and NBC's David Brinkley and Chet Huntley. Huntley and Brinkley's 1956 coverage of the major political conventions gave audiences an early glimpse of the power of television to cover news and history in the making.
- AT&T completed its national **coaxial cable** and **microwave relay** network for the distribution of television programming in the summer of 1951. The entire United States was now within the reach of the major television networks, and they came to dominate the medium.

Four other events from the 1950s would permanently shape how television operated: the quiz show scandal, the appearance of *I Love Lucy*, McCarthyism, and establishment of the ratings system.

The Quiz Show Scandal and Changes in Sponsorship   Throughout the 1950s the networks served primarily as time brokers, offering airtime and

Running from 1947 until 1958, NBC's *Kraft Television Theatre* aired some of the golden age's most respected live anthology dramas. *Top left,* Richard Kiley and Everett Sloane; *lower left,* Ossie Davis; *lower right,* Walter Matthau and Nancy Walker.

Quiz Show Scandal
www.
history.acusd.edu/gen/recording/
television7.html

distribution (their affiliates) and accepting payment for access to both. Except for their own news and sports coverage, the networks relied on outside agencies to provide programs. An advertising agency, for example, would hire a production company to produce a program for its client. That client would then be the show's sponsor—*The Kraft Television Theatre* and *Westinghouse Studio One* are two examples. The agency would then pay a network to air the program over its national collection of stations. This system had enriched the networks during the heyday of radio, and they saw no reason to change.

But in 1959 the quiz show scandal, enveloping independently produced, single advertiser–sponsored programs, changed the way the networks did business. Popular shows like *The $64,000 Question* and *Twenty-One* had been rigged by advertisers and producers to ensure that favored contestants would defeat unpopular ones and to artificially build tension where a mismatch was anticipated. Audiences were shocked to learn that winners had been provided with the quiz questions and answers before the broadcasts. Congress held hearings. The reputation of the new medium was being tarnished. The networks used this "embarrassment" as their excuse to eliminate the advertisers and ad agencies from the production and distribution processes. Because audiences held the networks responsible for what appeared under their names, the networks argued that they were obligated to control their schedules. The networks themselves began commissioning or buying the entertainment fare that filled their schedules. This has been the case ever since, but some historians claim that the networks realized quite early the wealth that could be made from **spot commercial sales** (selling individual 60-second spots on a given program to a wide variety of advertisers) and were simply looking for an excuse to remove the advertisers from content decision making.

In either case, the content of television was altered. Some critics argue that this change to spot sales put an end to the "golden age of television." When sponsors agreed to attach their names to programs, *Alcoa Presents* or the *Texaco Star Theater*, for example, they had an incentive to demand high-quality programming. Spot sales, with network salespeople offering small bits of time to a number of different sponsors, reduced the demand for quality. Because individual sponsors were not identified with a given show, they had no stake in how well it was made—only in how many viewers it attracted. Spot sales also reduced the willingness of the networks to try innovative or different types of content. Familiarity and predictability attracted more viewers and, therefore, more advertisers.

There is a counterargument, however. It goes like this. Once the financial well-being of the networks became dependent on the programming they aired, the networks themselves became more concerned with program quality, lifting television from its dull infancy (remembered now as the "golden age" only by those small, early audiences committed to serious character-driven televised drama). Different historians and critics offer arguments for both views.

I Love Lucy **and More Changes**   In 1951 CBS asked Lucille Ball to move her hit radio program, *My Favorite Husband,* to television. Lucy was willing but wanted her real-life husband, Desi Arnaz, to play the part of her video spouse. The network refused (some historians say the network objected to the prime-time presentation of an "interracial" marriage—Desi Arnaz was Cuban—but CBS denies this). But Lucy made additional demands. Television at the time was live—images were typically captured by three large television cameras, with a director in a booth choosing among the three available images. Lucy wanted her program produced in the same manner—in front of a live audience with three simultaneously running

I Love Lucy was significant for far more than its comedy. Thanks to Lucille Ball's shrewd business sense, it became the foundation for the huge off-network syndicated television industry.

cameras—but these cameras would be *film* cameras. Editors could then review the three sets of film and edit them together to give the best combination of action and reaction shots. Lucy also wanted the production to take place in Hollywood, the nation's film capital, instead of New York, the television center at the time. CBS was uncertain about this departure from how television was typically produced and refused these requests as well.

Lucy and Desi borrowed the necessary money and produced *I Love Lucy* on their own, selling the broadcast rights to CBS. In doing so the woman now best remembered as "that zany redhead" transformed the business and look of television:

- Filmed reruns were now possible, something that had been impossible with live television, and this, in turn, created the off-network syndication industry.

- The television industry moved from New York, with its stage drama orientation, to Hollywood, with its entertainment film mindset. More action, more flash came to the screen.

- Weekly series could now be produced relatively quickly and inexpensively. A 39-week series could be completed in 20 or 24 weeks, saving money on actors, crew, equipment, and facilities. In addition the same stock shots—for example, certain exterior views—could be used in different episodes.

McCarthyism: The Growing Power of Television   The red scare that cowed the movie business also touched television, aided by the publication in 1950 of *Red Channels: The Report of Communist Influence in Radio and Television*, the work of three former FBI agents operating a company called American Business Consultants. Its 200 pages detailed the pro-Communist sympathies of 151 broadcast personalities, including Orson Welles and newsman Howard K. Smith. Advertisers were encouraged to avoid buying time from broadcasters who employed these "red sympathizers." Like the movie studios, the television industry caved in. The networks employed security checkers to look into people's backgrounds, refused to hire "suspect" talent, and demanded loyalty oaths from performers. In its infancy television had taken the safe path. Many gifted artists were denied not only a paycheck but also the opportunity to shape the medium's content.

Ironically, it was this same red scare that allowed television to demonstrate its enormous power as a vehicle of democracy and freedom. Joseph McCarthy, the Republican junior senator from Wisconsin whose tactics

McCarthyism
WWW.
mccarthy.cjb.net/

The Army–McCarthy Hearings. Wisconsin's junior Republican Senator Joseph McCarthy (seated at the far right) begins his June 9, 1954, testimony before his fellow senators regarding his claims that the Army was rife with Communists, Reds, and "fellow travelers." Network coverage of the senator's erratic behavior helped bring the despot into disrepute.

gave this era its name, was seen by millions of viewers as his investigation of "Reds" in the U.S. Army was broadcast by all the networks for 36 days in 1954. Daytime ratings increased 50% (Sterling & Kittross, 1990). At the same time, Edward R. Murrow used his *See It Now* to expose the senator's lies and hypocrisy. As a consequence of the two broadcasts, McCarthy was ruined; he was censured by his Senate colleagues and later died the lonely death of an alcoholic. Television had given the people eyes and ears—and power—where before they had had little. The Army–McCarthy Hearings and Murrow's challenge to McCarthyism are still regarded as two of television's finest moments.

The Nielsen Ratings The concept of computing ratings was carried over from radio (see Chapter 7) to television, but the ratings as we know them today are far more sophisticated. The A. C. Nielsen Company began in 1923 as a product-testing company, which soon branched into market research. In 1936 Nielsen started reporting radio ratings and was doing the same for television by 1950.

Nielsen offers a variety of services. The best known are the *ratings*. It reports three types of ratings. **Overnights** are instant ratings gathered from homes in several major urban centers. **Pocketpieces** are ratings based on a national sample that are computed and reported every 2 weeks. **MNA reports** (multinetwork area reports) are computations based on the 70 largest markets (Walker & Ferguson, 1998). To produce the ratings, Nielsen selects 5,000 households thought to be representative of the entire U.S. viewing audience (the sample will grow to 10,000 homes in 2006). From its days as a radio ratings company, Nielsen used a measuring device called the **audimeter,** which recorded when the television set was turned on, the channel to which it was tuned, and the time of day. As discussed in the box "The Problem with the Nielsen Ratings," this was a most elementary counting—it said little about who was watching. In September 1987 Nielsen introduced the **peoplemeter,** a device requiring each member of a television home to press buttons to record his or her individual viewing. (Parents or guardians are responsible for recording children's choices.) The information recorded is sent to Nielsen by telephone lines, and the company can then determine the program watched, who was watching it, and the amount of time each viewer spent with it. But convergence is changing how ratings data will be gathered. Nielsen is experimenting with **portable peoplemeters,** pagerlike devices worn by audience members that "read" embedded audio signals in electronically delivered media content on radio, television, and the Web, no matter where a person may be— at home, in a car, at work, or at the corner bar. At night, the user plugs the small peoplemeter into a docking device that sends the day's results to the ratings company via phone lines. Nielsen promises to have its "PPM" out in summer of 2004.

To draw a more complete picture of the viewing situation and to measure local television viewing, Nielsen conducts diary surveys of viewing patterns four times a year. These **sweeps periods** are in February, May,

July, and November. During sweeps, diaries are distributed to thousands of sample households in selected markets. Viewers are asked to write down what they're watching and who is watching it. The diary data are then combined with the peoplemeter data to help stations set their advertising rates for the next 3 months.

Some people complain that a sample of 5,000 households (even 10,000) is simply too small to reflect the viewing patterns of millions of Americans. In truth, the sample is large enough, and is selected carefully enough, to ensure *statistical* accuracy within a few percentage points. For 50 years this had been good enough to warrant acceptance by the television industry. However, the entire conduct and value of the ratings has recently come under serious challenge from those same broadcasters, as you can see in the box "The Problem with the Nielsen Ratings."

A second, more important measure of television's audience is its *share*, which is a direct reflection of a particular show's competitive performance. Share doesn't measure viewers as a percentage of *all* television households (as do the ratings). Instead, the share measures a program audience as a percentage of the *television sets in use* at the time it airs. It tells us what proportion of the *actual* audience a program attracts, indicating how well a particular program is doing on its given night, in its time slot, against its competition (Figure 8.1). For example, *The Tonight Show with Jay Leno* normally gets a rating of around 4—terrible by prime-time standards—but because it's on when fewer homes are tuned in, its share of 15 (15% of the homes with sets in use) is very high.

Ratings and shares can be computed using these formulas:

$$\text{Rating} = \frac{\text{Households tuned in to a given program}}{\text{All households with television}}$$

$$\text{Share} = \frac{\text{Households tuned in to a given program}}{\text{All households tuned in to television at that time}}$$

Here's an example. Your talk show is aired in a market that has 1 million television households; 400,000 are tuned in to you. Therefore,

$$\frac{400,000}{1,000,000} = .40, \text{ or a rating of 40.}$$

At the time your show airs, however, there are only 800,000 households using television. Therefore, your share of the available audience is

$$\text{Share} = \frac{400,000}{800,000} = .50, \text{ or a rating of 50.}$$

If you can explain why a specific program's share is always higher than its rating, then you understand the difference between the two.

Figure 8.1 Computing Ratings and Shares.

Television and Its Audiences

The 1960s saw some refinement in the technical structure of television, which influenced its organization and audience. In 1962 Congress passed **all-channel legislation,** which required that all sets imported into or manufactured in the United States be equipped with both VHF and UHF receivers. This had little immediate impact; U.S. viewers were now hooked

The Problem with the Nielsen Ratings

From the very beginning television ratings have been criticized for factors other than the small number of homes used in their computation. More important questions have to do with what ratings are measuring in the first place and how the results are used. Audimeter ratings did not measure whether anyone was actually *watching* at a given time. Its replacement technology, the peoplemeter, also has limitations. Punch-in protocols for nonfamily members are sufficiently complex that many users simply fail to acknowledge the presence of additional viewers, or they substitute a family member's code for the guest code. The diary is flawed as well; its value is dependent on the active involvement of viewers. Lack of interest, forgetfulness, and lying can and do occur. Equally important, diaries offer viewers no opportunity to comment on likes and dislikes.

All three systems have an additional problem. Participation in the ratings distorts how and what people watch. Knowing that your viewing choices are being scrutinized, or, in the case of the diary, writing down bits of information before and after you watch, naturally changes the viewing situation. Moreover, 50% of those who are asked to participate refuse to do so. This raises the question of the representativeness of the sample, that is, how well it matches the entire viewing population.

The *use* of the ratings is also controversial. They are a device for setting advertising rates, not measures of program popularity or worth. The ratings say nothing about what a show means to its viewers. Yet industry and viewers alike often confuse these interpretations.

Still, the television industry was satisfied with the ratings until the introduction of cable and VCR divided the audience to such an extent that the ratings were in danger of becoming meaningless. The Nielsen Company had used a standard sample of 1,200 homes for 35 years. But as the audience became more and more fragmented, it increased the number of metered homes to 4,000. The increase in sample size and the use of the peoplemeter combined to produce more accurate figures, and in 1990 great declines in the number of viewers for ABC, CBS, and NBC were demonstrated.

Now the big networks, long enriched by the ratings, saw them as flawed. They should be "open to interpretation," they said. The sample is "too small," they complained. In early 1996 Nielsen increased the number of metered homes to 5,000. The networks then protested that the new ratings overrepresented the young and technically savvy because the peoplemeter was more complex than either the audimeter or diary and young people were more skilled at using it. This criticism may have been true, but these young people were in fact the very viewers who were abandoning the networks for cable, VCR, and satellite.

Just as the radio networks questioned the ratings system they had long embraced when television began to erode their audience (Chapter 7), the television networks are doing the same as they now lose audience to other media. NBC and Fox have threatened Nielsen with lawsuits over their falling numbers, and in December 1996 ABC, CBS, NBC, and Fox ran this full-page ad in the media industry's most important publications.

on the three national networks and their VHF affiliates (DuMont closed shop in 1955). Still, UHF independents and educational stations were able to at least attract some semblance of an audience. The UHF independents would have to wait for the coming of cable to give them clout. Now that the educational stations were attracting more viewers, they began to look less educational in the strictest sense of the word and began programming more entertaining cultural fare (see the box "The Creation of *Sesame Street*"). The Public Broadcasting Act of 1967 united the educational stations into an important network, the Public Broadcasting Service (PBS), which today has over 300 affiliates.

The 1960s also witnessed the immense social and political power of the new medium to force profound alterations in the country's consciousness and behavior. Particularly influential were the Nixon–Kennedy campaign debates of 1960, broadcasts of the aftermath of Kennedy's assassination and funeral in 1963, the 1969 transmission of Neil Armstrong's walk on the moon, and the use of television at the end of the decade by civil rights and anti–Vietnam War leaders.

The 1960s also gave rise to a descriptive expression often used today when television is discussed. Speaking to the 1961 convention of the National Association of Broadcasters, John F. Kennedy's new FCC chair, Newton Minow, invited broadcasters to

> sit down in front of your television set when your station goes on the air and stay there without a book, magazine, newspaper, profit and loss sheet, or ratings book to distract you, and keep your eyes glued to that set until the station signs off. I can assure you that you will observe a **vast wasteland.**

Whether one agrees or not with Mr. Minow's assessment of television, then or now, there is no doubt that audiences continue to watch:

- There are 106.7 million television households in the United States; 99.9% have color, 75% have more than one set.
- A television is on for an average of 7 hours, 40 minutes a day in each U.S. household.
- The average male watches 4 hours, 19 minutes a day; the average female 4 hours, 51 minutes; the average teen 3 hours, 4 minutes; and the average child, 3 hours, 12 minutes.
- A family of three or more people typically watches television 60 hours a week (all statistics from <www.nab.org>).

There can be no doubt, either, that television is successful as an advertising medium:

- Total 2001 billings were $56.4 billion, with approximately 40% in national network and national syndication sales, 30% in national non-network sales, 30% in local sales.

- The average 30-second prime-time network television spot costs $100,000 (spots on top-rated *Friends* cost $455,700).

- Average ad time on the 2004 Super Bowl Patriots–Panthers broadcast costs $2.3 million for 30 seconds.

- 82% of American consumers see television as the most influential ad medium; 67%, the most persuasive; 49%, the most authoritative; and 80%, the most exciting.

- A 30-second local spot can fetch up to $20,000 on a top-rated special in a major market (all statistics from http://www.tvb.org).

The great success of television as an advertising medium has as much to do with its scope and nature as it does with its public appeal.

Scope and Nature of the Television Industry

Today, as it has been from the beginning, the business of television is dominated by a few centralized production, distribution, and decision-making organizations. These **networks** link affiliates for the purpose of delivering and selling viewers to advertisers. The large majority of the 1,309 commercial stations in the United States are affiliated with a national broadcasting network: ABC, NBC, and CBS each have over 200 affiliates and Fox has close to that number. Many more stations are affiliated with UPN, the WB, and Pax, often referred to as "weblets." Although cable has introduced us to dozens of new "cable networks"—ESPN, MTV, Comedy Central, and A&E, to name a few—most programs that come to mind when we think of television were either conceived, approved, funded, produced, or distributed by the broadcast networks.

Local affiliates carry network programs (they are said to **clear time**) for a number of reasons.

1. Networks make direct payments to affiliates for airing their programs. For example, NBC pays **compensation** to its affiliates for airing *Frasier*. (Compensation has diminished dramatically in recent years as the networks have been losing audience to cable and other alternatives; many affiliates now receive no compensation.)

2. Networks allow affiliates to insert locally sold commercials in a certain number of specified spots in their programs. The affiliates are allowed to keep all the money they make from these local spots.

3. Financial risk resides with the network, not with the affiliate.

4. Affiliates enjoy the prestige of their networks and use this to their financial advantage. Not only do affiliates charge higher advertising rates for local programming that borders a network offering (for example, *Eyewitness News at 6* that immediately follows *CBS Evening News with Dan Rather*), but they typically charge more for local spots at other times of the day than can independent stations in the same market.

Two of syndication's biggest winners, urbane, off-network hit *Frasier* and sci-fi classic *Star Trek: The Next Generation*.

5. Affiliates get network-quality programming. Few local stations can match the promotional efforts of the networks; few locally produced programs can equal the budget, the glamour, and the audience appeal of network programming.

THE NETWORKS AND PROGRAM CONTENT

Networks control what appears on the vast majority of local television stations, but they also control what appears on non-network television, that is, when affiliates program their own content. In addition, they influence what appears on independent stations and on cable channels. This non-network material not only tends to be network-*type* programming but most often is programming that originally aired on the networks themselves (called **off-network** programs).

Why do network and network-type content dominate television? *Availability* is one factor. There is 50 years' worth of already successful network content available for airing on local stations. A second factor is that the *production and distribution* mechanisms that have long served the broadcast networks are well established and serve the newer outlets just as well as they did NBC, CBS, and ABC. The final reason is us, the audience. The formats we are most comfortable with—our television tastes and expectations—have been and continue to be developed on the networks.

Episodes of TV Shows
www.
epguides.com

CBS
www.
cbs.com

HOW A PROGRAM GETS ON THE AIR

The national broadcast networks look at about 4,000 proposals a year for new television series. Many, if not most, are submitted at the networks'

The Creation of *Sesame Street*

In 1968 a public affairs program producer for Channel 13 in New York City identified a number of related problems that she believed could be addressed by a well-conceived, well-produced television show.

Joan Ganz Cooney saw that 80% of 3- and 4-year-olds, and 25% of 5-year-olds, in the United States did not attend any form of preschool. Children from financially disadvantaged homes were far less likely to attend preschool at these ages than their better-off peers. Children in these age groups who did go to preschool received little academic instruction; preschool was the equivalent of organized recess. Large numbers of U.S. children, then, entered first grade with no formal schooling, even though education experts had long argued that preschool years were crucial in children's intellectual and academic development. In addition, the disparity in academic preparedness between poor and other children was a national disgrace.

What did these children do instead of going to preschool? Ms. Cooney knew that they watched television. But she also knew that "existing shows for 3- through 5-year-old children . . . did not have education as a primary goal" (Ball & Bogatz, 1970, p. 2). Her idea was to use an interesting, exciting, visually and aurally stimulating television show as an explicitly educational tool "to promote the intellectual and cultural growth of preschoolers, particularly disadvantaged preschoolers" and to "teach children how to think as well as what to think" (Cook et al., 1975, p. 7).

Ms. Cooney established a nonprofit organization, the Children's Television Workshop (CTW), and sought funding for her program. Several federal agencies, primarily the Office of Education, a number of private foundations including Carnegie and Ford, and public broadcasters contributed $13.7 million for CTW's first 4 years.

After much research into producing a quality children's television show and studying the best instructional methods for teaching preschool audiences, CTW unveiled *Sesame Street* during the 1969 television season. It was an instant hit with children and parents. The *New Republic* said, "Judged by the standards of most other programs for preschoolers, it is imaginative, tasteful, and witty" (cited in Ball & Bogatz, 1970, p. 3). *Reader's Digest* said, "The zooming popularity of *Sesame Street* has created a sensation in U.S. television" (p. 3). *Saturday Review* gave its "Television Award" *to Sesame Street* "for the successful illustration of the principle that a major allocation of financial resources, educational research and creative talent can produce a widely viewed and popular series of regular

Children's Television Workshop
www.
ctw.org

invitation or instigation. Of the 4,000, about 100 will be filmed as **pilots,** or trial programs. Perhaps 20 to 30 will make it onto the air. Only half of these will last a full broadcast season. In a particularly good year, at most 3 or 4 will succeed well enough to be called hits. For this reason, the networks prefer to see ideas from producers with established track records and financial and organizational stability—for example, David E. Kelley is the source of *L.A. Law, Picket Fences, Ally McBeal, Boston Public, Chicago Hope,* and *The Practice,* and 20th Century Fox produced 22 different primetime shows on the 1999–2000 schedules of the national networks.

The way a program typically makes it onto the air differs somewhat for those who have been asked to submit an idea and for producers who bring their concepts to the networks. First, a producer has an *idea;* or a network has an idea and asks a proven producer to propose a show based on it (possibly offering a **put,** a deal that guarantees the producer that the network will order at least a pilot or it has to pay a hefty penalty). The producer must then *shop* the idea to one of the networks; naturally, an invited producer submits the proposal only to the network that asked for it. In either case, if the network is persuaded, it *buys the option* and asks for a written *outline* in which the original idea is refined. If still interested, the network will order a full *script.*

programs for preschool children with an immediate pay-off in cognitive learning" (p. 4). Originally scheduled for one hour a day during the school week, within months of its debut *Sesame Street* was being programmed twice a day on many public television stations, and many ran the entire week's schedule on Saturdays and Sundays.

Did Ms. Cooney and her show make a difference? Several national studies demonstrated that academic performance in early grades was directly and strongly correlated with regular viewing of *Sesame Street.* The commercial networks began to introduce educational fare into their Saturday morning schedules. ABC's *Grammar Rock, America Rock* (on U.S. history), and *Multiplication Rock* were critical and educational successes at the time, and a traditional children's favorite, CBS's *Captain Kangaroo,* started airing short films influenced by *Sesame Street* on a wide variety of social and personal skills. *Sesame Street* went international and appears even today in almost every developed nation in the world.

Even *Sesame Street*'s primary failure was a product of its success. Research indicated that *all* children benefited socially and academically from regular viewing. But middle- and upper-class children benefited more than did the disadvantaged children who were a specific target for the

The Sesame Street *gang.*

show. *Sesame Street* was accused of widening the gap between these children, rather than improving the academic performance of those most in need.

If the network approves that script, it will order the production of a pilot. Because of increased production costs and dwindling profits, the networks have begun penny-pinching on pilots, demanding that pilots for 60-minute dramas be shot as shorter, less expensive presentations. Pilots are then subjected to rigorous testing by the networks' own and independent audience research organizations. Based on this research, networks will often demand changes, such as writing out characters who tested poorly or beefing up story lines that test audiences particularly liked.

If the network is still interested, that is, if it believes that the show will be a hit, it orders a set number of episodes and schedules the show. In television's early days, an order might be for 26 or 39 episodes. Today, however, because of escalating production costs, the convention is at first to order six episodes. If these are successful, a second order of nine more is placed. Then, if the show is still doing well, a final nine episodes (referred to as *the back nine*) will be commissioned. Untested program ideas or producers who are not fully established might get initial orders only for two or three episodes. This is called **short ordering.**

At any point in this process, the network can decline interest. Moreover, the network invests very little of its own money during the developmental stages of a program. Even when a network orders a package of episodes, including those for an established hit that has been on for years, it typically pays producers only half of the show's entire production costs. In other words, producers engage in deficit financing—they *lose* money throughout the development process and continue to lose even more the longer their show stays on the network schedule.

The reason television program producers participate in this expensive enterprise is that they can make vast amounts of money in syndication, the sale of their programs to stations on a market-by-market basis. Even though the networks control the process from idea to scheduling and decide how long a show stays in their lineups, producers continue to own the rights to their programs. Once enough episodes are made (generally about 50, which is the product of 4 years on a network), producers can sell the syndicated package to the highest bidder in each of the 210 U.S. television markets, keeping all the revenues for themselves. This is the legacy of Lucille Ball's business genius. The price of a syndicated program depends on the market size, the level of competition between the stations in the market, and the age and popularity of the program itself. The station buys the right to a specified number of plays, or airings. After that, the rights return to the producer to be sold again and again. A program that has survived at least 4 years on one of the networks has proven its popularity, has attracted a following, and has accumulated enough individual episodes so that local stations can offer weeks of daily scheduling without too many reruns. The program is a moneymaker. In its first 5 years of syndication (1998–2002), for example, *Frasier* earned Paramount TV $300,000,000. In 2002 that same producer was collecting $1 million per episode of *Star Trek: The Next Generation* from cable channel TNN alone, and Picard and crew were syndicated to scores of broadcast stations around the country and running on all Universal's UPN affiliates (Burlingame, 2002).

Many critics of television argue that it is this deficit financing system that keeps the quality of content lower than it might otherwise be. A producer must attract the interest of a network with an idea that is salable on the network's schedule today, while incurring years of financial loss in hopes of having content that will be of interest to syndication viewers 4, 5, or even 10 years in the future. There is little incentive to gamble with characters or story lines; there is little profit in pushing the aesthetic boundaries of the medium. See Figure 8.2 for the all-time most-watched television shows.

Trends and Convergence in Television

For more information on this topic, view *Television: Inside WSEE-TV*, #4 on the CD *Media Tours*.

The process by which programs come to our screens is changing because the central position of networks in that process has been altered. In 1978 ABC, CBS, and NBC drew 92% of all prime-time viewers. In 1988, they collected 70%. In 2002 their share fell "to an historic low: 47%. Not only is it a record low, but it's the first time the four-network share has dropped below 50%, a benchmark broadcasters dreaded to fall beneath" (McClellan,

UPN
www.
upn.com

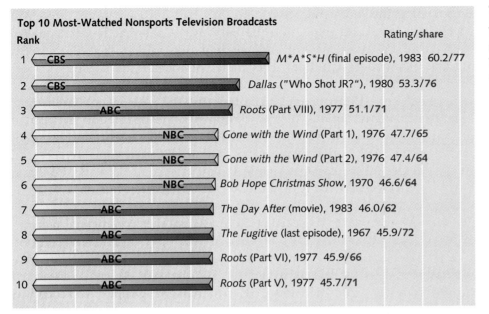

Top 10 Most-Watched Nonsports Television Broadcasts

Rank	Network		Rating/share
1	CBS	M*A*S*H (final episode), 1983	60.2/77
2	CBS	Dallas ("Who Shot JR?"), 1980	53.3/76
3	ABC	Roots (Part VIII), 1977	51.1/71
4	NBC	Gone with the Wind (Part 1), 1976	47.7/65
5	NBC	Gone with the Wind (Part 2), 1976	47.4/64
6	NBC	Bob Hope Christmas Show, 1970	46.6/64
7	ABC	The Day After (movie), 1983	46.0/62
8	ABC	The Fugitive (last episode), 1967	45.9/72
9	ABC	Roots (Part VI), 1977	45.9/66
10	ABC	Roots (Part V), 1977	45.7/71

Figure 8.2 Top 10 Most-Watched Nonsports Television Broadcasts. *Source:* Television Bureau of Advertising, *www.tvb.org*

2002, p. 6). New technologies—cable, VCR, DVD, digital video recorders, satellite, the Internet and digitalization, and even the remote control—have upset the long-standing relationship between medium and audience. Convergence is also reshaping that relationship.

CABLE

Cable television has reshaped the face of modern television. In 1948 television salesman John Walson erected a tower on a mountain to bring signals from Philadelphia to his town of Mahanoy City, Pennsylvania. He could not sell sets if people could not find channels. Within 2 years there were 14 such cable companies in the United States, all designed to improve reception through the **importation of distant signals** (delivering stations from distant locales). Today 67.4% of all U.S. television homes—72.1 million households—are wired. The precable television audience had very few choices—three commercial networks, public television, and an independent station or two sitting way out on the end of the UHF dial—but today's cable audience has 100 or more channel options. These new outlets provide channels for innovative, first-run series such as HBO's *Oz* and Showtime's *Soul Food*.

In addition, with the increased diffusion of **fiber optic** cable, which uses signals carried by light beams over glass fibers, 500-channel cable systems are becoming technologically feasible. By its mere existence, cable offers alternatives that were not available on broadcast networks. Chapter 9, "Cable and Other Multichannel Services," provides an in-depth look at these now-powerful delivery systems. Here we limit ourselves to cable's impact on the television industry as we knew . . . and now know it.

For more information on this topic, see NBC Video Clip #17 on the CD—*Future Television.*

The WB
www.
thewb.com

Empowering the Independents   Cable has had another, more subtle but every bit as powerful impact on the networks. Cable has helped equalize the size of the audience for independent and affiliated stations. NBC affiliate Channel 4 might appear as cable channel 11 and sit next to independent Channel 44 (cable channel 12). This erases the long-standing audience bias for the VHF channels. The fact that the network affiliate is now only one of many options further diminishes the distinction between it and its independent neighbors. Seventy-three independent stations were on the air in 1972. Today there are more than 400. These newly powerful independents helped create a viable fourth television network, Fox, and have nurtured development of the first-run syndication business.

Fox   In the early days of television there was another commercial network (DuMont), but only ABC, CBS, and NBC survived the 1950s. Ever since, speculators and dreamers have planned a "fourth network," but its development was hampered by the lack of available VHF channels. As cable eradicated the distinction between VHF and UHF, media magnate Rupert Murdoch was quick to move, uniting his own chain of stations with powerful independents in important markets. The new Fox Television Network won viewers away from its competitors with innovative and popular programming such as *The Simpsons, In Living Color, Melrose Place,* and *The X-Files.* The existence of Fox led to a change in the rules of program ownership.

In 1970, concerned that ABC, CBS, and NBC held a virtual monopoly over the production and distribution of television content, the FCC limited their ownership of the entertainment shows they aired, hoping that many independent producers bringing shows to the Big Three would result in a more diverse array of programming. Fox, however, was not bound by these limits when it began operation in 1985 because the FCC wanted to give the new network every chance to survive. Because the traditional networks

Gillian Anderson and David Duchovny in *The X-Files.* A hit on Fox, the program established the fourth network as a leader among young, urban viewers.

were losing audiences to cable and other alternatives, the Big Three lobbied the commission for change, pointing to Fox's success. Finally, in 1993, the FCC passed the **Financial Interest and Syndication Rules,** or **Fin-Syn.** Now the networks may produce and own the syndication rights to up to 50% of their prime-time entertainment fare. Warner Brothers TV, for example, owns 15 of the 18 pilots ordered by The WB for the 2002–2003 season. Disney-owned Touchstone TV produces all of Disney-owned ABC's comedies and owns a piece of 21 of the 23 pilots that network ordered for 2002–2003. NBC Studios owns all or part of 17 of the 20 pilots NBC ordered (Schlosser, 2002).

The impact of this change on what appears on television screens is unclear. The networks claim that content will get better. When it is their production money and potential syndication profits at risk, networks say they will be more likely to stay with a high-quality or innovative show until it finds an audience. Producers argue the opposite—that quality will suffer for two reasons. First, because independent producers will have less of a stake in future syndication money, they will not take innovative chances today. Second, because the networks are themselves only one part of larger, distant conglomerates, they, too, will naturally shy away from innovative or challenging programming. The Writers Guild of America, for example, points to the success of the controversial, groundbreaking *All in the Family,* one of the most influential television shows of all time. Its creator, Norman Lear, made two pilots for ABC in 1971, but the network kept demanding changes; they wanted it softened, watered down. "Lear refused and took the series to CBS, where he was allowed to follow his vision. . . . He could do that only because he owned it. Today, the network would have an ownership position and would be able simply to fire him and replace him with a writer and producer who would do what they wanted" (quoted in "Two Cheers," 2002, p. 4).

First-Run Syndication Syndicated programming is coming into viewers' homes in several new and important ways. In the era of network domination, **first-run syndication** was rarely attempted, except for game and talk shows. There was no need; a reservoir of already proven off-network fare was there for the choosing. But the increase in the number of independent stations hungry for quality fare, combined with their new financial clout, has made first-run syndication common. For several years, Paramount's *Star Trek: The Next Generation,* airing on more than 200 stations, would frequently beat network programming in the ratings. *Baywatch,* dubbed into 32 different languages, has 1 billion viewers in 141 countries. First-run syndication is attractive because producers do not have to run the gauntlet of the network programming process, and they keep 100% of the income.

Satellites have also boosted the number and variety of programs in first-run syndication. Game and talk shows, standard first-run fare in the past, have proliferated and been joined by programs such as *Judge Judy* and *Judge Joe Brown,* court shows distributed daily by satellite to hundreds of stations. These shows are inexpensive to make, inexpensive to distribute,

DirecTV
www.
directv.com

Audience and critic favorite *Malcolm in the Middle* became a syndication hit while original episodes were still aired on Fox.

and easily **stripped** (broadcast at the same time five nights a week). They allow an inexhaustible number of episodes with no repeats and are easy to promote ("Watch the case of the peeping landlord. Tune in at 7:30").

VCR

Introduced commercially in 1976, videocassette recorders (VCRs) now sit in more than 91% of U.S. homes. In some places, Flagstaff, Arizona, for example, they are in more than 97% of homes. There are approximately 30,000 video rental stores in the United States, and annual revenues for videocassette sales and rentals exceed $16 billion. Naturally, viewing rented and purchased videos further erodes the audience for traditional over-the-air television. The good news for the television industry, however, is that VCRs allow **time-shifting,** or taping a show for later viewing. Sixty-five percent of taping from television is from network-affiliated stations. Therefore, content (and commercials) that might otherwise have been missed can still be viewed. However, VCRs also permit **zipping**—that is, fast-forwarding through taped commercials, a practice used by 95% of all VCR owners (Evangelista, 2002).

DVD

In March 1996 DVD went on sale in U.S. stores. DVD might stand for digital video disc, digital versatile disc, or (according to its developers) it might stand for nothing at all, being merely a series of letters that sound "high tech" (Apar, 1997). The 4.7-inch DVD discs look exactly like audio CDs and deliver high-quality digital images and sound. Discs can be rented or purchased. Using a DVD player that looks much like a VCR machine, viewers can stop images with no loss of fidelity; can subtitle a movie in a number of languages; can search for specific scenes from an on-screen picture menu; and can access information tracks that give background on the movie, its production, and its personnel. Scenes and music not used in the theatrical release of a movie are often included on the disc. The 2001 DVD release of *Shrek* is indicative. Its studio, DreamWorks, added 11 *hours* of extra content to the 90-minute film. The two-disc set includes a 15-minute animated short created specifically for the DVD, and a new, 3-minute scene created specifically for insertion into the original movie. Technology was added that allows users to dub their voices in for those of any of the characters. Total cost: $19.95. DreamWorks even went as far as to skip video/DVD rental altogether, sending *Shrek* straight to home sales.

Innovations such as these have made DVD the fastest-growing consumer electronic product of all time. Sales of DVD players exceeded those of VCRs for the first time in September 2001. Machines now sit in more than 40% of all U.S. homes, and disc rental and sales exceed $8.1 billion a year (Lyman, 2002; Fraser, 2003). In June 2002, Circuit City, America's second-largest electronic chain, and Borders announced that they were dropping sales of videotapes in favor of exclusive sales of DVD. We are not likely to see the elimination of the VHS machine any time soon, however, because recordable DVD, while available, is still quite expensive, especially for those who already possess tape machines that can record.

REMOTE CONTROL

Another in-home technology the impact of which is being felt by the television industry is the remote control, currently in more than 90% of American homes. Viewers increasingly **zap** commercials, jumping to another channel with a mere flick of a finger. Two-thirds of all viewers zap commercials. The remote control also facilitates **grazing** (watching several programs simultaneously) and **channel surfing** or **cruising** (traveling through the channels focusing neither on specific programs nor on the commercials they house). The advertising industry estimates that at least half the audience manages to avoid television commercials.

DIRECT BROADCAST SATELLITE (DBS)

The technology for the direct delivery of television signals from satellites to homes has long existed. However, its diffusion has been hampered by the easy availability of cable, the cost and size of receiving dishes, and the inability to deliver local stations by satellite. With development of a small, affordable receiving dish, DirecTV began DBS service in 1994, offering 150 channels. Then, late in 1999, Congress passed legislation permitting DBS providers to carry local stations, erasing that problem. Today, because of mergers and failures, only two DBS providers operate in the United States, DirecTV and EchoStar/Dish Network. More on DBS can be found in Chapter 9.

The diffusion of DBS was initially slowed by people's unwillingness to install giant satellite dishes on their homes. The new breed of small receivers has overcome this problem.

DIGITAL VIDEO RECORDERS

New-technology writer John Quain (1999, p. 64) enthused, "The term *convergence* has been buzzing around the computer business for years. For the technology-bound digerati, it has represented the Holy Grail of acceptance: access to the mass-market audience for television. Despite many attempts, including Internet-on-your-TV boxes, video phones, and 'smart' cable converters, the marriage of computers and television has never been consummated—perhaps until now." This union produced the **digital video recorder (DVR**, sometimes called a **personal video recorder, or PVR).** In March 1999 Philips Electronics unveiled its version, TiVo, and soon after, Replay Networks introduced its ReplayTV. Both contain digital software that puts a significant amount of control over content in viewers' hands. What can viewers do with DVR? They can "rewind" and play back portions of a program while they are watching and recording it without losing any of that show. They can digitally record programs by simply telling the system their titles. By designating their favorite shows, viewers can instruct DVR to automatically record and deliver not only those programs but all similar content over a specified period of time. This application can even be used with the name of a favorite actor. Punch in Adam Sandler, and DVR will automatically record all programming in which he appears. The system accomplishes this through an automatically placed nightly, toll-free call to the service provider that lasts no more than 3 minutes. If a viewer should use the phone while this call is being placed, DVR hangs up and makes the necessary call later.

DVR does not deliver programming the way broadcasters, cablecasters, and DBS systems do. Rather, it is employed *in addition* to these content providers. To use either ReplayTV or TiVo, viewers must buy a special receiver, and TiVo requires a monthly service charge. It is too early in the life of this technology to predict its success or failure. Today there are 2.9 million DVR households, and industry predictions see 28.7 million by 2008 (Evangelista, 2002). The devices themselves are expensive. Both systems require access to a telephone jack, often a problem in rooms in which a television typically might sit, such as a den or living room, and the technology faces a copyright legal challenge from the broadcast and cable industries, both of which fear its commercial-skipping potential. But, as with DVD, its mere presence is additional evidence that television viewing, as we have long known and practiced it, is changing dramatically. See the box "Does DVR Make You a Thief?"

DIGITAL TELEVISION

Digitalization of video signals reduces their size; therefore, more information can be carried over telephone wires (belonging to either a cable or phone company) and stored. The traditional television broadcasters see digitalization of television signals as their salvation, because it would allow them to carry multiple forms of content on the spectrum space currently

TiVo
www.
tivo.com

ReplayTV
www.
sonicblue.com

used to carry their one broadcast signal. But digitalization for the purpose of transmitting multiple signals conflicts with the use of their spectrum space to transmit high-definition digital television (HDTV). This puts broadcasters in a bind, because viewers want beautiful, clear, wide-screen, high-definition images, but they also want a lot of channels of video and other data. If broadcasters opt to devote their entire spectrum space, as technologically required, to the transmission of high-definition images, they will lose audience share to cable, the Internet, and DBS, all of which offer multiple channels of programming and data. If they opt to use digitalization to divide their channels (called **multiplexing**) and in effect become minicable companies themselves, offering over-the-air services such as clearer digital video images (although not of HDTV quality), Internet access, paging services, and constant data flow of information such as stocks and sports scores, they will lose HDTV set owners who want the even crisper images of DVD.

The digital television revolution is progressing slowly for a number of reasons. First is the lack of availability of digital receivers. Even though many of today's sets are sold as *digital*, this refers to how the set itself constructs the image; they do not have digital tuners. The "vast majority of 'digital television sets' being manufactured, advertised, and sold at retail stores do not allow viewers to access local over-the-air digital stations," according to National Association of Broadcasters Edward Fritts (2002, p. 2). Viewers wanting to receive digital stations must either incur the additional cost of a set-top digital tuning box or pay much more for a true digital receiving set than they would for a more typical set. This problem should be overcome in a few years, given the FCC's August 2002 ruling that by 2007, all receivers imported into or made in the United States come equipped with digital tuners. Second is what Fritts calls the interoperability/compatibility issue. Telephone and computer companies want **progressive scanning,** that is, the format compatible with today's personal computers. In progressive scanning, the entire picture is built line by line in one scan of the television's electronic beam. Sets equipped to receive progressive signals can also use **interlaced scanning** (the electron beams sweep the picture tube twice, creating half the image's lines on the first pass and then filling in the gaps in the second). Many broadcasters want the standard to be interlaced scanning, the format compatible with their own current standards for manufacturing and broadcasting (although unable to accommodate progressive scanning). After intense lobbying by both sides, the FCC refused to set a standard, leaving the telecommunications industry to set a standard for itself. The operation of interlaced and progressive scanning is contrasted in Figure 8.3 on page 260.

A third problem in the diffusion of digital television is that cable operators too must be willing to change over to digital. It does broadcasters who have made the expensive conversion to digital no good if cable operators cannot or will not devote valuable channels to digital signals. Some small steps have been made to resolve this difficulty. Although the over-the-air broadcasters have long lobbied the FCC to pass

Does DVR Make You a Thief?

DVR, like VCR, permits viewers to record network and cable television programs for later viewing. And, of course, like 95% of all VCR owners, DVR users can skip the commercials. In fact, they can do so without having to zip (fast-forward) through them. They can simply (digitally) delete them altogether. Moreover, DVR viewers can *skip the commercials while they watch the shows* as they are broadcast or cablecast. This is possible because DVR permits viewers to digitally "rewind" and play the program they are watching while that program is still in progress. Half of the country's DVR owners "always" skip the commercials; a quarter skip them "frequently" (Evangelista, 2002).

Your favorite shows—*Friends, The Simpsons, ABC Monday Night Football, Malcolm in the Middle*—without commercials. You might think this is a great idea, but the broadcast and cable industries see things a bit differently. "The free television that we've all enjoyed for so many years is based on us watching these commercials," said Jamie Kellner, CEO of Turner Broadcasting. "There's no Santa Claus. If you don't watch the commercials, someone's going to have to pay for television and it's going to be you" (quoted in Harmon, 2002, p. C1). In another venue, Mr. Kellner upped the ante: "Your contract with the network when you get the show is you're going to watch the spots. Otherwise you couldn't get the show on an ad-supported basis. Any time you skip a commercial . . . you're actually stealing the programming" (quoted in "Soundbites," 2002, p. 2).

Comments such as these have put DVR, its ability to facilitate zipping, and even our "contract" with the broadcasters in the cultural forum. As for the technology itself, virtually all the major media conglomerates—Viacom, NBC, Disney, AOL/Time Warner, News Corp.—have sued the manufacturers of DVR in federal court, claiming that it facilitates copyright infringement. Their position is that they distribute a copyrighted piece of content (the program plus the commercials it houses) and that DVR allows violation of that copyright by encouraging the illegal alteration of that content. But how is this different from VCR? DVR makes zipping easier, but it's still zipping; and the Supreme Court rejected these same industry complaints against VCR in 1984. "What are they going to attack next, the mute button?" asks Ken Potashner, chief executive of Sonicblue, the company that makes ReplayTV machines, "We've provided an efficiency improvement for a consumer who is compelled to skip a commercial" (quoted in Harmon, 2002, p. C3).

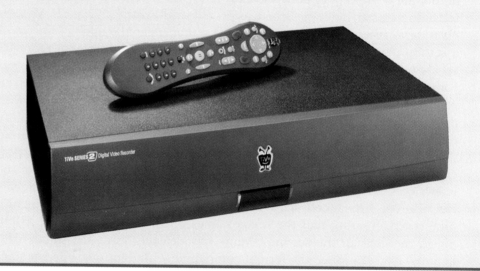

federal **digital must-carry rules** requiring cable operators to carry all digital, as well as analog, channels, some cable operators are making the move voluntarily.

These obstacles notwithstanding, the FCC requires all television stations to convert completely to digital transmission by 2006. At that time, they must return their analog licenses to the government.

Indeed, the changeover has begun. CBS introduced digital television on October 29, 1998, with its broadcast of the launch of the space shuttle *Discovery*. By October 2003, well over 1,060 local stations were

This, then, raises the question of our "contract" with the broadcasters and cablecasters. What if you are "compelled to skip a commercial" because you have to go to the bathroom, or because you are hungry and need a snack, or because your baby is crying? According to Turner Broadcasting's Kellner, you have a contract with the networks to watch their spots, and "any time you skip a commercial you're actually stealing." Do you think skipping a commercial is theft? If so, is it a smaller "crime" if you do so to care for your child than if you are simply annoyed by the constant, often imbecilic commercial interruptions?

Critics of the industry view also raise the issue of the broadcasters' contract with us, the public. As you saw in Chapter 7, broadcasters do not own the airwaves; they simply use them in exchange for their promise to serve our interest, convenience, and necessity. And despite numerous legal reiterations of this philosophy (see Chapter 14), public service, they contend, has virtually disappeared from many broadcasters' lexicons.

But ad-based broadcast and cable networks do provide us with entertainment and information, and if you can ignore the cost of advertising that is built into the price of the products we buy, they do so for free. Shouldn't they get something in return—specifically, ad dollars based on our viewing of their commercials? Critics of the industry view of DVR-as-crime-tool do not dispute the need for commercial broadcasters and cablecasters to make a profit. They contend, however, that these same companies build ads directly into their content in the form of product placements and other indirect advertising methods, such as the company logos and brand names that inundate most televised sporting events. We did not "contract" for these. In addition, TiVo and ReplayTV permit the transmission of commercials of any length, tailored to the specific individual viewer if he or she wishes to see them. For example, if a viewer is watching MTV, he or she can be sent an electronic tag that shows a 30-second Best Buy electronics commercial featuring singer Sheryl Crow visible only to DVR users. If a viewer wishes, he or she can click an icon in the spot and instantly be linked to a 12-minute Sheryl Crow miniconcert, sponsored by Best Buy, while the DVR automatically records the original MTV programming for subsequent viewing. Moreover, because DVR systems record users' viewing (and deletions), these data can be used to target even more specific spots for even more specific users. This is the market at work, they say, not some phony notion of theft or contracts.

What do you think? What, if any, obligation do you have to watch commercials? Do you draw a distinction between VCR and DVR based on DVR's more efficient zipping? Is this reasonable? Do you see DVR-abetted commercial avoidance as, if not a crime, at least somehow less proper than pressing the mute button on your remote or simply walking out of the room? Would you be willing to view specially tailored, presumably more useful commercials in exchange for the ability to avoid all those commercials that say nothing at all to you? Finally, throughout this book you have and will see efforts by an entrenched medium to derail the development and diffusion of a newer medium—newspapers would not give news to radio; the film studios would not rent their movies to television or permit their stars to appear on the tube; the recording industry fought DAT and continues to fight Internet file-sharing; television impeded the diffusion of cable for decades; cable continues to lobby Congress and the FCC against DBS and open access for Internet service providers; the broadcast and entertainment industries fought VCR all the way to the Supreme Court. Is this broadcast and cable industry challenge to DVR any different? If not, why not? If so, how so? Put your voice in the cultural forum.

broadcasting in digital. In the top 30 markets, nearly all network affiliates were digital. Ninety-nine percent of all U.S. television homes were in markets with at least one digital station, half in markets with four. As for HDTV, ABC and CBS were offering their prime-time lineups in high definition, as was PBS, and all networks were presenting high-profile sporting events such as the Olympics and the Kentucky Derby in hi-def. Cable movie channels HBO and Showtime were early HDTV leaders, and today, along with the Discovery Channel, offer HDTV 24 hours a day.

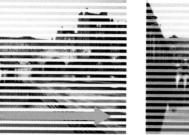

First scan

Second scan

Interlaced: Electron beams sweep across picture tube, creating half of the lines, then fill in the gaps on the second pass.

Progressive: The entire picture is built line by line in one scan.

Figure 8.3 Interlaced vs. progressive scanning.

WebTV
www.
webtv.com

Broadcast.com
www.
broadcast.yahoo.com

THE INTERNET ON TELEVISION

Although America OnLine, @Home, and Yahoo! all announced plans to begin offering the Internet over home television sets, the most aggressive advocate for accessing the Net on the home screen is Microsoft's WebTV. **WebTV** bet that the convergence of television and the Internet would be sufficiently attractive to viewers/users that they would pay $300 for a set-top receiving box and $20 a month for the service itself.

WebTV turns a television set into a computer screen, permitting access to the Internet. As such, it provides not only access to the Web but also several sites of its own, including one for children and another serving up local weather and news. But WebTV also offers several features that allow the Internet to enhance television viewing itself. For example, it provides a program-listing feature that takes viewers from a renewable screen schedule directly to a show with a simple click. Using the same feature, users can program a VCR with a click of the mouse/remote or instruct the technology to alert them that a favorite program is about to start.

Today, there are about one million subscribers to the service, not many more than there were 2 years ago. *Los Angeles Times* technology writers Edmund Sanders and Jon Healy labeled AOL's effort, AOLTV, "once considered the symbol of the combination of technology and entertainment . . . a failure" (2002, p. B3). Some observers feel that Net via television will never become popular because, even though innovators may converge technologies, they cannot force users to converge Internet use and television viewing habits. The computer and Internet, they argue, are task-oriented technologies that users are most comfortable using "up close and personal." But television is primarily a broad-based entertainment and information medium that viewers are most comfortable watching from several feet away.

TELEVISION AND VIDEO ON THE INTERNET

Television on the Internet has yet to take off. One problem is legal—local television stations are licensed to use network and syndicated material only in their local markets. Therefore, stations cannot stream content if it can be received outside their broadcast area. Advances in software technology promise to solve this problem within a few years. Another problem is the issue of piracy. If a program is sent on the Internet, it can be downloaded and copied infinitely. Again, technological solutions are in the offing. There is also the issue of **bandwidth,** space on the wires that bring content into people's homes. Most people do not have the necessary bandwidth or fast enough modems (see Chapter 7) for clear reception of television on their home computers. Finally, people simply seem unwilling to sit in front of their PCs to watch full-length television shows.

While television-over-the-Net is virtually nonexistent, video compression software does permit the downloading of high-quality moving images from the Internet. Broadcast.com, AtomFilms, RealNetwork, and similar companies offer a variety of specialty transmissions such as movie trailers, short independent films, music videos, space shuttle launches, feature films, and even old television shows. Providers such as CNN.com and ABCNews.com allow the downloading of video news clips. The true future of converged Internet/television technology, then, appears to be in the presentation of special events. Real Broadcast Network's general manager Mark Hall says, "Event programming is the Number 1 thing. Doing it on the Internet provides a unique benefit that you just wouldn't get on TV" (Tedesco, 1999, p. 22). That unique benefit includes not only exclusivity, but interactivity.

INTERACTIVE TELEVISION

It is not only the Internet that permits interactivity. Cable and satellite also allow viewers to "talk" back to content providers. Interactive television, already here for some, will eventually be a part of every viewer/user's media environment, providing a number of services:

- *Video-on-demand (VOD)*—viewers can access a virtually unlimited array of pay-per-view movies and other content that can be watched whenever they want; VOD also permits pausing, rewinding, and fast-forwarding as if the content were on videotape.

- *Web and Internet access*—we've already seen how WebTV works; other companies are joining this Microsoft innovator. E-mail, personal calendars, chat rooms, interactive game playing, everything users do online with their PCs, they can do with their interactive television sets.

- *One-click shopping*—television content, including commercials, can carry hidden graphics and text that can be called up with a remote control; once on screen, a simple click can automatically order the given product.

- *Local information on demand*—using a remote control, viewers can summon local information to their screens; for example, when watching political debates, viewers might call up information about the candidates' planned visits to their community, or the candidates' congressional voting record on issues of local importance.

AtomFilms
www.
atomfilms.shockwave.com

RealNetwork
www.
realnetwork.com

- *Program interactivity*—prompted by an on-screen cue, viewers can predict upcoming plays in a football game, choose camera angles in performances and sporting events, play along with game show contestants, or learn more about a favorite sitcom actor's career.
- *Interactive program guides*—viewers can navigate "smart" program schedules to plan viewing.

For now, however, greater diffusion of interactive television is hampered by lack of bandwidth (or, in the case of DBS, the electromagnetic spectrum) for viewer feedback. Fiber optic cable is making **broadband** (channels with broad information-carrying capacity) access more of a reality, and industry experts estimate that by 2005, 30 million Americans will have sufficient bandwidth for full interactivity (Amdur, 2003). Still, this is only a fraction of the total Web and television audience. Another problem potentially limiting the fuller diffusion of interactive television is that many people simply may not want it. As technology writer Bill Syken observed, "Television and work do not go together as naturally as, say, television and beer" (2000, p. 27). See Chapter 9 for more on broadband and interactive television.

DEVELOPING MEDIA LITERACY SKILLS

Recognizing Staged News

For years studies have shown that a majority of the American public turns to television as the source of most of its news and that viewers rank it as the most believable news source. Television news can be immediate and dramatic, especially when events being covered lend themselves to visual images. But what if they don't? News may be journalism, but television news is also a television *show,* and as such it must attract viewers. Television newspeople have an obligation to truthfully and accurately inform the public, but they also have an obligation to attract a large number of people so their station or network is profitable.

Even the best television journalists cannot inform a public that does not tune in, and the public tunes in to see pictures. Television professionals, driven to get pictures, often walk the fine ethical line of **news staging,** that is, re-creating some event that is believed to or could have happened. Sometimes news staging takes simple forms; for example, a reporter may narrate an account of an event he or she did not witness while video of that event is played. The intended impression is that the reporter is on the scene. What harm is there in this? It's common practice on virtually all U.S. television news shows. But how much of a leap is it from that to ABC's 1994 broadcast of reporter Cokie Roberts, wrapped tightly in winter clothes, seemingly reporting from Capitol Hill on a blustery January night when she was in fact standing in a nearby Washington studio, her "presence" at the scene staged by computer digital technology?

The broadcasters' defense is, "This is not staging in the sense that the *event* was staged. What does it matter if the reporter was not actually on

Did Geraldo Rivera engage in permissible or impermissible news staging when he reported from "sacred ground" although he was miles from the actual spot?

the spot? What was reported actually did happen." If you accept this view (the event *did* happen, therefore it's not news staging), how would you evaluate Fox News's Geraldo Rivera's reporting from "sacred ground," the scene of a battle in Afghanistan in which U.S. forces suffered heavy losses, even though he was miles from the actual spot? And if you accept digital alteration of news scenes to place network reporters "at the scene," how would you evaluate CBS's common practice of digitally inserting its network logo on billboards and buildings that appear behind its reporters and anchors (Poniewozik, 2000)? If this staging is acceptable to you, why not OK the digital enhancement of fires and explosions in the news?

Some media literate viewers may accept the-event-did-happen argument, but another form of news staging exists that is potentially more troublesome—re-creation. In 1992 the producers of *Dateline NBC* re-created the explosion of a GMC truck, justifying the move with the argument that similar explosions "had happened" (Chapter 14). In the mid-1990s a Denver news show ran footage of a pit bull fight it had arranged and defended its action on the ground that these things "do happen." *ABC Evening News* simulated surveillance camera recordings of U.S. diplomat Felix Bloch handing over a briefcase to a shady character on the street to accompany a 1989 report on Bloch's arrest on espionage charges. The simulation even had a surveillance camera's dark, grainy look and the time code numbers racing in the corner of the picture. This staging was justified with the claim that it "could have happened."

Where do media professionals draw the line? What happens to the public's trust in its favorite news source as the distinctions between fact and fiction, reality and illusion, what is and what is digital, and reporting and re-creating disappear?

Living Media Literacy

Turn Off Your TV

The Media Foundation (see Chapter 12) runs an annual campaign called TV Turn Off Week, typically in April. Hundreds of thousands of viewers around the world simply tune out for a week. There is a Web site (adbusters.org/campaigns/tvturnoff), posters, chat rooms, and contact lists, all designed to support communal action. You can involve yourself in the global community of TV-turn-offers by accessing the site and signing on.

But you, as a media literate individual, can test for yourself just how free you are of television's hold. In other words, whether you are a television fan or foe, you can see if you control your viewing or if your viewing controls you. To start, pick a 7-day period (or 5-day if that's how you choose to define a week) and simply stop watching. That means no television at all. No videos. No video games. If you are truly adventurous, enlist one or more friends, family, or roommates.

Now the hard part. Changing your routine viewing habits for a few days will not do very much for you unless you reflect on its meaning. Ask yourself, and any confederates you may have enlisted, these questions:

1. How easy or difficult was it to break away from television? Why?

2. What did you learn about your television consumption habits?

3. How did you use the freed-up time? Were you able to find productive activity, or did you spend your time longing for the tube?

4. Describe your interaction with other people during the week. Did your conversations change? That is, were there alterations in duration, depth, subject matter?

5. To which other media did you turn to replace your television viewing? Why those in particular? Did you learn anything about them as "TV substitutes"?

6. If you were unable to complete the week of nonviewing, describe why. How easy or difficult was it to come to the decision to give up? Why?

7. Do you consider it a failure to have resumed watching before the week was up? Why or why not?

8. Once you resume watching, either after the week has passed or when you abandon nonviewing, place yourself on a scale of 1 to 10, with 1 being I-Control-the-TV and 10 being The-TV-Controls-Me. Explain why you rated yourself as you did.

If you see a televised news story labeled as a re-creation or simulation, what leads you to trust the re-creator's or simulator's version? Media literate people develop strategies to analyze content, deciding where *they* draw the line and rejecting staged news that crosses it. The news producer must balance service to the public against ratings and profit, but viewers must balance their desire for interesting, stimulating visuals against confidence that the news is reported rather than manufactured.

Why did ABC feel compelled not only to have Ms. Roberts appear to report from in front of the Capitol Building but also to have it seem, by her dress, that she was quite cold? There are two possible explanations for staging such as this. One is the need to meet television audience demands for visuals. The second explanation is the assumption, widely held by television professionals, that people are incapable of reading, accepting, interpreting, and understanding important issues unless they are presented in a manner that meets viewers' expectations of the news. If this is accurate, media literate viewers must reconsider their expectations of the medium. If this assumption about viewers is incorrect, media literate people must make that clear to those who produce the news, either by choosing news programs that avoid staging or by protesting to those that do.

Chapter Review

Mechanical methods of television transmission were developed as early as 1884 by Paul Nipkow, but it was the electronic scanning developed by Zworykin and Farnsworth that moved the medium into its modern age. World War II delayed the diffusion of television but hastened its technical development. At the end of the war, a mature medium, complete with network structure, formats, stars, and economic base, was in place. By 1960, 559 stations were being watched by 90% of all homes in the United States. The quiz show scandal, Lucille Ball's production innovations, McCarthyism, and the onset of the ratings served to define the new medium's character.

The business of television is still dominated by the networks, although their power is in decline. New television technologies promise the greatest changes, not only in the business of television but in the relationship between medium and audience. Cable has eroded the network audience share by providing numerous alternatives for viewers, empowering the independents, allowing for creation of a powerful fourth network, and giving life to the first-run syndication business. VCRs have further eroded audiences by allowing viewers to time-shift and zip. And direct broadcast satellite, hampered at first by the success of cable and the size and cost of receiving dishes, is now a young but well-entrenched technology. DVD and DVR, too, are gaining in popularity.

Convergence, particularly in the form of digital television and Internet-based video, is also reshaping the television landscape. All stations are expected to convert completely to digital broadcasting by 2006, although the unavailability of digital receivers, disagreement over a technical standard, and cable's willingness to convert too are slowing digital television's full rollout. The convergence of television and the Internet, just under way, holds the potential to reinvent both media, particularly because of the promise of fuller interactivity.

News staging raises several issues for media literate viewers. Staging can be seemingly harmless, such as reporters narrating accounts of events they were not at to give the appearance that they are on the scene. But literate television viewers must make their own judgments about more questionable practices.

Key Terms

Use the text's CD-ROM and the Online Learning Center at www.mhhe.com/baran to further your understanding of the following terminology.

Questions for Review

1. What is the importance of each of the following to the history of television: Paul Nipkow, John Logie Baird, Vladimir Zworykin, Philo Farnsworth, and Newton Minow?
2. How do VCR, DVD, and DVR differ? How are they similar in the services they offer viewers?
3. What was the impact on television of the quiz show scandal, *I Love Lucy*, McCarthyism, and the Nielsen ratings?
4. How are the ratings taken? What are some complaints about the ratings system?
5. What is the network–affiliate relationship?
6. How does a program typically make it to the air? How does syndication figure in this process?
7. How have cable, VCR, DVD, DVR, and DBS affected the networks?
8. What are some of the changes in television wrought by cable?
9. What is first-run syndication?
10. What factors are delaying the fuller diffusion of digital television?
11. Is there a difference between HDTV and digital television? If so, what is it?
12. What are interlaced and progressive scanning?
13. What forms of Internet television or video do most viewers seem to favor? Why?
14. What are some of the forms that interactive television can take?
15. What is news staging?

Questions for Critical Thinking and Discussion

1. Do you think single-sponsorship of television programs necessarily produces quality fare? Do spot commercial sales necessarily produce mediocre fare? Defend your position.
2. Do you agree with Newton Minow's assessment of television? If so, what can be done to improve the medium's performance?
3. As an independent producer, what kind of program would you develop for the networks? How immune do you think you could be from the pressures that exist in this process?
4. Does the prospect of interactive television interest you? Why or why not? What aspects of interactive television most appeal to you, if any? Do you agree with the argument that television and work "don't mix"? If so, what future do you predict for interactive television?
5. Is news staging ever permissible? If not, why not? If yes, under what conditions? Have you ever recognized a report as staged when it was not so identified? Describe what you saw.

Important Resources

Broadcasting & Cable Magazine. This weekly magazine for radio, television, and cable offers insightful articles on regulation, economics, programming, and technology—virtually every aspect of contemporary broadcasting.

Barnouw, E. (1970). *The image empire: A history of broadcasting in the United States, from 1953.* **New York: Oxford University Press.** This third volume of the definitive study of broadcast history in the United States focuses on the beginning of television; it reads like a novel and is valuable to fans as well as scholars.

Barnouw, E. (1990). *Tube of plenty: The evolution of American television.* **New York: Oxford University Press.** This popular and readable book is Barnouw's effort to condense those parts of his landmark trilogy that deal with television into one volume. Barnouw also used this book to update the reader on what had happened in television between the publication of the trilogy and 1990.

MacDonald, J. F. (1993). *One nation under television: The rise and decline of network TV.* **Chicago: Nelson-Hall.** An entertaining examination of what the author calls "the most important social and cultural force in the United States during the last four decades." It is a history of television that centers on the networks. Particularly interesting is its insider look at how programming decisions were made during different stages of the medium's and the country's life.

Newcomb, H. (2000). *Television: The critical view.* **New York: Oxford University Press.** A collection of critical essays on most aspects of television's operation and programming, this book is meant for television-sophisticated readers. It has been through many editions, a testimony to its popularity and the timeliness of its contents.

Reel, A. F. (1979). *The networks: How they stole the show.* **New York: Charles Scribner's.** An excellent, readable, and opinionated study of how the networks took over television at a time when the medium was young. Special interest is given to the regulatory decisions that shaped television's early character. Don't let the date dissuade you.

Schwartz, E. I. (2002). *The last lone inventor.* **New York: HarperCollins** and **Stashower, D. (2002).** *The boy genius and the mogul.* **New York: Broadway.** Two "wonderful, riveting, and bittersweet" (according to *The New Yorker*) studies of the life and work of Philo Farnsworth. Equally important, they offer a detailed look at the personal side of the development of television and commentary on how science and invention have changed since Farnsworth's time.

Television History	www.mediahistory/umn.edu
Zworykin	www.ieee.org/organizations/history_center/ oral_histories/ transcripts/zworykin21.html
Farnsworth	www.invent.org/hall_of_fame/56.html
Quiz Show Scandal	www.history.acusd.edu/gen/recording/ television7.html
McCarthyism	www.mccarthy.cjb.net/
Radio Television News Directors Association	www.rtnda.org
A. C. Nielsen	www.nielsenmedia.com
Children's Television Workshop	www.ctw.org
National Association of Broadcasters	www.nab.org
ABC	www.abc.com
NBC	www.nbc.com
Episodes of TV Shows	www.epguides.com
CBS	www.cbs.com
Fox	www.fox.com
UPN	www.upn.com
The WB	www.thewb.com
DirecTV	www.directv.com
Dish Network	www.dishnetwork.com
TiVo	www.tivo.com
ReplayTV	www.sonicblue.com
WebTV	www.webtv.com
Broadcast.com	www.broadcast.yahoo.com
AtomFilms	www.atomfilms.shockwave.com
RealNetwork	www.realnetwork.com

Cable and Other Multichannel Services

LEARNING OBJECTIVES

Many observers inside and outside the media industries believe that, before long, most media content will be delivered to us by cable or other multichannel provider such as a satellite company. The implications for the existing media industries, for us as their audiences, and for our culture could not be more profound. After studying this chapter you should

- be familiar with the history and development of the cable and other multichannel industries and with cable and DBS themselves as media.

- understand in detail how content moves from originator to home via multichannel services.

- recognize how the organizational, regulatory, and economic nature of the multichannel industries shapes their relationship with their viewers.

- be aware of new and emerging multichannel video technologies and their potential impact.

- understand the significant implications for the mass media industries, for us as audience members, for our democracy, and for the culture of the migration of media from a broadcast to a telecommunications orientation.

- possess improved cable, DBS, and other multichannel service media literacy skills, especially in understanding pricing strategies.

ALL RIGHT, THIS IS IT! OPENING DAY—THE BOMBERS VERSUS the Birds in Baltimore. Major league baseball is back! You're a Yankees fan; your friends are at your place. The beer and soda are cold, the pizza hot. But there is no game. Using the remote, you click to the on-screen guide. Nope, not there. That's strange; you're sure it's on. You just talked to your upstate cousin and she has it. She's getting it on Cox Cable. You have cable; you watched the Yanks all last year. As your pals demand, "Waasssssuuuup?" you call your cable company, Cablevision. The lady answering the phone is polite enough, but all you get out of her is that the system does not carry the YES Network (owned by the Yankees and on which the team appears). Well, you say, you want the package that includes YES. Sorry, she says, Cablevision does not offer YES at all.

269

Three million New York area Cablevision customers were denied televised Yankee baseball in 2002 because of a dispute between their cable provider and the YES Network.

Next day. The Yanks lost anyway, so other than the embarrassment of assembling a half dozen of your friends to watch a game that was never on, you didn't miss too much. But you're still angry. You call the Consumers Union to complain. Their spokesman, David Butler, after a long explanation about cable deregulation, basic and premium packages, open access, court fights, rights to refunds, and similar battles in the recent past in your area between Time Warner Cable and Disney, sums it up for you: "This is essentially a fight between monopolists" (quoted in Berkowitz & Joshi, 2002, p. 2).

Monopolists? You don't care about monopolists! You don't read the business page. You're a baseball fan, and baseball is as much a part of television as commercials. Well, not quite. Baseball, now, is part of *cable* television—nationwide, 65% of all locally televised baseball games are unavailable unless you subscribe to cable, satellite, or some other **multichannel service**—that is, a fee-based provider of video content (Berkowitz & Joshi, 2002). The teams are looking to the future, and the future in sports (maybe in all television) is in cable.

In this chapter we will look at that future, one that, of necessity, will include Internet service providers and the telephone companies, because the future of television viewing—indeed, all telecommunications—is in the delivery of multiple channels of content by fat wires, that is, broadband. But before we get there, we have to look back at how the cable television with which we are familiar and that is now undergoing so much change evolved into its current nature. We will examine cable's technological and economic development and how confusing and contradictory regulation stunted and shaped its growth. We will see how a modern cable company operates and learn about the different types of cable programming, including pay cable and public access.

Because cable sits at the center of much of the convergence that we have been reading and will continue to read about, advances in cable technology that drive that convergence—fiber optics, digital cable, interactive cable, multiplexing, video compression, and video-on-demand—are presented in terms of both their current functioning and how they may shape the content we receive in the near future. Concentration of ownership, a factor in all our contemporary media, is an issue in cable, too. We study its various forms—**multiple system operators (MSOs),** vertical integration, and conglomeration—and the arguments for and against them. The interaction between the **telcos** (phone companies) and the cable industry promises even more convergence as telecommunications services are bundled into cable.

A Short History of Cable and Other Multichannel Services

John Walson

Mahanoy City, Pennsylvania, appliance salesman John Walson was having trouble selling televisions in 1948. The Pocono Mountains sat between his town and Philadelphia's three new stations. But Walson was also a power-line worker, so he convinced his bosses to let him run a wire from a tower he erected on New Boston Mountain to his store. As more and more people became aware of his system, he began wiring the homes of customers who bought his sets. In June of that year Walson had 727 subscribers for his **community antenna television (CATV)** system (Chin, 1978). Although no one calls it CATV anymore, cable television was born.

The cable Walson used was a twin-lead wire, much like the cord that connects a lamp to an outlet. To attract even more subscribers, he had to offer improved picture quality. He accomplished this by using *coaxial cable* and self-manufactured boosters (or amplifiers). Coaxial cable—copper-clad aluminum wire encased in plastic foam insulation, covered by an aluminum outer conductor, and then sheathed in plastic—had more bandwidth than did twin-lead wire. As a result, it allowed more of the original signal to pass and even permitted Walson to carry a greater number of channels.

As Walson continued to expand his CATV business, Milton Jerrold Shapp, later to become Pennsylvania's governor, noticed thousands of antennas cluttering the roofs of department stores and apartment buildings. Seeing Walson's success, he set up master antennas and connected the sets in these buildings to them, employing a signal booster he had developed. This was the start of **master antenna television (MATV).**

With expanded bandwidth and the new, powerful Jerrold boosters, these systems began experimenting with the importation of distant signals, using wires not only to provide improved reception but also to offer a wider variety of programming. They began delivering independent stations from as far away as New York to fill their then-amazing 7 to 10 channels. By 1962, 800 systems were providing cable television to more than 850,000 homes.

During cable's infancy, many over-the-air broadcasters saw it as something of a friend. It extended their reach, boosting both audience size and profits. Then, in November 1972, a company called Sterling Manhattan Cable launched a new channel, Home Box Office, or HBO. Only a handful of homes caught HBO's debut, but the broadcasters' mild concern over this development turned to outright antagonism toward cable in 1975, when new HBO owner Time, Inc. began distributing the movie channel by satellite. Now **pay cable** was eating into the broadcasters' audience by offering high-quality, nationally produced and distributed content. With the public's enthusiastic embrace of pay cable, the medium reached maturity.

The national distribution by satellite of HBO in 1975 changed cable television, all television in fact, for all time.

Figure 9.1 The Cable Signal—From Source to Home: A typical cable operation collects and distributes content in this manner from headend to homes.

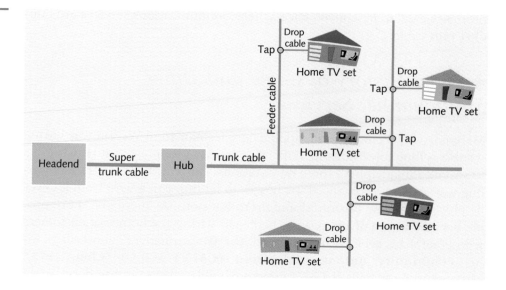

National Association of Minorities in Cable
www.
namic.com

CABLE RECEPTION AND DISTRIBUTION

The way cable systems receive and distribute programming has changed little since their earliest days. The process of getting a picture to a home screen begins at a receiving antenna, which includes microwave and satellite receiving equipment. The gathered signals are collected from these receivers at the **headend.** From there, they are sent over a **super trunk cable** to a **hub,** typically the cable system operation itself, at which they are processed and boosted for distribution. The cable that leads from the hub into the community is the **trunk cable,** which divides into **feeder cables** to access individual neighborhoods or areas. The line that runs from the feeder to our homes is a **drop cable.** The layout of a typical cable operation is presented in Figure 9.1.

CABLE'S ECONOMIC STRUCTURE

The economics of the cable industry were established once cable became a medium of expanded viewing options (rather than one of improved reception). At the outset, potential cable operators must make a substantial investment in the construction of their systems, with little hope of a quick return on those expenditures. New franchise operators (those with authority to offer cable service) spend heavily for such things as facility construction, receiving and distribution equipment, and wiring neighborhoods and homes—all before a single subscriber pays a dime. Operators can gauge their likelihood of success by weighing a number of factors. The first is **pass-by rate**—that is, the number of homes passed by or with the potential to take cable. Closely related is **density,** the number of households per mile of cable. A mile of cable costs the same whether it passes 10 homes or 2,500 homes. Therefore, greater density offers the potential for greater **penetration**—the number of homes passed by that cable that actually subscribe. Increased penetration not only means more income from **basic cable** (the "free" channels provided automatically by virtue of subscription) but also offers the promise of added income from pay cable, **pay-per-view, video-on-demand (VOD),** and other add-on services such as home security, various forms of data delivery, Internet access, and local and long-distance phone service. In a reversal of the typical economic structure in television (in which over-the-air stations make 90% of their income from ad sales), the typical cable operation earns only 10% of its revenue from advertising, with 90% coming from subscribers.

The promise of additional revenues from add-on subscriber services is so central to the future of the industry that in 2001 the National Cable Television Association changed its name to the National Cable and Telecommunications Association (NCTA), a move that reflects "cable's transformation from a one-way video service to supplier of a broad range of advanced, two-way services," according to the Association's president, Robert Sachs ("NCTA Name Change," 2001, p. 36). In addition, these advanced, two-way services are the factor that, more than any other, fuels the concentration and conglomeration rampant in contemporary cable. This is discussed in more detail later in the chapter.

National Cable & Telecommunications Association
www.
ncta.com

EARLY REGULATION OF CABLE

It is impossible to fully understand the development of cable without understanding the ups and downs of its regulatory history. The industry's size and shape and the content it offers have been variously limited and encouraged by frequently conflicting and shifting rules. As Joseph Fogarty and Marcia Spielholz (1985, p. 113) wrote in the *Federal Communications Law Journal,* "The history of FCC cable regulation is a complex interweaving of FCC opinions, court decisions, and technological advances, characterized by numerous shifts in opinion concerning both the source and scope of FCC cable jurisdiction and the value of new technology." This means that the FCC had to make the rules as it went along.

Federal Communications Commission
www.
fcc.gov

In the beginning the FCC ignored cable, seeing it as simply an aid to over-the-air television. But when cable operators began to import distant signals from outside their service areas, the commission—intent on fostering television diversity and local orientation—decided it was time to bring cable under its regulatory control. It did this in 1963 in a dispute between a microwave relay company, Carter Mountain Transmission Corporation, and a Wyoming television station. Station KWRB-TV objected to Carter Mountain picking up and delivering its signals to cable operators around the state. The FCC, concerned that cable would damage broadcasters' profitability, ruled that "when the impact of economic injury is such as to adversely affect the public interest . . . it is our duty to determine the ultimate effect . . . and act in a manner most advantageous to the public" (in Roman, 1983, p. 12).

Answering broadcasters' pleas for even more protection from the growing cable industry—there were now 1,325 systems operating nationally—the

FCC in 1965 expanded its regulatory control over cable. For example, it imposed restrictions that outraged cable operators, such as **local carriage rules,** which required cable systems to carry the signal of every television station within a 60-mile radius. The FCC based the new rules on two facts of cable life. First, the commission had a stake in ensuring the successful operation of the nation's broadcast system; a technology as significant as cable would surely have an impact. Second, cable systems enjoyed virtual monopoly positions in the areas in which they operated, and therefore they, like other monopolies (public utilities, for example), were subject to official oversight. The commission even began an effort to limit cable's expansion into the top 100 markets by passing restrictive rules on the use of microwave relays to bring distant signals to operators wishing to serve those areas. The effect of these rules was to slow the growth of cable.

Still, the FCC was not done with the upstart medium. In 1969 it ruled that operators make available not only channels but equipment and studios for the production of locally originated programming. Many systems programmed little more than time and weather, but others began what we now know as **public access channels,** cable channels reserved on a first-come, first-served, nondiscriminatory basis for use by groups or individuals who maintain editorial control of their programming. This imposed a financial burden on many systems already struggling to make a profit under the commission's restrictive rules. Even among operators attempting to meet the spirit of the FCC rules, there was resentment that the federal government was telling them how to use their facilities.

Finally, recognizing the inevitability of cable television, the FCC produced the 1972 Cable Television Report and Order. Hoping to shape rather than stop the medium's development, the goal was to limit cable to a secondary role, a supplement to over-the-air television. To that end, systems had to submit to local community franchising authority control over their rates; they were forbidden from importing *all* distant network and syndicated programming; telephone companies, local broadcasters, and television networks were forbidden to own cable operations; and pay channels could show only one feature film per week (which had to be more than 2 but less than 10 years old). In exchange, cable was allowed full entry into the top 100 markets.

National Telecommunications and Information Administration
www.
ntia.doc.gov

The cable industry fought mightily against the restrictions that limited its growth and profitability and, slowly, the FCC began to rescind many of the more onerous ones. But when local governments began to step up *their* demands on operators, the industry (ironically) turned to the commission for relief. It obliged with the Cable Franchise Policy and Communications Act of 1984, hoping to provide regulatory stability for the once-again-growing cable industry and to fix some of the problems created by the 1972 rules. Now, although operators still had to answer to municipal franchising authorities, the latter's control over rates and access programming was somewhat limited. In addition, it was now a federal offense to steal cable signals.

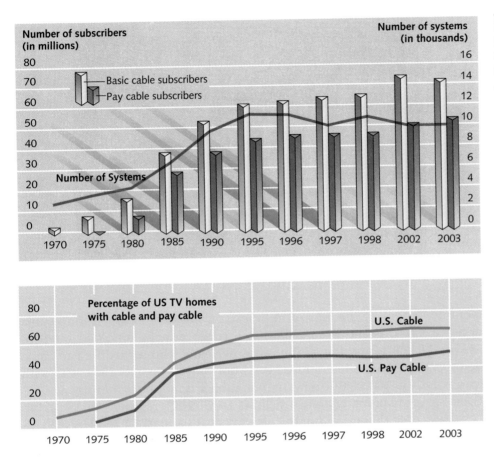

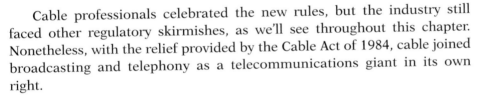

Figure 9.2 Cable Systems and Subscribers. *Sources:* National Cable Television Association, 1999; Paul Kagan Associates; *Marketing News Media,* March 16, 1998; *Cable TV Investor,* April 14, 1998; *Broadcasting & Cable Yearbook,* 1999; *Broadcasting & Cable Yearbook,* 2000; NCTA.com, 2003.

Cable professionals celebrated the new rules, but the industry still faced other regulatory skirmishes, as we'll see throughout this chapter. Nonetheless, with the relief provided by the Cable Act of 1984, cable joined broadcasting and telephony as a telecommunications giant in its own right.

Cable and Telecommunications Association for Marketing
www. ctam.com

Cable Today

Today that giant is composed of 9,947 individual cable systems serving 72.1 million homes subscribing to basic cable (67.4% of all television households). Seventy percent of these cable households, or 51% of all U.S. television homes, receive pay cable (see Figure 9.2). The industry employs nearly 131,000 people and generates annual revenues of $49.4 billion (NCTA, 2003).

PROGRAMMING

We saw in the previous chapter that cable's share of the prime time audience exceeded that of the Big Four broadcast networks for the first time in history in 2001. What attracted these viewers was programming, a

Revenues of cable shopping networks such as QVC exceed those of the traditional television networks.

Women in Cable &
Telecommunications
www.
wict.org

fact highlighted by the tens of millions of viewers who tuned in to cable network CNN as the drama of the terrorist attacks unfolded on September 11, 2001, and the 45% of all Americans who turned first to cable news, rather than other media, for information on the 2003 war with Iraq (Getting, 2003). But news is not cable's only programming success. Even home-shopping channels such as QVC (2001 revenues of $3.92 billion, exceeding that of traditional networks CBS and ABC) and HSN ($1.93 billion) have made their mark (Moss, 2002).

As we've seen, cable operators attract viewers through a combination of basic and pay channels, as well as with some programming of local origin. There are 287 national cable networks and scores of regional cable networks. We all know national networks such as CNN, Lifetime, HBO, and the History Channel. Regional network NorthWest Cable News serves Washington, Oregon, Idaho, Montana, northern California, and parts of Alaska; New England Cable News serves the states that give it its name; and several regional sports-oriented channels, including YES from the opening vignette, serve different parts of the country. The financial support and targeted audiences for these program providers differ, as does their place on a system's **tiers,** groupings of channels made available to subscribers at varying prices.

Basic Cable Programming   In recognition of the growing dependence of the public on cable delivery of broadcast service as cable penetration increased, Congress passed the Cable Television Consumer Protection and Competition Act of 1992. This law requires operators to offer a truly basic service composed of the broadcast stations in their area and their access channels. Cable operators also offer another form of basic service, **expanded basic cable,** composed primarily of local broadcast stations and services with broad appeal such as TBS, TNT, the USA Network, and the Family Channel. These networks offer a wide array of programming not

New England Cable News is one of the growing number of regional cable networks.

unlike that found on the traditional, over-the-air broadcast networks. The cable networks with the largest number of subscribers appear in Figure 9.3.

Because of concentration, operators are increasingly choosing to carry a specific basic channel because their owners (who have a financial stake in that channel) insist that they do. Multiple system operators (MSOs) are companies that own several cable franchises. Time Warner, Liberty, and Cablevision own Court TV. Comcast has an interest in numerous prime channels. Viacom owns BET. Naturally, these networks are more likely to be carried by systems controlled by the MSOs that own them and less likely to be carried by other systems. This pattern also holds true for MSO-owned premium channels such as HBO and Showtime.

Pay Cable   As the FCC lifted restrictions on cable's freedom to import distant signals and to show current movies, HBO grew and was joined by a host of other satellite-delivered pay networks. Today, the most familiar and popular pay cable networks are HBO, Showtime, the Spice Channel, the Sundance Channel, and Cinemax.

In addition to freedom from regulatory constraint, two important programming discoveries ensured the success of the new pay channels. After television's early experiments with over-the-air **subscription TV** failed, many experts believed people simply would not pay for television. So the first crucial discovery was that viewers would indeed pay for packages of contemporary, premium movies. These movie packages could be sold more inexpensively than could films bought one at a time, and viewers were willing to be billed on a monthly basis for the whole package rather than pay for each viewing.

The second realization boosting the fortunes of the pay networks was the discovery that viewers not only did not mind repeats (as many did with over-the-air television) but welcomed them as a benefit of paying for

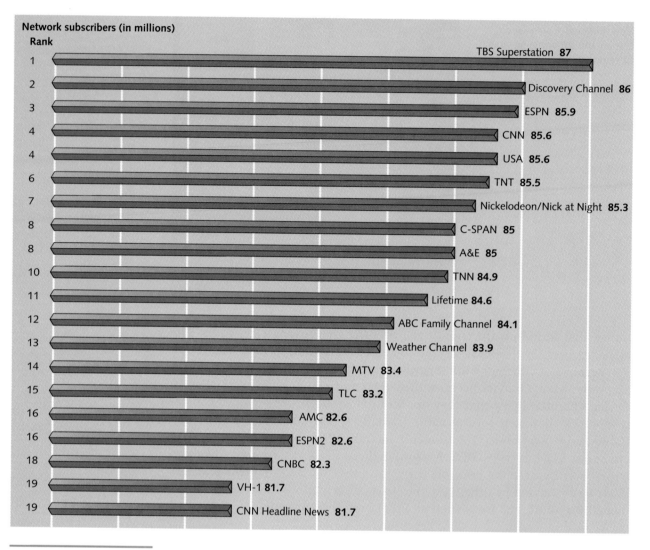

Network subscribers (in millions)

Rank

Rank	Network	Subscribers
1	TBS Superstation	87
2	Discovery Channel	86
3	ESPN	85.9
4	CNN	85.6
4	USA	85.6
6	TNT	85.5
7	Nickelodeon/Nick at Night	85.3
8	C-SPAN	85
8	A&E	85
10	TNN	84.9
11	Lifetime	84.6
12	ABC Family Channel	84.1
13	Weather Channel	83.9
14	MTV	83.4
15	TLC	83.2
16	AMC	82.6
16	ESPN2	82.6
18	CNBC	82.3
19	VH-1	81.7
19	CNN Headline News	81.7

Figure 9.3 Top 20 Cable Networks, 2002. *Source: NCTA, 2002b.*

the provider's slate of films. Pay channel owners were delighted. Replaying content reduced their programming costs and solved the problem of how to fill all those hours of operation.

Pay services come in two forms: movie channels (HBO, Starz!, and Encore, for example) that offer packages of new and old movies along with big sports and other special events—all available for one monthly fee—and pay-per-view channels, through which viewers choose from a menu of offerings (almost always of very new movies and very big sporting events) and pay a fee for the chosen viewing. In either case the subscriber must have a set-top converter to receive the paid-for channel, although most cable systems offer **addressable technology,** which enables pay services to be switched on and off at the hub. Many cable services are also experimenting with **interdiction technology,** which descrambles the signal outside the viewer's home, doing away with the set-top converter and even enabling operators to sell pay services to homes that are not already basic cable subscribers.

Boxing is a pay-cable standard. Even the fighters themselves, here for example Mike Tyson and Lennox Lewis battling in 2002, are "owned" by different cable networks.

People enjoy pay channels in the home for their ability to present unedited and uninterrupted movies and other content not usually found on broadcast channels—for example, adult fare and championship boxing and wrestling. Increasingly, however, that "content not usually found on broadcast channels" consists not of movies and sports but high-quality serial programming—content unencumbered by the need to attract the largest possible audience possessing a specific set of demographics. Pay cable series such as *The Sopranos, Arli$$, Sex and the City, Queer as Folk, Six Feet Under, Oz,* and *Soul Food* attract large and loyal followings. In fact, when the Academy of Television Arts and Sciences announced its 2002 prime-time Emmy nominations, 17 different cable networks recorded 191 nominations, and cable networks earned *all* the nominations in eight different categories. HBO alone had 93 nominations (its closest competitor was NBC with 89), and its *Six Feet Under* was the single most honored series, with nominations in 23 different categories (NBC's *West Wing* was second, with 21; NCTA, 2002a).

Keeping Subscribers But even this quality programming cannot satisfy all viewers. So one of the industry's largest ongoing problems is keeping subscribers once they have them, especially in the face of competition from other multichannel services, especially DBS. **Churn,** or turnover in subscribership whereby new subscriptions are offset by cancellations, is damaging to a system's financial well-being, and it is common. "Loyal cable subscribers may be an oxymoron," says cable industry consultant Dave Shepard (in Colman, 1998, p. 58). To keep customers, a variety of pricing

A typical set-top converter.

Viewers and critics agree that much of television's most sophisticated (and enjoyable) programming is available primarily on pay cable. Unafraid of offending advertisers, cable networks can present challenging often controversial content. Can you match the title with the image? *Oz, Soulfood, Six Feet Under, Sex and the City, The Sopranos, Queer as Folk, Arli$$.*

strategies is promoted. For example, a cable system may offer certain highly attractive basic channels from a higher tier to lower tier subscribers on an à la carte basis. Others provide FM radio service for free with basic cable, piping local stations into subscribers' homes. Other strategies include free subscriptions to monthly cable guides and access to on-screen programming schedules that offer constantly scrolling program and channel information and samples of the content available on those channels. Still others offer specialty pay channels such as DMX (talk- and commercial-free audio channels; see Chapter 7) and highly specialized text-based data and information channels.

Other Multichannel Services

There are multichannel services other than cable. We've already read about MATV. **Satellite master antenna (SMATV)** operates in the same fashion, but the signals are captured, logically, by a satellite dish and then distributed throughout the structure. **Microwave multidistribution systems (MMDS)** employ a home microwave receiver to collect signals and then pipe them through the house via internal wiring. DBS (see Chapter 8), however, is the multichannel system—other than cable—used by most viewers (see Figure 9.4).

It is DBS that most concerns cable professionals—DBS "has virtually halted cable's subscriber growth," according to *Broadcasting & Cable Magazine* (Higgins, 2001, p. 19). In fact, the relatively slow diffusion of DBS can be attributed to efforts by the cable industry to use its financial might (and therefore Congressional lobbying power) to thwart the medium. For example, federally mandated limitations on the importation by DBS of local over-the-air television stations remain in many parts of the country. Still, from the viewer's perspective, what is on a DBS-supplied screen differs little from what is on a cable-supplied screen.

DBS in the United States is, for now, the sole province of two companies, DirecTV, owned by Rupert Murdoch's News Corporation, and

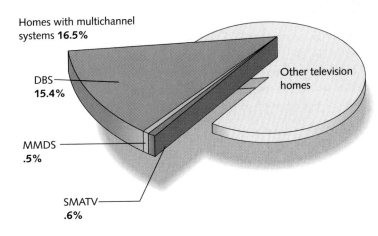

Homes with multichannel systems 16.5%

DBS 15.4%

Other television homes

MMDS .5%

SMATV .6%

Figure 9.4 Percentage of U.S. Television Homes with Multichannel Systems other than cable, 2002. *Source:* Television Bureau of Advertising, 2003.

*Society of Cable and Telecom-
munications Engineers*
www.
scte.org

DISH Network (owned by EchoStar, a publicly traded company). DirecTV has 11.9 million subscribers, DISH Network 8.5 million. In late 2001 EchoStar's offer to buy DirecTV was accepted by the latter's board of directors, but the deal was scuttled in late 2002 in the face of negative public and government reaction.

Trends and Convergence in Cable and Other Multichannel Services

Like all media, cable is experiencing convergence. DMX, for example, is radio plus cable. At the heart of much of the industry's convergence with other media is fiber optics, cable made of thin strands (less than one one-hundredth of an inch thick) of very pure glass fiber over which signals are carried by light beams. Because fiber optic wire offers a very wide bandwidth, permitting the passage of much more information, it can carry up to 600 times as much audio, video, or data information as the same size coaxial cable. Recent advances promise even more bandwidth—"1.6 trillion pieces of data on a single fiber optic strand with each tick of the clock" (Healey, 1999, p. 1F).

What is sent over fiber optics is pulses of light (Figure 9.5). Those pulses are the equivalent of a digital signal's binary on/off structure, making them perfectly suitable for carrying digital signals. As such, fiber optics sit at the very heart of the digital technologies that are reshaping cable.

One such advance is **digital cable television,** the delivery of digital images and other information to subscribers' homes. At present digital cable has more to do with the services a system can offer than with the picture subscribers receive, as we saw in Chapter 8's discussion of the public's unwillingness to buy expensive digital and HDTV receivers. Another impediment to more rapid diffusion of digital cable resides in cablecasters' dissatisfaction with digital must-carry rules, requirements that they carry both digital and analog channels offered by over-the-air broadcasters. Still, in 2002 there were 15.2 million digital cable subscribers in the United States, a number expected to grow to 38.6 million by 2006 (NCTA, 2002b). Many digital cable subscribers also use their cable connections to access the Internet. Currently there are 7.2 million users with **cable modems** connecting their computers to the Net via a specified Internet service provider, or ISP (NCTA, 2002b). As a result, "must-carry" has taken on new meaning in the Internet age, as you can see in the Cultural Forum box titled "Information or Telecommunications Service?"

INTERACTIVE CABLE

Cable's digital channels permit multiplexing, carrying two or more different signals over the same channel. This, in turn, is made possible by **digital compression,** which "squeezes" signals to permit multiple signals to be carried over one channel. Digital compression works by removing

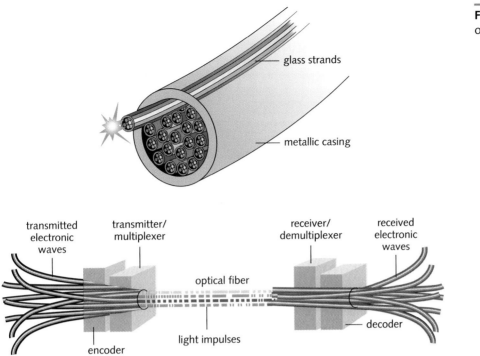

Figure 9.5 The operation of a fiber optic cable.

glass strands

metallic casing

transmitted electronic waves

transmitter/ multiplexer

receiver/ demultiplexer

received electronic waves

optical fiber

light impulses

encoder

decoder

redundant information from the transmission of the signal. For example, the set behind two actors in a movie scene might not change for several minutes. So why transmit the information that the set is there? Simply transmit the digital data that indicate what has changed in the scene, not what has not.

The expanded carrying capacity produced by fiber optics and digital compression makes possible **interactive cable,** that is, the ability of subscribers to talk back to the system operator (extra space on the channel is used for this back talk). And *this* permits video-on-demand (VOD; see Chapter 8). Interactivity is most often seen in electronic programming guides—use your remote to select a program from an on-screen list, and you are instantly taken to that content. True interactivity, as in true video-on-demand—choosing what you want when you want it from huge, digitally compressed databases maintained by a content provider—is still years away. Bandwidth is one obvious problem; the paucity of digital and HDTV television receivers is another (people won't watch full-length films and sports on their PCs, and the screens necessary to attractively display digitally compressed and stored video must have PC-like speed); and the cable industry itself, after years of experimenting with VOD, is experiencing "diminished expectations," having "learned one lesson from the billions of dollars incinerated in the financial fantasy of the Internet: that is, to spend money on products only when revenues are in clear sight" (Grotticelli & Kerschbaumer, 2001, p. 34). Nonetheless, all the major MSOs are moving ahead with plans for eventual greater interactivity and true VOD.

Cable Positive
www.
cablepositive.org

Cultural Forum

Information or Telecommunications Service?

"Must carry" found its way into the cultural forum in 2002 when the FCC ruled that cable was "an information service" rather than "a telecommunications service." Lawsuits quickly followed, pitting the cable industry and the commission against the Internet industry and public interest groups. The argument concerned how open a cable operator's wires should be. Although the debate may seem rather arcane, the province of lawyers and engineers, this issue will determine the future of the Internet and our access to it. As technology reporter Karen Charman argued, the Internet, rather than the "information commons" envisioned by its developers (see Chapter 10), will become "a conduit of commerce, booby-trapped with barriers and incentives designed to keep users where dollars can be wrung from them. As a result, a lot of freely accessible information and websites may become difficult or impossible to connect to—hindering the efforts of those posting that information to reach others" (2002, p. 22).

We saw earlier in this chapter that early cable operators resented local carriage rules and that current operators are resisting digital must-carry rules. The *new* must-carry fight is over the question of whether or not an operator should be required to carry any and all Internet service providers and Web sites that its subscribers choose—called "the key First Amendment issue for the 21st century" by Barry Steinhardt, associate director of the American Civil Liberties Union (quoted in McConnell, 2002c, p. 18).

By law, a technology classified as a "telecommunications service" is a **common carrier;** that is, like a phone company, it is required to carry the messages of others with no power to shape or restrict them. "An information service," on the other hand, like a television network, may control what passes through its technology. Why

The cable modem and its ability to connect users to the Net may be "the key First Amendment issue for the 21st century."

would the cable industry care what it is called? Why should we?

Free to control access to their fiber optic broadband wires, cable operators can charge as few or as many ISPs as they want however much money they want. Moreover, they can tell an ISP or a Web content provider that it cannot use their wires to deliver movies, video, audio—or any other information, for that matter—if that content competes directly with the movie, video, audio, or information services they themselves sell to their subscribers. As Stanford University communication professor François Bar explained, this would mean "an electronic marketplace which systematically favors the providers of content, services, or transactions who have a privileged financial relationship with the monopoly owner of the underlying infrastructure (the MSO). . . . The infrastructure owner will have strong incentives to configure its network to give superior performance to the preferred ISP and superior service to

PUBLIC ACCESS CABLE TELEVISION

Digitalization and compression have another effect on cable programming; they have renewed the debate over public access television.

We've already seen that public access channels were once required by the FCC, only to become negotiable between operators and their local franchising authorities. Media historian William Boddy (1994) wrote, "As the cable industry underwent a rapid consolidation from small owners to highly capitalized multiple systems operators in the late 1970s, the competition for large urban franchises became fierce. With channel capacity

the ISP's favored partners" (quoted in Chester & Larson, 2002, p. 7).

In other words, according to Blair Levin, chief of staff to former FCC chair Reed Hundt, "If you own the pipe, you can make a certain amount of money. If you can own the pipe *and* the content, you can make more money." He added, "It's a question of who owns the customer—who gets the customer dollar and how it's divided up between the different content providers" (quoted in Charman, 2002, p. 23). The vignette that opened this chapter is based precisely on this question—who owns cable-viewing Yankee fans' dollars, the MSO or the YES Network, and how should they divide it up?

The cable industry dismisses such concerns. Operators would never restrict the locations users can go to on the Internet, because it would alienate their customers. "That's like saying AOL/Time Warner Cable will only allow you to watch AOL/Time Warner channels," claims NCTA spokesperson Marc Smith. "But they also let you watch ESPN, which is owned by Disney, and MTV, which is owned by Viacom" (quoted in Charman, 2002, p. 24). In fact, critics counter, although an operator would be foolish to deny viewers their MTV or ESPN, MSOs do indeed favor channels (content providers) that they themselves own, a demonstrable fact (Crandall & Furchtgott-Roth, 1996). Moreover, an infinitely small number of the countless Web sites that exist could afford to pay the kinds of fees the cable industry would be able to command for access to their broad, but nonetheless limited, wires. Only the richest sites would have access, particularly shutting out citizen, community, and nonprofit groups.

Enter your voice in the cultural forum. Is a cable operator an information or a telecommunications service? Should it be required, like a common carrier, to make its pipes available to all comers, especially in this era of increased media concentration and conglomeration? Isn't the freedom to exchange ideas freely and openly at the heart of our democracy? But what of the cable companies? They have made the huge investment in the technology and infrastructure that have created this debate in the first place. Shouldn't they have the freedom to control their own wires? Stanford Law School professor Lawrence Lessig defines the dilemma this way:

> As the Internet moves from telephone wires to cable, which model should govern? When you buy a book from Amazon.com, you don't expect AOL to demand a cut. When you run a search at Yahoo!, you don't expect your MSN network to slow down anti-Microsoft sites. You don't expect that because the norm of neutrality on the Internet is so strong.
>
> But the same neutrality does not guide our thinking about cable. If the cable companies prefer some content over others, that's the natural image of a cable provider. If your provider declines to show certain stations, that's the sort of freedom we imagine it should have.
>
> So which model should govern when the Internet moves to cable? Freedom or control? (quoted in Johnson, 2001, p. 26).

What's at stake in your answers? The Center for Digital Democracy's executive director Jeff Chester says, "The infrastructure and rules for the next media system are being established now. We may not see the ultimate outcome of these decisions for 10 or more years. But if we want to ensure that we have as open a system as possible . . . we have to shape that system now" (quoted in Charman, 2002, p. 24).

---

exceeding available programming services, cable operators looked at public access as an inexpensive bargaining chip with franchise officials" (p. 356). But that was then. Today, "the continuing consolidation of the cable industry into a handful of giant multiple system operators, and their moves into ownership in cable programming firms, has created a growing hostility toward public access from vertically-integrated cable operators dizzy at the prospect of increasingly lucrative commercial cable program services" (p. 357).

What digitalization and compression have added to this hostility is the question of what to do with all those "extra" channels. Local franchising

Paper Tiger Television

Public access television has a bad reputation. Even the most committed local access devotee must admit that too much of what fills the nation's access channels is self-indulgent, infantile, or silly. There are too many amateurish skits, bad takeoffs on talk shows, and sophomoric *Star Trek* parodies.

Access also suffers from controversy. Its first-come, first-served nature, absence of censorship (other than restrictions on obscenity and libel), and almost full producer control leave public access television open to abuse by racists and other haters who have few other public outlets for their ideologies. But isn't this what public access is supposed to be about? Isn't it supposed to provide a forum for those whose message is either unwanted by, or unsuited for, the more mainstream media? In the 1990s, for example, local franchising authorities in Cincinnati, Ohio; Pocatello, Idaho; Jackson, Mississippi; and Kansas City, Missouri closed or attempted to close the access operations of their communities' cable providers rather than permit the cablecasting of a nationally distributed program by the Ku Klux Klan. But what of others who hold potentially unpopular opinions? What about animal rights activists? What about pro-choice organizations? What about pro-life groups? What about Chinese dissidents living on the West Coast? What about radicals on both the political right and left? You decide. Where would you draw the line? Or would you draw a line at all?

Now, read on and learn about one very successful public access producer whose message is invisible on commercial broadcast and cable television, not to mention offensive to many. Hoping to use access television to make a difference, Paper Tiger Television was founded in 1981 in New York City, and at that time issued its manifesto, which read in part:

> The power of mass culture rests on the trust of the public. This legitimacy is a paper tiger. Investigation into the corporate structures of the media and critical analysis of their content is one way to demystify the information industry. Developing a critical consciousness about the communications industry is a necessary first step toward democratic control of information resources ("Paper Tiger Manifesto," 2003).

The hundreds of episodes produced by Paper Tiger's "volunteer collective of media producers, educators, and activists" have and do appear on hundreds of public access channels across the United States, as well as on satellite-delivered Free Speech TV. Through its Deep Dish TV project, Paper Tiger collects the work of scores of access producers from around the country, repackages it into 60-minute shows on common themes such as labor, housing, women's issues, and disarmament, and redistributes the shows as a means of helping local access operations diversify and improve their offerings. The collective's goal is to "provide a model and network for other progressive public access programmers." Its guiding philosophy is drawn from the political far left. "The group's name recalls Mao's guerilla stance against superpower hegemony, and the manifesto's assertion of the importance of the reproduction of ideology is compatible with the ideas of . . . economic Marxism and anarchy" (Boddy, 1994, pp. 357–358). So, what kinds of shows does Paper Tiger produce and distribute?

authorities see growing channel capacity as the perfect argument for maintaining, or even expanding, public access service. Many cable operators see it as a way to meet a wide array of subscriber needs and interests, fortifying them in their battle for profits (and survival) against competing media. Confounding the debate is the operators' belief that no one is watching public access anyway. They point to the provision in the 1984 Cable Franchise Policy and Communications Act permitting them to reclaim "underused" public access channels.

The future of local access, then, comes down to whose perception will prevail. As the number of channels grows, franchising authorities argue that "underused" is defined downward; that is, a local channel that meets a public service function but draws a relatively small number of viewers is "well used" in a 500-channel environment. Many operators argue that the best use of these additional channels is to provide more sophisticated

PAPER TIGER TV
20 YEARS OF MEDIA REPAIR

Here are a few examples, including Paper Tiger's descriptions:

- *Turning Tragedy into War.* Counteracting the corporate media's war-driven and racist spin on the September 11 terrorist attacks on America, this show critiques the media's coverage while providing a background of the United States' involvement in the Middle East. It uncovers the ways in which media take advantage of the fear and confusion in U.S. public opinion and offers a look at the antiretaliation movement.

- *Operation Storm the Media.* In the media coverage of the Persian Gulf War, even the pretense of separation between the press and the state was abandoned. This show explores the relationship between corporate sponsorship and media censorship.

- *Mutiny on the Corporate Sponsorship.* This video looks at how mainstream media censor voices, not always through blatant censorship but sometimes through the rule of the status quo, which is dictated by the sponsors and mirrored by the corporate print and broadcasting elite.

- *How History Was Wounded: An Exclusive Report on Taiwanese Media.* This is an exclusive report from Taiwan investigating how Taiwanese news media covered the Tiananmen Square massacre. It compares coverage of the mainland clampdown with Taiwanese coverage of their own government's suppression of political movements.

- *A Cry for Freedom and Democracy.* Made in Chiapas, Mexico, this video follows human rights activists, journalists, and family members as they try to gain access to the region blockaded by the military. Residents of Chiapas who witnessed the Mexican army's indiscriminate brutality following the 1994 New Year's Day Zapatista uprising give their firsthand accounts.

Put yourself in the position of general manager of a public access channel. Do you air Paper Tiger on your channel? Why or why not? Now, imagine that you are a local franchising authority staff person. Do you welcome the series to the system under your authority? Why or why not? Now imagine that you are the owner of a large MSO. Do you fight to regain the access channel that's running Paper Tiger Television to put it to more profitable use, or do you support the access channel's use of its time for such programming? Why or why not?

Now consider this. Paper Tiger's far left ideology is offensive to many Americans. So, too, is the ideology of the KKK. How would you justify excluding Klan content (if you would) while accepting programming provided by Paper Tiger (if you did)?

---

services to information- and programming-hungry subscribers. The box titled "Paper Tiger Television" details the work of one access champion.

Paper Tiger Television
www.
papertiger.org

CONCENTRATION

Gone are the days when systems were "mom and pop" operations. Changes in the nature of cable system ownership parallel those in other media we've examined. As cable pioneer and current Time Warner executive Ted Turner explained, "We do have just a few people controlling all the cable companies in this country" (quoted in "All Together Now," 1997, p. 14).

Concentration initially came to cable in the form of MSOs. As cable experienced its greatest period of growth in the 1970s, only the biggest and richest corporations could afford to build, buy, and improve operations

Figure 9.6 Top 10 Cable MSOs, 2003. *Source:* Higgins, 2003.

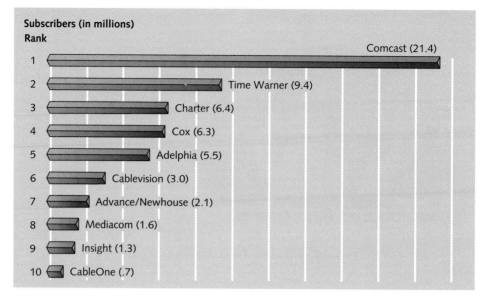

Cable TV Public Affairs Association
www.
ctpaa.org

in advance of the income they promised to generate. Today, five MSOs control 80% of all American cable households, and one MSO alone, Comcast, has 21.4 million subscribers in 41 states and systems in 17 of the top 20 television markets (Oppelaar, 2002a). Figure 9.6 lists the 10 largest MSOs and the size of their subscribership.

The second form of concentration in cable is vertical integration, wherein a company holds a financial interest in more than one aspect of the industry—production, distribution (the satellite service), and exhibition (local franchises). As we've seen, systems tend to carry cable networks owned by the MSOs that own them. Critics of cable concentration find this inherently unfair, limiting programming competition (and therefore variety). An MSO is more likely to initiate a new program service, because it has guaranteed channel space on at least its own systems. New, potentially innovative program services have no such guarantee. The counterargument, however, is that guaranteed channel availability encourages risk taking. MSOs point to innovative offerings such as BET, WE, Oxygen, and the Discovery Channel as examples of channels that never would have been developed without MSO investment. Still, the FCC is sufficiently wary of this concentration of power that it requires operators to dedicate no more than 40% of its first 75 channels to program services owned by their owners.

The third way in which concentration has come to cable is in the form of conglomeration, the ownership of large MSOs by even larger companies having both media and nonmedia holdings. General Electric, for example, not only owns NBC and 14 television stations but also owns outright or in part 27 cable television channels in the United States and abroad, including PAX, MSNBC, A&E, and Telemundo.

As we've seen in our discussions of other media, critics of conglomeration fear that the number of voices and variety of expression in the media (in this case, cable television) will be diminished as ownership is concentrated in fewer and fewer hands. Another fear is that the conglomerate's media holdings will become nothing more than profit centers, no different from its fruit-juice or diaper-supply businesses. Defenders of conglomeration argue that media companies will survive in the reality of today's world of converged telecommunications only if they are, in fact, parts of larger, integrated entities.

National Cable Television Center & Museum

www.
cablecenter.org

PHONE-OVER-CABLE AND BUNDLING

When the Telecommunications Act of 1996 made it legal for phone companies to enter the cable television business, there was a rush by the telcos to buy outright or strike partnerships with cable operations. Familiar names such as AT&T, Verizon, GTE, US West, and BellSouth entered the cable franchise business. But the telcos are interested in cable for reasons having little to do with television. Ever since 1984, when AT&T was forced to separate from the regional Bell operating companies (**BOCs,** often called "Baby Bells") to settle an antitrust suit brought by the federal government, it and other long-distance carriers such as MCI and Sprint have been barred from the local phone business. Likewise, the BOCs were barred from offering long-distance service.

In an effort to spur competition in the telecommunications industry, the 1996 Act opened all services to all comers. But because the BOCs owned the phone lines, companies wanting to provide local service had to find another way to enter people's homes. Cable, already in 73 million homes, offered the solution. Linking with a cable operation solved an additional problem for the long-distance companies. When they use a local carrier's lines to enter people's homes, they have to pay a connection fee to that local phone company for every call delivered over its lines. For a company such as AT&T, these fees can amount to $10 billion a year. Cable allows long-distance companies to avoid local phone networks entirely.

Despite this benefit to the telcos, phone-over-cable has spread very slowly. Currently there are only 1.5 million cable-delivered residential telephone subscribers (NCTA, 2002b). There are two reasons. The first is technical—although the technology for quality phone-over-cable exists, the problem is getting manufacturers to agree on compatibility standards. The second reason that phone-over-cable is slow in coming is consumer resistance. Many people, already dissatisfied with the level of service provided by their cable companies, are wary of relying on them for phone service as well.

But there is another, even more important reason that the telcos are interested in hooking up with cable—convergence. If telephone service can be delivered by the same cable that brings television into the home, so too can the Internet. And what's more, if the cable line is fiber optic broadband capable of handling digitally compressed data, that Internet service can be even faster than the service provided over traditional phone lines. Cable, in other words, can become a one-stop communications provider: television, VOD, audio, high-speed Internet access, long-distance and local phone service, multiple phone lines, and fax. This is **bundling.**

The Promise of Cable

As the medium was morphing from "CATV" to "cable" in the 1970s, "an ever expanding chorus of expert opinion [voiced] a new, hopeful view" for the medium (Streeter, 1997, p. 223), one echoed by today's Internet aficionados. As with the Internet, cable would make the United States a "wired nation"; cable would return television to the people—it would become the people's medium. Traditional television was the ill; cable television, the cure. With the coming of cable,

> television was no longer seen as an infant institution, and its problems were no longer interpreted as temporary foibles, amenable to correction with the existing overall structure. People in positions of authority and power were beginning to seek solutions to television's failings not in adjustments to the existing system, but in alternatives to the system itself. (Streeter, 1997, p. 232)

But by the early 1980s, talk had turned to the failed promise of cable. Cable had not become an alternative to dull, unchallenging, three-network-dominated television; rather, it had become simply more television: more movies, more sports, more commercials, more situation comedies.

But bundled cable service, providing all sorts of converged technologies, has rekindled what sociologist Thomas Streeter (1997) calls "utopian speculation" about cable's very near future. He samples contemporary comment:

- "Futurist" George Gilder predicts that, with the help of interactive television, "The human spirit—emancipated and thus allowed to reach its rarest talents and aspirations—will continue to amaze the world with heroic surprises" (Streeter, p. 238).

- Mitchell Kapor, cofounder of the Internet advocacy group Electronic Frontier Foundation, predicts that the convergence of Internet and cable will promote "grassroots democracy, diversity of users and manufacturers, true communications among the people, and all the dazzling goodies of home shopping, movies on demand, teleconferencing, and cheap, instant databases" (p. 239).

- The administration of President Bill Clinton predicted that the convergence of Internet and cable technologies would allow the arts and humanities to "play a vital role in creating a new sense of citizenship and community," would "bring new opportunities and resources to our nation's disadvantaged youth, allowing them to share their ideas, thoughts and creative energies, and to make new links with other young people throughout the nation," and would "give all Americans, of all races, ages, and locations, their cultural birthright: access to the highest quality thought and art of this and prior generations" (p. 238).

Maybe. Maybe not.

Despite all the criticism of television in the days of the Big Three (ABC, NBC, CBS), at least Americans shared a common culture (Chapter 2). Yes, it may have been a shallow culture of *I Love Lucy* and *My Favorite Martian,* but it was a widely shared culture. And it was also a culture boasting journalists of the caliber of Walter Cronkite and screenwriters the caliber of Rod Serling (*The Twilight Zone*). For better *and* for worse, precable television was the stock that helped flavor the American melting pot. So, will we really be better off when Americans are fragmented among 500 demographic, taste, and interest channels? Will we be better off when Americans are linked anonymously across fiber optic wires in virtual rather than actual communities, holding virtual rather than real conversations? This is not an argument against the new multichannel, bundled telecommunications universe, simply a reiteration of the classic warning, "Be careful what you wish for. You just may get it." Nor is it a warning specific to cable. It is echoed in the next chapter's discussion of technology haves and have-nots and the information and technology gaps.

What do you think? Have you considered what the future will really look like if "the promise of cable" is fulfilled? What kind of America will exist for all Americans, for the wired and the unwired, for those who look like you, for those who don't? Is it the kind of future you want to see? Or is all this concern simply an echo of the fears that have accompanied the introduction and diffusion of every new mass medium (Chapter 2)?

Cable Television Advertising Bureau
www.
cabletvadbureau.com

How valuable is a bundle-receiving subscriber to a cable/telco combination? The average American family currently spends $595 a year on the services likely to be bundled in the future, up from $175 in 1995. That's $49.58 a month ("Americans Are," 2001). Figure 9.7 shows one estimate, $170.13 per month, of the revenue that could be generated by an average bundled household.

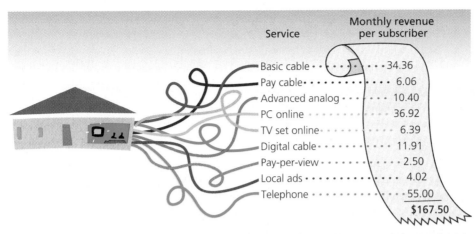

Service	Monthly revenue per subscriber
Basic cable	34.36
Pay cable	6.06
Advanced analog	10.40
PC online	36.92
TV set online	6.39
Digital cable	11.91
Pay-per-view	2.50
Local ads	4.02
Telephone	55.00
	$167.50

Figure 9.7 The Value of a Subscriber in a Bundled Cable World, 2002. High-speed cable service brings multiple communication services to subscribers. It is the promise of millions of homes buying multiple services that make cable franchises so attractive to telcos and others wanting to deliver bundled services. Here is one estimate (Higgins, 1999) of how much a typical cable home would have spent each month in 2002 if bundled.

Bundled services may be profitable for MSOs, but they raise the issue of concentration in a somewhat different form from that we've already discussed. Specifically, what risk for consumers does putting this much power into the hands of one company pose? The chairperson of the U.S. Senate Antitrust Subcommittee, Herb Kohl, Democrat from Wisconsin, sees an ominous future for "average consumers." He said that people "may find almost all of their personal communications and information dominated by a very few, large media companies. Their phone, their movies, their Internet, their cable, their link to the outside world will be priced, processed, and packaged for them by one company that faces virtually no competition" (quoted in Albiniak, 2002c, p. 7). You can develop your own thoughts on the potential of the "new cable" after reading the box titled "The Promise of Cable."

National Cable Television Cooperative
WWW.
cabletvco-op.org

DEVELOPING MEDIA LITERACY SKILLS
Understanding Cable Pricing

Cable rates are of interest to all cable viewers. In fact, when then-president George Bush vetoed the Cable Television Consumer Protection and Competition Act of 1992, Congress overrode that action, the only time it successfully challenged one of the president's vetoes. Congress knew that viewers were angry about their rising cable bills.

We saw earlier in this chapter that operators offer a variety of tiers to their customers. The pricing of those tiers may sometimes seem confusing to viewers, but they make perfect business sense for the operator. By law, systems must offer truly basic cable. But all operators, as we've seen, offer expanded basic cable, a tier that includes broadcast-network-type general programming. But operators often include more demographically

Living Media Literacy

Access Television

Cable or community access television offers the opportunity to make your media literacy a living enterprise. Most cable systems offer at least one access channel, and many offer two or more. Have you ever asked, "Why isn't there a show about …?" Have you ever said, "You know what would make a great show?" Do you want to write for television? Or would you like to edit, direct, program, manage, moderate, act, or engage in any of the scores of activities that go into producing a television program? Cable access is specifically designed to allow nonbroadcast professionals the opportunity to "make television." And because it is not commercial television, there is no mandate to attract as large an audience as possible. Therefore, media literate people who are involved in access can put their values and beliefs about mass communication into action. Portland Cable Access TV, for example, calls itself "Your Community Media First Amendment Forum" (www.pcatv.org), and this is the philosophy that motivates and sustains most access operations.

To get started, go to The Global Village CAT (www.openchannel.se/cat/linksus.htm), where you will find links to more than 600 different community access sites. Find one or more near you, either geographically, philosophically, or politically. Contact it (or them) to see how you can participate. Most access sites explain how to get involved as a volunteer and how to become a producer of an existing show or one of your own concept. Among the better sites for becoming acquainted with the potential of access are Chicago's CAN TV (www.cantv.org), Fairfax (Virginia) Public Access (www.fcac.org), and Burlington (Massachusetts) Cable Access Television (www.bcattv.org). Any one of these will show you the kinds of programs that are successful on access, so you can match your vision against that of those who are already involved. But no matter how you choose to proceed, there is no reason, if you are serious about testing your television/cable media literacy, to ignore access. It can give you what the commercial broadcasters will not, that is, access to a powerful medium of mass communication.

National Cable Television Institute
www.
ncta.com

targeted fare in expanded basic, networks such as the kids-oriented Nickelodeon and the upscale A&E, as an inducement to get us to sign up. The Sci-Fi Channel, Weather Channel, and American Movie Classics (AMC) are often used this way, as are Black Entertainment Television (BET) and Spanish-language Galavision. The goal is not only to garner higher monthly fees and to attract new viewers but also to make the "distance" between basic, expanded basic, and the premium options smaller, encouraging viewers to take that next, and next, and then that last step. For example, basic cable might cost you $18. Expanded basic, which might include the Discovery Channel and Disney ("Why not, they're good for the kids") and even a few more interesting options such as Comedy Central and E!, might cost "only" $10 more. Now, you're paying $28. The operator can now offer you a premium package that includes all the content from the lower tiers, as well as pay channels such as HBO and HBO Comedy, for $38. To you, that's "only $10 more," a seeming bargain. And then, for only $20 more, you can have digital cable, with DMX and on-screen program guide. Now you're at $58.

The media literate cable viewer needs to understand how quickly that bill can grow and just what value is received for what is now an average monthly basic cable price of $34.52 (NCTA, 2003). For example, when the Telecommunications Act of 1996 was being debated, Congress told voters that deregulating cable rates would create competition that would keep cable bills low. In fact, just the opposite happened, as rates have increased

45% since 1996, greatly outpacing inflation (Phillips, 2003). The media literate viewer, who understands that the average cable user watches only about six of the scores of available channels, must ask if that increase has produced a commensurate rise in value from the medium.

Chapter Review

The visions of two Pennsylvanians, John Walson and Milton Shapp, eventually became the mass communication giant we now call cable television. Initially conceived of as a way to deliver clear signals to people in remote areas, the medium quickly became more than that. Now local and distant signals, as well as a variety of pay channels, come to people's homes on systems composed of a headend, super trunk cable, hub, trunk cable, feeder cables, and drop cables.

The growth and development of cable has been shaped by often conflicting government regulation. The FCC entered cable oversight as a result of its Carter Mountain decision and regulated and reregulated to, at first, slow, then control, then free cable's growth. Nevertheless, rules governing local carriage, public access, and the power and operation of local franchising authorities remain today.

There are multichannel services other than cable. Satellite master antenna (SMATV) employs a satellite dish atop a building to capture signals and then distributes them throughout that structure. Microwave multidistribution systems (MMDS) employ a home microwave receiver to collect signals and then pipe them through the house via internal wiring.

DBS, however, is the multichannel system other than cable used by most viewers. Its operation in the United States is controlled by two companies, DirecTV and the DISH Network.

Cable programming exists in several forms. Basic cable typically fills systems' lower tiers and pay cable its upper tiers, with expanded basic falling somewhere in between, depending on the operator's needs. This content and newer services are made possible by a variety of sophisticated technologies. Fiber optics have greatly increased the efficiency and bandwidth of the cables that enter people's homes. Digital cable, especially when combined with digital compression, makes possible *multiplexing*, carrying two or more different signals over the same channel. Multiplexing, in turn, permits interactive cable and VOD.

Concentration, in the form of MSOs, vertical integration, and conglomeration, is widespread and controversial in cable and increasingly involves the telcos, eager to enter people's homes over the same wires that deliver video signals. These same wires can be used for a host of bundled services, from local and long-distance telephone to fax to high-speed Internet access.

Key Terms

Use the text's CD-ROM and the Online Learning Center at www.mhhe.com/baran to further your understanding of the following terminology.

multichannel service, 270
multiple system operator (MSO), 270
telco, 270
community antenna television (CATV), 271
master antenna television (MATV), 271
pay cable, 271
headend, 272
super trunk cable, 272

hub, 272
trunk cable, 272
feeder cable, 272
drop cable, 272
pass-by rate, 272
density, 272
penetration, 272
basic cable, 273
pay-per-view, 273
video-on-demand (VOD), 273
local carriage rules, 274

public access channels, 274
tier, 276
expanded basic cable, 276
subscription TV, 277
addressable technology, 278
interdiction technology, 278
churn, 279
satellite master antenna (SMATV), 281
microwave multidistribution systems (MMDS), 281

Questions for Review

OLC Go to the self-quizzes on the CD-ROM and the Online Learning Center to test your knowledge.

1. What were the contributions of John Walson and Milton Shapp to the development of cable television?
2. Differentiate between twin-lead, coaxial, and fiber optic cable.
3. What significance is there in the passage of the medium's name from CATV to cable television?
4. What are the elements involved in the reception and distribution of cable television signals?
5. What are pass-by rate, density, penetration, and churn?
6. What is the significance of the FCC's ruling in the Carter Mountain matter?
7. Explain the difference between basic cable, expanded basic cable, pay cable, and pay-per-view.
8. What are MATV, SMATV, MMDS, and DBS? How are they similar? How do they differ?
9. What are digital cable television, multiplexing, digital compression, and interactive cable, and how are they interrelated?
10. What are the three forms of concentration in cable television? What concerns are raised by each?
11. What are some of the factors leading to the telcos' interest in cable?
12. What is bundling? What is digital must-carry? What is their significance to cable's future?

Questions for Critical Thinking and Discussion

1. What do you think of digital must-carry rules? Why should a cable operator be forced to carry local stations' signals even if it doesn't want to? What gives the government the right to tell cable operators how to run their businesses?
2. Are you a cable subscriber? Why or why not? At what level? Why that level? Have you added to the industry's churn? Why or why not?
3. Does concentration in cable disturb you? Why or why not? What do you think of critics' fears? Are they realistic or overblown?
4. Have you ever watched public access cable? Have you seen programming that you thought was useful, or at least that was good television? Have you seen access content that was silly or offensive? Describe your cable access experience.
5. If you were a cable operator, how willing would you be to provide access to competitors? Why do you think it is proper (or improper) for the federal government to require open access should it do so?

Important Resources

Broadcasting & Cable, Electronic Media, and ***Variety.*** These media industry standards, introduced in earlier chapters, are as valuable for readers interested in cable and DBS as they are for those interested in all other media.

Bartlett, E. R. (2002). *Cable television handbook.* **New York: McGraw-Hill.** An excellent, thorough

look at cable history, regulation, economics, and technology. As such, some chapters are very detailed and sophisticated, but in all, it is probably the best overview available.

Lessig, L. (2001). *The future of ideas: The fate of the commons in a connected world.* **New York: Random House.** This is a sophisticated but readable treatise on the conflict between technological advance and individuals' ability to be heard and maintain control over their voices and ideas. It presents a thorough discussion of the differences between a telecommunications and an information society. It argues for greater public involvement in the balancing of control and freedom in a wired and interconnected world.

Multichannel News. A weekly trade publication focusing on cable and other multichannel service operations and their relationship to the larger telecommunications environment. Fact filled but readable.

National Association of Minorities in Cable	www.namic.com
National Cable & Telecommunications Association	www.ncta.com
Cable and Telecommunications Association for Marketing	www.ctam.com
Federal Communications Commission	www.fcc.gov
National Telecommunications & Information Administration	www.ntia.doc.gov
Women in Cable & Telecommunications	www.wict.org
Society of Cable and Telecommunications Engineers	www.scte.org
Cable Positive	www.cablepositive.org
Cable in the Classroom	www.ciconline.org
Paper Tiger Television	www.papertiger.org
Cable TV Public Affairs Association	www.ctpaa.org
National Cable Television Center & Museum	www.cablecenter.org
Cable Television Advertising Bureau	www.cabletvadbureau.com
National Cable Television Cooperative	www.cabletvco-op.org
National Cable Television Institute	www.ncta.com

CHAPTER 10

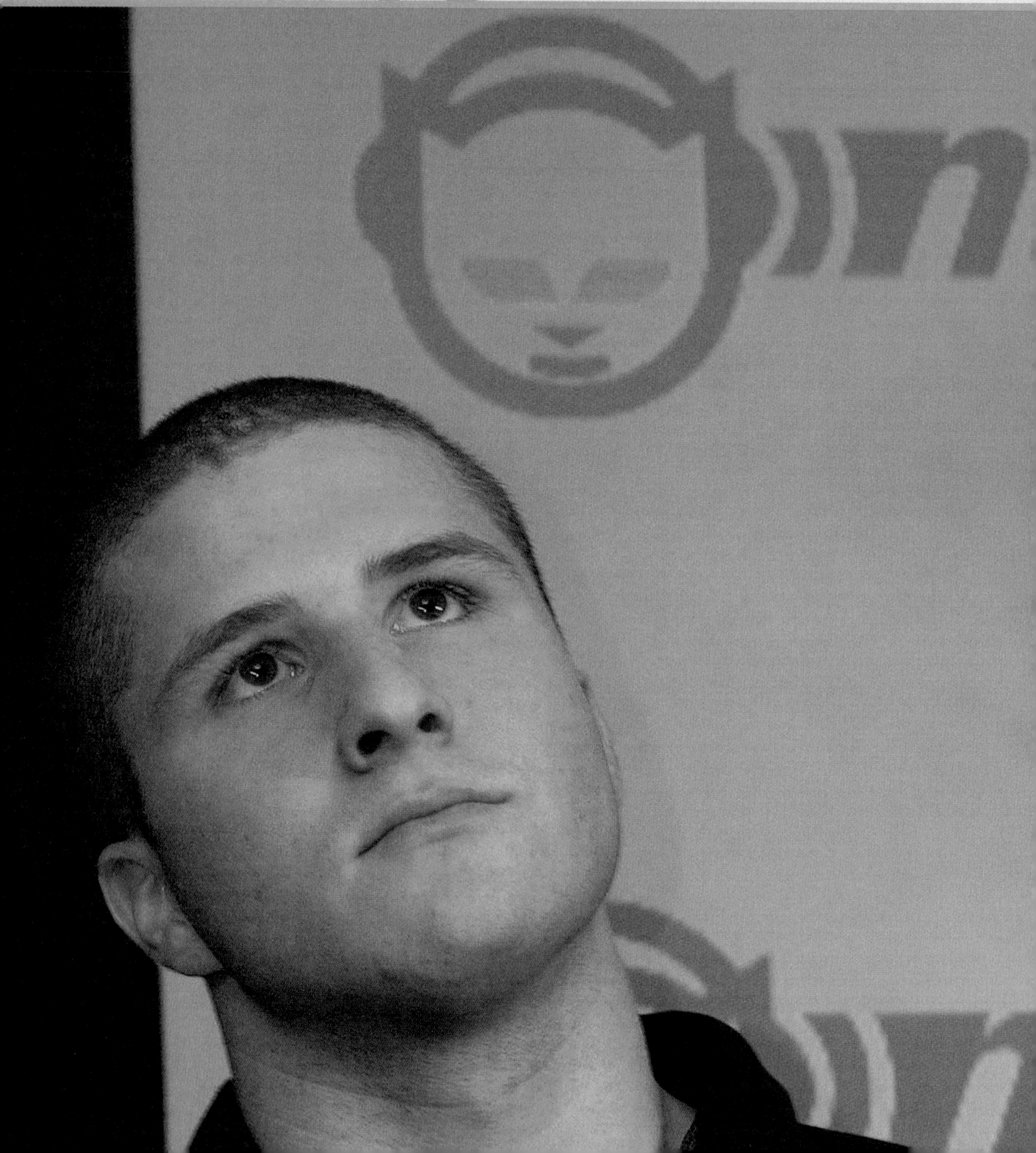

The Internet and the World Wide Web: Changing the Paradigm

LEARNING OBJECTIVES

It is not an overstatement to say that the Internet and World Wide Web have changed the world, not to mention all the other mass media. In addition to being powerful communication media themselves, the Net and the Web sit at the center of virtually all the media convergence we see around us. After studying this chapter you should

- be familiar with the history and development of the Internet and World Wide Web.

- recognize the potential cultural value of the Internet and World Wide Web and the implications of Web censorship and commercialization of the Internet.

- understand how the organizational and economic nature of the contemporary Internet and World Wide Web industries shapes their content.

- recognize alterations in the nature of mass communication made possible by the Internet and World Wide Web.

- develop an awareness of a number of social and cultural questions posed by the Internet, World Wide Web, and related emerging technologies.

- understand the relationship between these new media and their various users and audiences.

- possess improved Internet and World Wide Web media literacy skills, especially in protecting your privacy and reflecting on the Net's double edge of (potentially) good and troublesome change.

WILLIAM GIBSON AND MARSHALL MCLUHAN HAVE BEEN two of your intellectual heroes ever since you started college. Gibson is the "Godfather of Cyberspace" and author of *Neuromancer* and *Johnny Mnemonic,* and McLuhan is the author of *Understanding Media: The Extensions of Man* and originator of some of your favorite expressions such as "hot and cool media" and "the medium is the message." But now, as you see it, Gibson and McLuhan are in conflict.

For example, another of McLuhan's famous expressions is "the global village." You understood this to mean that as media "shrink" the world, people will become increasingly involved in

William Gibson

one another's lives. As people come to know more about others who were once separated from them by distance, they will form a new, beneficial relationship, a global village.

Then you saw Gibson interviewed on television. His vision of technology's impact on the globe was anything but optimistic. He said, "We're moving toward a world where all the consumers under a certain age will . . . identify more with their consumer status or with the products they consume than they would with an antiquated notion of nationality. We're increasingly interchangeable" (as cited in Trench, 1990).

Maybe you were wrong about McLuhan's ideas. He did his influential writing a long time ago. Where was it you read about the global village? In a magazine interview? You look it up at the library to confirm that you understood him correctly. There it is, just as you thought: "The human tribe can become truly one family and man's consciousness can be freed from the shackles of mechanical culture and enabled to roam the cosmos" ("A Candid Conversation," 1969, p. 158).

McLuhan's global village is an exciting place, a good place for people enjoying increased contact and increased involvement with one another aided by electronic technology. Gibson's nationless world isn't about involving ourselves in one another's lives and experiences. It's about electronic technology turning us into indistinguishable nonindividuals, rallying around products. We are united by buyable things, identifying not with others who share our common culture but with those who share some common goods. McLuhan sees the new communication technologies as expanding our experiences. Gibson sees them more negatively. You respect and enjoy the ideas of both thinkers. How can you reconcile the disagreement you have uncovered?

We begin this chapter with an examination of the Internet, the "new technology" that helped bring Gibson to prominence and gave renewed life to Marshall McLuhan's ideas. We study the history of the Internet, beginning with the development of the computer, and then we look at the Net as it exists today. We examine its formats and its capabilities, especially the popular World Wide Web. The number and nature of today's Internet users are also discussed, and we touch on the ongoing debate over the commercialization of the Internet.

Many of the issues discussed here will be familiar to you. Given the fundamental role that the Internet plays in encouraging and permitting convergence, concentration, audience fragmentation, globalization, and hypercommercialism, you should not be surprised that we've "met" the Internet and the Web before now in discussing the more traditional media. As Edgar Bronfman, Jr., CEO of multinational conglomerate Vivendi Universal, said of the Net, soon "a few clicks of your mouse will make it possible for you to summon every book ever written in any language, every movie ever made, every television show ever produced, every piece of music ever recorded" (as quoted in Mann, 2000, p. 41).

Media consultants Michael Wolf and Geoffrey Sands predict that the Internet-altered media

> will not just be broadcast networks, or cable news networks, or newspapers, or Websites. They will be entities that encompass all of them, and there will be only a few of them. They will deliver news anywhere, at any time you want it, through your TV, your laptop, even your Palm Pilot, as portable devices allowing online access revolutionize the way people get their news and entertainment. When you watch your favorite cable channel, the announcers will urge you not just to keep watching but to pick up its magazine, tune to its radio station, and log on to its Website. (1999, p. 110)

Marshall McLuhan

As the media with which we interact change, the role they play in our lives and the impact they have on us and our culture will likewise be altered. We will look at the new technology's double edge (its ability to have both good and bad effects), how to develop and maintain personal identity in the interconnected world, the Internet's ability to foster greater freedom of expression, efforts to control that expression, changes in the meaning of and threats to personal privacy, and the promise and perils of practicing democracy online.

Finally, our discussion of improving our media literacy takes the form of a primer for personal decision making and action in our increasingly media-saturated world. But first, the Internet.

A Short History of the Internet

There are conflicting versions about the origins of the Internet. The more common story is that the Net is a product of the Cold War. In this version, the Air Force in 1962, wanting to maintain the military's ability to transfer information around the country even if a given area was destroyed in an enemy attack, commissioned leading computer scientists to develop the means to do so. But many researchers and scientists dispute this "myth that (has) gone unchallenged long enough to become widely accepted as fact," that the Internet was initially "built to protect national security in the face of nuclear attack" (Hafner & Lyon, 1996, p. 10).

In the second version, as early as 1956 psychologist Joseph C. R. Licklider, a devotee of Marshall McLuhan's thinking on the power of communication technology, foresaw linked computers creating a country of

Joseph C. R. Licklider envisioned a national system of interconnected home computers as early as 1956.

citizens "informed about, and interested in, and involved in, the process of government" (p. 34). He foresaw "home computer consoles" and television sets connected in a nationwide network. "The political process would essentially be a giant teleconference," he wrote, "and a campaign would be a months-long series of communications among candidates, propagandists, commentators, political action groups, and voters. The key," he added, "is the self-motivating exhilaration that accompanies truly effective interaction with information through a good console and a good network to a good computer" (p. 34).

In what many technologists now consider to be the seminal essay on the potential and promise of computer networks, *Man-Computer Symbiosis*, Licklider, who had by now given up psychology and devoted himself completely to computer science, wrote in 1960, "The hope is that in not too many years, human brains and computing machines will be coupled . . . tightly, and the resulting partnership will think as no human brain has ever thought and process data in a way not approached by the information handling machines we know today" (as quoted in Hafner & Lyon, 1996, p. 35). Scores of computer experts, enthused by Licklider's vision (and many more who saw networked computers as a way to gain access to the powerful but otherwise expensive and unavailable computers just beginning to become available), joined the rush toward the development of what we know today as the **Internet,** a global network of interconnected computers that communicate freely and share and exchange information.

Development of the Computer

The title "Father of the Computer" resides with Englishman Charles Babbage. Lack of money and unavailability of the necessary technology stymied his plan to build an Analytical Engine, a steam-driven computer. But in the mid-1880s, aided by the insights of mathematician Lady Ada Byron Lovelace, Babbage did produce designs for a "computer" that could conduct algebraic computations using stored memory and punch cards for input and output. His work provided inspiration for those who would follow.

Internet Statistics
www.
glreach.com/globalstats/

Over the next 100 years a number of mechanical and electromechanical computers were attempted, some with success. But Colossus, developed by the British to break the Germans' secret codes during World War II, was the first electronic **digital computer.** It reduced information to a **binary code**—that is, a code made up of the digits 1 and 0. In this form information could be stored and manipulated. The first "full-service" electronic computer, ENIAC (Electronic Numerical Integrator and Calculator), based on the work of Iowa State's John V. Atanasoff, was introduced by scientists John Mauchly and John Presper Eckert of the Moore School

of Electrical Engineering at the University of Pennsylvania in 1946. ENIAC hardly resembled the computers we know today: 18 feet tall, 80 feet long, and weighing 60,000 pounds, it was composed of 17,500 vacuum tubes and 500 miles of electrical wire. It could fill an auditorium and ate up 150,000 watts of electricity. Mauchly and Eckert eventually left the university to form their own computer company, later selling it to the Remington Rand Corporation in 1950. At Remington they developed UNIVAC (Universal Automatic Computer), which, when bought for and used by the Census Bureau in 1951, became the first successful commercial computer.

Internet Statistics
www.
mids.org

The commercial computer explosion was ignited by IBM. Using its already well-entrenched organizational system of trained sales and service professionals, IBM helped businesses find their way in the early days of the computer revolution. One of its innovations was to sell rather than rent computers to customers. As a result of IBM's success, by 1960 the computer industry could be described as "IBM and the Seven Dwarfs"—Sperry, Control Data, Honeywell, RCA, NCR, General Electric, and Burroughs (Rosenberg, 1992, p. 60).

MILITARY APPLICATIONS

In 1957 the Soviet Union launched *Sputnik,* Earth's first human-constructed satellite. The once undisputed supremacy of the United States in science and technology had been usurped, and U.S. scientists and military officials were in shock. The Advanced Research Projects Agency (ARPA) was immediately established to sponsor and coordinate

The Soviet Union's 1-foot-long, 184-pound *Sputnik* was not only the first manmade satellite to orbit the Earth; it sent shudders throughout the American scientific and military communities.

sophisticated defense-related research. In 1962, as part of a larger drive to promote the use of computers in national defense (and giving rise to one of the stories of the Net's origins), ARPA commissioned Paul Baran of the Rand Corporation to produce a plan that would enable the U.S. military to maintain command over its missiles and planes if a nuclear attack knocked out conventional means of communication. The military thought a decentralized communication network was necessary. In that way, no matter where the bombing occurred, other locations would be available to launch a counterattack. Among Baran's plans was one for a "packet switched network." He wrote,

> Packet switching is the breaking down of data into datagrams or packets that are labeled to indicate the origin and the destination of the information and the forwarding of these packets from one computer to another computer until the information arrives at its final destination computer. This (is) crucial to the realization of a computer network. If packets are lost at any given point, the message can be resent by the originator. (As cited in Kristula, 1997, p. 1)

The genius of the system Baran envisioned is twofold: (1) common communication rules (called **protocols**) and common computer languages would enable any type of computer, running with any operating system, to communicate with another; and (2) destination or delivery instructions embedded in all information sent on the system would enable instantaneous "detours" or "rerouting" if a given computer on the network became unavailable.

Using Honeywell computers at Stanford University, UCLA, the University of California, Santa Barbara, and the University of Utah, the switching network, called ARPAnet, went online in 1969 and became fully operational and reliable within one year. Other developments soon followed. In 1972 an engineer named Ray Tomlinson created the first e-mail program (and gave us the ubiquitous @). In 1974 Stanford University's Vinton Cerf and the military's Robert Kahn coined the term "the Internet." In 1979 a graduate student at the University of North Carolina, Steve Bellovin, created Usenet and, independent of Bellovin, IBM created BITNET. These two networking software systems enabled virtually anybody with access to a Unix or IBM computer to connect to others on the growing network. By the time the Internet Society was chartered and the World Wide Web was released in 1992, there were more than 1.1 million **hosts**—computers linking individual personal computer users to the Internet. From 1995 to 1999, the number of hosts worldwide octupled. In Asia, the growth rate was double that (T. B. Allen, 2001). Today, there are more than 40 million hosts serving more than 300 million users across the globe (Hundt, 2002), including more than one-half of all households in the United States, in which there are 2 million new users every month (Barmann, 2002) and in which 80 million people log on every day (Charman, 2002).

A sixties-vintage IBM mainframe computer. The personal computer in your home probably carries more computing power than this giant machine.

An early computer chip on the right, and today's Pentium 4.

THE PERSONAL COMPUTER

A crucial part of the story of the Internet is the development and diffusion of personal computers. IBM was fantastically successful at exciting businesses, schools and universities, and other organizations about computers. But IBM's and other companies' **mainframe** and **minicomputers** employed **terminals,** and these stations at which users worked were connected to larger, centralized machines. As a result, the Internet at first was the province of the people who worked in those settings.

Definition of Internet Terms
WWW.
whatis.techtarget.com

When the semiconductor (or integrated circuit, or chip) replaced the vacuum tube as the essential information processor in computers, its tiny size, absence of heat, and low cost made possible the design and production of small, affordable **personal** or **microcomputers** (PCs). This, of course, opened the Net to anyone, anywhere.

The leaders of the personal computer revolution were Bill Gates and the duo of Steve Jobs and Stephen Wozniak. As a college freshman in 1975, Gates saw a magazine story about a small, low-powered computer, the MITS Altair 8800, that could be built from a kit and used to play a simple game. Sensing that the future of computing was in these personal computers and that the power of computers would reside not in their size but in the software that ran them, Gates dropped out of Harvard University and, with his friend Paul Allen, founded Microsoft Corporation. They licensed their **operating system**—the software that tells the computer how to work—to MITS. With this advance, people no longer had to know sophisticated operating languages such as FORTRAN and COBOL to use computers. At nearly the same time, in 1977, Jobs and Wozniak, also college dropouts, perfected Apple II, a low-cost, easy-to-use microcomputer designed specifically for personal rather than business use. It was immediately and hugely successful, especially in its development of **multimedia** capabilities—advanced sound and image applications. IBM, stung by its failure to enter the personal computer business, contracted with Microsoft to use the Microsoft operating system in its IBM PC, first introduced in 1981. All of the pieces were now in place for the home computer revolution.

The Internet Today

The Internet is most appropriately thought of as a "network of networks" that is growing at an incredibly fast rate. These networks consist of **LANs** (**L**ocal **A**rea **N**etworks), connecting two or more computers, usually within the same building, and **WANs** (**W**ide **A**rea **N**etworks), connecting several LANs in different locations. When people access the Internet from a computer in a university library, they are most likely on a LAN. But when several universities (or businesses or other organizations) link their computer systems, their users are part of a WAN.

Online White Pages
WWW.
whitepages.com

As the popularity of the Internet has grown, so has the number of Internet **providers** (sometimes called **ISPs,** or **I**nternet **s**ervice **p**roviders), companies that offer Internet connections at monthly rates depending on the kind and amount of access needed. There are 6,000 ISPs operating in the United States, including some of the better known, such as America Online, Prodigy, and the wireless provider Ricochet (Charman, 2002). Through providers, users can avail themselves of numerous services.

USING THE INTERNET

It is only a small overstatement to say that computers are rarely used for computing anymore because the Net has given the computer so much more versatility.

E-mail (Electronic Mail)   With an Internet **e-mail** account, users can communicate with anyone else online, any place in the world, with no long-distance fees (just applicable local phone connection charges). Most e-mail programs enable people to:

- List mail received and sent
- Read or delete an item from the list of documents received
- Print or save a document as a file
- Store frequently used names and addresses
- Automatically attach signatures at the end of letters
- Send replies, with portions of the original message in the reply
- Forward mail by simply readdressing it

Online Yellow Pages
WWW.
yellowpages.com

- Attach other files to mail
- Send a document to any number of people at once

Each person online has a unique e-mail address that works just like a telephone number. There are even online "Yellow Pages" and "White Pages" to help users find other people by e-mail.

Mailing Lists   E-mail can also be used to join mailing lists, bulletin boards, or discussion groups that cover a huge variety of subjects. The lists are often incorrectly called "listservs," which is the name of the free software program used to run most of them. Users simply subscribe to a group, and then all mail posted (sent) to that group is automatically forwarded to them by the host computer. The lists are typically produced by a single person or central authority such as a university, foundation, or public interest group. A listing of discussion groups can be obtained by e-mail from <listserv@ubvm.cc.buffalo.edu>.

Usenet   Also known as network news, **Usenet** is an internationally distributed bulletin board system. Users enter messages, and within a day or so the messages are delivered to nearly every other USENET host for everyone to read.

The best way to find a mailing list or discussion group is to access a document called "Publicly Accessible Mailing Lists," which is posted regularly on the Usenet newsgroup site <www.cs.uu.nl/cgi-bin/faqwais>. It is also available by anonymous FTP (file transfer protocol) at <ftp://rtfm.mit.edu/pub/usenet-by-group/news.answers/mail/mailing-lists>.

THE WORLD WIDE WEB

Another way of accessing information files is on the Internet via the **World Wide Web** (usually referred to as "the Web"). The Web is not a physical place, nor a set of files, nor even a network of computers. The heart of the Web lies in the protocols that define its use. The World Wide Web (WWW) uses hypertext transfer protocols (HTTP) to transport files from one place to another. Hypertext transfer was developed in the early 1990s by England's Tim Berners-Lee, who was working at Cern, the international particle physics laboratory near Geneva, Switzerland. Berners-Lee gave HTTP to the world for free. What makes the World Wide Web unique is the striking appearance of the information when it gets to your computer. In addition to text, the Web presents color, images, sounds, and video. This, combined with its ease of use, makes the Web the most popular aspect of the Internet for the large majority of users. Today there are more than 3 billion Web pages (Charman, 2002), but with estimates of up to 7.3 million new pages added every day ("Web Pages," 2000), there is really no way to precisely count the number of pages.

The ease of accessing the Web is a function of a number of components: hosts, URLs, browsers, search engines, and home pages.

Tim Berners-Lee
www.
w3.org/people/all

NASA's Pathfinder Web site welcomed millions of daily visitors from around the world during its July 1997 transmissions from the surface of Mars. The *New York Times* announced that, with this event, the World Wide Web had "arrived."

Hosts (Computers Connected to the Internet)   Other than e-mail transactions, most Internet activity consists of users accessing files on remote computers. To reach these files, users must first gain access to the Internet through "wired-to-the-Net" hosts. These hosts are often called servers.

NASA
www.
nasa.gov

When using the World Wide Web, it helps to understand how names are constructed. The rightmost part of the name is its **zone.** There are two kinds of zone information. One is *geographical,* such as *mx* for Mexico, *us* for the United States, and *uk* for the United Kingdom. The other is *organizational* and signifies the nature of the activity conducted by that site's creators. These include:

Zone	Type of Organization
com	Commercial organization
edu	Educational institution
gov	Government body or department
int	International organization (mostly NATO)
mil	Military site
net	Networking organization
org	Anything that doesn't fit elsewhere, such as a professional organization, especially nonprofit organizations
name	Personal Web sites

Once users gain access to a host computer on the Internet, they then have to find the exact location of the file they are looking for *on* the host.

Each file or directory on the Internet (that is, on the host computer connected to the Internet) is designated by a **URL** (**U**niform **R**esource **L**ocator). URLs, managed by the nonprofit International Corporation for Assigned Names and Numbers (ICANN), indicate:

- The program for accessing a file (or the protocol that will be used)
- The path to that file within the file directory of that computer
- The name of the file or directory in question

Here are some typical URLs:

Use	URL Identifier	Example
FTP	ftp://	ftp:/scholar.lib.vt.edu/
Gopher	gopher://	gopher://gopher.vt.edu
Telnet	telnet://	telnet://vtls.vt.edu
Usenet News	news:	news:comp.infosystems.www
WWW (HTTP)	http://	http://www.yahoo.com

As any user of the Web knows, however, sites are recognized by their **domain names** rather than by their URLs. Domain names presumably give some indication of the nature of a site's content or owner. For many years domain names were registered and licensed by a single company, Virginia-based Network Solutions, Inc. But in mid-1999, ICANN authorized several other firms, among them AOL and France Telecom, to do so in an attempt to spur competition and reduce the cost of registering domain names.

Browsers Software programs loaded onto the user's computer and used to download and view Web files are known as **browsers.** Browsers take separate files (text files, image files, and sound files) and put them all together for viewing. Netscape and Internet Explorer are two of the most popular Web browsers.

Search Engines Finding information on the Web is becoming easier thanks to the growing number of companies creating Web- or Net-search software. These programs are sometimes called **search engines, spiders,** or **Web crawlers.** They all provide on-screen menus that make their navigation as simple as pointing and clicking. The most popular search engines are:

Ask Jeeves	http://ask.com
AltaVista	http://www.altavista.com
AOL NetFind	http://search.aol.com
Excite	http://www.excite.com
Hotbot	http://hotbot.lycos.com
Go.com	http://www.go.com

A typical and often visited home page.

Lycos	http://www.lycos.com
Netscape	http://www.netscape.com
Webcrawler	http://www.webcrawler.com
Yahoo	http://www.yahoo.com
Google	http://www.google.com

Home Pages Once users reach the intended Web site, they are greeted by a **home page**—the entryway to the site itself. It not only contains the information the site's creators want visitors to know but also provides **hyperlinks** to other material in that site, as well as to material in other sites on other computers linked to the Net anywhere in the world.

The Internet and Its Users

We typically think of people who access a medium as audience members, but the Internet has *users*, not audience members. At any time—or even at the same time—a person may be both *reading* Internet content and *creating* content. E-mail and chat rooms are obvious examples of online users being both audience and creators, but others exist as well. For example, **multiple user domains (MUDs)** enable entire alternative realities to be simultaneously constructed and engaged, and computer screens that have multiple open windows enable users to "read" one site while creating another, sometimes using the just-read material. With ease we can access the Web, link from site to site and page to page, and even build our own sites. As former NBC and PBS president Lawrence K. Grossman wrote, "Gutenberg made us all readers. Radio and television made us all first-hand observers. Xerox made us all publishers. The Internet makes us all journalists, broadcasters, columnists, commentators, and critics" (1999, p. 17).

For more information on this topic, view *Internet: Inside Websites for Mass Media Outlets*, #5 on the CD *Media Tours*.

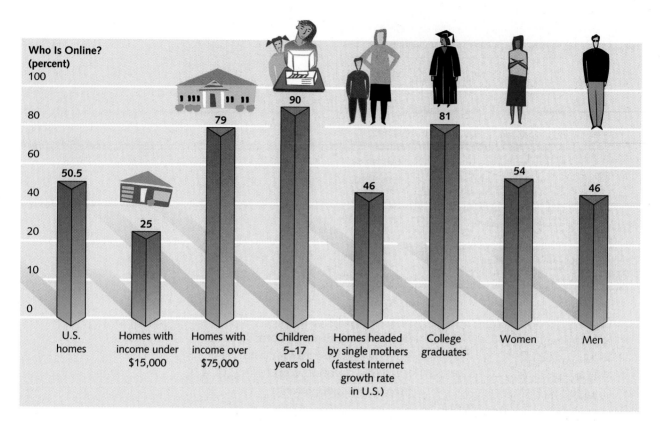

Figure 10.1 Internet User Profile, 2002. *Source: U.S. Census Bureau: A Nation Online: How Americans Are Expanding Their Use of the Internet* (www.ntia.doc.gov/).

U.S. Census Bureau
www.
census.gov

It is almost impossible to tell exactly how many users there are on the Internet. People who own computers are not necessarily linked to the Internet, and people need not own computers to use the Net. Some users access the Net through machines at school, the library, or work. Still, more than one-half of all U.S. homes regularly access the Internet (Barmann, 2002). The Net's demographics have undergone a dramatic shift in the last few years. In 1996, for example, 62% of U.S. Internet users were men. In 2000, women became the Net's majority gender for the first time (Hamilton, 2000). The Census Bureau offers some other interesting user data, as you can see in Figure 10.1.

Commercialization of the Internet

Today, 77% of American Internet users report making online purchases. A survey of 12 developed countries discovered that two-thirds of *all* users were using the Net to buy, up from 36% in 2000 (Gilbert, 2003). This growing number of users and their apparent willingness to go online to buy products have been at the heart of one important debate about the future of the Internet.

The Internet was developed, nurtured, and popularized by **hackers,** people interested in technology, information, and communication through computers. In *Road Warriors: Dreams and Nightmares Along the*

Information Highway (1995), Daniel Burstein and David Kline argue that the Internet and business are poor partners. They compared the characteristics of the Internet to those of the companies that were increasingly using the Internet to conduct their business:

Internet Characteristics	Business Characteristics
Free	For profit
Egalitarian	Hierarchical
Decentralized	Systematized
Ad hoc	Planned
Open	Proprietary
Experimental	Pragmatic
Autonomous	Accountable
Anarchic	Organized

These two sets of characteristics and the values they represent, Burstein and Kline wrote, would inevitably clash. Internet hackers, geeks, and innovators have ironically become the "traditionalists" in this debate. These users fear that business will turn the Internet into an electronic shopping mall and that this commercialization of what was once the freest of communication technologies will lead to growing privatization and control. Commerce, they claim, cannot function amid chaos and disorder, but it is just that anarchy that has made the Internet so exciting. Nobody needs permission to get on or off the Internet. Nobody can tell a user what to say.

Online traditionalists point to the history of television. In the medium's early stages, there were predictions and promises of a new medium of expression, education, and entertainment. Politics and political discourse, for example, would be transformed as people became aware of and involved in public affairs. The reality, the online traditionalists contend, is that television, with its commercial support, profit orientation, and lowest common denominator mentality, has cheapened politics and political discourse. Given this view, it is no surprise that a 1995 survey detailed in *Advertising Age* reported that two-thirds of the U.S. adult respondents said "No" when asked whether advertising should be allowed on the Internet (Fawcett, 1996). Online magazine founder David Talbot (Chapter 5) asks, "Where are the independent news voices on the Internet? Where's the great, flourishing media democracy? There's got to be room for a few independent voices" (quoted in Farhi, 2001, p. 36).

Defenders of online commerce argue, however, that the Internet will always be accessible and open. There is no spectrum scarcity to limit access, as there is in broadcasting, so the television analogy is inappropriate. In addition, because very small amounts of money are required for individuals to access and use the Internet, especially in contrast to the budget needed to start and run a broadcast or cable operation or a newspaper or magazine, the commercial orientation of those media will never fully overtake the Net. It is precisely this commercial potential of the Internet,

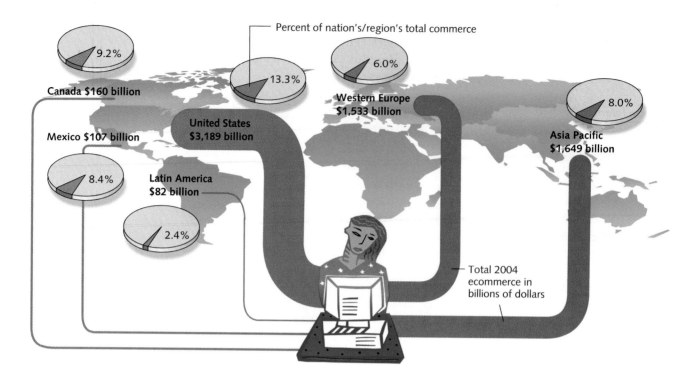

Percent of nation's/region's total commerce

Canada $160 billion — 9.2%

13.3%

United States
$3,189 billion

Western Europe
$1,533 billion — 6.0%

Asia Pacific
$1,649 billion — 8.0%

Mexico $107 billion — 8.4%

Latin America
$82 billion — 2.4%

Total 2004
ecommerce in
billions of dollars

Figure 10.2. Worldwide eCommerce Growth. By 2004, worldwide online commerce will reach $6.8 trillion. *Source:* Global Reach (www.glreach.com/eng/ed/art/2004.ecommerce.php3).

they contend, that will keep the cost of access low and its value high. Regardless of the position taken, there is little doubt that the online world is increasingly characterized by commercialization (Figure 10.2). And there is some indication that that commercialization *is* turning some users off. Recent declines in the average amount of time users spend online (Pastore, 2001) and the flight from the Internet by millions of former users (Pastore, 1999) have been attributed, in part, to overcommercialization and the intrusiveness of Internet advertising (see Chapter 12).

Possibly the most annoying form of commercialization of the Internet is **spam,** unsolicited commercial e-mail, and it threatens to alienate even more users. The typical e-mail user received 2,603 unsolicited commercial messages in 2003, or seven a day. By 2008, that number will reach 94 per day, 40 pieces of spam at work, 54 at home. By September 2004, some 400 billion pieces of spam will constitute a majority of all e-mail on the Internet (Agocs & Menduno, 2003). So serious had the problem become that in September 2003 California passed the nation's first anti-spam legislation. A month later, the U.S. Senate, in a 97 to 0 vote, followed suit.

Changes in the Mass Communication Process

In Chapter 2 we saw how concentration of ownership, globalization, audience fragmentation, hypercommercialism, and convergence were influencing the nature of the mass communication process. Each redefines the relationship between audiences and media industries. For example, we have discussed the impacts of concentration on newspaper readership; of globalization on the type and quality of films available to moviegoers; of audience fragmentation on the variety of channel choices for television viewers; of convergence on the record industry's reinvention; and of hyper-commercialism on all media.

The Internet is different from these more traditional media. Rather than changing the relationship between audiences and industries, the Net changes the *definition* of the different components of the process and, as a result, changes their relationship. On the Net a single individual can communicate with as large an audience as can the giant, multinational corporation that produces a network television program. That corporation fits our earlier definition of a mass communication source—a large, hier-archically structured organization—but the Internet user does not. Feed-back in mass communication is traditionally described as inferential and delayed, but online feedback can be, and very often is, immediate and direct. It is more similar to feedback in interpersonal communication than to feedback in mass communication.

This Internet-induced redefinition of the elements of the mass com-munication process is refocusing attention on issues such as freedom of expression, privacy, responsibility, and democracy.

THE DOUBLE EDGE OF TECHNOLOGY

The solution to the McLuhan versus Gibson dilemma in the opening vignette is one of perspective. McLuhan was writing and thinking in the relative youth of the electronic media. When *Understanding Media* was published in 1964, television had just become a mass medium, the personal computer wasn't even a dream, and Paul Baran was still envi-sioning ARPAnet.

Gibson, writing much later in the age of electronic media, was com-menting from a more experienced position and after observing real-world evidence. McLuhan was optimistic because he was speculating on what electronic media *could do*. Gibson is pessimistic because he is comment-ing on what he had seen electronic media *doing*.

Still, neither visionary is completely right nor completely wrong. Tech-nology alone, even the powerful electronic media that fascinated both, cannot create new worlds or new ways of seeing them. *We* use technology to do these things (see Figure 10.3 on p. 314). This, as we discussed briefly in Chapter 2, is why technology is a double-edged sword. Its power—for good and for bad—resides in us. The same aviation technology that we use to visit relatives halfway around the world can also be used to destroy the World Trade Center. The same communication technologies used to create a truly global village can be used to dehumanize and standardize the people who live in it.

© Hilary B. Price. Reprinted with special permission of King Features Syndicate.

Figure 10.3 Technology, even one with as much potential as the Internet, is only as good as the uses we make of it.

McLUHAN'S RENAISSANCE

Marshall McLuhan's ideas are in vogue again. The Canadian English professor was at the center of the early intellectual debate over electronic media. His books—especially *The Gutenberg Galaxy* (1962), *Understanding Media: The Extensions of Man* (1964), and *The Medium Is the Massage* (McLuhan & Fiore, 1967)—generated heated comment and earned McLuhan much criticism. His ideas satisfied almost no one. Critics from the humanities castigated him for wasting his time on something as frivolous as television. True culture exists in "real" literature, they argued. McLuhan fared just as badly among mass communication theorists. Social scientists committed to the idea of limited media effects (see Chapter 13) simply disagreed with his view of powerful media technologies, however optimistic. Others who were convinced of media's potential negative influence dismissed him as blindly in love with technology and overly speculative. Social scientists demanded scientific verification of McLuhan's ideas. Labeled the "High Priest of Popcult," the "Metaphysician of Media," the "Oracle of the Electronic Age," McLuhan may simply have been ahead of his time.

What has returned McLuhan to the forefront of the cultural discussion surrounding the mass media is the Internet. McLuhan's ideas resonate with those who believe the new medium can fulfill his optimistic vision of an involved, connected global village. Those who think the potential of the Internet, like that of television before it, will never fulfill McLuhan's predictions are forced to explain their reasoning in terms of his ideas. McLuhan is back, and, as before, he is controversial. *Wired* magazine, the self-proclaimed "Bible of Cyberspace," has anointed McLuhan its patron saint. But as we saw in the opening vignette, not everyone in the cyberworld trusts the technology as much as he did. Two of his concepts, however—the global village and media as extensions of our bodies—are receiving renewed discussion precisely because of the Net.

Marshall McLuhan
www.
mcluhan.ca

The Global Village Many concepts survive McLuhan's 1980 death and serve as his legacy. None is more often quoted than the **global village,** the

The books that put Marshall McLuhan at the center of the debate over electronic communication.

idea that the new communication technologies will permit people to become increasingly involved in one another's lives. Skeptics point out that McLuhan, with this notion, reveals his unrealistic, utopian infatuation with technology. But McLuhan himself never said all would be tranquil in the global village. Yes, he did believe electronic media would permit "the human tribe" to become "one family," but he also realized that families fight:

> There is more diversity, less conformity under a single roof in any family than there is with the thousands of families in the same city. The more you create village conditions, the more discontinuity and division and diversity. The global village absolutely insures maximal disagreement on all points. (McLuhan & Stearn, 1967, p. 279)

Involvement does not mean harmony, but it does mean an exchange of ideas. As McLuhan said, the global village is "a world in which people encounter each other in depth all the time" (p. 280).

Media as Extensions of Our Bodies Central to McLuhan's view of how media and cultures interact is the idea that media do not *bring* the world to us but rather permit us to experience the world with a scope and depth otherwise impossible. Media, then, are extensions of our bodies. Just as clothes are an extension of our skin, permitting us to wander farther from our warm caves into the cold world; just as the automobile is an extension of our feet, enabling us to travel farther than we could ever walk; television extends our vision and hearing, and computers extend our central nervous system. With television we can see and hear around the world, beyond the galaxy, into the future, and into the past. Computers process, sort, categorize, reconfigure, and clarify. McLuhan's message here is not

More McLuhan
www.
law.pitt.edu/hibbitts/mcl.htm

unlike Carey's (1975) ritual view of mass communication. Communication technologies do not deliver or transmit information; they fundamentally alter the relationship between people and their world, encouraging us to construct new meanings for the things we encounter with and through them.

Reconceptualizing Life in an Interconnected World

What happens to people in the global village? What becomes of audiences and users as their senses are extended technologically? How free are we to express ourselves? Does greater involvement with others mean a loss of privacy? What becomes of personal identity when it is built and extended through media? These are only a few of the questions confronting us as we attempt to find the right balance between the good and the bad that comes from the new communication technologies.

THE INTERNET AND FREEDOM OF EXPRESSION

By its very nature the Internet raises a number of important issues of freedom of expression. There is no central location, no on and off button for the Internet, making it difficult to control for those who want to do so. For free expression advocates, however, this freedom from control is the medium's primary strength. The anonymity of its users provides their expression—even the most radical, profane, and vulgar—great protection, giving voice to those who would otherwise be silenced. This anonymity, say advocates of strengthened Internet control, is a breeding ground for abuse. But opponents of control counter that the Net's affordability and ease of use make it our most democratic medium. Proponents of control argue that this freedom brings with it responsibilities that other media— and those who create their content—understand but that are ignored by many online. Internet freedom of expression issues, then, fall into two broad categories. The first is the Net's potential to make the First Amendment's freedom of the press guarantee a reality for greater numbers of people. The second is the problem of setting boundaries of control.

FREEDOM OF THE PRESS FOR WHOM?

Veteran *New Yorker* columnist A. J. Liebling, author of that magazine's "Wayward Press" feature and often called the "conscience of journalism," frequently argued that freedom of the press is guaranteed only to those who own one. Theoretically, anyone can own a broadcast outlet or cable television operation. But the number of outlets in any community is limited, and they are unavailable to all but the richest people and corporations. Theoretically, anyone can own a newspaper or magazine, but

The OCA's Web site gets 4,000 hits a day.
Reprinted with permission.

again the expense involved makes this an impossibility for most people. Newsletters, like a soap-box speaker on a street corner, are limited in reach, typically of interest to those who already agree with the message, and relatively unsophisticated when compared with the larger commercial media.

The Net, however, turns every user into a potential mass communicator. Equally important, on the Internet every "publisher" is equal. The Web sites of the biggest government agency, the most powerful broadcast network, the newspaper with the highest circulation, the richest ad agencies and public relations firms, the most far-flung religion, and the lone user with an idea or cause sit figuratively side by side. Each is only as powerful as its ideas.

In other words, the Net can give voice to those typically denied expression (see the box "Protest.org"). Writing for the alternative press news service Alternet, activist L. A. Kauffman said, "The Internet is an agitator's dream: fast, cheap, far-reaching. And with the planetary reach of the World Wide Web, activist networks are globalizing at nearly the pace of the corporate order they oppose" (as quoted in Cox, 2000, p. 14). The Organic Consumers Association is an instructive example. It is a public interest activist group focusing on food safety and the environment. Its director, Ronnie Cummins, says that 85,000 members receive its action alerts and newsletter, *BioDemocracy News,* by e-mail, and its Web site receives 4,000 hits a day, with visitors downloading an average of 10 pages of content. "A lot of our clout is being able to communicate cheaply to people," Cummins said, "If we had to revert back to telephones, faxes, the mail and leafleting, it would reduce our campaign power considerably" (quoted in Charman, 2002, p. 22). After instituting reforms in response to an Internet-led protest of labor practices in its Third World factories in 1998, a company spokesperson for athletic shoe manufacturer Nike

For more information on this topic, see NBC Video Clip #21 on the CD—*The Drudge Report.*

Protest.org

Many people are using the Internet to make a difference by employing its reach and anonymity to foster democracy and fight governmental repression. For example, when opponents to Slobodan Milosevic's regime won several municipal elections in 1996, the Yugoslavian dictator quickly moved to annul the vote. Popular independent radio station B92 immediately began coverage of the sometimes violent street protests that greeted the strongman's actions. With the flick of a switch of a state-owned transmitter, however, Milosevic had B92 put off the air.

But while radio stations can be shut down easily, the Internet is much harder to silence. B92 simply moved its broadcasts onto the Internet. The station used regular phone lines to send written and sound reports of the protests to servers in the Netherlands and the United States. Then the BBC downloaded the reports and broadcast them back into Yugoslavia, where there are few Internet users but almost universal access to radio. Why didn't the authorities simply shut down the phone lines over which B92 accessed the Net? The answer is simple—to do so would have meant shutting down the entire country's phone system. As a result, the government had no effective way of silencing the station. After a few weeks, Milosevic ordered the transmitter switched back on.

The Tibetan government-in-exile of the Dalai Lama uses the Internet from its base in India to garner international support for its fight against China's occupation of its homeland. Indonesian students successfully used the Internet to rally sentiment for the ouster of the repressive and corrupt government of President Suharto. But the most dramatic example of citizens using the Internet to fight government oppression comes from China. In that Communist country, Internet accounts have to be registered with the police. The state has established a 24-hour Internet task force to find and arrest senders of "counter-revolutionary" commentary. Popular bulletin boards are shut down when their chat becomes a bit too free. It is a crime to use the Internet to "spread rumors," "promote feudal superstitions," and "injure the reputation of state organs." Web sites such as Human Rights Watch, the *New York Times*, and publications about China that are independent of government control, such as *China News Digest*, are blocked. In January 1999, a 30-year-old computer engineer was sentenced to 2 years in prison for sending 30,000 Chinese e-mail addresses to an online dissident publication based in the United States. None of this repression, however, has swayed the creators of *Tunnel*, a Chinese-language Web journal of dissent (<http://www.geocities.com/CapitolHill/7288/tunn.htm>; be warned, however, this URL has changed a number of times, so if it does not get you to *Tunnel*, search for the publication by name).

Begun on June 3, 1997, the anniversary of the killing of hundreds of Chinese citizens by the People's Liberation Army in Beijing's Tiananmen Square in 1989, it hoped to make a difference by breaking "through the present lock on information and controls on expression" (*The Tunnel*, 2002). *Tunnel* is produced and edited in China, smuggled to the United States, and then carried back to China on the Internet. In this way, the staff is hidden from even the most diligent trackers. *Tunnel* turned to the Net, as it said in its first edition, because "the computer network . . . disseminates technology onto the desks of each and every one of us. It can undermine the two pillars of an autocratic society—monopoly and suppression" (Dobson, 1998, p. 20).

With its coverage of and commentary on international news and arguments for greater freedom penned anonymously by intellectuals and other dissidents, *Tunnel* has put the Chinese government in something of a bind. Communist Party and business leaders alike recognize that China will never gain full membership in the international community (and economy) unless its people and businesses are wired, but the more its people and businesses are wired, the greater difficulty the government will have in controlling expression, and therefore, dissent. The result will inevitably be more freedom.

said, "You make changes because it's the right thing to do. But obviously our actions have clearly been accelerated because of the World Wide Web" (as quoted in Klein, 1999, p. 392). At a 1998 conference of public relations professionals, Peter Verhille of public relations company Entente International told his colleagues, "One of the major strengths of pressure groups—in fact the leveling factor in their confrontation with powerful companies—is their ability to exploit the instruments of the telecommunication revolution. Their agile use of

Officials were caught off guard by the size and intensity of the protests against the World Trade Organization in Seattle in 1999. This massive gathering of protesters from scores of different groups from around the world was planned and organized on the Internet.

global tools such as the Internet reduces the advantage that corporate budgets once provided" (as quoted in Klein, 1999, p. 395).

This "agile use" is dramatically demonstrated by **flash mobs** (sometimes **smart mobs**), "large, geographically dispersed groups connected only by thin threads of communications technology . . . drawn together at a moment's notice like schools of fish to perform some collective action" (Taylor, 2003, p. 53). MoveOn.org is the best-known site for the coordination of flash mobs. Using e-mail and instant messaging, MoveOn led the February 15, 2003, worldwide anti-war protest, gathering 400,000 people in New York and 10 million more across the globe to protest the impending war in Iraq. To prove that flash mobs had become "the other superpower," according to the *New York Times*, 1 million people in 6,000 cities in 130 countries flash-mobbed an anti-war candle-light vigil on March 16, 2003, an action called in only 5 days (Boyd, 2003).

The Internet is also offering expanded expression through Weblogs, or **blogs.** Before September 11, 2001, blogs were typically personal online diaries. But after that horrible day, possibly because millions of people felt that the mainstream press had left them unprepared and clueless about what was really going on in the world, blogs changed. Blog now refers to a "Web journal that comments on the news—often by criticizing the media and usually in rudely clever tones—with links to stories that back up the commentary with evidence" (Seipp, 2002, p. 43). There are more than a million already on the Internet, and 1,000 new ones go online every day, some constructed by the famous, most by the not famous (Kloer, 2002). Technology writer Andrew Sullivan argues that "blogging is changing the media world and could foment a revolution in how journalism functions

Media Activist "Gripe Site"
WWW.
fair.org

Blogging
WWW.
blogger.com

in our culture." How? Blogs are

imbued with the temper of their writer. This personal touch is much more in tune with our current sensibility than (are) the opinionated magazines and newspapers of old. Readers increasingly doubt the authority of *The Washington Post* or *National Review*, despite their grand-sounding titles and large staffs. They know that behind the curtain are fallible writers and editors who are no more inherently trustworthy than a lone blogger who has earned a reader's respect. The second thing blogs do is—to invoke Marx [see Chapter 13]—seize the means of production. It's hard to underestimate what a huge deal this is. For as long as journalism has existed, writers of whatever kind have had one route to readers: They needed an editor and a publisher. Even in the most benign scenario, this process subtly distorts journalism. You find yourself almost unconsciously writing to please a handful of people—the editors looking for a certain kind of story, the publishers seeking to push a particular venture, or the advertisers who influence the editors and owners. Blogging simply bypasses this ancient ritual. (2002, pp. 43–44)

Sullivan, former editor of the *New Republic*, says this "means the universe of permissible opinions will expand, unconstrained by the prejudices, tastes or interests of the old-media elite" (quoted in Seipp, 2002, p. 43). In other words, because bloggers in effect own their own presses, they have freedom of the press. There is no more obvious example of the power of this freedom than the resignation in December 2002 of Trent Lott from his Senate leadership position. His nostalgia for segregation, expressed at the 100th birthday party of Senator Strom Thurmond, went unreported in the mainstream press. But bloggers, both liberal and conservative, spread the story, forcing the big media to pay attention. Lott could not survive the blog-inspired firestorm ("Blogs," 2003).

CONTROLLING INTERNET EXPRESSION

Freedom, or more specifically the abuse of freedom, is behind the argument for greater control of the Internet. The very same medium that can empower users who wish to challenge those more powerful than themselves can also be used to lie and cheat. The Internet does not distinguish between true and false, biased and objective, trivial and important. Once misinformation has been loosed on the Net, it is almost impossible to catch and correct it (Figure 10.4).

For example, in the summer of 2000, a fake Internet news release announcing the departure of Emulex's CEO sent the high-tech company's stock into freefall, costing it 50% of its value, or more than $2 billion, in a matter of minutes (Baranowski, 2001). More recently, in January 2002, Fox News anchorperson Brit Hume reported to his cableviewing audience:

It's deer hunting season out in Ohio, and People for the Ethical Treatment of Animals is trying to protect the animals by adorning them with bright orange vests. . . . PETA boasted it had succeeded in dressing more than 400 deer in vests, but Guy Lockley, owner of a sporting goods store in Youngstown,

Figure 10.4 Rumors, lies, and innuendo spread far, wide, and fast on the Internet. Jump Start reprinted by permission of United Feature Syndicate, Inc.

countered by offering a reward to hunters who could bag vested deer and bring home the vests. . . . State officials are said to be worried that the whole vest competition could get someone shot. (in Rosen, 2002b, p. 19)

The story, admittedly fairly interesting, quickly found its way onto numerous Web sites, including those of ESPN and the *Wall Street Journal*. This was only fitting, as the Web was where the story was born, an Internet-fed fictional urban legend. It was not deer season in Ohio, and there was no Guy Lockley in Youngstown. The people at Fox News could have checked with state officials. They could have tried to track down Mr. Lockley. They might have contacted PETA for comment. But why go through all that trouble? The "facts" were on the Internet.

Lies have always been part of human interaction; the Internet only gives them greater reach. There is little that government can do to control this abuse. Legal remedies already exist in the form of libel laws and prosecution for fraud. Users can help by teaching themselves to be more attentive to return addresses and by ignoring messages that are sent anonymously or that have suspicious origins. There is an Internet-based solution as well. Computer security specialists at the U.S. Department of Energy maintain a Web site designed to track and debunk online misinformation (http://hoaxbusters.ciac.org).

PORNOGRAPHY ON THE WORLD WIDE WEB

Most efforts at controlling the Internet are aimed at indecent or pornographic Web content. We will see in Chapter 14 that indecent and pornographic expression is protected. The particular concern with the Internet, therefore, is shielding children.

The Child Pornography Prevention Act of 1996 forbade online transmission of any image that "appears to be of a minor engaging in sexually explicit conduct." Proponents argued that the impact of child porn on the children involved, as well as on society, warranted this legislation. Opponents argued that child pornography per se was already illegal, regardless of the medium. Therefore they saw this law as an unnecessary and overly broad intrusion into freedom of expression on the Net. In April 2002 the Supreme Court sided with the act's opponents. Its effect would be too damaging to freedom of expression. "Few legitimate movie producers or book publishers, or few other speakers in any capacity, would risk distributing images in or near the uncertain reach of this law," wrote Justice Anthony Kennedy. "The Constitution gives significant protection from over-broad laws that chill speech within the First Amendment's vast and privileged sphere" (in "Justices Scrap," 2002, p. A3). Kennedy cited the antidrug film *Traffic*, Academy Award winner *American Beauty*, and Shakespeare's *Romeo and Juliet*, all works containing scenes of minors engaged in sexual activity, as examples of expression that would disappear from the Net.

The primary battleground, then, became protecting children from otherwise legal content. The Net, by virtue of its openness and accessibility, raises particular concerns. Children's viewing of sexually explicit material on cable television can theoretically be controlled by parents. Moreover, viewers must specifically order this content and typically pay an additional fee for it. The purchase of sexually explicit videos, books, and magazines is controlled by laws regulating vendors. But computers sit in homes, schools, and libraries. Children are encouraged to explore their possibilities. A search for the novel *Little Women*, for example, might turn up any number of pornographic sites.

Proponents of stricter control of the Net liken the availability of smut on the Internet to a bookstore or library that allows porn to sit side by side with books that children *should* be reading. In actual, real-world bookstores and libraries, professionals, whether book retailers or librarians, apply their judgment in selecting and locating material, ideally striving for appropriateness and balance. Children are the beneficiaries of their professional judgment. No such selection or evaluation is applied to the Internet. Opponents of control accept the bookstore/library analogy but argue that, as troubling as the online proximity of all types of content may be, it is a true example of the freedom guaranteed by the First Amendment.

The solution seems to be in technology. Filtering software, such as Net Nanny (www.netnanny.com), can be set to block access to Web sites by title and by the presence of specific words and images (see the box "Rating the Web"). Few free speech advocates are troubled by filters on home computers, but they do see them as problematic when used on more public machines, for example, in schools and libraries. They argue that software that can filter sexual content can also be set to screen out birth control information, religious sites, and discussions of racism. Virtually any content can be blocked. This, they claim, denies other users—adults and mature teenagers, for example—their freedoms.

Congress weighed in on the filtering debate, passing the Children's Internet Protection Act in 2000, requiring schools and libraries to install filtering software. But First Amendment concerns invalidated this act as well. A federal appeals court ruled in June 2002 that requiring these institutions to install

Net Nanny
WWW.
netnanny.com

Rating the Web

Proponents of a Web rating system see technology, in the form of filtering software, as an appropriate solution to the need to protect children. They see it as similar to the television content ratings system, which is tied to the blocking technology of the V-chip. Opponents of rating Web content call these filters **censorware,** but given that individual users can control the level of filtering they deem appropriate for their own households, there is less industry and user resistance to this screening method than there was to that used for television.

Rating proponents envision two forms of filtering—existing rating schemes and specific interest group ratings. As examples of the latter, the National Organization for Women can develop its own ratings scheme, the Catholic Diocese of St. Louis its own, and the Moral Majority its own. Software already exists for setting individual labeling and filtering codes.

Among preexisting filtering software, the three most utilized are the Recreational Software Advisory Council on the Internet (RSAC), SafeSurf, and Net Nanny.

RSAC is a nonprofit organization that asks Web sites to rate themselves on a scale from 0 to 4 for tolerance of sex, nudity, strong language, and violence. The higher the number, the more of each type of content is present. Users set their own screening levels on the RSAC-provided software.

SafeSurf is a commercial company that monitors a self-rating system that labels sites by suitable age ranges, as well as by the amount of such content as nudity and drug use. It has rated more than 50,000 sites.

Net Nanny can be set to screen out individual Web sites, newsgroups, chat rooms, even entire search engines. It can be customized for individual users of the same machine (so that what is filtered for the kids can be there

Reprinted with permission.

for mom and dad), and it maintains an account of Web and Net use.

The use of ratings, labels, and filters is generally accepted as a fact of life by both users and the Internet industry. Internet Explorer, Netscape Communicator, Yahoo, Excite, Lycos, Infoseek, and virtually all the well known browsers and search engines provide some form of built-in, easy-to-use filter. What has happened here in the online world echoes events in the film industry in 1968 and in television programming in 1996.

filters changes their nature from places that provide information to places that unconstitutionally restrict it. Nonetheless, in June 2003 a sharply divided Supreme Court upheld the Children's Internet Protection Act, declaring that Congress did indeed have the power to require libraries to install filters.

COPYRIGHT (INTELLECTUAL PROPERTY OWNERSHIP)

Another freedom-of-expression issue that takes on a special nature on the Internet is copyright. Copyright protection is designed to ensure that those who create content are financially compensated for their work (see Chapter 14). The assumption is that more "authors" will create more content if assured of monetary compensation from those who use it. When the content is tangible (books, movies, videotapes, magazines, CDs), authorship and use are relatively easy to identify. But in the cyberworld, things become a bit more complex. John Perry Barlow (1996), a cofounder of the Electronic Frontier Foundation, explains the situation:

> The riddle is this: If our property can be infinitely reproduced and instantaneously distributed all over the planet without cost, without our knowledge, without its even leaving our possession, how can we protect it? How are we going to get paid for the work we do with our minds? And, if we can't get paid, what will assure the continued creation and distribution of such work? (p. 148)

Technically, copyright rules apply to the Internet as they do to other media. Material on the Net, even on electronic bulletin boards, belongs to the author, so its use, other than fair use, requires permission and possibly payment. But because material on the Internet is not tangible, it is easily, freely, and privately copied. This renders it difficult, if not impossible, to police those who do copy.

Another confounding issue is that new and existing material is often combined with other existing material to create even "newer" content. This makes it difficult to assign authorship. If a user borrows some text from one source, combines it with images from a second, surrounds both with a background graphic from a third, and adds music sampled from many others, where does authorship reside?

To deal with these thorny issues, in 1998 the U.S. Congress passed the Digital Millennium Copyright Act. Its primary goal was to bring U.S. copyright law into compliance with that of the World Intellectual Property Organization (WIPO), headquartered in Geneva, Switzerland. The act does the following:

- Makes it a crime to circumvent antipiracy measures built into commercial software
- Outlaws the manufacture, sale, or distribution of code-breaking devices used to illegally copy software
- Permits breaking of copyright protection devices to conduct encryption research and to test computer security systems
- Provides copyright exemptions for nonprofit libraries, archives, and educational institutions under certain circumstances
- Limits the copyright infringement liability of Internet service providers for simply transmitting information over the Internet, but ISPs are required to remove material from users' Web sites that appears to constitute copyright infringement
- Requires Webcasters (Chapter 8) to pay licensing fees to record companies
- States explicitly that **fair use**—instances in which copyrighted material may be used without permission or payment, such as taking brief quotes from a book (see Chapter 14)—applies to the Internet

What the debate over Internet copyright represents—like concern about controlling content that children can access, commercialization of the Net, and efforts to limit troublesome or challenging expression—is a clash of fundamental values that has taken on added nuance with the coming of computer networks. Copyright on the Internet is discussed more fully in Chapter 14.

PERSONAL IDENTITY

As we discussed in Chapter 1, people develop their identities in part through interaction with their culture and with others in it. If that interaction changes, then so too must the identities it fosters. The question, then, is what kinds of identities people can build when new communication technologies infinitely extend the senses—sight, speech, and hearing—once used in more traditional interaction with the culture and others in it? Let's look at one example from the Internet.

A MUD (multiple user domain) is an online, virtual "community" in which users are encouraged to create their own identities, which then interact singly or in groups with other virtual citizens of that community. Individuals create their own look. They can appear tall, short, beautiful, or with the head of a lion and a mane of snakes. They also create their own rooms or spaces in the MUD. Users can then invite others into their virtual homes, condos, offices, or backyards. In MUDs, identity is constructed through communication with others who are always unseen (except as their MUD alter egos) and most often unknown. The purpose of the MUD is to allow people to experiment with their identities, to shed old ones and to try out new ones.

Links to MUDs
WWW.
godlike.com/muds

MUDs are virtual environments expressly designed for the creation of virtual identities. But they also serve as a metaphor for the way computer networks help modern people build their actual identities, according to MIT sociology professor Sherry Turkle (1995). Turkle writes of online "worlds without origin," places that "allow people to generate experiences, relationships, identities, and living spaces that arise only through interaction with technology" (p. 21). Rather than experiencing these things in everyday, actual environments, we experience them in a new environment, one characterized by "eroding boundaries between the real and virtual, the animate and inanimate, the unitary and multiple self" (p. 10).

Whether in a MUD, in a chat room, using e-mail, or in an interactive Web site conversation with an author, politician, or movie star, users are experiencing life—their own and others'—in ways markedly different from before. Are we as honest with our online friends as we are with our face-to-face cohorts? Are we less polite to those we cannot see? Are our cyberidentities more aggressive, more sexy, or less thoughtful than our real-world identities? The potential exists for the online expansion of individual personality, just as it exists for the online denial of who and what we really are (Figure 10.5). Individual users must make their own

Figure 10.5 Despite widespread enthusiasm for today's computer network technologies, some people *are* stopping to ponder how these changes will affect our experiences and ourselves.

decisions on the Net; and this, argue committed Internet users, is the medium's greatest promise.

PRIVACY

Privacy Site
WWW.
privacy.net

The issue of privacy in mass communication has traditionally been concerned with individuals' rights to protect their privacy from invasive, intrusive media (see Chapter 14). For example, should newspapers publish the names of rape victims and juvenile offenders? When does a person become a public figure and forfeit some degree of privacy? In the global village, however, the issue takes on a new character. Whereas Supreme Court Justice Louis Brandeis could once argue that privacy is "the right to be left alone," today privacy is just as likely to mean "the right to maintain control over our own data." Privacy in the global village has two facets. The first is protecting the privacy of communication we wish to keep private. The second is the use (and misuse) of private, personal information willingly given online.

Protecting Privacy in Communication The 1986 Electronic Communication Privacy Act guarantees the privacy of our e-mail. It is a criminal offense to either "intentionally [access] without authorization a facility through which an electronic communication service is provided; or intentionally [exceed] an authorization to access that facility." In addition, the law "prohibits an electronic communications service provider from knowingly divulging the contents of any stored electronic communication." The goal of this legislation is to protect private citizens from official abuse; it gives e-mail "conversations" the same protection that phone conversations enjoy. If a government agency wants to listen in, it must secure permission, just as it must get a court order for a telephone wiretap.

If a person or company feels that more direct protection of communication is necessary, encryption is one solution, but it is controversial. **Encryption** is the electronic coding or masking of information that can be deciphered only by a recipient with the decrypting key. According to the FBI and many other government officials, however, this total privacy is an invitation for terrorists, drug lords, and mobsters to use the Net to threaten national security. As such, in early January 2000 the Clinton administration proposed "relaxed" rules—relaxed from initial plans to allow the government to hold the key to *all* encryption technologies. The new rules require makers of encryption software to turn over a copy of their code to a designated third party. The government may access it only with a court order.

"Authorized" interception of messages is another problem for privacy. Courts have consistently upheld employers' rights to intercept and read their employees' e-mail. Employers must be able to guarantee that their computer systems are not abused by the people who work for them. Thoughtful companies solve the problem by issuing clear and fair guidelines on the use of computer networks. Therefore, when they do make unannounced checks of employees' electronic communication, the employee understands that these checks do occur, why they occur, and under what circumstances they can lead to problems.

Protecting Privacy of Personal Information   Every online act leaves a "digital trail," making possible easy "**dataveillance**—the massive collection and distillation of consumer data. . . . Information gathering has become so convenient and cost-effective that personal privacy has replaced censorship as our primary civil liberties concern" (Shenk, 1997, p. 146). Ironically, we participate in this intrusion into our privacy. Because of computer storage, networking, and cross-referencing power, the information we give to one entity is easily and cheaply given to countless, unknown others (See Figure 10.6 on p. 328).

One form of dataveillance is distributing and sharing personal, private information among organizations other than the one for whom it was originally intended. Information from every credit card transaction (online or at a store), credit application, phone call, supermarket or other purchase made without cash (for example, with a check, debit card, or "club" card), newspaper and magazine subscription, and cable television subscribership

Privacy Protection
www.
accessreports.com

Figure 10.6 In spite of his look of surprise, this consumer willingly gave away the personal information that is now stored and distributed by computers. Wilkinson/Cartoonists and Writers Syndicate/Cartoonweb.com. Reprinted with permission.

PHILADELPHIA DAILY NEWS Philadelphia USA

is digitally recorded, stored, and most likely sold to others. The increased computerization of medical files, banking information, job applications, and school records produces even more salable data. Eventually, anyone who wants to know something about a person can simply buy the necessary information—without that person's permission or even knowledge. These data can then be used to further invade people's privacy. Evening meals and family conversations at home can be interrupted by targeted phone solicitations. Employers can withhold jobs for reasons unknown to applicants. Insurance companies can selectively deny coverage to people based on data about their grocery choices. So troublesome has the problem become that the Federal Trade Commission "censured" the Internet industry in a June 1998 report to Congress "for doing little to insure adequate consumer privacy protection online" ("FTC Faults Net," 1998, p. 1C).

Recognizing the scope of data collection and the potential problems that it raises, Congress passed the 1974 Federal Privacy Act, restricting governments' ability to collect and distribute information about citizens. The act, however, expressly exempted businesses and other nongovernmental organizations from control. This stands in stark contrast to the situation across the Atlantic. In European Union countries it is illegal for an organization of any kind to sell the name and other personal information of a customer or client without permission. Both the FTC and Congress have recently attempted to address this inconsistency—if we have legislation to bring our copyright laws into compliance with those of other nations, why shouldn't we do the same with our privacy laws? In early 2002 the Senate Commerce, Science, and Transportation Committee passed an online privacy protection bill, requiring companies to get consumers' permission *before* they sold or otherwise disseminated their personal data (called **opt-in**), rather than providing that security

Fight ID Theft
www.
consumer.gov/idtheft

Whose Life Is It Anyway? Protecting Personal Privacy in the Digital Age

Our ability to protect our personal privacy has become increasingly difficult in an era of ubiquitous and networked computers and databases. As a result, protecting that privacy—how to do it for ourselves and how much we should depend on government to do it for us—are hotly debated issues in the cultural forum. A wealth of information has been made available to help people take greater control over their personal information. Three of the best Web sites offering privacy protection information are these:

- http://www.privacyrights.org
- http://www.consumer.gov/idtheft
- http://www.accessreports.com

Among the many books available are Beth Givens' 1997 *The Privacy Rights Handbook,* Edmund J. Pankau's 1999 *Hide Your A$$et$ and Disappear: A Step-by-Step Guide to Vanishing Without a Trace,* and Claire Wolfe's 1998 *I Am Not a Number! Freeing America from the ID State.* Commercial companies, such as Private Citizen (800-CUT-JUNK or <http://www.private-citizen.com>) will contact marketers to ensure that we are freer from identity theft and abuse than we might otherwise be. Using the combined wisdom of these and other privacy resources, we can take a number of steps (some controversial) to maintain control over our identities.

1. Contact the nation's three primary credit-reporting companies, Experian (888-397-3742), Trans Union (800-888-4213), and Equifax (800-685-1111). Order a copy of your credit report. Sometimes it can be had for free (if, for example, you have recently applied for some form of credit), but at worst it will cost only a few dollars. Once you have your report, contact these companies and correct any errors you may find, and be sure to close any unused credit accounts. Do this once a year.

2. Ascertain what is in your medical records. This information can be used against you when applying for a job or for insurance, for example. You can do this by contacting the Medical Information Bureau (617-426-3660 or <http://www.mib.com>). Do this every 3 years.

3. If you are a typical American, you are in more than 200 databases. Contact PrivacyScan at <http://www.privacyscan.com>. For about $30 PrivacyScan will search nearly 2,000 databases to see where you come up and what information on you is housed there.

4. Phone 888-5OPT-OUT and tell the credit bureaus to cease selling your name, address, Social Security number, and date of birth to credit card marketers. They are required by law to comply.

5. Destroy completely all "preapproved" credit card and other line-of-credit offers before you toss them out to foil trash snoopers who would steal your identity in this most offline manner.

6. Contact the Direct Marketing Association (DMA) at P. O. Box 9008, Farmingdale, New York, 11735 and ask to have your name removed from all its members' lists. The DMA is required by law to comply, but you must renew your request every 5 years.

7. You must decide if the few cents or dollars you save on your grocery bill is worth the distribution of your purchasing habits to countless marketers and other interested entities. If it is not, shop at card-free supermarkets.

8. When shopping or making purchases by phone, specify, "Do not rent, sell, or trade my personal information." Telemarketers are bound by law to honor your request.

9. If you use an 800 number to shop or buy, your phone number is automatically tagged and made available to telemarketers. Contact the Telephone Preference Service (a division of the DMA) at P.O. Box 9014, Farmingdale, New York, 11735 and ask to have your name removed from all its members' lists. Federal law says the service must comply.

10. The U.S. Postal Service sells your name and address to marketers when you fill out a change-of-address card. You can opt out of the National Change of Address System by calling the Postal Service's National Customer Support Center at 800-238-3150.

11. Refuse all "instant credit" offers. When you accept one of these offers, you grant the credit giver free rein ("a legitimate business need") to gain access to your credit history.

12. When dealing with any kind of business, read the fine print, or just ask if your Social Security number is required (for such things as getting cable or satellite service, for example). If it is not, don't give it. There is no law that says a company can't ask for your Social Security number or even deny you service if you don't comply. So if absolutely necessary, use 078-05-1120 (a discontinued

continued

Cultural Forum

Whose Life Is It Anyway? Protecting Personal Privacy in the Digital Age, *continued*

number), substitute 00 for the middle two digits of your actual Social Security number, or use 009-32-2317 (Maria von Trapp) or 472-14-4916 (Liberace). Never make up a Social Security number—you may cause problems for an innocent person.

13. To ensure your privacy, many companies ask for your mother's maiden name. Naturally, this information is added to the growing body of information about you that can be sold or traded. If asked, make one up, but remember to remember it. If asked for your date of birth, write or answer "legal age" or make one up that you can remember.

14. Reduce the contents of your wallet. Start by removing all material that carries your Social Security number. Several states print Social Security numbers on their driver's licenses. Those that do, however, allow drivers to substitute a generic number if requested.

15. Many retailers and service providers—face-to-face, telephone, and virtual—routinely ask for personal information. Develop the habit of asking if this is necessary. Be prepared to press. Ask why, for a cash purchase, a phone number or ZIP code is requested. If you are not given a satisfactory explanation, simply decline to provide the information. You can be sure that the vast majority of businesses and services will not risk losing your dollars.

16. When possible, avoid writing checks. They contain too much information—not only your bank and account number but typically your full name, address, and phone number. Never print your phone number on your check.

17. The Internet may be one of the engines driving the loss of privacy, but it is also a source of information on how to protect it. Go to <http://www.junkbusters. com> for instructions on how to disable cookies. You can surf anonymously using <http://www. anonymizer.com>. Use only four-star (contact with permission) rated TRUSTe sites. Avoid all others. You can check on a given site's ratings at <http://www.truste.org>.

18. Choose passwords and PINs carefully. Do not use birthdays or series of digits from your Social Security number. Always use passwords that contain both numbers and letters.

19. Never fill out marketing surveys, "registration of warranty," or sweepstakes applications. The surveys may promise better service for you, the consumer, but their primary function is gathering data that can be—and most likely is—sold and traded. When you buy a warrantied product, your warranty is in effect from the date of purchase. Period. Federal law prohibits the completion of a warranty card as a condition for warranty protection. And you're not going to win the

only if consumers specifically request to **opt-out.** Around that same time, the FTC asked Congress to support new rules creating a national "do not call" registry that would automatically include all consumers. Individuals who did not object to being called by telemarketers could ask to have their names removed. Congress approved the FTC plan in 2003, and 50 million Americans availed themselves of the do-not-call registry by dialing a toll-free phone number or through the Internet in its first 3 months (Mayer, 2003).

A second form of dataveillance is the electronic "tracking" of the choices we make when we are on the Web, called our **click stream.** Despite the anonymity online users think they enjoy, every click of a key can be, and often is, recorded and stored. This happens whether or not the user actually enters information, for example, a credit card number to make a purchase or a Social Security number to verify identity. Software exists that records what sites users visit, what they look at in those sites, and how long they stay at a given place in that site as they click

sweepstakes anyway. They are a primary means of collecting your personal data for sale to third (and fourth, fifth, and so on) parties.

These hints on protecting your privacy raise an important cultural question. Why must we go through all this trouble, and even expense in some cases, to protect our personal information? Another way to pose this question is to ask, Why is the loss of control over our personal information, so commonplace in our digitalized, mediated environment, strictly forbidden in almost all other developed, capitalist nations?

In the United States the Federal Trade Commission threatens federal regulation if Web sites do not clearly and prominently publish their policies on how personal data are used (*Financial Times,* 1999). Some companies sign on to TRUSTe, and others, such as IBM, announce that they will not advertise on any site that does not post its privacy policies or allow users to "opt out" of having their data sold or given to a third party without their permission ("Big Blue," 1999). Still, there is no nationwide standard for the protection of personal information. Countless online companies collect personal data on visitors to their Web sites and sell that information to countless others.

The situation in Europe is completely different. Countries that belong to the European Union (EU) require all companies, not only those doing online business, to guarantee their customers these rights:

- The right to see any and all information a company has about them.
- The right to be informed about how their personal information will be used.
- The right to access their personal information and make changes.
- The right to be notified before personal data are shared or sold.
- The right to veto any sharing or selling the individual does not want.
- The right to sue a company that violates these rules.

Enter your voice in the cultural forum. Why do you think this difference between the United States and the EU exists? Would you prefer that the United States adopt official government controls similar to those of the EU nations? Do you believe your personal data belong to you? If you do, what do you consider legitimate use of those data? Which of the personal means for protecting the privacy of your data listed here do you think are reasonable? Which are unreasonable (that is, you shouldn't have to go that far)? Do you accept industry arguments that it is income from the sale of customers' personal data that enables vendors to keep costs to consumers down or to provide interesting Web sites at no cost? Explain your answer.

from Web page to Web page. In and of itself, this is not a problem, because all the Web site reads about the user is a computer address. But once a user enters personal information, that "anonymous" address has a name.

Two forms of industry self-regulation are in place. One, offered by the Electronic Frontier Foundation and CommerceNet, a group of Internet businesses, is TRUSTe. Web sites, if they agree to certain restrictions on their collection and use of user information, will earn the TRUSTe "seal of approval," making them more attractive to privacy-conscious users.

TRUSTe
www.
truste.org

A second effort at self-regulation began in January 1998 when 14 companies, including Lexis-Nexis and the biggest credit-reporting companies in the United States, agreed to block dissemination of all personal information to anyone but "qualified customers." The 14 companies account for more than 90% of all online personal information selling. The voluntary plan has two serious handicaps, according to privacy advocates. First is the definition of "qualified." Government agencies and private investigators would seem to be qualified. But under *all* conditions and situations? Do all government agencies operate with the best of intentions all the time? Who can determine if a private investigator's inquiries are legitimate, or possibly the basis for blackmail? The second problem is that individual users must opt out rather than opt in (see the box "Whose Life Is It Anyway?").

For those uneasy with government regulation, as well as industry self-regulation, there is a technological solution. Users can download (for free) The Anonymizer (http://www.anonymizer.com), software that blocks information from the recording eyes of Web sites.

Privacy After September 11   The 9/11 terrorist attacks on America raised the stakes in the debate surrounding privacy. "Security and privacy are always in a balance, but since the attacks the equation has changed," said Harvard Law School privacy expert Jonathan Zittrain. "You don't want to have a committee meeting when your house is on fire" (quoted in Streitfeld & Piller, 2002, p. D6). No one disputes the need for more security, but finding the right balance in an emotional and dangerous time can be difficult.

Here are five examples. The nation was overwhelmingly against a national identity card before the attacks; now it is in favor of such a system (Carlson, 2002). In the immediate aftermath of the disaster, Congress passed the USA Patriot Act. Section 215 of the act allows the FBI, under secret warrant, to examine our library records. Those receiving the warrant, that is, librarians, are forbidden under threat of prosecution from telling anyone about the search, including the person whose records were examined (Flanders, 2002). That same Patriot Act makes it legal for the FBI to "monitor and infiltrate public meetings, libraries, churches, and mosques" (Hentoff, 2002, p. 30). President George W. Bush and Attorney General John Ashcroft proposed a program called Operation TIPS as part of their new Department of Homeland Security. It would enlist "civilians to inform on one another. Designed to develop 'a national system for reporting suspicious and potentially terrorist-related activity,'" its supporters called it "a sensible supplement to the vigilance of federal agencies" ("Nation of Snitches," 2002, p. B4). Finally, the Pentagon announced its Total Information Awareness office in December 2002. Its function is to collect and put in secret dossiers every phone call, e-mail, credit card purchase, local or long-distance trip, in fact, every piece of available data on every American, without their permission or knowledge (Barry, 2002; Congress killed the plan in early 2003).

National identity cards? Government secretly searching our reading habits? FBI infiltration of peaceful and legal church and town meetings? Neighbor squealing on neighbor? Secret government dossiers on innocent Americans? These were nearly unthinkable before September 11. But as Steward Baker, former general counsel to the National Security Agency, argued, "We as a people are willing to trade a little less privacy for a little more security" (quoted in Streitfeld & Piller, 2002, p. D6). But are we? Combine post-9/11 secret government investigations and record keeping *with* the massive amounts of commercial dataveillance already available *with* the ability of computers to store and instantly share information about any one of us to just about anybody with the need or desire to know. Does this make you feel more secure? Do you trust the government with secret warrants and secret searches? Does the demand, "Let me see your papers!" conjure up images of Nazi-occupied Europe? Do you trust that no neighbor, coworker, or other acquaintance will ever falsely accuse you of suspicious activity? Just what is suspicious behavior? Reading about Islam to better understand it? Do you agree with Mr. Baker's assertion that we as a people are willing to trade a little less privacy for a little more security? Or do you think Benjamin Franklin had it right when he said, "They that give up essential liberty to obtain a little temporary safety deserve neither safety nor liberty"?

VIRTUAL DEMOCRACY

The Internet is characterized by freedom and self-governance, which are also the hallmarks of true democracy. It is no surprise, then, that computer technology is often trumpeted as the newest and best tool for increased democratic involvement and participation. Presidential candidate Ross Perot used the promise of an "electronic town hall" as a centerpiece of his 1992 campaign. Vice President Al Gore conducted history's first interactive, computer network *news* conference on January 13, 1994. It was not a *press* conference, in the traditional sense, because the people themselves, rather than their representatives in the media, could query Mr. Gore. Virtually every politician of any standing, including the president, vice president, senate majority leader, and speaker of the house, maintains at least an e-mail address if not a full Web page. Internet voting, too, has become a limited reality. In 1999 the town of Shelton, Washington, allowed citizens to vote online for local candidates, and in March 2000 Arizona distributed PINs to 50,000 registered Democrats, permitting them to vote online in that state's presidential primary election.

This enthusiasm for a technological solution to what many see as increased disenchantment with politics and the political process mirrors that which followed the introduction of radio and television. A September 3, 1924, *New Republic* article, for example, argued that the high level of public interest in the broadcast of the 1924 political party conventions brought "dismay" to "the most hardened political cynic" (as cited in Davis, 1976, p. 351). The November 1950 *Good Housekeeping* claimed that television would bring greater honesty to politics because "television is a revealing medium, and it is impossible for a man or a woman appearing before those cameras to conceal his or her true self" (p. 359). In 1940 NBC founder and chairman David Sarnoff predicted that television would enrich democracy because it was "destined to provide greater knowledge to larger numbers of people, truer perception of the meaning of current events, more accurate appraisals of men in public life, and a broader understanding of the needs and aspirations of our fellow human beings" (as cited in Shenk, 1997, p. 60).

Some critics argue that the Internet will be no more of an asset to democracy than have been radio and television because the same economic and commercial forces that have shaped the content and operation of those more traditional media will constrain just as rigidly the new. Communication scientist Everette Dennis (1992) condensed the critics' concern into two overarching questions: (1) Will computer networks be readily accessible to all people—even if it means depending on institutions such as schools, churches, and community organizations—or only to some? and (2) Once the technology is in place and people have access to it, are they going to know how to use it?

The Technology Gap   An important principle of democracy is "one person, one vote." But if democracy is increasingly practiced online, those lacking the necessary technology and skill will be denied their vote. This is the **technology gap**—the widening disparity between the communication technology haves and have-nots. Even with its rapid diffusion, only half of the people in the United States use the Internet. This "democratization" of the Net still favors those who have the money to buy the hardware and software needed to access the Net as well as to pay for that connection. This leaves out many U.S. citizens—those on the wrong side of the **digital divide.**

The digital divide describes the lack of technological access among people of color, the poor, the disabled, and those in rural communities. And it is controversial. When asked in 2001 about his plans to bridge the divide, FCC Chair Michael Powell told reporters that the expression itself is "dangerous in the sense that it suggests that the minute a new and innovative technology is introduced in the market, there is a divide among every part of society, and that is just an unreal understanding of an American capitalistic system. . . . I'm not meaning to be completely flip about this—I think it's an important social issue—but it shouldn't be used to justify the notion of, essentially, the socialization of deployment of the infrastructure. . . . You know, I think there's a Mercedes divide. I'd like to have one; I can't afford one" (in Jackson, 2001a, p. 9). Critics pointed out that as the Internet becomes increasingly essential for full membership in America's economic and cultural life, those on the wrong side of the divide will be further disenfranchised. And, in the event that the Net becomes even more essential to the practice of democracy than it already may be, say through widespread online voting, those on the wrong side of the divide will be denied their basic democratic rights.

How real is the digital divide? You saw in Figure 10.1 that only 25% of U.S. homes with incomes under $15,000 were online, compared with 79% of homes with incomes over $75,000. Although more than 60% of all instructional classrooms in American schools are wired for the Internet, that percentage drops to 39% for schools in areas where poverty levels are highest (Malveaux, 2000). And according to the Census Bureau, there exists a large disparity in Internet usage between minorities and others. Internet use among African Americans and Hispanics is well below the national average: only 39% of African Americans and 31.6% of Hispanics are online (Barmann, 2002).

NTIA
www.
ntia.doc.gov

The Information Gap   Another important principle of democracy is that a self-governing people govern best with full access to information. This is the reason our culture is so suspicious of censorship. The technology gap feeds a second impediment to virtual democracy, the **information gap.** Those without the requisite technology will have diminished access to the information it makes available. In other words, they will suffer from a form of technologically imposed censorship.

Critics of the information gap point to troubling examples of other media failures to deliver important information to all citizens. Cable television subscribership is lowest among urban working-class and poor people. Many newspapers, uninterested in these same people because they do not possess the demographic profile coveted by advertisers, do not promote their papers in the neighborhoods in which they live and, in some large cities, do not even deliver there (Kirkhorn, 2000). For this same reason, there are precious few consumer magazines aimed at less well-off people. If the computer technology gap creates an even wider information gap than already exists between these audiences and other citizens, democracy will surely suffer.

Information, Knowledge, and Understanding   Some critics of the idea of online democracy are troubled by the amount of information available to contemporary citizens and the speed with which it comes. Add to this the difficulty of assessing the veracity of much online information, and they argue that the cyberworld may not be the best place to practice democracy.

For example, advocates of cyberdemocracy see the Internet as a way to let citizens have more direct access to politicians. Elected officials should hear what the people have to say. But does democracy necessarily benefit when its leaders respond directly, maybe even impulsively, to public sentiment? Until there is no more technology gap, certain voices—the poor, the uneducated, the elderly—will have less access to their leaders than those who are connected. Moreover, claim critics of cyberdemocracy, ours is a representative, deliberative democracy. It was intentionally designed to enable public representatives to talk to one another, to debate ideas and issues, to forge solutions that benefit not just their own but others' constituents as well. They claim that the political alienation felt by many citizens today is the product of politicians listening *too much* to the loudest voices (that is, special interests) and being *too responsive* to the polls. People often criticize politicians for "flip flopping" or "having no personal conviction." How can the situation improve if elected officials respond daily to the voices in the electronic town hall?

Critics also argue that cyberdemocracy, by its very virtual nature, is antidemocratic. Before the coming of VCR, cable, and satellite television, a president could ask for and almost invariably receive airtime from the three major television networks to talk to the people. Today, however, these technologies have fragmented us into countless smaller audiences. Should a president address the nation today, only a small proportion of citizens is likely to tune in. This fragmentation of the audience (Chapter 1) is exacerbated by the Internet. Not only is there now an *additional* medium to further divide the audience, but by simple virtue of the way it functions—chat rooms, bulletin boards, taste-specific Web sites—the Internet solidifies people into smaller, more homogeneous, more narrowly interested groups. This cannot be good for democracy, say some critics.

The Internet and the Web encourage people to splinter into virtual communities based on a shared interest in some given information. This renders actual communities irrelevant. No longer required to coexist with other people in the day-to-day world, cybercitizens have little need to examine their own biases. They need not question their own assumptions about the world and how it works. There is little benefit to seeking out and attempting to understand the biases and assumptions of others outside the self-chosen virtual community.

For example, writes media critic and scholar Robert McChesney, among the criteria that must be met if democracy is to serve the needs of its people are "a sense of community and a notion that an individual's well-being is determined to no small extent by the community's well-being" and "an effective system of political communication, broadly construed, that informs and engages the citizenry, drawing people meaningfully into the polity" (1997, p. 5). Where McLuhan would have seen the new electronic communication technologies doing just this, many others, often likening the Net and the Web to "talk radio writ large," fear the opposite, that the Internet has already become, in the words of *Time* environmental writer John Skow, "a stunning advance in the shoring up of biases, both benign (one's own views) and noxious (other views)" (1999, p. 61).

DEVELOPING MEDIA LITERACY SKILLS
Making Our Way in an Interconnected World

Questions raised by the Internet and the new communication technologies often lack clear-cut, satisfactory answers. For example, a world at peace with itself, its people sharing the common assumptions of a common culture, is a utopian dream. There are those who see it as attainable, but if the common culture that binds us is that of Mickey Mouse, is the harmony worth the loss of individual, idiosyncratic cultures?

Figure 10.7 on page 338 offers a primer, a self-study guide, to help media literate individuals examine their own beliefs about the double

POP for Privacy

Charlene Nelson, a politically conservative mother of three, made her media literacy a living enterprise and in the process made history. As a college student you, arguably, have the tools at your disposal—time, computers, classmates, education, sophistication—to do the same. Do you share Mrs. Nelson's commitment to privacy? To media literacy? Do you have her courage?

It all began in 1999 when the U.S. Congress passed the Gramm-Leach-Bliley Act. Few people are aware of the bill and its provision that permits banks, insurance companies, and other financial institutions to trade and sell your personal data without your knowledge or permission, unless you choose to opt out. Remember getting all those mailings from your bank and credit card companies, the ones that typically contained a thick leaflet "written in such indecipherable legalese that you either ignored it or passed out trying to read it" (Hightower, 2002, p. 8)? Those mailings contained the details of their privacy policies that companies were obligated to provide to inform you that you had the right to opt out. If you did not respond, that meant you gave them permission to use your personal data as they saw fit.

The problem in North Dakota was that the state already had its own opt-in law. That is, companies could not sell North Dakotans' personal data without their permission. To make North Dakota's law more closely resemble the Gramm-Leach-Bliley law, the state legislature wanted to repeal its own opt-in rules (something that was not required in the federal legislation).

Mrs. Nelson wrote to her representative expressing her opposition, as did thousands of other people. Nonethe-less, the legislature made opt-out the new standard. "I was just stunned when it passed," she said (quoted in Hightower, 2002, p. 8). Determined to protect her privacy in the age of dataveillance, Mrs. Nelson and a dozen friends and neighbors near Fargo started Protect Our Privacy (POP). POP used the Web, e-mail, talk radio, and the phones to marshal support for a citizens' petition to overturn the legislature's "treason." POP was able to get hundreds of volunteers to build a left-right coalition, easily putting a binding referendum, something unheard of in North Dakota, on the June 11, 2002, ballot.

The opposition's media budget was five times larger than POP's; it hired public relations firms and television campaign experts. It attacked Mrs. Nelson in the press as "a right-wing wacko." It said that business would flee the state, already troubled by a weak agricultural economy. On election day, POP prevailed, 73% to 27%. Newspapers as far away as the East Coast editorialized, "True to their heritage, North Dakotans took a pioneering stand on privacy this month, in a vote that curbs the power of banks to sell personal data. The referendum was the first in the nation letting citizens directly challenge a 1999 federal banking law" that requires people to opt out. Mrs. Nelson's "example should encourage all of us" ("Victory," 2002, p. B6).

If you are encouraged by Mrs. Nelson's example, you can e-mail her at <r.cnelson@juno.com> to discuss with her how to put your media literacy values into action. POP's Web site offers information on how to fight for privacy rights in your state, as well as the story of its historic victory. Visit it at <www.protectourprivacy.net>.

---

edge of communication technologies. As we saw in Chapter 2, among the elements of media literacy are the development of an awareness of the impact of the media on individuals and society and an understanding of the process of mass communication. Use the primer's good news/bad news format to answer for yourself the questions that are raised, to build your awareness of media's impact, and to examine the possible influence media have on the process of mass communication.

It is important to remember that culture is neither innate nor inviolate. *We* construct culture—both dominant and bounded. Increasingly, we do so through mass communication. Before we can enter the forum in which those cultures are constructed and maintained, we must understand where we stand and what we believe. We must be able to defend our positions. The hallmarks of a media literate individual are analysis and self-reflection; the primer provides a framework for exactly that.

THE ISSUE	THE GOOD NEWS	THE BAD NEWS	THE QUESTIONS
Technological advances have made communication easier and more democratic.	People can consume some media as wanted and needed rather than allowing media producers to schedule consumption time and content. The consumer, rather than the producer, has more control over meaning making. New technology enables participation by groups previously media-neglected (blind, handicapped, etc.). Users can participate anonymously, which leads to less prejudice (you never know who you might really be communicating with). In some cases, new technology enables communication to be accomplished at a fraction of the cost previously established by older media.	Control of much of the most influential content is in the hands of fewer and fewer people (namely, large multinational corporations). This is not democratic. Content decisions are made to fulfill economic or marketing goals, which define users of communication as simply consumers of content. Source anonymity makes it difficult to document and prosecute illegal acts. Electronic communication could lead to social fragmentation (society divided into the information rich and poor). In the information age, hardware, software, and the education to use them cost money. The difference between the "haves" and the "have-nots" will increase, placing a strain on democracy.	Can a smaller number of powerful people create havoc or revolution online (i.e., shutting down governments, bugging worldwide systems)? Should law enforcement have encryption codes on file to use under court order? Or is this an infringement of privacy and First Amendment rights? Will new technology be available to everyone? Will an information underclass form? Who will pay for information technology as it develops (private corporations, governments, users)? Who will control and regulate the information technology? Is official control necessary to ensure equal access and opportunity? Do advancements in technology result from societal need or market demands? Or is there a "technological push"—technologies logically producing the next innovation? What is the public's role in each situation?
Technological advances have made the *creation* and *distribution* of media content easier.	Content can be duplicated and transmitted easily and without loss of quality. Individuals, *themselves,* can now be producers of media. Easier creation and distribution of content leads to more choice for media consumers. People can seek out and receive content they are interested in while ignoring other content. Information can be transmitted in "real time." A person can communicate to anywhere, from anyplace, at anytime. This affords freedom of movement and more convenience in terms of space and time. Individuals will have access to other people despite lack of physical proximity. We can finally, truly, be a global village.	Destructive (false, hateful, libelous, etc.) or even illegal communication content is also more easily created and distributed. Piracy is easier and more widespread. Questions of copyright and intellectual property are more complex, more difficult to define, and even more difficult to regulate. Too much choice leads to information overload. There is a big difference between having more information and having more understanding or comprehension. Important decisions are made based on instant information (whether it is accurate or not). There is little time for reflection and analysis. Content is sent and received without context. Reliability of sources becomes questionable. Context and continuity are lost; they are simply replaced by more "instant" content. Who wants to be available *all the time?* This "convenience" will add additional stress to life because "time off" becomes more difficult to find.	How can producers of content (corporations, artists, etc.) receive compensation for their work in a digital world of unlimited production and distribution possibilities? What will happen to security of personal information if content can be so easily copied and transmitted (privacy and security issues)? How much choice do audience members *really* want? From where is the information coming? Who will be the "authorities" creating, providing, and regulating the information (setting the agenda, etc.)? How much connection is too much? What kind of physical damage (headaches, carpal tunnel syndrome, etc.) and psychological damage (cyberaddiction, alienation, etc.) can be done by using communication too much or too often?

Figure 10.7 The New Communication Technology Media Literacy Primer.

THE ISSUE	THE GOOD NEWS	THE BAD NEWS	THE QUESTIONS
New technology allows seamless alteration of sound and pictures.	Production and postproduction are less expensive than in older media and allow unlimited possibilities for altering content. Creativity is limited only by one's imagination because technology can create the ways and means.	Images and sounds can be digitally (and invisibly) manipulated, so truth and reality are difficult to ascertain.	How will people be able to tell what is real and what is not? Will the definition of "reality" change?
New technology allows communication to be presented in a nonlinear way.	New communication technologies allow for more user control in the creation of content. Form, function, and time take on new meaning.	When immersed in a sea of data, audience members may not see a beginning, middle, or end. Communication errors are likely.	What will be the storytelling, narrative, and aesthetic conventions of the virtual real world?

Chapter Review

The first electronic digital computer was developed during World War II to break secret code. The first full-service electronic computer, introduced in 1946, was ENIAC. Computers quickly made their way into U.S. business and commercial life, largely through the efforts of IBM.

The Internet is in part the product of the military's desire to maintain U.S. defenses after a nuclear attack. Decentralization was the key to enabling communication to continue no matter where an attack occurred, and the solution was a network of computer networks—the Internet. Once personal or microcomputers entered the picture, the Internet became accessible to millions of noninstitutional users. Its capabilities include e-mail, mailing lists, Usenet, and FTP. But its fastest growing application is the World Wide Web. The Web's popularity is fueled by its ease of use.

It is difficult to accurately measure the number of Internet users, but more than half of all U.S. homes are online.

The growing number of people online has inevitably led to efforts to advertise on and sell by the Internet. This commercialization of the online world is greeted with disdain by traditional Net users, who fear that their medium will lose its freedom and energy to corporate takeover. Spam, too, is turning many users away from Net use.

The diffusion of the Internet raises a number of important cultural issues, not the least of which is the question of technology's benefits and drawbacks,

technology's double edge. The Net transforms every user into a potential mass communicator, making freedom of the press a reality for everyone, especially through the use of flash mobs and blogs. But critics contend that this freedom is often abused because individuals are not bound by the kinds of economic and legal restraints that tend to impose responsibility on larger, commercially oriented media. The major free expression battles in cyberspace revolve around containing online pornography, protecting children from inappropriate content, and protecting copyright. None is easily resolved, but improved technology may provide some solutions.

We see technology's touch in how people use online communication to develop meaningful personal identities, MUDs being only the most obvious example. Privacy, too, takes on new meaning online. Privacy of communication—freedom from the snooping of others, including the government—can be accomplished in a number of ways, one being encryption. This secret coding, however, is problematic for many government officials. Online privacy has a second dimension—protecting the privacy of important personal information. People often willingly give such information to unknown others, and technological data surveillance exists as well.

The new communication technologies are often touted as a boon to democracy because they permit greater citizen involvement. Yet a more pessimistic view is that the commercialization of the Internet will make it as ineffective as more traditional media in serving participatory democracy. Critics also point to the technology and information gaps to argue that many people will be shut out of the electronic debate. Another question raised about cyberdemocracy revolves around the distinction between information and understanding. The Net's

wealth of data may not necessarily produce a better-informed electorate.

The rapid changes that characterize today's communication technologies and the mass communication they foster demand that we increase our media literacy skills and that we keep ourselves aware of and open to change.

Key Terms

Use the text's CD-ROM and the Online Learning Center at www.mhhe.com/baran to further your understanding of the following terminology.

Internet, 300
digital computer, 300
binary code, 300
protocols, 302
host, 303
mainframe, 304
minicomputer, 304
terminal, 304
personal or microcomputer, 304
operating system, 304
multimedia, 305
LAN, 305
WAN, 305
ISP (Internet service provider), 305

e-mail, 305
Usenet, 306
World Wide Web, 306
hosts, 307
zone, 307
URL, 308
domain name, 308
browser, 308
search engine, 308
spider, 308
Web crawler, 308
home page, 309
hyperlinks, 309
multiple user domains (MUDs), 309

hacker, 310
spam, 312
global village, 314
flash mob, 319
blogs, 319
copyright, 323
censorware, 323
fair use, 324
encryption, 327
dataveillance, 328
opt-in/opt-out, 328, 330
click stream, 330
technology gap, 334
digital divide, 334
information gap, 335

Questions for Review

Go to the self-quizzes on the CD-ROM and the Online Learning Center to test your knowledge.

1. What is the importance of each of these people to the development of the computer: Charles Babbage, John Atanasoff, John Mauchly, and John Presper Eckert?
2. What were the contributions of Joseph C. R. Licklider, Paul Baran, Bill Gates, Steve Jobs, and Steve Wozniak to the development and popularization of the Internet?
3. What are digital computers, microcomputers, and mainframe computers?
4. What are the services or capabilities offered by the Internet?
5. What factors have led to the popularity of the World Wide Web?
6. What are the differing positions on the commercialization of the Internet?

7. What are the differing positions on Internet copyright?
8. Both proponents and opponents of greater control over Internet content see advances in technology as one solution to their disagreement. What are they? How do they work?
9. Why is there renewed interest in Marshall McLuhan? What does he mean by the global village and media as extensions of our bodies?
10. What is a MUD? How does it operate?
11. What are the two primary privacy issues for on-line communication?
12. What is a flash mob? A blog? How might they alter citizen action and journalism?
13. What are some of the arguments supporting the idea that the Internet will be a boost to

participatory democracy? What are some of the counterarguments?

14. What are the technology and information gaps? What do they have to do with virtual or cyber-democracy? What is the digital divide?

Questions for Critical Thinking and Discussion

1. Do you believe commercialization of the Internet is a worthy price to pay for its continued success and diffusion? Explain.
2. What controls should be placed on gripe sites, if any? Do you see them, by whatever name, as a way of distributing power in the culture between traditional media outlets and ordinary individuals? Why or why not?
3. Have you ever participated in a MUD? If so, what was your experience? If not, what identity do you think you might adopt? Why?

4. Do you ever make personal information available online? If so, how confident are you of its security? Do you take steps to protect your privacy?
5. Do you believe the new communication technologies will improve or damage participatory democracy? Why? Can you relate a personal experience of how the Net increased or limited your involvement in the political process?
6. Do you agree with the FCC's Michael Powell that no one has a "right" to Internet access? Why or why not?

Important Resources

Aspray, W., & Campbell-Kelly, M. (1997). *Computer: A history of the information machine.* **New York: Basic Books.** This is a thorough examination of the technological and entrepreneurial successes in the development of the computer. It also offers interesting histories of other facets of the computer world, for example, inside looks at companies like IBM and Microsoft and applications like the Web.

InfoWorld. Calling itself "the voice of enterprise computing," this publication is clearly oriented toward people working in the computer industry. Despite (or as a result of) that, it is a good source for finding out what is next in hardware, software, and networking.

internet world. This slick magazine calls itself "the Internet Authority." It offers monthly articles on Web development, Internet business, and other Internet-related news. Aimed more at companies that do business online than at everyday users, it is still a valuable resource for users.

Hafner, K., & Lyon, M. (1996). *Where wizards stay up late: The origins of the Internet.* **New York: Simon & Schuster.** Written by two journalists, this important look at the origins of the Net offers evidence that its founders had an optimistic, McLuhanesque goal for their innovation. Accessible and fun.

the net. Continuing the trend of Internet magazines to ignore uppercase letters, this self-proclaimed "ultimate Internet guide" is slick, readable, and targeted at users.

Rosen, J. (2000). *The unwanted gaze: The destruction of privacy in America.* **New York: Random House.** This book presents a "powerful and sobering look at the degree to which personal privacy has been invaded by both technology and the law," according to the *San Jose Mercury News.* Rosen writes, "At the beginning of the twenty-first century, new technologies of communication have increased the danger that intimate personal information originally disclosed to our friends and colleagues may be exposed to and misinterpreted by a less understanding audience. As thinking and writing increasingly take place in cyberspace, the part of our life that can be monitored and searched has vastly expanded."

Shenk, D. (1997). *Data smog: Surviving the information glut.* **New York: Harper Edge.** About the people and societies of the information age, this book focuses on the impact of too much data (information overload) on the culture.

Wired. Either "the hottest magazine in computing" or a jumbled mess of self-aggrandizing ruminations by hackers with attitude, depending on whom you speak with. Worth a look, nonetheless. Its essays on free speech issues are particularly provocative.

Internet Statistics	www.glreach.com/globalstats/
Internet Statistics	www.mids.org
Internet History	www.isoc/internet/history
Definition of Internet Terms	www.whatis.techtarget.com
Online White Pages	www.whitepages.com
Online Yellow Pages	www.yellowpages.com
Tim Berners-Lee	www.w3.org/people/all
NASA	www.nasa.gov
U.S. Census Bureau	www.census.gov
Marshall McLuhan	www.mcluhan.ca
More McLuhan	www.law.pitt.edu/hibbitts/mcl.htm
Media Activist "gripe site"	www.fair.org
Blogging	www.blogger.com
Net Nanny	www.netnanny.com
Electronic Frontier Foundation	www.eff.org
Links to MUDS	www.godlike.com/muds
Privacy Site	www.privacy.net
Privacy Protection	www.accessreports.com
Fight ID Theft	www.consumer.gov/idtheft
TRUSTe	www.truste.org
Surf Anonymously	www.anonymizer.com
NTIA	www.ntia.doc.gov

PART three

Supporting Industries

UNITED we will wi

Public Relations

TIMELINE

1800 George Washington hires Mason Weems to burnish his reputation

1833 Andrew Jackson hires Amos Kendall, first presidential press secretary

1889 Westinghouse establishes first corporate public relations department

1896 William Jennings Bryan and William McKinley launch first national political campaigns

1906 The Publicity Bureau, first publicity company

1913 Lee's *Declaration of Principles*

1917 President Wilson establishes Committee on Public Information

1938 Foreign Agents Registration Act

1941 Office of War Information

1946 Federal Regulation of Lobbying Act

1947 Public Relations Society of America (PRSA)

1954 PRSA Code of Ethics

1962 PRSA accreditation program

LEARNING OBJECTIVES

It is no small irony that PR has such poor PR. We criticize the "flacks" who try to "spin" the truth, because PR is most obvious when used to reclaim the reputation of someone or some organization in need of such help. But PR can be much more than that. Good PR is invisible, and much invisible PR is used for good. After studying this chapter you should

- be familiar with the history and development of the public relations industry.

- be aware of the controversies surrounding unethical public relations practices.

- recognize how the organizational and economic nature of the contemporary public relations industry shapes the messages with which publics interact.

- be familiar with different types of public relations and the different publics each is designed to serve.

- understand the relationship between public relations and its various publics.

- possess improved media literacy skills when consuming public relations messages, especially crisis public relations.

YOU WANT TO RUN; YOU HAVE TO RUN! YOU'VE BEEN TRAINING for 2 months, and next week's 5K through the hills outside campus seems like a reasonable test of your newfound athletic prowess. When your race packet arrives in the mail, it contains your number, 1071; pre- and postrace instructions, a map of the route, and a lot of other material you hadn't expected—a pamphlet on breast cancer self-examinations, for one thing, and a fact sheet explaining that you are part of something a little bigger than a simple road race behind your school. You knew you were running in a Race for the Cure 5K, underwritten by a local radio station and the newspaper, but until you read the mailing you had no idea that it was a cure for breast cancer for which you were running; that something called the Susan G. Komen Breast Cancer Foundation was behind this and 100 other 5Ks in the United States and other countries; and that 1.3 million people like you would be racing

Kellogg and American Airlines are two of the corporations whose support of Race for the Cure helps others while helping us better understand them as companies.

for the cure. You're curious, so you check out the Foundation's Web site (www.komen.org). The site itself is sponsored by Lee Jeans' National Denim Day. That's nice. A big company like that donating time, money—and even a day—to such a good cause. You link to the site devoted specifically to the race and *its* sponsors. That group reads like a veritable Who's Who of corporate America—the employment firm Adecco, RE/MAX Realtors, Johnson & Johnson, Kellogg, Ford, New Balance Shoes, Yoplait Yogurt, American Airlines. That's pretty cool, you think, these folks getting involved, doing good, especially at a time when Enron, WorldCom, and other big companies seem to be doing their best to shake your confidence in the corporate world, the very world you hope to enter when you graduate.

In this chapter we investigate the public relations industry and its relationship with mass media and their audiences. We first define public relations. Then we study its history and development as the profession matured from its beginnings in hucksterism to a full-fledged, communication-based industry. We see how the needs and interests of the profession's various publics became part of the public relations process. We also define exactly who those publics are. The scope and nature of the industry are detailed. Types of public relations activities and the organization of a typical public relations operation are described. Trends such as globalization and specialization are studied, as is the impact of new communication technologies on the industry. Finally, we discuss trust in public relations. As our media literacy skill, we learn how to evaluate PR messages from organizations in crisis.

Defining Public Relations

The Komen Foundation, like Mothers Against Drunk Driving, Save Venice, Handgun Control, Incorporated, the National Environmental Trust, and countless other nonprofit organizations, is an interest group that uses a variety of public relations tools and strategies to serve a variety of publics. It wants to use public relations to do good. The companies that sponsor its activities also want to do good—do good for their communities *and* for themselves. Even the most cynical person must applaud their efforts on behalf of finding a cure for breast cancer.

But for many people, efforts such as these serve to demonstrate one of the ironies of public relations, both as an activity and as an industry: Public relations has terrible public relations. We dismiss information as "just PR." Public relations professionals are frequently equated with snake oil salespeople, hucksters, and other willful deceivers. They are referred to both inside and outside the media industries as **flacks.** Yet virtually every organization and institution—big and small, public and private, for-profit and volunteer—uses public relations as a regular part of its operation. Many have their own public relations departments. The term "public relations" carries such a negative connotation that most independent companies and company departments now go by the name "public affairs," "corporate affairs," or "public communications."

The problem rests, in part, on confusion over what public relations actually is. There is no universally accepted definition of public relations because it can be and is many things—publicity, research, public affairs, media relations, promotion, merchandising, and more. Much of the contact media consumers have with public relations occurs when the industry defends people and companies who have somehow run afoul of the public. The Saudi Arabian government hired two American PR firms, Patton Boggs and Akin, Gump, Strauss, Hauer, and Feld, to burnish its image after it was learned that the majority of the September 11 terrorists were Saudi citizens and that it had financially supported groups close to Osama bin Laden and Al Qaeda. Starbucks similarly sought PR help after reports

odwalla

IN THIS SEASON OF THANKS,
YOU'VE MADE US REALIZE HOW MUCH
WE HAVE TO BE THANKFUL FOR.

As you probably know, the last few weeks have been very challenging for everyone here

at Odwalla. These times have made us especially grateful for the overwhelming

support we've received from the entire community, including our customers, retail

partners, friends and families. The thousands of letters, phone calls and e-mails

we've received have truly inspired us. We thank you very much for that. We are

feeling optimistic and energized. More than ever, we are committed to bringing

you the healthiest and best-tasting juices on the planet. From all of us at Odwalla,

thank you for your blessings and have a wonderful Thanksgiving.

120 Stone Pine Road, Half Moon Bay, CA, 94019   1-800-odwalla or www.enw.com/odwalla

Odwalla's prompt, honest public relations campaign to communicate with its public may have saved additional lives. It did save the 16-year-old company and the jobs of its employees.

MADD
www.
madd.org

that one of its store managers forced rescue crews to pay for bottled water as they worked to save lives on that horrible day. Ford and Firestone waged a PR war against one another in mid-2000 when Firestone's tires were implicated in rollovers of Ford's Explorer SUVs, Exxon used a vast PR army to minimize its responsibility for the environmentally disastrous 1989 oil spill from its tanker *Exxon Valdez,* and politicians and partisan groups habitually use public relations to shape the news. The University of Maryland's College of Journalism even went so far as to drop its public relations program in the late 1990s because it thought that the goals of PR and journalism clashed.

Yet when seven people died from cyanide poisoning after taking tainted Tylenol capsules in 1982, a skilled and honest public relations campaign by Johnson & Johnson (makers of Tylenol) and its public relations firm, Burson-Marsteller, saved the brand and restored trust in the product. In late 1996, when Odwalla fresh apple juice was linked to the death of a young child, that company's instant, direct, and honest campaign to identify and eliminate the source of the contamination and rebuild public confidence saved the company and thousands of jobs. The public relations campaign by Mothers Against Drunk Driving (MADD) led directly to passage of tougher standards in virtually every state to remove drunk drivers from the road and to provide stiffer sentences for those convicted of driving under the influence. Dramatic reductions in the number of alcohol-related traffic accidents resulted from this effort (see the box "The MADD Campaign").

The industry itself recognizes the confusion surrounding what public relations actually is. Various public relations professional organizations have made efforts over the years to develop a succinct yet thorough definition of this industry. In one such effort, that of the Foundation for Public Relations Research and Education, 65 public relations professionals sifted through 472 different definitions (Harlow, 1976). The definition that we will use, however, is that offered by marketing educator William F. Arens (1999). This definition includes two elements that individually appear in almost all other definitions, *communication* and *management:*

> Public relations is the management function that focuses on the relationships and communications that individuals and organizations have with other groups (called publics) for the purpose of creating mutual goodwill. (p. 310)

The MADD Campaign

After Candy Lightner's child was killed in a drunk-driving accident in 1980, she sought out others like herself, mothers who had lost children to the volatile mix of cars and alcohol. What she hoped they could do was provide each other with emotional support and campaign to ensure that other parents would never know their grief. Thus, Mothers Against Drunk Driving (MADD) was born.

There are now more than 400 chapters of MADD in the United States and a number of foreign groups as well. Individuals and businesses contribute over $40 million a year to MADD's efforts, which include a variety of educational, public relations, and victims' assistance programs. MADD's primary public information campaign, Project Red Ribbon, which runs throughout the Thanksgiving to New Year's holiday season, annually distributes more than 30 million red ribbons. People tie them to the rearview mirrors, door handles, and radio antennae of their cars. This reminder encourages people not to drive if under the influence of drugs or alcohol, to call a cab if necessary, or even to take away a friend's car keys if he or she is drunk. The ribbon also serves as a sign of solidarity against the terrors of drunk driving. MADD has enlisted in Project Red Ribbon such major corporations as Welch's, 7-Eleven Stores, and the national trucking company Consolidated Freightways Motorfreight.

Among MADD's publics are teenagers. With its parallel organization, Students Against Drunk Driving (SADD), MADD targets this high-risk group through various educational campaigns and in the media aimed at teen audiences. The organization also conducts public information campaigns aimed at adult drivers and repeat drunk drivers, often in conjunction with state and other authorities. It also assists legislators in their efforts to pass drunk-driving legislation. Finally, two more of MADD's publics are public servants such as police and paramedics, who must deal with the effects of drunk driving, and the families and friends who have lost loved ones in alcohol- or drug-related driving accidents.

Has MADD made a difference? Since 1988, numerous prime-time television programs have featured episodes about the dangers of drunk driving. MADD's professional staff has served as script advisors to these programs. MADD was instrumental in passage of the federal Drunk Driving Prevention Act of 1988, offering states financial

MADD reaches its various publics in a variety of ways.

incentives to set up programs that would reduce alcohol- and drug-related automobile fatalities. This legislation also made 21 the national minimum legal drinking age. MADD successfully campaigned for the Victim's Crime Act of 1984, making compensation from drunk drivers to victims and their families federal law.

There are two even more dramatic examples of how successful Lightner's group has been. According to the National Commission Against Drunk Driving (2002), there have been significant reductions in the number of alcohol- and drug-related auto fatalities in every year since MADD was founded. But MADD's cultural impact shows most strongly in the way people treat drunk drivers. It is no longer "cool" to talk about how smashed we got at the party, or how we can't believe we made it home. Almost every evening out with a group of friends includes a designated driver. Drunk drivers are considered nearly as despicable as child molesters. Many in public relations, traffic safety, and law enforcement credit MADD's public relations efforts with this change.

A Short History of Public Relations

The history of this complex field can be divided into four stages: early public relations, the propaganda-publicity stage, early two-way communication, and advanced two-way communication. These four stages have combined to shape the character of this industry.

SADD
www.
sadd.org

The December 16, 1773, Boston Tea Party was one of the first successful pseudo-events in the new land. Had cameras been around at the time, it would also have been a fine photo op.

EARLY PUBLIC RELATIONS

Archaeologists in Iraq have uncovered a tablet dating from 1800 B.C. that today we would call a public information bulletin. It provided farmers with information on sowing, irrigating, and harvesting their crops. Julius Caesar fed the people of the Roman Empire constant reports of his achievements to maintain morale and to solidify his reputation and position of power. Genghis Khan would send "advance men" to tell stories of his might, hoping to frighten his enemies into surrendering.

Public relations campaigns abounded in colonial America and helped to create the Colonies. Merchants, farmers, and others who saw their own advantage in a growing colonial population used overstatement, half-truths, and lies to entice settlers to the New World. *A Brief and True Report of the New Found Land of Virginia,* by John White, was published in 1588 to lure European settlers. The Boston Tea Party was a well-planned media event organized to attract public attention for a vital cause. Today we'd call it a **pseudo-event,** an event staged specifically to attract public attention. Benjamin Franklin organized a sophisticated campaign to thwart the Stamp Act, the Crown's attempt to limit colonial press freedom (Chapter 3), using his publications and the oratory skills of criers. *The Federalist Papers* of John Jay, James Madison, and Alexander Hamilton were originally a series of 85 letters published between 1787 and 1789, which were designed to sway public opinion in the newly independent United States toward support and passage of the new Constitution, an early effort at issue management. George Washington employed the public relations skills of Mason Weems in 1800 to burnish his reputation in a glowing and often fictitious biography of the Father of Our Country. (Among Weems's inventions was the cherry tree / "I cannot tell a lie" myth.) In all these examples, people or organizations were using communication to inform, to build an image, and to influence public opinion.

THE PROPAGANDA-PUBLICITY STAGE

Mass circulation newspapers and the first successful consumer magazines appeared in the 1830s, expanding the ability of people and organizations to communicate with the public. In 1833, for example, Andrew Jackson hired former newspaperman Amos Kendall as his publicist and the country's first presidential press secretary in an effort to combat the aristocrats who saw Jackson as too common to be president.

Abolitionists sought an end to slavery. Industrialists needed to attract workers, entice customers, and enthuse investors. P. T. Barnum, convinced that "a sucker is born every minute," worked to lure them into his shows. All used the newspaper and the magazine to serve their causes.

Politicians recognized that the expanding press meant that a new way of campaigning was necessary. In 1896 presidential contenders William Jennings Bryan and William McKinley both established campaign headquarters in Chicago from which they issued news releases, position papers, and pamphlets. The modern national political campaign was born.

It was during this era that public relations began to acquire its deceitful, huckster image. PR was associated more with propaganda than with useful information. A disregard for the public and the willingness of public relations experts to serve the powerful fueled this view, but public relations began to establish itself as a profession during this time. The burgeoning press was its outlet, but westward expansion and rapid urbanization and industrialization in the United States were its driving forces. As the railroad expanded to unite the new nation, cities exploded with new people and new life. Markets, once small and local, became large and national.

Public Relations History
www.
public-relations-online.net/
history.htm

As the political and financial stakes grew, business and government became increasingly corrupt and selfish—"The public be damned" was William Vanderbilt's official comment when asked in 1882 about the effects of changing the schedule of his New York Central Railroad. The muckrakers' revelations badly tarnished the images of industry and politics. Massive and lengthy coal strikes led to violence and more antibusiness feeling. In the heyday of the journalistic exposé and the Progressive movement (Chapter 5), government and business both required some good public relations.

In 1889 Westinghouse Electric established the first corporate public relations department, hiring a former newspaper writer to engage the press and ensure that company positions were always clear and in the public eye. Advertising agencies, including N. W. Ayer & Sons and Lord and Thomas, began to offer public relations services to their clients. The first publicity company, The Publicity Bureau, was opened in Boston in 1906 and later expanded to New York, Chicago, Washington, St. Louis, and Topeka to help the railroad industry challenge federal regulations that it opposed.

The railroads had still other problems, and they turned to *New York World* reporter Ivy Lee for help. Beset by accidents and strikes, the Pennsylvania Railroad usually responded by suppressing information. Lee

Cadillac
Standard of the World

The PENALTY OF LEADERSHIP

IN every field of human endeavor, he that is first must perpetually live in the white light of publicity. ¶Whether the leadership be vested in a man or in a manufactured product, emulation and envy are ever at work. ¶In art, in literature, in music, in industry, the reward and the punishment are always the same. ¶The reward is widespread recognition; the punishment, fierce denial and detraction. ¶When a man's work becomes a standard for the whole world, it also becomes a target for the shafts of the envious few. ¶If his work be merely mediocre, he will be left severely alone—if he achieve a masterpiece, it will set a million tongues a-wagging. ¶Jealousy does not protrude its forked tongue at the artist who produces a commonplace painting. ¶Whatsoever you write, or paint, or play, or sing, or build, no one will strive to surpass, or to slander you, unless your work be stamped with the seal of genius. ¶Long, long after a great work or a good work has been done, those who are disappointed or envious continue to cry out that it can not be done. ¶Spiteful little voices in the domain of art were raised against our own Whistler as a mountebank, long after the big world had acclaimed him its greatest artistic genius. ¶Multitudes flocked to Bayreuth to worship at the musical shrine of Wagner, while the little group of those whom he had dethroned and displaced argued angrily that he was no musician at all. ¶The little world continued to protest that Fulton could never build a steamboat, while the big world flocked to the river banks to see his boat steam by. ¶The leader is assailed because he is a leader, and the effort to equal him is merely added proof of that leadership. ¶Failing to equal or to excel, the follower seeks to depreciate and to destroy—but only confirms once more the superiority of that which he strives to supplant. ¶There is nothing new in this. ¶It is as old as the world and as old as the human passions—envy, fear, greed, ambition, and the desire to surpass. ¶And it all avails nothing. ¶If the leader truly leads, he remains—the leader. ¶Master-poet, master-painter, master-workman, each in his turn is assailed, and each holds his laurels through the ages. ¶That which is good or great makes itself known, no matter how loud the clamor of denial. ¶That which deserves to live—lives.

Cadillac Motor Car Co. Detroit, Mich.

Copyright 1915 Cadillac Motor Car Co.

recognized, however, that this was dangerous and counterproductive in a time when the public was already suspicious of big business, including the railroads. Lee escorted reporters to the scene of trouble, established press centers, distributed press releases, and assisted reporters in obtaining additional information and photographs.

When a Colorado coal mine strike erupted in violence in 1913, the press attacked the mine's principal stockholder, New York's John D. Rockefeller, blaming him for the shooting deaths of several miners and their wives and children. Lee handled press relations and convinced Rockefeller to visit the scene to talk (and be photographed) with the strikers. The strike ended, and Rockefeller soon was being praised for his sensitive intervention. Eventually Lee issued his *Declaration of Principles,* arguing that public relations practitioners should be providers of information, not purveyors of publicity.

Not all public relations at this time was damage control. Henry Ford began using staged events such as auto races to build interest in his cars, started *Ford Times* (an in-house employee publication), and made heavy use of image advertising.

Public relations in this stage was typically one-way, from organization to public. Still, by the outbreak of World War I, most of the elements of today's large-scale, multifunction public relations agency were in place.

EARLY TWO-WAY COMMUNICATION

Because the U.S. public was not particularly enthusiastic about the nation's entry into World War I, President Woodrow Wilson recognized the need for public relations in support of the war effort (Zinn, 1995, pp. 355–357). In 1917 he placed former newspaperman George Creel at the head of the newly formed Committee on Public Information (CPI). Creel assembled opinion leaders from around the country to advise the government on its public relations efforts and to help shape public opinion. The committee sold Liberty Bonds and helped increase membership in the Red Cross. It engaged in public relations on a scale never before seen, using movies, public speakers, articles in newspapers and magazines, and posters.

About this time public relations pioneer Edward Bernays began emphasizing the value of assessing the public's feelings toward an organization. He would then use this knowledge as the basis for the development of the public relations effort. Together with Creel's committee, Bernays's work was the beginning of two-way communication in public relations—that is, public relations talking to people and, in return, listening to them when they talked back. Public relations professionals began representing their various publics to their clients, just as they represented their clients to those publics.

There were other advances in public relations during this stage. During the 1930s, President Franklin D. Roosevelt, guided by advisor Louis McHenry Howe, embarked on a sophisticated public relations campaign to win support for his then-radical New Deal policies. Central to Roosevelt's effort was the new medium of radio. The Great Depression that plagued the country throughout this decade once again turned public opinion against business and industry. To counter people's distrust, many more corporations established in-house public relations departments; General Motors opened its PR operation in 1931. Public relations professionals turned increasingly to the newly emerging polling industry founded by George Gallup and Elmo Roper to better gauge public opinion as they constructed public relations campaigns and to gather feedback on the effectiveness of those campaigns. Gallup and Roper successfully applied newly refined social science research methods—advances in sampling, questionnaire design, and interviewing—to meet the business needs of clients and their publics.

The growth of the industry was great enough and its reputation sufficiently fragile that the National Association of Accredited Publicity Directors was founded in 1936. The American Council on Public Relations was

Canadian Public Relations Society
WWW.
cprs.ca

World War I brought government into large-scale public relations. Even today, the CPI's posters—like this one encouraging citizens to support the war effort through war bonds—are recognized.

established three years later. They merged in 1947, creating the Public Relations Society of America (PRSA), the principal professional group for today's public relations professionals.

World War II saw the government undertake another massive campaign to bolster support for the war effort, this time through the Office of War Information (OWI). Employing techniques that had proven successful during World War I, the OWI had the additional advantage of public opinion polling, fully established and powerful radio networks and their stars, and a Hollywood eager to help. Singer Kate Smith's war bond radio telethon raised millions, and director Frank Capra produced the *Why We Fight* film series for the OWI.

During this era both public relations and Ivy Lee suffered a serious blow to their reputations. Lee was the American public relations spokesman for Germany and its leader, Adolf Hitler. In 1934 Lee was required to testify before Congress to defend himself against the charge that he was a Nazi sympathizer. He was successful, but the damage had been done. As a result of Lee's ties with Germany, Congress passed the Foreign Agents Registration Act in 1938, requiring anyone who engages in political activities in the United States on behalf of a foreign power to register as an agent of that power with the Justice Department.

Better known for hits such as *Mr. Smith Goes to Washington* and *It's a Wonderful Life*, director Frank Capra brought his moviemaking talents to the government's efforts to explain U.S. involvement in World War II and to overcome U.S. isolationism. His *Why We Fight* documentary series still stands as a classic of the form.

ADVANCED TWO-WAY COMMUNICATION

Post–World War II U.S. society was confronted by profound social change and expansion of the consumer culture. It became increasingly important for organizations to know what their clients were thinking, what they liked and disliked, and what concerned and satisfied them. As a result, public relations turned even more decidedly toward integrated two-way communication, employing research, advertising, and promotion.

As the public relations industry became more visible, it opened itself to closer scrutiny. Best-selling novels such as *The Hucksters* and *The Man in the Gray Flannel Suit* (and the hit movies made from them) painted a disturbingly negative picture of the industry and those who worked in it. Vance Packard's best-selling book *The Hidden Persuaders*, dealing with both public relations and advertising, further eroded PR esteem. As a result of public distrust of the profession, Congress passed the Federal Regulation of Lobbying Act in 1946, requiring, among other things, that those who deal with federal employees on behalf of private clients disclose those relationships. And as the industry's conduct and ethics came under increasing attack, the PRSA responded with a code of ethics in 1954 and an accreditation program in 1962. Both, with modification and improvement, stand today.

The modern era of public relations is characterized by other events as well. More people buying more products meant that greater numbers of people were coming into contact with a growing number of businesses.

Public Relations Students Society of America
www.
prssa.org

Criticism of public relations found its way into popular culture through a number of popular films and books. This scene is from the movie *The Hucksters*.

As consumer markets grew in size, the basis for competition changed. Texaco, for example, used advertising to sell its gasoline. But because its products were not all that different from those of other oil companies, it also sold its gasoline using its good name and reputation. Increasingly, then, advertising agencies began to add public relations divisions. This change served to blur the distinction between advertising and PR.

Women, who had proved their capabilities in all professional settings during World War II, became prominent in the industry. Anne Williams Wheaton was associate press secretary to President Eisenhower; Leone Baxter was president of the powerful public relations firm Whitaker and Baxter. Companies and their executives and politicians increasingly turned to television to burnish their images and shape public opinion. Nonprofit, charitable, and social activist groups also mastered the art of public relations. The latter used public relations especially effectively to challenge the PR power of targeted businesses. Environmentalist, civil rights, and women's rights groups and safety and consumer advocate organizations were successful in moving the public toward their positions and, in many cases, toward action.

SHAPING THE CHARACTER OF PUBLIC RELATIONS

Throughout these four stages in the development of public relations, several factors combined to shape the identity of public relations, influence the way the industry does its job, and clarify the necessity for PR in the business and political world. These factors include:

Advances in technology. Advances in industrial technology made possible mass production, distribution, and marketing of goods. Advances in communication technology (and their proliferation) made it possible to communicate more efficiently and effectively with ever larger and more specific audiences.

Growth of the middle class. A growing middle class, better educated and more aware of the world around it, required information about people and organizations.

Growth of organizations. As business, organized labor, and government grew bigger after World War II, the public saw them as more powerful and more remote. As a result, people were naturally curious and suspicious about these forces that seemed to be influencing all aspects of their lives.

Better research tools. The development of sophisticated research methodologies and statistical techniques allowed the industry to know its audiences better and to better judge the effectiveness of public relations campaigns.

Professionalization. Numerous national and international public relations organizations helped professionalize the industry and clean up its reputation.

Public Relations and Its Audiences

Virtually all of us consume public relations messages on a daily basis. Increasingly, the video clips we see on the local evening news are provided by a public relations firm or the PR department of some company or organization. The content of many of the stories we read in our daily newspaper or hear on local radio news comes directly from PR-provided press releases. As one media relations firm explained in a promotional piece sent to prospective clients, "The media are separated into two categories. One is content and the other is advertising. They're both for sale. Advertising can be purchased directly from the publication or through an ad agency, and the content space you purchase from PR firms" (quoted in Jackson & Hart, 2002, p. 24). In addition, the charity food drive we support, the poster encouraging us toward safe sex, the corporation-sponsored art exhibit we attend, and the 5K race we run are all someone's public relations effort. Public relations professionals interact with seven categories of publics (Arens, 1999):

PRSA Foundation
www.
tampa.prsa.org

Employees. An organization's employees are its life blood, its family. Good public relations begins at home with company newsletters, social events, and internal and external recognition of superior performance.

Stockholders. Stockholders own the organization (if it is a public corporation). They are "family" as well, and their goodwill is necessary for the business to operate. Annual reports and stockholder meetings provide a sense of belonging as well as information.

Communities. An organization has neighbors where it operates. Courtesy, as well as good business sense, requires that an organization's neighbors be treated with friendship and support. Information meetings, company-sponsored safety and food drives, and open houses strengthen ties between organizations and their neighbors.

For more information on this topic, view *Advertising and Public Relations: Inside Ogilvy*, #6 on the CD *Media Tours.*

Media. Very little communication with an organization's various publics can occur without the trust and goodwill of professionals in the mass media. Press packets, briefings, and facilitating access to organization newsmakers build that trust and goodwill.

Government. Government is "the voice of the people" and, as such, deserves the attention of any organization that deals with the public. From a practical perspective, governments have the power to tax, regulate, and zone. Organizations must earn and maintain the goodwill and trust of the government. Providing information and access through reports, position papers, and meetings with personnel keeps government informed and builds its trust in an organization. The government is also the target of many PR efforts, as organizations and their lobbyists seek favorable legislation and other action.

Investment community. Corporations are under the constant scrutiny of those who invest their own money, invest the money of others, or make recommendations on investment. The value of a business and its ability to grow are functions of the investment community's respect for and trust in it. As a result, all PR efforts that build an organization's good image speak to that community.

Customers. Consumers pay the bills for companies through their purchase of products or services. Their goodwill is invaluable. That makes good PR, in all its forms, invaluable.

Scope and Structure of the Public Relations Industry

PR Statistics and Commentary **www.** odwyerpr.com

Today some 200,000 people identify themselves as working in public relations, and more than 80% of major U.S. companies have public relations departments, some housing as many as 400 employees (Figure 11.1). There are over 4,000 public relations firms in the United States, the largest employing as many as 2,000 people. Most, however, have fewer, some as few as four employees.

There are full-service public relations firms and those that provide only special services. Media specialists for company CEOs, newspaper clipping services, and makers of video news releases are special service providers. Public relations firms bill for their services in a number of ways. They may charge an hourly rate for services rendered, or they may be on call, charging clients a monthly fee to act as their public relations counsel. Hill and Knowlton, for example, has a minimum $5,000 a month charge. Third are **fixed-fee arrangements,** wherein the firm performs a

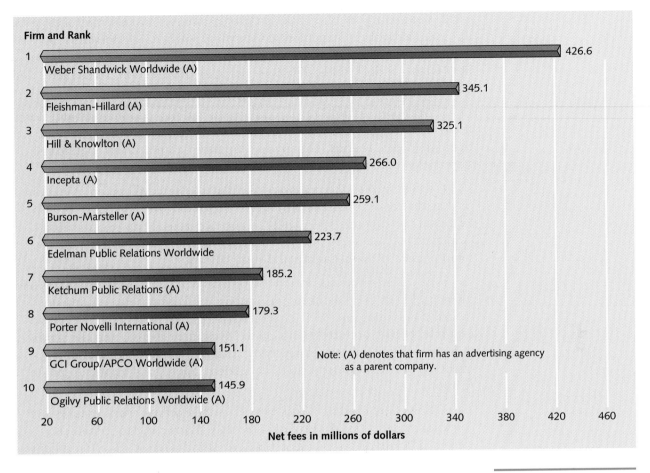

Firm and Rank

1 Weber Shandwick Worldwide (A) — 426.6
2 Fleishman-Hillard (A) — 345.1
3 Hill & Knowlton (A) — 325.1
4 Incepta (A) — 266.0
5 Burson-Marsteller (A) — 259.1
6 Edelman Public Relations Worldwide — 223.7
7 Ketchum Public Relations (A) — 185.2
8 Porter Novelli International (A) — 179.3
9 GCI Group/APCO Worldwide (A) — 151.1
10 Ogilvy Public Relations Worldwide (A) — 145.9

Note: (A) denotes that firm has an advertising agency as a parent company.

20 60 100 140 180 220 260 300 340 380 420 460

Net fees in millions of dollars

Figure 11.1. Ten Largest PR Firms in the United States, 2001. *Source:* Online, http://www.odwyerpr.com (September 2002).

specific set of services for a client for a specific and prearranged fee. Finally, many firms bill for **collateral materials,** adding a surcharge as high as 17.65% for handling printing, research, and photographs. For example, if it costs $3,000 to have a poster printed, the firm charges the client $3,529.50 ($3,000 + [$3,000 × .1765] = $3,000 + $529.50).

PUBLIC RELATIONS ACTIVITIES

Regardless of the way public relations firms bill their clients, they earn their fees by offering all or some of these 13 interrelated services identified by the PRSA (2002). The PRSA alphabetizes the presentation of these functions to indicate that none is more important than the others (Public Relations Society of America, 2002).

1. *Community relations.* This type of public affairs work focuses on the communities in which the organization exists. If a city wants to build a new airport, for example, those whose land will be taken or devalued must be satisfied. If they are not, widespread community opposition to the project may develop.

2. *Counseling.* Public relations professionals routinely offer advice to an organization's management concerning policies, relationships, and communication with its various publics. Management must tell its publics "what we do." Public relations helps in the creation, refinement, and presentation of that message.

3. *Development/fund raising.* All organizations, commercial and non-profit, survive through the voluntary contributions in time and money of their members, friends, employees, supporters, and others. Public relations helps demonstrate the need for those contributions.

4. *Employee/member relations.* Similar to the development function in that the target public is employees and members, this form of public relations responds specifically to the concerns of an organization's employees or members and its retirees and their families. The goal is maintenance of high morale and motivation.

5. *Financial relations.* Practiced primarily by corporate organizations, financial PR is the enhancement of communication between investor-owned companies and their shareholders, the financial community (for example, banks, annuity groups, and investment firms), and the public. Much corporate strategy, such as expansion into new markets and acquisition of other companies, is dependent upon good financial public relations.

6. *Government affairs.* This type of public affairs work focuses on government agencies. **Lobbying**—directly interacting to influence elected officials or government regulators and agents—is often a central activity.

Annual reports are the most visible product of financial public relations.

Figure 11.2 The fictitious Acme Fishhook Research Council in this Robotman & Monty cartoon is a good example of an organization that engages in industry relations activities. Robotman reprinted by permission of Newspaper Enterprise Association, Inc.

7. *Industry relations.* Companies must interact not only with their own customers and stockholders but also with other companies in their line of business, both competitors and suppliers. In addition, they must also stand as a single voice in dealing with various state and federal regulators. For example, groups as disparate as the Texas Restaurant Association, the American Petroleum Institute, and the National Association of Manufacturers all require public relations in dealing with their various publics. The goal is the maintenance and prosperity of the industry as a whole (Figure 11.2).

8. *Issues management.* Often an organization is as interested in influencing public opinion about some larger issue that will eventually influence its operation as it is in the improvement of its own image. Issues management typically uses a large-scale public relations campaign designed to move or shape opinion on a specific issue. Usually the issue is an important one that generates deep feelings. Death penalty activists, for example, employ a full range of communication techniques to sway people to their side. Exxon Mobil frequently runs advertorials that address environmentalism and public transportation—important issues in and of themselves, but also important to the future of a leading manufacturer of gasoline. For a close look at a controversial issues management campaign, see the Cultural Forum box titled "The Office of Strategic Influence: The Pentagon Does PR."

For more information on this topic, see NBC Video Clip #18 on the CD—*Pentagon Planning to Plant Misinformation in Foreign News Sources.*

9. *Media relations.* As the number of media outlets grows and as advances in technology increase the complexity of dealing with them, public relations clients require help in understanding the various media, in preparing and organizing materials for them, and in placing those materials. In addition, media relations requires that the public relations professional maintain good relationships with professionals in the media, understand their deadlines and other restraints, and earn their trust.

10. *Marketing communication.* This is a combination of activities designed to sell a product, service, or idea. It can include the creation of advertising; generation of publicity and promotion; design of packaging, point-of-sale displays, and trade show presentations; and design and execution of special events. It is important to note that PR professionals often use advertising but that the two are not the same. The difference is

The Office of Strategic Influence: The Pentagon Does PR

"The Office of Strategic Lying" and "Office of Strategic Disinformation" were two of the kinder names attached to the proposed Office of Strategic Influence (OSI) that put public relations in general and government-sponsored public relations in particular into the cultural forum in 2002. After a series of leaks to the press in February of that year, Secretary of Defense Donald Rumsfeld was forced to announce the creation of this new division in the Pentagon, the purpose of which would be "to provide news items, possibly even false ones, to foreign media organizations in order to influence public sentiment and policy makers in both friendly and unfriendly countries. . . .

The secretive new office envisions using a mix of truthful news releases, phony stories, and e-mails from disguised addresses to encourage the kinds of news coverage abroad that the Pentagon considers advantageous, while using clandestine activities, including computer network attacks, to disrupt coverage it opposes" ("Would I," 2002, p. 1).

Reaction from the American journalism and public relations industries and our international allies was immediate and universally negative, forcing the scrapping of the plan. "The office is done," a clearly upset Secretary Rumsfeld told a press conference held 8 days after the story first broke, "It's over. What do you want, blood?" (quoted in MacArthur, 2002, p. B4).

But what could the objections be? Why wouldn't we want an office in the Pentagon running our country's public relations efforts after September 11 and as our soldiers and sailors continued the war against terrorism? The objections varied, depending on the source. The public relations industry, sensitive about its reputation, saw the governmentally sanctioned disinformation campaign as reinforcing people's most negative stereotype of it and its practitioners. Arguing that misinformation breeds distrust

one of control. Advertising is controlled communication—advertisers pay for ads to appear in specific media exactly as they want. PR tends to be less controlled. The PR firm cannot control how or when its press release is used by the local paper. It cannot control how the media react to Nike's ongoing insistence that it has rectified reported worker abuses in its overseas shops. Advertising becomes a public relations function when its goal is to build an image or to motivate action, as opposed to the usual function of selling products. The Smokey Bear forest fire prevention campaign is a well-known successful public relations advertising campaign.

Advertising and public relations obviously overlap even for manufacturers of consumer products. Chevrolet must sell cars, but it must communicate with its various publics as well. Exxon sells gasoline. But in the wake of the *Valdez* disaster, it needed serious public relations help. One of the misinformers, Dr. Steve Pieczenik, a psychological warfare expert who had done work for the State Department, said, "I find it commendable that the administration reversed the decision. What would have happened would have been an incredible disaster in increasing the American public's distrust toward the presidency and the Pentagon" (quoted in "Real News," 2002, p. A5). Then there is the issue of "blowback." That is, the U.S. press, especially in the age of the Internet and satellites, often gets its leads from foreign stories. How much of what we see and read here at home would be the product of our own government's lies and half-truths originally fed to foreign reporters? Paul McMasters, the Freedom Forum's First Amendment ombudsman, raised the additional issue of the credibility of American reporters working overseas: "Even our allies sometimes allege that our press and our government are in cahoots" (quoted in Mundy, 2002, p. 26). How can U.S. journalists do their jobs if they are suspected agents of disinformation? Even worse, they could become marked for death, as was the *Wall Street Journal*'s Daniel Pearl, suspected of being a U.S. government agent by Muslim radicals in Pakistan.

But the most telling criticism, echoed by scores of commentators from all walks of American life, was that an operation such as the OSI is simply beneath the world's greatest democracy, one supposedly committed to free and robust public discourse. Said Al Cross, president of the Society of Professional Journalists, "Here we are trying to encourage the formation of a free press in some of these emerging democracies, and now we're going to make the press untrustworthy? We've done damage to our credibility just by considering this" (quoted in Mundy, 2002, p. 26). Case Western Reserve University journalism professor Ted Gup wrote in *Columbia Journalism Review* that the OSI was the product of

> a low esteem for the public's maturity and its rights to the facts. [It] alternately regards truth as something to be feared or something too anemic to convince others of the rightness of the U.S. cause. . . . With the revelations about the OSI, the government inadvertently handed its enemies a powerful weapon. Cynics may argue that the U.S. is rarely believed even when it is telling the truth, so what does it matter? It matters, perhaps not to the hardened fanatic, but to the hundreds of millions of fencesitters exposed only to the toxic lies of their own repressive regimes. And it matters to us at home. In an age of global information, falsehoods are swept up like wind-borne radiation back to our shores and to those who stand with us. (2002, pp. 74–75)

Enter your voice in the cultural forum. Should we expect our government to tell the truth? After all, that government is us—government of the people, by the people, for the people. Or do you agree with Solicitor General Theodore Olson, who argued before the Supreme Court that "it's easy to imagine an infinite number of situations where the government might legitimately give out false information" (quoted in Gup, 2002, p. 75)? Or is it permissible to lie to "foreigners" if we can somehow ensure that those lies do not come home? PR professionals argue that all they have is their credibility, so lying is never permissible in a public information effort. Do you see this as naïve, especially in our dangerous, post-September 11 world? If you were in the Pentagon when plans for the OSI were being drawn up, how might you have advised your colleagues?

result of the overlap of advertising and public relations is that advertising agencies increasingly own their own public relations departments or firms or associate closely with a PR company. Nine of the top 10 highest-earning public relations firms are subsidiaries of advertising agencies (see Figure 11.1). For example, Burson-Marsteller is owned by Young & Rubicam.

Another way that advertising and public relations differ is that advertising people typically do not set policy for an organization. Advertising people *implement* policy after organization leaders set it. In contrast, public relations professionals usually are part of the policy decision process because they are the liaison between the organization and its publics. Effective organizations have come to understand that even in routine decisions the impact on public opinion and subsequent consequences can be of tremendous importance. As a result, public relations

Our Children's Stories

Tanya liked to play outside at the House while she recovered from a bone marrow transplant.

Tanya is a bright and joyful seven year old from Sonora, but already in second remission with rhabdomyosarcoma. She was referred to Lucile Salter Packard Children's Hospital at Stanford when a bone marrow transplant was considered.

The transplant was done in early October and Tanya was released from the Hospital a few days before Halloween. At the Ronald McDonald House Tanya pirouetted around in her ballerina costume, climbed the big oak in the courtyard and enjoyed the warmth and support of the House, while recovering from her bone marrow transplant operation.

Four-month old Alex was having difficulty breathing. He was tentatively diagnosed with asthma and underwent a chest x-ray and sonogram to evaluate his situation. He was found to have a birth defect, with an artery connected to the wrong chamber of his heart. His breathing difficulties were due to his heart using only two chambers instead of the necessary four. He was brought to the Lucile Salter Packard Children's Hospital for corrective surgery.

The surgery to repair the artery was not complicated, but when it was time to remove Alex from the heart-lung bypass machine, his repaired heart would not beat, and Alex had to be put on full life support. His parents were notified of his dire situation. The only hope was a heart transplant with a

Alex, who owes his life to an emergency heart transplant, returns to the Hospital, and security of the Ronald McDonald house, several times a year to be evaluated. He is a vibrant, active six year old who enjoys being read to by his mom...truly a miracle of medicine.

RONALD McDONALD HOUSE at Lucile Salter Packard Children's Hospital at Stanford
1993 Annual Report

The best public relations can serve both client and the public, as demonstrated by this Ronald McDonald House promotional material.

PR Watch
www.
prwatch.org

has become a management function, and a public relations professional typically sits as a member of a company's highest level of management.

11. *Minority relations/multicultural affairs.* Public affairs activities are directed toward specific racial minorities in this type of work. When Denny's restaurant chain was beset by numerous complaints of racial discrimination during the 1990s, it undertook an aggressive campaign to speak to those who felt disenfranchised by the events. A secondary goal of its efforts, which were aimed largely at the African American community, was to send a message to its own employees and the larger public that this was the company line, that discrimination was wrong, that everybody was welcome in Denny's.

12. *Public affairs.* The public affairs function includes interacting with officials and leaders of the various power centers with whom a client must deal. Community and government officials and leaders of pressure groups are likely targets of this form of public relations. Public affairs emphasizes social responsibility and building goodwill, such as when a company donates money for a computer lab to the local high school.

13. *Special events and public participation.* As you saw in the opening vignette, public relations can be used to stimulate interest in an organization, person, or product through a well-planned, focused

"happening," activities designed to facilitate interaction between an organization and its publics.

ORGANIZATION OF A PUBLIC RELATIONS OPERATION

Public relations operations come in all sizes. Regardless of size, however, the typical PR firm or department will have these types of positions (but not necessarily these titles):

Executive. This is the chief executive officer who, sometimes with a staff, sometimes alone, sets policy and serves as the spokesperson for the operation.

Account executives. Each account has its own executive who provides advice to the client, defines problems and situations, assesses the needs and demands of the client's publics, recommends a communication plan or campaign, and gathers the PR firm's resources in support of the client.

Creative specialists. These are the writers, graphic designers, artists, video and audio producers, and photographers—anybody necessary to meet the communication needs of the client.

This is a very successful, long-running advertising campaign. It is also a very successful, long-running public relations campaign.

Media specialists. Media specialists are aware of the requirements, preferences, limitations, and strengths of the various media used to serve the client. They find the right media for clients' messages.

Larger public relations operations may also have these positions as need demands:

Research. The key to two-way public relations communication rests in research—assessing the needs of a client's various publics and the effectiveness of the efforts aimed at them. Polling, one-on-one interviews, and **focus groups,** in which small groups of a targeted public are interviewed, provide the PR operation and its client with feedback.

Government relations. Depending on the client's needs, lobbying or other direct communication with government officials may be necessary.

Financial services. Very specific and sophisticated knowledge of economics, finance, and business or corporate law is required to provide clients with dependable financial public relations.

Trends and Convergence in Public Relations

GLOBALIZATION AND SPECIALIZATION

For more information on this topic, see NBC Video Clip #19 on the CD—*Why Is the United States Viewed So Poorly in the Arab World?*

As it has in the media industries themselves, globalization has come to public relations, both in the form of foreign ownership and in the reach of PR firms' operations into foreign countries. For example, three of the world's top-10-earning PR firms, despite their U.S. roots, are owned by London-based WPP Group—Hill and Knowlton, Burson-Marsteller, and Ogilvy PR Worldwide. Hill and Knowlton alone has 2,000 employees working in 66 offices in 35 countries on all the inhabited continents. Rowland Company Worldwide is owned by English advertising agency Saatchi & Saatchi. Weber Shandwick, the highest-earning PR firm in the United States, is based in London.

A second trend in public relations is specialization. As we've seen, the PRSA identifies 13 activities of public relations professionals, but it also acknowledges that specialization could expand that list. This specialization takes two forms. The first is defined by issue. Environmental public relations is attracting ever larger numbers of people, both environmentalists and industrialists. E. Bruce Harrison Consulting attracts corporate clients in part because of its reputation as a firm with superior **greenwashing** skills. That is, Harrison is particularly adept at countering the public relations efforts aimed at its clients by environmentalists.

CONVERGENCE

The second impetus driving specialization has to do with the increasing number of media outlets used in public relations campaigns that rely on new and converging technologies. Online information and advertising are a growing part of the total public relations media mix, as are **video news releases** (see Figure 11.3) and videoconferencing. Television, in the form of the **satellite-delivered media tour,** in which spokespeople can be simultaneously interviewed by a worldwide audience connected to the on-screen interviewee via telephone, has further extended the reach of public relations. In addition, desktop publishing has greatly expanded the number and type of available print outlets. All require professionals with quite specific skills.

The public relations industry is responding to the convergence of traditional media with the Internet in other ways as well. One is the development of **integrated marketing communications (IMC).** We saw earlier how advertising and PR often overlap, but in IMC, firms actively combine public relations, marketing, advertising, and promotion functions into a more or less seamless communication campaign that is as at home on the Web as it is on the television screen and magazine page. The goal of this integration is to provide the client and agency with greater control over communication (and its interpretation) in an increasingly fragmented but synergized media environment. For example, a common IMC tactic is to employ **viral marketing,** a strategy that relies on targeting specific Internet

Figure 11.3 This Tom Tomorrow comic satirizes one of the most controversial tools used by public relations firms—the self-promoting video news release. Legal, and sometimes providing useful information, these video clips test the viewer's media literacy skills. © Tom Tomorrow. Reprinted with permission.

users with a given communication and relying on them to spread the word through the communication channels with which they are most comfortable. This is IMC, and it is inexpensive and effective.

The industry has had to respond to the Internet in another way. The Net has provided various publics with a new, powerful way to counter even the best public relations effort (Chapter 10). Tony Juniper of the British environmental group Friends of the Earth calls the Internet "the most potent weapon in the toolbox of resistance." As Peter Verhille of PR giant Entente International explains, "One of the major strengths of pressure groups—in fact the leveling factor in their confrontation with powerful companies—is their ability to exploit the instruments of the telecommunication revolution. Their agile use of global tools such as the Internet reduces the advantages that corporate budgets once provided" (both quotes from Klein, 1999, pp. 395–396). The Internet, for example, was central in activists' 1999 efforts to shame Nike into improving conditions for its overseas workers; and in 1995 use of the Net played a prominent part in forcing Shell Oil to find environmentally sensitive ways to dispose of its outdated Atlantic Ocean drilling platforms. Public relations agencies and in-house PR departments have responded in a number of ways. One is IMC. Another is the hiring of in-house Web monitors; a third is the growth of specialty firms such as eWatch, whose function is to alert clients to negative references on the Web and suggest effective countermeasures.

TRUST IN PUBLIC RELATIONS

Edward Bernays
www.
lib.uwo.ca/business/bernays.html

We began our discussion of public relations with the admission that the profession bears a negative reputation (see the box "Boosting Smoking among Women"). Edward Bernays's call for greater sensitivity to the wants and needs of the various publics and Ivy Lee's insistence that public relations be open and honest were the industry's first steps away from its huckster roots. The post–World War II code of ethics and accreditation programs were a second and more important step. Yet Bernays himself was dissatisfied with the profession's progress. The "Father of Public Relations" died in 1995 at the age of 103. He spent the greater part of his last years demanding that the industry, especially the PRSA, police itself. In 1986 Bernays wrote:

> Under present conditions, an unethical person can sign the code of the PRSA, become a member, practice unethically—untouched by any legal sanctions. In law and medicine, such an individual is subject to disbarment from the profession. . . . There are no standards. . . . This sad situation

The Father of Public Relations, Edward Bernays, used the last years of his long career and life to campaign for improved industry ethics.

Boosting Smoking among Women

Into the early 1900s, smoking was seen as an unsavory habit, permissible for men, never for women. But with the turn of the century, women too wanted to light up. Advertising campaigns first began targeting female smokers in 1919. The American Tobacco Company slogan "Reach for a Lucky instead of a sweet," along with ads designed to help women understand that they could use cigarettes to keep their figures, was aimed at this new market. The rush to smoke was also fueled by the fight for suffrage; women wanted equality. The right to vote was an important goal, but if men could smoke without a fight, why couldn't women?

As more women began to smoke, antismoking crusades attempted to deter them. The protection of women's morality, not their health, inspired the crusaders. Many cities forbade the use of tobacco by women in public places. Yet the number of women who started smoking continued to grow. George Washington Hill, head of American Tobacco, wanted this lucrative market to continue to expand, and he wanted to own as large a part of it as possible. He turned to public relations and Edward Bernays.

A nephew of Sigmund Freud, Bernays was employed to conduct psychological research aimed at understanding the relationship between women and cigarettes. He learned that women saw cigarettes as symbols of freedom, as the representation of their unfair treatment in a man's world,

"There's none so good as LUCKIES"

SHE'S MISCHIEVOUS, RESTLESS AND 20, WEIGHS 112 POUNDS. Miss Harlow has smoked Luckies for two years—and one can't win paid for her signed statement. She took to stardom in "Hell's Angels" ... and if you've seen her new COLUMBIA PICTURE, "THREE WISE GIRLS," you'll understand why thousands of girls are trying to match her riotous platinum blonde locks. We appreciate all she writes of Luckies, and so we say, "Thanks, Jean Harlow."

"I've tried all cigarettes and there's none so good as LUCKIES. And incidentally I'm careful in my choice of cigarettes. I have to be because of my throat. Put me down, as one who always reaches for a LUCKY. It's a real delight to find a Cellophane wrapper that opens without an ice pick." *Jean Harlow*

"It's toasted"
Your Throat Protection—against irritation—against cough
And Moisture-Proof Cellophane Keeps that "Toasted" Flavor Ever Fresh

Lucky Strike used advertising and an effective public relations campaign to break the taboo on women smokers.

and as a sign of their determination to be accepted as equal.

Bernays had several objectives: (1) to let the public know that it was quite all right for women to smoke; (2) to undercut the bans on public smoking by women that existed in many places; and (3) to position Lucky Strike cigarettes as a progressive brand.

In meeting these goals, Bernays perpetrated a publicity stunt that is still heralded as a triumphant coup among public relations practitioners. New York City had a ban on public smoking by females. Because of, rather than despite, this, Bernays arranged for 10 socially prominent young women to enter the 1929 annual Easter Parade down Fifth Avenue as the "Torches of Liberty Contingent." As they marched, the debutantes lit their Lucky "torches of freedom" and smilingly proceeded to puff and walk. For reporters on the scene, this made for much better news and photos than the usual little kids in their spring finery. The blow for female emancipation was front-page news, not only in New York, but nationally. The taboo was dead.

Later in his life, Bernays would argue that had he known of the link between cigarette smoking and cancer and other diseases, he would never have taken on American Tobacco as a client. We will see in Chapter 12 whether his strategy—and his later misgivings—are echoed in contemporary efforts to expand the market for cigarettes.

makes it possible for anyone, regardless of education or ethics, to use the term "public relations" to describe his or her function. (p. 11)

Many people share Bernays's concern. In the United States the number of public relations people exceeds the number of journalists (200,000 to 130,000). Estimates from both inside and outside the industry claim that from 50% to 90% of the stories we read in the paper or see on television originate entirely or in part from a public relations operation in the form of either a printed or a video news release. Critics further contend that 40% of what we read and see appears virtually unedited, leading PR professionals to boast that "the best PR is invisible" and "the best PR ends up looking like news" (Stauber & Rampton, 1995, p. 2).

This state of affairs led journalist and former *Mother Jones* editor Mark Dowie to write in his introduction to John Stauber and Sheldon Rampton's *Toxic Sludge Is Good for You: Lies, Damn Lies and the Public Relations Industry:*

> PR has become a communications medium in its own right, an industry designed to alter perception, reshape reality, and manufacture consent. It is run by a fraternity carefully organized so that only insiders can observe their peers at work. . . . It is critical that consumers of media in democratic societies understand the origin of information and the process by which it is mediated, particularly when they are being deceived. (1995, pp. 2–4)

If it is true that the public is being systematically deceived by public relations, the cultural implications could not be more profound. What becomes of the negotiation function of culture, wherein people debate and discuss their values and interests in the cultural forum, if public relations gives some voices advantages not available to others? Dowie suggests the remedy for this potential problem: Consumers must make themselves aware of "the origin of information and the process by which it is mediated" (p. 4). As we've seen throughout this book, we would expect nothing less of a media literate person.

DEVELOPING MEDIA LITERACY SKILLS

Judging Crisis PR

There is no greater challenge for an organization than having to communicate its position (and reclaim its good name) after a significant public failure. We've already seen that Tylenol and Odwalla survived situations in which their products were involved in the deaths of their users. On the other hand, Hooker Chemical (dumping toxins in western New York's Love Canal), Nestlé (selling useless baby formula to Third World countries), Nike (maintaining sweatshops in Southeast Asia), the Catholic Church (a pedophile scandal), Exxon (the *Exxon Valdez* oil spill), Union Carbide (4,000 people killed by a gas leak in Bhopal, India), and Bridgestone/Firestone (failing tires on Ford SUVs) all suffered PR disasters to compound

Early in the Catholic Church's recent pedophile scandal, its spokespeople committed the crisis PR sin of blaming the victims. Here, U.S. Cardinal Theodore McCarrick talks to journalists in front of St. Peter's Basilica in Rome in 2002.

the disasters that PR was designed to solve. It is this questionable reaction to bad news that, more than anything, gives PR its sometimes less-than-laudable reputation. What did Tylenol and Odwalla do right? Basically, they immediately told the truth. What did the others do wrong? Hooker and Nike denied responsibility. Nestlé claimed that what it did was not illegal. The Catholic Church blamed the victims, Exxon blamed the ship's skipper, Union Carbide blamed a disgruntled employee, and Bridgestone/Firestone blamed Ford.

But there is more to saving an organization's reputation than telling the truth. Nestlé told the truth. What it had done was not illegal. Exxon told the truth. The skipper was drinking. The media literate consumer of crisis PR should be skilled at evaluating the nature of an organization's PR messages, in part to judge those messages as good, fair, and honest mass communication but also to judge the organization itself. Does this company respect us and our intellects? Is it a good company, worthy of our business (and respect)? How do we do this?

Practice Public Relations

We've read in this chapter that despite its sometimes conflicted reputation, public relations often serves quite noble ends. We saw this, for example, in the Race for the Cure campaign from the opening vignette. But media literate individuals can decide for themselves about the value of PR by making it a living enterprise, that is, by actually engaging in the practice of public relations.

There are a number of ways that this can be done. First, every college and university has a public relations office. It might be called Public Information or Relations with Schools or some similar name, but your campus has one. Visit it and talk to the professionals there about what it is they do, how they operate, whom they identify as their primary publics, what different strategies they employ to reach each public, and what you can do to help. You may want to volunteer for a specific period of time, say 2 weeks on a campaign that interests you—for example, an effort to get older alums to reconnect with the campus—or a specific event, for example, an open-house weekend for prospective students. You may even want to sign on for a formal internship with that office, as many campuses encourage their students to gain preprofessional experience right on campus.

A second way to experience public relations is to contact the Public Relations Student Society of America (www.prssa.org). The PRSSA is a preprofessional PR organization with 7,000 members in chapters on 230 campuses. Its primary goal is to connect student and professional PR practitioners. The PRSSA runs an annual competition—the Bateman Case Study—that allows students to engage in "real world" strategic planning and creative execution. If your campus does not have a chapter, you can connect with one that does (you will be welcomed) or begin a chapter at your own school. The groups' Web site tells you how.

1. *Consider what you thought about the company before it found itself in crisis.* That is, was it an organization that you considered a good corporate citizen, fair to its clients and customers, treating its employees well, doing the right thing when not in crisis? When cable giant Adelphia found itself embroiled in an accounting scandal in 2002, few people had sympathy. Who could love "the cable company"? But consider your thinking about Yoplait, the yogurt maker that sponsors Race for the Cure.

2. *Was this an organization that had foreseen the problem and taken the necessary steps to ensure that it would not find itself in crisis?* For example, Bridgestone/Firestone's case before the public was considerably weakened when it was revealed that dozens of people had already died in overseas accidents involving its tires.

3. *How did the company initially react?* The Catholic Church's public relations people spoke ominously of "shared responsibility" between priests and boys in its pedophile scandal. Nike claimed it was not responsible for the labor practices of its subcontractors. Both organizations eventually accepted responsibility and took steps to correct the problems that had led to crisis, but now they were suspect. However, Johnson & Johnson, the maker of Tylenol, was immediately honest with the public, explaining what it did and did not know about the tampered-with capsules that had killed.

4. *Did the company tell the truth?* Nike found itself in even deeper crisis when it was revealed that it did, indeed, have control over its subcontractors if it wanted to exercise it. The Catholic Church and Bridgestone/Firestone found the public increasingly difficult to convince of their

rectitude when once-secret documents revealed their postcrisis obfuscation. More generally, is this an organization that has been and continues to be open to scrutiny? Exxon, Union Carbide, and the Catholic Church were seen as secretive before and after crisis. Odwalla and Johnson & Johnson have always been seen as open with their publics.

5. *Did the organization do the right thing once the crisis erupted?* Tylenol was immediately pulled from the shelves, and the product was redesigned. Odwalla destroyed all its existing product, whether implicated or not, closed its plants, and reopened only after safety was assured. Nestlé destroyed all the baby formula that remained and underwrote infant care programs for Third World mothers. When Denny's was faced with charges of racism, it immediately apologized for its failure to properly train its personnel, set up an 800-number hotline to field complaints, and redoubled its minority-recruiting efforts. But Ford blamed Bridgestone/Firestone. Bridgestone/Firestone blamed Ford (and more people died as they played the blame game). The Catholic Church attacked the press that was reporting victims' complaints. Nike promised to send basketball player Michael Jordan to review the plants where sneakers were being made.

6. *Did the organization indicate that it had learned from its mistakes?* Nike reclaimed its good name, in large part because it let its public know that it had corrected the problems and would police its subcontractors more closely. The Catholic Church suffered continued criticism and loss of supporters because its laypeople, priests, and hierarchy argued publicly for years about the best solution to its high-profile problems.

The job of a PR professional faced with a crisis, especially in the Internet/tabloid journalism age, is not an easy one. But neither is the task of the consumers of that professional's messages. There is so much information "out there," and it is often of questionable worth. Therefore, there is much at stake in literate reading of crisis public relations—not just our ability to make good decisions for ourselves but also the fates of the crisis-bound organizations and the employees.

Chapter Review

Because public relations is and does many different things, there is no universally accepted definition of this industry. In this chapter we define public relations as a management function that focuses on the relationships and communications that individuals and organizations have with other groups (called publics) for the purpose of creating mutual goodwill.

Public relations has matured from a huckster's activity into an industry attempting to develop and maintain professionalism among its practitioners. It has passed through four stages in this process: early public relations, the propaganda-publicity stage, early two-way communication, and advanced two-way communication.

Some 200,000 people work in contemporary public relations in the United States. There are more than 4,000 public relations firms, and most major companies have in-house PR operations. The 13 activities typically carried out by PR operations are community relations, counseling, development/fund raising, employee/member relations, financial relations, government affairs, issues management, industry relations, media relations, marketing communication, minority relations/multicultural affairs, public affairs, and special events and public participation. One way public relations differs from advertising is that public relations typically has a policymaking or management function in an organization, which advertising lacks.

The publics addressed by public relations include employees of the organization, its stockholders, the communities in which it operates, the media it depends on, the government, the investment community, and its customers.

Public relations operations typically employ an executive, account executives, creative specialists, and media specialists. Some larger operations will also have people in research, government relations, and financial services.

Globalization and specialization are altering the nature of the industry. Convergence, too, especially that of traditional media with the Internet, is having its impact on PR. Integrated marketing communications, seamlessly meshing several communication functions, is designed to provide firms with greater control over communication and its interpretation in a fragmented and converged media environment. The Net, too, has empowered those publics who wish to challenge corporations and their PR spokespeople. Still, one thing that has not changed since the earliest days of the industry is the question of trust. Evaluating an organization's crisis PR is not only a test of our media literacy, it can also be a service to that organization.

Key Terms

Use the text's CD-ROM and the Online Learning Center at www.mhhe.com/baran to further your understanding of the following terminology.

flack, 347
pseudo-event, 350
fixed-fee arrangement, 358
collateral materials, 359
lobbying, 360

focus group, 365
greenwashing, 366
video news release, 366
satellite-delivered
   media tour, 366

integrated marketing
   communications (IMC), 366
viral marketing, 366

Questions for Review

Go to the self-quizzes on the CD-ROM and the Online Learning Center to test your knowledge.

1. Good definitions of public relations should contain what two elements?
2. What are the four stages in the development of the public relations industry?
3. Who are Ivy Lee, George Creel, and Edward Bernays?
4. What are the CPI and OWI? What is their importance to the development of public relations?
5. Who are George Gallup and Elmo Roper?
6. What is the difference between public relations and advertising?
7. What are some specific divisions of public relations' public affairs activities?
8. Who are public relations' publics? What are their characteristics?
9. What positions typically exist in a public relations operation?
10. How have new communication technologies influenced the public relations industry?
11. What is integrated marketing communications? What is its goal?
12. What is viral marketing? How does it work?

Questions for Critical Thinking and Discussion

1. Are you familiar with any of the companies identified in the opening vignette that are associated with Race for the Cure? What was your opinion of those companies before you read of their support for the fight against breast cancer? What is your opinion now? Does community relations such as

this really work, or do most people see it as self-serving? Do you agree or disagree that a company's precrisis reputation can help it weather a crisis should one occur? Why or why not?

2. Have you ever been part of an Internet-fueled movement against the activities of an organization or in support of some good cause? If you were, you were engaged in public relations. Measure your experience against the lessons in this chapter. What kind of public relations activities did you undertake? Who were your publics? Were you successful? Why or why not?

3. Propaganda is avoided by ethical PR people because it depends on an automatic, nonreflective reaction to a message or symbol. Can you think of industry, government, or interest group propaganda efforts that do exist? What symbols or messages typically generate these automatic responses?

4. Reread the Dowie quote from page 370. Do you agree with his assessment of the profession? What is your feeling about public relations? When do you think it is useful for the culture? When do you think it is harmful?

5. Would you consider a career in public relations? If not, why not? If yes, what attracts you to this profession? Is there a specific aspect of its operation that interests you more than others? Why?

Important Resources

International Public Relations Review. Calling itself the "international journal of corporate and public affairs," this quarterly presents articles on both public relations within specific countries and public relations in countries other than one's own.

Public Relations Quarterly. A half-scholarly, half-trade journal that specializes in applied research and serious commentary on the profession from within and without.

Public Relations Review. A journal of research and commentary, published five times a year, that presents applied industry research and critical comment from academics.

pr reporter. This weekly typically takes on a specific public relations problem—for example, a hoax aimed at Girl Scout Cookies or public dissatisfaction with colleges and universities—for each of its issues and either details how one campaign addressed it or offers several opinions on how the problem might be handled.

It bills itself as a "cutting edge newsletter of public relations, public affairs, and communication strategies."

PR Watch. Published quarterly by the Center for Media and Democracy, a public interest advocacy group, this publication offers, in its own words, "public interest reporting on the PR and Public Affairs industry." It is very critical of PR, but the reporting is well researched, well documented, and well written.

Rampton, S., & Stauber, J. (2001). *Trust us, we're experts! How industry manipulates science and gambles with your future.* New York: Tarcher/Putnam. This is a meticulously researched and delightfully written assessment of the use of experts in public relations. Like the other books by this Center for Media and Democracy duo, *Toxic Sludge Is Good For You* and *Mad Cow USA: Could the Nightmare Happen Here?,* it is part history lesson, part civics lesson, and laugh-out-loud funny. But the

Public Relations Society of America   www.prsa.org

MADD   www.madd.org

SADD   www.sadd.org

Public Relations History   www.public-relations-online.net/history.htm

Canadian Public Relations Society   www.cprs.ca

Public Relations Students Society of America   www.prssa.org

PRSA Foundation   www.tampa.prsa.org

PR Watch   www.prwatch.org

PR Statistics and Commentary   www.odwyerpr.com

Edward Bernays   www.lib.uwo.ca/business/bernays.html

CHAPTER 12

Advertising

LEARNING OBJECTIVES

Advertising is everywhere. And as it becomes more ubiquitous, we tend to ignore it. But as we tend to ignore it, advertisers find new ways to make it more ubiquitous. As a result, and as with television, no one is neutral about advertising. We love it or we hate it. Many of us do both. After studying this chapter you should

- be familiar with the history and development of the advertising industry.

- understand contemporary criticisms and defenses of advertising.

- recognize how the organizational and economic nature of the contemporary advertising industry shapes the content of advertising.

- be familiar with different types of advertising and their goals.

- understand the relationship between advertising content and its consumers.

- possess improved media literacy skills when consuming advertising, especially when interpreting intentional imprecision.

YOUR ROOMMATES, BOTH ADVERTISING MAJORS, CHALLENGE YOU. "We bet you $10 that you can't go all of tomorrow without seeing an ad." You think, "I'll just stay away from radio and television—no problem, considering I have a CD player in my car and tons of homework to do." That leaves newspapers and magazines, but you can avoid their ads simply by not reading either for 24 hours. Online ads? You'll simply stay unlinked. "What about billboards?" you counter.

"We won't count them," your roomies graciously concede, "but everything else is in."

You shake hands and go to bed planning your strategy. This means no cereal in the morning—the Cheerios box has a McDonald's ad on it. There'll be no bus to school. Not only are the insides packed with ads, but a lot of buses are now covered in vinyl wrap ads that let riders see out the windows but turn buses into gigantic rolling commercials. Can't walk either. There are at least two ad kiosks on the way. It'll cost you more than $10 to take a cab, but this is about winning the bet, not about money. Cab it will be! You sleep well, confident victory is yours.

The next evening, over pizza, you hand over your $10.

"What was it?" gloats one of your companions. "Sneak a peek at TV?"

"No," you say, and then you begin the list: The cab had an ad for a radio station on its trunk and a three-sided sign on its roof touting the pizza joint you're sitting in, a chiropractor, and American Airlines. Inside, it had an electronic digital display hanging from the ceiling, pushing the lottery. The sidewalk near campus had the message "From here it looks like you could use some new underwear—Bamboo Lingerie" stenciled on it in water-soluble iridescent red paint. The restrooms on campus have Volkswagen ads pasted on their walls. Your ATM receipt carried an ad for a brokerage firm. You encountered a Domino's Pizza ad on the back of the cash register receipt you got at the store; the kiwi you bought there had a sticker on it reminding you to buy Snapple. The shopping basket had a realtor's pitch pasted to the side; even the little rubber bar you used to separate your kiwi and mineral water from the groceries of the shopper in front of you had an ad on each of its four sides.

"Easiest $10 we ever made," smile your roommates.

In this chapter we examine the history of advertising, focusing on its maturation with the coming of industrialization and the Civil War. The development of the advertising agency and the rise of professionalism within its ranks are detailed, as is the impact of magazines, radio, World War II, and television.

We discuss the relationship between consumers and contemporary advertising in terms of how advertising agencies are structured, how various types of advertising are aimed at different audiences, and which trends—converging technologies, audience segmentation, globalization—promise to alter those relationships.

We study the controversies that surround the industry. Critics charge that advertising is intrusive, deceptive, inherently unethical when aimed at children, and corrupting of the culture. We look at industry defenses, too.

Finally, in the media literacy skills section, we discuss advertisers' use of intentional imprecision and how to identify and interpret it.

A Short History of Advertising

Your roommates had the advantage. They know that U.S. advertisers spend $236 billion a year trying to get your attention and influence your decisions (Eisenberg, 2002). They also know that the typical person sees 3,000 advertising messages a day ("It's an Ad," 2001) and more than 2 million ads by the time he or she is 25 years old. There are a lot of ads and a lot of advertisers, so pitches are showing up in some unusual places. Many public schools sell ad space on their lunch menus. Some golf courses sell ads at the bottom of the plastic cup that sits in the holes. Skatertizers, in-line skaters who earn as much as $40 an hour for wearing a lightweight, flat-screen television monitor around their necks that displays videotaped commercials, are appearing in many cities. Television network ABC installs motion sensor–activated promotional ads above urinals in men's rooms that pitch its shows as users do their business. Several companies, among them FreeCar.com and Autowraps.com, offer various inducements to drivers to turn their cars into vinyl-wrapped moving ads. A New Jersey company sculpts clients' logos into fresh beach sand so that their ad greets morning beachgoers. Sports stadiums now carry sponsors' names—take me out to BankOne Ballpark! Qualcomm Stadium! International Edison Stadium! PSINet Stadium! Coke is the official drink of Ocean City, Maryland. Nissan is the official truck, Speedo the official bathing suit, and Naya Canadian the official bottled water of Los Angeles County's Department of Beaches and Harbors. MasterCard is the official credit card of South Orange, New Jersey. In August 2001, IBM was fined by Chicago authorities for defacing public sidewalks with graffiti at 100 different locations. The company had paid a man to paint ads on the ground for a new operating system. The man was arrested. We see ads on door hangers, on urinal deodorant cakes, in the mail, behind the batter at a baseball game, on basketball backboards in city parks, on suspended video monitors as we wait in line at the amusement park. We hear ads when we're on hold on the telephone. It wasn't always like this, but advertising itself has been with us for a long time.

This narrow street in Salzburg, Austria, still exhibits evidence of early European advertising, which often took the form of artistically designed signs announcing the nature of the business below.

EARLY ADVERTISING

Babylonian merchants were hiring barkers to shout out goods and prices at passersby in 3000 B.C. The Romans wrote announcements on city walls. This ad was discovered in the ruins of Pompeii:

> The Troop of Gladiators of the Aedil
> Will fight on the 31st of May
> There will be fights with wild animals
> And an Awning to keep off the sun. (Berkman & Gilson, 1987, p. 32)

Advertising History
www.
scriptorium.lib.duke.edu/hartman

By the 15th century, ads as we know them now were abundant in Europe. **Siquis**—pinup want ads for all sorts of products and services—were common. Tradespeople promoted themselves with **shopbills,** attractive, artful business cards. Taverners and other merchants were hanging eye-catching signs above their businesses. In 1625 the first **newsbook** containing ads, *The Weekly News*, was printed in England. From the beginning, those who had products and services to offer used advertising.

Advertising came to the Colonies via England. British advertising was already leaning toward exaggeration and hyperbole, but colonial advertising

was more straightforward. We saw in Chapter 4 that Ben Franklin was selling advertising space in his *Pennsylvania Gazette*. This 1735 ad is typical:

> A Plantation containing 300 acres of good Land, 30 cleared, 10 or 12 Meadow and in good English Grass, a house and barn & c. [creek] lying in Nantmel Township, upon French-Creek, about 30 miles from Philadelphia. Inquire of Simon Meredith now living on the said place. (Sandage, Fryburger, & Rotzoll, 1989, p. 21)

Advertising, however, was a small business before the Civil War. The United States was primarily an agricultural country at that time, with 90% of the population living in self-sufficiency on farms. Advertising was used by local retailers primarily to encourage area residents to come to their businesses. The local newspaper was the major advertising medium.

INDUSTRIALIZATION AND THE CIVIL WAR

The Industrial Revolution and the Civil War altered the social and cultural landscape and brought about the expansion of advertising. By the

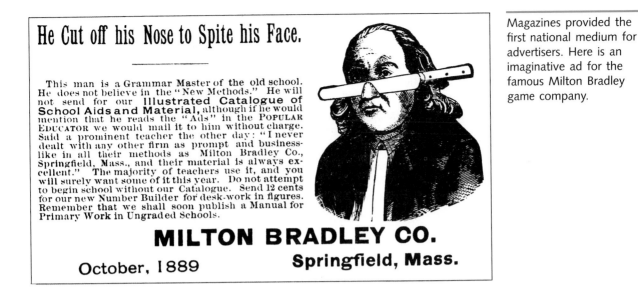

He Cut off his Nose to Spite his Face.

This man is a Grammar Master of the old school. He does not believe in the "New Methods." He will not send for our **Illustrated Catalogue of School Aids and Material,** although if he would mention that he reads the "Ads" in the POPULAR EDUCATOR we would mail it to him without charge. Said a prominent teacher the other day: "I never dealt with any other firm as prompt and business-like in all their methods as Milton Bradley Co., Springfield, Mass., and their material is always excellent." The majority of teachers use it, and you will surely want some of it this year. Do not attempt to begin school without our Catalogue. Send 12 cents for our new Number Builder for desk-work in figures. Remember that we shall soon publish a Manual for Primary Work in Ungraded Schools.

MILTON BRADLEY CO.

October, 1889   **Springfield, Mass.**

Magazines provided the first national medium for advertisers. Here is an imaginative ad for the famous Milton Bradley game company.

1840s the telegraph made communication over long distances possible. Railroads linked cities and states. Huge numbers of immigrants were welcomed to the United States to provide labor for the expanding factories. Manufacturers wanted access to larger markets for their goods. Advertising copywriter Volney B. Palmer recognized in 1841 that merchants needed to reach consumers beyond their local newspaper readership. He contacted several Philadelphia newspapers and agreed to broker the sale of space between them and interested advertisers. Within 4 years Palmer had expanded his business to Boston, and in 1849, he opened a branch in New York. The advertising agency had been invented.

The Civil War sped industrialization. More factories were needed to produce war material, and roads and railroads were expanded to move that material as well as troops. As farm workers went to war or to work in the new factories, more farm machinery was needed to compensate for their departure. That meant that more factories were needed to make more machinery, and the cycle repeated.

By the early 1880s the telephone and the electric light had been invented. That decade saw numerous innovations in manufacturing as well as an explosion in the type and availability of products. In one year alone, 1880, there were applications for more than 13,000 U.S. copyrights and patents. Over 70,000 miles of new railroad track were laid in the 1880s, linking cities and towns of all sizes. With more producers chasing the growing purchasing power of more consumers, manufacturers were forced to differentiate their products—to literally and figuratively take the pickle out of the barrel and put it in its own recognizable package. Brands were born: Quaker Oats, Ivory Soap, Royal Baking Powder, and many more. What advertisers now needed was a medium in which to tell people about these brands.

MAGAZINE ADVERTISING

We've seen in Chapter 5 how expansion of the railroads, the rise in literacy, and advantageous postal rates fueled the explosive growth of the popular magazine just before the end of the 19th century. The marriage of magazines and advertising was a natural. Cyrus H. K. Curtis, who founded the *Ladies' Home Journal* in 1883, told a group of manufacturers:

Audit Bureau of Circulations
WWW.
accessabc.com

> The editor of the Ladies' Home Journal thinks we publish it for the benefit of American women. This is an illusion, but a very proper one for him to have. The real reason, the publisher's [Curtis's] reason, is to give you who manufacture things American women want, a chance to tell them about your product. (Sandage et al., 1989, p. 32)

By the turn of the century magazines were financially supported primarily by their advertisers rather than by their readers, and aspects of advertising we find common today—creativity in look and language, mail-order ads, seasonal ads, and placement of ads in proximity to content of related interest—were already in use.

THE ADVERTISING AGENCY AND PROFESSIONALISM

Reaction to the deception and outright lies of patent medicine advertising—such as this 1880 piece for Pratts Healing Ointment—led to important efforts to professionalize the industry.

In the years between the Civil War and World War I, advertising had rapidly become more complex, more creative, and more expensive, and it was conducted on a larger scale. Advertising agencies had to expand their operations to keep up with demand. Where Palmer offered merely to broker the sale of newspaper space, F. Wayland Ayer (whose firm is now the oldest ad agency in the United States) began his "full service" advertising agency in 1869. He named his firm N. W. Ayer and Sons after his father because, at only 20 years old, he felt that clients would not trust him with their business. Ayer (the son) provided clients with ad campaign planning, created and produced ads with his staff of artists and writers, and placed them in the most appropriate media. Some other big agencies still operating today started at this time, including J. Walter Thompson, William Esty, and Lord & Thomas.

During this period, three factors combined to move the advertising industry to establish professional standards and to regulate itself. First was the reaction of the public and the medical profession to the abuses of patent medicine advertisers. These charlatans used fake claims and medical data in their ads to sell tonics that at best were useless, and at worst, deadly. The second was the critical examination of most of the country's important institutions, led by the muckrakers (Chapter 5). The third factor was the establishment in 1914 of the Federal Trade Commission (FTC), which had among its duties monitoring and regulating advertising. A number of leading advertising agencies and publishers mounted a crusade against gross exaggeration, false testimonials, and other misleading forms of advertising. The Audit Bureau of Circulations was established to verify circulation claims. The Advertising Federation of America (now the American Advertising Federation), the American Association of Advertising Agencies, the Association of National Advertisers, and the Outdoor Advertising Association all began operation at this time.

*National Advertising
Review Board*
WWW.
bbb.org/advertising/narb.asp

ADVERTISING AND RADIO

The first radio ad, as we've seen in Chapter 7, was broadcast on WEAF in 1922 (the cost was $50 for a 10-minute spot). Radio was important to advertising in many ways. First, although people both inside and outside government were opposed to commercial support for the new medium, the general public had no great opposition to radio ads. In fact, in the prosperous Roaring Twenties, many welcomed them; advertising seemed a natural way to keep radio "free." Second, advertising agencies virtually took over broadcasting, producing the shows in which their commercials appeared. The ad business became show business. The 1923 variety show *The Eveready Hour*, sponsored by a battery maker, was the first regularly broadcast sponsored series. Ad agency Blackett-Sample-Hummert even developed a new genre for its client Proctor & Gamble—the radio soap opera. Finally, money now poured into the industry. That money was used to expand research and marketing on a national scale, allowing advertisers access to sophisticated nationwide consumer and market information for the first time. The wealth that the advertising industry accrued from radio permitted it to survive during the Depression.

A Plymouth hard-sell ad from 1931. The hard sell made its debut during the Depression as advertisers worked to attract the little consumer money that was available.

The Depression did have its effect on advertising, however. The stock market crashed in 1929, and by 1933 advertising had lost nearly two thirds of its revenues. Among the responses were the hard sell—making direct claims about why a consumer *needed* a product—and a tendency away from honesty. At the same time, widespread unemployment and poverty bred a powerful consumer movement. The Consumers Union, which still publishes *Consumer Reports*, was founded in 1936 to protect people from unscrupulous manufacturers and advertisers. And in 1938 Congress passed the Wheeler-Lea Act, granting the FTC extended powers to regulate advertising.

...Yank friendliness comes back to Leyte

Naturally Filipinos thrilled when their Yankee comrades-in-arms came back to the Philippines. Freedom came back with them. Fair play took the place of fear. But also they brought back the old sense of friendliness that America stands for. You find it quickly expressed in the simple phrase *Have a Coke*. There's no easier or warmer way to say *Relax and be yourself*. Everywhere *the pause that*

refreshes with ice-cold Coca-Cola has become a symbol of good will—an everyday example of how Yankee friendliness follows the flag around the globe.

*　　*　　*

Our fighting men meet up with Coca-Cola many places overseas, where it's bottled on the spot. Coca-Cola has been a globe-trotter "since way back when".

"Coke" = Coca-Cola

You naturally hear Coca-Cola called by its friendly abbreviation "Coke". Both mean the quality product of The Coca-Cola Company.

-the global high-sign

COPYRIGHT 1945, THE COCA-COLA COMPANY

WORLD WAR II

The Second World War, so important in the development of all the mass media, had its impact on advertising as well. Production of consumer products came to a near halt during the war (1941–1945), and traditional advertising was limited. The advertising industry turned its collective skills toward the war effort, and the limited product advertising typically adopted a patriotic theme.

In 1941 several national advertising and media associations joined to develop the War Advertising Council. The council used its expertise to promote numerous government programs. Its best-known campaign, however, was on behalf of the sale of war bonds. The largest campaign to date for a single item, the war bond program helped sell 800 million bonds,

Saving the Grand Canyon

Advertising can often move people to do good. Robert Glatzer (1970) recounts the story of how advertising saved the Grand Canyon. In 1966 the Bureau of Reclamation of the U.S. Department of the Interior sought congressional approval to build two dams on the Colorado River that would back water up 100 miles, creating a vast lake stretching upstream into the Grand Canyon. The lake would have ended at a spot just below the national park's stunning and justly famous South Rim. With a coalition of House and Senate members backing the plan, its passage was virtually assured.

David Brower, executive director of the Sierra Club, a small conservation group, was horrified. He went to advertising professionals Jerry Mander and Howard Gossage and asked their help in derailing the plan through advertising. Mander wrote the first ad, "Now Only You Can Save the Grand Canyon From Being Flooded—For Profit," and spent $10,000 to place it in the June 9 *New York Times* and *Washington Post.* Not only do these two papers have a sizable readership of educated people, but they are read by virtually every legislator and government official in Washington, D.C. Within 1 week, 3,000 new memberships had flowed into the Sierra Club. At $14 each, they boosted the available campaign funds—at the time down to $8,000—to $50,000.

A second effect of the ad was that by noon of the day it appeared, the Internal Revenue Service announced that it would investigate, and possibly revoke, the tax-exempt status of the Sierra Club for its "substantial" political activity. It was the first time the IRS had taken such an action against a nonprofit group. In response, thousands of new members joined to support the club in the months that followed.

In July Mander penned an eloquent, now famous ad that he placed in a number of intellectual magazines, from *The National Review* on the political right to *Ramparts* on the left. Almost immediately *Scientific American* and dozens of other magazines and newspapers asked permission to reprint the ad at no cost to the Sierra Club. The piece generated enough money for Mander and Gossage to buy a third ad in the *Times.*

Did the ads make a difference? Several congresspeople reported that the volume of mail they received on this issue exceeded that on all other topics, including the war in Vietnam. Sierra Club membership reached 50,000, and the club received more than a quarter of a million dollars in new memberships and gifts. These events combined to make it a political power. When the allocation of money for the dams finally came to a vote in the spring of 1967, it was defeated in the Senate 70 to 12.

---

totaling $45 billion. When the war ended, the group, now called the Advertising Council, directed its efforts toward a host of public service campaigns on behalf of countless nonprofit organizations (see the box "Saving the Grand Canyon"). Most of us have read or heard, "This message is brought to you by the Ad Council."

Ad Council
www.
adcouncil.org

The impact of World War II on the size and structure of the advertising industry was significant. A high excess-profits tax was levied on manufacturers' wartime profits that exceeded prewar levels. The goal was to limit war profiteering and ensure that companies did not benefit too greatly from the death and destruction of war. Rather than pay the heavy tariff, manufacturers reduced their profit levels by putting income back into their businesses. Because the lack of raw materials made expansion or recapitalization difficult, many companies invested in corporate image advertising. They may not have had products to sell to the public, but they knew that the war would end someday and that stored-up goodwill would be important. One result, therefore, was an expansion in the number and size of manufacturers' advertising departments and of advertising agencies. A second result was a public primed by that advertising anticipating the return of consumer goods.

Among the earliest demonstration ads, Timex took many a licking but kept on ticking.

ADVERTISING AND TELEVISION

There was no shortage of consumer products when the war ended. The nation's manufacturing capacity had been greatly expanded to meet the needs of war, and now that manufacturing capability was turned toward the production of consumer products for people who found themselves with more leisure and more money (Chapter 2). People were also having more children and, thanks to the GI Bill, were able to think realistically about owning their own homes. They wanted products to enhance their leisure, please their children, and fill their houses.

Advertising was well positioned to put products and people together, not only because agencies had expanded during the war but also because of television. Radio formats, stars, and network structure had moved wholesale to the new medium. Television soon became the primary national advertising medium. Advertisers bought $12 million in television time in 1949; 2 years later they spent $128 million.

Television commercials, by virtue of the fact that consumers could see and hear the product in action, were different from the advertising of all other media. The ability to demonstrate the product—to do the torture test for Timex watches, to smoothly shave sandpaper with Gillette Foamy—led to the **unique selling proposition (USP)**—that is, highlighting the aspect of a product that sets it apart from other brands in the same product category. Once an advertiser discovered a product's USP, it could drive it home in repeated demonstration commercials. Inasmuch as most brands in a given product category are essentially the same—that is, they are **parity products**—advertisers were often forced to create a product's USP. Candy is candy, for example, but M&Ms are unique—they melt in your mouth, not in your hand.

Some observers were troubled by this development. Increasingly, products were being sold not by touting their value or quality but by emphasizing their unique selling propositions. Ads were offering little information about the product, yet people were increasing their spending. This led to growing criticism of advertising and its contribution to the consumer culture (more on this controversy later in the chapter). The immediate impact was the creation of an important vehicle of industry self-regulation. In response to mounting criticism in books such as *The Hidden Persuaders* (Packard, 1957), and concern over increasing scrutiny from the FTC, the industry in 1971 established the National Advertising Review Board (NARB) to monitor potentially deceptive advertising. The NARB, the industry's most important self-regulatory body, investigates consumer complaints as well as complaints made by an advertiser's competitors.

THE EVOLUTION OF TELEVISION COMMERCIALS

The history of television commercials themselves is interesting because it highlights the interdependence between medium and advertising message. We saw in Chapter 8 how advertisers and their ad agencies produced early television shows, only to lose that function after the quiz show scandal in 1959. Once advertisers no longer owned program content, it became impossibly expensive to be the sole sponsor of a network broadcast. The networks were demanding a great deal of money to offset their investment in a program. In this climate it was more efficient and more profitable for advertisers to spread commercials across a number of programs, reaching many more viewers. The networks, profiting from this new state of affairs, began selling commercial time in 60-second segments. With many different "spot" commercials for many different products in the same show, the nature of the commercials themselves changed. A spot had to stand out and be remembered—greater creativity came to television advertising.

In addition, because a number of commercials in an individual program or on a given night of television were selling the same or similar products, and because many of these products were essentially the same in quality and cost, the USP became even more important, as did the need to boost **brand awareness**—identification of a product with a particular manufacturer. Brand identification was achieved through slogans and jingles: "You'll wonder where the yellow went when you brush your teeth with Pepsodent."

In television's early days commercials were highly product-oriented. This focus changed, however, as a result of government regulation of cigarette companies, then television's biggest advertisers. Responding to mounting challenges from health groups, in 1971 the FCC banned cigarette commercials from the airwaves. With the loss of this important

Television Advertising Bureau
www.
tvb.org

category of advertisers, the networks quickly discovered that too few advertisers could afford to buy a 60-second spot on a popular prime-time program.

Lowering the price of advertising time was a possible solution, but rising production costs for network shows made this difficult. In 1953, for example, a 1-hour episode of *Studio One* cost CBS $30,000 to produce. In 1975, *Gunsmoke* cost that same network $230,000 for 1 hour. The networks' solution was to split the 60-second spots into more affordable 30-second segments. Now an even greater number of advertisers could afford television. At the same time, the networks could make more money by selling two 30-second spots at more than the price of one full minute. Each minute of advertising time became more profitable. The networks had solved *their* problem, but advertisers had a new one—their commercials were now aired among twice as many competing messages. In 1965 every network television commercial was a full 60 seconds, although 23% were **piggybacked** (that is, a single sponsor presented two products in the same minute). By 1975 only 6% were a full minute long.

The number of commercial spots grew, and so too did the number of commercial minutes allowed on television. In 1967, for example, there were an estimated 100,000 commercial minutes aired on the networks. By 1974 there were 105,622 commercial minutes—5,600 *additional* minutes on the three commercial networks alone. As the number of spots grew and their length shrank, commercials became less about the products—there was too little time to give any relevant information—and more about the people who use them. Image advertising came to television.

Today the price of commercial time continues to rise, production costs for programming continue to increase, the number of commercials on the air continues to grow, the air time available for advertising continues to expand, and as a result, the length of commercial spots continues to shrink. Fifteen- and even 10-second spots are now common. One-second spots, **blink ads,** now appear on some stations and networks (Christopher, 1998). More and more spots crammed into a commercial break produces **clutter** (see Figure 12.1). How does an advertiser get heard and seen above

Figure 12.1 Length of Television Commercials, 2002. The vast majority of television commercials, 91.8%, are 30 seconds or shorter. *Source:* Television Advertising Bureau, 2002.

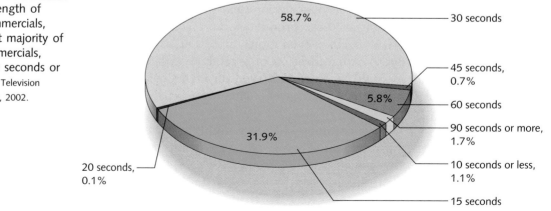

58.7% — 30 seconds
45 seconds, 0.7%
5.8% — 60 seconds
90 seconds or more, 1.7%
10 seconds or less, 1.1%
31.9%
20 seconds, 0.1%
15 seconds

the clutter? The answer for many contemporary television advertisers is to give even less information about the product and place greater emphasis on style, image, graphics, and look. Today's television ads can cost as much as $1 million a minute to produce.

Advertising and Its Audiences

The typical individual living in the United States will spend more than one year of his or her life just watching television commercials. It is a rare moment when we are not in the audience of some ad or commercial. This is one of the many reasons advertisers have begun to place their messages in many venues beyond the traditional commercial media (called **ambient advertising**), hoping to draw our attention. We confront so many ads every day that we overlook them, and they become invisible. As a result, many people become aware of advertising only when it somehow offends them.

Better Business Bureau's Ad Division
www.
bbb.org/advertising

CRITICISMS AND DEFENSES OF ADVERTISING

Advertising does sometimes offend, and it is often the focus of criticism. But industry defenders argue that:

- Advertising supports our economic system; without it new products could not be introduced and developments in others could not be announced. Competitive advertising of new products and businesses powers the "engine" of our economy, fostering economic growth and creating jobs in many industries.
- People use advertising to gather information before making buying decisions.
- Ad revenues make possible the "free" mass media we use not only for entertainment but for the maintenance of our democracy.
- By showing us the bounty of our capitalistic, free enterprise society, advertising increases national productivity (as people work harder to acquire more of these products) and improves the standard of living (as people actually acquire more of these products).

The first defense is a given. Ours is a capitalistic society whose economy depends on the exchange of goods and services. Complaints, then, have less to do with the existence of advertising than with its conduct and content, and they are not new. At the 1941 founding meeting of the Advertising Council, J. Walter Thompson executive James Webb Young argued that such a public service commitment would go far toward improving the public's attitude toward his industry, one "rooted very deep. It is a sort of repugnance for the manifestations of advertising—or its banality, its bad taste, its moronic appeals, and its clamor" (quoted in "Story of the Ad

Council," 2001). The second defense assumes that advertising provides information. But much—critics would say most—advertising is void of useful information about the product. Grant Leach, managing director of the ad agency The Revo Group, declares, "Consumers no longer buy products but rather lifestyles and the stories, experiences, and emotions products convey" (quoted in Williams, 2002, p. 17). The third defense assumes that the only way media can exist is through commercial support, but many nations around the world have built fine media systems without heavy advertiser support (see Chapter 15). To critics of advertising, the fourth defense—that people work hard only to acquire more things and that our standard of living is measured by what material things we have—draws an unflattering picture of human nature.

SPECIFIC COMPLAINTS

Antitobacco Advertising
www.
badadvertising.org

Specific complaints about advertising are that it is often intrusive, deceptive, and, in the case of children's advertising, inherently unethical. Advertising is said to demean or corrupt the culture.

Advertising Is Intrusive   Many critics fault advertising for its intrusiveness. Advertising is everywhere, and it interferes with and alters our experience. Giant wall advertisements change the look of cities. Ads beamed by laser light onto night skies destroy evening stargazing. School learning aids provided by candy makers that ask students to "count the Tootsie Rolls" alter education. Many Internet users complain about the commercialization of the new medium and fear advertising will alter its free, open, and freewheeling nature.

Advertising Is Deceptive   Many critics say that much advertising is inherently deceptive in that it implicitly and sometimes explicitly promises to improve people's lives through the consumption or purchase of a sponsor's products. Jamieson and Campbell (1997) described this as the "If . . . then" strategy: "A beautiful woman uses a certain brand of lipstick in the ad, and men follow her everywhere. Without making the argument explicit, the ad implies that if you use this product you will be beautiful, and if you are beautiful (or use this product), you will be more attractive to men" (p. 242). They called the opposite strategy "If not . . . then not." When Hallmark says "When you care enough to send the very best," the implication is that when you do not send Hallmark you simply do not care.

Advertising promises health, long life, sexual success, financial success, companionship, popularity, and acceptance. Industry defenders argue that people understand and accept these as allowable exaggerations, not as deception.

Advertising Exploits Children   The average child sees more than 30,000 television commercials and magazine ads a year; ads increasingly appear even on school materials (Consumers Union, 2000). Critics contend that

This gym may be the home of Cougar pride, but it is also home to a large Wendy's ad. Advertising in schools and on educational materials is now common—and quite controversial.

children are simply not intellectually capable of interpreting the intent of these ads, nor are they able before the age of 7 or 8 to rationally judge the worth of the advertising claims (see the box "Boosting Smoking among Children" on p. 392). This makes children's advertising inherently unethical. Television advertising to kids is especially questionable because children consume it in the home—with implicit parental approval, and most often without parental supervision. The question ad critics ask is, "If parents would never allow living salespeople to enter their homes to sell their children products, why do they allow the most sophisticated salespeople of all to do it for 20 minutes every hour every Saturday morning?" Rowan Williams, upon his installation as Archbishop of Canterbury in 2002, spoke not of the ethics of advertising to kids but of the morality. "If a child is a consumer, the child is an economic subject. And what economic subjects do is commit their capital, limit their options by doing so, take risks for profit or gratification." His argument, according to education writer Laura Barton (2002, p. 2), is that "at a time in our lives when the future should be wide open (that is, childhood), we are increasingly encouraged to hem ourselves in, to define ourselves by the trainers [sneakers] we wear and the yogurts we eat. As such, advertising campaigns aimed directly at children amount to a perversion of innocence."

Advertising Demeans and Corrupts Culture   In our culture we value beauty, kindness, prestige, family, love, and success. As human beings we need food, shelter, and the maintenance of the species, in other words, sex. Advertising succeeds by appealing to these values and needs. The basis for this persuasive strategy is the **AIDA approach**—to persuade

Boosting Smoking among Children

In the 1980s as U.S. levels of smoking continued to decline, RJR Nabisco introduced a new ad campaign for its Camel brand cigarettes. The campaign featured a sun-bleached, cool, and casual camel who possessed human qualities. Joe Camel, as he was called, was debonair, in control, and the center of attention, whether in a pool hall, on a dance floor, leaning against his convertible, or lounging on the beach. He wore the hippest clothes. He sported the best sunglasses. RJR Nabisco said it was trying a new campaign to boost brand awareness and corner a larger portion of a dwindling market. But anti-smoking groups saw in Joe Camel the echo of Edward Bernays's strategy to open smoking to an untapped market (Chapter 11). They accused the company of attempting to attract young smokers—often adding that these were the lifelong customers the tobacco company needed to replace those it was killing.

The battle heated up in 1991, and an entire issue of the *Journal of the American Medical Association* was devoted to the impact of smoking on the culture. One of the articles reported on a study of Joe Camel's appeal to youngsters. Researcher Dr. Joseph DiFranza had discovered that Joe Camel was the single most recognizable logo in the country. Children as young as 3 years old could recognize Joe, and more kids could identify him than could identify Mickey Mouse.

RJR Nabisco attempted to discredit the study and its author and claimed that it had a First Amendment right to advertise its legal product any way it wanted. Nonetheless, soon after the publication of the *JAMA* issue, anti-smoking activist Janet Mangini filed a lawsuit in San Francisco against the tobacco company. Several California counties and cities joined the suit, alleging that the Joe Camel campaign violated state consumer protection laws designed to protect minors from false or misleading tobacco advertising.

Just before it was to go to trial in 1997, the country's second largest tobacco company, while admitting no wrongdoing, agreed to settle out of court with a payment

Joe Camel was ubiquitous . . . and controversial.

of $10 million. It also agreed to a court order to suspend the Joe Camel campaign, the first time in history that a tobacco company had done so. What may have encouraged the cigarette company to cooperate were internal memos in the hands of the court that would later be made public. An R. J. Reynolds Tobacco memo from 1975 said: "To ensure increased and long-term growth for Camel Filter, the brand must increase its share penetration among the 14–24 age group" ("Kids Are Getting Lost," 1998, p. 10A). Other memos identified target smokers as young as 12 years old.

Edward Bernays said that had he known about the health risks involved with smoking he would not have planned the Lucky Strike "Torches of Liberty" campaign back in 1929. What justification for the Joe Camel campaign would you give if you were part of the ad team that developed the character, or if you worked for an ad agency that placed the ads, or if you were the editor at a magazine that ran them?

consumers, advertising must attract *attention,* create *interest,* stimulate *desire,* and promote *action.* According to industry critics, however, problems arise when important aspects of human existence are reduced to the consumption of brand-name consumer products. Freedom is choosing between a Big Gulp and a canned soda at 7-Eleven. Being a good mother is as simple as buying a bottle of Downy Fabric Softener. Prestige is driving an Oldsmobile. Success is drinking Chivas Regal. Love is giving your husband a shirt without ring-around-the-collar or your fiancée a diamond

Large advertisers such as Nike have come under much criticism for their intrusion into virtually all aspects of people's lives. Here Garry Trudeau ponders life on Planet Nike.

worth 2 months' salary (see the box "Challenging Advertising: Adbusters and Uncommercials").

Critics argue that ours has become a **consumer culture**—a culture in which personal worth and identity reside not in ourselves but in the products with which we surround ourselves. The consumer culture is corrupting because it imposes new definitions that serve the advertiser and not the culture on traditionally important aspects of our lives. If love, for example, can be bought rather than being something that has to be nurtured, how important can it be? If success is not something an individual values for the personal sense of accomplishment but rather is something chased for the material things associated with it, how does the culture evaluate success? Name the five most successful people you know. How many teachers did you name? How many social workers? How many wealthy or famous people did you name?

Advertising critics fear that our growing consumer culture will produce people who define their self-worth and personal identity by the products they own rather than by who they are, as portrayed in this *Jump Start* cartoon.

Challenging Advertising: Adbusters and Uncommercials

The Media Foundation operates out of Vancouver, British Columbia, with the goal of increasing public awareness of overconsumption and overcommercialization. Naturally, advertising is one of its primary targets. The group publishes a quarterly magazine called *Adbusters,* maintains an active Web site (http://www.adbusters.org), and sponsors events like the annual late-November "Buy Nothing Day" and the mid-April "TV Turnoff Week" (26 state governors officially endorsed this event in 1997). The group also makes print and video "uncommercials" (public service announcements that challenge well-known actual commercials), which are available at no cost to those who wish to use them to, as the Media Foundation likes to call it, "culturejam," or challenge the prevailing commercial culture.

Sometimes this anticommercial advocacy has trouble getting its ideas into the cultural forum. All four major American television networks and all the commercial networks of both Australia and France refuse to sell airtime to the group for its 30-second uncommercials announcing Buy Nothing Day and TV Turnoff Week, despite its willingness to pay full commercial rates. NBC's vice president for advertising standards Richard Gitter told *The Wall Street Journal,* "We don't want the business. We don't want to take any advertising that's inimical to our legitimate business interests" (quoted in Media Foundation, 2002). In a letter to the Media Foundation, the General Electric–owned network explained its position more fully, saying that Buy Nothing Day "is in opposition to the current economic policy in the United States" (quoted in Media Foundation, 2002). A spokesperson for Australian television was more

to the point, asking the foundation, "Who do you think you are, trying to harm our business? Do you think we're stupid? Why would we agree to air an ad our advertisers might not like?" (quoted in Media Foundation).

Other times, however, the Media Foundation has had more success. CNN willingly carries the foundation's spots. After 30 seconds of Media Foundation–sponsored blank screen during a 2001 airing of *Wolf Blitzer Reports,* network spokesperson Steven Haworth explained, "We should make our commercial space available to debate issues of the day" (Media Foundation, 2002). In the fall of 1997 the foundation was the subject of an hour-long PBS documentary called *Affluenza.* Its Joe Chemo uncommercials and antismoking posters (parodying Joe Camel) appear in thousands of stores, schools, medical and health offices, and other public places. Many cable access stations run the uncommercials, and they occasionally appear on local commercial stations as well.

Whether or not you believe this effort is effective or even necessary, if you believe in freedom of expression, you have to ask yourself whether it is proper for the commercial television networks to refuse to carry Media Foundation uncommercials. Overcommercialization is a sometimes controversial public issue. If broadcasters feel comfortable refusing to air a side of the debate that they feel is "inimical" to their "legitimate business interests," several questions arise. First, what other expressions do they deny because they run counter to their business interests? Second, if broadcasters refuse to air material that challenges a "current policy" of the nation, as many did before the invasion

Critics contend that the consumer culture also demeans the individuals who live in it. A common advertising strategy for stimulating desire and suggesting action is to imply that we are inadequate and should not be satisfied with ourselves as we are. We are too fat or too thin, our hair is in need of improvement, our clothes are all wrong, and our spouses don't respect us. Personal improvement is only a purchase away.

Ad Forum
www.
adforum.com

The ad-created consumer culture, according to former Wieden + Kennedy and Martin Agency executive Jelly Helm (his clients include Nike, Coke, and Microsoft), has produced an America that is "sick. . . . We work too hard so that we can buy things we don't need, made by factory workers who are paid too little, and produced in ways that threaten the very survival of the earth." It has produced an America that "will be remembered as the greatest wealth-producer ever. It will be a culture remembered for its promise and might and its tremendous achievements in technology

Images courtesy of www.adbusters.org.

of Iraq in rejecting anti-war spots (Tienowitz, 2003), how will democratic debate over any significant issues ever enter the public forum? Finally, what issue *will ever* be discussed if broadcasters refuse to air material that their advertisers might not like? Measure the attitudes of the NBC and Australian television executives against that of the man from CNN. With which are you most comfortable? Which promises to serve the cultural forum (and therefore democracy) better? What, ask the activists at the Media Foundation, will you do about it? At the very minimum, are you willing to buy nothing during the Friday after Thanksgiving or turn your television off for a week? Why or why not?

and health. It also will be remembered as a culture of hedonism to rival any culture that has ever existed, a culture of materialism and workaholism and individualism, a culture of superficiality and disposability, of poverty and pollution and vanity and violence, a culture denuded of its spiritual wisdom" (Helm, 2002).

Scope and Nature of the Advertising Industry

The proliferation of the different types of sales pitches described in the opening vignette is the product of an avalanche of advertising. Advertisers are exploring new ways to be seen and heard, to stand out, to be remembered, and to be effective. With so many kinds of commercial messages, the definition of advertising must be very broad. For our purposes, advertising is mediated messages paid for by and identified with a business or

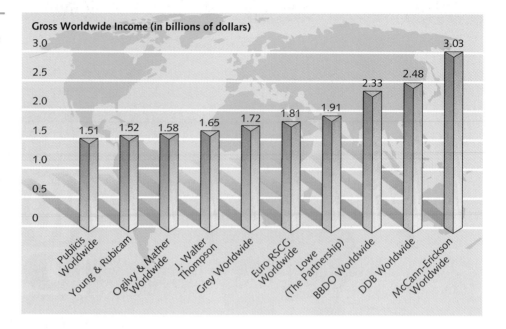

Figure 12.2 Largest U.S. Ad Agencies, 2001. *Source:* Adage.com, 2002.

Gross Worldwide Income (in billions of dollars)

Publicis Worldwide	1.51
Young & Rubicam	1.52
Ogilvy & Mather Worldwide	1.58
J. Walter Thompson	1.65
Grey Worldwide	1.72
Euro RSCG Worldwide	1.81
Lowe (The Partnership)	1.91
BBDO Worldwide	2.33
DDB Worldwide	2.48
McCann-Erickson Worldwide	3.03

American Association of Advertising Agencies
www.
aaaa.org

institution that seeks to increase the likelihood that those who consume those messages will act or think as the advertiser wishes.

In 2002 advertisers spent over $236 billion to place their messages before the U.S. public, more than $400 billion to reach the world's consumers. These amounts do not include the billions of dollars spent in the planning, production, and distribution of those ads. An overwhelming proportion of all this activity is conducted through and by advertising agencies.

THE ADVERTISING AGENCY

There are approximately 6,000 ad agencies operating in the United States, employing roughly half a million people (Figure 12.2). Fewer than 500 agencies annually earn more than $1 million. Many agencies also produce the ads they develop, and virtually all buy time and space in various media for their clients. Production is billed at an agreed-upon price called a **retainer;** placement of advertising in media is compensated through **commissions,** typically 15% of the cost of the time or space. Commissions account for as much as 75% of the income of larger agencies.

Ad agencies are usually divided into departments, the number determined by the size and services of the operation. Smaller agencies might contract with outside companies for the services of these typical ad agency departments:

- *Administration* is the agency's management and accounting operations.
- *Account management* is typically handled by an account executive who serves as liaison between agency and client, keeping communication

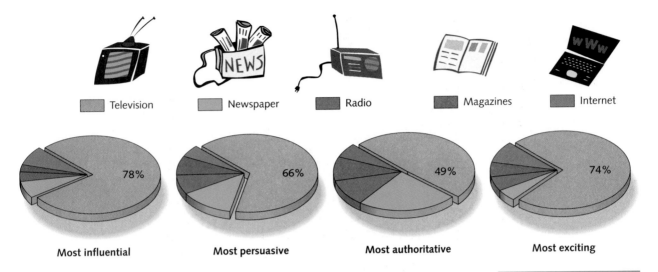

| Television | Newspaper | Radio | Magazines | Internet |

Most influential 78% **Most persuasive** 66% **Most authoritative** 49% **Most exciting** 74%

flowing between the two and heading the team of specialists assigned by the agency to the client.

- The *creative department* is where the advertising is developed from idea to ad. It involves copywriting, graphic design, and often the actual production of the piece, for example radio, television, and Web spots.

- The *media department* makes the decisions about where and when to place ads and then buys the appropriate time or space (see Figure 12.3). The effectiveness of a given placement is judged by its **cost per thousand (CPM),** the cost of reaching 1,000 audience members. For example, an ad that costs $20,000 to place in a major newspaper and is read by 1 million people has a CPM of $20.

- *Market research* tests product viability in the market, the best venues for commercial messages, the nature and characteristics of potential buyers, and sometimes the effectiveness of the ads.

- As we saw in Chapter 11, many larger agencies have *public relations departments* as well.

TYPES OF ADVERTISING

The advertising produced and placed by ad agencies can be classified according to the purpose of the advertising and the target market. Some types of advertising you may be familiar with include:

> *Institutional or corporate advertising.* Companies do more than just sell products; companies also promote their names and reputations. If a company name inspires confidence, selling its products is easier. Some institutional or corporate advertising promotes only the organization's image, such as "FTD Florists support the U.S. Olympic Team." But some advertising sells the image at the same time it sells the product: "You can be sure if it's Westinghouse."

Figure 12.3 Image of Advertising in Major Media. How do consumers rate the different advertising media in terms of their influence, persuasiveness, authority, and excitement?
Source: Television Advertising Bureau, 2002, online.

Association of National Advertisers
www.
ana.net

Through this industrial ad, appearing in *Broadcasting & Cable Magazine,* a program syndicator hopes to sell its series to local stations.

"Get ready to howl!"
– Los Angeles Times

"It's irreverent, totally riotous and cheerfully rude."
– TV Guide

"Genius!"
– Entertainment Weekly

"This is one smart family comedy."
– USA Today

"Wickedly hilarious at every turn, much like its animated cousin, The Simpsons."
– San Francisco Chronicle

"Making sitcom history."
– Newsweek

"Unaccountably funny."
– New York Times

"It's full of belly laughs."
– Time Magazine

Malcolm in the Middle

AVAILABLE FALL 2004

great **ratings.** great **press.** great **opportunity.**

Advertising World
www.
advertising.utexas.edu/world

For more information on this topic, view *Advertising and Public Relations: Inside Ogilvy,* #6 on the CD *Media Tours.*

Trade or professional advertising. Typically found in trade and professional publications, messages aimed at retailers do not necessarily push the product or brand but rather promote product issues of importance to the retailer—volume, marketing support, profit potential, distribution plans, and promotional opportunities.

Retail advertising. A large part of the advertising we see every day focuses on products sold by retailers like Sears and Macy's. Ads are typically local, reaching consumers where they live and shop.

Promotional retail advertising. Typically placed by retailers, promotional advertising does not focus on a product but rather on a promotion, a special event held by a retailer. "Midnight Madness Sale" and "Back to School Sale" are two promotions that often benefit from heavy advertising, particularly in newspapers.

Industrial advertising. Advertising products and services directed toward a particular industry is usually found in industry trade publications. For example, *Broadcasting & Cable,* the primary trade magazine for the television industry, runs ads from program syndicators hoping to sell their shows to stations. It also runs ads from transmitter and camera manufacturers.

National consumer advertising. National consumer advertising constitutes the majority of what we see in popular magazines and on television. It is usually product advertising, commissioned by the manufacturer—McDonald's, Honda, Cheerios, Sony, Nike—aimed at potential buyers.

Direct market advertising. Product or service advertising aimed at likely buyers rather than at all consumers is called direct market

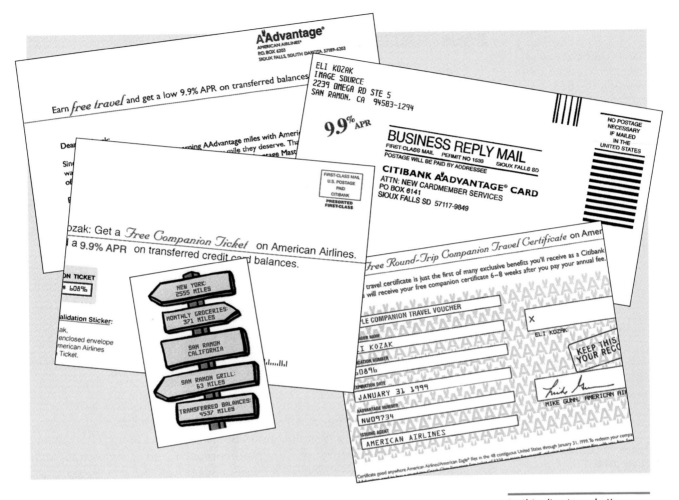

advertising. These targeted consumers are reached through direct mail, catalogues, and telemarketing. This advertising can be personalized—"Yes, BRUCE FRIEDBERG, you can drive a Lexus for less than you think"—and customized. Computer data from credit card and other purchases, zip codes, telephone numbers, and organizational memberships are a few of the ways consumers are identified.

Public service advertising. Advertising that does not sell commercial products or services but promotes organizations and themes of importance to the public is public service advertising. The Heart Fund, the United Negro College Fund, and ads for MADD are typical of this form. They are usually carried free of charge by the medium that houses them.

In this direct marketing package, the advertiser has not only personalized the pitch—Dear Eli Kozak—but targeted this consumer's particular interests in restaurants, travel, and other consumer goods and services. American Airlines reserves the right to change the AAdvantage program at any time without notice. American Airlines is not responsible for products or services offered by other participating companies.

THE REGULATION OF ADVERTISING

The FTC is the primary federal agency for the regulation of advertising. The FCC regulates the commercial practices of the broadcasting industry, and individual states can police deceptive advertising through their own regulatory and criminal bureaucracies. In the deregulation movement of 1980,

Public service advertising allows advertisers to use their skills to serve society. Here is a still from a spot for Doctors without Borders.

Commercial Production

Despite belt-tightening, blurbmeisters' shorthand tells stories in an increasingly imaginative way

Simple messages for tough times

Doc filmmakers eschew flash for honesty

By CHRIS GROVE

HOLLYWOOD Despite the often sky-high budgets, even higher concepts and a plethora of visual effects in many commercials these days, the most effective ads are usually the plain, old vanilla variety. You know, the ones with "real people," testimonials and simple my-toothpaste-is-better-than-yours appeals.

"Ninety percent of commercials are a waste of time," says James Twitchell, professor of

UNFLINCHING: *Marcel Langenegger's spot for Nobel Peace Prize-winning org Doctors Without Borders, which provides medical aid wherever needed, is a follow-up to Langenegger's Cannes Gold Lion-winning "Borderline." The agency is Advico/Young & Rubicam.*

Federal Trade Commission
www.
ftc.gov

oversight by the FTC changed from regulating unfair and deceptive advertising to regulating and enforcing complaints *against* deceptive advertising.

The FTC has several options for enforcement when it determines that an advertiser is guilty of deceptive practices. It can issue a **cease-and-desist order** demanding that the practice be stopped. It can impose fines. It can order the creation and distribution of **corrective advertising.** That is, a new set of ads must be produced by the offender that corrects the original misleading effort. Offenders can challenge FTC decisions in court, and they are innocent until proven guilty. Meanwhile, the potentially unethical advertising remains in the marketplace.

One of the greatest difficulties for the FTC is finding the line between false or deceptive advertising and **puffery**—that little lie that makes advertising more entertaining than it might otherwise be. "Whiter than white" and "stronger than dirt" are just two examples of puffery. On the assumption that the public does not read commercials literally—the Jolly Green Giant does not exist; we know that—the courts and the FTC allow a certain amount of exaggeration.

The FTC and courts, however, do recognize that an advertisement can be false in a number of ways. An advertisement is false if it:

- Lies outright. For years Wonder Bread was the bread that "builds strong bodies 12 ways." When the FTC asked Wonder Bread to name them, it could not. Listerine mouthwash was long advertised as "preventing colds and sore throats or lessening their severity." It does neither.

- Does not tell the whole truth. "Each slice of Profile Bread contains half the calories of other breads" was the claim of this brand. True, each slice did have about half the calories. But each slice was half as thick as a normal slice of bread.

- Lies by implication, using words, design, production device, sound, or a combination of these. Television commercials for children's toys now end with the product shown in actual size against a neutral background (a shot called an **island**). This is done because production techniques such as low camera angles and close-ups can make these toys seem larger or better than they actually are.

MEASURING THE EFFECTIVENESS OF ADVERTISING

It might seem reasonable to judge the effectiveness of an ad campaign by a subsequent increase in sales. But many factors other than advertising influence how well a product fares, including changes in the economy, product quality, breadth of distribution, and competitors' pricing and promotion strategies. As a result, "for most advertisers most of the time, the answer to the essential question, 'What are you getting for your advertising expenditure?' must be 'I'm not sure'"(Sandage et al., 1989, p. 370). Agency clients, however, find this a less than comforting response. Advertisers, therefore, turn to research to provide greater certainty.

A number of techniques may be used before an ad or ad campaign is released. **Copy testing**—measuring the effectiveness of advertising messages by showing them to consumers—is used for all forms of advertising. It is sometimes conducted with focus groups, collections of people brought together to see the advertising and discuss it with agency and client personnel. Sometimes copy testing employs **consumer juries.** These people, considered to be representative of the target market, review a number of approaches or variations of a campaign or ad. **Forced exposure,** used primarily for television advertising, requires advertisers to bring consumers to a theater or other facility (typically with the promise of a gift or other payment), where they see a television program, complete with the new commercials. People are asked their brand preferences before the show, and then after. In this way, the effectiveness of the commercials can be gauged.

Once the campaign or ad is before the public, a number of different tests can be employed to evaluate the effectiveness of the ad. In **recognition tests** people who have seen a given publication are asked, in person or by phone, whether they remember seeing specific ads. In **recall testing** consumers are asked, again in person or by phone, to identify which print or broadcast ads they most easily remember. This recall can be unaided, that is, the researcher offers no hints ("Have you seen any interesting commercials or ads lately?"), or aided, that is, the researcher identifies a specific class of products ("Have you seen any interesting pizza commercials lately?"). In recall testing, the advertisers assume that an easily recalled ad is an effective ad. **Awareness tests**

Adage
www.
adage.com

make this same assumption, but they are not aimed at specific ads. Their goal is to measure the cumulative effect of a campaign in terms of "consumer consciousness" of a product. A likely question in an awareness test, usually made by telephone, is: "What brands of laundry detergent can you name?"

What these research techniques lack is the ability to demonstrate the link that is of most interest to the client—did the ad move the consumer to buy the product? Their value lies in helping advertisers understand how people react to specific ads and advertising strategies, aiding advertisers in avoiding costly mistakes, and assisting advertisers in planning and organizing immediate and later campaigns.

Trends and Convergence in Advertising

For more information on this topic, see NBC Video Clip #20 on the CD—*Your Ad Here: Pizza Hut Places Billboard on Spacecraft.*

Many of the same forces reshaping the media industries are having an impact on the advertising industry as well.

NEW AND CONVERGING TECHNOLOGIES

The production of advertising has inevitably been altered by computers. Computer graphics, morphing (digitally combining and transforming images), and other special effects are now common in national retail television advertising. Computer databases and computerized printing have fueled the rapid growth of direct market advertising, and we saw in Chapter 5 that computerized printing has made possible zoned and other specialized editions of national magazines. But it is **cyberadvertising**—the convergence of print and broadcast advertising with the Internet—that has recently attracted a large amount of industry interest. In 1996 companies spent $300 million on online advertising; in 2002, $8.1 billion; and, according to industry estimates, that number was $9.2 billion in 2003 (see Figure 12.4; Gaffney, 2002).

Online advertising has matured over the last few years, moving well beyond static online billboards placed across the top (**banners**) or down the side (**skyscrapers**) of a Web page. Banners and skyscrapers represented 84% of all Web advertising in 2002 (Gaffney, 2002). Users today are likely to confront what the industry refers to as **contextual advertising,** that is, ads that automatically intrude into users' Web sessions whether wanted or not. Among this new breed of online advertising are:

- **interstitial ads**—images that appear on the screen and then disappear as users click from one page to the next
- **pop-outs**—ads that appear in a smaller window at the border of the Web page being read
- **extramercials**—columns of ad content that slide down over the page's content

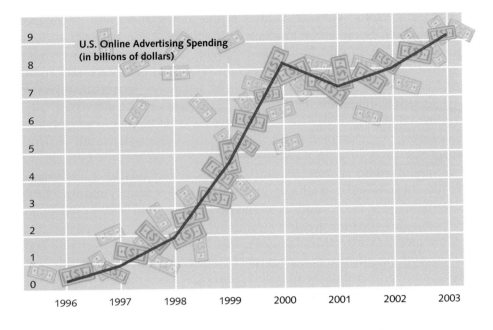

Figure 12.4 U.S. Online Advertising Spending.

Source: eMarketer: Interactive Advertising Bureau (Gaffney, 2002).

- **intermercials**—attractive, lively commercials that run while people wait for Web pages to download
- **targeted keyword buys**—ads that pop up on the screen every time a user types in a sponsor's name or other word or phrase
- **shoshkeles**—animated objects, like a car or Homer Simpson, that run across the screen (sometimes called **floating ads**)
- **large rectangles**—oversized ads that appear in the center of the page, over existing text
- **surround sessions**—users are served a steady stream of ads from one sponsor during their entire visit to a site
- **text ad**—ads that appear alongside search results that somehow relate to the search
- **advergames**—free, downloadable games that center on a sponsor's product (e.g., The Ford Truck Racing Experience) or have commercial product placements

We saw in Chapter 10 that online advertising was turning many Web users off, and Figure 12.3 suggests that online advertising is among the least effective and appreciated commercial forms. But the Net's true value to an advertiser is in its low cost and great reach (in other words, good CPM), excellent audience demographics, ability to target specific consumers with specific messages, and interactivity.

A final form of online advertising is **transaction journalism,** the direct linking of editorial content to sales, which takes several forms and is quite controversial. The *New York Times* online newspaper, for example, places links to bookseller barnesandnoble.com next to its book reviews. The *Times* gets paid every time a reader links from this page to

Adweek
www.
adweek.com

the Barnes & Noble Web site. Other online newspapers and magazines are even bolder. Some embed links to advertisers *in* the editorial content they run. Others sell specific stories or pages, for example sports or business, to advertisers; those advertisers naturally then have exclusive rights to all links from those pages. Still others sell users' search histories to advertisers. If sufficiently interested in a given user, the advertiser pays the online content provider for the right to have its banners and pop-outs appear on that user's screen as he or she searches through the site (Effron, 1999b).

As many online advertisers work to make their ads look and sound more like those found on radio and television, others are expanding a form of advertising that is far more at home on the Net than it is on radio and television—classified advertising.

Sites such as Classifieds.2000.com, match.com, and messagemates.com offer general classifieds. Kbb.com, cars.com, and autoweb.com sell cars. Monster.com, careerpath.com, and careermosaic.com present job listings. Realtor.com, homefair.com, and apartments.com list real estate.

In 1998, online classified advertising represented only 1.3% of the total of all print-based classified advertising and 14% of all online advertising. But industry experts predict that by 2003, online classifieds will make up 27% of all cyberadvertising (Stone, 1999) and one-third of all classified advertising, pulling in more than $6 billion a year (Brown, 1999).

INCREASED AUDIENCE SEGMENTATION

As the number of media outlets for advertising grows, and as audiences for traditional media are increasingly fragmented, advertisers have refined their ability to reach and speak to ever narrower audience segments. Computer technology facilitates this practice, but segmentation exists apart from the new technologies. The ethnic composition of the United States is changing, and advertising is keeping pace. African Americans constitute just over 12% of the total U.S. population, and

Critics of cyberadvertising may be correct in their prediction that the Internet will become little more than "more TV," but advertisers relish its reach, efficiency, and interactivity.

© 1997 The Washington Post Writers Group. Reprinted with permission.

The growing U.S. Hispanic population is increasingly targeted by advertisers, both in English and Spanish. Here, Latin diva Shakira sings the praises of Pepsi.

Hispanics 11%. The Census Bureau reports that middle- and upper-income African Americans and Hispanics are indistinguishable from Whites in terms of such economic indicators as home ownership and consumer purchasing. It also reports that the average household income for African Americans exceeded all previous levels and that that of Hispanic households was growing at a rate five times faster than that of all other citizens. The average rate of growth in household income for African Americans exceeds that of White households (Century, 2001). Asians and Pacific Islanders constitute the fastest-growing ethnic segment of the population, and 65% of the Native American population lives in the general community rather than on reservations. Together these groups control billions of dollars of discretionary income and are increasingly targeted by advertisers.

American Advertising Federation
www.
aaf.org

PSYCHOGRAPHICS

Demographic segmentation—the practice of appealing to audiences defined by varying personal and social characteristics such as race/ethnicity, gender, and economic level—has long been part of advertisers' strategy. But advertisers are making increased use of **psychographic segmentation**—that is, appealing to consumer groups with similar lifestyles, attitudes, values, and behavior patterns.

Psychographics entered advertising in the 1970s and is receiving growing attention as advertisers work to reach increasingly disparate consumers in increasingly segmented media. **VALS,** a psychographic segmentation strategy that classifies consumers according to values and lifestyles, is indicative of this lifestyle segmentation. Developed by SRI International, a California consulting company, VALS II divides consumers into eight VALS segments. Each segment is characterized by specific values and lifestyles, demographics, and, of greatest importance to advertisers, buying patterns (Television Advertising Bureau, 2002). The segments, including some of their demographic identifiers, are:

Actualizers: Like using their heads. Resent manipulation. They seek technical and social information to help them act responsibly.

Fulfilleds: Respect and appreciate authority. Are decidedly nonimpulsive. Serious and conservative.

Believers: Very traditional, holding strong home and family values. Ignore flash and style.

Achievers: Want every symbol of success. Seek the very best and work hard to pay for it.

Strivers: Look for ways to simplify their lives. Want directness in commercial appeals.

Experiencers: Self-centered, trendy, and demanding. Look for ways to meet *their* needs.

Makers: Self-sufficient, hardworking. Value is important.

Strugglers: Very cautious, having limited income. Tend to be suspicious.

GLOBALIZATION

Institute of Practitioners in Advertising
www.
ipa.co.uk

As media and national economies have globalized, advertising has adapted. Figure 12.5 shows the world's 10 largest ad organizations—agencies and their international subsidiaries (regardless of local name). U.S. agencies are increasingly merging with, acquiring, or affiliating with agencies from other parts of the world. In addition to the globalization of media and economies, a second force driving this trend is the demographic fact that today 80% of the world's population lives in developing countries. The advertising industry is prepared to put its clients in touch with these consumers. As Martin Sorrell, CEO of the WPP Group, the world's largest ad agency, explained, "Look, you've got 1 billion people in India, 1.3 billion in China. By 2014, two-thirds of the world's population will be in Asia" (quoted in Garland, 2002, p. 66).

DEVELOPING MEDIA LITERACY SKILLS
Interpreting Intentional Imprecision

Advertisers often use intentional imprecision in words and phrases to say something other than the precise truth, and they do so in all forms of advertising—profit and nonprofit, scrupulously honest and less so. There are three categories of intentional imprecision: unfinished statements, qualifiers, and connotatively loaded words and expressions.

We are all familiar with *unfinished statements,* such as the one for the battery that "lasts twice as long." Others include "You can be sure if it's Westinghouse," "Magnavox gives you more," and "Easy Off makes oven cleaning easier." A literate advertising consumer should ask, "Twice as long

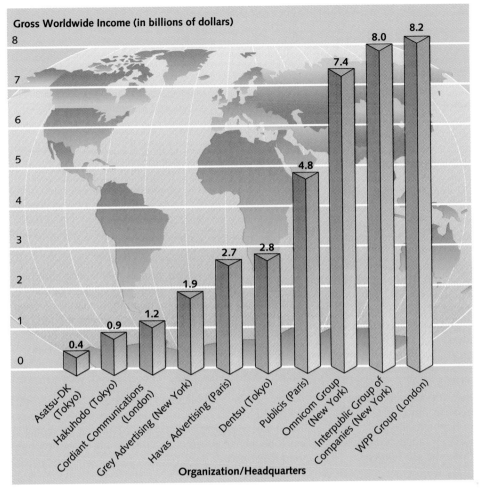

Gross Worldwide Income (in billions of dollars)

Figure 12.5 World's 10 Largest Ad Organizations, 2001. *Source:* Ad Age Data-place, online: <http://adage.com>.

Bars (left to right):
- Asatsu-DK (Tokyo): 0.4
- Hakuhodo (Tokyo): 0.9
- Cordiant Communications (London): 1.2
- Grey Advertising (New York): 1.9
- Havas Advertising (Paris): 2.7
- Dentsu (Tokyo): 2.8
- Publicis (Paris): 4.8
- Omnicom Group (New York): 7.4
- Interpublic Group of Companies (New York): 8.0
- WPP Group (London): 8.2

Organization/Headquarters

as *what*?" "Of *what* can I be sure?" "Gives me more of *what*?" "Easier than *what*?" Better, more, stronger, whiter, faster—all are comparative adjectives whose true purpose is to create a comparison between two or more things. When the other half of the comparison is not identified, intentional imprecision is being used to create the illusion of comparison.

Qualifiers are words that limit a claim. A product *helps* relieve stress, for instance. It may not relieve stress as well as rest and better planning and organization. But once the qualifier "helps" appears, an advertiser is free to make just about any claim for the product because all the ad really says is that it helps, not that it does anything in and of itself. It's the consumer's fault for misreading. A product that makes a task *virtually* effort-free is not one that saves you work. In fact, the qualifier "virtually" does not mean "almost" or "the same as"; it means "not the same as"—as in "virtual reality." A product may *fight* grime, but there is no promise that it will win. In the statement "Texaco's coal gasification process could mean you won't have to worry about how it affects the environment," "could" relieves the advertiser of all responsibility. "Could" does not mean "will." Moreover, the fact that you *could stop worrying about the environment* does

BadAds.org

An interesting fact about the Media Foundation and its Adbusters program (see the box "Challenging Advertising: Adbusters and Uncommercials") is that a large proportion of its members are themselves current or former advertising professionals. Some are critical of their profession, or at least its excesses, as are many of us. But some of these disaffected advertising practitioners recognize that advertising cannot be effective if it is not respected. Their membership in the Media Foundation, then, is an expression of their commitment to their profession. They want to preserve its effectiveness. You'll remember from earlier in the chapter that this sentiment played a part in the founding of the Ad Council.

Another activist group interested in improving advertising is BadAds.org (www.badads.org). Its particular targets are intrusive and deceptive advertising. This group attracts parents and teachers more than industry professionals. It maintains archives of what it considers bad ads, a BadAd Blog, links to other advertising activist sites, and discussions of advertising's excesses. It also provides how-to sections. For example, there are instructions on how parents should deal with their children when confronted by the kids' ad-fueled demands for specific brands or products (www.badads.org/teachers.shtml).

BadAds also offers advice on how to write an effective letter of complaint about a piece of advertising (www.badads.org/letter.shtml). Here's what its site suggests:

1. How? Choose your format: mail, fax, or e-mail; complete the company's online feedback form; or leave a message on the company president's voice mail.

2. Where? BadAds provides addresses of what it considers some of the more egregious ad offenders, and it provides links to *Hoovers* and *Big Yellow,* two national business directories.

3. Who? BadAds suggests that complaints *not* be sent to the customer service department. As it explains, "The big cheese (a.k.a chief executive officer, president, or chairman) has the most power to solve your problem. You can find out his or her name when you get the company address. While you may not hear from the CEO personally, you're more likely to get action than if you send your letter to anyone else."

4. What? Identify what you're complaining about and why you're upset. Offer a means of making it better (stop running the campaign, clean up the language, and so on). Explain what your next step is if you are not satisfied with the response. The Better Business Bureau or FTC or FCC. Spread your dissatisfaction to friends and family. Stop using the brand. But always be polite (and no typos). Thank the company for dealing with your complaint.

No one is neutral about advertising. We are often delighted by its successes, distressed by its excesses. These two organizations provide the means for media literate people to engage advertising and advertisers in a productive way.

not mean the product does not harm the environment—only that you could stop worrying about it.

Some qualifiers are more apparent. "Taxes not included," "limited time only," "only at participating locations," "prices may vary," "some assembly required," "additional charges may apply," and "batteries not included" are qualifiers presented after the primary claims have been made. Often these words are spoken quickly at the end of radio and television commercials, or they appear in small print on the screen or at the bottom of a newspaper or magazine ad.

Other qualifiers are part of the product's advertising slogan. Boodles gin is "the ultra-refined British gin that only the world's costliest methods could produce. Boodles. The world's costliest British gin." After intimating that the costliest methods are somehow necessary to make the best gin, this advertiser qualifies its product as the costliest "British" gin. There may be costlier, and possibly better, Irish, U.S., Russian, and Canadian gins. Many sugared children's cereals employ the tactic of displaying the cereal on a table with fruit, milk, and toast. The announcer says or the copy reads, "Coco Yummies are *a part of* this complete breakfast"—so is the tablecloth. But the cereal, in and of itself, adds little to the nutritional completeness of the meal. It is "a part of" it.

Advertising is full of words that are *connotatively loaded*. Best Western Hotels never has to explain what makes them "best." A *best-selling product* may not be the best in its product class, only the one with the best advertising campaign and distribution system. A product that has more of "the pain-relieving medicine doctors prescribe most" merely contains more aspirin. Products that are "cherry-flavored" have no cherries in them. A product that is high in "food energy" is in fact high in calories. Advertisers want consumers to understand the connotations of these words and phrases, not their actual meanings.

Intentional imprecision is puffery. It is not illegal; nor is it sufficiently troubling to the advertising industry to warrant self-regulatory limits. But puffery is neither true nor accurate, and its purpose is to deceive. This means that the responsibility for correctly and accurately reading advertising that is intentionally imprecise rests with the media literate consumer.

Chapter Review

Advertising has been practiced for thousands of years and came to the Colonies via England. Industrialization and the Civil War led to more leisure, more discretionary income, and greater urbanization and industrialization, all of which fueled the growth of advertising. Magazines provided a national medium for ads, and advertising agencies quickly developed to meet the needs of the industry's growing scale. As the industry matured during this time, it began to professionalize itself.

Radio moved advertising closer to show business and also allowed the industry to survive the Depression, a period in which advertising came under additional scrutiny from dollar-conscious consumers.

World War II reduced the number of consumer products that could be advertised, but advertising continued in the form of image advertising, another boon to the ad agency business. Then came television, which changed the nature of advertising content just as the commercials themselves changed the nature of the medium.

The 6,000 U.S. advertising agencies make money through retainers or commissions for placing ads. They have some or all of these departments: admin-istration, account management, creative, media, market research, and public relations. They place some or all of these types of ads: institutional or corporate, trade or professional, retail, promotional retail, industrial, national consumer, direct market, and public service. Advertisers judge the effectiveness of their work in a number of ways, but understanding the vital link between consumers' seeing the ad and their buying behavior is at best tenuous.

Agencies and the industry as a whole are being reshaped by new communication technologies, such as computerized databases, computerized printing, and online advertising. Audiences for advertising, as for most media, are increasingly fragmented along demographic and psychographic lines, and globalization has come to advertising as well.

Despite its central role in the U.S. economy, advertising is often criticized for being intrusive and deceptive, for unethically targeting children, and for debasing the culture. These criticisms are supported by citing the industry's practice of using words and phrases that do not mean what the audience is led to believe they mean.

Key Terms

Use the text's CD-ROM and the Online Learning Center at www.mhhe.com/baran to further your understanding of the following terminology.

siqui, 379

shopbill, 379

newsbook, 379

unique selling proposition (USP), 386

parity product, 387

brand awareness, 387

piggyback, 388

blink ad, 388

clutter, 388

ambient advertising, 389

AIDA approach, 391

consumer culture, 393

retainer, 396

commission, 396

cost per thousand (CPM), 397

cease-and-desist order, 400

corrective advertising, 400

puffery, 400

island, 401

copy testing, 401

consumer jury, 401

forced exposure, 401

recognition tests, 401

recall testing, 401

awareness test, 401

cyberadvertising, 402

banners, 402

skyscrapers, 402

contextual advertising, 402

interstitial ads, 402

pop-out, 402

extramercial, 402

intermercial, 403

targeted keyword buy, 403

shoshkeles (floating ad), 403

large rectangle, 403

surround session, 403

text ad, 403

advergames, 403

transaction journalism, 403

demographic segmentation, 405

psychographic segmentation, 405

VALS, 405

Questions for Review

Go to the self-quizzes on the CD-ROM and the Online Learning Center to test your knowledge.

1. Why are we seeing so many ads in so many new and different places?
2. What are siquis, shopbills, and newsbooks?
3. What impact did industrialization and the Civil War have on the advertising industry?
4. What impact did the coming of magazines, radio, and television have on the advertising industry?
5. What is USP? A parity product? Brand awareness? Piggybacking? Clutter?
6. Why do some people consider advertising to children unethical? Immoral?
7. What is the AIDA approach? The consumer culture?
8. In what ways can an ad be false?
9. What was the excess-profits tax? How did it benefit advertising agencies?
10. What are the departments in a typical advertising agency? What does each do?
11. What are the different categories of advertising and the goal of each?
12. What is a cease-and-desist order? Corrective advertising? Puffery?
13. What are copy testing, consumer juries, forced exposure, recognition tests, recall testing, and awareness tests? How do they differ?
14. What are banners, skyscrapers, interstitials, pop-outs, extramercials, transaction journalism, intermercials, shoshkeles, large rectangles, surround sessions, text ads, and targeted keyword buys? How do they differ?
15. What are demographic and psychographic segmentation?
16. How can words be used to deceive in advertising?

Questions for Critical Thinking and Reflection

1. If you owned an advertising agency, would you produce advertising aimed at children? Why, or why not?

2. If you were an FTC regulator, to what extent would you allow puffery? Where would you draw the line between deception and puffery? Give examples.

3. Do you think U.S. culture is overly materialistic? If you do, what role do you think advertising has had in creating this state of affairs? Do you find it surprising that much of the criticism of our consumer culture comes from people (Jelly Helm and Kalle Lasn, founder of the Media Foundation [see p. 394] are two examples) who are or were in the advertising industry? Why or why not?

4. Can you identify yourself among the VALS segments? If you can, how accurately does that segment describe your buying habits?
5. What do you think of contemporary television advertising? Are its creativity and technological sophistication adequate substitutes for information about the product?

Important Resources

Alfino, M., Caputo, J. S., & Wynard, R. (Eds.). (1998). *McDonaldization revisited: Critical essays on consumer culture.* **New York: Praeger.** A collection of essays from scholars representing different disciplines, different theoretical approaches, and different countries. Each examines the latest thinking about commercialism and the consumer culture.

Advertising Age. The self-proclaimed "international newspaper of marketing," this weekly tabloid examines advertising from both agency and media sides from a global perspective.

Adweek. The very latest in industry news with much insider information about advertising people and agencies. The magazine contains a lot of attractive and interesting ads for magazines and other media hoping to attract the business of its readers.

Journal of Advertising. This quarterly scientific journal publishes academic and scholarly articles on many aspects of advertising—legal issues, ethics, effects, practices, and ad effectiveness. Some essays are very technical, but many make for interesting, challenging reading.

Kern-Foxworth, M. (1994). *Aunt Jemima, Uncle Ben, and Rastus: Blacks in advertising, yesterday, today, and tomorrow.* **New York: Praeger.** As the title suggests, a detailed study of racial stereotyping in advertising. It provides important historical contexts, as well as an analysis of how the ad industry will handle this sensitive issue in the future.

Moses, E. (2000). *The $100 billion allowance: How to get your share of the global teen market.* **New York: John Wiley** and **Del Vecchio, G. (1997).** *Creating ever-cool: A marketer's guide to a kid's heart.* **New York: Penguin.** These two books offer an ad industry how-to for reaching kids. They are an excellent means to seeing how it is done and judging for yourself the merits of the different sides in the advertising-to-children debate.

Schudson, M. (1984). *Advertising, the uneasy persuasion: Its dubious impact on American society.* **New York: Basic Books.** Only a little dated, the classic critical examination of advertising's contribution to the consumer culture.

Advertising History	www.scriptorium.lib.duke.edu/hartman
Audit Bureau of Circulations	www.accessabc.com
National Advertising Review Board	www.bbb.org/advertising/narb.asp
American Advertising Federation	www.aaf.org
Ad Council	www.adcouncil.org
Television Advertising Bureau	www.tvb.org
Better Business Bureau's Ad Division	www.bbb.org/advertising
Antitobacco Advertising	www.badadvertising.org
Adbusters	www.adbusters.org
Ad Forum	www.adforum.com
American Association of Advertising Agencies	www.aaaa.org
Association of National Advertisers	www.ana.net

Advertising World	www.advertising.utexas.edu/world
Federal Trade Commission	www.ftc.gov
Adage	adage.com
Outdoor Advertising Association	www.oaaa.org
Adweek	www.adweek.com
American Advertising Federation	www.aaf.org
Institute of Practitioners in Advertising	www.ipa.co.uk

PART four

Mass-Mediated Culture in the Information Age

Theories and Effects of Mass Communication

TIMELINE

~1900–1938 Era of mass society theory

~1930s The Frankfurt School

1938 Welles's *War of the Worlds*

~1938–1945 Era of the scientific perspective on mass communication

1941 Office of War Information; persuasion studies

1945 Allport and Postman rumor study

~1945–1975 Era of limited effects theories

1955 Two-step flow

1960 Klapper's *The Effects of Mass Communication*/ reinforcement theory; Nixon/Kennedy debates

~1960s Social cognitive theory; symbolic interaction; social construction of reality; British Cultural Studies

~1970s Cultivation analysis

1972 Agenda setting; Surgeon General's Report on Television and Social Behavior

1975 Uses and gratifications; dependency theory

~1975–today Era of cultural theory

LEARNING OBJECTIVES

Media have effects. People may disagree about what those effects might be, but media do have effects. Advertisers would not spend billions of dollars a year to place their messages in the media if they did not have effects, nor would our Constitution, in the form of the First Amendment, seek to protect the freedoms of the media if the media did not have important consequences. We attempt to understand and explain these effects through mass communication theory. After studying this chapter you should

- be familiar with the history and development of mass communication theory.

- understand what is meant by theory, why it is important, and how it is used.

- be familiar with some of the most influential traditional and contemporary mass communication theories.

- be conversant in a number of controversial effects issues, such as violence, media's impact on drug and alcohol consumption, media's contribution to racial and gender stereotyping, and the media's impact on the electoral process.

- possess improved skill at applying mass communication theory to your own use of media.

"I KNOW THIS ISN'T LISTED ON THE SYLLABUS. BUT LET'S CALL IT A pop quiz." Your instructor has surprised you. "Will this count in our final grade?" you ask. You are seared by the professorial stare.

"Put everything away except a piece of paper and a pen."

You do as instructed.

"Number your paper from 1 to 6. Items 1 through 3 are true–false. One. Most people are just looking out for themselves. Two. You can't be too careful in dealing with people. Three. Most people would take advantage of you if they got the chance. Now, number four. How much television do you watch each week?"

Not too tough, you think, you can handle this.

Your prof continues, "You must answer number 5 out loud. What's the moon made of?"

You and several classmates respond, "Cheese!"

"Finally, number 6. Draw the outline of a dime as close to actual size as possible."

In this chapter we examine mass communication theory. After we define theory and discuss why it is important, we see how the various theories of mass communication that are prevalent today developed. We then study several of the most influential contemporary theories before we discuss the relationship between media literacy and mass communication theory. These theories and their application form the basis of our understanding of how media and culture affect one another, the effects of mass communication.

The Effects Debate

Whether the issue is online hate groups, televised violence, the absence of minority characters in prime-time television programming, or a decline in the quality of political discourse, the topic of the effects of mass communication is—and has always been—hotly debated. Later in this chapter we will take detailed looks at such effects issues as media's impact on violence, the use of drugs and alcohol, the nature of our political process, and stereotyping. But before we can examine specific effects issues, we must understand that there exists fundamental disagreement about the presence, strength, and operation of effects. Many people still hold to the position that media have limited or minimal effects. Here are their arguments, accompanied by their counterarguments.

1. *Media content has limited impact on audiences because it's only make-believe; people know it isn't real.*

The counterarguments: (a) News is not make-believe (at least it's not supposed to be), and we are supposed to take it seriously. (b) Most film and television dramas (for example, *CSI: Crime Scene Investigation* and *NYPD Blue*) are intentionally produced to seem real to viewers, with documentary-like production techniques such as handheld cameras and uneven lighting. (c) Much contemporary television is expressly *real*—reality shows such as *Cops* and *America's Most Wanted* and talk shows such as *The Jerry Springer Show* purport to present real people. (d) Advertising is supposed to tell the truth. (e) Before they develop the intellectual and critical capacity to know what is not real, children confront the world in all its splendor and vulgarity through television, what television effects researchers call the **early window.** To kids, what they see is real. (f) To enjoy what we consume, we **willingly suspend disbelief;** that is, we willingly accept as real what is put before us.

2. *Media content has limited impact on audiences because it is only play or just entertainment.*

The counterarguments: (a) News is not play or entertainment (at least it's not supposed to be). (b) Even if media content is only play,

The mirror that media hold up to culture is like a fun-house mirror—some things appear bigger than they truly are, some things appear smaller, and some disappear altogether.

play is very important to the way we develop our knowledge of ourselves and our world. When we play organized sports, we learn teamwork, cooperation, the value of hard work, obedience to authority, and respect for the rules. Why should play be any less influential if we do it on the Internet or at the movies?

3. *If media have any effects at all, they are not the media's fault; media simply hold a mirror to society and reflect the status quo, showing us and our world as they already are.*

The counterargument: Media hold a very selective mirror. The whole world, in all its vastness and complexity, cannot possibly be represented, so media practitioners must make choices. For example, according to the Parents Television Council, 47% of television's families are headed by married couples. The Census Bureau, however, tells us that in the real world, 72% of all families enjoy the presence of a mom and dad. On television, 14% of the families are headed by a single father. In the real world, 6% are (Elber, 2002). And when was the last time you saw a car explode in an accident? At best, media hold a fun-house mirror to society and distort what they reflect. Some things are overrepresented, others underrepresented, and still others disappear altogether.

4. *If media have any effect at all, it is only to reinforce preexisting values and beliefs. Family, church, school, and other socializing agents have much more influence.*

The counterarguments: (a) The traditional socializing agents have lost much of their power to influence in our complicated and fast-paced world. (b) Moreover, reinforcing effects are not the same as having no effects. If media can reinforce the good in our culture, media can just as easily reinforce the bad. Is racism eradicated yet? sexism? disrespect for others? If our media are doing no more than reinforcing the values and beliefs that already exist, then they are as empty as many critics contend. Former Federal Communications Commission member Nicholas Johnson has long argued of television in particular that the real crime is not what television is doing *to* us but what it could be doing *for* us, but isn't.

5. *If media have any effects at all, they are only on the unimportant things in our lives, such as fads and fashions.*

The counterarguments: (a) Fads and fashions are not unimportant to us. The car we drive, the clothes we wear, and the way we look help define us; they characterize us to others. In fact, it is media that have helped make fads and fashions so central to our self-definition and happiness. Kids don't kill other kids for their $150 basketball shoes because their mothers told them that Air Jordans were cool. (b) If media influence only the unimportant things in our lives, why are billions of dollars spent on media efforts to sway opinion about social issues such as universal health care, nuclear power, and global warming (Chapter 11)?

Defining Mass Communication Theory

Whether you accept the limited effects arguments or their counterarguments, all the positions you just read are based in one or more **mass communication theories,** explanations and predictions of social phenomena that attempt to relate mass communication to various aspects of our personal and cultural lives or social systems. Your responses to the six quiz questions that opened the chapter, for example, can be explained (possibly even predicted) by several different mass communication theories.

The first four items are a reflection of **cultivation analysis**—the idea that people's ideas of themselves, their world, and their place in it are shaped and maintained primarily through television. People's responses to the three true–false items can be fairly accurately predicted by the amount of viewing they do (question 4). The more people watch, the more likely they are to respond "true" to these unflattering comments about others.

Your response to the question about the moon's composition can be explained by a theory called **social construction of reality,** which argues that people learn to behave in their social world through interaction with it. In other words, people in a given society or culture communicate, using signs and symbols, to construct a common reality that allows them to act meaningfully and efficiently in different settings. Many of us said "cheese" because we respond according to the "reality" that we constructed using our media's stories. We know intellectually that the moon is not made of cheese, but in this quiz setting we respond not as we've been educated but as we've been enculturated.

The solution to the dime-drawing task is predicted by **attitude change theory.** Almost everyone draws the dime too small. Because a dime is an inconsequential coin, we perceive it as smaller than it really is, and our perceptions guide our behavior. Even though every one of us has real-world experience with dimes, our attitudes toward that coin shape our behavior regarding it.

To understand mass communication theory, you should recognize these important ideas:

1. As we've just seen, *there is no one mass communication theory.* There is a theory, for example, that describes something as grand as how we give meaning to cultural symbols and how these symbols influence our behavior (symbolic interaction), and there is a theory that explains something as individual as how media influence people in times of change or crisis (dependency theory). Mass communication theorists have produced a number of **middle-range theories** that explain or predict specific, limited aspects of the mass communication process (Merton, 1967).

2. *Mass communication theories are often borrowed from other fields of science.* The social construction of reality theory (the cheese question) comes from sociology. Attitude change theory (the dime question) is borrowed from psychology. Mass communication theorists adapt these borrowed theories to questions and issues in communication. People's behavior with regard to issues more important than the size of a dime—democracy, ethnicity, government, and gender roles, for example—is influenced by the attitudes and perceptions presented by our mass media.

3. *Mass communication theories are human constructions.* People create them, and therefore their creation is influenced by human biases—the times in which we live, the position we occupy in the mass communication process, and a host of other factors. Broadcast industry researchers, for example, have developed somewhat different theories to explain how violence is learned from television than have university researchers.

4. Because theories are human constructions and the environments in which they are created constantly change, *mass communication theories are dynamic;* they undergo frequent recasting, acceptance, and rejection. For example, theories that were developed before television and computer networks became mass media outlets have to be reexamined and sometimes discarded in the face of these new media.

A Short History of Mass Communication Theory

The dynamic nature of mass communication theory can be seen in its history. All bodies of knowledge pass through various stages of development. Hypotheses are put forth, tested, and proven or rejected. Eventually a uniform theory or **paradigm** results—that is, a theory that summarizes and is consistent with all known facts. However, over time, new facts come to light and our knowledge and understanding increase. This often leads to a **paradigm shift**—a fundamental, even radical, rethinking of what we believe to be true (Kuhn, 1970). Mass communication theory is particularly open to such paradigm shifts due to three factors:

■ *Advances in technology or the introduction of new media* fundamentally alter the nature of mass communication. The coming of radio and movies, for example, forced rethinking of theories based on a print-oriented mass communication system.

Agnes Ayers swoons in Rudolph Valentino's arms in the 1921 movie *The Sheik*. Mass society theorists saw such common entertainment fare as debasing the culture through its direct and negative effects on helpless audience members.

- *Calls for control or regulation* of these new technologies require, especially in a democracy such as ours, an objective, science-based justification.
- As a country committed to protecting *democracy and cultural pluralism*, we ask how each new technology or medium can foster our pursuit of that goal.

The paradigm shifts that have resulted from these factors have produced four major eras of mass communication theory: the era of mass society theory, the era of the scientific perspective, the era of limited effects theory, and the era of cultural theory. The first three may be considered early eras; the last is the era in which we currently find ourselves.

THE ERA OF MASS SOCIETY THEORY

As we've seen, several important mass media appeared or flourished during the second half of the 19th century and the first decades of the 20th century. Mass circulation newspapers and magazines, movies, talkies, and radio all came to prominence at this time. This was also a time of profound change in the nature of U.S. society. Industrialization and urbanization spread, African Americans and poor southern Whites streamed northward, and immigrants rushed across both coasts in search of opportunity and dignity. People in traditional seats of power—the clergy, politicians, and educators—feared a disruption in the status quo. The country's peaceful rural nature was beginning to slip further into history. In its place was a cauldron of new and different people with new and different habits, all crammed into rapidly expanding cities. Crime grew, as did social and political unrest. Many cultural, political, educational, and religious leaders thought the United States was becoming too pluralistic. They charged that the mass media catered to the low tastes and limited reading and language abilities of these newcomers by featuring simple and sensationalistic content. The media needed to be controlled to protect traditional values.

The successful use of propaganda by totalitarian governments in Europe, especially Germany's National Socialist Party (the Nazis), provided further evidence of the overwhelming power of media. Media needed to be controlled to prevent similar abuses at home.

The resulting paradigm was **mass society theory**—the idea that the media are corrupting influences that undermine the social order and that "average" people are defenseless against their influence. To mass society theorists, "average" people were all those who did not hold their (the theorists') superior tastes and values. The fundamental assumption of this paradigm is sometimes expressed in the **hypodermic needle theory** or the **magic bullet theory.** The symbolism of both is apparent—media are a dangerous drug or a killing force that directly and immediately penetrates a person's system.

Orson Welles directs *War of the Worlds.* The 1938 Halloween eve broadcast of this science fiction classic helped usher in the era of the scientific study of mass communication.

Mass society theory is an example of a **grand theory,** one designed to describe and explain all aspects of a given phenomenon. But clearly not all average people were mindlessly influenced by the evil mass media. People made consumption choices. They interpreted media content, often in personally important ways. Media did have effects, often good ones. No single theory could encompass the wide variety of media effects claimed by mass society theorists, and the theory eventually collapsed under its own weight.

THE ERA OF THE SCIENTIFIC PERSPECTIVE

Paradigm shifts usually happen over a period of time, and this is true of the move away from mass society theory. But media researchers often mark the beginning of the scientific perspective on mass communication as occurring on the eve of Halloween 1938. On that night actor and director Orson Welles broadcast his dramatized version of the H. G. Wells science fiction classic, *The War of the Worlds,* on the CBS radio network. Produced in what we would now call docudrama style, the realistic radio play in which Earth came under deadly Martian attack frightened thousands. People fled their homes in panic. Proof of mass society theory, argued elite media critics, pointing to a radio play with the power to send people into the hills to hide from aliens.

Research by scientists from Princeton University demonstrated that, in fact, 1 million people had been frightened enough by the broadcast to take some action, but the other 5 million people who heard the show had not, mass society theory notwithstanding. More important, however, these scientists determined that different factors led some people to be influenced and others not (Lowery & DeFleur, 1995).

The researchers had the benefit of advances in survey research, polling, and other social scientific methods developed and championed by Austrian immigrant Paul Lazarsfeld. The researchers were, in fact, his students and colleagues. Lazarsfeld (1941) argued that mere speculation about the impact of media was insufficient to explain the complex interactions that mass communication comprised. Instead, well-designed, sophisticated studies of media and audiences would produce more valuable knowledge.

Limited Effects Theories   Using Lazarsfeld's work, researchers identified those individual and social characteristics that led audience members to be influenced (or not) by media. What emerged was the view that media influence was limited by *individual differences* (for example, in intelligence and education), *social categories* (such as religious and political affiliation), and *personal relationships* (such as friends and family). The theories that emerged from this era of the first systematic and scientific study of media effects, taken together, are now called **limited effects theories.**

Two-Step Flow Theory   Lazarsfeld's own **two-step flow theory** of mass media and personal influence is a well-known product of this era and an example of a limited effects theory (Katz & Lazarsfeld, 1955). His research on the 1940 presidential election indicated that media influence on people's voting behavior was limited by **opinion leaders**—people who initially consumed media content on topics of particular interest to them, interpreted it in light of their own values and beliefs, and then passed it on to **opinion followers,** people like them who had less frequent contact with media (Figure 13.1).

Roper Center for Public Opinion Research **www.** ropercenter.uconn.edu

Two-step flow theory has been rethought since Lazarsfeld's time. For example, television, virtually unavailable in 1940, has given everyone a more or less equal opportunity to consume media content firsthand. There is no doubt that opinion leaders still exist—we often ask friends what they've read or heard about a certain movie, book, or CD—but their centrality to the mass communication process has diminished.

THE ERA OF LIMITED EFFECTS THEORY

During and after World War II, the limited effects paradigm and several theories it supported became entrenched, controlling research and thinking about media until well into the 1960s. And as was the case with virtually

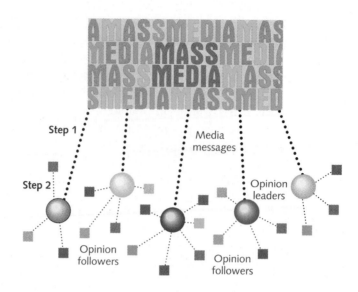

Figure 13.1 Model of Two-Step Flow of Media Influence. Media influence passes from the mass media through opinion leaders to opinion followers. Because leaders and followers share common personal and social characteristics, the potential influence of media is limited by their shared assumptions, beliefs, and attitudes. *Source:* After E. Katz & P. F. Lazarsfeld (1955), *Personal Influence*, New York: Free Press.

all the media and support industries we've studied, the war itself was crucial to the development of mass communication theory during this era.

Memories of World War I were still very much alive, and not all Americans were enthused about entering another seemingly remote world conflict. Those who joined or were drafted into the armed forces apparently knew very little about their comrades-in-arms from different regions of the country and from different backgrounds. German propaganda seemed to prove the view of mass society theorists who claimed that mass media wielded remarkable power. The Office of War Information (OWI), therefore, set out to change public opinion about the wisdom of entering the war, to educate the military about their fellow soldiers and sailors, and to counter Nazi propaganda. Speeches and lectures failed. So, too, did informational pamphlets. The OWI then turned to filmmakers such as Frank Capra (see Chapter 6) and radio personalities such as Kate Smith for their audience appeal and looked to social scientists to measure the effectiveness of these new media campaigns.

The Army established the Experimental Section inside its Information and Education Division, staffing it with psychologists who were expert in issues of attitude change. Led by Carl Hovland, these researchers tested the effectiveness of the government's mass communication campaigns. Continuing its work at Yale University after the war, this group produced some of our most influential communication research. Their work led to development of *attitude change theory*, which explains how people's attitudes are formed, shaped, and changed through communication and how those attitudes influence behavior (Hovland, Lumsdaine, & Sheffield, 1949).

Attitude Change Theory Among the most important attitude change theories are the related ideas of dissonance and selective processes. **Dissonance theory** argues that when confronted by new or conflicting information people experience a kind of mental discomfort, a dissonance. As a result, we consciously and subconsciously work to limit or reduce that discomfort through three interrelated **selective processes.** These processes help us "select" what information we consume, remember, and interpret in personally important and idiosyncratic ways:

- **Selective exposure** (or **selective attention**) is the process by which people expose themselves to or attend to only those messages consistent with their preexisting attitudes and beliefs. How often do you read the work of a newspaper columnist who occupies a different place on the political spectrum from you? You're more likely to read those articles that confirm what you already believe. It's quite common for someone who buys a new car, electronic component, or other expensive item to suddenly start to see more of that product's advertising. You've spent a lot of money; that creates dissonance. The ads confirm the wisdom of your decision, reducing dissonance.

- **Selective retention** assumes that people remember best and longest those messages that are consistent with their preexisting attitudes and beliefs. Television viewers, for example, remember much more detail from the convention broadcasts of the political party to which they are philosophically closer than they do the broadcasts of competing parties.

- **Selective perception** predicts that people will interpret messages in a manner consistent with their preexisting attitudes and beliefs. When your favorite politicians change positions on an issue, they're flexible and heeding the public's will. When those you don't like do so, they're flip-flopping and have no convictions.

American Psychological Association
www.
apa.org

Line drawing used in the 1945 Allport and Postman study of rumor. Psychologists Allport and Postman demonstrated the operation of the selective processes. When groups of White Americans were asked to whisper from one to another the subject of this drawing, the razor invariably shifted from the hand of the White aggressor to that of the African American defender. Can you explain this result in terms of dissonance theory and the selective processes? Reprinted from "The Basic Psychology of Rumor," Transactions of the New York Academy of Sciences, 1945, VIII, 61–81. Used with permission.

The dominant paradigm at the time of the development of dissonance theory was limited effects theory; thus, the selective processes were seen as limiting media impact because content is selectively filtered to produce as little attitude change as possible. Contemporary mass communication theorists accept the power of the selective processes to limit the influence of media content when it is primarily informational. But because so much content is symbolic rather than informational, other theorists see the selective processes as relatively unimportant when it comes to explaining media's contribution to some important cultural effects. You will recognize these differing perspectives on media's power in the distinction made in Chapter 1 between the transmissional and ritual views of mass communication.

Here is an example of the distinction between informational and symbolic content and the way they relate to the selective processes. Few television stations would broadcast lecture programs by people who openly espouse the racist opinion that people of color are genetically more prone to commit crime. If we were to see such a show, however, the selective processes would likely kick in. We would change to another channel (selective exposure). If we did watch, we would interpret the ideas as loony or sick (selective perception); later we would quickly forget the arguments (selective retention).

Fortunately, the media rarely offer such overtly racist messages. The more likely situation in contemporary television is that the production

Susan Smith had the country fooled for 9 days after claiming that an African American carjacker had stolen her car and drowned her children. The Associated Press wire service caption for this photo read, "David and Susan Smith arrive at the Union County Sheriff's office in Union, SC, Thursday, October 27, 1994. The Smiths' children were kidnapped Tuesday night after a carjacker took Mrs. Smith's car at gunpoint and told her to get out, but would not allow her to remove her two children, Alexander, 14 months old and Michael, 3 years." It was eventually learned that Smith had murdered her own children.

conventions and economic and time demands of television news production lead to the common portrayal of certain people as more likely to be involved in violence and crime. It is easier and cheaper, for example, for stations to cover downtown violent crime—it's handy, it's visual, and it needs no significant research or writing—than to cover nonviolent crime, even though 90% of all felonies in the United States are nonviolent. As a result of these largely symbolic portrayals of crime, our selective processes do not have an opportunity to reshape the "information" in these news reports. There is little information, only a variety of interesting images.

Cultural theorists (we'll meet them later in this chapter) point to the 1989 shooting by Charles Stuart of his pregnant wife and the 1994 drowning by Susan Smith of her own two children as proof of the power of television to shape attitudes toward race. In both crimes most of the public and police—even thoughtful people of goodwill—easily accepted Stuart's and Smith's claims that African Americans had committed these crimes, although in both cases the murders were actually perpetrated by these White "victims." Before the truth was uncovered, Stuart—who killed his wife and unborn child to free himself for an affair with a coworker—was visited in the hospital by a parade of politicians lamenting urban violence. Smith—who killed her children because her boyfriend did not want kids—was front-page news as a mother who had suffered the ultimate loss, the death of her children—even appearing on *The Today Show* to weepily accept the nation's sympathy.

Reinforcement Theory The selective processes, however, formed the core of what is arguably the most influential book ever published on the impact of mass communication. In *The Effects of Mass Communication*, written in 1960 by the eminent scientist and eventual head of social research for CBS Broadcasting Joseph Klapper, the core of the limited effects paradigm is articulated firmly and clearly. Klapper's theory is based on social science evidence developed prior to 1960 and is often called **reinforcement theory.** It was very persuasive at a time when the nation's social fabric had yet to feel the full impact of the cultural change brought about by the war. In addition, flush with enthusiasm and optimism for the technology

Family, school, and church do not have the same socializing power they did in Klapper's time.

© Baby Blues Partnership. Reprinted with special permission of King Features Syndicate.

and science that had helped the United States defeat the Axis powers, the public could see little but good coming from the media technologies, and they trusted the work of Klapper and other scientists.

In retrospect, the value of reinforcement theory may have passed with its 1960 publication date. With rapid postwar urbanization, industrialization, and the increase of women in the workplace, Klapper's "nexus of mediating factors and influences" (church, family, and school) began to lose its traditional socializing role for many people. During the 1960s, a decade both revered and reviled for the social and cultural changes it fostered, it became increasingly difficult to ignore the impact of media. Most important, however, all the research Klapper had studied in preparation for his book was conducted before 1960, the year in which it is generally accepted that television became a mass medium. Almost none of the science he examined in developing his reinforcement theory considered television.

The Uses and Gratifications Approach   Paradigms do not shift easily. Limited effects researchers were unable to ignore obvious media effects such as the impact of advertising, the media's role in sustaining sentiment against the war in Vietnam and in spreading support for civil rights and the feminist movement, and increases in real-world crime that appeared to parallel increases in televised violence. They turned their focus to media consumers to explain how influence is limited. The new body of thought that resulted, called the **uses and gratifications approach,** claimed that media do not do things *to* people; rather, people do things *with* media. In other words, the influence of media is limited to what people allow it to be.

Because the uses and gratifications approach emphasizes *audience members'* motives for making specific consumption choices and the consequences of that intentional media use, it is sometimes seen as being too apologetic for the media industries. In other words, when negative media effects are seen as the product of audience members' media choices and use, the media industries are absolved of responsibility for the content they produce or carry. Media simply give people what they want. This approach is also criticized because it assumes not only that people know why they make the media content choices they do but also that they can clearly articulate those reasons to uses and gratifications researchers. A third criticism is that the approach ignores the fact that much media consumption is unintentional—when we read the newspaper for election news, we can't help but see ads. When we go to an action movie, we are presented with various representations of gender and ethnicity that have nothing to do with our choice of that film. A fourth criticism is that the approach ignores media's cultural role in shaping people's media choices and use (Figure 13.2).

Despite these criticisms, the uses and gratifications approach served an important function in the development of mass communication theory by stressing the reciprocal nature of the mass communication process. That is, scientists began to take seriously the idea that people

DENNIS THE MENACE

"BOY! SHE SURE HAS A LOT OF SKIN, HUH, DAD?"

Figure 13.2 This Dennis the Menace cartoon demonstrates two criticisms of the uses and gratifications approach. Someone who chooses to read the newspaper may not intentionally select this cartoon but see it nonetheless. In addition, someone who chooses to read this cartoon for its humor will still be confronted with the idealized cultural image of women. Dennis the Menace ® used by permission of Hank Ketcham Enterprises and © by North America Syndicate.

are important in the process—they choose content, they make meaning, they act on that meaning.

Agenda Setting   During the era of limited effects, several important ideas were developed that began to cast some doubt on the assumption that media influence on people and cultures was minimal. These ideas are still respected and examined even today. Among the most influential is **agenda setting,** a theory that argues that media may not tell us what to think, but media certainly tell us what to think *about*. Based on their study of the media's role in the 1968 presidential election, Maxwell McCombs and Donald Shaw wrote in 1972,

> In choosing and displaying news, editors, newsroom staff, and broadcasters play an important part in shaping political reality. Readers learn not only about a given issue, but how much importance to attach to that issue from the amount of information in a news story and its position. . . . The mass media may well determine the important issues—that is, the media may set the "agenda" of the campaign. (p. 176)

The agenda-setting power of the media resides in more than the amount of space or time devoted to a story and its placement in the broadcast or on the page. Also important is the fact that there is great consistency between media sources across all media in the choice and type of coverage they give an issue or event. This consistency and repetition signal to people the importance of the issue or event.

Researchers Shanto Iyengar and Donald Kinder (1987) tested the application of agenda-setting theory to the network evening news shows in a series of experiments. Their conclusions supported McCombs and Shaw. "Americans' views of their society and nation" they wrote, "are powerfully shaped by the stories that appear on the evening news" (p. 112). But Iyengar and Kinder took agenda setting a step or two further. They discovered that the position of a story affected the agenda-setting power of television news. As you might expect, the lead story on the nightly newscast had the greatest agenda-setting effect, in part because first stories tend to have viewers' full attention—they come before interruptions and other distractions can occur. The second reason, said the researchers, is that viewers accept the broadcasters' implicit categorization of the lead story as the most important. Iyengar and Kinder also tested the impact of vivid video presentations, discovering that emotionally presented, powerful images tended to undercut the agenda-setting power of television news because the images focused too much attention on the specific situation or person in the story, rather than on the issue.

Dependency Theory In 1975 Melvin DeFleur and Sandra Ball-Rokeach offered a view of potentially powerful mass media, tying that power to audience members' dependence on media content. Their **dependency theory** is composed of several assertions:

- The basis of media's influence resides in the "relationship between the larger social system, the media's role in that system, and audience relationships to the media" (p. 261).
- The degree of our dependence on media and their content is the "key variable in understanding when and why media messages alter audience beliefs, feelings, or behavior" (p. 261).
- In our modern industrial society we are increasingly dependent on media (a) to understand the social world; (b) to act meaningfully and effectively in society; and (c) to find fantasy and escape or diversion.
- Our level of dependency is related to (a) "the number and centrality (importance) of the specific information-delivery functions served by a medium"; and (b) the degree of change and conflict present in society (p. 263).

Limited effects theory has clearly been left behind here. Dependency theory argues that, especially in our complex and changing society, people become increasingly dependent on media and media content to understand what is going on around them, to learn how to behave meaningfully, and for escape. Think of a crisis, a natural disaster, for example. We immediately turn to the mass media. We are dependent on the media to understand what is going on around us, to learn what to do (how to behave), and even sometimes for escape from the reality of the situation. Now think of other, more personal crises—reaching puberty, attending high school, beginning dating, or having a child. Dependency theory can explain or predict our media use and its impact in these situations as well.

Social Cognitive Theory   While mass communication researchers were challenging the limited effects paradigm with ideas such as agenda setting and dependency theory, psychologists were expanding **social cognitive theory**—the idea that people learn through observation—and applying it to mass media, especially television.

Social cognitive theory argues that people model (copy) the behaviors they see and that **modeling** happens in two ways. The first is **imitation,** the direct replication of an observed behavior. For example, a child might see cartoon cat Tom hit cartoon mouse Jerry with a stick and then hit his sister with a stick. The second form of modeling is **identification,** a special form of imitation in which observers do not copy exactly what they have seen but make a more generalized but related response. For example, the child might still be aggressive toward his sister but dump a pail of water on her head rather than hit her with a stick.

The idea of identification was of particular value to mass communication theorists who studied television's impact on behavior. Everyone admits that people can imitate what they see on television. But not all do, and when this imitation does occur in dramatic instances—for example, when someone hijacks a plane after seeing it done on a made-for-TV movie—it is so outrageous that it is considered an aberration. Identification, although obviously harder to see and study, is the more likely way that television influences behavior.

Social cognitive theorists demonstrated that imitation and identification are products of three processes:

Observational learning. Observers can acquire (learn) new behaviors simply by seeing those behaviors performed. Many of us who have never fired a handgun can do so because we've seen it done.

Inhibitory effects. Seeing a model, a movie character, for example, punished for a behavior reduces the likelihood that the observer will perform that behavior. In the media we see Good Samaritans sued for trying to help someone, and it reduces our willingness to help in similar situations. That behavior is inhibited by what we've seen.

Disinhibitory effects. Seeing a model rewarded for prohibited or threatening behavior increases the likelihood that the observer will perform that behavior. This is the basis for complaints against the glorification of crime and drugs in movies, for example. Behaviors that people might not otherwise make, those that are inhibited, now become more likely to occur. The behaviors are disinhibited.

Controversy over the children's show *The Teletubbies* proves that mass society theory was alive and well in 1999, as critics accused the program of encouraging homosexuality. The purple Teletubbie was said to be representative of and a glorification of the gay lifestyle.

The Era of Cultural Theory

The obvious and observable impact television has on our culture; the increased sophistication of media industries and media consumers; entrenched social problems such as racial strife; the apparent cheapening of the political process; and the emergence of calls for controls on new technologies such as cable, VCR, satellite, and computer networks are only a few of the many factors that have forced mass communication theorists to rethink media's influence. Clearly, the limited effects idea is inadequate to explain the media impact we see around us every day. But just as clearly, mass society theory tells us very little.

It's important to remember that prominent theories never totally disappear. Joseph McCarthy's efforts to purge Hollywood of communists in the 1950s, for example, were based on mass society notions of evil media and malleable audiences, as were the 1991 attacks on CNN reporter Peter Arnett's broadcasts from Baghdad during the first Persian Gulf War. Unsuspecting viewers would be swayed by this obvious Iraqi propaganda, said the critics (who never explained why they themselves were resistant to it, a perfect example of the third-person effect discussed in Chapter 2). In the 1996 congressional debates and hearings leading up to the Telecommunications Act requirements of a television ratings system and the V-chip, broadcast industry spokespeople consistently raised limited effects and reinforcement theory arguments.

But the theories that have gained the most support among today's media researchers and theorists are those that accept the potential for powerful media effects, a potential that is *either* enhanced or thwarted by audience members' involvement in the mass communication process. Important to this perspective on audience–media interaction are the **cultural theories.** Stanley Baran and Dennis Davis (2003) wrote that these theories share

> the underlying assumption that our experience of reality is an ongoing, social construction, not something that is only sent, delivered, or otherwise transmitted to a docile public. . . . Audience members don't just passively take in and store bits of information in mental filing cabinets, they actively process this information, reshape it, and store only what serves culturally defined needs. (pp. 244–245)

This book's focus on media literacy is based on cultural theories, which say that meaning and, therefore, effects are negotiated by media and audiences as they interact in the culture. Several theories of mass communication reside under the cultural theories umbrella.

SYMBOLIC INTERACTION

Mass communication theorists borrowed another important theory from the psychologists, **symbolic interaction.** This is the idea that cultural symbols are learned through interaction and then mediate that interaction. In other words, people give things meaning, and that meaning controls their behavior. The flag is a perfect example. We have decided that an array of red, white, and blue cloth, assembled in a particular way, represents not only our nation but its values and beliefs. The flag has meaning because we have given it meaning, and that meaning now governs certain behavior toward the flag. We are not free to remain seated when a color guard carries the flag into a room. We are not free to fold it any way we choose. We are not free to place it on the right side of a stage in a public meeting. This is symbolic interaction.

Communication scholars Don Faules and Dennis Alexander (1978) define communication as "symbolic behavior which results in various degrees of shared meaning and values between participants" (p. 23). In their view, symbolic interaction is an excellent way to explain how mass communication shapes people's behaviors. Accepting that these symbolic meanings are negotiated by participants in the culture, mass communication scholars are left with the questions, What do the media contribute to these negotiations, and how powerful are they?

Symbolic interaction theory is frequently used when the influence of advertising is being studied because advertisers often succeed by encouraging the audience to perceive their products as symbols that have meaning beyond the products' actual function. This is called **product positioning.** For example, what does a Cadillac mean? Success. A Porsche? Virility. General Foods International Coffees? Togetherness and intimacy.

Critical Theory
www.
127.pair.com/critical/index2.htm

SOCIAL CONSTRUCTION OF REALITY

If we keep in mind James Carey's cultural definition of communication from Chapter 1—communication is a symbolic process whereby reality is produced, maintained, repaired, and transformed—we cannot be surprised that mass communication theorists have been drawn to the ideas of sociologists Peter Berger and Thomas Luckmann. In their 1966 book, *The Social Construction of Reality,* they never mention mass communication, but they offer a compelling theory to explain how cultures use signs and symbols to construct and maintain a uniform reality.

Social construction of reality theory argues that people who share a culture also share "an ongoing correspondence" of meaning. Things generally mean the same to me as they do to you. A stop sign, for example, has just about the same meaning for everyone. Berger and Luckmann call these things that have "objective" meaning **symbols**—we routinely interpret them in the usual way. But there are other things in the environment to which we assign "subjective" meaning. These things they call **signs.** In social construction of reality, then, a car is a symbol of mobility, but a Cadillac or Mercedes Benz is a sign of wealth or success. In either case the meaning is negotiated, but for signs the negotiation is a bit more complex.

Through interaction in and with the culture over time, people bring together what they have learned about these signs and symbols to form **typification schemes**—collections of meanings assigned to some phenomenon or situation. These typification schemes form a natural backdrop for people's interpretation of and behavior in "the major routines of everyday life, not only the typification of others . . . but typifications of all sorts of events and experiences" (Berger & Luckmann, 1966, p. 43). When you enter a classroom, you automatically recall the cultural meaning of its various elements—desks in rows, chalkboard, lectern. You recognize this as a classroom and impose your "classroom typification scheme." You know how to behave: address the person standing at the front of the room with courtesy, raise your hand when you have a question, talk to your neighbors in whispers. These "rules of behavior" were not published on the classroom door. You applied them because they were appropriate to the "reality" of the setting in your culture. In other cultures, behaviors in this setting may be quite different.

Social construction of reality is important to researchers who study the effects of advertising for the same reasons that symbolic interaction has proven valuable. But it is also widely applied when looking at how media, especially news, shape our political realities.

Crime offers one example. What do politicians mean when they say they are "tough on crime"? What is their (and your) reality of crime? It is likely that "crime" signifies (is a sign for) gangs, drugs, and violence. But the statistical (rather than the socially constructed) reality is that there is 10 times more white-collar crime in the United States than there is violent crime. Now think "welfare." What reality is signified? Is it big corporations seeking money and tax breaks from the government? Or, is it unwed, unemployed mothers, unwilling to work, looking for a handout? Social construction theorists argue that the "building blocks" for the construction of these "realities" come primarily from the mass media.

CULTIVATION ANALYSIS

Symbolic interaction and social construction of reality provide a strong foundation for *cultivation analysis*, which says that television "cultivates" or constructs a reality of the world that, although possibly inaccurate, becomes accepted simply because we as a culture believe it to be true. We then base our judgments about and our actions in the world on this cultivated reality provided by television.

Although cultivation analysis was developed by media researcher George Gerbner and his colleagues out of concern over the effects of television violence, it has been applied to countless other television-cultivated realities such as beauty, sex roles, religion, the judicial process, and marriage. In all cases the assumptions are the same—television cultivates realities, especially for heavy viewers.

Cultivation analysis is based on five assumptions:

1. *Television is essentially and fundamentally different from other mass media.* Unlike books, newspapers, and magazines, television requires no reading ability. Unlike the movies, television requires no mobility or cash; it is in the home, and it is free. Unlike radio, television combines pictures and sound. It can be consumed from people's very earliest to their last years of life.

2. *Television is the "central cultural arm" of U.S. society.* Gerbner and his colleagues (Gerbner, Gross, Jackson-Beeck, Jefferies-Fox, & Signorielli, 1978) wrote that television, as our culture's primary story-teller, is "the chief creator of synthetic cultural patterns (entertainment and information) for the most heterogeneous mass publics in history, including large groups that have never shared in any common public message systems" (p. 178). The product of this sharing of messages is the **mainstreaming** of reality, moving individual and different people toward a shared, television-created understanding of how things are.

3. *The realities cultivated by television are not necessarily specific attitudes and opinions but rather more basic assumptions about the "facts" of life.* Television does not teach facts and figures; it builds general frames of reference. Return to our earlier discussion of the portrayal of crime on television. Television newscasts never say, "Most crime is violent, most violent crime is committed by people of color, and you should be wary of those people." But by the choices news producers make, television news presents a broad picture of "reality" with little regard for how its "reality" matches that of its audience.

4. *The major cultural function of television is to stabilize social patterns.* That is, the existing power relationships of the culture are reinforced and maintained through television images. Gerbner and his colleagues made this argument:

> The repetitive pattern of television's mass-produced messages and images forms the mainstream of the common symbolic environment that cultivates the most widely shared conceptions of reality. We live in terms of the stories we tell—stories about what things exist, stories about how things work, and stories about what to do—and television tells them all through news, drama, and advertising to almost everybody most of the time. (1978, p. 178)

Because the media industries have a stake in the political, social, and economic structures as they exist, their stories rarely challenge the system that has enriched them.

5. *The observable, measurable, independent contributions of television to the culture are relatively small.* This is not a restatement of limited effects theory. Instead, Gerbner and his colleagues explained its meaning with an "ice-age analogy":

> Just as an average temperature shift of a few degrees can lead to an ice age . . . so too can a relatively small but pervasive influence make a crucial difference. The "size" of an effect is far less critical than the direction of its steady contribution. (Gerbner, Gross, Morgan, & Signorielli, 1980, p. 14)

In other words, even though we cannot always see media effects, they do occur and eventually will change the culture in possibly profound ways.

CRITICAL CULTURAL THEORY

A major influence on modern mass communication theory comes from European scholarship on media effects. **Critical cultural theory**—the idea that media operate primarily to justify and support the status quo at the expense of ordinary people—is openly political and is rooted in **neo-Marxist theory.** "Old-fashioned" Marxists believed that people were oppressed by those who owned the factories and the land (the means of production). They called the factories and land the *base*. Modern neo-Marxist theorists believe that people are oppressed by those who control the culture, the *superstructure*—in other words, the mass media.

Modern critical cultural theory encompasses a number of different conceptions of the relationship between media and culture. But all share these identifying characteristics:

- *They tend to be macroscopic in scope.* They examine broad, culturewide media effects.
- *They are openly and avowedly political.* Based on neo-Marxism, their orientation is from the political left.

- *Their goal is at the least to instigate change in government media policies; at the most, to effect wholesale change in media and cultural systems.* Critical cultural theories logically assume that the superstructure, which favors those in power, must be altered.

- *They investigate and explain how elites use media to maintain their positions of privilege and power.* Issues such as media ownership, government–media relations, and corporate media representations of labor and disenfranchised groups are typical topics of study for critical cultural theory because they center on the exercise of power.

The Frankfurt School The critical cultural perspective actually came to the United States in the 1930s when two prominent media scholars from the University of Frankfurt escaped Hitler's Germany. Theodor Adorno and Max Horkheimer were at the heart of what became known as the **Frankfurt School** of media theory (Arato & Gebhardt, 1978). Their approach, centered in neo-Marxism, valued serious art (literature, symphonic music, and theater) and saw consumption of art as a means to elevate all people toward a better life. Typical media fare—popular music, slapstick radio and movie comedies, the soft news dominant in newspapers—pacified ordinary people while assisting in their repression.

Adorno and Horkheimer's influence on U.S. media theory was minimal during their lifetimes. The limited effects paradigm was about to blossom, neo-Marxism was not well received, and their ideas sounded a bit too much like mass society theory claims of a corrupting and debasing popular media. More recently, though, the Frankfurt School has been "rediscovered," and its influence can be seen in the two final examples of contemporary critical theory, British cultural theory and news production research.

British Cultural Theory There was significant class tension in England after World War II. During the 1950s and 1960s, working-class people who had fought for their country were unwilling to return to England's traditional notions of nobility and privilege. Many saw the British media—with broadcasting dominated by graduates of the best upper-crust schools, and newspapers and magazines owned by the wealthy—as supporting long-standing class distinctions and divisions. This environment of class conflict produced theorists such as Stuart Hall (1980), who first developed the idea of media as a public forum (Chapter 1) in which various forces fight to shape perceptions of everyday reality. Hall and others in British cultural studies trusted that the media *could* serve all people. However, because of ownership patterns, the commercial orientation of the media, and sympathetic government policies toward media, the forum was dominated by the reigning elite. In other words, the loudest voice in the give-and-take of the cultural forum belonged to those already well entrenched in the power structure.

British cultural theory today provides a home for much feminist research and research on popular culture both in Europe and in the United States.

News Production Research   Another interesting strand of critical cultural theory is **news production research**—the study of how economic and other influences on the way news is produced distort and bias news coverage toward those in power. W. Lance Bennett (1988) identified four common news production conventions used by U.S. media that bolster the position of those in power:

1. *Personalized news.* Most news stories revolve around people. If a newspaper wants to do a report on homelessness, for example, it will typically focus on one person or family as the center of its story. This makes for interesting journalism (and increased ratings or circulation), but it reduces important social and political problems to soap opera levels. The two likely results are that these problems are dismissed by the public as specific to the characters in the story and that the public is not provided with the social and political contexts of the problem that might suggest avenues of public action.

2. *Dramatized news.* News, like other forms of media content, must be attractively packaged. Especially on television, this packaging takes the form of dramatization. Stories must have a hero and a villain, a conflict must be identified, and there has to be a showdown. Again, one problem is that important public issues take on the character of a soap opera or a Western movie. But a larger concern is that political debate is trivialized. Fundamental alterations in tax law or defense spending or any of a number of important issues are reduced to George W. Bush versus Nancy Pelosi, the White House versus Congress. This complaint is often raised about media coverage of campaigns. The issues that should be at the center of the campaign become lost in a sea of stories about the "horse race"—who's ahead; how will a good showing in New Hampshire help Candidate X in her battle to unseat Candidate Y as the front-runner?

3. *Fragmented news.* The daily time and cost demands of U.S. journalism result in newspapers and broadcasts composed of a large number of brief, capsulated stories. There is little room in a given report for perspective and context. Another contributor to fragmented news, according to Bennett (1988), is journalists' obsession with objectivity. Putting any given day's story in context—connecting it to other events of the time or the past—would require the reporter to make decisions about which links are most important. Of course, these choices would be subjective, and so they are avoided. Reporters typically get one comment from somebody on one side of the issue and a second comment from the other side, juxtapose them as if they were equally valid, and then move on to tomorrow's assignment.

4. *Normalized news.* The U.S. newswriting convention typically employed when reporting on natural or man-made disasters is to seek out and report the opinions and perspectives of the authorities. When an airplane crashes, for example, the report invariably concludes with the words "The FAA was quickly on the scene. The cockpit recorder has

Pennsylvania Governor Mark Schweiker manned the press conference microphones throughout the rescue ordeal of the 9 Que Creek coal miners in July, 2002. Here he celebrates the rescue of the trapped miners. But what was he doing there in the first place? He did not direct the effort. He had no expertise in mine safety or rescue. News production researchers would argue that his presence was designed to normalize the news—to remind us that the system, as it exists, works.

been retrieved, and the reason for this tragedy will be determined soon." In other words, what happened here is bad, but the authorities will sort it out. Journalists give little independent attention to investigating any of a number of angles that a plane crash or flood might suggest, angles that might produce information different from that of officials.

The result of news produced according to these conventions is daily reassurance by the media that the system works if those in power are allowed to do their jobs. Any suggestions about opportunities for meaningful social action are suppressed.

For more information on this topic, see NBC Video Clip #19 on the CD—*Why Is the United States Viewed So Poorly in the Arab World?*

The Effects of Mass Communication

Scientists and scholars use these theories, the earliest and the most recent, to form conclusions about the effects of mass communication. You no doubt are familiar with the long-standing debate over the effects of television violence. But there are other media effects that occupy thinkers' interest.

VIOLENCE

No media effects issue has captured public, legislative, and industry attention as has the relationship between media portrayals of violence

Ernest Borgnine in Sam Peckinpah's *The Wild Bunch* (1969). In trying to differentiate itself from the television industry, the movie industry turned to graphic violence, fueling the debate over media violence and subsequent real-world aggression.

and subsequent aggressive behavior. Among the reasons for this focus are the facts that violence is a staple of both television and movies and that the United States experienced an upsurge in real violence in the 1960s, just about the time television entrenched itself as the country's dominant mass medium, and that movies turned to increasingly graphic violence to differentiate themselves from and to compete with television.

The prevailing view during the 1960s was that *some* media violence affected *some* people in *some* ways *some* of the time. Given the dominance of the transmissional perspective of communication (Chapter 1) and the limited effects paradigm, researchers believed that for "normal" people— that is, those who were not predisposed to violence—*little* media violence affected *few* people in *few* ways *little* of the time. However, increases in youth violence, the assassinations of Robert F. Kennedy and Reverend Martin Luther King Jr., and the violent eruption of cities during the civil rights, women's rights, and anti–Vietnam War movements led to creation of the Surgeon General's Scientific Advisory Committee on Television and Social Behavior in 1969. After 2 years and $1 million worth of research, the committee (whose members had to be approved by the television networks) produced findings that led Surgeon General Jesse L. Steinfield to report to the U.S. Senate:

> While the . . . report is carefully phrased and qualified in language acceptable to social scientists, it is clear to me that the causal relationship

These scenes from Albert Bandura's media violence research are typical of the laboratory response to portrayals of media violence that social learning researchers were able to elicit from children.

between televised violence and antisocial behavior is sufficient to warrant appropriate and immediate remedial action. The data on social phenomena such as television and violence and/or aggressive behavior will never be clear enough for all social scientists to agree on the formulation of a succinct statement of causality. But there comes a time when the data are sufficient to justify action. That time has come. (Ninety-Second Congress, 1972, p. 26)

Despite the apparent certainty of this statement, disagreement persists over the existence and extent of the media's contribution to aggressive behavior. Few would argue that media violence *never* leads to aggressive behavior. The disagreement is about what circumstances are needed for such effects to occur, and to whom.

Under What Circumstances? A direct causal relationship between violent content and aggressive behavior—the **stimulation model**—has been scientifically demonstrated in laboratory experiments. So has the **aggressive cues model**—the idea that media portrayals can suggest that certain classes of people, for example, women or foreigners, are acceptable targets for real-world aggression, thereby increasing the likelihood that some people will act violently toward people in these groups.

For more information on this topic, see NBC Video Clip #16 on the CD—*Violence in the Media and Its Effects on Children.*

Both the stimulation and aggressive cues models are based on social cognitive theory. Fueled by the research of psychologists such as Albert Bandura, social cognitive theory has made several additional contributions to the violence debate.

Social cognitive theory deflated the notion of **catharsis,** the idea that watching violence in the media reduces people's innate aggressive drive. Social scientists were already skeptical: Viewing people eating does not reduce hunger; viewing people making love does not reduce the drive to reproduce. But social cognitive theory provided a scientific explanation for the research that did show a reduction in aggression after viewing violence. This phenomenon was better explained not by some cathartic power of the media but by inhibitory effects. That is, as we saw in our discussion of social cognitive theory, if media aggression is portrayed as punished or prohibited, it can indeed lead to the reduced likelihood that that behavior will be modeled.

Some people, typically media industry practitioners, to this day defend catharsis theory. But 30 years ago, respected media researcher and theorist Joseph Klapper, who at the time was the head of social research for CBS television, told the U.S. Senate, "I myself am unaware of any, shall we say, hard evidence that seeing violence on television or any other medium acts in a cathartic . . . manner. There have been some studies to that effect; they are grossly, greatly outweighed by studies as to the opposite effect" (Ninety-Second Congress, 1972, p. 60).

Using Media to Make a Difference

Television and the Designated Driver

Television's ability to serve prosocial ends is obvious in the public service messages we see sprinkled throughout the shows we watch. For example, dozens of national broadcast and cable channels simultaneously ran a 30-second PSA in August 1999 that featured President Clinton urging parents to talk to their kids about violence. And "This is your brain; This is your brain on drugs" is familiar to everyone who can operate a remote control.

But there is a movement among television writers and producers to more aggressively use their medium to produce prosocial effects by embedding important cultural messages in the entertainment fare they create. The one-time ABC series *The Hughleys* is indicative. This 30-minute comedy opened its 1999 season with an episode centering on the show's lead, D. L. Hughley, discovering his children playing with a gun he keeps in the house. Neither pro- nor antigun, this "program-length PSA" was intentionally designed to keep alive the gun debate that began with the horrific string of murderous shootings that blighted 1998 and 1999. *Mad About You* offers another example. Directed to a dealer by the Environmental Media Association, its producers made an electric car part of its series-ending, farewell episode in 1999.

This "prime time activism" can be traced to Harvard professor Jay Winsten and his 1988 campaign to get Hollywood to push his novel "designated driver" idea. You know what a designated driver is—he or she is the person among a group of friends who is selected to remain alcohol-free during a get-together and then to drive everyone else home. The concept, much less the term, did not even exist until Professor Winsten, through the intervention of CBS executive Frank Stanton, contacted Stanton's friend Grant Tinker, then chairman of NBC, to ask for help. Intrigued by Winsten's plan to develop a new social norm, Tinker put his considerable clout behind the effort, writing letters to the heads of the 13 production companies that did the most business with the networks. If they did not reply quickly enough to suit Tinker, he called them on the phone. Once everyone was in line, Tinker personally escorted Professor Winsten, director of Harvard's Center for Health Communication, to meetings with all 13 producers.

442

Social cognitive theory introduced the concept of **vicarious reinforcement**—the idea that observed reinforcement operates in the same manner as actual reinforcement. This helped direct researchers' attention to the context in which media violence is presented. Theoretically, inhibitory and disinhibitory effects operate because of the presence of vicarious reinforcement. That is, seeing the bad guy punished is sufficient to inhibit subsequent aggression on the part of the viewer. Unfortunately, what researchers discovered is that in contemporary film and television, when the bad guys are punished, they are punished by good guys who out-aggress them. The implication is that even when media portray punishment for aggressive behavior they may in fact be reinforcing that very same behavior.

Social cognitive theory introduced the concept of **environmental incentives**—the notion that real-world incentives can lead observers to ignore the negative vicarious reinforcement they have learned to associate with a given behavior.

In 1965 Bandura conducted a now classic experiment in which nursery school children saw a video aggressor, a character named Rocky, punished for his behavior. The children subsequently showed lower levels of

In the four network television seasons that followed these meetings, designated drivers were part of the story-lines of 160 different prime-time shows seen by hundreds of millions of viewers. Professor Winsten was successful in placing his message in entertainment programming, but did his message make a difference? Absolutely. Within one year of the introduction of the idea of the designated driver in these television shows, 67% of U.S. adults said they were aware of the concept, and by 1991, 52% of adults under 30 years old said they had served as a designated driver. From 1988, the campaign's first year, to 1997, the number of drunk driver fatalities in the United States dropped by 32% (Cox, 1999). But Professor Winsten acknowledges that embedding public service messages in prime-time television "isn't a magic bullet. It's one component of a larger strategy" (Cox, 1999, p. 22), as can be seen in the work of Mothers Against Drunk Driving, a group of committed women, much like Dr. Winsten, who

recognize that mass communication can be used by media literate people to make a real cultural difference (see Chapter 11).

Storylines touting responsible drinking and designated drivers are frequently embedded in many prime-time shows. Do you recognize this type of action from shows such as Party of Five?

aggressive play than did those who had seen Rocky rewarded. This is what social cognitive theory would have predicted. Yet Bandura later offered "sticker-pictures" to the children who had seen Rocky punished if they could perform the same actions they had seen him perform. They all could. Vicarious negative reinforcement may reduce the likelihood that the punished behavior will be performed, but that behavior is still observationally learned. It's just that, at the same time it is observed and learned, observers also learn not to make it. When the real world offers sufficient reward, the originally learned behavior can be demonstrated.

For Whom? The compelling evidence of social learning researchers aside, it's clear that most people do not exhibit aggression after viewing film or video violence. There is also little doubt that those predisposed to violence are more likely to be influenced by media aggression. Yet viewers need not necessarily be predisposed for this link to occur, because at any time anyone can become predisposed. For example, experimental research indicates that frustrating people before they view media violence can increase the likelihood of subsequent aggressive behavior.

But the question remains, who, exactly, is affected by mediated violence? If a direct causal link is necessary to establish effects, then it can indeed be argued that some media violence affects some people in some ways some of the time. But if the larger, macro-level ritual view is applied, then we all are affected because we live in a world in which there is more violence than there might be without mass media. We live in a world, according to cultivation analysis, in which we are less trusting of our neighbors and more accepting of violence in our midst. We experience **desensitization.** This need not be the case. As researcher Ellen Wartella (1997) said, "Today, we find wide consensus among experts that, of all the factors contributing to violence in our society, violence on television may be the easiest to control" (p. 4). And in a clear sign of that wide consensus, the American Medical Association, the American Academy of Pediatrics, the American Psychological Association, and the American Academy of Child & Adolescent Psychiatry issued a joint report in summer 2000 offering their combined view that the effects of violent media are "measurable and long lasting" and that "prolonged viewing of media violence can lead to emotional desensitization toward violence in real life" (as quoted in Wronge, 2000, p. 1E).

DRUGS AND ALCOHOL

Concern about media effects reaches beyond the issue of violence. The claims and counterclaims surrounding media portrayals of drugs and alcohol parallel those of the violence debate.

The wealth of scientific evidence linking media portrayals of alcohol consumption, especially in ads, to increases in youthful drinking and alcohol abuse led the U.S. Department of Health and Human Services' National Institute of Alcohol Abuse and Alcoholism to report, "The preponderance

For more information on this topic, see NBC Video Clip #14 on the CD—*Debating the Effects of TV Violence.*

Center on Alcohol Advertising
WWW.
tf.org/tf/alcohol2.htm

of the evidence indicates that alcohol advertising stimulates higher consumption of alcohol by both adults and adolescents" and "There is sufficient evidence to say that alcohol advertising is likely to be a contributing factor to overall consumption and other alcohol-related problems in the long term" (Center for Science in the Public Interest, 2002, p. 2). The National Institute on Media and the Family (2002) reports that:

- by the time teenagers reach driving age, they will have seen 75,000 alcohol ads
- beer ads are a strong predictor of adolescents' knowledge, preference, and loyalty to beer brands and of their intention to drink
- young people report more positive feelings about drinking and their own likelihood to drink after watching alcohol commercials
- 56% of children in grades 5 through 12 say that alcohol advertising encourages them to drink
- 10 million people ages 12 to 20 report drinking "in the last month." Seven million are classified as "binge drinkers"
- the average age of first alcohol use is 13.1 years old

What does this magazine ad say about drinking? About attractiveness? About people of color? About having fun? About men? About women? Are you satisfied with these representations of important aspects of your life?

Yet there is a good deal of scientific research—typically from alcohol industry scientists—that discounts the causal link between media portrayals and real-world drinking. Again, researchers who insist on the demonstration of this direct causal relationship will rarely agree on media's influence on behavior. The larger cultural perspective, however, suggests that media portrayals of alcohol, both in ads and in entertainment fare, tell stories of alcohol consumption that predominantly present it as safe, healthy, youthful, sexy, necessary for a good time, effective for dealing with stress, and essential to ceremonies and other rites of passage.

The same scenario exists in the debate over the relationship between media portrayals of nonalcohol drug use and behavior. Relatively little contemporary media content presents the use of illegal drugs in a glorifying manner. In fact, the destructive power of illegal drugs is often the focus of television shows such as *NYPD Blue* and *ER* and a central theme in movies such as *Traffic* and *Boyz N the Hood*. Scientific concern has centered therefore on the impact of commercials and other media portrayals of legal over-the-counter drugs. Again, impressive amounts of experimental research suggest a causal link between this content and subsequent abuse of both legal and illegal drugs; however, there also exists research that discounts the causal link between media portrayals and the subsequent abuse of drugs. It cannot be denied, however, that media often present legal drugs as a cure-all for dealing with that pesky mother-in-law, those screaming kids, that abusive boss, and other daily annoyances.

GENDER AND RACIAL/ETHNIC STEREOTYPING

National Institute of Media and the Family
WWW.
mediaandthefamily.org

Stereotyping is the application of a standardized image or concept to members of certain groups, usually based on limited information. Because media cannot show all realities of all things, the choices media practitioners make when presenting specific people and groups may well facilitate or encourage stereotyping.

Numerous studies conducted over the last 40 years have demonstrated that women and people of color are consistently underrepresented in all media (among the new series introduced by CBS in 2002, for example, were *CSI: Miami,* having only one recurring Hispanic character, and *Presidio Med,* set in San Francisco and having no Asian characters); that when they are portrayed they are more often than not presented in traditional, inferior roles (actor Danny Hoch was removed from his *Seinfeld* role as a "Puerto Rican 'pool guy' who cleans up towels and jumps around like an idiot and talks with a 'funny Spanish accent'" when he argued with producers that the portrayal was offensive because "people in Idaho, Australia, even in government were already forming their opinions about Latinos, blacks, Asians, Native Americans from the one-dimensional image 'opportunities' that existed for them in film and television"; Hoch, 2000 p. 25.); that women are more likely to be presented as the victims of aggression than is the case in the real world; and that people of color are more likely to be presented as the perpetrators of crime and aggression than is the case in the real world (Dixon & Linz, 2000). When women and minorities are presented favorably, they are often stereotyped as "perfect"—the "perfect Asian student" or the "perfect African American social worker." These portrayals are as narrow and limiting as the "dumb blonde" or "dangerous dark outsider."

Center for Science in the Public Interest
WWW.
cspinet.org

Any of a number of theories, especially cultivation analysis, symbolic interaction, and social construction of reality, can predict the probable outcome of repeated and frequent exposure to these limited and limiting representations. They influence people's perceptions, and people's perceptions influence their behaviors. Examine your own perceptions not only of women and people of color but of the elderly, lawyers, college athletes, and people sophisticated in the use of computers. What images or stereotypes come immediately to mind?

Sure, you're skeptical. You're a smart, progressive, college-educated individual. Use four more quiz questions to test yourself on your stereotypes of big cities, women, teens, and illegal drug users:

1. True or false: A woman is more likely to be the victim of forcible rape in big urban cities such as New York City and Washington, D.C. than she is in "heartland" towns such as Oklahoma City or Rapid City, South Dakota.

These three images—Barbara Billingsley as Beaver Cleaver's mom, the female leads from *Sister, Sister*, and Charlie's Angels—show how women have been portrayed over time on television. Researchers believe that repeated and frequent exposure to such representations as these influences people's perceptions of, and therefore their behaviors toward, women. The question that is typically raised when talking about media stereotypes is "Which came first, the culture's representation or the media representation?" Clearly, television's image of women has changed over the years, but were these different cultural views of women simply mirrored by television, or did television's constant reliance on a limited array of images of women create—or at least reinforce—the stereotypes? And even if the media do create or reinforce stereotypes, why should anyone care? Do all cultures have stereotypes of their people? What do you think?

Embedding Antidrug Messages in Prime-Time Television

We saw on pages 442–443 that network television programmers often willingly insert important prosocial messages and themes in their content. Their efforts on behalf of the designated driver proved to be very effective and earned them much praise. But a similar effort on behalf of the federal government's antidrug campaign had a very different outcome and revealed the practice of embedding prosocial messages in prime-time content as a highly controversial issue in the cultural forum.

In January 2000, online magazine *Salon* revealed that the White House's Office of National Drug Control Policy (ONDCP) had entered into an agreement with five of the six national television networks, allowing them to avoid a 1997 law requiring them to provide 1 free PSA minute for every minute the federal government bought to run its antidrug messages. When the networks had trouble finding sufficient time for the free PSAs, they were permitted to avoid the payback by inserting "an aggressive antidrug message" in their prime-time entertainment fare (Kurtz & Waxman, 2000). Among the shows involved were *Beverly Hills 90210, ER, Chicago Hope, The Drew Carey Show, Sports Night, Sabrina the Teenage Witch,* and *The Practice.* In all, 109 programs earned credit for their networks in 1999 (Albiniak, 2000a).

Salon further reported that some scripts were being submitted *in advance* for approval by the ONDCP, and that ONDCP staff even worked with producers in preparing storylines and scripts. In later stories, the online magazine revealed that the ONDCP had similar arrangements with magazines such as *U.S. News & World Report* and *Seventeen,* and with movie theaters.

Criticism was swift and strong, and it incorporated two main arguments. The first, specific to broadcasters, objected to the fact that the networks, already the beneficiaries of the use of the public's airwaves, were avoiding their legally mandated responsibility, while at the same time further enriching themselves. In other words, licensed broadcasters should not have to be paid to do what is right and responsible. But the second, possibly greater concern was that the government had no business suggesting storylines, approving scripts, and inserting messages of any kind into media fare—broadcast, magazine, or film—especially without public knowledge.

Media watchdog group FAIR editorialized that such arrangements "give media corporations a financial incentive to transmit what is essentially government propaganda. Unsuspecting audiences have no way of knowing that the messages they are receiving are designed to conform to the official federal line on drugs. The promotion of undisclosed government propaganda is incompatible with the First Amendment and the idea of a free press" (2000, p. 1). The editors of *Broadcasting & Cable,* after renaming the ONDCP the "Office of National Media Control Policy," complained, "What if the next administration wants to discourage different kinds of behavior? What if _____ gets elected and decides that _____ is a threat to the republic (fill in somebody you don't like and something you favor)? With the bribe-the-media model in place, the way has been cleared" (*Lights, Camera,* 2000, p. 90). *Time*'s Richard Lacayo asked, "If Washington can offer financial incentives to work antidrug dialogue into *Drew Carey,* why not induce *NYPD Blue* to have Sipowicz plug gun control every time he plugs a suspect? Even worse, depending on who runs Congress, *Buffy the Vampire Slayer* could end up pro-life one season and pro-choice the next" (2000, p. 67). Robert Corn-Revere, a First Amendment lawyer, added, "It's an unprecedented level of government involvement into the content of entertainment programming. Most

2. True or false: Teen pregnancy and out-of-wedlock birth rates continue to climb.

3. A two-parter: How tall is the average American woman—5'3" or 5'7"? How much does she weigh—110 or 152 pounds?

4. Of all the illegal drug users in the United States, what proportion are people of color—30%, 50%, or 70%?

Are you surprised to learn that the FBI reports that the incidence of rape is 3 times higher in Oklahoma City than in New York City and Washington, D.C., and that Rapid City has the nation's highest rate of forcible rape (Zoellner, 1995)? That teen birth rates and pregnancies are at historic lows

NYPD Blue *and* Buffy the Vampire Slayer *are only two of the many television shows that use government-approved antidrug messages in their stories.*

would agree that it is unseemly for the government to be involved in a secret proceeding to insert anti-drug messages into programming even if it's a good thing to be informing the public about" (quoted in Albiniak, 2000a, p. 3).

But not everyone saw it as unseemly. ONDCP head General Barry McCaffrey insisted to Congress that the program would continue (although he said content would be evaluated only *after* it appeared), and Dick Wolf, producer of NBC's *Law & Order*, spied a mole hill where critics saw a mountain. "It's a slow-news-day story," he said, "a boondoggle" (quoted in Albiniak, 2000b, p. 24).

This debate was in the public forum for months; what do you think? What is the difference between embedding designated driver themes and antidrug themes? Might it be that while no one opposes designated drivers, there is considerable debate over the development of an effective national drug policy? Is the difference government involvement? A do-gooder is a do-gooder, whether it is a nonprofit group or a government agency, right?

Enter your voice in the public forum. Is the "bribe-the-media model" "unseemly" or "a boondoggle"?

(Males, 2002)? That the average American woman is 5′3¾″ tall and weighs 152 pounds (Irving, 2001)? That 72% of all illegal drug users are White (or, conversely, that only 28% are people of color; Williams, 2002)? How did you develop your stereotypes of these people? Where did you find the building blocks to construct your realities of their lives?

POLITICAL CAMPAIGNS AND VOTING

Media impact on political campaigns and voting was at the center of some of mass communication's earliest research. The two-step flow model, for example, was the product of research on the 1940 presidential election conducted by Paul Lazarsfeld and his colleagues. Given that television had yet to develop into a true mass medium and that the notion of limited effects held sway, the overall conclusion drawn from this early work was that media had little *direct* impact on campaigns and voting and, when and if they did, that the impact was in the form of reinforcement.

But with the fuller diffusion of television and the interest generated in that medium by the 1960 Kennedy–Nixon debates, thinking about media and campaigns began to change. For example, research after those inaugural televised debates began to focus on how candidates used media for image building and the subsequent "cheapening" of campaigns as personalities became more important than issues. Another important development in contemporary thinking about media and campaigns was agenda setting, introduced after research on the 1968 presidential elections. Agenda setting was used to explain how media can influence campaigns and voting. Media helped set the issue agenda for the campaign, and that agenda dictated the issues on which many people ultimately based their voting decisions.

The growing influence of television news throughout the 1960s and 1970s naturally turned attention to its role in the electoral process. Early thinking saw news reports as more important than political ads in shaping preferences because of the perceived impartiality of news reporting. But recent research has demonstrated dramatic declines in the amount of time given to candidates' positions in typical news programs. In 1968 the average on-screen comment by presidential candidates lasted 43 seconds; in 2000 it was 7.8 seconds. The amount of all air time devoted to campaign coverage on the three major broadcast networks in 2000 was 28% lower than it was in 1988 (Hickey, 2002a).

But content-free political campaigns, coupled with the increase in negative campaign commercials, may be creating an apathetic and alienated public, rather than the involved and informed citizens necessary for democracy (Grossman, 2003). A paradox exists, however. The public often complains about shoddy campaign coverage and negative ads, yet the great majority of Americans identify television—often seen as the prime culprit in encouraging both phenomena—as its primary source of public affairs information. Moreover, although Americans consider negative campaign advertising unethical, uninformative, deceptive, and lacking in credibility (Pinkelton, 1997), research indicates that negative campaigns are more memorable than positive ones, and voters' decision making is influenced to a greater degree by negative than by positive campaign information (Richardson, 2001). So, what is an office seeker to do? To run an "information lite," negative campaign might ultimately damage democracy, and voters declare they want better from their candidates, but candidates want to win.

This situation has given rise to a number of proposals for improvement. Primary among them is campaign reform. Because the media, again, especially television, have become essential to modern campaigning, raising money to buy media time and space is a full-time obsession

Presidential debates have become the focus of much research on the media's contribution to the electoral process. Here, John F. Kennedy and Richard M. Nixon face off in history's first series of televised presidential debates.

for many politicians. This state of affairs has led to widespread suspicion among voters that the money raised to buy media access for a candidate ultimately buys access to the candidate for the source of the money, a suspicion reinforced by the disclosure of huge campaign contributions to both political parties by Enron executives in the investigations following the failure of the one-time energy giant. It was public outrage at these revelations that helped move the John McCain–Russ Feingold campaign finance bill from Congressional disinterest to swift passage in 2002 (Nichols, 2002).

A second suggestion—one embraced by the Fox television network among others—is that broadcasters should make free time available to candidates and campaigns, reducing the influence of money and increasing the length of time candidates have to present full, cogent explanations of their positions. In fact, in the 2000 elections, CBS, NBC, and Fox began airing 5 minutes a night of free political time on their stations. A third suggestion is that the United States should follow the British election practice of not only granting free air time to candidates but also limiting all campaigning—personal and mediated—to a specified period, say 3 or 6 months, before election day. Campaigning outside this "run up" to the election would be illegal.

PROSOCIAL EFFECTS

Virtually every argument that can be made for the harmful or negative effects of media can also be applied to the ability of media to do good. A sizable body of science exists that clearly demonstrates that people, especially children, can and will model the good or prosocial behaviors they see in the media, often to a greater extent than they will the negative behaviors. Research on the impact of media portrayals of cooperation and constructive problem solving (Baran, Chase, & Courtright, 1979) and other "good" behaviors indicates that much more than negative behavior can be

Gerbner's Three Bs of Television

After years of developing cultivation analysis theory, George Gerbner (1990, p. 261) was able to articulate the "three Bs of television":

1. Television BLURS the traditional distinctions of people's view of their world.

2. Television BLENDS people's realities into the cultural mainstream.

3. Television BENDS that mainstream reality to its own and its sponsors' institutional interests.

He then wrote of this power:

> The historical circumstances in which we find ourselves have taken the magic of human life—living in a universe erected by culture—out of the hands of families and small communities. What has been a richly diverse handcrafted process has become—for better or worse, or both—a complex manufacturing and mass-distribution enterprise. This has abolished much of the provincialism and parochialism, as well as some of the elitism, of the pretelevision era. It has enriched parochial cultural horizons. It also gave increasingly massive industrial conglomerates the right to conjure up much of what we think about, know, and do in common. (p. 261)

Gerbner's tone gives away his opinion as to whether television's impact has been "for better or worse, or both." Discussion of the effects of television has been in

George Gerbner

the cultural forum since this medium was first developed. What is your opinion?

---

socially learned from the media (see the boxes "Television and the Designated Driver" and "Embedding Antidrug Messages in Prime-Time Television").

DEVELOPING MEDIA LITERACY SKILLS

Applying Mass Communication Theory

There are many more theories of mass communication and effects issues than we've covered here. Some apply to the operation of media as part of specific social systems. Some examine mass communication at the most micro level; for example, How do viewers process individual television scenes? This chapter has focused on a relatively small number of theories and effects that might prove useful to people trying to develop their media literacy skills. Remember Art Silverblatt's (1995) elements of media literacy in Chapter 2. Among them were understanding the process of mass

Be a Media Effects Researcher

The debate over media effects means little if it does not produce effects itself. In other words, the experts on all sides of the various effects issues can write and lecture all they want, but until people (and their representatives in the media and government) take up the discussion, nothing will change (if, indeed, you even think it should).

One way, then, for media literate individuals to make the debate over media effects a living enterprise is to take the effects conversation to their friends and family; they can become media effects researchers themselves. This chapter gives you the tools.

First, take the six-question quiz that opens the chapter. Now, add the stereotype questions from page p. 446. Type them onto a page, followed by a few demographic questions you might want to ask your respondents. Some examples are gender; age; level of education; marital status; number of children; favorite medium; amount of time per day with radio, television, newspapers, magazines, and the Internet; and number of movies attended per month. Choose the ones you are interested in or add any others you think might be important.

Then, select a sample of a reasonable size. If you have a spreadsheet or statistical program on your computer, you can use quite a few respondents, maybe 30 to 50. If you have to do your computations by hand, you may want to talk to 10 or 15 people. Interview those you've chosen and note their responses.

What do you do with the data? First, once your respondents have completed your survey, tell them the significance of the first six questions and the correct answers to the stereotype items. Ask them if this information changes what they think about media effects. Does it reinforce their existing belief that media have strong effects? Does it move them, even a little bit, from a limited to a strong effects perspective? Do they remain convinced that media have limited effects? Challenge and debate your respondents. See how strong your convictions are and how well you can articulate the lessons of this chapter.

Analyze your data. Get raw scores; that is, identify the percentage of respondents who answered each item a specific way. What do these results say to you? Then reanalyze your results in terms of respondents' demographics. That is, did men show different patterns than did women? Parents versus nonparents? Heavy versus light television viewers, and so on? What do these data suggest? Then think about the discussions you had with your respondents following the survey. Who seemed most reluctant to accept your effects arguments? Who was most receptive?

Another way to find value in your work is to use it as the basis for an article or essay for your campus or local paper. You may not want to claim your effort as strong science, but your results and the interactions they generated with your respondents should provide the grist for some interesting observations on media and media effects.

communication and accepting media content as a "text" providing insight into ourselves and our culture. Among the media literacy skills we identified was an understanding of and respect for the power of media messages. Good mass communication theory speaks to these elements and skills. Good mass communication theorists understand media effects. Media literate people, then, are actually good mass communication theorists. They apply the available conceptions of media use and impact to their own content consumption and the way they live their lives.

George Gerbner's ideas are described a bit further in the box "Gerbner's Three Bs of Television," which also makes clear how important Gerbner believes it is to be a literate television viewer, that is, to understand the medium's power. Awareness of television's influence led this distinguished and influential mass communication theorist to become one of the founders of the Cultural Environment Movement, an activist media literacy organization introduced in Chapter 2.

Chapter Review

The debate over media effects focuses on a number of issues. Are media effects limited by the fact that audiences know content is only make-believe? Is impact limited because media are used only as entertainment? Does media content simply reflect society as it is? Do media effects typically exist only in the form of reinforcement? Can media affect more than the unimportant aspects of people's lives?

There is no one mass communication theory. Instead, there are many mass communication theories, explanations and predictions of social phenomena relating mass communication to various aspects of our personal and cultural lives or social systems. Many are borrowed from other disciplines. They are human constructions, and they are dynamic.

Theories are often identified by paradigms; mass communication theory paradigms shift because new technologies and media are introduced, because there needs to be an objective basis for their control, and because media's impact must be understood in a nation committed to preserving democracy and pluralism.

Mass communication theory has passed through four eras. The era of mass society theory includes such notions as magic bullet and hypodermic needle theory. Both see media as all-powerful and audiences as more or less defenseless. The era of the scientific perspective, ushered in by the 1938 *War of the Worlds* radio broadcast, saw the development of objective, social science–based mass communication theories such as two-step flow theory. Taken together, the theories from this era are called limited effects theories.

The era of limited effects saw the entrenchment of limited effects beliefs. Attitude change theory, including dissonance theory and the selective processes, is typical of this time, as is Joseph Klapper's reinforcement theory. When limited effects theorists could no longer ignore seemingly powerful media influence, they turned to the uses and gratifications approach to explain how audience members allow media to affect them or not. Important theories claiming powerful media effects began during this era. Agenda setting (the media may not tell us what to think, but what to think about) and dependency theory (media influence is a function of people's dependence on media content) are applied even today. So, too, is social

cognitive theory—the idea that people can learn behaviors by observing them.

Contemporary mass communication theory can be called the era of cultural theory. Potentially powerful media effects are seen as either enhanced or thwarted by audience members' involvement in the mass communication process. Viewing media influence as negotiated between media and audience members, these theories see reality as socially constructed. Symbolic interaction is the idea that people give symbols meaning and that those symbols control behavior. Social construction of reality argues that reality is a social construction that depends on a correspondence of people's meanings for things in their shared world.

Cultivation analysis, developed by George Gerbner and his colleagues, claims that television "cultivates" or constructs a reality of the world that, although possibly inaccurate, becomes the accepted reality simply because we as a culture believe it to be the reality. Heavy viewers are more susceptible to cultivation than are light viewers.

Critical cultural theory, based on neo-Marxism, sees media as agents used in the cause of entrenched elites. Two interesting examples, British cultural studies and news production research, demonstrate the core philosophy of this theory, that regular people are disadvantaged by media systems as they currently exist.

There are many more mass communication theories than can be discussed in one textbook chapter, but media literate people, like mass communication theorists, develop their awareness of the impact of media, understand the process of mass communication, and accept media content as a text that provides insight into ourselves and our culture.

The impact of mediated violence is the best-known effects issue. The causal relationship between violent media content and subsequent aggressive behavior has been demonstrated for decades, giving rise to the stimulation and aggressive cues models of media's influence on aggressive behavior. Social cognitive theory has been central to demonstrating the operation of both vicarious reinforcement and environmental incentives. Catharsis, the idea that viewing mediated aggression reduces people's innate aggressive drives, has been discredited.

Effects researchers have also made important discoveries, paralleling the discoveries of the violence researchers, about the relationship between media representations of drugs and alcohol and subsequent behavior. Disagreement exists, however, regarding the interplay of content and behavior. Those who adopt the wider, macro-level ritual view of mass communication more readily accept media's influence on people's behavior than do those who hold to more transmissional views.

Two other effects issues that have attracted scientific attention are the impact of media portrayals of different groups of people (stereotyping) and the impact of media, especially television, on political campaigns. Links between attitudes and media portrayals have been demonstrated. None of this, however, is meant to imply that media content cannot have good or prosocial effects.

Key Terms

Use the text's CD-ROM and the Online Learning Center at www.mhhe.com/baran to further your understanding of the following terminology.

early window, 416
willing suspension of
   disbelief, 416
mass communication
   theory, 418
cultivation analysis, 418
social construction of
   reality, 418
attitude change theory, 419
middle-range theories, 419
paradigm, 420
paradigm shift, 420
mass society theory, 421
hypodermic needle theory, 421
magic bullet theory, 421
grand theory, 422
limited effects theory, 423
two-step flow theory, 423
opinion leaders, 423

opinion followers, 423
dissonance theory, 424
selective processes, 425
selective exposure
   (attention), 425
selective retention, 425
selective perception, 425
reinforcement theory, 427
uses and gratifications
   approach, 428
agenda setting, 429
dependency theory, 430
social cognitive theory, 431
modeling, 431
imitation, 431
identification, 431
observational learning, 431
inhibitory effects, 431
disinhibitory effects, 431

cultural theory, 433
symbolic interaction, 433
product positioning, 433
symbols, 434
signs, 434
typification schemes, 434
mainstreaming, 435
critical cultural theory, 436
neo-Marxist theory, 436
Frankfurt School, 437
British cultural theory, 437
news production research, 438
stimulation model, 441
aggressive cues model, 441
catharsis, 442
vicarious reinforcement, 443
environmental incentives, 443
desensitization, 444
stereotyping, 446

Questions for Review

Go to the self-quizzes on the CD-ROM and the Online Learning Center to test your knowledge.

1. What are paradigms and paradigm shifts?
2. What are the four eras of mass communication theory?
3. Who are Paul Lazarsfeld, Carl Hovland, Joseph Klapper, and George Gerbner? What is the contribution of each to mass communication theory?
4. How did *The War of the Worlds* radio broadcast influence the development of mass communication theory?
5. What are dissonance theory and the selective processes?
6. What is agenda setting?
7. What is dependency theory?

8. According to uses and gratifications, what is the relationship between media and audience members?
9. What is the distinction between imitation and identification in social cognitive theory?
10. What assumptions about people and media are shared by symbolic interaction and social construction of reality?
11. What are the five assumptions of cultivation analysis?
12. What are the three Bs of television?
13. What is the ice-age analogy?
14. What four common news production conventions shape the news to suit the interests of the elite?
15. What are the characteristics of critical cultural studies?
16. What are the early window and willing suspension of disbelief?
17. What is the mirror analogy as it relates to media effects? The fun-house mirror analogy?
18. What are the stimulation and aggressive cues models of media violence? What is catharsis?
19. What are vicarious reinforcement and environmental incentives? How do these ideas figure in the media violence debate?
20. What is meant by desensitization?
21. What is stereotyping? How might media contribute to it?

Questions for Critical Thinking and Discussion

1. Did you draw your dime too small? Whether you did or not, can you explain your behavior in this seemingly simple situation?
2. Many observers today hold to limited effects theories. Are you one? If you are, why? If you are not, why not?
3. Do media set the agenda for you? If not, why not? If they do, can you cite examples from your own experience?
4. Can you find examples of magazine or television advertising that use ideas from symbolic interaction or social construction of reality to sell their products? How do they do so?
5. Can you give examples of Gerbner's three Bs of television from your own viewing? How do you think they affect your and others' views of the world?
6. Do you pay attention to alcohol advertising? Do you think it influences your level of alcohol consumption?
7. How did you do on the Stereotype Quiz on page 446? Why do you think you responded as you did?

Important Resources

Arato, A., & Gebhardt, E. (1978). *The essential Frankfurt School reader*. New York: Urizen Books. The classic collection of original writing from and commentary on the Frankfurt School. People interested in issues from the effects of popular music to the use of the Internet will find useful commentary here.

Bandura, A. (1971). *Psychological modeling: Conflicting theories*. Chicago, IL: Aldine Atherton. The classic articulation of social cognitive theory written by its dominant thinker and researcher. Not only are all aspects of social cognition thoroughly covered, but alternative views are aired.

Blumer, H. (1969). *Symbolic interactionism*. Englewood Cliffs, NJ: Prentice Hall. The classic expression of symbolic interaction.

Blumler, J. G., Katz, E., & Gurevitch, M. (1974). Utilization of mass communication by the individual. In J. G. Blumler & E. Katz (Eds.), *The uses of mass communications: Current perspectives on gratifications research*. Beverly Hills, CA: Sage. The original articulation of uses and gratifications from the researchers who developed and championed the theory.

***Critical Studies in Mass Communication*.** One of the best mass communication journals, publishing much significant theoretical and effects research.

Hall, S. (1982). The rediscovery of "ideology": Return of the repressed in media studies. In M. Gurevitch, T. Bennett, J. Curran, & J. Woollacott (Eds.), *Culture, society and the media*. New York: Methuen. A provocative and readable essay in which

Hall lays out the theoretical as well as the political basis for British cultural studies.

Hovland, C. I., Janis, I. L., & Kelley, H. H. (1953). *Communication and persuasion.* **New Haven, CT: Yale University Press.** This collection of essays and original research is the classic work on which a generation of attitude change and dissonance theory research and theory is based.

Journal of Broadcasting and Electronic Media. Another important mass communication journal, this one focusing on broadcasting and other electronic media.

Journal of Communication. A publication of the International Communication Association offering many scholarly and commentary articles from a wide variety of perspectives on many mass communication issues.

Journalism and Electronic Media Quarterly. A fine scholarly journal presenting research that goes well beyond issues of the impact of journalistic content.

American Communication Association	www.americancomm.org
International Communication Association	www.icahdq.org
National Communication Association	www.natcom.org
American Sociological Association	www.asanet.org
Roper Center for Public Opinion Research	www.ropercenter.uconn.edu
American Psychological Association	www.apa.org
Critical Theory	www.127.pair.com/critical/index2.htm
Surgeon General	www.surgeongeneral.gov
Center on Alcohol Advertising	www.tf.org/tf/alcohol2.htm
National Institute of Media and the Family	www.mediaandthefamily.org
Center for Science in the Public Interest	www.cspinet.org

CHAPTER 14

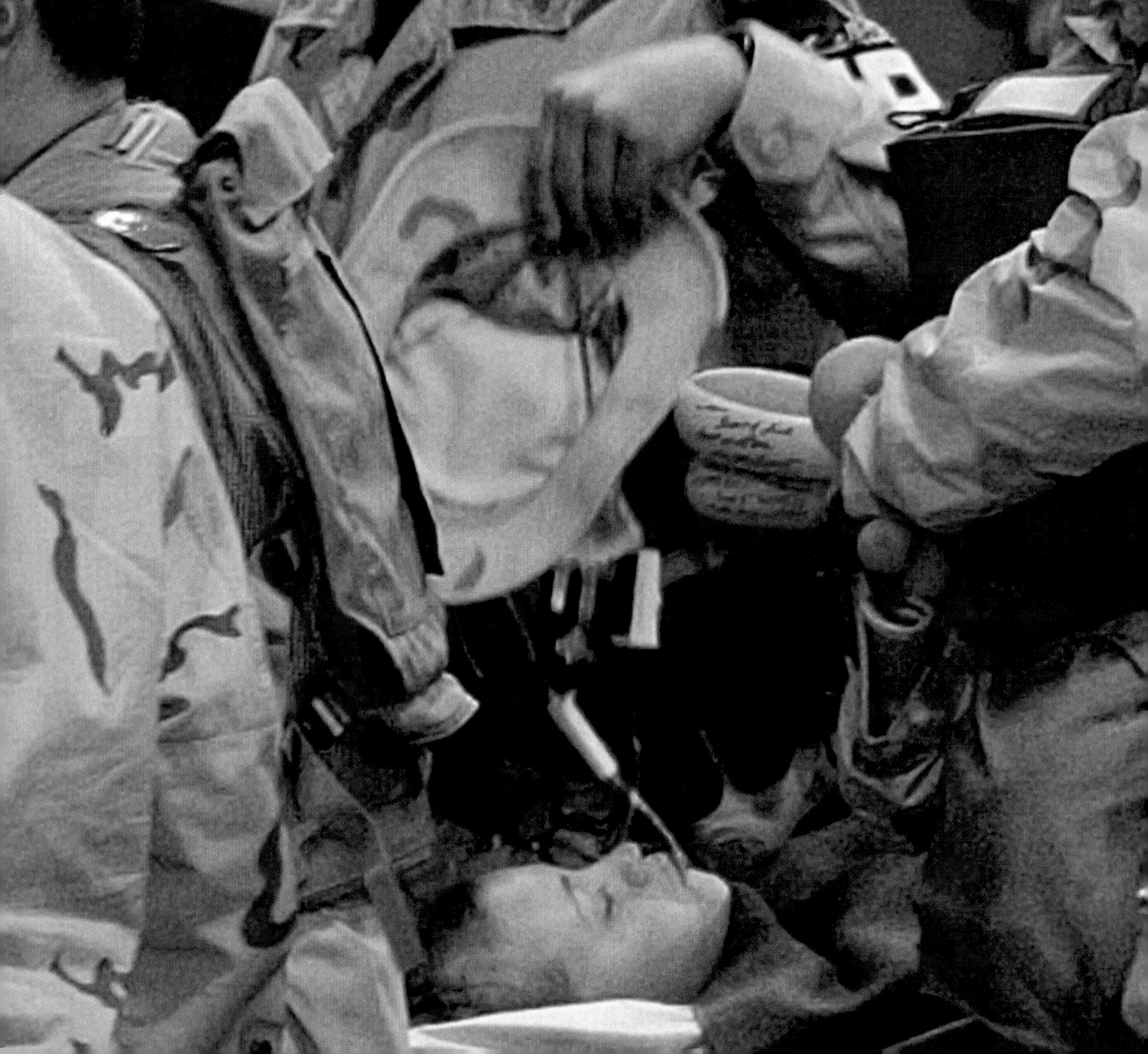

Media Freedom, Regulation, and Ethics

LEARNING OBJECTIVES

Our democracy exists on a foundation of self-governance, and a free and responsible mass media are essential to both. But media, because of their power and the often conflicting demands of profit and service under which they operate, are (and should be) open to some control. The level and sources of that control, however, are controversial issues for the media, in the government, and in the public forum. After studying this chapter you should

- be familiar with the history and development of our contemporary understanding of the First Amendment.

- understand the justification for and exercise of media regulation.

- differentiate between a media system that operates under a libertarian philosophy and one that operates under a social responsibility philosophy.

- be conversant in the changes in copyright occasioned by the new digital media and what they mean for content consumers and democracy.

- be able to effectively define and discuss media ethics and how they are applied.

- make personally relevant judgments about media practitioners' conduct in the face of ethical dilemmas.

- understand the operation and pros and cons of self-regulation.

- possess improved skill at discerning the ethical use of anonymous sources.

TIMELINE

- **1644** Milton's *Areopagitica*
- **1790** Bill of Rights
- **1919** "Clear and present danger" ruling
- **1931** *Near v. Minnesota* prior restraint ruling
- **1935** Hauptmann/Lindbergh trial
- **1943** NBC "traffic cop" decision
- **1947** *Social Responsibility Theory of the Press*
- **1964** *New York Times v. Sullivan* public figure ruling
- **1969** Red Lion decision
- **1971** Pentagon Papers
- **1973** Miller decision defines obscenity
- **1979** *Progressive* hydrogen bomb case
- **2001** U.S. Patriot Act

UP UNTIL NOW, EVERYTHING HAD BEEN RIGHT ABOUT THE JOB. Editor of a major college daily newspaper makes a great resumé entry, you are treated like royalty at school events, you get to do something good for your campus, and, if you do your job well, even for the larger world out there. But as the tension around you grows, you start to wonder if it's all worth it.

First there was September 11. Your staff wanted you to run an award-winning photo of a man jumping from the North Tower of the World Trade Center. You questioned its appropriateness; too soon, you said. Scores of papers around the world had already passed on the Associated Press–provided image (Artusa, 2002). "This picture is part of the story. We have no right to shield our readers from it," argued your staff.

Then there was the David Horowitz controversy. The conservative columnist wanted to place a full-page ad arguing against reparations for slavery. The piece, entitled "Ten Reasons Why Reparations Are a Bad Idea for Black People—And Racist, Too," had already been rejected by 41 of the 73 college papers to which it had been submitted. Students at Brown University had seized and destroyed the entire run in which it had appeared (Jeffrey, 2001). You saw the ad as inflammatory and divisive and even questioned the veracity of some of its claims. But, argued many of your top staff, not only does Mr. Horowitz have a right to his say, but also college is supposed to be a place of debate and inquiry.

There was also the dustup with your editorial page editor. She wanted to editorialize against a state law that had sent a man to jail on a gun charge for violating rules against using "human images" for target practice. Why, you ask, should we editorialize on a gun case? It's not a gun case, replies your trusted colleague, it's a First Amendment case. The human images were those of Saddam Hussein and Osama bin Laden. This guy was simply expressing a political viewpoint ("High Court," 2002). But then, you counter, the paper should editorialize in support of antiabortion groups that disseminate "Wanted: Dead or Alive" posters of doctors and their families, complete with reward amounts (Mintz, 2000). It's simply their expression of a political viewpoint, you explain. She curses you and storms away.

In each of these situations you decide in favor of more, rather than less, freedom. After all, it's your legal, First Amendment–guaranteed right.

Would you have run this award-winning photo on September 12, 2001?

You use the photo. You get 161 angry phone calls and e-mails. You place the antireparations ad. Nine long-time advertisers abandon the paper. You run the editorial, but with your own counterpoint essay. Someone puts a brick through the windshield of your car, and your colleague quits the paper. These events, all recently faced by real college and professional editors, highlight two important lessons offered in this chapter. First, what is legal may not always be what is right. Second, when media practitioners do try to do the right thing, they have to consider the interests, needs, and values of others besides themselves.

In this chapter we look at how the First Amendment has been defined and applied over time. We study how the logic of a free and unfettered press has come into play in the area of broadcast deregulation. We also detail the shift in the underlying philosophy of media freedom from libertarianism to social responsibility theory. This provides the background for our examination of the ethical environment in which media professionals must work as they strive to fulfill their socially responsible obligations.

A Short History of the First Amendment

The U.S. Constitution mentions only one industry by name as deserving special protection, the press. Therefore, our examination of media regulation, self-regulation, and ethics must begin with a discussion of this "First Freedom."

First Amendment
www.
freedomforum.org

As we saw in Chapter 4, the first Congress of the United States made freedom of the press a priority. The First Amendment to the new Constitution expressly stated that "Congress shall make no law . . . abridging the freedom of speech, or of the press." As a result, government regulation of the media must not only be unobtrusive but also must be sufficiently justified to meet the limits of the First Amendment. Media industry self-regulation must be sufficiently effective to render official restraint unnecessary, and media practitioners' conduct should be ethical in order to warrant this special protection.

EARLY SENTIMENT FOR A FREE PRESS

Democracy—government by the people—requires a free press. The framers of the Bill of Rights understood this because of their experience with the European monarchies from which they and their forebears had fled. They based their guarantee of this privileged position to the press on **libertarianism,** the philosophy that people cannot govern themselves in a democracy unless they have access to the information they need for that governance. Libertarian philosophy is based on the **self-righting principle,** which was forcefully stated in 1644 by English author and poet John Milton in his book *Areopagitica*. Milton argued from two main points:

- The free flow or trade of ideas serves to ensure that public discourse will allow the truth to emerge.
- Truth will emerge from public discourse because people are inherently rational and good.

But as we also saw in Chapter 4, even the First Amendment and libertarian philosophy did not guarantee freedom of the press. The Alien and Sedition Acts were passed a scant eight years after the Constitution was ratified. And Milton himself was to become the chief censor of Catholic writing in Oliver Cromwell's English government.

DEFINING AND REFINING THE FIRST AMENDMENT

Clearly the idea of freedom of the press needed some clarification. One view was (and is) housed in the **absolutist position,** which is expressed succinctly by Supreme Court Justice Hugo Black: "No law means no law." Yet the absolutist position is more complex than this would suggest. Although absolutists accept that the First Amendment provides a central and fundamental wall of protection for the press, several questions about its true meaning remained to be answered over time. Let's look at some of history's answers.

What Does "No Law" Mean?   The First Amendment said that the U.S. Congress could "make no law," but could state legislatures? City councils? Mayors? Courts? Who has the power to proscribe the press? This issue was settled in 1925 in a case involving the right of a state to limit the publication of a socialist newsletter. The Supreme Court, in *Gitlow v. New York*, stated that the First Amendment is "among the fundamental personal rights and 'liberties' protected by the due process clause of the Fourteenth Amendment from impairment by the states" (Gillmor & Barron, 1974, p. 1). Given this, "Congress shall make no law" should be interpreted as "government agencies shall make no law." Today, "no law" includes statutes, laws, administrative regulations, executive and court orders, and ordinances from government, regardless of locale.

What Is "The Press"?   Just what "press" enjoys First Amendment protection? We saw in Chapter 6 that the Supreme Court in its 1952 *Burstyn v. Wilson* decision declared that movies were protected expression. In 1973 Justice William O. Douglas wrote in *CBS v. Democratic National Committee*:

> What kind of First Amendment would best serve our needs as we approach the 21st century may be an open question. But the old fashioned First Amendment that we have is the Court's only guideline; and one hard and fast principle has served us through days of calm and eras of strife, and I would abide by it until a new First Amendment is adopted. That means, as I view it, that TV and radio . . . are all included in the concept of "press" as used in the First Amendment and therefore are entitled to live under the laissez faire regime which the First Amendment sanctions. (Gillmor & Barron, 1974, pp. 7–8)

Advertising, or commercial speech, enjoys First Amendment protection. This was established by the Supreme Court in 1942. Despite the fact that the decision in *Valentine v. Christensen* went against the advertiser, the Court wrote that just because expression was commercial did not mean that it was necessarily unprotected. Some justices argued for a "two-tiered" level of protection, with commercial expression being somewhat less worthy of protection than noncommercial expression. But others argued that this was illogical because almost all media are, in fact, commercial, even when they perform a primarily journalistic function. Newspapers, for example, print the news to make a profit.

In its 1967 *Time, Inc. v. Hill* decision the Supreme Court applied similar logic to argue that the First Amendment grants the same protection to entertainment content as it does to nonentertainment content. Is an entertainingly written news report less worthy of protection than one that is dully written? Rather than allow the government to make these kinds of narrow and ultimately subjective judgments, in the last six decades of media development the Supreme Court has consistently preferred expanding its definition of protected expression to limiting it.

What Is "Abridgment"?   Even absolutists accept the idea that limits can be placed on the time, place, and manner of expression—as long as the restrictions do not interfere with the substance of the expression. Few, for example, would find it unreasonable to limit the use of a sound truck to broadcast political messages at 4 o'clock in the morning. But the Supreme Court did find unconstitutional an ordinance that forbade all use of sound amplification except with the permission of the chief of police in its 1948 decision in *Saia v. New York*. The permissibility of other restrictions, however, is less clear-cut.

Clear and present danger   Can freedom of the press be limited if the likely result is damaging? The Supreme Court answered this question in 1919 in *Schenck v. United States*. In this case involving the distribution of a pamphlet urging resistance to the military draft during World War I, Justice Oliver Wendell Holmes wrote that expression could be limited when "the words used are used in such circumstances and are of such a nature as to create a clear and present danger that they will bring about the substantive evils that Congress has a right to prevent." Justice Holmes added, "Free speech would not protect a man in falsely shouting fire in a theater and causing panic." This decision is especially important because it firmly established the legal philosophy that there is no absolute freedom of expression; the level of protection is one of degree.

Balancing of interests   This less-than-absolutist approach is called the **ad hoc balancing of interests.** That is, in individual First Amendment cases

Is the man here accused of rape guilty or innocent? If he is guilty, he should want to cover his face to hide his identity. But if he is innocent, wouldn't he be just as likely to want to hide his identity? These so-called perp walks raise the issue of unfair pretrial publicity.

several factors should be weighed in determining how much freedom the press is granted. In his dissent to the Court's 1941 decision in *Bridges v. California*, a case involving a *Los Angeles Times* editorial, Justice Felix Frankfurter wrote that free speech and press is "not so absolute or irrational a conception as to imply paralysis of the means for effective protection of all the freedoms secured by the Bill of Rights. . . . In the cases before us, the claims on behalf of freedom of speech and of the press encounter claims on behalf of liberties no less precious."

Free press versus fair trial   One example of the clash of competing liberties is the conflict between free press (First Amendment) and fair trial (Sixth Amendment). This debate typically takes two forms: (1) Can pretrial publicity deny citizens judgment by 12 impartial peers, thereby denying them a fair trial? (2) Should cameras be allowed in the courtroom, supporting the public's right to know, or do they so alter the workings of the court that a fair trial is impossible?

Courts have consistently decided in favor of fair trial in conflicts between the First and Sixth Amendments. But it was not until 1961 that a conviction was overturned because of pretrial publicity. In *Irvin v. Dowd* the Court reversed the death sentence conviction of confessed killer Leslie Irvin because his right to a fair trial had been hampered by press coverage that labeled him "Mad Dog Irvin" and reported crimes he had committed as a juvenile, his military court-martial, his identification in a police lineup, his failure to pass a lie detector test, his confession to six

Media intrusion during the 1935 Bruno Hauptmann kidnapping trial led to the banning of radio transmissions and photographers from the courtroom. Hauptmann is seated in the center, hands crossed.

killings and numerous robberies, and his willingness to trade a guilty plea for a life sentence. Of 430 potential jurors screened before the trial by attorneys, 370 said they already were convinced Irvin was guilty. Nonetheless, although "tainted" by pretrial publicity, four of the 370 were seated as jurors. The Court determined that Irvin's trial was therefore unfair.

Print reporters have long enjoyed access to trials, but broadcast journalists have been less fortunate. In 1937, after serious intrusion by newspaper photographers during the 1935 trial of Bruno Hauptmann, accused of kidnapping the baby of trans-Atlantic aviation hero Charles Lindbergh, the American Bar Association (ABA) adopted canon 35 as part of its Code of Judicial Ethics. This rule forbade cameras and radio broadcasting of trials. In 1963 the ABA amended the canon to include a prohibition on television cameras. This, however, did not settle the issue of cameras in the courtroom.

Texas was one of three states that did not subscribe to canon 35. When the conviction for theft, swindling, and embezzlement of Texas financier Billy Sol Estes was overturned by the Supreme Court because of "the insidious influence" (Justice William Douglas's words) of cameras on the conduct of the trial, the debate flared again. Justice Tom Clark wrote for the majority:

> The free press has been a mighty catalyst in awakening public interest in governmental affairs, exposing corruption among public officers and employees and generally informing the citizenry of public events and occurrences, including court proceedings. While maximum freedom must be allowed the press in carrying on this important function in a democratic society its exercise must necessarily be subject to the maintenance of absolute fairness in the judicial process. *(Estes v. State of Texas, 1965)*

Television cameras, then, were out. But Justice Clark continued, "When advances in [broadcast journalism] permit reporting . . . by television without their present hazards to a fair trial we will have another case." Cameras were back in if they posed no hazard to the principle of fair trial.

In 1972 the ABA replaced canon 35 with canon 3A(7), allowing some videotaping of trials for specific purposes but reaffirming its opposition to the broadcast of trial proceedings. But in 1981 the Supreme Court, in *Chandler v. Florida,* determined that television cameras in the courtroom were not inherently damaging to fairness. Today, different states have adopted different standards on the issue, and the U.S. Congress is debating opening up federal courts, including the Supreme Court, to cameras. As for now, photography and broadcast of federal trials is banned by Federal Rule of Criminal Procedure 53. Still, so common has the televising of court proceedings become that Court TV, a cable channel programming nothing but real trials and commentary on them, was launched in 1991.

Libel and slander **Libel,** the false and malicious publication of material that damages a person's reputation, and **slander,** the oral or spoken defamation of a person's character, are not protected by the First

Amendment. The distinction between libel and slander, however, is sufficiently narrow that "published defamation, whether it is in a newspaper, on radio or television, in the movies, or whatever, is regarded since the 1990s as libel. And libel rules apply" (Pember, 1999, p. 134). Therefore, if a report (a) defames a person, (b) identifies that person, and (c) is published or broadcast, it loses its First Amendment protection.

A report accused of being libelous or slanderous, however, is protected if it meets any one of three tests. The first test is *truth*. Even if a report damages someone's reputation, if it is true, it is protected. The second test is *privilege*. Coverage of legislative, court, or other public activities may contain information that is not true or that is damaging to someone's reputation. The press cannot be deterred from covering these important news events for fear that a speaker or witness's comments will open it to claims of libel or slander. The third test is *fair comment*; that is, the press has the right to express opinions or comment on public issues. For example, theater and film reviews, however severe, are protected, as is commentary on other matters in the public eye.

For public figures, however, a different set of rules applies. Because they are in the public eye, public figures are fair game for fair comment. But does that leave them open to reports that are false and damaging to their reputations? The Supreme Court faced this issue in 1964 in *New York Times Co. v. Sullivan*. In 1960 the Committee to Defend Martin Luther King bought a full-page ad in the *New York Times* asking people to contribute to Dr. King's defense fund. The ad detailed abuse of Dr. King and other civil rights workers at the hands of the Montgomery, Alabama, police. L. B. Sullivan, one of three elected commissioners in that city, sued the *Times* for libel. The ad copy was not true in some of its claims, he said, and because he was in charge of the police, he had been "identified."

The Supreme Court ruled in favor of the newspaper. Even though some of the specific facts in the ad were not true, the *Times* had not acted with **actual malice.** The Court defined the standard of actual malice for reporting on public figures as *knowledge of its falsity or reckless disregard* for whether it is true or not.

Prior restraint   There is much less confusion about another important aspect of press freedom, **prior restraint.** This is the power of the government to *prevent* the publication or broadcast of expression. U.S. law and tradition make the use of prior restraint relatively rare, but there have been a number of important efforts by government to squelch content before dissemination.

In 1931 the Supreme Court ruled in *Near v. Minnesota* that freedom from prior restraint was a general, not an absolute, principle. Two of the four exceptions it listed were in times of war when national security was involved and when the public order would be endangered by the incitement to violence and overthrow by force of orderly government. These exceptions were to become the basis of two landmark prior restraint decisions. The first, involving the *New York Times*, dealt with national security in times of war; the second, focusing on protecting the public order, involved publishing instructions for building an atomic bomb.

On June 13, 1971, at the height of the Vietnam War, the *New York Times* began publication of what commonly became known as the Pentagon Papers. The papers included detailed discussion and analysis of the conduct of that unpopular war during the administrations of Presidents Kennedy and Johnson. President Nixon's National Security Council (NSC) had stamped them Top Secret. Believing that this was an improper restriction of the public's right to know, NSC staff member Daniel Ellsberg gave copies to the *Times*. After the first three installments had been published, the Justice Department, citing national security, was able to secure a court order stopping further publication. Other newspapers, notably the *Washington Post* and *Boston Globe*, began running excerpts while the *Times* was silenced until they, too, were enjoined to cease.

On June 30 the Supreme Court ordered the government to halt its restraint of the *Times*'s and other papers' right to publish the Pentagon Papers. Among the stirring attacks on prior restraint written throughout its decision was Justice Hugo Black's:

> In the First Amendment the Founding Fathers gave the free press the protection it must have to fulfill its essential role in our democracy. The press was to serve the governed, not the governors. The Government's power to censor the press was abolished so that the press would remain forever free to censure the Government. The press was protected so that it could bare the secrets of government and inform the people. Only a free and unrestrained press can effectively expose deception in government. *(New York Times v. United States)*

U.S. Supreme Court News
WWW.
oyez.nwu.edu

The New York Times

SUPREME COURT, 6-3, UPHOLDS NEWSPAPERS ON PUBLICATION OF THE PENTAGON REPORT; TIMES RESUMES ITS SERIES, HALTED 15 DAYS

Nixon Says Turks Agree To Ban the Opium Poppy

By JOHN HERBERS
Special to The New York Times

WASHINGTON, June 30— President Nixon announced today that Turke- had agreed to eliminate with a year her product, on of opium poppies, which account for about two-thirds of the illegal heroin reaching the United States.

Mr. Nixon, in a brief announcement delivered in the White House press room, said Premier Erim for "courageous, that as a result of negotiations between the United States and Turkish Governments, Premier Nihat Erim had agreed to halt altogether the cultivation of farmers shift to other crops opium poppies by June, 1972.

He said the joint announcement, made simultaneously in Washington and Ankara, "rep-resents by far the most significant breakthrough that has been achieved in stopping the source of supply of heroin n our P. Rogers, who helped work worldwide offensive against dangerous drugs."

Continued on Page 22, Column 1

Soviet Starts an Inquiry Into 3 Astronauts' Deaths

By BERNARD GWERTZMAN

PRESIDENT CALLS STEEL AND LABOR TO WHITE HOUSE

He Asks Both Sides to Meet With Him Tuesday Before Contract Talks Start

By PHILIP SHABECOFF
Special to The New York Times

WASHINGTON, June 30—President Nixon has called negotiators of the steel companies and steelworkers union to meet with him next Tuesday, before they sit down to begin contract negotiations, a White House spokesman announced today.

It will be the first time that the President will have met with labor and management in any industry prior to nationwide contract negotiations, according to Ronald L. Ziegler, the White House press secretary.

Discussion Issues Listed

Mr. Ziegler said that the President had called the meeting to discuss general economic developments and trends in the world steel markets.

Earlier today, the chairman

Pentagon Papers: Study Reports Kennedy Made 'Gamble' Into a 'Broad Commitment'

By HEDRICK SMITH

The Pentagon's study of the Vietnam war concludes that President John F. Kennedy transformed the "limited-risk gamble" of the Eisenhower Administration into a "broad commitment" to prevent Communist domination of South Vietnam.

Although Mr. Kennedy resisted pressures for putting American ground-combat units into South Vietnam, the Pentagon analysts say, he took a series of actions that significantly expanded the American military and political involvement in Vietnam but nonetheless left President Lyndon B. Johnson with had a situation as Mr. Kennedy inherited.

"The dilemma of the U.S. involvement dating from the Kennedy era," the Pentagon study observes, was to use "only limited means to achieve excessive ends."

Moreover, according to the study, prepared in 1967-68 by Government analysts, the Kennedy tactics deepened the American involvement in Vietnam piecemeal, with each step minimizing public recognition that the American role was growing.

The expansion of that role, over three decades, is traced in the 3,000 pages of the Pentagon's study, which is ac-

companied by 4,000 pages of documents on the Vietnam era. Previous articles in The Times's presentation of this material have recounted President Johnson's movement to war in 1964 and 1965.

President Kennedy made his first fresh commitments to Vietnam secretly. The Pentagon study discloses that in the spring of 1961 the President ordered 400 Special Forces troops and 100 other American military advisers sent to South Vietnam. No publicity was given to either move.

Small as the numbers seem in retrospect, the Pentagon study comments that even the first such expansion "signaled a willingness to go beyond the 685-man limit on the size of the U.S. [military] mission in Saigon, which, if it were done openly, would be the first formal breach of the Geneva agreement."

Under the interpretation of that agreement in effect since 1956, the United States was limited to 685 military advisers in Vietnam. Washington, while it did not sign the accord, pledged not to undermine it.

On May 11, 1961, the day on which President Kennedy decided to send the Special Forces, he also ordered the start of a campaign of clandestine warfare against North Vietnam, to be conducted by South Vietnamese agents directed and trained by the Central Intelligence Agency and some American Special Forces troops. [See text, action memorandum, May 11, 1961, Page 3.]

The President's instructions, as quoted in the documents, were, "In North Vietnam ... [to] form networks of resistance, covert bases and teams for

Continued on Page 6, Column 1

The Times today resumes its series of articles on the Pentagon's secret study of the Vietnam war. The study was obtained through the investigative reporting of Neil Sheehan, and the articles were researched and written over three months by Mr. Sheehan and other staff members. The fourth and fifth articles, both by Hedrick Smith, are published today and form an account of decisions in the Kennedy Administration.

Three pages of documentary material covering the Kennedy policy begin on Page 3, and documents on the 1963 coup begin on Page 9. A summary of the three earlier articles, covering the substance, covert bases and teams for sistance, appears on Page 15.

BURGER DISSENTS

First Amendment Rule Held to Block Most Prior Restraints

Decision, concurring opinions, dissents start on Page 17.

By FRED P. GRAHAM
Special to The New York Times

WASHINGTON, June 30 — The Supreme Court freed The New York Times and The Washington Post today to resume immediate publication of articles based on the secret Pentagon papers on the origins of the Vietnam war.

By a vote of 6 to 3 the Court held that any attempt by the Government to block news articles prior to publication bears "a heavy burden" of presumption against its constitutionality.

In a historic test of that principle — the first effort by the Government to enjoin publication on the ground of national security — the Court declared that "the Government had not met that burden."

The brief judgment was read to a hushed court room by Chief

Then came the case of the magazine *The Progressive*. In 1979 the magazine announced its intention to publish instructions on how to make a hydrogen bomb. President Jimmy Carter's Justice Department successfully obtained a court order halting publication, even though the article was based on information and material freely obtained from public, nonclassified sources. Before the case could come to court, several newspapers published the same or similar material. The Justice Department immediately abandoned its restraint, and six months later *The Progressive* published its original article.

Obscenity and pornography   Another form of press expression that is not protected is **obscenity.** Two landmark Supreme Court cases established the definition and illegality of obscenity. The first is the 1957 *Roth v. United States* decision. The court determined that sex and obscenity were not synonymous, a significant advance for freedom of expression. It did, however, legally affirm for the first time that obscenity was unprotected expression. The definition or test for obscenity that holds even today was expressed in the 1973 *Miller v. State of California* decision. Chief Justice Warren Burger wrote that the basic guidelines must be:

> (a) whether the average person, applying contemporary community standards, would find that the work, taken as a whole, appeals to the prurient interest, (b) whether the work depicts or describes, in a patently offensive way, sexual conduct specifically defined by the applicable state law, and (c) whether the work, taken as a whole, lacks serious literary, artistic, political, or scientific value.

The problem for the courts, the media, and the public, of course, is judging content against this standard. For example, what is patently offensive to one person may be quite acceptable to others. What is serious art to one may be serious exploitation to another. And what of an erotic short story written online by an author in New York City but accessed and read by people in Peoria, Illinois? Whose community standards would apply?

An additional definitional problem resides in **pornography,** expression calculated solely to supply sexual excitement. Pornography is protected expression. The distinction between obscenity and pornography may, however, be a legal one. Sexually explicit content is pornography (and protected) until a court rules it illegal; then it is obscene (and unprotected). The difficulty of making such distinctions can be seen in Justice Potter Stewart's famous declaration, "I may not be able to come up with a definition of pornography, but I certainly know it when I see it," and his dissent in *Ginzburg v. United States* (1966), "If the First Amendment means anything, it means that a man cannot be sent to prison merely for distributing publications which offend a judge's sensibilities, mine or any others" (as cited in Gillmor & Barron, 1974, p. 362).

Clearly, the issues of the definition and protection of obscenity and pornography may never be clarified to everyone's satisfaction (see the box "Larry Flynt and Protection for Expression We Don't Like").

OTHER ISSUES OF FREEDOM AND RESPONSIBILITY

The First Amendment has application to a number of specific issues of media responsibility and freedom.

Indecency   Obscenity and pornography are rarely issues for broadcasters. Their commercial base and wide audience make the airing of such potentially troublesome programming unwise. However, broadcasters frequently do confront the issue of **indecency.** According to the FCC, indecent language or material is that which depicts sexual or excretory activities in a way that is offensive to contemporary community standards.

An increase in the number of indecency complaints recently led the commission to modify, much to broadcasters' dissatisfaction, its way of handling indecency complaints, making it easier for listeners and viewers to challenge questionable content. Official statistics say the FCC receives 40 indecency complaints a month, but Commissioner Michael Copps disputes his own agency's count: "It's become a rare morning when I don't walk into my office and find 30 in one day," he said. The real number is probably closer to "hundreds of thousands" a year. As such, stations must now prove they are innocent. "If the station can't refute information in the

The music of such bands as the Diesel Queens is relegated to the safe harbor of late-night radio to which children are not usually listening.

Larry Flynt and Protection for Expression We Don't Like

In the 18th century, newspaper publisher John Peter Zenger's freedom to publish was tested in a famous court case, as we saw in Chapter 4. In the late 20th century, admitted pornographer Larry Flynt has had more than one day in court, but his 1988 Supreme Court appearance might be the most important for the First Amendment.

The November 1983 issue of Flynt's raunchy magazine *Hustler* included a parody of a series of Campari Liqueur ads. The real ads featured celebrities talking about their "first time" trying the drink, clearly a play on the more usual understanding of the expression. The *Hustler* take-off depicted an intoxicated Jerry Falwell—minister, tele-vangelist, and founder of the Moral Majority—confessing that his "first time" was with his mother in an outhouse. Falwell sued for $45 million, eventually winning $200,000 for intentional infliction of emotional distress. A federal court of appeals upheld the judgment.

Flynt appealed to the Supreme Court. The justices' 1988 unanimous decision supported the man who, in an earlier trial, had worn only an American flag used as a diaper. The case reaffirmed the protection of parody. But *Hustler Magazine v. Falwell*, called by Flynt "the most important First Amendment case in the history of this country," made an even stronger point. As Flynt himself stated, "If the First Amendment will protect a scumbag like me, then it will protect all of you. Because I'm the worst."

Chief Justice Rehnquist made the case for the protection of expression we don't like a bit more delicately:

At the heart of the First Amendment is the recognition of the fundamental importance of the free flow of ideas. Freedom to speak one's mind is not only an aspect of individual liberty, but essential to the quest for truth and the vitality of the society as a whole. In the world of debate about public affairs, many things done with motives that are less than admirable are nonetheless protected by the First Amendment.

Larry Flynt before the Supreme Court.

What do you think of this Supreme Court decision? Shouldn't there be limits on what can appear in the media? For example, was the attack on Falwell's mother necessary? Where should a media outlet draw the line? Where should the courts? Where should the culture?

complaint, we'll assume that the complainant got it right" said Enforcement Bureau Chief David Solomon (both quoted in McConnell, 2002d). Broadcasters see this "guilty until proven innocent" approach as an infringement of their First Amendment rights, as it requires that they keep tapes of all their content in the event they are challenged, even in the absence of evidence that a complaint has merit.

Situations such as these have led to the development of the concept of **safe harbor,** times of the broadcast day (typically 10 P.M. to 6 A.M.)

First Amendment Cyber-Tribune

WWW.

w3.trib.com/FACT

when children are not likely to be in the listening or viewing audience. In the concept of safe harbor, the FCC recognizes that potentially offensive content, because it is in fact protected expression, should be available to those who wish to see and hear it. But in its role of trustee (Chapter 7), the commission feels it has not only the right but also the obligation to protect those listeners and viewers who do not want such content for themselves or their children.

Deregulation   The difficulty of balancing the public interest and broadcasters' freedom is at the heart of the debate over deregulation and the relaxation of ownership and other rules for radio and television. As we saw in Chapter 8, changes in ownership rules have been controversial, but relaxation of the regulation of broadcasters' public service obligations and other content controls have provided even more debate.

The courts have consistently supported the FCC's right to evaluate broadcasters' performance in serving the public interest, convenience, and necessity. Naturally, that evaluation must include some judgment of the content broadcasters air. Broadcasters long argued that such "judgment" amounted to unconstitutional infringement of their First Amendment freedom. Many listeners and viewers saw it as a reasonable and quite small price to pay for the use of their (the public's) airwaves.

The Supreme Court resolved the issue in 1943 in *National Broadcasting Co. v. United States*. NBC argued that the commission was no more than a traffic cop, limited to controlling the "flow of traffic." In this view, the regulation of broadcasters' frequency, power, times of operation, and other technical matters was all that was constitutionally allowable. Yet the Court turned what is now known as the **traffic cop analogy** against NBC. Yes, the justices agreed, the commission is a traffic cop. But even traffic cops have the right to control not only the flow of traffic but its composition. For example, drunk drivers can be removed

Broadcast deregulation produced a rush of toy-based children's television shows such as *The Powerpuff Girls*, which critics contend are inherently unfair to children who cannot recognize them as program-length commercials.

The *Red Lion* Decision and the Rights of the Audience

Throughout this book we've seen how media have been used to make a difference, for example, to fight for causes or to alert people to problems. In the specific case of broadcasting, however, it was not decided until the 1960s exactly how much power individuals had in gaining access to broadcasting so they could use it to make a difference. The question was a simple one: Did broadcasters hold their licenses for the purpose of satisfying their own goals, economic and otherwise, or could ordinary citizens expect that they, too, would have access to radio and television?

In November 1964, small AM/FM radio station WGCB in Red Lion, Pennsylvania, aired its weekly installment of "The Christian Crusade." The show's host, Reverend Billy James Hargis, offered his review of a book written by a man named Fred J. Cook. Hargis did not enjoy Cook's book, *Goldwater—Extremist of the Right,* an analysis of the career of conservative politician Barry Goldwater. In his comments on the work, Hargis accused Cook of a number of offenses—lying, being fired from his job as a reporter, being left wing. To Cook this amounted to a personal attack, and under FCC rules he was entitled to time to reply.

The station owner, Red Lion Broadcasting Company, offered to sell time to Cook or, if the writer would plead poverty, to give him free time. Cook refused, claiming the *right* to reply. FCC rules said that reply time must be free in cases of personal attack. The station (and virtually the entire broadcast industry that bankrolled its defense) argued that this free time requirement was an infringement of broadcasters' First Amendment rights. As a result, the stakes were high. The question before the courts was nothing less than an affirmation or denial of the FCC's

power to promulgate rules regarding public access to airwaves that the public, in fact, owned.

In 1966 the United States Court of Appeals for the Seventh Circuit in Chicago District ruled in favor of the station. But the FCC persisted and, in 1967, the United States Court of Appeals for the District of Columbia overturned that decision, siding with Cook and the commission. Red Lion Broadcasting and the Radio Television News Directors Association appealed to the Supreme Court.

On June 9, 1969, the justices delivered what has become known as the *Red Lion* decision. Justice Byron White expressed the Court's support for Mr. Cook and the FCC this way:

> There is nothing in the First Amendment which prevents the Government from requiring a licensee to share his frequency with others and to conduct himself as a proxy or fiduciary with obligations to present those views and voices which are representative of his community and which would otherwise, by necessity, be barred from the airwaves. . . . [T]he people as a whole retain their interest in free speech by radio and their collective right to have the medium function consistently with the ends and purposes of the First Amendment. . . . It is the purpose of the First Amendment to preserve an uninhibited marketplace of ideas in which truth will ultimately prevail, rather than to countenance monopolization of that market, whether it be by the Government itself or a private licensee. *(Red Lion Broadcasting v. United States)*

Justice White's most memorable and meaningful comment on the clash between broadcaster and audience rights remains: *"It is the right of the viewers and listeners, not the right of the broadcasters, which is paramount."*

from the road. Potentially dangerous "content," like cars with faulty brakes, can also be restricted. It was precisely this traffic cop function that required the FCC to judge content. The commission was thus free to promulgate rules such as the **Fairness Doctrine,** which required broadcasters to cover issues of public importance and to be fair in that coverage, and **ascertainment,** which required broadcasters to ascertain or actively and affirmatively determine the nature of their audiences' interest, convenience, and necessity (see the box "The *Red Lion* Decision and the Rights of the Audience").

The Fairness Doctrine, ascertainment, and numerous other regulations, such as rules on children's programming and overcommercialization, disappeared with the coming of deregulation during the Reagan Administration. License renewal, for example, was once a long and diffi-

Fairness and Accuracy in Reporting
www.
fair.org

cult process for stations, which had to generate thousands of pages of documents to demonstrate that they not only knew what their audiences wanted and needed but had met those wants and needs. The burden of proof in their efforts to keep their licenses rested with them. Had they been fair? Had they kept commercial time to acceptable levels? What was their commitment to news and public affairs? Now deregulated, renewal is conducted through a much less onerous process. Broadcasters simply file brief quarterly reports with the commission indicating compliance with technical and other FCC rules. Then, when their licenses are up for renewal (every 8 years), they file a short, postcard-like renewal application.

The deregulation drive began in earnest with President Reagan's FCC Chair Mark Fowler in the 1980s. Fowler rejected the trustee model of broadcast regulation. He saw many FCC rules as an unconstitutional infringement of broadcasters' rights and believed that "the market" was the audience's best protector. He said that special rules for the control of broadcasting were unnecessary, likening television, for example, to just another home appliance. He called television no more than "a toaster with pictures."

Current FCC Chair Michael Powell, too, is a strong advocate of deregulation. Of the public interest, he has said that he "has no idea" what it is. "It is an empty vessel," he added, "in which people pour whatever their preconceived views or biases are" (quoted in Hickey, 2002b, p. 33). In another press conference he called regulation of telecommunications "the oppressor" (Coen & Hart, 2002, p. 4).

This view of deregulation is not without its critics. Republican and Democratic congressional leaders, liberal and conservative columnists, and numerous public interest groups from across the political spectrum have continued to campaign against such fruits of deregulation as concentration, conglomeration, overcommercialization, the abandonment of children, and the lowering of decency standards (Hickey, 2002b). As media law attorney Charles Tillinghast argued, "Deregulation of broadcasting means freeing that medium from one of its major obligations to the public—to inform and educate. As ownership of media outlets, including those in broadcasting, becomes more concentrated in the hands of large corporations, unless there is some regulation of content by government (where else can 'public' regulation come from?), broadcasters cannot be trusted to fulfill these obligations" (2000, pp. 150–151).

Copyright The First Amendment protects expression. *Copyright*—identifying and granting ownership of a given piece of expression—is designed to protect the creator's financial interest in that expression. Recognizing that the flow of art, science, and other expression would be enhanced by authors' financial interest in their creation, the framers of the Constitution wrote Article I, Section 8 (8), granting authors exclusive rights to their "writings and discoveries." A long and consistent history of

Fight for Fair Use
www.
digitalconsumer.org

Supreme Court decisions has ensured that this protection would be extended to the content of the mass media that have emerged since that time.

The years 1978 and 1998 saw extensive rewritings of U.S. copyright law. Copyright now remains with creators (in all media) for the span of their lives, plus 70 years. During this time, permission for the use of the material must be obtained from the copyright holder and, if financial compensation (a fee or royalty) is requested, it must be paid. Once the copyright expires, and if the creator does not renew it, the material passes into **public domain,** meaning it can be used without permission.

The exception to copyright is *fair use*, instances in which material can be used without permission or payment. Fair use includes (1) limited noncommercial use, such as photocopying a passage from a novel for classroom use; (2) use of limited portions of a work, such as excerpting a few lines or a paragraph or two from a book for use in a magazine article; (3) use that does not decrease the commercial value of the original, such as videotaping a daytime football game for private, at-home evening viewing; and (4) use in the public interest, such as an author's use of line drawings of scenes from an important piece of film. This latter situation occurred in a dispute over the Zapruder home movie of the 1963 assassination of President Kennedy. A writer used sketches based on the Zapruder film in a book examining the investigation of the Kennedy killing.

Two specific applications of copyright law pertain to recorded music and cable television. Imagine the difficulty cable companies would have in obtaining permission from all the copyright holders of all the material they import and deliver to their subscribers. Yet the cable operators do make money from others' works—they collect material from original sources and sell it to subscribers. The solution to the problem of compensating the creators of the material carried by cable systems was the creation of the Copyright Royalty Tribunal, to which cable companies paid a fee based primarily on the size of their operations. These moneys were then distributed to the appropriate producers, syndicators, and broadcasters. Congress abolished the Copyright Royalty Tribunal in 1993, leaving cable copyright issues in the hands of several different arbitration panels under the auspices of the Library of Congress.

Now imagine the difficulty songwriters would have in collecting royalties from all who use their music—not only film producers and radio and television stations, but bowling alleys, supermarkets, and restaurants. Here the solution is the **music licensing company.** The two biggest are the American Society of Composers, Authors and Publishers (ASCAP) and Broadcast Music Inc. (BMI). Both collect fees based on the users' gross receipts and distribute the money to songwriters and artists.

The Internet and Expanding Copyright   The Internet, as we saw in Chapter 7 with MP3 and in Chapter 10 with file sharing, is forcing a significant rethinking of copyright, one that disturbs many advocates of free expression. They fear that efforts to protect the intellectual property rights of copyright holders are going too far. The expansion of copyright, argues technology writer Dan Gillmor, gives "the owners of intellectual property vast new authority, simultaneously shredding users' rights" (2000, p. 1C).

For example, in January 2000, a California Superior Court, citing the Digital Millennium Copyright Act (Chapter 10), ruled the posting of DVD decryption software to be illegal. The defendants argued that they did not violate copyright. The court ruled against them because they posted "tools" on the Web that would allow others to violate copyright. Tech writer Gillmor scoffed, "Let's ban cars next. Were you aware that bank robbers use them for getaways?" (2000, p. 6C). In August of that same year, a New York court reaffirmed the ban on posting decryption software, adding that even posting links to sites offering the software was a violation of copyright. And we've already seen the controversy surrounding MP3 and file sharing, neither of which copies anybody's intellectual property, but both of which allow the sharing of copyrighted material.

Copyright exists, say critics of its expansion, to encourage the flow of art, science, and expression, and it grants financial stake to creators, not to enrich those creators but to ensure that there is sufficient incentive to keep the content flowing. "It's always important to remember that copyright is a restriction on free speech, and it's a constitutionally granted restriction on free speech. Therefore, we need to be careful when we play with copyright, because it can have some serious effects on public discourse and creativity," argued copyright expert Siva Vaidhyanathan (as quoted in Anderson, 2000, p. 25). In other words, tightening copyright restrictions can have the effect of inhibiting the flow of art, science, and expression.

Some free-expression champions see the tightening of copyright, or **digital rights management (DRM),** as something other than the justifiable protection of intellectual property. Rather, they argue, it is the drive for more control over and therefore profit from the distribution of content (Harmon, 2003). Congressman Rick Boucher (D-Virginia), arguing that "fair use is a First Amendment right," declared that DRM "has moved our nation one step closer to a 'pay per use' society that threatens to advance the narrow interests of copyright owners over the broader public interest of information consumers" (quoted in Chester & Larson, 2002, p. 4). Technology writer Gilmor says that new copy-protected digital content and copyright rules combine to "help the entertainment cartel grab absolute control over customers' reading, viewing, and listening" (2002, p. F1). *Wired*'s Jeff Howe (2001, p. 140) writes of technology and copyright-enabled "refrigerators" that will "hold music, movies, books, videogames, and anything else that's digital and salable. Like the perishables stored in that most mundane of household appliances, a media refrigerator's contents will come with expiration dates. They'll need to be refreshed periodically by the shifting of 1s and 0s out of your bank account into [a media company's]. Otherwise, your license to use them will go stale, and the songs, stories, and shows that constitute your daily media diet will wilt like week-old lettuce." And although current copyright law grants you unlimited private use of the media content you legally buy (*and* gives you the right to play it on whatever device you want wherever you want) *and* protects your freedom to copy it for your own private use, "the record companies and Hollywood are scheming to drastically erode your freedom to use legally purchased CDs and videos, and they are doing it behind your back. The only parties represented in the debate are media and technology companies, lawyers, and politicians. Consumers aren't invited. . . . In the new world sought by the media companies," warns *Wall Street Journal* technology columnist Walter Mossberg, you will "not be able to buy a CD or DVD and play it back on your PC. You might not be able to copy to your hard disk, or to a custom-made CD, the few songs you really like from a CD you bought. You might not be able to tape, or to digitally record, any TV program you like" (2002a, p. D7). Admitted one DRM executive who wished to remain anonymous, "DRM isn't about piracy. It's about driving revenue" (quoted in Howe, 2001, p. 142).

This DRM "threat" to consumers' rights to copy has led to the issuance in 2002 of a *Digital Consumers Bill of Rights* (www.digitalconsumer.org). It specifies:

- The right to "time shift" audio and video content, that is, to record it for later playback
- The right to "space shift" music and videos, that is, to copy content to blank CDs, multiple PCs, or portable players in different locations
- The right to make backup copies
- The right to use content on any platform you choose—a Windows PC, a Macintosh, a DVD player, whatever the consumer wishes
- The right to translate content into different formats (CD to tape, for example)

Social Responsibility Theory

As we saw at the beginning of this chapter, the First Amendment is based on the libertarian philosophy that assumes a fully free press and a rational, good, and informed public. But we have also seen in this and previous chapters that the media are not necessarily fully free. Government control is sometimes allowed. Corporate control is assumed and accepted. During the 1930s and 1940s, serious doubts were also raised concerning the public's rationality and goodness. As World War II spread across Europe at the end of the 1930s, libertarians were hard pressed to explain how Nazi propaganda could succeed if people could in fact tell right from wrong. As the United States was drawn closer to the European conflict, calls for greater government control of press and speech at home were justified by less-than-optimistic views of the "average American's" ability to handle difficult information. As a result, libertarianism came under attack for being too idealistic.

Time magazine owner and publisher Henry Luce then provided money to establish an independent commission of scholars, politicians, legal experts, and social activists who would study the role of the press in U.S. society and make recommendations on how it should best operate in support of democracy. The Hutchins Commission on Freedom of the Press, named after its chairperson, University of Chicago Chancellor Robert Maynard Hutchins, began its work in 1942 and, in 1947, produced its report, "The Social Responsibility Theory of the Press" (see Davis, 1990).

Social responsibility theory is a **normative theory**—that is, it explains how media should *ideally* operate in a given system of social values—and it is now the standard for U.S. media. Other social and political systems adhere to different normative theories, and these will be detailed in Chapter 15.

Social responsibility theory asserts that media must remain free of government control, but in exchange media must serve the public. The core assumptions of this theory are a cross between libertarian principles of freedom and practical admissions of the need for some form of control on the media (McQuail, 1987):

- Media should accept and fulfill certain obligations to society.
- Media can meet these obligations by setting high standards of professionalism, truth, accuracy, and objectivity.
- Media should be self-regulating within the framework of the law.
- Media should avoid disseminating material that might lead to crime, violence, or civil disorder or that might offend minority groups.
- The media as a whole should be pluralistic, reflect the diversity of the culture in which they operate, and give access to various points of view and rights of reply.
- The public has a right to expect high standards of performance, and official intervention can be justified to ensure the public good.
- Media professionals should be accountable to society as well as to their employers and the market.

In rejecting government control of media, social responsibility theory calls for responsible, ethical industry operation, but it does not free audiences from their responsibility. People must be sufficiently media literate to develop firm yet reasonable expectations and judgments of media performance. But ultimately it is practitioners, through the conduct of their duties, who are charged with operating in a manner that obviates the need for official intrusion.

Media Industry Ethics

A number of formal and informal controls, both external and internal to the industry, are aimed at ensuring that media professionals operate in an ethical manner consistent with social responsibility theory. Among the external formal controls are laws and regulations, codified statements of what can and can't be done and what content is permissible and not permissible, and industry codes of practice. Among the external informal controls are pressure groups, consumers, and advertisers. We have seen how these informal controls operate throughout this text. Our interest here is in examining media's internal controls, or ethics.

DEFINING ETHICS

Thomas Jefferson Center for Free Expression
WWW.
tjcenter.org

Ethics are rules of behavior or moral principles that guide our actions in given situations. The word comes from the Greek *ethos,* which means the customs, traditions, or character that guide a particular group or culture. In our discussion, ethics specifically refer to the application of rational thought by media professionals when they are deciding between two or more competing moral choices.

For example, it is not against the law to publish the name of a rape victim. But is it ethical? It is not illegal to stick a microphone in a crying father's face as he cradles the broken body of his child at an accident scene. But is it ethical?

The application of media ethics almost always involves finding the *most morally defensible* answer to a problem for which there is no single correct or even best answer. Return to the grieving father. The reporter's job is to get the story; the public has a right to know. The man's sorrow is part of that story, but the man has a right to privacy. As a human being he deserves to be treated with respect and to be allowed to maintain his dignity. The reporter has to decide whether to get the interview or leave the grief-stricken man in peace. That decision is guided by the reporter's ethics.

THREE LEVELS OF ETHICS

Because ethics reflect a culture's ideas about right and wrong, they exist at all levels of that culture's operation. **Metaethics** are fundamental cultural values. What is justice? What does it mean to be good? Is fairness possible? We need to examine these questions to know ourselves. But as valuable as they are for self-knowledge, metaethics provide only the broadest foundation for the sorts of ethical decisions people make daily. They define the basic starting points for moral reasoning.

Normative ethics are more or less generalized theories, rules, and principles of ethical or moral behavior. The various media industry codes of ethics or standards of good practice are examples of normative ethics. They serve as real-world frameworks within which people can begin to weigh competing alternatives of behavior. Fairness is a metaethic, but journalists' codes of practice, for example, define what is meant by fairness in the world of reporting, how far a reporter must go to ensure fairness, and how fairness must be applied when being fair to one person means being unfair to another.

Ultimately, media practitioners must apply both the big rules and the general guidelines to very specific situations. This is the use of **applied ethics,** and applying ethics invariably involves balancing conflicting interests.

BALANCING CONFLICTING INTERESTS

In applying ethics, the person making the decisions is called the **moral agent.** For moral agents, sticky ethical issues invariably bring together conflicting interests, for example, those of the editor, readers, and advertisers in this chapter's opening vignette.

Media ethicist Louis Day (1997) identified six sets of individual or group interests that often conflict:

Media Ethics Watchdog
www.
mediawhoresonline.com

- The interests of the moral agent's *individual conscience;* media professionals must live with their decisions.

- The interests of *the object of the act;* a particular person or group is likely to be affected by media practitioners' actions.

- The interests of *financial supporters;* someone pays the bills that allow the station to broadcast or the newspaper or magazine to publish.

- The interests of *the institution;* media professionals have company loyalty, pride in the organization for which they work.

- The interests of *the profession;* media practitioners work to meet the expectations of their colleagues; they have respect for the profession that sustains them.

- The interests of *society;* media professionals, like all of us, have a social responsibility. Because of the influence their work can have, they may even have greater responsibilities than do many other professionals.

In mass communication, these conflicting interests play themselves out in a variety of ways. Some of the most common, yet thorniest, require us to examine such basic issues as truth and honesty, privacy, confidentiality, personal conflict of interest, profit and social responsibility, and protection from offensive content.

Truth and Honesty   Can the media ever be completely honest? As soon as a camera is pointed at one thing, it is ignoring another. As soon as a video editor combines two different images, that editor has imposed his or her definition of the truth. Truth and honesty are overriding concerns for media professionals. But what is truth? Take the case of Las Vegas television station KLAS. It wanted to use surveillance footage of a fatal shooting at a casino. The video was dramatic—a full-scale shoot-out in a crowded gambling hall resulting in one death. The images were truthful, but for the evening news they were too "dull, silent" (Rosen, 2002a, p. 12). So the station dubbed in casino sounds—slot machines ringing, laughter and chatter, gunfire. These sounds were in the casino when the gunplay occurred, so all the station did was show the truth.

Privacy   Do public figures forfeit their right to privacy? in what circumstances? Are the president's marital problems newsworthy if they do not get in the way of the job? Who is a public figure? When are people's sexual orientations newsworthy? Do you report the names of women who have been raped or the names of juvenile offenders? What about sex offenders? How far do you go to interview grieving parents? When is secret taping permissible?

Our culture values privacy. We have the right to maintain the privacy of our personal information. We use privacy to control the extent and nature of interaction we have with others. Privacy protects us from unwanted government intrusion.

The media, however, by their very nature, are intrusive. Privacy proves to be particularly sensitive because it is almost a metaethic, a fundamental value. Yet the applied ethics of the various media industries allow, in fact sometimes demand, that privacy be denied.

The media have faced a number of very important tests regarding privacy over the last few years. Media pursuit of celebrities and the propriety of **ride-alongs** have generated much comment both inside and outside the media industries.

The death of John F. Kennedy, Jr., in July 1999 put the issue of media ethics—the balancing of press freedom and privacy—squarely in the public spotlight. Hundreds of still and video photographers descended on the grieving family of Kennedy, who, with his wife and her sister, died when the plane he was flying crashed on the way to Martha's Vineyard. The particular ethical issue became the privacy of young members of the Kennedy clan. Reputable media organizations such as CBS's *48 Hours* aired aerial video footage of the family's home as loved ones gathered to console one another. *People* magazine ran cover and inside pictures of the distraught young relatives. Even the venerable *New York Times* later

The ethical issue of personal privacy was thrust into open debate with the media frenzy that followed the plane crash that killed John F. Kennedy, Jr. Here, a pack of reporters swarms around the Reverend Edward Byington, the priest of the church where the Kennedy family worships when summering on Cape Cod.

Reality shows such as *Cops* may be popular with viewers, but ride-alongs that provide their footage raise important ethical questions concerning the rights of the accused.

printed a photograph of one of the Kennedy children leaving the church memorial service on its front page.

Another privacy issue, *ride-alongs*—the practice of allowing television reporters to accompany police in the conduct of their duty—became a hotly debated ethical issue because of a 1999 Supreme Court decision. Ride-alongs are a staple of low-budget reality television shows such as *Cops,* but it was lawsuits against two well-respected media companies, CNN and the *Washington Post,* that forced the Supreme Court to decide if the practice posed a legal rather than an ethical problem. Media professionals need access to police activities, argued the media, and journalists are also a powerful check on police abuse. The decision when to ride along with police and when to enter an alleged crime scene with them should depend on the media professional's moral judgment.

In the case of CNN, reporters accompanied federal agents from the Department of the Interior's Fish and Wildlife Division on a raid against Montana ranchers suspected of poisoning eagles. CNN ran the footage of the raid numerous times. The ranchers were eventually acquitted of killing eagles but found guilty of misusing pesticides. The *Post* case involved a reporter and photographer accompanying Maryland police to the home of a couple whose son they were hunting. The *Post* never used photos of the couple—the father in his underwear, the mother in her nightgown—forced to the floor at gunpoint. The respective lawsuits

Find the journalist. Vanessa Leggett (top left) spent 168 days in jail rather than violate her promise of confidentiality to her sources. But the Texas Attorney General said she wasn't a journalist, only an "aspiring writer." As such, she could not claim reporter's privilege. But what makes one a journalist? Would you trust (moving counterclockwise) Leeza Gibbons, Stone Phillips, Katie Couric, or Dan Rather to spend more than 5 months in jail to protect you?

brought by both the ranchers and the couple (whose son did not live with them) produced a unanimous Supreme Court decision taking ride-alongs out of the realm of ethics and making them illegal unless subjects grant permission for the use of the collected pictures which, of course, is unlikely in these situations. In balancing the public's right to know against the privacy interests of those suspected of wrongdoing, privacy prevailed.

Confidentiality An important tool in contemporary news gathering and reporting is **confidentiality,** the ability of media professionals to keep secret the names of people who provide them with information. Without confidentiality, employees could not report the misdeeds of their employers for fear of being fired; people would not tell what they know of a crime for fear of retribution from the offenders or unwanted police attention. The anonymous informant nicknamed "Deep Throat" would never have felt free to divulge the Nixon White House involvement in the Republican break-in of the Democratic Party's Watergate campaign offices were it not for the promise of confidentiality from *Washington Post* reporters Carl Bernstein and Bob Woodward.

But how far should reporters go in protecting a source's confidentiality? Should reporters go to jail rather than divulge a name? Thirty-one states and the District of Columbia have established **shield laws,** legislation that expressly protects reporters' rights to maintain sources' confidentiality in courts of law. There is no shield law in federal courts, and most journalists want it that way. Their fear is that once Congress makes one "media law" it may want to make another. For example, media professionals do not want the government to legislate the definition of "reporter" or "journalist." The 168 days Vanessa Leggett spent in jail highlight the dilemma for media professionals. Ms. Leggett, who had never published a piece of journalism, was working on a book about a high-profile Texas murder. In her research she interviewed several people to whom she promised confidentiality. A federal grand jury demanded her notes. She said no, basing her refusal on the First Amendment, claiming reporter's privilege. But, responded the Attorney General's office, she was not a journalist, only an "aspiring writer." When she was released in 2002, her $5\frac{1}{2}$ months in prison made her the longest-jailed journalist in U.S. history—*if* she is a journalist. But what makes a journalist? Can you think of a well-known "journalist," for example, Leeza Gibbons, Deborah Norville, Stone Phillips, Katie Couric, or Dan Rather, who would be willing to spend half a year in prison to protect your confidentiality?

The ethics of confidentiality are also tested by reporters' frequent use of quotes and information from "unnamed sources," "sources who wish to remain anonymous," and "inside sources." Often the guarantee of anonymity is necessary to get the information, but is this fair to those who are commented on by these nameless, faceless newsmakers? Don't these people—even if they are highly placed and powerful themselves—have a right to know their accusers?

Personal Conflict of Interest   As we've seen, ethical decision making requires a balancing of interests. But what of a media professional's own conflicts of interest? Should media personalities accept speaking fees, free travel, and other gifts from groups and corporations that they may later have to examine? Is it proper for media personalities to fail to disclose the sources and amounts of such gifts? The bankruptcy of Enron and the resulting financial damage to millions of Americans recently put a harsh spotlight on journalists' personal conflicts of interest. Online postings were calling into question the company's financial practices and stability as early as 1997 (for example, Yahoo message boards were calling Enron "not just a dog but a hybrid cur whose genetics were suspect"; in Reno, 2002, p. B4). Other hints of the company's questionable practices abounded (Sherman, 2002), but where was the mainstream press, not to mention the business press? Many, it seems, were working for Enron. *New York Times* financial columnist Paul Krugman received $50,000 as an Enron adviser before joining the paper. Also earning payment from Enron for various services were Irwin Stelzer (who refused to reveal the amount of his payment) and William Kristol of *The Weekly Standard* ($100,000), Lawrence Kudlow of CNBC and *National Review* ($50,000), and the *Wall Street Journal*'s Peggy Noonan ($25,000 to $50,000) (Kurtz, 2002). There is no evidence that Enron's money bought it favorable coverage and commentary from these journalists, but media professionals should, in the words of media ethics reporter Joshua Lipton, "think twice about what companies really want when they pay for advice" (2002, p. 13). Media critic Howard Kurtz explained that these journalists "have put themselves in a weird box. If they recused themselves and wrote nothing, as some critics suggest, then the company would in effect have bought their silence. By writing on Enron, they risk the appearance of biting the hand that fed them just to flaunt their journalistic courage" (Kurtz, 2002, p. B4). Enron "was not the press's finest hour," editorialized *Business Week* (in Sherman, 2002, p. 23).

Other conflict-of-interest issues bedevil media professionals. The 2003 war in Iraq raised the problem of **embedding,** reporters accepting military control over their output in exchange for close contact with the troops. The interests in conflict here are objectivity and access—do reporters pay too high a price for their exciting video or touching personal interest stories? Conflicts of interest also arise when media professionals' personal values, if put into action (for example, marching in a pro-choice demonstration), conflict with their obligation to show balance (for example, in reporting on a series of pro-life protests). The September 11, 2001, terrorist attacks on New York City and Washington, D.C., put the ethical question of personal versus professional values into the cultural forum as have few events, as you can see in the box entitled "Journalist or American? Media Ethics and 9/11" on pages 489–491.

Profit and Social Responsibility   The media industries are just that, industries. They exist not only to entertain and inform their audiences but also to make a profit for their owners and shareholders. What happens when serving profit conflicts with serving the public?

The conflict between profit and responsibility was the subject of the Academy Award–nominated 1999 movie *The Insider*. In late 1995, CBS executives killed an exclusive *60 Minutes* interview with Jeffrey Wigand, a former Brown & Williamson tobacco company executive, who told anchor Mike Wallace that cigarette manufacturers manipulated nicotine levels and had lied under oath before Congress. Network officials claimed they only wished to save CBS from a multibillion-dollar lawsuit brought by Brown & Williamson, with whom Wigand had signed a nondisclosure agreement. Many observers at the time—and many moviegoers 4 years later—believed that the company's real fear was that such a lawsuit would reduce the value of the executives' CBS stock.

Concentration and conglomeration raise serious questions about media professionals' willingness to choose responsibility over profit. As media law expert Charles Tillinghast commented:

> One need not be a devotee of conspiracy theories to understand that journalists, like other human beings, can judge where their interests lie, and what risks are and are not prudent, given the desire to continue to eat and feed the family. Nor does one have to be possessed of such theories to understand that wealthy media corporations often share outlooks common to corporations in many different fields, as a result of their status, not of any 'agreements.' It takes no great brain to understand one does not bite the hand that feeds—or that one incurs great risk by doing so. (2000, pp. 145–146)

Balancing profit and social responsibility is a concern not just for journalists. Practitioners in entertainment, advertising, and public relations often face this dilemma. Does an ad agency accept as a client the manufacturer of sugared children's cereals even though doctors and dentists consider these products unhealthy? Does a public relations firm accept as a client the trade office of a country that forces prison inmates to manufacture products in violation of international rules? Does a production company distribute the 1950s television show *Amos 'n' Andy* knowing that it embodies many offensive stereotypes of African Americans?

Moreover, balancing profit and the public interest does not always involve big companies and millions of dollars. Often, a media practitioner

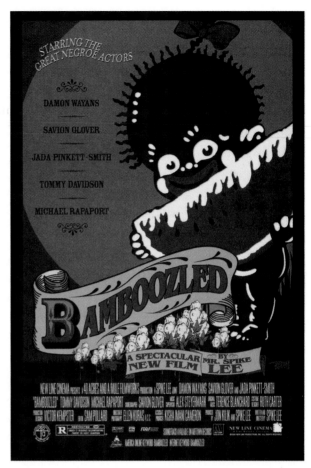

Many newspapers across the country refused to run this ad for Spike Lee's movie *Bamboozled* (2000). Even though the film attacked racist media stereotypes, editors at the newspapers found it socially irresponsible to run an ad featuring such an offensive stereotype.

will face an ethical dilemma at a very personal level. What would you do in this situation? The editor at the magazine where you work has ordered you to write an article about the 14-year-old daughter of your city's mayor. The girl's addiction to amphetamines is a closely guarded family secret, but it has been leaked to your publication. You believe that this child is not a public figure. Your boss disagrees, and the boss *is* the boss. By the way, you've just put a down payment on a lovely condo, and you need to make only two more installments to pay off your new car. Do you write the story?

Offensive Content Entertainment, news, and advertising professionals must often make decisions about the offensive nature of content. Other than the particular situation of broadcasters discussed earlier in this chapter, this is an ethical rather than a legal issue.

Offensive content is protected. Logically, we do not need the First Amendment to protect sweet and pretty expression. Freedom of speech and freedom of the press exist expressly to allow the dissemination of material that *will* offend. But what is offensive? Clearly, what is offensive to one person may be quite satisfactory to another. Religious leaders on the political right have attacked the children's television show *Teletubbies* for supposedly promoting homosexuality, and critics from the political left have attacked the film *Star Wars Episode I: The Phantom Menace* for racist stereotyping. Television stations and networks regularly bleep cuss words that are common on cable television and in the schoolyard but leave untouched images of stabbings, beatings, and shootings. Our culture sanctions the death penalty but is unwilling to view it on television. Where do we draw the line? Do we consider the tastes of the audience? Which members of the audience—the most easily offended? These are ethical, not legal, determinations.

CODES OF ETHICS AND SELF-REGULATION

To aid practitioners in their moral reasoning, all major groups of media professionals have established formal codes or standards of ethical behavior. Among these are the Society of Professional Journalists' *Code of Ethics,* the American Society of Newspaper Editors' *Statement of Principles,* the Radio-Television News Directors Association's *Code of Broadcast News Ethics,* the American Advertising Federation's *Advertising Principles of American Business,* and the Public Relations Society of America's *Code of Professional Standards for the Practice of Public Relations.* These are prescriptive codes that tell media practitioners what they should do.

To some, these codes are a necessary part of a true profession; to others, they are little more than unenforceable collections of clichés that restrict constitutional rights and invite lawsuits from outsiders. They offer at least two important benefits to ethical media practitioners: They are an additional source of information to be considered when making moral judgments, and they represent a particular media industry's best expression of its shared wisdom. To others, however, they are meaningless and needlessly restrictive. Ethicists Jay Black and Ralph Barney (1985), for example, argue, "The fact should be evident that the First Amendment has a primary purpose of protecting the distribution of ideas . . . from restriction efforts by legions of 'regulators.' Ethics codes should be considered among those 'regulators'" (p. 28). They continue, "It is indeed not difficult to find examples of codified professional ethics that ultimately become self-serving. That is, they tend to protect the industry, or elements of the industry, at the expense of individuals and other institutions, even of the full society" (p. 29).

Another criticism of ethics codes is that they are an open invitation to lawsuits from outsiders. Media industry lawyers "worry that plaintiffs' lawyers will focus on deviations from the guidelines as evidence of actual malice, negligence, or some other fault standard. Depending on how the guidelines are worded, you might even cobble together a breach-of-contract theory based on 'I promised my (audience) I would do X, I didn't, and therefore, I breached my contract with my (audience),'" explained Jane Kirtley, executive director of the Reporters Committee for Freedom of the Press. This argument, she continued, "would probably be thrown out and could be averted by careful wording . . . but in these days of crazy lawsuits, I don't think I would rule it out" (as quoted in Noack, 1999, p. 9). In other words, the fear is that published codes or standards could be used against the organization as evidence that it failed to follow its own rules.

In addition to industry professional codes, many media organizations have formulated their own institutional policies for conduct. In the case of the broadcast networks, these are enforced by **Standards and Practices Departments.** Local broadcasters have what are called **policy books.** Newspapers and magazines standardize behavior in two ways: through **operating policies** (which spell out standards for everyday operations) and **editorial policies** (which identify company positions on specific issues). Many media organizations also utilize **ombudsmen,** practitioners internal to the company who serve as "judges" in disputes between the public and the organization. Some media organizations subscribe to the small number of existing **media councils,** panels of people from both the media and the public who investigate complaints against the media from the public and publish their findings.

These mechanisms of normative ethics are a form of self-regulation, designed in part to forestall more rigorous or intrusive government regulation. In a democracy dependent on mass communication, they serve an important function. We are suspicious of excessive government involvement in media. Self-regulation, however, has certain limitations:

- *Media professionals are reluctant to identify and censure colleagues who transgress.* To do so might appear to be admitting that

UNITED COLORS
OF BENETTON.

This Benetton ad was offensive to many readers. Yet its message—that race should not matter—certainly is not offensive. Why do you think the ad was so controversial and, eventually, pulled from distribution?

problems exist; whistle-blowers in the profession are often met with hostility from their peers.

- *The standards for conduct and codes of behavior are abstract and ambiguous.* Many media professionals see this flexibility as a necessary evil; freedom and autonomy are essential. Others believe the lack of rigorous standards renders the codes useless.

- *As opposed to those in other professions, media practitioners are not subject to standards of professional training and licensing.* Again, some practitioners view standards of training and licensing as limiting media freedom and inviting government control. Others argue that licensing has not had these effects on doctors and lawyers.

- *Media practitioners often have limited independent control over their work.* Media professionals are not autonomous, individual professionals. They are part of large, hierarchically structured organizations. Therefore, it is often difficult to punish violations of standards because of the difficulty in fixing responsibility.

Critics of self-regulation argue that these limitations are often accepted willingly by media practitioners because the "true" function of self-regulation

Journalist or American? Media Ethics and 9/11

Boondocks © 2001 Aaron McGruder. Distributed by Universal Press Syndicate. Reprinted with permission. All rights reserved.

The September 11, 2001, terrorist attacks on America put our mass media and their operation squarely in the cultural forum. We've already seen in Chapter 1 that the media have been faulted for their lack of international news and commentary, essentially leaving citizens in the dark about external threats. But as we also saw at the opening of this chapter, that horrific event and its aftermath raised several vexing ethical dilemmas. Choice of images was only one. Would you have run the photo of the falling man?

Other serious debates arose surrounding the issues of patriotism versus journalism, of determining acceptable levels of government censorship, of coverage of combat, of acceptable levels of criticism in wartime, and of commercialization of the tragedy. What each contains is a legitimate conflict between the interests identified earlier in this chapter. As such, none of these dilemmas has an easy solution.

Patriotism versus Journalism

CBS newsman Dan Rather, tears filling his eyes, told David Letterman's national television audience, "George Bush is the president, he makes the decisions and, you know, as just one American, he wants me to line up, just tell me where." ABC's Cokie Roberts told the late-night viewers, "Look, I am, I will just confess to you, a total sucker for the guys who stand up with all the ribbons on and stuff and they say it's true and I'm ready to believe it" (both quoted in Hart & Ackerman, 2001, pp. 6–7). Anchors and reporters wore American flag lapel pins on the air. Station and network logos were literally draped in digitally waving Stars and Stripes. What became of journalistic detachment, multiple tongues and antagonistic voices (Chapter 4), skepticism, objectivity?

Regardless of what you personally believed at that terrible time, was there not legitimate debate over the root causes of the terrorist attacks? The nation's preparedness for such attacks? The wisdom of war in Afghanistan? Do you accept the argument "We're Americans first, journalists second"?

Or do you agree with Michael Massing, *Columbia Journalism Review* contributing editor, who wrote that those who confuse patriotism and journalism "have violated every canon of good journalism. They have also snuffed out any whiff of debate and dissent" (2001, p. 6)?

continued

Journalist or American? Media Ethics and 9/11, *continued*

Does the argument of Russ Baker, another *Columbia Journalism Review* contributing editor, move you? He wrote:

> Flag-waving is not surprising in the aftermath of a full-scale attack on American civilians. As individuals we are all part of a severely traumatized body politic. But it is precisely during the most trying periods that journalists must distance themselves from their emotions if they are to do their best work. . . . The need for tough-minded reporting has never been clearer. When journalists hold themselves back—in deference to their own emotions or to the sensitivities of the audience or through timidity in the face of government pressure—America is weakened. Journalism has no more important service to perform than to ask tough, even unpopular questions when our government wages war. (2002, pp. 78–79)

Acceptable Levels of Criticism in Wartime

Not everyone agreed with Mr. Baker's definition of journalism's "no more important service" or with the title of his essay, "Want To Be A Patriot? Do Your Job." Attorney General John Ashcroft told reporters that media professionals who question his decisions "aid terrorists" and "give ammunition to America's enemies" (quoted in Naureckas, 2002, p. 2). When a guest on late-night ABC talk show *Politically Incorrect* called the hijackers "cowards," host Bill Maher commented that whatever those madmen were, they were not cowards. Military men who lob missiles from the safety of thousands of miles, he suggested, are cowards. Despite Maher's next-night apology, numerous affiliates dropped the show, several sponsors withdrew their ads, and the network did not renew the popular program for the next season. Commenting on the controversy over *Politically Incorrect,* White House press secretary Ari Fleischer told reporters that the events surrounding the show "are reminders to all Americans that they need to watch what they say, watch what they do, and this is not a time for remarks like that" (quoted in Hart & Ackerman, 2001, p. 6).

Elsewhere, several newspapers dropped the comic strip *Boondocks* because it was critical of American foreign policy; reporters Dan Guthrie of the *Oregon Daily Courier* and Tom Gutting of the *Texas City Sun* were fired from their papers for writing columns critical of President Bush's actions on the day of the attacks; and syndicated radio host Peter Werbe's show was dropped from a Santa Cruz, California, AM/FM combo after he criticized U.S. foreign policy. The station owner's mother explained in an on-air editorial, "We are all Americans now. . . . We cannot afford the luxury of political divisiveness" (quoted in Hart & Ackerman, 2001, p. 6). But the *Washington Post* editorialized that our mass media "will be judged in time by how robustly they resist a climate of intolerance. . . . It is America's strength to encourage contrarian viewpoints and tolerate distasteful remarks, especially when political discourse matters" (quoted in Hentoff, 2001, p. 26). How many "contrarian viewpoints and distasteful remarks" are proper (or even necessary) in time of war? How much "divisiveness" can a democracy accommodate? If a democracy cannot accommodate divisiveness, can it call itself a democracy?

Determining Acceptable Levels of Government Censorship

How far should the media go in accepting government requests to limit or otherwise shape their performance to meet legitimate government ends? This is the same question asked in Chapter 13's discussion of government-sponsored antidrug messages in television programming. First Amendment advocates demand a strict separation of government and media. Others rely on the philosophy of clear and present danger, saying that extraordinary times demand extraordinary concessions.

For example, soon after September 11, as Osama bin Laden and Al Qaeda videotapes began appearing on the Middle East's Al Jazeera television network, administration officials asked American cable and broadcast networks to edit them for removal of possible "inflammatory language" and "secretly encoded messages." They made a similar request of the nation's newspapers, asking that they not print full texts of bin Laden's taped messages. President Bush's political strategist Karl Rove met with Hollywood studio heads to enlist their aid in the war on terrorism. Reaction from media professionals was mixed. CBS News president Andrew Heyward said, "Journalists always have to be wary about any government guidance in the editorial process" (in McClintock, 2001, p. 50). *The New York Times* editorialized, "the White House effort is ill advised" (quoted in Hart & Ackerman, 2001, p. 8). But CNN said, "In deciding what to air, CNN will consider guidance from appropriate authorities" (quoted in Hart & Ackerman, 2001, p. 8). How would you have responded to government requests that you shape your news judgments to meet what it saw as the greater good? How can you defend your decision?

Coverage of Combat

The wartime ethical dilemma with which we are most familiar is that of the degree of access that media professionals should have to military information and action; we saw this dilemma during the Vietnam War, the invasions of Panama and Granada, and in the 1991 Gulf War. Few would question limits on information that would endanger the lives of soldiers. Few would question limits on information that might signal possible places and dates of action. But, said an Army public affairs officer who supports greater access for the media, "We cheat history if we don't permit reporters upfront" (quoted in Easton, 2002, p. 37). More than cheating history, we cheat democracy, says *American Journalism Review*'s Nina Easton: A "sanitized version of the country's first 21st-century war doesn't give the public and policymakers a realistic accounting of the difficulties, failures, and setbacks of U.S. military ventures abroad. . . . Just as problems are kept under wraps, so too are the heroic stories—and the soldiers behind them" (2002, p. 39). Her argument is that democratic support for this and the next war relies on access to full and accurate information, good *and* bad.

The conflict between the government's legitimate need to wage war and the press's and the people's legitimate need to know are encapsulated in these two quotes from Secretary of Defense Donald Rumsfeld. He recognizes the need, he said, "to provide the press—and through [them], the American people—with information to the fullest extent possible. . . . Defending our freedom and way of life is what this conflict is all about, and that certainly includes freedom of the press" (in Shaw, 2001, p. C7). But the same Secretary Rumsfeld opened his October 18, 2001, military press briefing with this introduction: "Let's hear it for the essential daily briefing, however hollow and empty it might be" (in MacArthur, 2001, p. 5). Where do you strike the balance? How much hollowness and emptiness do you accept? How much First Amendment right do you demand?

Commercialization of the Tragedy

It was not just journalists who were forced to face their ethics by the terrorist attacks. All media and their adver-

tisers had to determine just how much reference to the tragedy to make in their commercial messages. Budweiser's Clydesdale horses bowed before the New York skyline; Kenneth Cole ads reminded a sad nation that "On September 12, fewer men spent the night on the couch"; General Motors promised to "Keep America Rolling," and Ford asked car buyers to "Help Move America Forward"; airlines, most notably Southwest, equated travel with patriotism; gun makers introduced new models—Ithaca's Homeland Security shotgun, Tromix's 50-caliber Turban Chaser, Beretta's 9mm United We Stand pistol; ESPN used New York City police officers and firefighters in its promotional spots. Where do you draw the line?

On one hand, the use of the tragedy in ads is a business decision. DDB Chicago creative director Robert Scarpelli argues, "Anything that refers to September 11 is dangerous. When people think you're using patriotism to sell products, they'll turn you off in a second" (quoted in Winters, 2002, p. 13). But, counters Marian Salzman of ad agency Euro RSCG, mentioning 9/11 in commercial messages is good business because, "now more than ever, consumers want the sense of security and community that comes from emotional linkages with a brand. Let them know that your brand had always been there for them, and always will be" (in Levere, 2001, p. C8). But what of the morality of using a national tragedy to sell products? Advertisers always use Americans' common experiences to define their brands, and isn't 9/11 an obvious example of a shared experience? Are advertisers on safer ethical ground using the tragedy for some products rather than others? In other words, would you be more comfortable with a 9/11-based commercial for an airline than for pet food?

Commercialization of September 11 reentered the cultural forum 1 year after the attacks, when scores of newspapers declined to run any ads at all in their anniversary coverage of the tragedy. In the newspaper business, "everybody's really clear there's a huge interest in all things September 11, but they don't want to merchandise it," said Mort Goldstrom of the Newspaper Association of America (in Moses, 2002a, p. 5). Are papers that refuse to run ads adjacent to their 9/11 anniversary coverage being too cautious, or are they being appropriately sensitive? Is this a business or an ethical decision? Given the interests of the organization and those of the audience, can these sometimes be the same, or must they always be in conflict?

Confront and Complain

Media literate people can and should judge the ethical performance of media professionals. Remembering that the application of media ethics almost always involves finding the most morally defensible solution to a problem that has no right or wrong answer, we can evaluate media performance by weighing *our* values against *theirs*. Put the microphone in the grieving father's face? You consider the interests of the object of the act. The local station gives priority to the ratings, in other words, the interests of its financial supporters. The station's decision is not wrong. It simply does not match *your* definition of ethical performance in that circumstance. Dan Rather is not wrong in pledging blind loyalty to his government in time of war. He may make his decision based on the interests of society. But you, too, using society's interests, might demand more objectivity. Disagreeing with the judgments made in these two examples, you may choose to find a different local news station and look somewhere other than CBS for war reporting.

But what happens when *you* are the object of the act; that is, when the media outlet's ethical decision personally affects you or someone close to you? You can use your media literacy and understanding of the rights and responsibilities of media practitioners to confront those who have made you the object of their act. As businesses that rely in part on their reputations to attract audiences and readers, they will more often than not listen.

This is exactly what happened to Melissa Nathaniel. In late 2001 the athletic 20-something Ms. Nathaniel was

Rape victims Tamara Brooks and Jacqueline Marris chose to be identified in the media. Others refuse. But does the public have a right to know? And if so, how much? Whose ethics should prevail? Here Ms. Marris speaks with reporters outside her home.

the victim of a sexual assault in southern Rhode Island. A state-employed corrections worker, she held off her attacker, a registered sex offender, managing to hold him captive until police arrived.

For more information on this topic, see NBC Video Clip #20 on the CD—*Your Ad Here: Pizza Hut Places Billboard on Spacecraft.*

is "to cause the least commotion" for those working in the media industries (Black & Whitney, 1983, p. 432). True or not, the decision to perform his or her duties in an ethical manner ultimately rests with the individual media professional. As Black and Barney (1985) explain, an ethical media professional "must rationally overcome the status quo tendencies . . . to become the social catalyst who identifies the topics and expedites the negotiations societies need in order to remain dynamic" (p. 36).

DEVELOPING MEDIA LITERACY SKILLS
Accepting Reports Based on Anonymous Sources

We have seen how culture is created and maintained through communication, and that, increasingly, mass communication is central to that process. The need for literacy among media consumers, and for ethical performance among media industry practitioners, should be obvious. Yet neither is a simple enterprise. Developing sophisticated media literacy

Much to her surprise, she found herself identified by name in the *Providence Journal*'s account of the crime. Unfazed by the warning, "Don't get into an argument with someone who buys ink by the barrel," she confronted the paper and complained. She was told that the *Journal* had a policy of not printing victims' names in the case of first-degree sexual assault, but inasmuch as her success in fending off her attacker made the charge against him *only* attempted sexual assault, she did not warrant that protection. In other words, had she let herself be raped, the paper would have protected her identity. Because she was not raped, her identity was fair game. Later she wrote:

> This is reckless, dangerous, and devoid of common sense. The reporting [of the attack and arrest] would have the same appeal and impact without divulging my name. . . . During my assault, I experienced intense feelings of fear, vulnerability, and anger. When I discovered that my name and address were in the newspaper, I relived those feelings. I was terrified that my assailant now knows who I am and where I live. If, and when, he is released from prison, what is going to prevent him from coming to my house and hurting me again? What about my right to privacy and to feel safe within my home? (Nathaniel 2001, p. B7)

Ms. Nathaniel was faced with an ethical dilemma. She knew that if she were to successfully challenge the paper, she would bring even more notoriety to herself, exactly what she had complained about to the paper. But she chose to put the interests of others—other attack victims—above her own. The paper, to its credit, printed her challenge to it and its policies. Would you have been this brave, this ethical? Would you have confronted and complained? In defense of yourself or someone whom you feel was treated unethically, have you ever engaged in action against a media outlet—for example, writing letters to the editor, addressing a complaint to an ombudsman or media council, canceling a subscription (and telling the publication why), or registering an official complaint with an appropriate self-regulatory or official agency such as the FCC, FTC, or Better Business Bureau?

There are a number of good Web sites that can guide you should you choose to confront a media outlet that you think has not met your ethical standards. San Francisco State University maintains <www.journalism.sfsu.edu/www/ethics.html>. The Society for Professional Journalists offers advice at <www.spj.org/ethics.asp>. Two linksoriented ethics sites are Media Ethics Online (www.stlouisspj.org/ethics.htm) and Social Communication and Journalism Resources (www.journalism.uts.edu.au/subjects/jres/ethics.html). Finally, if you are involved in college journalism through a campus publication or broadcast facility and want more on your own ethical operation, go to Ethics On Campus, <members.tripod.com/Islander/indyethics.html>.

skills is hampered by a number of impediments, and even when media practitioners *do* make ethical decisions, they are not always the right or best decisions for everyone involved.

Many major news operations, for example, avoid the use of unidentified or anonymous sources, although they can sometimes be quite valuable, as we have seen earlier in this chapter. The danger is that sources' requests for anonymity might be based more on their desire to disguise inaccuracy and falsehood than on their need for protection. When the use of such a source is necessary to a journalistic investigation, these organizations will not use the information the anonymous sources provide unless there is corroboration from at least one other source. In addition, major journalistic operations have a series of internal checks and balances—reporters, a hierarchy of editors, and ombudspeople—to ensure that the material they publish is factual, even when the source cannot be identified. As a result, media literate people can make their own decisions on whether to accept the account. They can evaluate the ethical standards applied by media professionals. Some readers and viewers may not accept information from anonymous sources; some may. But at least all understand that the publication or station that produced a given story did its best to ensure veracity and accuracy. The Internet and war, however, pose particular challenges to media literate people.

We saw in Chapter 10 that the Net makes everyone a potential journalist, but they are "journalists" without benefit of the traditional news industry's internal checks and balances. For example, Matt Drudge, at the time an independent "online journalist" with no media background, reported many of the alleged moral lapses of the Clinton White House. His sources were usually unnamed, always without corroboration, and frequently wrong. But because his allegations were "on the Net," traditional media outlets were forced to repeat them. Unchecked allegations therefore became news.

War, when the normal rules are often obscured, poses another challenge. Does a journalist need corroboration from other sources if the original source is the military? Some media literate observers might answer "No," because in times of conflict we all need to back the war effort. Moreover, much of what these sources claim cannot be corroborated because they are the only ones with the information. Other media literates, however, might argue that corroboration is all the more necessary in times of war, specifically because of the high station of these sources. Why, they ask, would the powerful—the government, the military—fear identification other than to mislead in the shaping of policy?

Two dramatic instances of anonymously sourced stories, both associated with the war in Iraq, highlight the dilemma. When Pvt. Jessica Lynch was captured by Iraqi soldiers, "unnamed Pentagon sources" fed reporters false accounts of her bravery—fired her gun until empty, shot and stabbed, mistreated by her captors. Reporters belatedly understood that their "unnamed Pentagon sources" fabricated the tale in their search for a hero to rally the public when support for the controversial war was wavering (Eviatar, 2003).

Much of the controversy surrounding that conflict resided in questions about Iraq's possession of weapons of mass destruction (WMD). Many who believed in their existence based their judgment on the reporting of the *New York Times's* Judith Miller. For example, the Pulitzer Prize–winning Miller reported the claims of "unnamed experts" and an Iraqi scientist whom the Pentagon "declined to identify" in her accounts of the discovery of WMD. Unfortunately, much of her reporting was subsequently discredited, not only by the failure of the military to find the weapons in question, but by other reporters. Jack Shafer, Slate.com media writer, called Miller's reporting "faulty and biased," offering "no independent confirmation," and asked, "Is the *New York Times* breaking the news—or flacking for the military" (quoted in Layton, 2003, p. 34).

Different media professionals apply varying professional and ethical standards when they decide to use anonymous sources in their reports. But the challenges for media literate people who confront these accounts are twofold. First, they must develop their own standards for *accepting* these anonymously sourced reports; and then, they must decide how and when to apply those standards to different media and different situations.

For more information on this topic, see NBC Video Clip #21 on the CD—*The Drudge Report.*

Chapter Review

The First Amendment, based on libertarian philosophy, guarantees freedom of press and speech. It protects the press from official intrusion by all levels of government. That protection carries to all media but can be suspended in cases of clear and present danger and when competing interests must be balanced, for example, in free press versus fair trial conflicts. Some expression, primarily libel, slander, and obscenity, is not protected. Pornography, however, is protected expression. In almost no case is prior restraint acceptable.

Indecent expression, although protected, is limited in broadcasting and is typically relegated to late-night hours. Yet broadcasters' First Amendment rights were at the heart of deregulation, resulting in, among other things, the demise of the Fairness Doctrine and ascertainment.

Copyright does not protect the expression of ideas; rather, it protects the creator's financial interest in that expression, considered an important incentive in maintaining the free and ongoing flow of art, science, and other public speech. The 1978 and 1998 copyright laws set new rules and formalized exceptions such as use of material once it has passed into the public domain and fair use. The Internet has created significant copyright controversy, especially in the realm of digital rights management.

Because the press is not totally free, libertarianism gave way in the 1940s to social responsibility theory, the idea that to earn their freedom the media must perform responsibly. Self-regulation demands that media professionals balance conflicting interests. This balancing often produces dilemmas best resolved by applying ethics, rules of behavior or moral principles that guide actions in given situations. Ethics operate at three levels: metaethics, normative ethics, and applied ethics. Applying ethics requires balancing the conflicting interests of moral agents' consciences, people affected by their actions, their financial supporters, the institutions for which they work, their profession, and society as a whole. In mass communication these interests sometimes collide in the areas of truth and honesty, privacy, confidentiality, personal conflict of interest, profit and social responsibility, and offensive content.

Media practitioners are aided in their moral decision making by formal codes of conduct and their own institutional policies of conduct. These forms of self-regulation are controversial, however. They are seen by some as necessary and by others as limiting, abstract, and unenforceable.

Key Terms

Use the text's CD-ROM and the Online Learning Center at www.mhhe.com/baran to further your understanding of the following terminology.

democracy, 461
libertarianism, 461
self-righting principle, 461
absolutist position, 461
ad hoc balancing of
   interests, 463
libel, 465
slander, 465
actual malice, 466
prior restraint, 466
obscenity, 468
pornography, 468
indecency, 469

safe harbor, 470
traffic cop analogy, 471
Fairness Doctrine, 472
ascertainment, 472
public domain, 474
music licensing company, 474
digital rights management, 475
normative theory, 477
social responsibility theory, 477
ethics, 478
metaethics, 478
normative ethics, 478
applied ethics, 479

moral agent, 479
ride-along, 480
confidentiality, 483
shield law, 483
embedding, 484
Standards and Practices
   Departments, 487
policy book, 487
operating policies, 487
editorial policies, 487
ombudsman, 487
media council, 487

Questions for Review

 Go to the self-quizzes on the CD-ROM and the Online Learning Center to test your knowledge.

1. What are the basic tenets of libertarianism? How do they support the First Amendment?
2. What is the absolutist position on the First Amendment?
3. Name important court cases involving the definition of "no law," "the press," "abridgment," clear and present danger, balancing of interests, and prior restraint.
4. What are libel and slander? What are the tests of libel and slander? How do the rules change for public officials?
5. Define obscenity, pornography, and indecency.
6. What is safe harbor?
7. What is the traffic cop analogy? Why is it important in the regulation of broadcasting?
8. What is copyright? What are the exceptions to copyright? What is DRM?
9. What is normative theory?
10. What are the basic assumptions of social responsibility theory?
11. What are ethics? What are the three levels of ethics?
12. What are some of the individual and group interests that often conflict in the application of media ethics?
13. What is confidentiality? Why is confidentiality important to media professionals and to democracy?
14. What are some examples of personal and professional conflict of interest faced by media practitioners?
15. What are the different grounds on which critics object to media codes of conduct?
16. What are some forms of media self-regulation? What are the strengths and limitations of self-regulation?

Questions for Critical Thinking and Discussion

1. Are you a libertarian? That is, do you believe that people are inherently rational and good and that they are best served by a fully free press? Defend your position.
2. What is your position on pornography? It is legally protected expression. Would you limit that protection? When?
3. How much regulation or, if you prefer, deregulation do you think broadcasters should accept?
4. Of all the groups whose interests must be balanced by media professionals, which ones do you think would have the most influence over you?
5. In general, how ethical do you believe media professionals to be? Specifically, print journalists? Television journalists? Advertising professionals? Public relations professionals? Television and film writers? Direct mail marketers?

Important Resources

Bittner, J. R. (1994). *Law and regulation of electronic media.* Englewood Cliffs, NJ: Prentice-Hall. A thorough explanation of the political, economic, and technological bases for U.S. regulation of the electronic media. This college textbook is strong on history and on contemporary analysis.

Broadcasting and the Law, Censorship News, and *Media Law Bulletin.* Three excellent periodicals that, among them, offer reprints, condensations, and commentary on current and ongoing media law and regulation topics.

Foerstel, H. N. (1997). *Free expression and censorship in America.* Westport, CT: Greenwood Publishing. A thorough encyclopedia of names, cases, and issues involving the First Amendment and censorship that presents the history of this ongoing conflict as well as its contemporary status.

Media Law Reporter. This monthly publication reprints most and digests some federal court, state court, and administrative agency (such as the FCC) decisions regarding the mass media. Reprints and digests are then collected and published in an annual volume.

Seib, P., & Fitzpatrick, K. (1997). *Journalism ethics.* **New York: Harcourt Brace College Publishers.** Written for college students, this text deals with the human side of ethics, that is, how those making the decisions do so. Two of its most useful chapters are on the compassionate journalist and developing more ethical journalism.

First Amendment	www.freedomforum.org
Media Watchdog	www.mediatransparency.org
Journalism Watchdog	www.onlinejournal.org
U.S. Supreme Court News	www.oyez.nwu.edu
Center for Democracy and Technology	www.cdt.org
First Amendment Cyber-Tribune	www.w3.trib.com/fact
Fairness and Accuracy in Reporting	www.fair.org
Fight for Fair Use	www.digitalconsumer.org
Electronic Frontier Foundation	www.eff.org
Thomas Jefferson Center for Free Expression	www.tjcenter.org
Media Ethics Watchdog	www.mediawhoresonline.com
Electronic Privacy Information Center	www.epic.org
ACLU	www.aclu.org

Global Media

TIMELINE

1901 Marconi sends wireless signal trans-Atlantic

~mid-1920s European colonial powers use shortwave radio to connect holdings

1923 Radio comes to China

1928 Baird sends television image from London to New York

1940 Voice of America goes on air

1957 *Sputnik* goes into orbit

1960s British pirate broadcasters go on air

1962 *Telstar I* goes into orbit; COMSAT founded

1965 INTELSAT founded

1980 MacBride Report calls for New World Information Order

1984 German RTL goes on air

1985 Radio Martí goes on air

1989 Fall of European Communism

1990 TV Martí goes on air

LEARNING OBJECTIVES

Satellites and the Internet have made mass media truly global. The Earth has become a global village. But not all countries use mass media in the same ways. Moreover, many people around the world resent the "Americanization" of their indigenous media systems. After studying this chapter you should

- be familiar with the development of global media.
- be familiar with the practice of comparative analysis.
- be familiar with different media systems from around the world.
- be aware of the debate surrounding the New World Information Order and other controversies raised by the globalization of media.
- understand the global nature of the media literacy movement and be familiar with other countries' efforts to improve their citizens' ability to engage the media.

HENRI AND YOU HAVE BEEN PEN PALS SINCE SEVENTH grade. He's visited you here in the United States, and you've been to his house in the small walled village of Alet, near Carcassonne in southern France. You treat each other like family. Which means you sometimes fight. But unlike siblings living under the same roof, you have to carry on your dispute by e-mail.

Dear Henri,

What's with you guys and your language police? For everyone else it's *e-mail*. For you it's *courrier electronique*. People around the world are getting rich with Internet *start-ups*. You have *jeune-pousses*. My French isn't as good as yours, but doesn't that mean little flower or something?

Mon ami,

Close, *mais pas de cigare* (but no cigar, my linguistically challenged friend). I admit that we may seem a little foolish to the rest of you, but the Académie Française (what you called the language police) is simply trying to protect our language because it represents the deepest expression of our national identity. The French speak French, our popular culture reflects and is reflected in French, and our history and literature are preserved in French. Maybe as an American speaking another country's language (English from England) you don't understand.

499

Dear Henri,

You dissin' the USA? Check it out. English is the first language of 400 million people and the second of another 400 million. The world's air traffic control systems all use English for their communication. Three quarters of all the world's mail is written in English. English is the primary language for the publication of scientific and scholarly reports and for many international organizations such as the European Union and the Association of South-East Nations. Protecting the culture of a country that reveres Jerry Lewis is one thing, but keeping up with the rest of the planet is another.

Mon ami,

You just don't get it. Maybe you will know how it feels the next time you come to Europe. If you want to conduct any official business there in the future you will have to do it in Euro English. As for the European Union, its member countries just voted to make Euro English their official language. These are some of the changes to your "dominant" language that will be phased in over the next five years:

soft c will replace *s*   *k* will replace *hard c*

f will replace *ph*   double letters will be removed

z will replace *th*   the *silent e* will be dropped

v will replace *w*

ou will become *o,* and
other letter combinations
will be halved

Nov, ask yorcelf hov komfortabl yu vuld be and hov vel yu culd komunikat using zis langag? Vuld yu stil fel Amerikan? So, ze qeston remanz, ar ze French pepl making to much ovr ze deklin of zer nativ tong?

Euro English is real ("Let Them," 1999). So is the cultural conflict surrounding global communication inherent in this exchange of e-mails (or *courrier electronique,* if you prefer). Throughout this text we have seen how globalization is altering the operation of the various mass media industries, as well as the process of mass communication itself. In this chapter, we focus specifically on this globalization and its impact.

In doing so we will look at the beginnings of international media and examine the impact of satellites in creating truly global mass media systems. To study today's global media we will use comparative analyses, looking at the media systems of Britain (the Western concept), Honduras (the development concept), Poland (the revolutionary concept), and China (the authoritarian and communist concepts). Naturally, we will discuss the programming available in other countries. And because global media influence the cultures that use them both positively and negatively, we visit the debate over cultural imperialism. Finally, our media literacy discussion deals with practicing media literacy in our global village.

A Short History of Global Media

In Chapters 7 and 8 we saw that radio and television were, in effect, international in their earliest days. Guglielmo Marconi was the British son of an Italian diplomat, and among his earliest successes was the 1901 transmission of a wireless signal from England to Newfoundland. American inventors, in the persons of Philo Farnsworth and Russian immigrant Vladimir Zworkyin, met and eventually overcame the challenge posed by Scotsman John Logie Baird, among whose greatest achievements was the successful transmission of a television picture from London to New York in 1928. But both the Marconi and Baird transmissions were experimental, designed to attract attention and money to their infant technologies.

However, it was not much later in the development of radio and television that these media did indeed become, if not truly global, at least international. To understand best how this happened, we divide our discussion into two eras, before satellites and after satellites.

INTERNATIONAL MASS MEDIA BEFORE SATELLITES

Almost from the very start, radio signals were broadcast internationally. Beginning in the mid-1920s, the major European colonial powers—the Netherlands, Great Britain, and Germany—were using **shortwave radio** to connect with their various colonies in Africa, Asia, and the Middle East, as well as, in the case of the British, North America (Canada) and the South Pacific (Australia). Shortwave was (and still is) well suited for transmission over very long distances, because its high frequencies easily and efficiently reflect—or **skip**—off the ionosphere, producing **sky waves** that can travel vast distances.

Radio Caroline
www.
radiocaroline.com.uk

Clandestine Stations   It was not only colonial powers that made use of international radio. Antigovernment or antiregime radio also constituted an important segment of international broadcasting. These **clandestine stations** typically emerged "from the darkest shadows of political conflict. They [were] frequently operated by revolutionary groups or intelligence agencies" (Soley & Nichols, 1987, p. vii). In World War II, for example, stations operating from Britain and other Allied nations encouraged German soldiers and sailors to sabotage their vehicles and vessels rather than be killed in battle. Allied stations, such as the Atlantic Station and Soldiers' Radio Calais, also intentionally broadcast misleading reports. Posing as two of the many official stations operated by the German army, they frequently transmitted false reports to confuse the enemy or to force official Nazi radio to counter with rebuttals, thus providing the Allies with exactly the information they sought.

But it was in the Cold War that clandestine broadcasting truly flowered. In the years between the end of World War II and the fall of European communism in 1989, thousands of radio, and sometimes television, pirates took up the cause of either revolutionary (pro-communist) or

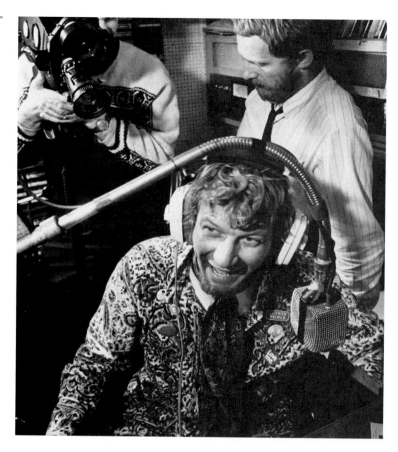

counterrevolutionary (anti-communist) movements. In addition, other movements tangentially related to this global struggle—especially the growing anticolonial movements in South and Central America and in Africa—made use of clandestine broadcasting.

During the Cold War the unauthorized, clandestine opposition stations typically operated outside the nations or regions to which they broadcast to avoid discovery, capture, and imprisonment or death. Today the relatively few clandestine operations functioning inside the regions to which they transmit can be classified as **indigenous stations,** whereas those operating from outside are **exogenous stations.** Radio Free Iraq is an example of an exogenous (or international) station. It broadcast from Czechoslovakia in opposition to the despotic rule of Saddam Hussein.

Pirate Broadcasters Another type of broadcast operation transmitting from outside its desired audience's geographic location involved something a bit more benign than war and revolution. These were stations that began broadcasting into Great Britain in the 1960s. Called **pirate broadcasters,** they were illegally operated stations broadcasting to British audiences from offshore or foreign facilities. Among the more notable were Radio Caroline, which reached a daily audience of a million listeners with its signal broadcast from the *MV Frederika* anchored $3\frac{1}{2}$ miles off the Isle of Man, and Radio Veronica, broadcasting from a ship off the coast of the Netherlands.

These pirates, unlike their politically motivated clandestine cousins, were powerful and well subsidized by advertisers and record companies. Moreover, much like the commercial radio stations with which we are now familiar, they broadcast 24 hours a day, every day of the year. These pirates offered listeners an alternative to the controlled and low-key programming of the British Broadcasting Corporation's (BBC) stations. Because the BBC was noncommercial, pirate stations represented the only opportunity for advertisers who wanted to reach British consumers. Record companies intent on introducing Britain's youth to their artists and to rock 'n' roll also saw the pirates as the only way to reach their audience, which the staid BBC all but ignored.

Enterprising broadcasters also made use of foreign locales to bring commercial television to audiences otherwise denied. The top-rated network in Germany today, for example, is RTL. Now broadcasting from the German city of Cologne, it began operations in January 1984 in Luxembourg, transmitting an American-style mix of children's programming, sports, talk shows, and action-adventure programming into Germany to compete with that country's two dominant public broadcasters, ARD and ZDF.

For more information on this topic, see NBC Video Clip #19 on the CD—*Why Is the United States Viewed So Poorly in the Arab World?*

The United States as International Broadcaster   World War II brought the United States into the business of international broadcasting. Following the lead of Britain, which had just augmented its colonial broadcast system with an **external service** called the BBC World Service, the United States established in 1940 what would eventually be known as the Voice of America (VOA) to counter enemy propaganda and disseminate information about America. The VOA originally targeted countries in Central and South America friendly to Germany, but as the war became global, it quickly began broadcasting to scores of other nations, attracting, along with Britain's World Service, a large and admiring listenership, first in countries occupied by the Axis powers, and later by those in the Soviet sphere of influence.

It was this Cold War with the Soviets that moved the United States into the forefront of international broadcasting, a position it still holds today. To counter the efforts of the Soviet Union's external service, Radio Moscow, the United States established three additional services. Radio in the American Sector (RIAS), broadcasting in German, served people inside East Berlin and East Germany; Radio Free Europe (RFE) broadcast to all of the other Communist-bloc Eastern European countries in their native languages; and Radio Liberty (RL) was aimed at listeners in the Soviet Union itself. When these services were initiated, people in both the United States and abroad were told that they were funded by contributions from American citizens. However, as a result of the furor that arose when it was revealed in 1971 that they were in fact paid for by the Central Intelligence Agency, they were brought openly under

Voice of America
www.
voa.gov

The Voice of America logo

Radio Martí's homepage

AFRTS
WWW.
afrts.osd.mil

For more information on this topic, see NBC Video Clip #18 on the CD—*Pentagon Planning to Plant Misinformation in Foreign News Sources.*

government control and funded and administered by the Board of International Broadcasting, whose members were appointed by the president.

The communist nations targeted by these services attempted to jam their signals by broadcasting on the same frequencies at higher powers, but they were only minimally successful in keeping their people from listening to these Western broadcasts. It was the success of these **surrogate services**—broadcast operations established by one country to substitute for another's own domestic service—that prompted President Ronald Reagan in 1985 to establish a special division of the VOA, Radio Martí, to broadcast into Communist Cuba. Radio Martí, still in operation, was joined by TV Martí in 1990.

A final United States external service established during World War II and the Cold War, Armed Forces Radio and Television Service (AFRTS), remains active today. Maintained by the American military, its stated mission is "to deliver Department of Defense internal information and radio and television programming services which provide 'a touch of home' to Department of Defense personnel and their families serving overseas" (AFRTS, 2000). Its more than 100 stations reach listeners in 70 countries with commercial-free fare.

The VOA Today Today, 91 million listeners a day tune in to VOA broadcasts in 53 languages, and another 20 million people in 23 developing countries listen to its surrogate operations, RFE, RL, Radio Martí, and the recently added Radio Free Asia (McClintock, 2002). Throughout its history, the VOA has frequently vacillated between two roles in response to world events and political pressures at home: (1) disseminating Western propaganda and (2) providing objective information. With the threat of Communist world domination now almost nonexistent, it attempts to meet the far less contradictory goals of spreading American culture and disseminating health and social information.

The VOA's commitment to the spread of American culture is evidenced by the establishment in 1992 of a 24-hour-a-day top 40–style service, VOA Europe, and in 1998 of a 24-hour, all-news English-language worldwide radio service characterized by a snappy style reminiscent of domestic commercial stations. The VOA's focus on transmitting health and other practical information can be seen in the increased efforts it devotes to programs aimed at Third World nations on AIDS prevention, nutrition, and vaccination. In pursuit of this humanitarian goal, the VOA now frequently strikes agreements with local stations in these countries to broadcast its programs over their AM and FM stations, making them accessible to those people who listen on these rather than on the shortwave band. Still, not everyone is comfortable with the role of the VOA and other American surrogate services, as you can see from the box "The United States as International Propagandist."

SATELLITES AND GLOBAL MASS MEDIA

We saw in Chapter 8 how satellites turned cable television from primarily an importer of distant signals into a provider of original programming, setting off a revolution in television. The impact of satellites on international mass communication was no less profound. With the coming of satellites, signals could be distributed not only internationally, that is, between two specific countries, as had previously been the case, but all over the world.

Voice of America Online
www.
voanews.com

The satellite revolution began in 1957 with the successful launch and orbit of the Soviet Union's *Sputnik*. *Sputnik* had no real function other than to prove (especially to the United States) that the Soviets could indeed produce the world's first artificial satellite. But it fulfilled this function admirably—shaking the confidence of the Western nations and leading the United States to redouble its efforts to conquer space.

The United States placed the second satellite, AT&T's Telstar I, in orbit in 1962. In that same year, Congress established the Communications Satellite Corporation (COMSAT) to coordinate ownership and operation of America's communications satellite system. It was clear even at the time, however, that satellites' greatest potential was in their ability to globalize telecommunications. To this end, President John F. Kennedy convened a consortium of Western and nonaligned countries to establish the International Telecommunications Satellite Organization (INTELSAT). Kennedy had two goals in mind: first, to effect the creation and maintenance of a global communication satellite system serving its many member nations; and second, to ensure that its leadership remained with the United States.

U.S. leadership in global satellites was ensured when COMSAT was declared managing agent of INTELSAT's system, begun on April 6, 1965, with the launch of INTELSAT I, better known in the United States as Early Bird. Within one year of that success, 55 nations had joined INTELSAT, and Early Bird allowed the first regularly scheduled transmission of live television between Europe and North America.

INTELSAT's role as a facilitator of global mass communication began slowly but rapidly expanded. Early Bird contained 240 voice/data circuits and one television channel, but by the time the INTELSAT VI generation of satellites was operational in 1989, each had the capacity to handle 120,000 voice/data circuits and three television channels (Stevenson, 1994). However, 1982 is considered the benchmark year for global media; it was then that INTELSAT's system became large and technologically sophisticated enough to begin offering its television customers full-time leases rather than the customary single-show service. Now, satellites not only enabled global distribution of media content, they encouraged it— once a company had paid for its lease, it incurred no additional cost no matter how much additional content it sent.

The United States as International Propagandist

September 11, 2001, and the subsequent war on terrorism thrust the VOA into the cultural forum, although it was rarely free of controversy before its October 2001 broadcast of an interview with Taliban leader Mullah Mohammad Omar—the equivalent, according to North Carolina Republican Senator Jesse Helms, of granting "equal time for Hitler" (in Wenner, 2001, p. 11).

The VOA offers Afghanistan and Pakistan services in two languages, Dari and Pashto (the language of the Taliban). Eighty percent of all Afghan men listen to the transmissions (Wenner, 2001). Just as the VOA-conducted interview with Omar was to be broadcast, the U.S. State Department stopped it. Taking the words of acting director Myrna Whitworth to heart—she urged her staff "not to fall under the spell of 'self-censorship.' If you do, 'they have won.' Continue to interview, *anyone, anywhere*" (quoted in Hentoff, 2001, p. 26)—VOA reporters and editors threatened mass resignation. The State Department relented, and the interview, in part, was eventually aired.

The difficulty that repeatedly returns the VOA to the cultural forum resides in the question of whether it should operate as an independent news organization or as an arm of American foreign policy. When it went on the air in the 1940s, its pledge to foreign listeners was straightforward: The news may be good. The news may be bad. We shall tell you the truth. Even today, VOA external affairs director Joseph O'Connell says that the best way to present the United States in the "best possible light" is "by telling the whole story. That by itself says something about us as a country. We're not afraid to let people make up their own minds." Robert Reilly, who replaced Myrna Whitworth soon after her demand for independence for her staff, agrees, telling the *American Journalism Review* that he'd be "stupid to squander the reputation and trust that almost 60 years of accurate news reporting has created around the world" (both quoted in Wenner, 2001, pp. 10–11). Still, incidents such as the interference with the Omar interview and practices such as mandatory State Department approval of all VOA editorials lead critics, such as former VOA Moscow bureau chief Mark Hopkins to charge that the VOA consistently places "the truth" second to "political programming with clear ideological agendas" (1999, p. 44). Current VOA news director Andre de Nesnera says he feels the pressure: "There are quite a lot of people on Capitol Hill who would like this to be the office of war information" (quoted in Wenner, 2001, p. 10).

The argument of a VOA language service director that "as a government broadcaster, you can't be neutral" (quoted in Hopkins, 1999, p. 46) is unconvincing to those who want America's premier surrogate service, the VOA, to be more like the highly regarded BBC World Service or the smaller but respected German Deutsche Welle. These critics want a unified, objective American international radio and television service, free of political objectives, that commands an audience because of its reliability and credibility.

Their arguments are several. First, a worldwide propaganda system is unnecessary in an era of global telecommunications. Why would anyone tune in to a propaganda channel when they can receive objective, high-quality content not only from the BBC World Service but from other American and Western sources? Critics point to Radio and TV Martí, both of which are ignored by a Cuban audience within easy reach of American commercial broadcasters. Second, propagandistic broadcasts can alienate the leadership of targeted countries. The president of the VOA's Radio Free Europe/Radio Liberty, Thomas Dine, says that his service aims to "foster democracy, promote free market reforms"; indeed, Radio Free Asia focuses its news reports on dissidents who challenge regimes considered unfriendly to the United States (Hopkins, 1999, p. 46). Neither RFE/RL's goals nor Radio Free Asia's practice endear the United States to leaders in eastern Europe and China who, regardless of their political orientations, are our global neighbors. Finally, the cost—nearly $400 million a year—is simply too high to engage in practices that would not only be considered offensive at home but also belie the American ideal of free media open to all shades of opinion.

Enter your voice in the cultural forum. Is $400 million not a particularly steep price to ensure that people around the world have access to the American point of view? Do you think any international service, commercial or surrogate, should produce and distribute content specifically designed to transmit its government's "official" viewpoint? Does it concern you that Congress, in exchange for its funding, requires the VOA to broadcast U.S. State Department–approved editorials? How free of government influence should any taxpayer-supported international telecommunications service be? Would you have run the Mullah Mohammad Omar interview? If yes, what defense would you offer to those who said you were giving equal time to Hitler?

In 1973 COMSAT gave up control of INTELSAT, and the latter became an independent consortium of member nations, each paying a yearly fee. However, at the 1999 INTELSAT Assembly of Parties, the official meeting of all 143 member governments, the consortium unanimously decided to privatize its service, largely in response to the growing number of competing systems. Among these are Europe's EUTELSAT and several regional and national systems. Most significant, though, are the numerous private, commercial systems that commenced operation in 1984. Today, companies such as Globalstar (partners with Loral and Qualcomm), Inmarsat (partners with Lockheed Martin and Matra Marconi Space), Hughes Electronics' Spaceway, and Lockheed Martin's Astrolink manage the majority of the globe's nearly 800 working communication satellites (Lo, 1998). And the capacity of these satellites has grown to the point at which a single provider such as PanAmSat carries more than 100 television transmissions a day, charging customers as much as $200,000 a month for a dedicated transponder, the part of the satellite that receives and retransmits a specific telecommunications service (Littleton, 1999b).

The 1965 launch of INTELSAT I, better known as Early Bird, made possible the first regularly scheduled transmission of live television between Europe and North America and established the United States's leadership in global satellites.

INTELSAT
www.
intelsat.com

Shown here on its launch pad in French Guiana, this French Ariane-5 rocket took two more communications satellites—Asia Star and Insat 3B—into geostationary orbit in March 2000.

Global Media Today

After *Who Wants to Be a Millionaire?* became the hot new show on American television, native-language versions of the game show were soon being broadcast in 29 other countries, and the producers made plans to extend the franchise into 50 more. The Cartoon Network is satellite- and cablecast in 145 countries in 14 languages. It is the Number 1 kids' network in Argentina, Mexico, France, and the Philippines. In addition to *The Jerry Springer Show* with which we are familiar, Mr. Springer has two other series, one in Great Britain, the other in South Africa. The latter, *Jerry Springer Saturday Night,* is received in 40 different African countries. All but six of the top 125 world-wide box office leaders in 2002 were American-made movies. Britain's Channel 4 *alone* pays Fox Television $1 million per episode for *The Simpsons,* and the half-hour comedy makes another $600,000 per episode from other foreign broadcasters. Fox also collects $1.5 million per episode in foreign sales for *The X-Files* and Warner Brothers $1.4 million per episode for *ER* (Guider, 2002). Britain's BBC has a channel on hundreds of American cable systems, and its storied *BBC Television News* can be watched by some 36 million American PBS viewers. If you're in the right place, you can join the 366 million households worldwide that watch MTV Latin America, MTV Asia, MTV Australia, MTV Brazil, MTV Japan, MTV Europe, or other MTV (see Figure 15.1). TV France International, that country's umbrella distribution organization, has partnership agreements with Fox, Warner Brothers, the Discovery and Sundance channels, and Bravo. Its all-French channel is available to viewers in the United States on satellite provider DirecTV. Close to 200 nations receive CNN by satellite. Radio Beijing broadcasts to a worldwide audience in 40 languages. Hundreds of millions of Internet users spread throughout scores of countries can tune in to thousands of Web radio stations originating from every continent except Antarctica. AT&T, the United States' largest

Figure 15.1 They Want Their MTV. The number of households that receive MTV, 2001. *Source:* Burlingame, 2001.

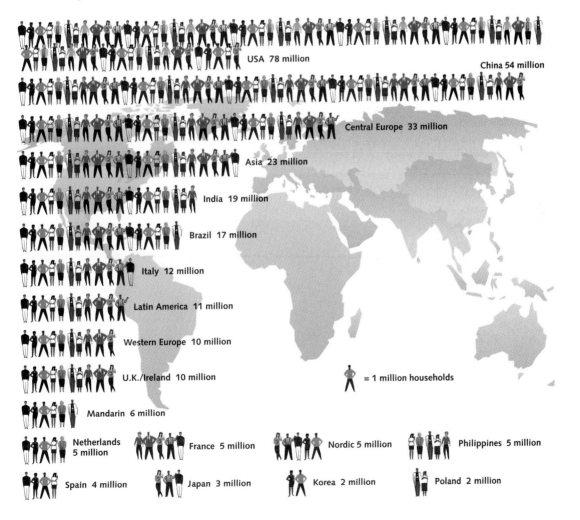

USA 78 million
China 54 million
Central Europe 33 million
Asia 23 million
India 19 million
Brazil 17 million
Italy 12 million
Latin America 11 million
Western Europe 10 million
U.K./Ireland 10 million
Mandarin 6 million
Netherlands 5 million
France 5 million
Nordic 5 million
Philippines 5 million
Spain 4 million
Japan 3 million
Korea 2 million
Poland 2 million

= 1 million households

Maintaining Gross National Happiness

High in the Himalayas, in a country half the size of Indiana, the 600,000 citizens of the monarchy of Bhutan try to eke out an existence. The country is poor—the majority of its people are yak herders and monks—and anxious to maintain its Buddhist culture and identity. But global media, as they have everywhere else, are coming to this tiny land sitting between China and India. King Jigme Singye Wangchuck has declared that he intends to bring modern technology to his country while at the same time preserving its guiding principle, Gross National Happiness. The king's goal is to bring his "spartan rural society into the high-tech world without surrendering its soul." In calling for Gross National Happiness, the king hopes to ensure the "equitable distribution of health care and education; environmental protection; and, good government" (Zielenziger, 2000, p. 6AA). To accomplish his goals he wants his people to use media, rather than be used by them. "We felt the compulsion of globalization," explains Foreign Minister Jigme Thinley. "We see ourselves as a society that must change. [But] we are very conscious of the fact that certain aspects of our culture need to be preserved. Culturally we are changing, but we want to remain Bhutanese" (as quoted in Zielenziger, 2000, p. 6AA).

This is a country whose capital, Thimphu, has no traffic lights. Not a single McDonald's or Starbucks is to be found anywhere in Bhutan. It is a nation that strictly limits the number of foreign visitors it allows inside its bor-

Remote and picturesque, the tiny nation of Bhutan sees the new communication technologies as its avenue to involvement with the larger world.

ders, charging those who do come $200 a day just for the honor. But it is also a land that offers its citizens free public education in English and sends its best students overseas to do advanced study. When they have completed their studies, 99% return home to render service, along with compassion and individual enlightenment, a primary precept of the country's Mahayanan Buddhism.

E.R. earns Warner Brothers $1.4 million per episode from foreign broadcasters.

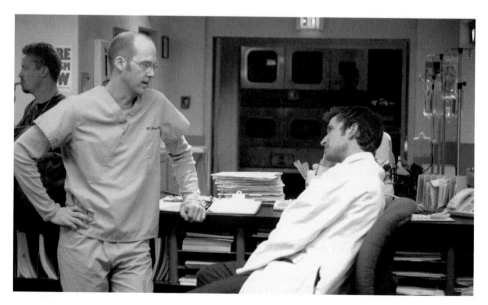

In 1999, to commemorate his 25-year reign—and to start the process of (slow and controlled) modernization—King Wangchuck removed the country's ban on television (within one year there were 3,500 homes with television), permitted private ownership of DBS receivers, started the Bhutan Broadcasting Service—it broadcasts in Bhutan's national language, Dzongkha, and in English—and opened Bhutan's first ISP. "We would not want to be an outcast in the global village. We want to be a part; but by being a part we also want to be ourselves," explained Foreign Minister Thinley (Zielenziger, 2000, p. 6AA).

There is little doubt that media will make a difference in this poor, traditional land. But the nature of that difference is still in question. Bhutan is meeting the world and the world is meeting it. "I have never set foot outside of Bhutan," said 23-year-old student Chhodup. "But now I've been to almost every country through the Internet" (Zielenziger, 2000, p. 6AA). Yet it is precisely these online visits that frighten many older Bhutanese. "We are a people who are trained to say, 'We have enough; this is enough,' which is so very anti-development," says writer Kunzang Choden. But television and the Internet present a different worldview. "We have to be prudent and careful in how we open up. If we lose our culture and our identity, we lose everything" (Zielenziger, 2000, p. 6AA).

Still, the majority of the country's people welcome the new communication technologies. True to the spirit of

Will satellite television bring Gross National Happiness or destruction of traditional culture to Bhutan?

Gross National Happiness, they base their optimism on Buddhist belief. Lama P. S. Dorjie explained, "It all depends on the purity of the perceptions in your mind. If you are a wise person, then television will not change you. If you are an evil person, TV will not make you good. You will still be evil. So the inner happiness is what counts. The rest is just illusion" (Zielenziger, 2000, p. 6AA).

telecommunications and cable company, and British Telecom, Britain's biggest telecommunications provider, have merged their international operations into a single $10 billion unit. Media know few national borders.

But the global flow of expression and entertainment is not welcomed by everyone. French law requires that 40% of all music broadcast by its radio stations be in French. The Israeli government considered a law requiring all "radio stations to devote half their airtime to songs sung in Hebrew in order to slow down Israel's cultural shift toward Americanization" (Zachary, 1999, p. 56). Sri Lanka forbade the import and distribution of foreign movies until 2000, and in the kingdom of Bhutan, near India and Tibet, television was illegal until June 1999 (to read more about Bhutanese media, see the box "Maintaining Gross National Happiness"). To ensure that its people do not access "foreign" or otherwise "counterrevolutionary" Internet content, the Chinese government requires all Internet accounts to be registered with the police. Media may know few national borders, but there is growing concern that they at least respect the cultures within them.

One traditional way to understand the workings of the contemporary global media scene is to examine the individual media systems of the different countries around the world. In doing so, we can not only become familiar with how different folks in different places use media but also better evaluate the workings of our own system. Naturally, not every media system resembles that of the United States. As a result, such concepts as audience expectations, economic foundations, and the regulation of mass media differ across nations. The study of different countries' mass media systems is called **comparative analysis** or **comparative studies.**

COMPARATIVE ANALYSES

Different countries' mass media systems reflect the diversity of their levels of development and prosperity, values, and political systems. Often, a country's geography also influences the type of media system it embraces. The level of diffusion of different communication technologies in different countries offers a clear example. The United States is prosperous, and its people enjoy considerable mobility and leisure. Americans also tend to live in bigger homes than do their counterparts in most other lands. As a result, the United States has two radios for every citizen and almost one television per person. Australia, a prosperous country, is very large. Many of its people live in quite remote parts of this continent nation. It, too, has more than one radio per person, but only one television for every two people. Uganda, a developing African nation, has almost no television, and despite the remote locations in which many of its people live, its lack of prosperity makes even radio ownership a rarity. In the oil-rich desert nation of Oman, on the other hand, even though only one in eleven people has a telephone (the hostile terrain makes the stringing and maintenance of phone lines difficult), there is one television (served by a domestic satellite system) for every two people (Peterson, 1998; Hilliard & Keith, 1996).

That a country's political system will be reflected in the nature of its media system is only logical. Authoritarian governments need to control the mass media to maintain power. Therefore, they will institute a media system very different from that of a democratic country with a capitalistic, free economy. The overriding philosophy of how media ideally operate in any given system of social values is called a normative theory (Chapter 14). The classic work on normative theory is *The Four Theories of the Press* by Fred Siebert, Theodore Peterson, and Wilbur Schramm, but because so much has changed in the world of mass communication since it was written in 1956, these "Four Theories" have required "a little sprucing up" (Stevenson, 1994, p. 108), carried out by media scholar William Hachten.

Hachten (1992) offered "five concepts" that guide the world's many media systems—Western, Development, Revolutionary, Authoritarianism, and Communism. We'll examine each and provide a look at examples that exemplify them.

The Western Concept: Great Britain The **Western concept** is an amalgamation of the original libertarian and social responsibility models (Chapter 14). It recognizes two realities: There is no completely free (libertarian) media system on Earth, and even the most commercially driven systems include the expectation not only of public service and responsibility but also of "significant communication-related activities of government" to ensure that media professionals meet those responsibilities (Stevenson, 1994, p. 109).

Great Britain offers a good example of a media system operating under the Western concept. The BBC was originally built on the premise that broadcasting was a public trust (the social responsibility model). Long before television, BBC radio offered several services—one designed to provide news and information; another designed to support high or elite culture such as symphony music and plays; and a third designed to provide popular music and entertainment. To limit government and advertiser control, the BBC was funded by license fees levied on receivers (currently about $165 a year), and its governance was given over to a nonprofit corporation. Many observers point to this goal-oriented, noncommercial structure as the reason that the BBC developed, and still maintains, the most respected news operation in the world.

Eventually, Britain, like all of Western Europe, was forced by public demand to institute more American-style broadcasting. It now has local commercial radio stations in addition to the BBC's six radio networks: Radio 1 (pop and rock music), Radio 2 (popular music such as folk and other regional music), Radio 3 (live music and arts), Radio 4 (drama and talk), Radio 5 (news and sports), and Radio 1xtra (new Black music). In addition to television networks BBC1 (more popular) and BBC2 (more serious), there are commercial Channels 4 and 5 and several regional commercial networks operating under the auspices of the Independent Television Authority (ITA). ITA has regional channels for Ireland, Scotland, Wales, southern England, and so on. But even these must accept limits on the amount of advertising they air and agree to specified amounts of public affairs and documentary news programming in exchange for their licenses to broadcast. This is referred to as their **public service remit.**

Cable was slow to develop in Great Britain for two reasons. First, many people simply did not want their beautiful or historic towns sullied by cable's overhead wires, nor did they want their cobbled streets dug up to accommodate underground cables. The second reason is that virtually all of the country has long had access to Rupert Murdoch's DBS system, SkyTV. Murdoch pioneered the mini-dish receiver, which not only gave viewers multiple channels, but satisfied Britons' traditional aesthetic sensibilities (no big, obtrusive dish, no unsightly wires, and no excavated streets). Today, satellite provider

Unlike U.S. media, British media do not enjoy First Amendment protections, but as their notorious tabloids demonstrate, they nonetheless do operate with a great deal of freedom.

BSkyB has 5.7 million viewers in Great Britain, whereas total cable subscribership is 3.5 million in a country of 24.5 million television households (Westcott, 2002).

In terms of regulation, the media in Great Britain do not enjoy a First Amendment–like guarantee of freedom. Prior restraint does occur, but only when a committee of government officials and representatives of the media industry can agree on the issuance of what is called a **D-notice.** British media are also forbidden to report on court trials in progress, and Parliament can pass other restrictions on the media whenever it wishes, for example the ban, imposed in 1988 and maintained for several years, on broadcasting the voice of anyone associated with the Irish Republican or other paramilitary movements.

The Development Concept: Honduras The media systems of many Third World or developing African, Asian, Latin and South American, and Eastern European nations formerly part of the Soviet bloc best exemplify the **development concept.** Here government and media work in partnership to ensure that media assist in the planned, beneficial development of the country. Content is designed to meet specific cultural and societal needs, for example, teaching new farming techniques, disseminating information on methods of disease control, and improving literacy. This isn't the same as authoritarian control. There is less censorship and other official control of content.

Honduras offers one example. This Central American country has government as well as privately owned commercial radio and television stations. A government-authorized and -controlled private commission, the Honduran Contractors of Television, coordinates much of the commercial outlets' operation. In addition, HONDUTEL, the Honduran equivalent of the FCC, exerts tight regulatory control over all broadcasting. Together these two bodies ensure that Honduran broadcasting meets the nation's developmental needs, as determined by the government.

The Honduran government is forbidden by its constitution from taking over or shutting down media outlets because of the content they distribute. Control, however, comes in other forms. One is the requirement that media professionals hold membership in a government-run "official press organization." Naturally, if the government decides who can and cannot function in media organizations, it can easily control those organizations. Another resides in "the close ties of the owners of the most powerful media to the military and to government leaders. The media, therefore, by and large operate with little freedom despite strong constitutional guarantees" (Hilliard & Keith, 1996, p. 161).

The Revolutionary Concept: Poland No country "officially" embraces the **revolutionary concept** as a normative theory, but this does not mean that a nation's media will never serve the goals of revolution. Stevenson (1994) identified four aims of revolutionary media: ending government monopoly over information, facilitating the organization of opposition to the incumbent powers, destroying the legitimacy of a standing government,

and bringing down a standing government. In Yugoslavia, for example, 33 radio and 18 television stations combined in 1998 to form the Association of Independent Electronic Media (ANEM) for the purpose of challenging the regime of President Slobodan Milosevic and asserting Serbian independence. ANEM operated with significant public support despite repressive legislation, threats of jail and huge fines, and even military and police confiscation of members' equipment (Aumente, 1999). Milosevic's ouster in October 2000 is testimony to ANEM's effectiveness. The experience of the Polish democracy movement Solidarity, however, offers a better-known example of the use of media as a tool of revolution.

The Polish workers' and democracy movement, Solidarity, was greatly aided by media, both official outlets from beyond Poland's borders and its own extensive network of clandestine new and old communication technologies.

By the first years of the 1980s, the Polish people had grown dissatisfied with the domination of almost all aspects of their lives by a national Communist Party perceived to be a puppet of the Soviet Union. This frustration was fueled by the ability of just about all Poles to receive radio and television signals from neighboring democratic lands (Poland's location in central Europe made it impossible for the authorities to block what the people saw and heard). In addition, Radio Free Europe, the Voice of America, and the BBC all targeted Poland with their mix of Western news, entertainment, and propaganda. Its people's taste for freedom thus whetted, Solidarity established an extensive network of clandestine revolutionary media. Much of it was composed of technologies traditionally associated with revolution—pamphlets, newsletters, audiotapes and videocassettes—but much of it was also sophisticated radio and television technology used to disrupt official broadcasts and disseminate information. Despite government efforts to shut the system down, which went as far as suspending official broadcasting and mail services in order to deny Solidarity these communication channels, the revolution was a success, making Poland the first of the Eastern-bloc nations to defy the Party apparatus and install a democratically elected government.

The Authoritarianism and Communism Concepts: China Because only three communist nations remain and because the actual operation of the media in these and other **authoritarian systems** is quite similar, we can discuss authoritarianism and communism as a single concept. Both call for the subjugation of media for the purpose of serving the government. China is not only a good example of a country that operates its media according to the authoritarian/communist concepts, it also demonstrates how difficult it is becoming for authoritarian governments to maintain strict control over media and audiences.

The Chinese media system is based on that of its old ideological partner, the now-dissolved Soviet Union. For a variety of reasons, however, it has developed its own peculiar nature. China has more than a billion people living in more than a million hamlets, villages, and cities. Despite sophisticated life in many big cities, there is nearly universal illiteracy in the countryside. Because good pulp wood is not native to China and importing it from abroad is too expensive, newspapers are printed on costly but poor-quality paper made from bamboo. Daily circulation is 116 million copies, around one paper for every 100 citizens. As a result, print is not a major national medium. In fact, face-to-face communication remains a primary means of transmitting news and information among the country's enormous personal communication system. This process is aided by the wide distribution of **wired radio,** centrally located loudspeakers, for example in a town square, that deliver primarily political and educational broadcasts.

The media exist in China to serve the government. Chairman Mao Zedong, founder of the Chinese Communist Party, clarified the role of the media very soon after coming to power in 1949. The media exist to propagandize the policies of the Party and to educate, organize, and mobilize the masses. These are still their primary functions.

Radio came to China via American reporter E. C. Osborn, who established an experimental radio station in China in 1923. Official Chinese broadcasting began 3 years later. Television went on the air in 1958, and from the outset it was owned and controlled by the Party in the form of Central China Television (CCTV), which in turn answers to the Ministry of Radio and Television. Radio, now regulated by China People's Broadcasting Station (CPBS), and television stations and networks develop their own content, but it must conform to the requirements of the Propaganda Bureau of the Chinese Communist Party Central Committee.

Financially, Chinese broadcasting operates under direct government subsidy. But in 1979 the government approved commercial advertising for

A Chinese reading wall. The newspaper is not a major national mass medium in China—there is only one copy for every 100 people. Most read the newspaper at public postings such as this one.

broadcasting, and it has evolved into an important means of financial support—television billings are at $8 billion a year, for example (Jones, 2002). Coupled with the Chinese government's desire to become a more active participant in the international economy, this commercialization has led to increased diversity in broadcast content. Today, China's 400 million television households are served by eight CCTV and hundreds of local and satellite channels. Foreign content is purchased by the state's China TV Programming Agency, which can buy no more than 500 hours a year. Stations can devote no more than 25% of their time to imported content. MTV and the Children's Television Workshop coproduce content with local Chinese broadcasters, and among imported favorites are *The Teletubbies (Antenna Babies* in China) and *Little House on the Prairie.* CNN and other satellite-delivered services are also available to China's 100 million cable and 150 million satellite television households (Jones, 2002).

Basic government control over major media and the Internet remains, however. In December 1997 the government began enforcing criminal sanctions against those who would use the Net to "split the country," "injure the reputation of state organs," "defame government agencies," "promote feudal superstitions," or otherwise pose a threat to "social stability" ("China Adopts," 1997, pp. C1, C4; Dobson, 1998, p. 20). Internet accounts have to be registered with the police. The state has established a 24-hour Internet task force to find and arrest senders of "counterrevolutionary" commentary. Popular bulletin boards are shut down when their chat becomes a bit too free. Web sites such as Human Rights Watch, the *New York Times,* and publications about China that are independent of government control, such as *China News Digest,* are officially blocked, but not very successfully, as

Media Echoes

Freedom of the Press in Iran

John Peter Zenger went to jail for his exercise of free expression, and his name is forever linked to the fight against official intrusion into journalism. Larry Flynt spent millions of dollars on legal fees to protect his magazine's right to publish unpopular expression. He was immortalized in a big-budget Hollywood movie. Few people outside Iran, however, know the names of Latif Safari, Akbar Ganji, Mahmoud Shams, and Saeed Hajjarian.

In 1999 Safari, director of the Iranian daily *Neshat,* was sentenced to 27 months in prison for insulting Islam, police, and lawmakers. His paper was shut down. Ganji, an investigative reporter and a national hero for his writings on the murder of Iranian dissidents by hard-line Islamic officials, was imprisoned. Shams, editor-in-chief of the newspaper *Asr-e-Azadegan* and a leader of Iran's free press movement, was sentenced to $2\frac{1}{2}$ years in prison for "insulting religious sanctities" (Dareini, 2000, p. A12). His paper was shuttered. Hajjarian, another respected reform journalist, was shot in the face, allegedly by hard-line supporters of Iran's ruling theocracy.

The events that brought these men to martyrdom began in 1997, when reform-minded Mohammad Khatami won a decisive victory over the Islamic clergy–backed incumbent in the presidential election. Believing that reform in Iran would be best served by a free and open press, the new president used his "bully pulpit" to encourage more outspoken media expression than the country had ever known. Journalists soon felt free to take on once-forbidden topics such as Iran's secret police and the all-powerful agents of the ruling clerics, the Revolutionary Guards. Then, when parliamentary elections in February 2000 showed even more support for Iran's reform movement, an emboldened Khatami proposed a new Iranian press law explicitly permitting the greater

Latif Safari (on his way into court in April 2000) was sentenced to 27 months in prison for his newspaper writing. His crime, according to fundamentalist lawmakers, was insulting Islam.

freedoms he desired. Whereas the existing press law gave the religious courts summary power to shut down newspapers and decide who can own and run them, the proposed law sought to give media professionals increased freedom and to require a hearing before any publication could be closed.

This possibility proved too much for Iran's supreme religious leader, the Ayatollah Ali Khamenei, and his

---

skilled Internet users can easily access the Web by routing themselves through distant servers or at one of the country's 150,000 unlicensed Internet cafés (Beech, 2002). The box "Freedom of the Press in Iran" offers a glimpse of media operation in another authoritarian system.

PROGRAMMING

Regardless of the particular concept guiding media systems in other countries, those systems produce and distribute content, in other words, programming. In most respects radio and television programming throughout the world looks and sounds much like that found in the United States. There are two main reasons for this situation: (1) the United States is a world

cleric-populated Guardian Council. The Ayatollah sent a letter to the parliament declaring his opposition to the proposed new press freedoms, which he saw as a threat to clergy rule in Iran. Read aloud, it warned, "It will be a great danger to the national security and people's faith if the enemies of the Islamic revolution control or infiltrate the press. The present press law has prevented such disaster so far" (as quoted in "Setback," 2000, p. 8A).

Within weeks 22 newspapers unsympathetic to the ruling ayatollahs were closed and Safari, Ganji, Shams, and Hajjarian met their fates. The seven remaining newspapers in this Middle East theocracy were all loyal to the Ayatollah. Iran's reformers called the closings and arrests clear violations of the Iranian constitution. Elahe Hicks of Human Rights Watch called the actions "not only a violation of Iranian law, but a violation of Iran's obligation to uphold freedom of expression" (as quoted in Sachs, 2000, p. 21A). Iran's college students boycotted classes and held on-campus demonstrations in protest.

Freedoms that are taken for granted in the United States and in other free countries simply do not exist for many of the world's people. Shouldn't you be concerned about what happens to media professionals in places such as Iran? Is it enough to know that abuses such as these cannot occur in traditional democracies? Or can and do they? What restrictions on American media would move you to boycott and demonstrate? How do you explain the results of a 2002 First Amendment Center poll demonstrating that 49% of adult Americans believe that the First Amendment "goes too far in the rights it guarantees" and that 42% believe that "the press has too much freedom" (Paulson, 2002, p. 30)? Things are different in times of war and national crisis,

College students across Iran staged protests condemning their government's repression of the nation's newly emerging free press.

you say? Then how do you explain the outcome of a similar poll taken *before* September 11, 2001, that showed that only 53% of American adults agreed that "newspapers should be allowed to publish freely without government approval of the story" and that 71% of your fellow citizens believed that "it is important for the government to hold the media in check" (Hentoff, 2001, p. 26)?

leader in international distribution of broadcast fare, and (2) very early in the life of television, American producers flooded the world with their programming at very low prices. Foreign operators of emerging television systems were delighted to have access to this low-cost content, because they typically could not afford to produce their own high-quality domestic material. For American producers, however, this strategy served the dual purpose of building markets for their programming and ensuring that foreign audiences would develop tastes and expectations similar to those in the United States, further encouraging future sales of programs originally produced for American audiences (Barnouw, 1990). The success of this approach is evident from comments made by actress-producer Pamela Anderson Lee in discussing her globally syndicated *V.I.P.*: "I took a lower salary on this show

V.I.P., a first-run syndication hit in the U.S., has been quite successful in foreign distribution, largely because it requires little dubbing of dialogue, and it offers its international audiences "a lot of physical gags and comedy, explosions, and beautiful scenery." Other countries export their media too. Here is an ad for a Spanish distribution company that appeared in *Variety*.

because I felt the back end could really be meaningful. I know a lot about syndication and what appeals to the international market. I make sure there are a lot of physical gags and comedy, explosions and beautiful scenery" (as quoted in J. Stein, 1999, p. 134). Lee might also have added that action shows such as *V.I.P.* are easily dubbed into local languages.

Naturally, programming varies somewhat from one country to another. The commercial television systems of most South American and European countries are far less sensitive about sex and nudity than are their counterparts in the United States. In Brazil, for example, despite a constitutional requirement that broadcasters "respect society's social and ethical values" (Epstein, 1999, p. A11), television networks such as SBT, TV Record, and TV Globo compete in what critics call the *guerra da baixaria*, the war of the lowest common denominator. Guests on variety shows wrestle with buxom models dressed only in bikinis and eat sushi off other women's naked bodies. On game shows, male contestants who give wrong answers can be punished by having patches of leg hair ripped out, while those who answer correctly are rewarded by having a nearly naked model sit in their laps. European commercial operations regularly air shows featuring both male and female nudity, sometimes because it is integral to the plot, sometimes simply for titillation.

Another difference between American programming and that of its global neighbors is how that content is utilized in different places. As telecommunications professors Robert Hilliard and Michael Keith observed, "In systems relying on commercial advertising for their support, the value of programming is based on how many viewers any given presentation attracts. . . . In systems operated by public corporations that rely on sources of funding other than advertising, the purpose of programming is oriented principally to the educational, social, and/or political purpose of the operating entity" (1996, p. 109). And in general, this is the case. But many nations, even those with commercially supported systems, use a particular genre, the soap opera, for educational and social purposes. For example, American-style soap operas in countries from Mexico to Kenya are used to encourage greater use of birth control and family planning. Typically aired in the evening, soap operas, rather than comedies or dramas, are used to this end primarily because they are inexpensive to produce, a sine qua non in developing nations.

The Debate over Cultural Imperialism

There are few physical borders between countries in a globally mediated world. Governments that could once physically prohibit the introduction and distribution of unwanted newspapers, magazines, and books had to work harder at jamming unwanted radio and television broadcasts. But they could do it, until satellite came along. Governments cannot disrupt satellite signals. Only lack of the necessary receiving technology can limit their reach. Now, with the Internet, a new receiving technology is cheap, easy to use, and on the desks of more and more millions of people in every corner of the world (see Chapter 10). As a result, difficult questions of national sovereignty and cultural diversity are being raised anew.

THE MacBRIDE REPORT AND THE NWIO

The debate reached its height with the 1980 release of The MacBride Report by the United Nations Educational, Scientific, and Cultural Organization (UNESCO). The report was named after the chairman of the commission set up to study the question of how to maintain national and cultural sovereignty in the face of rapid globalization of mass media. At the time, many Third World and Communist countries were concerned that international news coverage was dominated by the West, especially the United States, and that Western-produced content was overwhelming the media of developing countries, which lacked sufficient resources to create their own quality fare (Figure 15.2). The fear was that Western cultural values, especially those of the United States, would overshadow and displace those of other countries. These countries saw this as a form of colonialization, a **cultural imperialism**—the invasion of an indigenous people's culture by powerful foreign countries through mass media.

UNESCO
WWW.
unesco.org

The MacBride Report, endorsed by UNESCO, called for establishment of a New World Information Order (NWIO) characterized by several elements problematic to Western democracies. In arguing that individual nations should be free to control the news and entertainment that entered their lands, it called for monitoring of all such content, monitoring and licensing of foreign journalists, and requiring that prior government permission be obtained for direct radio, television, and satellite transmissions into foreign countries.

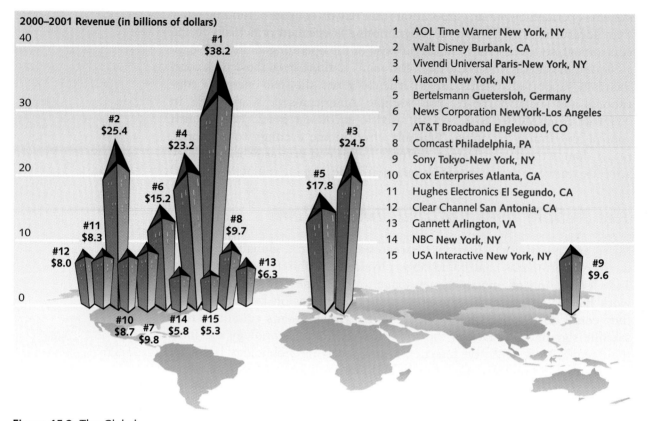

2000–2001 Revenue (in billions of dollars)

1	AOL Time Warner New York, NY
2	Walt Disney Burbank, CA
3	Vivendi Universal Paris-New York, NY
4	Viacom New York, NY
5	Bertelsmann Guetersloh, Germany
6	News Corporation NewYork-Los Angeles
7	AT&T Broadband Englewood, CO
8	Comcast Philadelphia, PA
9	Sony Tokyo-New York, NY
10	Cox Enterprises Atlanta, GA
11	Hughes Electronics El Segundo, CA
12	Clear Channel San Antonia, CA
13	Gannett Arlington, VA
14	NBC New York, NY
15	USA Interactive New York, NY

Figure 15.2 The Global Top-10 Media Conglomerates, 2002. Fourteen out of fifteen of the world's biggest media companies list the U.S. as their headquarters (although two list dual headquarter sites). *Source:* "Variety's Global 50," 2002.

Western nations rejected these rules as a direct infringement on the freedom of the press.

Western allies of the United States may have agreed that the restrictions of the NWIO were a threat to the free flow of information, yet virtually every one had in place rules (in the form of quotas) that limited U.S. media content in their own countries. Canada, our closest cultural neighbor, required that specific proportions of all content—print and broadcast—either be produced in Canada or reflect Canadian cultural identity. The French made illegal the printing of certain U.S. words, including "hamburger" and "cartoon" (France maintains an official office to prosecute those who would "debase" its language, the Académie Française, mentioned in our opening vignette). In 1989 the European Union, then called the European Community, established "Television Without Frontiers," which mandates that 50% of all content on all television channels in Europe be produced in its member countries. In 1998 the cultural ministers of 20 countries, among them Brazil, Mexico, Sweden, Canada, and Italy, met in Ottawa to develop "ground rules" to protect their nations' cultures from "the Hollywood juggernaut" (Turner, 1998, p. 1A). South Korean law mandates that movie houses show native films at least 146 days out of each year (Kim, 2002). British law forbids foreign (read American) ownership in its commercial broadcasting channels (Ashley, 2002).

The resistance to U.S. media would not exist among our international friends if they did not worry about the integrity of their own cultures. It is

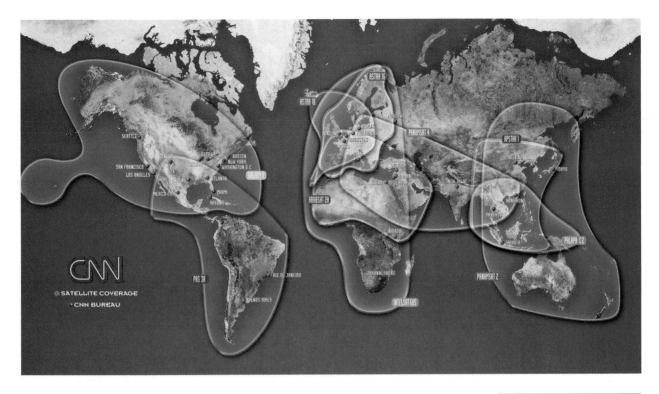

folly, then, to argue that nonnative media content will have no effect on local culture—as do many U.S. media content producers. The question today is "How much influence will countries accept in exchange for fuller membership in the global community?" In light of instant, inexpensive, and open computer network communication, a parallel question is "Have notions such as national sovereignty and cultural integrity lost their meaning?" For

CNN uses 14 satellites to transmit to a billion viewers in almost 200 countries.

What does it say about American "cultural integrity" when the most popular magazine among college men in the U.S. is *Maxim*, a direct copy of England's *Maxim*? Can you tell which cover is from which nation? Hint: look for the price.

To limit cultural intrusion, the South Korean government requires that movie houses in its country screen Korean-made films, such as *The Way Home*, at least 146 days out of the year.

example, ESPN is carried on 20 networks in 21 languages to 155 million television households in 183 different countries. *The Simpsons* is drawn in South Korea. The BBC broadcasts daily to a worldwide audience in 40 languages, as does Radio Beijing from China. CNN uses 14 satellites to transmit to a billion viewers in almost 200 countries. Mexican soap operas dominate the television schedules of much of Latin and South America. Three of the four largest U.S. record companies have international ownership. Hollywood's Universal Studios is owned by French Vivendi, Columbia Pictures by Japanese Sony, and 20th Century Fox by Rupert Murdoch's Australian corporation. As Thomas Middelhoff, former CEO of Bertelsmann, a German company that controls a large proportion of the U.S. book publishing market (Chapter 3) and earns more money from the United States than from any other nation, including its homeland, explained, "We're not foreign. We're international. I'm an American with a German passport" (as quoted in McChesney, 1999a, p. 104).

THE CASE FOR THE GLOBAL VILLAGE

Globalvision News Network
WWW.
gvnews.net

There are differing opinions about the benefits of this trend away from nation-specific cultures. Global village proponents see the world community coming closer together as a common culture is negotiated and, not incidentally, as we become more economically interconnected. "We are witnessing the revolution of the empowerment of the media consumer," argues Reuters Television Director Enriqué Jara (as cited in Hilliard & Keith, 1996, p. 1). There should be little fear that individual cultures and national identities will disappear, because the world's great diversity will ensure that culture-specific, special-interest fare remains in demand. Modern media technology makes the delivery of this varied content not only possible but profitable. For example, native-language versions of *Jeopardy* and *Wheel of Fortune* exist in virtually every Western European country.

Abaya-clad Saudi Arabian women line up at the women-only counter of a McDonald's in a mall in Dhahran. Although critics of cultural imperialism see this as an intrusion of Western culture into the lives of these people, defenders of the globalization of culture see the expansion of opportunity for both the "sending" and the "receiving" cultures.

THE CASE AGAINST THE GLOBAL VILLAGE

The global village is here, say those with a less optimistic view, and the problem is what it looks like. *Time* media writer James Poniewozik (2001, p. 69) calls it "the new cold war—between the Hollywood/Mickey D's axis and every other world culture." Professor Richard Rosenberg (1992) predicts the erosion of national sovereignty. "The advanced nations of the world, through their multi-national corporations, will greatly expand their control over the international flow of information. As a result, much of the world may become even more heavily dependent on the Western nations and Japan" (p. 331). He also predicts the demise of native cultures. "The ongoing assault on national cultures will continue, fostered by direct satellite broadcasts and worldwide information distribution networks" (p. 332).

Media critic Robert McChesney (1997) fears for worldwide democracy. "The present course," he writes, "is one where much of the world's entertainment and journalism will be provided by a handful of enormous firms, with invariably pro-profit and pro-global market political positions on the central issues of our times. The implications for political democracy, by any standard, are troubling" (p. 23).

He elaborated elsewhere:

> The global commercial-media system is radical in that it will respect no tradition or custom, on balance, if it stands in the way of profits. . . . The global media system is better understood as one that advances corporate and commercial interests and values and denigrates or ignores that which cannot be incorporated into its mission. There is no discernible difference in the firms' content, whether they are owned by shareholders in Japan or Belgium or have corporate headquarters in New York or Sydney. (1999b, pp. 13–14)

There is no simple answer to the debate over protecting the integrity of local cultures. As we've just seen, there is even disagreement over the wisdom of doing so. Media literate people should at least be aware of the debate and its issues.

DEVELOPING MEDIA LITERACY SKILLS
Making Our Way in the Global Village

Questions raised by the new communication technologies often lack clear-cut, satisfactory answers. In fact, as the major controversy addressed in this chapter—the impact of new communication technologies on national sovereignty and culture—demonstrates, different answers flow from different perspectives. For example, a world at peace with itself, its people sharing the common assumptions of a common culture, is a utopian dream. There are those who see it as attainable. But if the common culture that binds us is that of Mickey Mouse, is the harmony worth the loss of individual, idiosyncratic cultures?

There may be no easy—or even correct—solution to the problem of protecting the integrity of local cultures in our increasingly interconnected, mediated world. But at the very least, the simple existence of the problem requires that we remain open to and appreciative of the cultures of all our neighbors in the global village. The new communication technologies will put them and us together in ways that were unimaginable in pre-Internet times. Are you ready?

The hallmarks of a media literate individual are surely analysis and self-reflection. Revisit the primer on pages 338–339. Reread its good news and bad news and answer again the questions it raises. Have any of your answers changed? If they have, which ones, how, and most important, why? Are you a media literate, competent citizen of the global village? What contribution can you and will you make?

Support the Media Literacy Movement

One of the ironies of contemporary mass communication is that the United States, no doubt the world's most media saturated country, lags behind most of the developed world in its commitment to media literacy. We saw in Chapter 2, for example, that many countries not only have aggressive and active media literacy movements but also that these movements are supported and funded by those countries' media companies and governments.

But the United States may be catching up. As you saw in Chapter 14, there is growing dissatisfaction from across the political and social spectrum with the operation of the American media, especially on the issues of privacy, concentration, and the pace and products of deregulation. This dissatisfaction, according to media activists John Nichols and Robert McChesney (2002), is producing the basis for a true media literacy movement in the United States. "During the 1990s," they wrote, media literacy "activists began to recognize the need to do more than just critique increasingly monopolized and monotonous media. Local groups formed across the nation to monitor the local news media, keep commercialism out of schools, and banish liquor billboards from working-class and minority neighborhoods. In the past several years, media activism has blossomed at both the local and national levels" (Nicholas & McChesney, 2002, p. 26). Media literacy has become a bipartisan issue, they continue, because "no more than leftists do sincere conservatives want their children's brains marinated in advertising; they do not want political campaigns to be centered entirely around expensive, inaccurate, and insulting political advertising; and they do not want America's democratic discourse reduced to poll-tested soundbites and arguments about which television anchor is wearing the biggest flag pin" (p. 27).

Live your media literacy by actively promoting a true American media literacy movement. There is a lot of help available from overseas, because if media are globalized, there is no reason that a strong American media literacy movement should not be, too. Examine the organization and efforts of these nations' movements to inform your own living media literacy:

Canada

Canadian Association of Media Education Organizations (CAMEO)

interact.uoregon.edu/MediaLit/CAMEO/index.htm

Ontario Media Literacy

www.angelfire.com/ms/MediaLiteracy/index.html

United Kingdom

The United Kingdom Media Education Website

www.mediaed.org.uk/home.htm

Media and Communication Studies Site

www.aber.ac.uk/media/Functions/mcs.html

South Africa

Media Institute of South Africa (MISA)

www.misanet.org

Australia

Australian Children's Television Foundation

www.actf.com.au/

Chapter Review

International telecommunications has its roots in the clandestine radio stations operated during World War II and the Cold War, as well as the pirate radio stations that challenged the dominance of Europe's noncommercial broadcasters. These efforts, based originally on shortwave radio, gave rise to international broadcasting that is still with us today, such as the Voice of America and the BBC World Service. The United States in fact maintains several surrogate services in addition to the VOA, including Radio Martí and Radio Free Europe/Radio Liberty.

Satellites made truly global telecommunications possible. COMSAT, representing the United States, managed the first global system of telecommunications satellites, INTELSAT, which has since been joined by many other commercial and government-run satellite providers.

Comparative analysis traditionally examines different countries' media systems in terms of the normative theories that guide them: Western, for example, the United States and Great Britain; development, for example, Honduras; revolutionary, as practiced by Poland's Solidarity movement; and authoritarianism and communism, still in place in the world's few remaining communist countries.

Regardless of the nature of a country's media system, that system carries programming. Most of the world's radio and television programming looks much like that found in the United States. The United States was among the first countries to distribute its media fare to other countries, setting audience expectations around the globe. It remains a world leader. The global spread of American and other Western media content raises questions about cultural imperialism, that is, concerns over smaller countries' ability to maintain national sovereignty and control over their own cultures. Critics of cultural imperialism argue that non-native fare inevitably debases native cultures and that global media companies exert undue influence over the flow of information. Others, however, see little to fear in the globalization of media content, claiming that the world might indeed be a better place if its people shared a more common culture and that, besides, most nations demand culture-specific content.

Key Terms

OLG · Use the text's CD-ROM and the Online Learning Center at www.mhhe.com/baran to further your understanding of the following terminology.

Euro English, 500
shortwave radio, 501
skip, 501
sky waves, 501
clandestine stations, 501
indigenous station, 502
exogenous station, 502

pirate broadcaster, 502
external service, 503
surrogate service, 504
comparative analysis (studies), 512
Western concept, 512
public service remit, 513

D-notice, 514
development concept, 514
revolutionary concept, 514
authoritarian systems, 516
wired radio, 516
cultural imperialism, 521

Questions for Review

OLG · Go to the self-quizzes on the CD-ROM and the Online Learning Center to test your knowledge.

1. What are clandestine broadcast stations? Differentiate between indigenous and exogenous stations.
2. What are pirate broadcasters? What differentiates them from traditional clandestine operators?
3. How did World War II and the Cold War shape the efforts of the United States in terms of its external and surrogate services?
4. Describe the goals of the Voice of America, Radio and TV Martí, Armed Forces Radio and Television Services, and Radio Free Europe/Radio Liberty?
5. What are COMSAT and INTELSAT? How are they related?
6. What is comparative analysis?
7. What are the main characteristics of media systems operating under Hachten's Western concept?
8. What are the main characteristics of media systems operating under Hachten's development concept?

9. What are the main characteristics of media systems operating under Hachten's revolutionary concept?
10. What are the main characteristics of media systems operating under Hachten's authoritarianism and communism concepts?
11. In British media, what is the public service remit? What is a D-notice?
12. What is meant by wired radio?
13. What is cultural imperialism? What two telecommunications technologies fuel current concern over its operation?
14. What was the MacBride Report? Why did most Western nations reject it?
15. What is meant by the New World Information Order?

Questions for Critical Thinking and Discussion

1. Britain's external service, the BBC, is available on shortwave radio and American cable and satellite television. Listen to or watch the BBC. How does its content compare to the homegrown radio and television with which you are familiar? Think especially of news. How does its reporting differ from that of cable networks such as CNN and from broadcast networks such as ABC, CBS, and NBC? Why do you think differences exist? Similarities?

2. Do you have experience with another country's media? If so, which one? Can you place that system's operation within one of the concepts listed in this chapter? Describe how that system's content was similar to and different from that with which you are familiar in the United States. Do you favor one system's fare over another's? Why or why not?

3. Do you think countries, especially developing nations, should worry about cultural imperialism? Would you argue that they should use low-cost Western fare to help their developing system get "off the ground," or do you agree with critics that this approach unduly influences their system's ultimate content?

4. Compared with the United States, much of the rest of the world allows more sex and nudity in television programming. What does this tell us about these other countries and their people? About American audiences? Would you favor more sex and nudity on American television? Why or why not?

Important Resources

Galtung, J., & Vincent, R. C. (1992). *Global glasnost: Toward a new world information and communication order?* **Cresskill, NJ: Hampton Press.** A historical overview of the 1970–1980 worldwide debate over the free flow of information and national sovereignty, covering all sides of the dispute while suggesting possible solutions: technological, economic, and political.

Gordon, W. T. (1997). *McLuhan for beginners.* **New York: Writers and Readers Publishing.** A funny, iconoclastic homage to one of media's great thinkers.

It doesn't gloss over McLuhan's too optimistic infatuation with technology, but it does give the man his due.

Mohammadi, A. (Ed.). (1997). *International communication globalization.* **Thousand Oaks, CA: Sage.** A collection of essays from scholars representing several countries and several philosophies about communication and national development and cultural sovereignty. There are interesting essays on global communication ethics and worldwide communication deregulation.

Radio Free Europe/Radio Liberty	www.rferl.org
Radio Caroline	www.radiocaroline.com.uk
Clandestine Radio	www.clandestineradio.com
RIAS	www.scripps.ohiou.edu/rias/history.htm
Voice of America	www.voa.gov
AFRTS	www.afrts.osd.mil
Voice of America Online	www.voanews.com
INTELSAT	www.intelsat.com
Center for Global Media Studies	www.cgms.org
BBC	www.bbc.co.uk
UNESCO	www.unesco.org
Globalvision News Network	www.gvnews.net

Glossary

absolutist position regarding the First Amendment, the idea that no law means no law

acquisitions editor the person in charge of determining which books a publisher will publish

Acta Diurna written on a tablet, account of the deliberations of the Roman senate; an early "newspaper"

actual malice the standard for libel in coverage of public figures consisting of "knowledge of its falsity" or "reckless disregard" for whether it is true or not

ad hoc balancing of interests in individual First Amendment cases, several factors should be weighed in determining how much freedom the press is granted

addressable technology technology enabling a program provider to switch access to pay services on and off at the hub

administrative research studies of the immediate, practical influence of mass communication

advergames free, downloadable computer games with commercial product placements

advertorials ads in magazines and newspapers that take on the appearance of genuine editorial content

affiliate a broadcasting station that aligns itself with a network

agenda setting the theory that media may not tell us what to think but do tell us what to think about

aggressive cues model of media violence; media portrayals can indicate that certain classes of people are acceptable targets for real-world aggression

AIDA approach the idea that to persuade consumers advertising must attract **A**ttention, create **I**nterest, stimulate **D**esire, and promote **A**ction

Alien and Sedition Acts series of four laws passed by 1798 U.S. Congress making illegal the writing, publishing, or printing of "any false scandalous and malicious writing" about the president, the Congress, or the U.S. government

aliteracy possessing the ability to read but being unwilling to do so

all-channel legislation 1962 law requiring all television sets imported into or manufactured in the United States to be equipped with both VHF and UHF receivers

ambient advertising advertising content appearing in nontraditional venues

AM/FM combo two stations, one AM and one FM, simultaneously broadcasting identical content

applied ethics the application of metaethics and normative ethics to very specific situations

ascertainment requires broadcasters to ascertain, or actively and affirmatively determine, the nature of their audiences' interest, convenience, and necessity; no longer enforced

attitude change theory theory that explains how people's attitudes are formed, shaped, and changed and how those attitudes influence behavior

audimeter device for recording when the television set is turned on, the channel to which it is tuned, and the time of day; used in compiling ratings

audion tube vacuum tube developed by DeForest that became the basic invention for all radio and television

authoritarian/communism system a national media system characterized by authoritarian control

average quarter-hour how many people are listening to a broadcast station in each 15-minute day part

awareness test ad research technique that measures the cumulative effect of a campaign in terms of a product's "consumer consciousness"

basic cable television channels provided automatically by virtue of subscription to a cable provider

B-movie the second, typically less expensive, movie in a double feature

bandwidth a communication channel's information-carrying capacity

banners online advertising messages akin to billboards

Bill of Rights the first 10 amendments to the U.S. Constitution

billings total sale of broadcast airtime

Biltmore Agreement settled the press war between newspapers, which had refused their services to their electronic competitors, and radio

binary code information transformed into a series of digits 1 and 0 for storage and manipulation in computers

bitcasters "radio stations" that can be accessed only over the World Wide Web

blink ads television commercials lasting one second

block booking the practice of requiring exhibitors to rent groups of movies (often inferior) to secure a better one

blockbuster mentality filmmaking characterized by reduced risk taking and more formulaic movies; business concerns are said to dominate artistic considerations

blogs Web journal that comments on the news with links to stories that back up the commentary with evidence

BOC regional Bell operating company

bounded cultures (co-cultures) groups with specific but not dominant cultures

brand awareness an advertising goal when a number of essentially similar brands populate a given product category

brand magazine a consumer magazine published by a retail business for readers having demographic characteristics similar to those consumers with whom it typically does business

broadband a channel with broad information-carrying capacity

broadcast spectrum that portion of the electromagnetic spectrum on which the FCC grants permission to transmit

broadsides (sometimes **broadsheets**) early colonial newspapers imported from England, single-sheet announcements or accounts of events

browsers software programs loaded on personal computers and used to download and view Web files

bundling delivering television, VOD, audio, high-speed Internet access, long-distance and local phone service, multiple phone lines, and fax via cable

cable modem modem connecting a computer to the Internet via a specified Internet service provider

calotype early system of photography using translucent paper from which multiple prints could be made

catalogue albums in record retailing; albums more than 3 years old

catharsis theory that watching mediated violence reduces people's inclination to behave aggressively

cease-and-desist order demand made by a regulatory agency that a given illegal practice be stopped

censorware unflattering name given to Web content-filtering software by its opponents

chained Bibles Bibles attached to church furniture or walls by early European church leaders

channel surfing traveling through the television channels focusing neither on specific programs nor on the commercials they house

churn in cable, turnover in subscribership, whereby new subscriptions are offset by cancellations

cinematographe Lumière brothers' device that both photographed and projected action

circulation the number of issues of a magazine or newspaper that are sold

civic journalism modern practice of newspapers actively engaging the community in their reporting of important civic issues

clandestine stations illegal or unlicensed broadcast operations frequently operated by revolutionary groups or intelligence agencies for political purposes

clear time when local affiliates carry a network's program

click stream the series of choices made by a user on the Web

clutter in television, when many individual commercials share one commercial break

coaxial cable copper-clad aluminum wire encased in plastic foam insulation, covered by an aluminum outer conductor, and then sheathed in plastic

collateral materials printing, research, and photographs that PR firms handle for clients, charging as much as 17.65% for this service

commissions in advertising, placement of advertising in media is compensated, at typically 15% of the cost of the time or space, through commissions

common carrier technology required to carry the messages of others with no power to shape or restrict them

communication the process of creating shared meaning

community antenna television (CATV) outmoded name for early cable television

community publishing Web pages built by local schools, clubs, and nonprofit groups carried on online newspaper Web sites

comparative analysis the study of different countries' mass media systems

comparative studies see **comparative analysis**

compensation network payments to affiliates for clearing content

complementary copy newspaper and magazine content that reinforces the advertiser's message, or at least does not negate it

concentration of ownership ownership of different and numerous media companies concentrated in fewer and fewer hands

concept films movies that can be described in one line

confidentiality the ability of media professionals to keep secret the names of people who provide them with information

conglomeration the increase in the ownership of media outlets by nonmedia companies

consumer culture in which personal worth and identity reside not in the people themselves but in the products with which they surround themselves

consumer juries ad research technique in which people considered representative of a target market review a number of approaches or variations of a campaign or ad

contextual advertising in online advertising, ads that automatically intrude into users' Web sessions whether wanted or not

controlled circulation a magazine is provided at no cost to readers who meet some specific set of advertiser-attractive criteria

conventions in media content, certain distinctive, standardized style elements of individual genres

convergence the erosion of traditional distinctions among media due to concentration of ownership, globalization, hypercommercialism, and increased audience fragmentation

co-op placements paid-for features (commercials) on given books that appear on the Web pages of some online booksellers

copy testing measuring the effectiveness of advertising messages by showing them to consumers; used for all forms of advertising

copyright identifying and granting ownership of a given piece of expression to protect the creators' financial interest in it

corantos one-page news sheets on specific events, printed in English but published in Holland and imported into England by British booksellers; an early "newspaper"

corrective advertising a new set of ads required by a regulatory body and produced by the offender that correct the original misleading effort

cost per thousand (CPM) in advertising, the cost of reaching 1,000 audience members, computed by the cost of an ad's placement divided by the number of thousands of consumers it reaches

cottage industry an industry characterized by small operations closely identified with their personnel

cover rerecording of one artist's music by another

critical cultural theory idea that media operate primarily to justify and support the status quo at the expense of ordinary people

critical research studies of media's contribution to the larger issues of what kind of nation we are building, what kind of people we are becoming

cruising see **channel surfing**

cultivation analysis idea that television "cultivates" or constructs a reality of the world that, although possibly inaccurate, becomes the accepted reality simply because we as a culture believe it to be the reality

cultural definition of communication communication is a symbolic process whereby reality is produced, maintained, repaired, and transformed; from James Carey

cultural imperialism the invasion of an indigenous people's culture, through mass media, by outside, powerful countries

cultural theory the idea that meaning and therefore effects are negotiated by media and audiences as they interact in the culture

culture the world made meaningful; socially constructed and maintained through communication, it limits as well as liberates us, differentiates as well as unites us, defines our realities and thereby shapes the ways we think, feel, and act

cume the cumulative audience, the number of people who listen to a radio station for at least 5 minutes in any one day

cyberadvertising placement of commercials on various online sites

d-book a book that is downloaded in electronic form from the Internet to a computer or handheld device

D-notice in Great Britain, an officially issued notice of prior restraint

daguerreotype process of recording images on polished metal plates, usually copper, covered with a thin layer of silver iodide emulsion

dataveillance the massive electronic collection and distillation of consumer data

decoding interpreting sign/symbol systems

democracy government by the people

demographic segmentation advertisers' appeal to audiences composed of varying personal and social characteristics such as race, gender, and economic level

density number of households per mile of cable

dependency theory idea that media's power is a function of audience members' dependency on the media and their content

deregulation relaxation of ownership and other rules for radio and television

desensitization the idea that viewers become more accepting of real-world violence because of its constant presence in television fare

desktop publishing small-scale print content design, layout, and production made possible by inexpensive computer hardware and software

development concept of media systems; government and media work in partnership to ensure that media assist in the planned, beneficial development of the country

digital audio radio service (DARS) direct home or automobile delivery of audio by satellite

digital audio tape (DAT) introduced in the early 1970s, offers digital-quality sound purity in a cassette tape format

digital cable television delivery of digital video images and other information to subscribers' homes

digital compression "squeezing" of digital signals to permit multiple signals to be carried over one channel

digital computer a computer that processes data reduced to a binary code

digital delivery daily the online distribution of entire versions of printed newspapers

digital divide the lack of technological access among people of color, the poor, the disabled, and those in rural communities

digital must-carry rules in cable television, rules requiring that cable systems carry the signal of every television station, both analog and digital, within a specified radius

digital recording recording based on conversion of sound into 1s and 0s logged in millisecond intervals in a computerized translation process

digital rights management (DRM) protection of digitally distributed intellectual property

digital video recorder (DVR) video recording device attached to a television, that gives viewers significant control over content

dime novels inexpensive late 19th- and early 20th-century books that concentrated on frontier and adventure stories; sometimes called **pulp novels**

disinhibitory effects in social cognitive theory, seeing a model rewarded for prohibited or threatening behavior increases the likelihood that the observer will perform that behavior

dissonance theory argues that people, when confronted by new information, experience a kind of mental discomfort, a dissonance; as a result, they consciously and subconsciously work to limit or reduce that discomfort through the selective processes

diurnals daily accounts of local news printed in 1620s England; forerunners of our daily newspaper

DMX (Digital Music Express) home delivery of audio by cable

domain name on the World Wide Web, an identifying name, rather than a site's formal URL, that gives some indication of the nature of a site's content or owner

dominant culture (mainstream culture) the culture that seems to hold sway with the large majority of people; that which is normative

double feature two films on the same bill

drop cable cable television line that runs from the feeder to people's homes

duopoly single ownership and management of multiple radio stations in one market

e-book digital book having the appearance of traditional books but with content that is digitally stored and accessed

e-mail (electronic mail) function of Internet allowing communication via computer with anyone else online, anyplace in the world, with no long-distance fees

e-publishing the publication and distribution of books initially or exclusively online

early window the idea that media give children a window on the world before they have the critical and intellectual ability to judge what they see

economies of scale concept that relative cost declines as the size of the endeavor grows

editorial policy newspapers' and magazines' positions on certain specific issues

embedding when war correspondents exchange control of their output for access to the front

encoding transforming ideas into an understandable sign/symbol system

encryption electronic coding or masking of information on the Web that can be deciphered only by a recipient with the decrypting key

environmental incentives in social learning theory, the notion that real-world incentives can lead observers to ignore negative vicarious reinforcement

ethics rules of behavior or moral principles that guide actions in given situations

Euro English official language of the European Union

exogenous stations clandestine broadcast operations functioning from outside the regions to which they transmit

expanded basic cable in cable television a second, somewhat more expensive level of subscription

external service in international broadcasting, a service designed by one country to counter enemy propaganda and disseminate information about itself

extramercials in cyberadvertising, columns of ad content that slide down over a Web page's content

factory studios the first film production companies

fair use in copyright law, instances in which material may be used without permission or payment

Fairness Doctrine requires broadcasters to cover issues of public importance and to be fair in that coverage; abolished in 1987

feature syndicates clearinghouses for the work of columnists, cartoonists, and other creative individuals, providing their work to newspapers and other media outlets

feedback the response to a given communication

feeder cables television cables that run from the trunk cable into individual neighborhoods or areas

fiber optics signals carried by light beams over glass fibers

Financial Interest and Syndication Rules FCC rules delineating the amount of ownership the television networks are allowed in the programming they air

Fin-Syn see **Financial Interest and Syndication Rules**

First Amendment Congress shall make no law respecting an establishment of religion, or prohibiting the free exercise thereof; or abridging the freedom of speech, or of the press; or the right of the people peacefully to assemble, and to petition the Government for a redress of grievances

first-run syndication original programming produced specifically for the syndicated television market

fixed fee arrangements when PR firms perform a specific set of services for a client for a specific and prearranged fee

flack a derogatory name sometimes applied to public relations professionals

flash mobs (sometimes **smart mobs**) large, geographically dispersed groups connected only by communications technology, quickly drawn together to perform collective action

floating ads see **shoshkeles**

focus groups small groups of people who are interviewed, typically to provide advertising or public relations professionals with detailed information

forced exposure ad research technique used primarily for television commercials, requiring advertisers to bring consumers to a theater or other facility where they see a television program, complete with the new ads

format a radio station's particular sound or programming content

franchise films movies produced with full intention of producing several sequels

Frankfurt School media theory, centered in neo-Marxism, that valued serious art, viewing its consumption as a means to elevate all people toward a better life; typical media fare was seen as pacifying ordinary people while repressing them

genre a form of media content with a standardized, distinctive style and conventions

global village a McLuhan concept; new communication technologies permit people to become increasingly involved in one another's lives

grand theory a theory designed to describe and explain all aspects of a given phenomenon

grazing watching several television programs simultaneously

green light process the process of deciding to make a movie

greenwashing public relations practice of countering the public relations efforts aimed at clients by environmentalists

griots the "talking chiefs" in orally based African tribes

hackers people interested in technology, information, and communication through computers

hard news news stories that help readers make intelligent decisions and keep up with important issues

HDTV digital compression of television signals allowing transmission of six or seven channels of programming in a single band

headend place or equipment necessary for cable television to receive and process a signal

home page entryway into a Web site, containing information and hyperlinks to other material

hosts computers linking individual personal computer users to the Internet

hub cable system operation itself, in which signals are processed and boosted for distribution

hypercommercialism increasing the amount of advertising and mixing commercial and noncommercial media content

hyperlink connection, embedded in Internet or Web site, allowing instant access to other material in that site as well as to material in other sites

hypodermic needle theory idea that media are a dangerous drug that can directly enter a person's system

iconoscope tube first practical television camera tube, developed in 1923

identification in social cognitive theory, a special form of imitation by which observers do not exactly copy what they have seen but make a more generalized but related response

ideogrammatic alphabet a symbol- or picture-based alphabet

imitation in social cognitive theory, the direct replication of an observed behavior

importation of distant signals delivery of distant television signals by cable television for the purpose of improving reception

in-band-on-channel (IBOC) digital radio technology that uses digital compression to "shrink" digital and analog signals, allowing both to occupy the same frequency

indecency in broadcasting, language or material that depicts sexual or excretory activities in a way offensive to contemporary community standards

indigenous stations clandestine broadcast operations functioning from inside the regions to which they transmit

inferential feedback in the mass communication process, feedback is typically indirect rather than direct; that is, it is inferential

information gap the widening disparity in amounts and types of information available to information haves and have-nots

information society a society in which the creation and exchange of information is the predominant social and economic activity

inhibitory effects in social cognitive theory, seeing a model punished for a behavior reduces the likelihood that the observer will perform that behavior

instant books books published very soon after some well-publicized public event

integrated marketing communications (IMC) combining public relations, marketing, advertising, and promotion into a seamless communication campaign

interactive cable ability of subscribers to talk back to cable system operators on the same wire used by operators to deliver content

interdiction technology technology that descrambles pay channel cable television signals outside the home

interlaced scanning television format in which electron beams sweep the picture tube twice, creating half the image's lines on the first pass and then filling in the gaps in the second

intermercials attractive, lively commercials that run while people are waiting for Web pages to download

Internet a global network of interconnected computers that communicate freely and share and exchange information

Internet service provider (ISP) see **provider**

interpersonal communication communication between two or a few people

interstitial ads in cyberadvertising, images that seem to appear and disappear mysteriously on the screen as users click from one page to the next

islands in children's television commercials, the product is shown simply, in actual size against a neutral background

joint operating agreement (JOA) permits a failing paper to merge most aspects of its business with a successful local competitor, as long as editorial and reporting operations remain separate

kinescope improved picture tube developed by Zworykin for RCA

kinetograph William Dickson's early motion picture camera

kinetoscope peep show devices for the exhibition of kinetographs

LANs (Local Area Networks) networks connecting two or more computers, usually within the same building

large rectangles in online advertising, oversized ads that appear in the center of the page, over existing text

libel the false and malicious publication of material that damages a person's reputation (typically applied to print media)

libertarianism philosophy of the press that asserts that good and rational people can tell right from wrong if presented with full and free access to information; therefore censorship is unnecessary

limited effects theory media's influence is limited by people's individual differences, social categories, and personal relationships

linotype technology that allowed the mechanical rather than manual setting of print type

liquid barretter first audio device permitting the reception of wireless voices; developed by Fessenden

literacy the ability to effectively and efficiently comprehend and utilize a given form of communication

literate culture a culture that employs a written language

lobbying in public relations, directly interacting with elected officials or government regulators and agents

local carriage rules rules requiring cable systems to carry specific sets of television signals

macro-level effects media's wide-scale social and cultural impact

magalogue a designer catalogue produced to look like a consumer magazine

magic bullet theory the idea from mass society theory that media are a powerful "killing force" that directly penetrates a person's system

mainframe computer a large central computer to which users are connected by terminals

mainstreaming in cultivation analysis, television's ability to move people toward a common understanding of how things are

mass communication the process of creating shared meaning between the mass media and their audiences

mass communication theories explanations and predictions of social phenomena relating mass communication to various aspects of our personal and cultural lives or social systems

mass medium (pl. **mass media**) a medium that carries messages to a large number of people

mass society theory the idea that media are corrupting influences; they undermine the social order, and "average" people are defenseless against their influence

master antenna television (MATV) connecting multiple sets in a single location or building to a single, master antenna

media councils panels of people from both the media and the public who investigate complaints against the media and publish their findings

media literacy the ability to effectively and efficiently comprehend and utilize mass communication

medium (pl. **media**) vehicle by which messages are conveyed

metaethics examination of a culture's understanding of its fundamental values

microcomputer a very small computer that uses a microprocessor to handle information (also called a **personal computer** or **PC**)

microcinema filmmaking using digital video cameras and desktop digital editing machines

micro-level effects effects of media on individuals

microwave multidistribution system (MMDS) video distribution system employing a home microwave receiver to collect signals and pipe them through a house via internal wiring

microwave relay system audio and video transmitting system in which super-high-frequency signals are sent from land-based point to land-based point

middle-range theories ideas that explain or predict only limited aspects of the mass communication process

minicomputers a relatively large central computer to which users are connected by terminals; not as large as a mainframe computer

MNA reports multinetwork area television ratings based on the 70 largest markets

modeling in social cognitive theory, learning through imitation and identification

modem a device that translates digital computer information into an analog form so it can be transmitted through telephone lines

montage tying together two separate but related shots in such a way that they take on a new, unified meaning

moral agent in an ethical dilemma, the person making the decision

MP3 file compression software that permits streaming of digital audio and video data

muckraking a form of crusading journalism that primarily used magazines to agitate for change

multichannel service fee-based provider (such as cable and DBS) of video content

multimedia advanced sound and image capabilities for microcomputers

multiple points of access ability of a literate media consumer to access or approach media content from a variety of personally satisfying directions

multiple system operator (MSO) a company owning several different cable television operations

multiple user domain (MUD) an online, virtual "community" in which users are encouraged to create their own identities, which then interact with other virtual citizens of that community

multiplexing the practice of using one channel to transmit multiple forms of content; in television and cable, through signal compression

music licensing company an organization that collects fees based on recorded music users' gross receipts and distributes the money to songwriters and artists

narrowcasting aiming broadcast programming at smaller, more demographically homogeneous audiences

neo-Marxist theory the theory that people are oppressed by those who control the culture, the superstructure, as opposed to the base

network centralized production, distribution, decision-making organization that links affiliates for the purpose of delivering their viewers to advertisers

news production research the study of how economic and other influences on the way news is produced distort and bias news coverage toward those in power

news staging re-creation on television news of some event that is believed to have happened or which could have happened

newsbook early weekly British publications that carried ads

newshole that portion of a newspaper devoted to news

newspaper chains businesses that own two or more newspapers

niche marketing aiming media content or consumer products at smaller, more demographically homogeneous audiences

nickelodeons the first movie houses; admission was one nickel

Nipkow disc first workable device for generating electrical signals suitable for the transmission of a scene

noise anything that interferes with successful communication

nonduplication rule mid-1960s FCC ruling that AM and FM license holders in the same market must broadcast different content at least 50% of the time

normative ethics generalized theories, rules, and principles of ethical or moral behavior

normative theory an idea that explains how media should ideally operate in a given system of social values

O&O a broadcasting station that is owned and operated by a network

obscenity unprotected expression determined by (a) whether the average person, applying contemporary community standards, would find that the work, taken as a whole, appeals to the prurient interest, (b) whether the work depicts or describes, in a patently offensive way, sexual conduct specifically defined by the applicable state law, and (c) whether the work, taken as a whole, lacks serious literary, artistic, political, or scientific value

observational learning in social cognitive theory, observers can acquire (learn) new behaviors simply by seeing those behaviors performed

off-network broadcast industry term for syndicated content that originally aired on a network

offset lithography late-19th-century advance making possible printing from photographic plates rather than from metal casts

oligopoly a media system whose operation is dominated by a few large companies

ombudsman internal arbiter of performance for media organizations

open source software freely downloaded software

operating policy spells out standards for everyday operations for newspapers and magazines

operating system the software that tells the computer how to work

opinion followers people who receive opinion leaders' interpretations of media content; from **two-step flow theory**

opinion leaders people who initially consume media content, interpret it in light of their own values and beliefs, and then pass it on to opinion followers; from **two-step flow theory**

opt-in/opt-out consumers giving permission to companies to sell personal data or consumers requesting that companies do not sell personal data

oral (or **preliterate**) **culture** a culture without a written language

overnights television ratings data gathered from homes connected by phone lines to Nielsen computers

P2P person-to-person software that permits direct Internet-based communication or collaboration between two or more personal computers while bypassing centralized servers

papyrus early form of paper composed of pressed strips of sliced reed

paradigm a theory that summarizes and is consistent with all known facts

paradigm shift fundamental, even radical rethinking of what people believe to be true for a given body of knowledge

parchment writing material made from prepared animal skins

parity products products generally perceived as alike by consumers no matter who makes them

pass-along readership measurement of publication readers who neither subscribe nor buy single copies but who borrow a copy or read one in a doctor's office or library

pass-by rate number of homes passed by, or with the potential to take cable

pay cable cable television channels delivered to those viewers who pay a fee over and above their basic service charge

payola payment made by recording companies to DJs to air their records

pay-per-view cable television viewers pay a set fee for delivery of a specific piece of content

penetration number of homes passed by cable that actually subscribe

penny press newspapers in the 1830s selling for one penny

peoplemeter remote control keypad device for recording television viewing for taking ratings

personal video recorder see **digital video recorder**

persistence of vision images our eyes gather are retained by our brains for about $\frac{1}{24}$ of a second, producing the appearance of constant motion

personal computer (PC) see **microcomputer**

piggybacking in television advertising, a single sponsor presents two products in the same commercial

pilot a sample episode of a proposed television program

piracy the illegal recording and sale of copyrighted material

pirate broadcasters unlicensed or otherwise illegally operated broadcast stations

pixels the smallest picture element in an electronic imaging system such as a television or computer screen

platform rollout opening a movie on only a few screens in the hope that favorable reviews and word-of-mouth publicity will boost interest

playlist predetermined sequence of selected records to be played by a disc jockey

pocketpieces television ratings based on a national sample, computed and reported every 2 weeks

policy book delineates standards of operation for local broadcasters

pop-outs in cyberadvertising, ads that appear in a smaller window at the border of the Web page being read

pornography expression calculated solely to supply sexual excitement

portable peoplemeter pager-like ratings device worn by audience members that "reads" embedded audio signals in electronically delivered media content

preliterate culture see **oral culture**

print on demand publishing method whereby publishers store books digitally for instant printing, binding, and delivery once ordered

prior restraint power of the government to *prevent* publication or broadcast of expression

product positioning the practice in advertising of assigning meaning to a product based on who buys the product rather than on the product itself

production values media content's internal language and grammar; its style and quality

progressive scanning digital television format compatible with personal computers in which the entire picture is built line by line in one scan of the television's electronic beam

protocols common communication rules and languages for computers linked to the Internet

providers (Internet) companies that offer Internet connections at monthly rates depending on the kind and amount of access needed; also called **Internet service providers**

pseudo-events events that have no real informational or issue meaning; they exist merely to attract media attention

psychographic segmentation advertisers' appeal to consumer groups of varying lifestyles, attitudes, values, and behavior patterns

public access channel cable channel reserved on a first-come, first-served, nondiscriminatory basis for use by groups or individuals who maintain editorial control of their programming

public domain in copyright law, the use of material without permission once the copyright expires

public journalism see **civic journalism**

public service remit limits on advertising and other public service requirements imposed on Britain's commercial broadcasters in exchange for the right to broadcast

puffery the little lie or exaggeration that makes advertising more entertaining than it might otherwise be

pulp novels see **dime novels**

put agreement between a television producer and network that guarantees that the network will order at least a pilot or pay a penalty

rating percentage of a market's total population that is reached by a piece of broadcast programming

recall testing ad research technique in which consumers are asked to identify which ads are most easily remembered

recent catalogue albums in record retailing, albums out for 15 months to 3 years

recognition tests ad research technique in which people who have seen a given publication are asked whether they remember seeing a given ad

reinforcement theory Joseph Klapper's idea that if media have any impact at all it is in the direction of reinforcement

remainders unsold copies of books returned to the publisher by bookstores to be sold at great discount

retainer in advertising, an agreed-upon amount of money a client pays an ad agency for a specific series of services

ride-alongs the practice of allowing television reporters to accompany police in the conduct of their duty

ritual perspective the view of media as central to the representation of shared beliefs and culture

safe harbor times of the broadcast day (typically 10 P.M. to 6 A.M.) when children are not likely to be in the listening or viewing audience

satellite-delivered media tour spokespeople can be simultaneously interviewed by a worldwide audience hooked to the interviewee by telephone

satellite master antenna (SMATV) video distribution system in which signals are captured by a satellite dish and then distributed throughout a structure

search engines (sometimes called **spiders**, or **Web crawlers**) Web- or Net-search software providing on-screen menus

secondary service a radio station's second, or nonprimary, format

selective attention see **selective exposure**

selective exposure the idea that people expose themselves or attend to those messages that are consistent with their preexisting attitudes and beliefs

selective perception the idea that people interpret messages in a manner consistent with their preexisting attitudes and beliefs

selective processes people expose themselves to, remember best and longest, and reinterpret messages that are consistent with their preexisting attitudes and beliefs

selective retention assumes that people remember best and longest those messages that are consistent with their existing attitudes and beliefs

self-righting principle John Milton's articulation of libertarianism

share the percentage of people listening to radio or of homes using television tuned in to a given piece of programming

shield laws legislation that expressly protects reporters' rights to maintain sources' confidentiality in courts of law

shopbills attractive, artful business cards used by early British tradespeople to promote themselves

short ordering network practice of ordering only one or two episodes of a new television series

shortwave radio radio signals transmitted at high frequencies that can travel great distances by skipping off the ionosphere

shoshkeles in online advertising, animated objects, such as a car or Homer Simpson, that run across the screen; sometimes called **floating ads**

signs in social construction of reality, things that have subjective meaning

siquis pinup want ads common in Europe before and in early days of newspapers

Sixth Report and Order fundamental blueprint for the technical operation of television, issued in 1952

skip ability of radio waves to reflect off the ionosphere

skyscrapers online billboards placed down the side of a Web page

sky waves radio waves that are skipped off the ionosphere

slander oral or spoken defamation of a person's character (typically applied to broadcasting)

social cognitive theory idea that people learn through observation

social construction of reality theory for explaining how cultures construct and maintain their realities using signs and symbols; argues that people learn to behave in their social world through interaction with it

social responsibility theory (or **model**) normative theory or model asserting that media must remain free of government control but, in exchange, must serve the public

soft news sensational stories that do not serve the democratic function of journalism

spam unsolicited commercial e-mail

spectrum scarcity broadcast spectrum space is limited, so not everyone who wants to broadcast can; those who are granted licenses must accept regulation

spiders see **search engines**

split runs special versions of a given issue of a magazine in which editorial content and ads vary according to some specific demographic or regional grouping

spot commercial sales in broadcasting, selling individual advertising spots on a given program to a wide variety of advertisers

Standards and Practices Department the internal content review operation of a television network

stereotyping application of a standardized image or conception applied to members of certain groups, usually based on limited information

stimulation model of media violence; viewing mediated violence can increase the likelihood of subsequent aggressive behavior

streaming the simultaneous downloading and accessing (playing) of digital audio or video data

stripping broadcasting a syndicated television show at the same time five nights a week

subscription TV early experiments with over-the-air pay television

subsidiary rights the sale of a book, its contents, even its characters to outside interests, such as filmmakers

super trunk cable television cable that leads from the headend to the hub

surrogate service in international broadcasting, an operation established by one country to substitute for another's own domestic service

surround sessions in online advertising, users are served a steady stream of ads from one sponsor during their entire visit to a site

sweeps periods special television ratings times in February, May, July, and November in which diaries are distributed to thousands of sample households in selected markets

syllable alphabet a phonetically based alphabet employing sequences of vowels and consonants, that is, words

symbolic interaction the idea that people give meaning to symbols and then those symbols control people's behavior in their presence

symbols in social construction of reality, things that have objective meaning

syndicates feature services that operate as clearinghouses for the work of columnists, essayists, cartoonists, and other creative individuals

syndication sale of radio or television content to stations on a market-by-market basis

synergistic magazine magazine explicitly designed to generate stories that will become movies, television programs, or content for other media

synergy the use by media conglomerates of as many channels of delivery as possible for similar content

targeted keyword buys in cyberadvertising, a sponsor buys the right from an Internet service provider to have its ads pop up on the screen every time a user types in the sponsor's name

targeting aiming media content or consumer products at smaller, more specific audiences

taste publics groups of people or audiences bound by little more than their interest in a given form of media content

technological determinism the idea that machines and their development drive economic and cultural change

technology gap the widening disparity between communication technology haves and have-nots

telcos phone companies

telenovellas Spanish-language soap operas

television freeze 1948 freeze in authorization of new television stations while the FCC resolved a number of technical problems

terminals user workstations that are connected to larger centralized computers

text ad in online advertising, ads that appear alongside search results that somehow relate to the search

theatrical films movies produced primarily for initial exhibition on theater screens

third person effect the common attitude that others are influenced by media messages, but we are not

tier groupings of channels made available by a cable or satellite provider to subscribers at varying prices

time-shifting taping a show on a VCR for later viewing

trade books hard- or softcover books including fiction and most nonfiction and cookbooks, biographies, art books, coffee-table books, and how-to books

traffic cop analogy in broadcast regulation, the idea that the FCC, as a traffic cop, has the right to control not only the flow of broadcast traffic but its composition

transaction journalism in cyberadvertising, the direct linking of editorial content to sales

transmissional perspective the view of media as senders of information for the purpose of control

trunk cable television cable that leads from the head-end into the community

trustee model in broadcast regulation, the idea that broadcasters serve as the public's trustees or fiduciaries

two-step flow theory the idea that media's influence on people's behavior is limited by opinion leaders—people who initially consume media content, interpret it in light of their own values and beliefs, and then pass it on to opinion followers, who have less frequent contact with media

typification schemes in social construction of reality, collections of meanings people have assigned to some phenomenon or situation

unique selling proposition (USP) the aspect of an advertised product that sets it apart from other brands in the same product category

URL (**U**niform **R**esource **L**ocator) the designation of each file or directory on the host computer connected to the Internet

Usenet also known as network news, an internationally distributed Internet bulletin board system

uses and gratifications approach the idea that media don't do things *to* people; people do things *with* media

V-chip popular name for television set technology allowing parents to program out specific categories of content

VALS advertisers' psychographic segmentation strategy that classifies consumers according to values and lifestyles

vast wasteland expression coined by FCC Chair Newton Minow in 1961 to describe television content

vertical integration a system in which studios produced their own films, distributed them through their own outlets, and exhibited them in their own theaters

vicarious reinforcement in social cognitive theory, the observation of reinforcement operates in the same manner as actual reinforcement

video-on-demand (VOD) service allowing television viewers to access pay-per-view movies and other content that can be watched whenever they want

video news release preproduced report about a client or its product that is distributed on video-cassette free of charge to television stations

viral marketing PR strategy that relies on targeting specific Internet users with a given communication and relying on them to spread the word

virtue ethics emphasize the moral agent's character

WANs (**W**ide **A**rea **N**etworks) networks that connect several LANs in different locations

Web crawlers see **search engines**

Web radio the delivery of "radio" over the Internet directly to individual listeners

WebTV online delivery of high-definition television to special home receivers

Webzines online magazines

Wi-Fi wireless Internet

willing suspension of disbelief audience practice of willingly accepting the content before them as real

wire services news-gathering organizations that provide content to members

wired radio employed in remote areas of many developing countries; centrally located loudspeakers that deliver radio broadcasts

World Wide Web a tool that serves as a means of accessing files on computers connected via the Internet

yellow journalism early-20th-century journalism emphasizing sensational sex, crime, and disaster news

zapping using the remote control to switch to other content when a commercial appears

zipping fast-forwarding through taped commercials on a VCR

zone Internet address information, typically either geographic or descriptive of the type of organization

zoned editions suburban or regional versions of metropolitan newspapers

zoopraxiscope early machine for projecting slides onto a distant surface

References

A candid conversation with the high priest of popcult and metaphysician of media. (1969, March). *Playboy*, 53–74, 158.

Adams, M. (1996). The race for radiotelephone: 1900–1920. *AWA Review*, *10*, 78–119.

Add it up. (2001, November). *American Journalism Review*, p. 11.

AFRTS. (2000). Mission statement. Online, *http://www.eucom.mil/programs/afrts/index.htm*.

Agocs, C.S. & Menduno, M. (2003, September). Losing the war on spam. *Wired*, p. 50.

Albiniak, P. (1999, May 3). Media: Littleton's latest suspect. *Broadcasting & Cable*, pp. 6–15.

Albiniak, P. (2000a, January 17). TV's drug deal. *Broadcasting & Cable*, pp. 3, 148.

Albiniak, P. (2000b, January 24). Congress eyes PSA trade-off. *Broadcasting & Cable*, pp. 3, 148.

Albiniak, P. (2002a, January 28). Clear Channel challenged. *Broadcasting & Cable*, p. 12.

Albiniak, P. (2002b, February 4). It's all over for ALTV. *Broadcasting & Cable*, p. 11.

Albiniak, P. (2002c, April 29). Railing—but no derailing. *Broadcasting & Cable*, p. 7.

All together now. (1997, December 15). *Electronic Media*, p. 14.

Allen, B. (2001, July/August). Two—make that three—cheers for the chain bookstores. *The Atlantic Monthly*, pp. 148–151.

Allen, T. B. (2001, December). The future is calling. *National Geographic*, pp. 76–83.

Alterman, E. (2002, May 20). Bad work. *The Nation*, p. 10.

Amdur, M. (2003, March 10–16). What's the holdup with VOD? *Variety*, p. 13, cont. 26.

Americans are increasingly "wired." (2001, July 7). *Providence Journal*, p. A2.

Anderson, M. K. (2000, May/June). When copyright goes wrong. *Extra!*, p. 25

Angell, R. (2002, March 11). Read all about it. *The New Yorker*, pp. 27–28.

Apar, B. (1997, summer). DaViD meets Goliath. *Video Business DVD Supplement*, 10.

Arato, A., & Gebhardt, E. (1978). *The essential Frankfurt School reader*. New York: Urizen Books.

Arbitron. (2001, February 7). Study shows rise in streaming media consumption. Online: *www.arbitron.com/newsroom/archive/2_8_01_1745.htm?inframe*.

Arbitron. (2002, June 18). Radio listening highest among well-educated, upper-income consumers. Online: *www.arbitron.com/newsroom/archive/06_18_02.htm*.

Arens, W. F. (1999). *Contemporary advertising*. Boston: Irwin McGraw-Hill.

Artusa, M. (2002, July/August). Did you run this photo? *Columbia Journalism Review*, p. 47.

Ashley, J. (2002, July 31). Puttnam is right to want broadcasting to stay British. *The Guardian*, p. 16.

Auletta, K. (2001, December 10). Battle stations. *The New Yorker*, pp. 60–67.

Aumente, J. (1999, January/February). Cracking down: Yugoslavia's campaign against an independent media harkens back to the Cold War era. *American Journalism Review*, pp. 40–43.

Baker, R. (1997, September/October). The squeeze. *Columbia Journalism* Review, 30–36.

Baker, R. (1999, October 20). Profits vs. truth. *San Jose Mercury News*, p. 6B.

Baker, R. (2002, May/June). Want to be a patriot? Do your job. *Columbia Journalism Review*, pp. 78–79.

Baker, W. F. (2002, March 15). Media deregulation hurts the public. *Providence Journal*, p. B4.

Ball, S., & Bogatz, G. A. (1970). *The first year of* Sesame Street: *An evaluation*. Princeton, NJ: Educational Testing Service.

Bandura, A. (1965). Influence of model's reinforcement contingencies on the acquisition of imitative responses. *Journal of Personality and Social Psychology, 1*, 589–595.

Baran, S. J., Chase, L. J., & Courtright, J. A. (1979). *The Waltons*: Television as a facilitator of prosocial behavior. *Journal of Broadcasting, 23* (3), 277–284.

Baran, S. J., & Davis, D. K. (2003). *Mass communication theory: Foundations, ferment and future*. Belmont, CA: Wadsworth.

Baranowski, M. (2001, February 1). When all hell breaks loose. *American Way*, pp. 94–96.

Barlow, J. P. (1996). Selling wine without bottles: The economy of mind on the global Net. In L. H. Leeson (Ed.), *Clicking in: Hot links to a digital culture*. Seattle, WA: Bay Press.

Barmann, T. C. (2002, January 7). The information highway is getting more crowded. *Providence Journal*, pp. E1, E3.

Barnouw, E. (1966). *A tower in Babel: A history of broadcasting in the United States to 1933*. New York: Oxford University Press.

Barnouw, E. (1990). *Tube of plenty: The evolution of American television*. New York: Oxford University Press.

Bart, P. (2000, January 3–9). The big media blur. *Variety*, pp. 4, 95.

Barton, L. (2002, July 30). Cereal offenders. *Guardian Education*, pp. 2–3.

Beam, A. (2002, January 10). Attack of the teeny books. *Boston Globe*, p. D1.

Beck, D. (2000, July 2). Top U.S. book release ever is a thriller. *San Jose Mercury News*, pp. 1A, 17A.

Beech, H. (2002, July 22). Living it up in the illicit Internet underground. *Time*, p. 4.

Bennett, W. L. (1988). *News: The politics of illusion*. New York: Longman.

Berelson, B. (1949). What "missing the newspaper" means. In P. F. Lazarsfeld & F. N. Stanton (Eds.), *Communication research, 1948–1949*. New York: Harper.

Berger, P. L., & Luckmann, T. (1966). *The social construction of reality: A treatise in the sociology of knowledge*. Garden City, NY: Doubleday.

Berkman, H. W., & Gilson, C. (1987). *Advertising: Concepts and strategies*. New York: Random House.

Berkowitz, H., & Joshi, P. (2002, March 31). Cablevision quiz: YES Network or no? *Newsday.com*. Online: *www.newsday.com/templates/misc/printstory.jsp?slug=ny%2Dsunspec312647699ma*.

Big Blue vs. Big Brother. (1999, April 12). *San Jose Mercury News*, p. 6B.

Bittner, J. R. (1994). *Law and regulation of electronic media*. Englewood Cliffs, NJ: Prentice Hall.

Black, J. (2001). Hardening of the articles: An ethicist looks at propaganda in today's news. *Ethics in Journalism, 4*, 15–36.

Black, J., & Barney, R. D. (1985/86). The case against mass media codes of ethics. *Journal of Mass Media Ethics, 1*, 27–36.

Black, J., & Whitney, F. C. (1983). *Introduction to mass communications*. Dubuque, IA: William C. Brown.

Blais, J. (2003, July 23). Harry Potter casts a record-breaking spell. *USA Today*, p. 1D.

Blogs: The newest new journalism. (2003, January 10). *The Week*, p. 11.

Boddy, W. (1994). Alternative television in the United States. In H. Newcomb (Ed.), *Television: The critical view*. New York: Oxford University Press.

Bogle, D. (1989). *Toms, coons, mulattos, mammies, & bucks: An interpretive history of Blacks in American films*. New York: Continuum.

Booth, C. (1999, November 15). Worst of *Times*. *Time*, p. 79.

Boucher, G. (1999, April 7). New hits don't age gracefully. *San Jose Mercury News*, p. 12E.

Boutin, P. (2002, December). Burn, baby, burn. *Wired*, 91–92.

Boyd, A. (2003, August 4/11). The Web rewires the movement. *The Nation*, pp. 13–18.

Bradbury, R. (1981). *Fahrenheit 451*. New York: Ballantine. (Originally published in 1956.)

Bridges v. California 314 U.S. 252 (1941).

Brill S. (2000, April). The mega threats. *Brill's Content*, pp. 23–27.

Bronski, M. (2003, July 2). What is it about Harry? *Boston Phoenix*. Online: *http://www.alternet.org/printhtml?StoryID=16314*.

Burlingame, J. (2001, October 8–14). Crossing Euro borders changes content. *Variety*, p. A6.

Burlingame, J. (2002, July 15–21). The write stuff. *Variety*, pp. 59–60.

Burstein, D., & Kline, D. (1995). *Road warriors: Dreams and nightmares along the information highway*. New York: Dutton.

Cappella, J. N., & Jamieson, K. H. (1997). *Spiral of cynicism: The press and the public good*. New York: Oxford University Press.

Carey, J. W. (1975). A cultural approach to communication. *Communication, 2*, 1–22.

Carlson, M. (2002, January 21). The case for a national ID card. *Time*, p. 52.

Case, T. (2001, April 30). The last mass medium? *Editor & Publisher*, pp. SR16–SR18.

CBS v. Democratic National Committee 412 U.S. 94 (1973).

Center for Science in the Public Interest. (2002). Booze news. Online: *www.cspinet.org/booze/alcad.htm*.

Century, D. (2001, March). Black publishing's new colors. *Brill's Content*, pp. 84–87, 141.

Chandler v. Florida 449 U.S. 560 (1981).

Charman, K. (2002, July/August). Recasting the Web. *Extra!*, pp. 22–24.

Chester, J., & Larson, G. (2002, July 26). A 12-step program for media democracy. *The Nation*. Online: *www.alternet.org/print.html?StoryID=13687*.

Chin, F. (1978). *Cable television: A comprehensive bibliography*. New York: IFI/Plenum.

China adopts new Net curbs. (1997, December 31). *San Jose Mercury News*, pp. C1, C4.

Christ, W. G., & W. J. Potter (1998). Media literacy, media education, and the academy. *Journal of Communication, 48*, 5–15.

Christopher, A. (1998, August 3). Blink of an ad. *Time*, p. 51.

Cieply, M. (2001, February 6). Who will save Hollywood? *[Inside]*, pp. 46–56.

Clueless. (2002, May 27). *Broadcasting & Cable*, p. 50.

Coen, R., & Hart, P. (2002, April). Last media ownership limits threatened by judicial action. *Extra! Update*, p. 4.

Cohen, W. (2002, June 20). CD burning. *Rolling Stone*, pp. 43–44.

Colman, P. (1998, December 7). Keeping the customer, period. *Broadcasting & Cable*, p. 58.

Compaine, B. M., & Gomery, D. (2000). *Who owns the media? Competition and concentration in the mass media industry*. Mahwah, NJ: Lawrence Erlbaum.

Consumers Union. (2002). *Captive kids*. Online: *www.media-awareness.ca/eng/med/class/edissue/cecapti2.html*.

Cook, T. D., Appleton, H., Conner, R. F., Shaffer, A., Tamkin, G., & Weber, S. J. (1975). Sesame Street *revisited*. New York: Russell Sage Foundation.

Corliss, R. (1999, October 11). Putting on the Dogme. *Time*, p. 84.

Cox, C. (1999, September/October). Prime-time activism. *Utne Reader*, pp. 20–22.

Cox, C. (2000, July/August). Plugged into protest? *Utne Reader*, pp. 14–15.

Crandall, R. W., & Furchtgott-Roth, H. (1996). *Cable TV: Regulation or competition.* Washington, DC: The Brookings Institute.

Dalton, T. A. (1997, September/October). Reporting on race: A tale of two cities. *Columbia Journalism Review, 36,* 54–57.

Dareini, A. A. (2000, April 24). Iran closes 5 newspapers in crackdown. *San Francisco Chronicle*, p. A12.

Davis, D. K. (1990). News and politics. In D. L. Swanson & D. Nimmo (Eds.), *New directions in political communication.* Newbury Park, CA: Sage.

Davis, R. E. (1976). *Response to innovation: A study of popular argument about new mass media.* New York: Arno Press.

Day, L. A. (1997). *Ethics in media communications: Cases and controversies.* Belmont, CA: Wadsworth.

DeFleur, M. L., & Ball-Rokeach, S. (1975). *Theories of mass communication* (3rd ed.). New York: David McKay.

Denby, D. (1999, September 13). Dog days. *New Yorker*, pp. 107–109.

Dennis, E. E. (1992). *Of media and people.* Newbury Park, CA: Sage.

DiOrio, C. (2002a, March 11–17). High price of peddling pix. *Variety*, p. 11.

DiOrio, C. (2002b, June 10–16). Promo blitz fuels booming biz. *Variety*, p. 9.

Dixon, T. L., & Linz, D. (2000). Overrepresentation and underrepresentation of African Americans and Latinos as lawbreakers on television news. *Journal of Communication, 50,* 131–154.

Dobson, W. J. (1998, July 6). Protest.org. *The New Republic*, pp. 18–21.

Dowd, D. (1997). *Against the conventional wisdom.* Boulder, CO: Westview Press.

Drucker, P. E. (1999, October). Beyond the information revolution. *Atlantic Monthly*, pp. 47–57.

Easton, N. J. (2002, March). Blacked out. *American Journalism Review*, pp. 36–40.

Editor & Publisher International Yearbook. (1998). New York: Editor & Publisher Company.

Effron, E. (1999a, November). Taking the sin out of synergy. *Brill's Content*, pp. 47–48.

Effron, E. (1999b, July/August). Journalism.commerce. *Brill's Content*, pp. 56–57.

Effron, S. (1997, January/February). The North Carolina experiment. *Columbia Journalism Review, 35,* 12–14.

Eisenberg, D. (2002, September 2). It's an ad, ad, ad, ad world. *Time*, pp. 38–41.

Elber, L. (2002, July 25). TV parents: Two's a crowd. *Providence Journal*, p. G1.

Enns, A. (2001, November/December). No matches found. *Adbusters*, p. 27.

Epstein, J. (1999, June 26). Sex and sleaze put Brazil's television viewers in a tizzy. *San Francisco Chronicle*, pp. A10, A12.

Estes v. State of Texas 381 U.S. 532 (1965).

Evangelista, B. (2002, July 15). Commercial skipping is key factor in Sonicblue's DVR. *San Francisco Chronicle*, p. E1.

Eviatar, D. (2003, July 7). The press and Private Lynch. *The Nation*, pp. 18–20.

Ewen, S. (2000). Memoirs of a commodity fetishist. *Mass Communication & Society, 3,* 439–452.

FAIR. (2000a, July 31). Drug czar continues assault on First Amendment. Online: *<fair-1-request@LISTSERVE. AMERICAN.EDU>.*

FAIR. (2000b, August 30). NAB 2000: Speak out for media democracy. Online: *FAIRL@FAIR.org.*

Farhi, P. (2001, March). Can *Salon* make it? *American Journalism Review*, pp. 36–41.

Faules, D. F., & Alexander, D. C. (1978). *Communication and social behavior: A symbolic interaction perspective.* Reading, MA: Addison-Wesley.

Fawcett, A. W. (1996, October 16). Interactive awareness growing. *Advertising Age*, p. 20.

Feldman, G. (2001, February 12). Publishers caught in a Web. *The Nation*, pp. 35–36.

Filler, L. (1968). *The muckrakers: Crusaders for American liberalism.* Chicago: Henry Regnery.

Fitzgerald, M. (1999, October 30). Robert Sengstake Abbot. *Editor & Publisher*, p. 18.

Fitzgerald, M., Shields, T., & Strupp, J. (2001, April 9). Creed vs. Greed: Harris reports from the front. *Editor & Publisher*, pp. 7–8.

Flanders, L. (2002, August 5/12). Librarians under siege. *The Nation*, pp. 42–43.

Flint, J., & Nelson, E. (2002, April 20). Revlon joins the plot of *All My Children. The Providence Journal*, pp. G7, G12.

Foerstel, H. N. (1994). *Banned in the U.S.A.: A reference guide to book censorship in schools and public libraries.* Westport, CT: Greenwood Press.

Fogarty, J. R., & Spielholz, M. (1985). FCC cable jurisdiction: From zero to plenary in twenty-five years. *Federal Communications Law Journal, 37,* 113.

Fogel, M. (2001, May/June). Hard numbers. *Columbia Journalism Review*, p. 25.

Fonda, D. (2003, March 24). National Prosperous Radio. *Time*, pp. 49–51.

Ford, M. (2001, March 29). Shoot to fame. *The Guardian*, p. 11.

Fraser, R. (2003, March 17). DVD players: cheaper and getting cheaper. *TV Guide*, pp. 42–43.

Friend, T. (2000, April 24). Mickey Mouse Club. *The New Yorker*, pp. 212–214.

Fritts, E. O. (2002, May 15). Broadcasters moving forward on DTV. Online: *http://www.nab.org/Newsroom/Pressrel/ speeches/051502.htm.*

FTC faults Net on privacy. (1998, June 4). *San Jose Mercury News*, pp. 1C, 4C.

The future of communication. (2001, October 29). *Broadcasting & Cable*, p. 12A.

Gaffney, J. (2002, June). The online advertising comeback. *Business 2.0*. Online: *www.business2.com/articles/mag/print/0,1643,40430,00.html*.

Garchik, L. (2000, July 25). Death and hobbies. *San Francisco Chronicle*, p. D10.

Garland, E. (2002, April). Can this man save advertising? *Wired*, pp. 65–70.

Garriga, R. (2001, December). The Hispanic challenge. *American Journalism Review*, pp. 58–61.

Gerbner, G. (1990). Epilogue: Advancing on the path of righteousness (maybe). In N. Signorielli & M. Morgan (Eds.), *Cultivation analysis: New directions in media effects research*. Newbury Park, CA: Sage.

Gerbner, G., Gross, L., Jackson-Beeck, M., Jeffries-Fox, S., & Signorielli, N. (1978). Cultural indicators: Violence profile no. 9. *Journal of Communication, 28*, 176–206.

Gerbner, G., Gross, L., Morgan, M., & Signorielli, N. (1980). The "mainstreaming" of America: Violence profile no. 11. *Journal of Communication, 30*, 10–29.

Gerhart, A. (2000, February 22). Teen angst. *San Jose Mercury News*, pp. 1E, 3E.

Germain, D. (2000, March 9). Film distributors learn to think internationally. *San Jose Mercury News*, p. 3AA.

Getting the News. (2003, March 24). *Broadcasting & Cable*, p. 58.

Gilbert, A. (2003, February 13). Survey: Web use trends ever upward. *CNET News.Com*. Online: *http://news.com.com/ 2102-1017-984566.html*.

Gillmor, D. (2000, August 18). Digital Copyright Act comes back to haunt consumers. *San Jose Mercury News*, pp. 1C, 6C.

Gilmor, D. (2002, July 21). Hollywood, tech make suspicious pairing. *San Jose Mercury News*, pp. 1F, 7F.

Gillmor, D. M., & Barron, J. A. (1974). *Mass communication law: Cases and comments*. St. Paul, MN: West.

Ginsberg, T. (2002, January/February). Rediscovering the world. *American Journalism Review*, pp. 48–53.

Ginzburg v. United States 383 U.S. 463 (1966).

Gitlin, T. (1997, March 17). The dumb-down. *The Nation*, 28.

Gitlow v. New York 268 U.S. 652 (1925).

Glatzer, R. (1970). *The new advertising*. New York: Citadel Press.

Goldsmith, J. (2002, June 10). With billions in play, studios keep toying with pic wares. *Variety*, p. 7.

Goldstein, P. (2002a, June 5). Melting-pot action stars. *Providence Journal*, pp. G9, G14.

Goldstein, P. (2002b, March 14). Health group campaigns for a smoke-free screen. *Providence Journal*, pp. G1, G3.

Goldstein, T. (1998, September/October). Does big mean bad? *Columbia Journalism Review*, pp. 52–53.

Goodman, E. (2000, September 13). Hollywood hitmen. *San Jose Mercury News*, p. 10B.

Gow, D. (2002, August 3). Power steering: Spy spoof revs up Jaguar sales. *The Guardian*, p. 20.

Graser, M. (2001, October 8). Digital pics flying with Boeing. *Variety*, pp. 7, 72.

Grossman, L. K. (2003, January/February). Who took the body out of the body politic? *Columbia Journalism Review*, pp. 49–50.

Grotticelli, M., & Kerschbaumer, K. (2001, July 9). Slow and steady. *Broadcasting & Cable*, pp. 32–43.

Guider, E. (2001, June 4). Global B.O. projection: $24 bil by '10. *Variety*, p. 10.

Guider, E. (2002, April 15). Top shows still fly first class. *Variety*, pp. A1–A2.

Gup, T. (2002, May/June). The short distance between secrets and lies. *Columbia Journalism Review*, pp. 74–75.

Hachten, W. A. (1992). *The world news prism* (3rd ed.). Ames, IA: Iowa State University Press.

Hafner, K., & Lyon, M. (1996). *Where wizards stay up late: The origins of the Internet*. New York: Simon & Schuster.

Hall, E. T. (1976). *Beyond culture*. New York: Doubleday.

Hall, S. (1980). Cultural studies: Two paradigms. *Media, Culture and Society, 2*, 57–72.

Hamilton, A. (2000, August 21). Meet the new surfer girls. *Time*, p. 67.

Harlow, R. F. (1976). Building a public relations definition. *Public Relations Review, 2*, 36.

Harmon, A. (2002, May 23). Skip-the-ads TV has Madison Ave. upset. *New York Times*, pp. C1, C3.

Harmon, A. (2003, January 5). The digital future is coming with locks attached. *Providence Journal*, pp. A-1, A-9.

Harper, R. (2003, October). The CD's sad song. *Wired*, p. 58.

Harris, J. T. (2001, May/June). Excerpt from 2001 ASNE address. *Columbia Journalism Review*, pp. 20–21.

Harris, M. (1983). *Cultural anthropology*. New York: Harper & Row.

Hart, P., & Ackerman, S. (2001, November/December). Patriotism and censorship. *Extra!*, pp. 6–9.

Hayes, D. (2002, February 25). Color of success. *Variety*, p. 6.

Healey, J. (1999, May 4). Demand for data: More, more, faster, faster. *San Jose Mercury News*, pp. 1F, 4F.

Healey, J. (2000, January 28). Lights, camera, online! Hollywood plans Web shows. *San Jose Mercury News*, pp. 1A, 23A.

Helm, J. (2002, March/April). When history looks back. *Adbusters*.

Hentoff, N. (2001, November 5). Attacks on freedom. *Editor & Publisher*, p. 26.

Hentoff, N. (2002, July 1). The heirs of liberty. *Editor & Publisher*, p. 30.

Hettrick, S. (2002, February 25). Tale of the tape favors studios. *Variety*, p. 71.

Hickey, N. (2002a, September/October). TV's big stick. *Columbia Journalism Review*, pp. 50–53.

Hickey, N. (2002b, May/June). Media monopoly Q&A. *Columbia Journalism Review*, pp. 30–33.

Higgins, J. M. (1999, May 10). All for just $5,000. *Broadcasting & Cable*, pp. 16–18.

Higgins, J. M. (2003, November 10). A pause in consolidation. *Broadcasting & Cable*, p. 32.

High court again poised to decide free-speech cases. (2002, August 20). *Providence Journal*, p. A10.

Hightower, J. (2002, July 22/29). POP-ing the bankers. *The Nation*, p. 8.

Hilliard, R. L., & Keith, M. C. (1996). *Global broadcasting systems*. Boston: Focal Press.

Hoch, D. (2000, April 3). Mr. Hoch goes to Hollywood. *The Nation*, pp. 25–30.

Hoover v. Intercity Radio Co., Inc. 286 F. 1003 (1923).

Hopkins, M. (1999, July/August). A babel of broadcasts. *Columbia Journalism Review*, pp. 44–47.

Hovland, C. I., Lumsdaine, A. A., & Sheffield, F. D. (1949). *Experiments on mass communication*. Princeton, NJ: Princeton University Press.

Howe, J. (2001, October). Licensed to bill. *Wired*, pp. 140–149.

Huang, E. S. (2001). Readers' perception of digital alteration in photojournalism. *Journalism Monographs*, pp. 148–182.

Hundt, R. (2002, January). Keeping the Net secure. *The Atlantic Monthly*, pp. 26–27.

Hustler Magazine v. Big Jerry Falwell 485 U.S. 46 (1988).

International Marketing Data and Statistics. (2002). London: EUROMONITOR.

Internet Movie Database. (2004). Top grossing movies of all time at the USA box office. Online: *us.imdb.com/charts/usatopmovies*.

Irvin v. Dowd 366 U.S. 717 (1961).

Irving, L. M. (2001). Media exposure and disordered eating: Introduction to the special section. *Journal of Social and Clinical Psychology, 20*, 259–265.

Italie, H. (2003, July 26). Whirlwind, record sales of Harry Potter. *Providence Journal*, p. G3.

It's an ad, ad, ad, ad world. (2001, July 9). *Time*, p. 17.

Iyengar, S., & Kinder, D. R. (1987). *News that matters: Television and American opinion*. Chicago: University of Chicago Press.

Jackson, J. (2001a, September/October). Their man in Washington. *Extra!*, pp. 6–9.

Jackson, J. (2001b, September/October). Wall Street's gain is journalism's loss. *Extra!*, pp. 20–21.

Jackson, J., & Hart, P. (2001, May/June). Fear and favor 2000. *Extra!*, pp. 15–22.

Jackson, J., & Hart, P. (2002, March/April). Fear and favor 2001. *Extra!*, pp. 20–27.

Jamieson, K. H., & Campbell, K. K. (1997). *The interplay of influence: News, advertising, politics, and the mass media*. Belmont, CA: Wadsworth.

Jeers. (2002, February 16). *TV Guide*, p. 13.

Jeffrey, S. (2002, August 7). Playing college newspaper editors for dupes. *Providence Journal*, p. B5.

Jesdanun, A. (2002, August 4). E-mail accounts gagging on spam. *Providence Journal*, pp. A1, A15.

Jessell, H. A. (2000, March 6). A mess of clutter. *Broadcasting & Cable*. p. 14.

Johnson, S. (2001, December 17). Marketplace of ideas or tag sale? *The Nation*, pp. 25–27.

Jones, A. (2002, April 15–21). China hits $8 billion in ads. *Variety*, p. A12.

Justices scrap Internet child porn law. (2002, April 17). *Providence Journal*, p. A3.

Katz, E., & Lazarsfeld, P. F. (1955). *Personal influence: The part played by people in the flow of communications*. New York: Free Press.

Kava, B. (1996, July 12). Longing for the days when DJs made the calls. *San Jose Mercury News*, p. 22.

Kava, B. (1999, October 12). Internet poised to make your CD collection obsolete. *San Jose Mercury News*, pp. 1E, 6E.

Kava, B. (2003, September 4). With goal of $10 CDs, record giant cuts price. *San Jose Mercury News*, Online: *http://bayarea.com/mld/mercurynews/business/6688650.htm?template=contentModule*.

Kelly, M. (2002, January). A renaissance of liberalism. *The Atlantic Monthly*, pp. 18–19.

Kennedy, L. (2002, June). Spielberg in the Twilight Zone. *Wired*, pp. 106–113, 146.

Kids are getting lost in the tobacco deal shuffle. (1998, January 16). *USA Today*, p. 10A.

Kim, B. H., Pasadeos, Y., & Barban, A. (2001). On the deceptive effectiveness of labeled and unlabeled advertorial forms. *Mass Communication and Society, 4*, 265–281.

Kim, M. H. (2002, January 28–February 3). Filmmakers won't budge an iota on screen quotas. *Variety*, p. 16.

Kirk, L. M. (2003, February 16). Smaller and smaller. *Providence Journal Lifestyles*, pp. 8–10.

Kirkhorn, M. J. (2000, February 20). Media increasingly ignore poor. *San Jose Mercury News*, p. 3C.

Kirsner, S. (1999, April). Do newspapers have a future on the Net? Online: *mediainfo.com*.

Klapper, J. T. (1960). *The effects of mass communication*. New York: Free Press.

Klein, N. (1999). *No logo: Taking aim at the brand bullies*. New York: Picador.

Kloer, P. (2002, May 19). With online journals, the Web gets personal. *Providence Sunday Journal Lifestyles*, p. 7.

Kohut, A. (2000, May/June). Self-censorship: Counting the ways. *Columbia Journalism Review*, pp. 42–43.

Konner, J. (1999, March/April). Of Clinton, the Constitution & the press. *Columbia Journalism Review*, p. 6.

Krantz, M. (2000, July 24). Online music ready to rock. *Marin Independent Journal*, p. B1.

Kristula, D. (1997, March). *The history of the Internet*. Online: *http://www.davesite.com/webstation/net-history.shtml*.

Kuhn, T. (1970). *The structure of scientific revolutions* (2nd ed.). Chicago: University of Chicago Press.

Kuralt, C. (1977). *When television was young* (videotape). New York: CBS News.

Kurtz, H. (2000, January 17). When the news is all in the family. *Washington Post National Weekly Edition*, p. 7.

Kurtz, H. (2002, February 1). Pundits at the corporate trough. *Providence Journal*, p. B4.

Kurtz, H., & Waxman, S. (2000, January 14). Antidrug shows pay off for TV. *San Jose Mercury News*, pp. 1A, 24A.

L.A. Times takes itself to task over arena deal. (1999, December 21). *San Francisco Chronicle*, pp. A1, A7.

Lacayo, R. (2000, January 24). A drug deal goes bad. *Time*, p. 67.

Lasswell, H. D. (1948). The structure and function of communication in society. In L. Bryson (Ed.), *The communication of ideas*. New York: Harper.

Lawson, T. (2002, April 29). Once reviled, geek becomes marketing force. *Providence Journal*, pp. D1, D4.

Layton, C. (2003, August/September). Miller brouhaha. *American Journalism Review*, pp. 30–35.

Lazarsfeld, P. F. (1941). Remarks on administrative and critical communications research. *Studies in Philosophy and Social Science, 9*, 2–16.

Lester, J. (2002, Spring). Carved runes in a clearing. *Umass*, pp. 24–29.

Let them eat vowels. (1999, January/February). *Utne Reader*, p. 33

Levere, J. L. (2001, November 27). Advertising. *New York Times*, p. C8.

Levitas, D. (2002, July 22, 29). The radical right after 9/11. *The Nation*, pp. 19–23.

Lights, Camera, Government. (2000, July 17). *Broadcasting & Cable*, p. 90.

Lindlof, T. R. (1987). *Natural audiences: Qualitative research of media uses and effects*. Norwood, NJ: Ablex.

Lipton, J. (2002, March/April). Ethics: Enron's helpers. *Columbia Journalism Review*, p. 13.

Littleton, C. (1999a, January 25–31). Sinclair's way is to pay-to-play. *Variety*, pp. 53, 57.

Littleton, C. (1999b, March 29–April 4). U.S. birds made to get local for TV businesses. *Variety*, p. 58.

Lo, C. (1998, October). Space jam. *Wired*, pp. 142–143.

Lohse, D. (2000b, September 12). Violence knowingly marketed to kids. *San Jose Mercury News*, pp. 1A, 10A

Lopez, S. (2002, January/February). What channel is this? *American Journalism Review*, p. 14.

Lovell, G. (1997, December 21). Branded. *San Jose Mercury News*, pp. 7G, 14G.

Lowery, S. A., & DeFleur, M. L. (1995). *Milestones in mass communication research*. White Plains, NY: Longman.

Lyman, R. (2002, August 25). How DVDs came to dominate home entertainment so quickly. *Providence Journal*, pp. A1, A5.

MacArthur, J. R. (2001, November 19). Unleash the press. *The Nation*, pp. 5–6.

MacArthur, J. R. (2002, March 5). A classic Rumsfeld maneuver. *Providence Journal*, p. B4.

Magazine Publishers of America. (2002). Resources. Online: *http://www.magazine.org/resources/fact_sheets/html*.

Males, M. (2002, July/August). A cold shower for the "teen sex" beat. *Extra!*, p. 30.

Malveaux, J. (2000, August 27). Looking at the digital divide from the global perspective. *San Francisco Examiner*, p. B2.

Mann, C. C. (2000, September). The heavenly jukebox. *The Atlantic*, pp. 39–59.

Marsh, A. (1998, June 15). Rewriting the book of journalism. *Forbes*, pp. 47–48.

Massing, M. (2001, October 15). Press watch. *The Nation*, pp. 6, 31.

Mast, G., & Kawin, B. F. (1996). *A short history of the movies*. Boston: Allyn & Bacon.

Mayer, C. E. (2003, September 25). Hold the phone: Judge puts do-not-call list in doubt. *Providence Journal*, pp. A1, A19.

McChesney, R. W. (1997). *Corporate media and the threat to democracy*. New York: Seven Stories Press.

McChesney, R. W. (1999). *Rich media poor democracy*. Urbana, IL: University of Illinois Press.

McClellan, S. (2001, October 22). Eyes wide shut. *Broadcasting & Cable*, pp. 20–24.

McClellan, S. (2002, May 27). Winning, and losing too. *Broadcasting & Cable*, pp. 6–7.

McClintock, P. (2001, October 15–21). Battle lines drawn in propaganda war. *Variety*, p. 50.

McClintock, P. (2002, March 4–10). White House struggles with o'seas image. *Variety*, p. 26.

McCombs, M. E., & Shaw, D. L. (1972). The agenda-setting function of mass media. *Public Opinion Quarterly, 36*, 176–187.

McConnell, B. (2002a, May 3). Big media, big targets. *Broadcasting & Cable*, pp. 19–22.

McConnell, B. (2002b, April 8). Radio giants want more turf. *Broadcasting & Cable*, p. 34.

McConnell, B. (2002c, March 4). New rules for risque business. *Broadcasting & Cable*, p. 5.

McConnell, B. (2003, November 3). Study: young kids "immersed" in TV. *Broadcasting & Cable*, p. 22.

McCowan, K. (2002, March 20). Films set off smoke alarms. Online: *www.registerguard.com/news/20020320/1d.cr. mccowan. 0320.html*.

McKenna, K. (2000, August). John Malkovich interview. *Playboy*, pp. 65–78.

McLuhan, M. (1962). *The Gutenberg galaxy: The making of typographic man*. London: Routledge & Kegan Paul.

McLuhan, M., & Fiore, Q. (1967). *The medium is the massage*. New York: Random House.

McNamara, T. (2000, July/August). Hard numbers, now and then. *Columbia Journalism Review*, p. 25.

McQuail, D. (1987). *Mass communication theory: An introduction*. Beverly Hills, CA: Sage.

McQuail, D., & Windahl, S. (1986). *Communication models for the study of mass communications*. New York: Longman.

Media Foundation. (2002). Campaigns. Online: *adbusters.org/ campaigns*.

Merton, R. K. (1967). *On theoretical sociology*. New York: Free Press.

Miller, M. C. (1997, March 17). The crushing power of big publishing. *The Nation*, 11–18.

Miller v. State of California 413 U.S. 463 (1966).

Mintz, H. (2000, September 10). Abortion foes pursue appeal over Net freedom. *San Jose Mercury News*, pp. 1A, 10A.

Mitchell, G. (1999, December 4). Two-way street: Gatekeepers still on guard, but editorial, advertising talking more than ever. *Editor & Publisher*, pp. 20–30.

Mitchell, G. (2001, April 9). Poll finds profits rule. *Editor & Publisher*, pp. 16–17.

Moore, F. (1999, June 7). Free speech isn't free, reports PBS special. *Santa Cruz County Sentinal*, p. A11.

Morton, J. (2002, January/February). Why circulation keeps dropping. *American Journalism Review*, 64.

Moses, L. (2001, July 23). Newspapers get a fair share. *Editor & Publisher*, p. 19.

Moses, L. (2002a, August 19). Around Sept. 11, ads a tough sell. *Editor & Publisher*, pp. 5–6.

Moses, L. (2002b, June 3). Youth must be served . . . but how? *Editor & Publisher*, pp. 12–14, 21.

Moses, L. (2002c, December 2). Alternative approaches. *Editor & Publisher*, pp. 14–17.

Moss, L. (2002, July 15). What recession? *Broadcasting & Cable*, pp. 24–32.

Mossberg, W. S. (2002a, March 17). It's time for consumers to stand up for technology rights. *Providence Journal*, p. D7.

Mossberg, W. S. (2002b, February 10). Two efforts to replace Napster play out as feeble. *Providence Journal*, p. E4.

Mundy, A. (2002, February 25). Ministry of truth? *Editor & Publisher*, p. 26.

Mutual Film Corp. v. Ohio Industrial Commission 236 U.S. 230 (1915).

Nathaniel, M. (2001, November 10). You shouldn't print my name. *Providence Journal*, p. B7.

Nation of snitches. (2002, July 25). *Providence Journal*, p. B4.

National Broadcasting Company v. United States 319 U.S. 190 (1943).

National Cable and Telecommunications Association. (2002a). Cable networks receive record number of primetime Emmy nominations. Online: *www.ncta.com/ptess/press.cfm?Prid=287&showArticles=ok*.

National Cable and Telecommunications Association (2002b). Industry statistics. Online: *www.ncta.com/industry_overview/indStat.cfm?indOverviewID=2*.

National Cable and Telecommunications Association (2003). Industry statistics. Online: *http://www.ncta.com/docs/PageContent.cfm?pageID86*.

National Commission Against Drunk Driving. (2002). Alcohol-related fatality rates. Online: *www.ncadd.com/alcrate. htm*.

National Communication Association (1996). *Speaking, listening, and media literacy: Standards for K through 12 education*. Annandale, VA: NCA.

National Institute on Media and the Family. (2002). Alcohol advertising and youth. Online: *www.mediaandthefamily.org/research/fact/alcohol.shtml*.

Naureckas, J. (2002, January/February). Patriotism vs. jingoism. *Extra!*, 2

NCTA name change. (2001, February 12). *Broadcasting & Cable*, p. 36.

Near v. Minnesota 283 U.S. 697 (1931).

New York Times v. Sullivan 376 U.S. 254 (1964).

New York Times v. United States 403 U.S. 713 (1971).

News and profits. (2001, May 28). *The Nation*, p. 3.

Nichols, J. (2002, April 29). Campaign finance: The sequel. *The Nation*, pp. 16–20.

Nichols, J., & McChesney, R. W. (2002, August). On the verge in Vermont. *Extra!*, pp. 26–27.

Ninety-Second Congress. (1972). *Hearings before the Subcommittee on Communications on the Surgeon General's Report by the Scientific Advisory Committee on Television and Social Behavior*. Washington, DC: U.S. Government Printing Office.

Noack, D. (1999, June 19). Gannett pushes ethics. *Editor & Publisher*, p. 9.

Norsigian, J., Diskin, V., Doress-Worters, P., Pincus, J., Sanford, W., & Swenson, N. (1999). The Boston Women's Health Book Collective and *Our bodies ourselves:* A brief history and reflection. *Journal of the American Medical Women's Association*. Online: <*http://www.ourbodiesourselves.org*>.

Numbers. (2003, March 17). *Time*, p. 16.

N.Y. shock jocks canned over cathedral sex stunt. (2002, August 23). *Providence Journal*, p. A8.

O'Connor, R. J., & Wasserman, E. (1996, November 25). E-commerce isn't yet an e-ssential way of life. *San Jose Mercury News*, pp. 1A, 13A.

Oppelaar, J. (2000, October). Expensive lessons. *eV*, pp. 18, 20.

Oppelaar, J. (2001, July 30–August 5). Majors fight Napster spawn. *Variety*, p. 16.

Oppelaar, J. (2002, December 24–January 6). Comcast's cable colossus. *Variety*, p. 15.

Oppelaar, J. (2003, May 12–18). Will Apple for pay keep doldrums away? *Variety*, p. 42.

O'Shaughnessy, W. (2003, February 3). You have to trust in the market. *Broadcasting & Cable*, p. 36.

Packard, V. O. (1957). *The hidden persuaders*. New York: David McKay.

Palmeri, C. (2001, December 3). Boffo at the box office, scarce on the shelves. *Business Week*, p. 53.

Paper Tiger Manifesto. (2003, January). Online: *www.papertiger.org/index.php?name=roar-chap1*.

Pareles, J. (1998, November 15). With a click, a new era of music dawns. *New York Times*, pp. 1, 22.

Parks, M. (2002, January/February). Foreign news: What's next? *Columbia Journalism Review*, pp. 52–57.

Pastore, M. (1999). US Internet audience growth slowing. Online: *cyberatlas.internet.com/big_picture/geographics*.

Pastore, M. (2001). Gone fishin'. Online: *www.internetnews.com/IAR*.

Paulson, K. (2002, September). Too free? *American Journalism Review*, pp. 30–35.

Pember, D. (1999). *Mass media law*. Boston: McGraw-Hill.

The People's Communication Charter. (1996, Fall). *Cultural Environment Monitor*, 1, 3–6.

Peraino, V. (1999, August). The law of increasing returns. *Wired*, pp. 144–147.

Peterson, I. (1997, November 17). At *Los Angeles Times*, a debate on news-ad interaction. *New York Times*, pp. C1, C11.

Peterson, L. C. (1998, November). The *Wired* world atlas. *Wired*, pp. 162–167.

Phillips, H. F. (2003, February 10). Brave new program. *San Jose Mercury News*, p. 1E, cont. 5E.

Pielke, R. G. (1986). *You say you want a revolution: Rock music in American culture*. Chicago: Nelson-Hall.

Pincus, J. (1998). Introduction. In Boston Women's Health Book Collective (Eds.), *Our bodies ourselves for the new century* (pp. 21–23). New York: Touchstone.

Pinkelton, B. E. (1997). The effects of negative comparative political advertising on candidate evaluations and advertising evaluations: An exploration. *Journal of Advertising, 26,* 19–29.

Poll says Americans relax with lots of media at once. (2000, June 29). *San Jose Mercury News*, p. 11A.

Poniewozik, J. (2000, January 24). A trick of the Eye. *Time*, p. 67.

Poniewozik, J. (2001, Fall). Get up, stand up. *Time*, pp. 68–70.

Poniewozik, J. (2002, January 28). The day the *Talk* dies out. *Time*, p. 54.

Pope, J. (2001, December 6). A leap toward video you can bend. *Providence Journal*, pp, A1, A18.

Potter, W. J. (1998). *Media literacy*. Thousand Oaks, CA: Sage Publications.

Public Relations Society of America. (2002). Public relations: An overview. Online: *tampa.prsa.org*.

Publishers Information Bureau. (2002). *Ad revenue up 12.6%, pages up 6.9%*. Retrieved December 10, 2002, from www.magazine.org/news/press_releases/02_nov_pib.html.

Quain, J. R. (1999, September). Fast-forward, rewind—and take control. *Brill's Content*, pp. 64–65.

Quindlen, A. (2000, July 17). Aha! Caught you reading. *Newsweek*, p. 64.

Quittner, J. (1999, May 17). Coinless jukebox. *Time*, p. 94.

Rathburn, E. A. (2000, August 28). Clutter, clutter everywhere. *Broadcasting & Cable*, p. 58.

Real news is: Pentagon closes office. (2002, February 27). *Providence Journal*, p. A5.

Red Lion Broadcasting v. United States 395 U.S. 367 (1969).

Reno, R. (2002, May 7). Enron fallout will persist. *Providence Journal*, p. B4.

Richardson, G. W. (2001). Looking for meaning in all the wrong places: Why negative advertising is a suspect category. *Journal of Communication, 51,* 775–800.

Ridder, T. (2001, May/June). Excerpt from April 6 column in *Mercury News*. *Columbia Journalism Review*, p. 21.

Rieder, R. (2001, May). A sacred profession? *American Journalism Review*, p. 6.

Risser, J. (2000, January/February). The wall is heading back. *Columbia Journalism Review*, pp. 26, 29.

Robins, W. (2001, July 16). Newspapers get real. *Editor & Publisher*, pp. 16–18.

Rock Out Censorship. (1998, January). Online: <http://www.theroc.org>.

Roman, J. W. (1983). *Cablemania: The cable television sourcebook*. Englewood Cliffs, NJ: Prentice-Hall.

Rosaldo, R. (1989). *Culture and truth: The remaking of social analysis*. Boston: Beacon.

Rosen, J. (2002a, April). Making some noise. *American Journalism Review*, pp. 12–13.

Rosen, J. (2002b, March). D'oh, a deer. *American Journalism Review*, p. 19.

Rosenberg, R. S. (1992). *The social impact of computers*. Boston: Harcourt Brace Jovanovich.

Ross, A. (2000, March 14). Community losing out to e-commerce. *San Francisco Chronicle*, p. A21.

Roth v. United States 354 U.S. 476 (1957).

Rubin, A. M. (1998). Editor's note: Media literacy. *Journal of Communication, 48,* 3–4.

Sachs, S. (2000, April 28). Hard-liners escalate attack. *San Jose Mercury News*, p. 21A.

Saia v. New York 334 U.S. 558 (1948).

Sampson, H. T. (1977). *Blacks in black and white: A source book on Black films*. Metuchen, NJ: Scarecrow Press.

Sandage, C. H., Fryburger, V., & Rotzoll, K. (1989). *Advertising theory and practice*. New York: Longman.

Sanders, E., & Healy, J. (2002, July 19). AOL had tools, not synergy. *Los Angeles Times*, pp. B1, B3.

Sarnoff, D. (1953, September 21). Address to NBC Radio Affiliates Committee in Chicago. *Broadcasting/Telecasting*, pp. 108–112.

Schenck v. United States 249 U.S. 47 (1919).

Schiffrin, A. (1996, June 3). The corporatization of publishing. *The Nation*, pp. 29–32.

Schiffrin, A. (1999, July 5). Random acts of consolidation. *The Nation*, p. 10.

Schlosser, J. (2002, February 11). Do-it-yourself development. *Broadcasting & Cable*, p. 12.

Schwarzbaum, L. (1997, November/December). Independents' day. *Entertainment Weekly*, pp. 8–9.

Scott, D. K., & Gobetz, R. H. (1992). Hard news/soft news content of the national broadcast networks, 1972–1987. *Journalism and Mass Communication Quarterly, 69,* 406–412.

Scribner, S. (2001, February 7). Conspiracy to limit the films we see. *Hartford Courant*, pp. D1, D3.

Seipp, C. (2002, June). Online uprising. *American Journalism Review*, pp. 42–47.

Setback for Iran's Reform. (2000, August 7). *San Jose Mercury News*, p. 8A.

Shaw, D. (2001, November 4). Media relying on military. *Atlanta Journal Constitution*, p. C7.

Shenk, D. (1997). *Data smog: Surviving the information glut*. New York: Harper Edge.

Sherman, S. (2002, March/April). Enron: Uncovering the uncovered story. *Columbia Journalism Review*, pp. 22–27.

Siebert, F. S., Peterson, T., & Schramm, W. (1956). *Four theories of the press*. Urbana, IL: University of Illinois Press.

Silverblatt, A. (1995). *Media literacy*. Westport, CT: Praeger.

Skow, J. (1999, April 26). Lost in cyberspace. *Time*, p. 61.

Sloan, W., Stovall, J., & Startt, J. (1993). *Media in America: A history*. Scottsdale, AZ: Publishing Horizons.

Smiley, J. (1999, December 2). Everything I never really wanted. *San Jose Mercury News*, p. 10B.

Smoke Free Movies. (2002). Act now! Online: *smokefreemovies. ucsf.edu.*

Soley, L. C., & Nichols, J. S. (1987). *Clandestine radio broadcasting: A study of revolutionary and counterrevolutionary electronic communication.* New York: Praeger.

Soundbites. (2002, June). Channel surfing is theft. *Extra!*, p. 2.

Spector, J. (2001, March 6). Cheap shot artists. *[Inside]*, pp. 56–58.

Statistical Abstracts of the United States. (2002). Online: *www.census.gov/statab.*

Stauber, J. C., & Rampton, S. (1995). *Toxic sludge is good for you: Lies, damn lies and the public relations industry.* Monroe, ME: Common Courage Press.

Stein, J. (1999, November 8). Babe tube. *Time*, pp. 133–135.

Steinberg, S. H. (1959). *Five hundred years of printing.* London: Faber & Faber.

Sterling, C. H., & Kitross, J. M. (1990). *Stay tuned: A concise history of American broadcasting.* Belmont, CA: Wadsworth.

Stevenson, R. L. (1994). *Global communication in the twenty-first century.* New York: Longman.

Stone, M. L. (1999, May 8). Sticking to the Web. *Editor & Publisher*, p. 20.

The story of the ad council. (2001, October 29). *Broadcasting & Cable*, pp. 4–11.

Strauss, N. (2000, August 6). Toeing a slim, shady line on explicit lyrics. *San Jose Mercury News*, p. 5G.

Streeter, T. (1997). Blue skies and strange bedfellows: The discourse of cable television. In L. Spigel & M. Curtis (Eds.), *The revolution wasn't televised: Sixties television and social conflict.* New York: Routledge.

Streitfeld, D. (1998, January 8). Hit writers strike anew while presses are hot. *San Jose Mercury News*, p. 9E.

Streitfeld, D., & Piller, C. (2002, March 3). Identity crisis: That's what happens when high tech meets Big Brother. *Providence Journal*, pp. D1, D6.

Strupp, J. (2002, April 15). Editors call for forum on profits/quality question. *Editor & Publisher*, p. 3.

Sullivan, A. (2002, May). The blogging revolution. *Wired*, pp. 43–44.

Surowiecki, J. (2000, June 5). Can the record labels survive the Internet? *The New Yorker*, p. 35.

Surowiecki, J. (2001, November 26). The paranoia principle. *New Yorker*, p. 46.

Sutherland, J. (2002, July 29). Shame on Amazon for selling the "bible of the racist right"—but at least the fascist who wrote it is dead. *Guardian*, p. 7.

Szatmary, D. P. (2000). *Rockin' in time: A social history of rock-and-roll* (4th ed.). Upper Saddle River, NJ: Prentice Hall.

Taylor, C. (2003, March 10). Day of the smart mobs. *Time*, p. 53.

Taylor, D. (1991). Transculturating TRANSCULTURATION. *Performing Arts Journal*, *13*, 90–104.

Tebbel, J. (1987). *Between covers: The rise and transformation of American book publishing.* New York: Oxford University Press.

Tebbel, J., & Zuckerman, M. E. (1991). *The magazine in America 1741–1990.* New York: Oxford University Press.

Tedesco, R. (1999, March 8). Who'll control the video streams? *Broadcasting & Cable*, pp. 20–24.

Teinowitz, I. (2003, January 29). FCC Chairman ho-hums anti-war ad controversy. *AdAge.com.* Online: http://www. adage.com/news.cms?newsId-37016.

Television Bureau of Advertising. (2003). TV basics. Online: *www.tvb.org/tvfacts/tvbasics.html.*

Tessler, J., & Heim, K. (2000, August 29). Novel ideas for selling digital books. *San Jose Mercury News*, pp. 1C, 7C.

Tillinghast, C. H. (2000). *American broadcast regulation and the First Amendment: Another look.* Ames, IA: Iowa State University Press.

Time, Inc. v. Hill 385 U.S. 374 (1967).

Trench, M. (1990). *Cyberpunk.* Mystic Fire Videos. New York: Intercon Production.

Trigoboff, D. (2002, April 22). The news not out of Topeka. *Broadcasting & Cable*, p. 12.

The Tunnel. (2002). *The Tunnel:* Where is it? Online: *www.geocities.com/Capito1Hill/7288/tunn.htm.*

Turkle, S. (1995). *Life on the screen: Identity in the age of the Internet.* New York: Simon & Schuster.

Turner, C. (1998, July 1). 19 nations join to counter spread of U.S. culture. Madison (WI) *Capital Times*, p. 1A.

Two cheers for our side. (2002, March 18). *Nation*, p. 4.

USA Today. (2000, July 9). The *Potter* phenomenon: It's just magic. *Honolulu Advertiser*, p. E4.

U.S. Census Bureau. (2001). *Statistical abstract of the United States.* Washington, DC: U.S. Government Printing Office.

U.S. v. Zenith Radio Corp. et al. 12 F. 2d 616 (1926).

Valentine v. Christensen 316 U.S. 52 (1942).

Vane, S. (2002, March). Taking care of business. *American Journalism Review*, pp. 60–65.

Variety's Global 50. (2002, August 26). *Variety*, p. B12.

Verbatim. (2002, August 19). *Time*, p. 16.

Victory for privacy. (2002, June 29). *Providence Journal*, p. B6.

Walker, J., & Ferguson, D. (1998). *The broadcast television industry.* Boston: Allyn & Bacon.

Waller, D. (2000, April 10–16). Epoch of the Rolling Clones. *Variety*, pp. 1, 78.

Walser, R. (1993). *Running with the devil: Power, gender, and madness in heavy metal.* Hanover, NH: University Press of New England.

Ward, E., Stokes, G., & Tucker, K. (1986). *Rock of Ages: The Rolling Stone history of rock & roll.* New York: Rolling Stone Press.

Warner, B. (2002, April 15). Piracy in spotlight at annual music sales event. Online: *http://digitalmass.boston.com/ news/2002/04/15/piracy.html.*

Wartella, E. A. (1997). *The context of television violence.* Boston: Allyn & Bacon.

Web pages grow by billions. (2000, July 16). *Honolulu Advertiser*, p. G1.

Wenner, K. S. (2001, December). Just how independent a voice? *American Journalism Review*, pp. 10–11.

Westcott, T. (2002, April 15). Brits step up for right fare. *Variety*, p. A9.

Whitcomb, I. (1972). *After the ball*. New York: Allen Lane.

Whitty, S. (1999, October 24). Hollywood waste line too big. *San Jose Mercury News*, p. 9G.

Why Elvis still lives. (2002, August 9). *The Week*, p. 9.

Wigand, R. (2002, July). Online privacy protection for consumers. *ICA News*, pp. 11, 15.

Williams, P. J. (2002, March 25). Virtual reality. *Nation*, p. 9.

Williams, T. (2002, January/February). Dream society. *Adbusters*, p. 17.

Winokur, S. (1999, November 28). News, ads: Do twain ever meet? *San Francisco Examiner*, p. D3.

Winters, R. (2002, February 4). Those patriotic ads: Thrown for a loss. *Time*, p. 13.

Wolf, M. J., & Sands, G. (1999, July/August). Fearless predictions: The content world, 2005. *Brill's Content*, pp. 109–113.

Would I lie to you? (2002, August 14). *O' Dwyer's PR Daily*. Online: *www.odwyerpr.com/0814comm_rumsfeld.htm*.

Wronge, Y. S. (2000, August 17). New report fuels TV-violence debate. *San Jose Mercury News*, pp. 1E, 3E.

Wulfemeyer, K. T. (1982). A content analysis of local television newscasts: Answering the critics. *Journal of Broadcasting, 26*, 481–486.

Yi, M. (2003, August 25). Wi-Fi hits the spot. *San Francisco Chronicle*, pp. E1, E7.

Zachary, G. P. (1999, January/February). The world gets in touch with its inner American. *Mother Jones*, pp. 50–56.

Zielenziger, M. (2000, July 23). Small nation takes journey to happiness. *San Jose Mercury News*, pp. 1AA, 6AA.

Zinn, H. (1995). *A people's history of the United States, 1492–present*. New York: HarperPerennial.

Zoellner, D. B. (1995, September/October). The truth about the Heartland. *Columbia Journalism Review*, p. 8.

Acknowledgments

Photo Credits

Front matter Author photo courtesy of the author

Part Opener 1 p. 1, © Paul Grebliunas/Getty Images/ Stone

Chapter 1 p. 2, Photo by Mary Ellen Matthews/Corbis Outline from Rolling Stone, December 12, 2002. © 2002 Rolling Stone LLC. All rights reserved. Reprinted by permission.; p. 11TL, Photofest; p. 11TR, © Reuters NewMedia, Inc./Corbis; p. 11ML, © Michael Newman/ PhotoEdit; p. 11MR, © AP/Wide World Photos; p. 11BL, © Reuters NewMedia, Inc./Corbis; p. 13L, © 2001 ABC Photography Archives; p. 13M, © Reuters NewMedia, Inc./ Corbis; p. 13R, © Reuters NewMedia, Inc./Corbis; p. 14TL, Photofest; p. 14TR, The Kobal Collection/NBC/ Paramount Television; p. 14B, © 2001 ABC Photography Archives; p. 15, © Reuters NewMedia, Inc./Corbis; p. 17, Everett Collection; p. 19, Skyy Spirits; p. 20, Photofest; p. 30, © Koren Ziv/Corbis Sygma

Chapter 2 p. 36, © Miramax/Courtesy Everett Collection; p. 40, 41, © The Granger Collection, New York; p. 42, © Bettmann/Corbis; p. 43, © The Granger Collection, New York; p. 45, © Erich Lessing/ Art Resource, NY; p. 47, © UPI/ Corbis-Bettmann; p. 48, © Amy Ramey/PhotoEdit; p. 49, © The Granger Collection, New York; p. 52T, The Kobal Collection; p. 52B, © Twentieth Century Fox and DreamWorks L.L.C./Everett Collection; p. 58, Everett Collection; p. 59, © Big Feats! Entertainment/ Courtesy Photofest

Part 2 p. 65, © Mark Peterson/Corbis Saba

Chapter 3 p. 66, Harry Potter, characters, names, and all related indicia are trademarks of Warner Brothers, © 2001; p. 68, The Kobal Collection; p. 69, © The Granger Collection, New York; p. 71, © Culver Pictures, Inc.; p. 74, © Ancient Art & Architecture Collection; p. 75T, © The Granger Collection, New York; p. 75BL, BR, Courtesy Random House, Inc.; p. 76, Courtesy Boston Women's Health Book Collective; p. 84, Courtesy MySimon.com; p. 85T, © Ian Mainsbridge/PPL Photo Agency; p. 85B, Courtesy Random House, Inc.; p. 88T, Courtesy Ten Speed Press, Berkeley, CA; p. 88B, Courtesy TV Books, Inc.; p. 91, © Michael Newman/ PhotoEdit; p. 93, © Greg Smith/Corbis Saba; p. 95, Harry Potter, characters, names, and all related indicia are trademarks of Warner Brothers, © 2001

Chapter 4 p. 100, © Mug Shots/Corbis; p. 104, Courtesy John Frost Newspapers; p. 105, 106, 107, 109, © The Granger Collection, New York; p. 112, Reprinted by permission of USA Today; p. 114TL, © 2002 by the San Francisco Chronicle. Reproduced with permission of the San Francisco Chronicle; p. 114TR, Copyright © 2002 San Jose Mercury News. All rights reserved. Reproduced with permission.; p. 114B, Courtesy Santa Cruz Sentinel; p. 115L, Reproduced by permission of the Pacific Sun; p. 115M, Reprinted by permission of the Providence Phoenix; p. 115R, Reprinted by permission of Metro Publishing Company; p. 120, © 2002 San Jose Mercury News; p. 121L, © Washington Post. Newsweek Interactive. www.washingtonpost.com; p. 121R, © The Atlanta Journal Constitution. ajc.com; p. 125, North County Telegram & Gazette; p. 127L, Reprinted Courtesy of the Boston Globe; p. 127R, Providence Journal

Chapter 5 p. 132, © Kevin Fleming/Corbis; p. 136, © The Granger Collection, New York; p. 137, © 1923 Time, Inc./ Time Life Pictures/Getty Images; p. 139T, Theodore Roosevelt Collection, Harvard College Library; p. 139B, © Alán Gallegos/AG Photograph; p. 140T, Printed by permission of the Norman Rockwell Family Agency. © 1958 The Norman Rockwell Family Entities; p. 140M, Mark Selinger/GQ, Condé Nast Publications; p. 140B, People Weekly is a registered trademark of Time, Inc., used with permission.; p. 146L, R, Courtesy of American Airlines; p. 146M, Courtesy of Voyageur, Carlson Hospitality World-wide's In-room Magazine. Cover Photograph by Jonathan Orenstein; p. 149T, The Kobal Collection/ Universal/John P. Johnson; p. 149M, The Kobal Collection/ Bel-Air/Castle Rock/Ralph Nelson; p. 149B, The Kobal Collection/Warner Brothers; p. 150, Courtesy Psychologie Heute; p. 152, This advertisement is reprinted by arrangement with Sears, Roebuck and Co. and is protected under copyright. No duplication is permitted; p. 153, Jason Bell © GQ/The Condé Nast Publications Ltd.; p. 154, Courtesy of Cosmo Girl!

Chapter 6 p. 158, © Warner Brothers/Courtesy Everett Collection; p. 161, The Kobal Collection; p. 162, © The Granger Collection, New York; p. 163, © Culver Pictures, Inc.; p. 164, Photofest; p. 165, © Edison Co. 1903/MP & TV Photo Archive; p. 167, 168, Everett Collection; p. 169, © 1927 Warner Brothers/MP & TV Photo Archive; p. 170, © Walt Disney. Courtesy Everett Collection; p. 173, 174, Photofest; p. 178, 180, 183L, Everett Collection; p. 183R, © Miramax. Courtesy Everett Collection; p. 186T,

Index

Page numbers in **bold** denote glossary terms. Page numbers in *italic* denote illustrations.